AI, Personalization, Equity, and the Future of Learning

Viktor Wang
California State University, San Bernardino, USA

IGI Global
Scientific Publishing
Publishing Tomorrow's Research Today

Vice President of Editorial Melissa Wagner
Director of Acquisitions Mikaela Felty
Director of Book Development Jocelynn Hessler
Production Manager Mike Brehm
Cover Design Jose Rosado

Published in the United States of America by
IGI Global Scientific Publishing
701 East Chocolate Avenue
Hershey, PA, 17033, USA
Tel: 717-533-8845
Fax: 717-533-7115
Website: https://www.igi-global.com E-mail: cust@igi-global.com

Library of Congress Cataloging-in-Publication Data

LCCN: 2025026193 (CIP Data Pending)
ISBN13: 9798337350974
Isbn13Softcover: 9798337350981
EISBN13: 9798337350998

British Cataloguing in Publication Data
A Cataloguing in Publication record for this book is available from the British Library.

Table of Contents

Detailed Table of Contents

down equally to all groups; lack of access to technology and biases in algorithms may exclude some groups. AI tools therefore need to be transparent, explainable and ethically grounded. This chapter examines the dimensions of the digital divide, the contributions of AI, the effects of algorithmic biases, and teachers' AI literacy, and offers recommendations for inclusive AI design and policy.

This chapter investigates the role of AI chatbots in pre-service language teacher education using data from 134 trainees in Vietnam. Applying the AI-CITE framework, the study examines how a customized chatbot, Mizou, influenced learning across six areas: individualization, interactivity, engagement, decision-making, lesson planning, and barriers. Findings show that chatbots support instructional design, feedback, and learner motivation but struggle with contextual sensitivity and emotional nuance. While effective as supplementary tools, chatbots cannot replace human mentorship. The chapter concludes with practical strategies for integrating AI responsibly into teacher education, emphasizing the need for culturally aware and ethically designed systems.

This chapter explores the role of artificial intelligence (AI) in fostering inclusive education for students with disabilities, focusing on how AI-powered assistive technologies like speech-to-text, text-to-speech, screen readers, and real-time captioning can improve accessibility and engagement. It examines personalized learning platforms, AI-driven tutoring systems, and adaptive assessments tailored to individual needs. Ethical challenges such as algorithmic bias, data privacy, and infrastructural disparities are also addressed. The chapter offers recommendations for effective AI integration, including comprehensive needs assessments, phased implementation, collaborative ecosystems, and an emphasis on affordability and accessibility. It highlights the importance of inclusive AI policies, data governance, and educator training to ensure responsible use of AI. The chapter stresses AI's transformative potential but emphasizes the need for ongoing research, interdisciplinary collaboration, and human-centered design to ensure AI tools promote equity and empower all learners.

Artificial intelligence (AI) is transforming the future of work, education, and innovation, particularly in the realms of career and technical education (CTE) and science, technology, engineering, and mathematics (STEM). This chapter examines how AI reshapes roles across industries from software engineering to healthcare by democratizing programming through no-code platforms and intelligent coding assistants. Educators are incorporating AI to personalize learning, promote equitable access, and prepare students for evolving technical careers. Emphasizing both technical fluency and ethical responsibility, the chapter explores AI's role in cloud-native development, lifelong learning, and educational transformation. Through analysis of current tools, workforce trends, and instructional strategies, it demonstrates how AI augments, rather than replaces, human capability. The discussion highlights the importance of interdisciplinary collaboration and continuous upskilling to ensure a resilient, inclusive, and innovative future shaped by intelligent technology.

Artificial intelligence (AI) is transforming academic research by streamlining methodologies, accelerating discovery, and expanding analytical capabilities across disciplines. In STEM, AI enables efficient data analysis, predictive modeling, and automation of complex processes. In medicine, it aids diagnostics and drug development, while in the humanities and social sciences, it supports large-scale text analysis and cultural interpretation. Disciplines like law, education, business, archaeology, and psychology are also leveraging AI for precision, efficiency, and innovation. AI-generated tools assist in drafting, modeling, and decision-making, enhancing both productivity and collaboration. However, these benefits come with challenges—bias, opacity, and ethical concerns surrounding authorship and data privacy. This chapter provides a comprehensive overview of AI's cross-disciplinary applications, examines its ethical implications, and offers practical strategies and future directions for integrating AI responsibly within academic research ecosystems.

the integration of AI into adult education, exploring its role in personalized learning, upskilling, and reskilling the workforce. By leveraging AI technologies such as adaptive learning systems, intelligent tutoring, and predictive analytics, educators can address the unique needs of adult learners and create more inclusive and accessible learning environments. The chapter delves into the potential of AI to align adult education programs with evolving industry demands, fostering workforce readiness in an era of rapid technological change. Additionally, the ethical considerations, challenges of implementation, and strategies for equitable AI integration in adult education are discussed. The chapter concludes by presenting a vision for the future of AI in lifelong learning and its impact on empowering individuals and advancing global workforce development.

Machine translation (MT) systems like Google Translate, Baidu Translate, and DeepL Translator have become popular for bridging linguistic and cultural divides. These platforms use neural machine translation models to deliver instantaneous, multilingual translation services. This study aimed to compare the translation quality of Google Translate, Baidu Translate, and DeepL Translate in translating texts from Chinese to Indonesian. A mixed-methods strategy was used, involving 100 samples of Chinese source HSK vocabulary and business-related sentences. The findings indicated distinct variations in the efficacy of the three machine translation systems. Google Translate demonstrated the highest performance, attaining scores of 86% in accuracy, 85% in faithfulness, and 87% in naturalness. This superiority may not just indicate superior translation algorithms; its extensive popularity and regular use among Indonesian users undoubtedly contribute to improved output quality, notably through user data and feedback mechanisms that perpetually refine the system.

This chapter explores the transformative potential of artificial intelligence (AI) to advance educational equity specifically for Black, Indigenous, and People of Color (BIPOC) learners, who have historically navigated systemic barriers within traditional education systems. Arguing that AI offers a unique opportunity to disrupt entrenched inequities, we examine its capacity to foster just and inclusive learning environments. The chapter delves into how AI-driven personalized learning platforms can cater

Speech recognition helps students by translating voice-to-text. It is helpful for the person who is disabled or learning impaired. It helps with reading, writing, and learning. It helps visually impaired, physically challenged, or non-native speakers through increased accessibility. It makes classes more inclusive and offers better communication. It helps teachers with individualized comments and saves time. Although helpful, it has to be precise, confidential, and cost-effective for mass application.

The rapid rise of Artificial Intelligence (AI) has significantly impacted both education and software development, particularly in coding instruction. AI-powered tools like GitHub Copilot, ChatGPT, and intelligent tutoring systems are transforming traditional teaching methods by offering personalized learning, real-time feedback, and enhanced debugging. While these tools show promise in supporting novice programmers and improving coding skills, concerns exist about their potential to undermine critical cognitive skills like problem-solving and creativity. This chapter examines the effectiveness of AI-driven coding tools in achieving educational and professional goals, exploring their impact on cognitive development and workforce readiness. It also addresses the societal implications of AI in education, including algorithmic biases, tool accessibility, and ethical considerations. Through empirical research and case studies, this chapter provides a nuanced view of AI's role in shaping coding education and the software industry.

Foreword

As global policymakers and innovators grapple with the ethical, economic, and social implications of artificial intelligence, the education sector remains a critical arena for both opportunity and responsibility. In this context, Dr. Viktor Wang's latest book stands out as a pioneering contribution—one that bridges the gap between policy vision and practical implementation in classrooms and institutions around the world.

For those of us engaged in shaping national and international strategies around workforce development, digital inclusion, and educational access, this volume offers indispensable insight. Dr. Wang not only introduces cutting-edge tools that harness AI for pedagogical innovation, but he also grounds these tools in principles of lifelong learning, global equity, and ethical application. It is this blend of technological fluency and human-centered purpose that makes the book especially timely.

Around the globe, ministries of education, multilateral organizations, and non-governmental stakeholders are asking the same questions: How do we prepare learners for the jobs of tomorrow? How can AI support rather than displace human educators? And how do we ensure that AI-enhanced education systems promote inclusion rather than deepen existing divides? This book does not shy away from these challenges. Instead, it embraces them head-on, offering strategies and insights that are both forward-looking and grounded in experience.

Dr. Wang's work reminds us that the future of AI in education is not just a technological issue—it is a governance issue, a values issue, and ultimately, a human development issue. The policy community will find this book to be a valuable asset in developing frameworks that guide the ethical integration of AI into national and regional education systems.

I commend this volume to all who are invested in building educational systems that are future-ready and learner-focused. Whether you are a minister, policymaker, or leader in a global education NGO, this book provides the insight and inspiration needed to take meaningful action. Dr. Wang has given us not only a scholarly text, but a roadmap for international cooperation and human-centered innovation.

William J. Rothwell
The Pennsylvania State University, USA

Preface

INTRODUCTION

The idea for this book, *AI, Personalization, Equity, and the Future of Learning*, emerged from the convergence of two lifelong passions: my dedication to advancing adult, career, and higher education, and my deep curiosity about the potential of artificial intelligence to reshape the ways we teach, learn, and lead. As an educator, researcher, and mentor with more than two decades of global academic engagement, I have had the privilege of witnessing—and contributing to—many waves of educational reform. Yet none has been as rapid, as disruptive, or as full of possibility as the current era of AI innovation.

My academic foundation is rooted in one of the most influential departments in the history of adult education—the Department of Vocational and Adult Education at the University of Arkansas, where I earned both my doctoral degree in education and a master's degree in educational technology. This is the same department where the late Dr. Malcolm Knowles, the father of andragogy, taught until his passing in 1997. It is a profound honor to have graduated from a department so deeply connected to the origins of adult learning theory. I have proudly carried Dr. Knowles' torch of andragogical leadership forward, guiding research across disciplines and continents, and advancing his legacy through my own teaching, writing, and mentorship.

To date, I have published over 240 refereed works, including approximately 80 volumes of scholarly books. My publications are held in the libraries of leading universities such as Stanford, New York University, and Princeton, a testament to their relevance and scholarly impact. I have had the privilege of publishing articles and book chapters authored by some of the most respected figures in the field of education, including Dr. Stephen Brookfield. Furthermore, my *Encyclopedia of Strategic Leadership and Management* drew contributions from over 300 scholars worldwide, reflecting a truly global conversation around leadership and learning in a changing world.

I also take great pride in my long-standing relationship with Dr. John A. Henschke, one of Malcolm Knowles' own doctoral students and a towering figure in his own right. Dr. Henschke has been both a mentor and a friend, and it is with deep gratitude that I acknowledge his contribution of a foreword to this volume. His lifelong dedication to andragogical principles and international education has deeply shaped my thinking and my work.

The inspiration for this work also draws from a career in teaching that spans continents. I have had the distinct honor of teaching in both China and across many states in the United States, including California, Florida, Arizona, and Montana. My classrooms have included doctoral candidates, educational leaders, adult learners, and pre-service teachers—all eager to make sense of the complexities of learning in the 21st century. Across all these settings, a common thread emerged: the desire to understand how technology, when guided by values and vision, can support deeper, more inclusive learning experiences.

This book is the result of ongoing conversations with colleagues, students, institutional leaders, and policymakers from around the world. It is built upon decades of work in instructional leadership, curriculum development, and the integration of andragogical principles in both physical and virtual learning environments. Over time, I began to realize that while AI was gaining traction in the fields of industry, healthcare, and business, its application in education was often misunderstood, oversimplified, or siloed. There was—and still is—a need for thoughtful, ethical, and strategically guided exploration of what AI can actually do to support and uplift teaching and learning.

My intent with this book is not to celebrate technology for its own sake. Rather, it is to invite educators, leaders, and learners into a dialogue about how AI can be used to advance the values we hold most dear: access, inclusion, equity, adaptability, and lifelong learning. I firmly believe that AI tools, when integrated intentionally and reflectively, can serve as catalysts for educational transformation—not only enhancing instructional efficiency, but also deepening human connection and creativity in ways that support the full spectrum of learning.

ORGANIZATION OF THE BOOK

The book is organized into several volumes, each focused on a specific aspect of AI in education—from practical tools and case studies to theoretical frameworks and future-facing models of leadership. The contributors to this work represent a wide range of disciplines and global perspectives. Together, we aim to highlight both the promise and the limitations of AI, always with the understanding that technology must serve human development—not replace it.

Chapter 1: AI-Driven Personalized Learning: Revolutionizing Student-Centered Education

In our opening chapter, we explore the transformative power of artificial intelligence in shaping student-centered education. This contribution delves into how AI technologies—particularly within the frameworks of Education 4.0 and 5.0—are revolutionizing learning through real-time adaptation and personalization of content. Drawing from both extensive literature and empirical data from 317 respondents, the authors illuminate how AI fosters individualized learning experiences, enhances student performance, and boosts satisfaction. However, the chapter does not shy away from the pressing concerns of algorithmic bias, data privacy, and equitable access. Strategic recommendations for ethically grounded AI integration are offered to guide future educational environments toward inclusivity and responsibility.

Chapter 2: Artificial Intelligence and Equal Opportunity in Education

Chapter 2 turns our attention to the imperative of equity in educational access and how AI can serve as both a bridge and a barrier. The authors analyze how AI tools can mitigate disparities caused by geography, disability, socioeconomic status, and linguistic diversity. Through personalized instruction and early identification of learning challenges, AI offers tremendous promise. However, unequal access to technology and embedded algorithmic biases threaten to exacerbate existing inequities. The chapter presents a compelling case for transparent, explainable, and ethically informed AI, while also emphasizing the crucial role of teachers' AI literacy and inclusive policy design in creating truly equitable learning systems.

Chapter 3: Harnessing AI Chatbots in Pre-Service Teacher Education

Focusing on the evolving landscape of teacher education, this chapter examines how AI chatbots like Mizou are being used in the training of pre-service language teachers. Drawing from the experiences of 134 teacher trainees in Vietnam, the authors apply the AI-CITE framework to evaluate the chatbot's impact on areas such as engagement, planning, and pedagogical decision-making. The findings reveal that while chatbots enhance learning design and motivation, they still lack emotional intelligence and contextual sensitivity. This chapter offers thoughtful strategies for incorporating AI tools as supplements—rather than replacements—in teacher training, with a strong emphasis on ethical, culturally aware integration.

Chapter 4: Ensuring Equity and Access for Students with Disabilities

This chapter provides a critical lens into how AI technologies can foster inclusive education for students with disabilities. Highlighting tools like speech-to-text systems, screen readers, and adaptive assessments, the chapter showcases how AI can enhance both accessibility and learning personalization. Yet, it also addresses the complex ethical terrain, including issues of bias, privacy, and infrastructure gaps. Offering actionable strategies—from needs assessments to educator training and collaborative ecosystems—the authors call for inclusive AI policy frameworks and human-centered design that ensure every learner has an equitable opportunity to succeed.

Chapter 5: The New Era of Artificial Intelligence: Empowering Coders, Non-Coders, and Shaping Future Workforce Creativity

As we move further into the digital age, this chapter captures the dynamic role AI plays in reshaping the future of work, particularly in STEM and CTE education. The authors explore how AI tools, from intelligent coding assistants to no-code platforms, democratize access to programming and innovation. With a focus on personalized instruction and lifelong learning, this chapter outlines the importance of preparing students not just for today's technical demands, but for a future where ethical awareness and interdisciplinary agility will define success. It advocates for continuous upskilling and emphasizes collaboration between educators, technologists, and policymakers.

Chapter 6: AI for Academic Research: Transforming the Research Landscape

AI is rapidly transforming the nature of academic inquiry, and this chapter offers a panoramic view of its impact across diverse disciplines. From predictive modeling in STEM to text mining in the humanities, the authors demonstrate how AI augments analysis, discovery, and collaboration. Yet with this power comes responsibility—issues of data transparency, authorship, and bias are scrutinized with rigor. The chapter offers a practical roadmap for researchers and institutions seeking to responsibly integrate AI into their work, promoting a future where AI complements human intellect rather than overshadowing it.

Chapter 7: AI and the Elderly: Empowering Lifelong Learning

In an era of global aging, AI presents new possibilities for supporting education and well-being among older adults. This chapter examines the deployment of AI-driven tools such as virtual assistants, cognitive training apps, and immersive technologies that address challenges like cognitive decline, mobility, and digital exclusion. Emphasizing the social and cognitive benefits of lifelong learning, the chapter also addresses critical ethical and equity concerns. It advocates for inclusive design, policy reform, and intergenerational collaboration to ensure that AI empowers—not marginalizes—elder learners in a rapidly changing educational ecosystem.

Chapter 8: AI and the Future of STEM Education: Transforming Pedagogy, Curriculum, and Workforce Readiness

This chapter reimagines the STEM classroom through the lens of artificial intelligence. By exploring how AI enables adaptive assessments, virtual labs, and individualized learning pathways, the authors reveal a future where pedagogy is both deeply personalized and aligned with industry needs. The discussion spans curriculum design, critical thinking, and innovation, while also acknowledging the barriers to equitable access and ethical use. This forward-thinking chapter underscores AI's potential as a powerful agent for creativity, inclusion, and excellence in STEM education—preparing learners not just for today's jobs but for tomorrow's challenges.

Chapter 9: AI in Adult Education: Transforming Lifelong Learning and Workforce Development

Our final chapter brings the spotlight to adult education and workforce transformation, where AI is catalyzing new pathways for lifelong learning and reskilling. By analyzing adaptive learning systems, intelligent tutoring, and predictive analytics, the authors show how AI can meet the unique demands of adult learners. With an eye on workforce alignment, the chapter examines how AI supports agility and inclusion amid rapid technological change. It calls for ethically guided implementation strategies, stressing that inclusive and accessible design is essential for ensuring that all adults—not just the digitally privileged—benefit from the opportunities of an AI-enhanced world.

Chapter 10: A Comparative Study on Chinese-Indonesian Translation Quality of Three AI-based Translators (Google, Baidu, and DeepL)

Chapter 10 presents a rigorous comparative analysis of three widely used AI-based machine translation platforms—Google Translate, Baidu Translate, and DeepL Translate—within the specific linguistic pairing of Chinese to Indonesian. Employing a mixed-methods approach and drawing from 100 sample translations of HSK vocabulary and business-related content, the study reveals notable variations in translation quality. Google Translate emerged as the most accurate, natural, and faithful system, a result attributed not only to algorithmic superiority but also to extensive user feedback loops in the Indonesian context. This chapter provides essential insight into the capabilities and limitations of neural machine translation and offers a nuanced view of how data-driven optimization and user engagement shape translation outcomes in multilingual education.

Chapter 11: AI In Color: Examining Educational Technology Through a BIPOC Lens

In Chapter 11, we confront the intersection of artificial intelligence and educational equity for BIPOC (Black, Indigenous, and People of Color) communities. This chapter makes the compelling case that AI can become a vehicle for justice, offering tools to disrupt systemic inequities long entrenched in traditional education. Through the lens of culturally responsive pedagogy, the authors explore AI-driven personalization, bias detection, and targeted student support. Yet, they also caution against overlooking data privacy and the replication of bias within AI systems. The chapter invites educators, technologists, and policymakers to reimagine how AI can be harnessed ethically and equitably to ensure that technological innovation advances—not obstructs—racial and educational justice.

Chapter 12: Adaptive Learning Systems: Revolutionizing Student-Centered Education

Chapter 12 explores the power of adaptive learning systems to transform educational experiences into dynamic, personalized journeys. By aligning AI with pedagogical responsiveness, the authors detail how these systems adjust in real-time to learners' progress and preferences, promoting greater engagement and achievement. The chapter covers use cases across diverse educational environments, discusses implementation strategies, and critically addresses challenges such as ethical constraints, digital infrastructure gaps, and equitable access. With actionable recommendations, this chapter provides a roadmap for educators and institutions seeking to responsibly adopt adaptive learning to meet the ever-evolving needs of 21st-century learners.

Chapter 13: Personalized Education in the Age of AI: Innovations and Implications

Chapter 13 delves into the widespread educational shifts ushered in by artificial intelligence, particularly in the domain of personalized learning. The authors synthesize literature and emerging practices to highlight AI's impact on content delivery, pacing, formative assessments, and policymaking. This chapter emphasizes that personalization can elevate inclusivity and student agency while supporting educators in crafting more effective instructional strategies. However, it also calls attention to the pressing need for ethical safeguards concerning algorithmic fairness, data privacy, and access equity. This comprehensive discussion equips stakeholders with a thoughtful lens on how to align personalization with ethical responsibility in educational innovation.

Chapter 14: Speech Recognition Tools in Education: Enhancing Accessibility

Chapter 14 offers a focused exploration of speech recognition technologies as tools for advancing educational accessibility. Highlighting applications for students with disabilities, non-native speakers, and learners with reading or writing challenges, this chapter emphasizes the inclusive power of converting spoken language into written text. It also considers benefits for educators through time-saving feedback mechanisms. Despite its promise, the chapter calls for careful attention to cost, accuracy, and data confidentiality to ensure the responsible and scalable use of speech recognition systems. This contribution reinforces the value of inclusive design in educational technologies.

Chapter 15: AI-Driven Coding: Transforming Education and Industry

Chapter 15 investigates the transformative influence of AI in the realm of coding education and software development. Tools such as GitHub Copilot and AI-powered tutoring platforms are reshaping how programming is taught and learned, offering real-time support, error correction, and scaffolded instruction. This chapter examines how these tools benefit novice coders while also interrogating their impact on critical thinking, creativity, and problem-solving. Through empirical evidence and industry case studies, the chapter highlights both opportunities and concerns, including algorithmic bias and accessibility. It offers a balanced and informed view of how AI is reshaping the digital literacy landscape across education and industry.

Chapter 16: Artificial Intelligence in Personalized Education: Revolutionizing Learning Paths and Student Engagement

Chapter 16 presents a sweeping survey of how artificial intelligence is redefining personalized education. Exploring intelligent tutoring systems, recommendation engines, real-time feedback mechanisms, and reinforcement learning, the chapter underscores AI's capacity to craft individualized learning paths. Drawing from current trends and forward-looking technologies like augmented reality and advanced analytics, it explores both opportunities and implementation challenges. Privacy concerns, technical complexity, and algorithmic fairness emerge as key issues. This chapter is an essential contribution for those envisioning a future where education is deeply personalized, data-informed, and ethically attuned.

Chapter 17: Transformative AI Tools for Inclusive and Holistic Learning Environments

Chapter 17 emphasizes the human side of AI integration in education, particularly in addressing diversity, equity, and inclusion (DEI). Drawing on real-world case studies from institutions like Georgia Tech and the University of Michigan, the authors show how AI-driven platforms can create psychologically safe, culturally competent learning spaces. This chapter highlights the role of AI in building holistic environments that support both academic and emotional intelligence. Ethical concerns such as data privacy and digital equity are given thoughtful attention, with a consistent call to preserve human-centered values in technology-enhanced learning design.

Chapter 18: Chatbots and AI Tutors: Enhancing Student Engagement and Learning Management

Concluding this section, Chapter 18 explores the integration of chatbots and AI tutors in India's evolving educational landscape. These tools, powered by natural language processing, are increasingly vital in addressing student queries, offering instant feedback, and fostering continuous engagement. The chapter details how such systems enhance both teaching and learning by supporting individualized instruction and automating administrative tasks. It also examines how these technologies are redefining student-teacher dynamics and contributing to more scalable and efficient educational ecosystems. This final chapter is a powerful testament to AI's role in reshaping global education through context-specific, learner-centric innovation.

CONCLUSION

It is no coincidence that this work includes contributions from educators and thought leaders across continents. We are in a moment of global transformation, and our responses must be equally global. AI is not a trend—it is an inflection point. And the choices we make now, as educators and institutions, will determine whether we amplify opportunity or exacerbate inequality. This book is a humble offering in service of the former.

I would like to express my deepest gratitude to my co-authors, contributors, reviewers, and institutional partners who have supported this project. Your insights and commitment have shaped every chapter. I also want to thank the students and doctoral candidates I've mentored over the years—you continue to inspire me with your questions, your resilience, and your determination to make education more inclusive and more effective for future generations.

I also wish to extend my heartfelt appreciation to IGI Global, the publisher of this volume, for their enduring commitment to scholarly excellence and their support in bringing this multi-volume work to fruition. Their dedication to disseminating transformative research in education and leadership has been instrumental throughout this process.

Special thanks are also due to the many reviewers whose critical feedback helped refine the clarity, depth, and coherence of the chapters included. Your thoughtful engagement enriched the work in ways too numerous to count.

To the global network of contributors who lent their voices, perspectives, and expertise—thank you. Your diverse insights and dedication to educational advancement have shaped this book into a truly international and collaborative effort.

Finally, I wish to express deep gratitude to the university libraries around the world—including Stanford University, New York University, and Princeton University—that continue to catalog and share my work. Your support ensures that knowledge remains accessible, visible, and impactful for future generations of learners and researchers.

To the readers: whether you are a faculty member rethinking your curriculum, a dean or provost leading systemic change, a policymaker designing new frameworks, or a student exploring the frontiers of digital learning—I hope you find in these pages not only knowledge, but encouragement. This is your invitation to engage, to question, and to lead. The future of education is not just about digital tools or predictive algorithms—it's about the people who wield them with wisdom and care.

In closing, I offer this book as both a scholarly resource and a starting point for transformation. May it spark ideas, challenge assumptions, and serve as a guide for all who believe in the power of education to shape a better, more equitable world—one learner, one classroom, one innovation at a time.

This book, *AI, Personalization, Equity, and the Future of Learning* is part of the *Transformative AI Tools for Use in Education and Learning* series. It focuses on the practical integration of AI into curriculum, instruction, and assessment. Drawing on global case studies, emerging tools, and pedagogical models, this book highlights how educators and researchers are applying AI to reimagine the teaching and learning experience in classrooms, training programs, and higher education environments.

Viktor Wang
California State University, San Bernardino, USA

Chapter 1
AI-Driven Personalized Learning:
Revolutionizing Student-Centered Education

Patcha Bhujanga Rao
https://orcid.org/0000-0003-4736-8497
Jain University, Bangalore, India

G. Shrijith
Mcom (IFA), School of Commerce, Jain University, Bangalore, India

Khushi Desai
School of Commerce, Jain University, Bangalore, India

Muneer Ahmad
School of CS & IT, Jain University, Bangalore, India

Nasratullah Nejat
School of CS & IT, Jain University, Bangalore, India

ABSTRACT

The incorporation of artificial intelligence (AI) in learning environments has caused a significant shift in pedagogical practices, culminating in the development of learning systems that are adaptive as well as personalized. This research investigates the paradigm shift and explores how artificial intelligence enable real-time customization of learning trajectories and content to the specific requirements of individual learners. This research is based on the Education 4.0 and Education 5.0 paradigms. An exhaustive analysis of conceptual and empirical literature is supplemented with primary data collected from 317 respondents measuring the effects of artificial intelligence's on student learning, performance, and satisfaction towards personalized learning. The findings focus on a multitude of concerns including algorithmic prejudice, data confidentiality, and accessibility in equal amounts. The research provides strategic recommendations for incorporating ethical artificial intelligence models into future learning environments in the area of AI-based learning.

DOI: 10.4018/979-8-3373-5097-4.ch001

INTRODUCTION

The convergence of pedagogic change and electronic technology is now affecting a sensational transformation in the learning environment.

Artificial intelligence (AI) is at the center to guide the reformation of education with the facility for having learning experience customized especially for individuals.

The education system has forever been limited by standard and uniform curricula and teaching styles which cannot hold the varied learning styles, pace, and needs of learners. The solution to this has been increased use of personalized learning models among teachers and schools. These models seek to tailor training, content, and feedback to the unique individual learner.

Whereas customized learning has long been an education dream, using artificial intelligence made it a realizable option at scale only within recent years. AI may study students' learning patterns, dynamically adapt content, and provide customized paths that enhance motivation and learning outcomes. This is realized through the employment of machine learning algorithms, smart tutoring systems, natural language processing, and predictive analytics. This convergence is a transition from Education 3.0, typified by collective, web-driven education, to Education 4.0 and 5.0, wherein intelligent systems take part in active decision-making, curriculum design, and real-time individualization.

Education 4.0 corresponds to Industry 4.0's main aims through the support of lifelong learning, adaptive skills, and evidence-based education by the use of emerging technologies.

Education 5.0 progresses by focusing on humanistic AI assimilation to enhance emotional intelligence, creativity, and global education. For such perspectives, artificial intelligence is not only a tool but also a teaching companion that maximizes the learning outcomes and redefines the student-teacher relationship and schools.

Artificial intelligence-enabled personalized learning creates gargantuan hurdles when it comes to its implementation, even when it has the potential to transform. Solving ethical use of data issues, equitable access to digital resources, and algorithmic bias will be crucial to protect the use of technology so that it does not isolate but elevates and empowers the people. This paper addresses both the promise and threat artificial intelligence (AI) has in student-centered education to solve these issues. This study tries to shed light on the real-world implications, advantages, and difficulties of AI-driven personalized learning based on a comprehensive literature review and hypothesis-driven empirical study with 317 participants.

The goal is to empower educators, policymakers, and technologists dedicated to building an inclusive and prosperous education enhanced by artificial intelligence through reflective ideas.

CONCEPTUAL FRAMEWORK

Conceptual framework of this research is based on the convergence of three vital pillars: the application of artificial intelligence (AI) in learning, the principle of customized learning, and the learning paradigms of Education 4.0 and Education 5.0.

Together, these elements provide a model that demonstrates how artificial intelligence technology can support student-centered learning by facilitating the personalization of teaching to each student's unique preferences, pace, and abilities.

Artificial Intelligence in Education

An artificial intelligence (AI) system is a computer that can simulate human intelligence through learning, reasoning, and problem-solving abilities.Artificial intelligence (AI) is implemented in education as adaptive learning systems, intelligent tutoring systems (ITS), learning analytics, predictive modeling, and natural language processing (NLP). Gligorea et al. (2023) say that these systems can give students immediate personalized learning experience by assessing the data of the students such as behavioral indicators, performance indicators, and engagement actions. AI encompasses far more than simply presenting content in the classroom. Mahmoud and Sørensen (2024) describe it as a feedback cycle that can respond to student input and forecast future needs, thus enabling teachers to respond in advance to develop tailored lesson plans. This ability to adapt dynamically is the foundation for smart education systems that contribute to increased engagement, improved performance, and readiness for lifelong learning.

Personalized Learning Theory

Followers of the personalized learning theory claim that students are presented with increased scholastic success whenever lessons are tailored to fit their respective strengths, strengths, weaknesses, interests, and learning dispositions. Choice, student agency, and multiple pathways form the pillars of personalized learning which derive their strength from constructivist and student-centered paradigms.

Hashim et al. (2022) affirm that AI made it possible for personalized learning to become a data-driven, scale-able, and realizable phenomenon.

The related features encapsulate the most important aspects of AI-powered personalized learning:

1. Personalization of activities and content according to learner profiles
2. Self-directed learning paths that advance at the pace of the student
3. Feedback loops that react to encourage mastery learning
4. Ongoing formative assessment to provide timely support

By integrating AI with learning theory personalized learning allows one to build a predictive and adaptive model of learning that boosts motivation, retention, and academic performance.

Education 4.0 and 5.0 as Structural Paradigms

The integration of digital technologies into the learning space is what sets Education 4.0 apart from other methods of education. The technologies involved are artificial intelligence, the internet of things, big data, and cloud computing.

More specifically, it supports education that is competence-based, virtual, collaborative, and adaptable learning environments. Artificial intelligence is leveraged within this paradigm in order to generate learning experiences which are immersive, scalable, and outcomes-driven (Rane et al., 2023). Such a paradigm has been coined as the experiential learning paradigm.

Furthermore, Education 5.0, which emphasizes ethics, diversity, and the capacity to feel empathy, is developed upon this basis. Consequently, it puts human values at the forefront of innovation in technology and leads the construction of artificial intelligence systems that consider the diversity of learners, protect confidentiality of information, and encourage the development of socioemotional skills. Application of artificial intelligence in Education 5.0 goes beyond the level of a facilitator; it is a co-educator that not only supports the development of the individual as a complete being but also reduces the negative effects of algorithmic processes to the maximum extent possible. The merging of these paradigms, according to which artificial intelligence (AI) can and ought to be applied to build equity, participation, and critical thinking in a world dominated by digital technology, reinforces the conceptual underpinning of this study. These paradigms proclaim that AI can and ought to be applied to tailor education, but also to build equity, participation, and critical thinking.

THEORETICAL FOUNDATIONS OF PERSONALIZED LEARNING DRIVEN BY ARTIFICIAL INTELLIGENCE

Educational psychology, constructivist learning theories, and intelligent system design are the theoretical foundations of AI-driven personalized learning. This section provides a more in-depth analysis of the key concepts that underlie the creation and application of AI-driven personalization in educational settings, with far-reaching implications for the research subject: Personalized learning, driven by artificial intelligence, is revolutionizing student-centered education.

Developed Constructivist Theory Of Learning

Constructivism forms the core of personalized learning, a theory which argues that learners should actively construct information for themselves instead of acquiring it passively. Jean Piaget (2013) spoke of cognitive development stages and argued that learning must be related to the learner's existing developmental stage. During this time, Lev Vygotsky (1978) came up with the idea of the Zone of Proximal Development (ZPD), which refers to the gap between an individual's independent ability and his or her capacity for doing so with guidance. It accomplishes this with the offering of scaffolded aid through personalization systems that rely on artificial intelligence, in like fashion to an educator within the ZPD.

As an instance, adaptive programs are able to measure a learner's existing amount of skill level and then proceed to challenge the learner to break past it slightly. It does this with the offering of materials or guidance that is reflective of Vygotsky's theory of learning.

Theory of Mastery Learning

Benjamin Bloom created the Mastery Learning hypothesis in 1968, which focuses on the importance of individualized feedback and pace.

Bloom's theory suggests that almost all students can learn effectively if they are provided with sufficient time and individualized instruction.

To mimic this idea, artificial intelligence constantly evaluates the degree of knowledge that students have and immediately provides corrections before moving on to new topics. Examples of technologies that illustrate mastery learning in practice include Carnegie Learning's MATHia and Knewton Alta. These technologies allow students to progress only after they have ascertained that they have reached a degree of understanding that is sufficient.

Theory of Multiple Intelligences

Individuals are able to exhibit a range of intelligences, including linguistic, logical-mathematical, spatial, bodily-kinesthetic, musical, interpersonal, intrapersonal, and naturalistic intelligences, as per Howard **Gardner's theory in 1983**. Most traditional training tends to emphasize only a limited number of them.

Artificial intelligence (AI) deepens the personalization of learning through the tailoring of the format of content to the main intelligences of a learner. For instance, abundant infographic courses can be presented to learners who are visual, while AI chatbots based on conversation, like Khanmigo, might be more effective for verbal learners. Gardner's model is exactly in sync with this variety, making education more inclusive and interactive.

Learning Analytics Theory

George Siemens and Phil Long (2011) presented the idea of Learning Analytics, where pupil data is measured and analyzed to improve learning. Artificial intelligence systems are designed to function in line with this principle, which involves data collection on learner behavior, engagement patterns, and assessment results to suggest individualized interventions and forecast performance.

Teachers can monitor the progress of their students in real time using dashboards that are integrated with artificial intelligence. This allows them to create an education paradigm that is data-driven and aligned with the basic principles of learning analytics theory.

Heutagogy

Lisa Marie Blaschke (2012) developed the theory of heutagogy, otherwise known as self-determined learning. Blaschke's work went beyond the limitations of pedagogy and andragogy. Under the heutagogical model, which has a focus on autonomy, the development of competence and responsiveness, learners must have a capacity to decide what they learn and how they learn it.

Artificial intelligence (AI) supports heutagogical learning through enabling students to choose their own learning routes, explore subjects based on their interest, and engage with resources as and when they want. Two such platforms that are driven by artificial intelligence and offer flexibility are EdApp and Duolingo. These platforms shift the focus of control from the teacher to the student.

Cognitive Load Theory

In 1988, John Sweller's first presented Cognitive Load Theory. The theory suggests that instructional design needs to be developed in such a way that the working memory of the learner is not overloaded. Artificial intelligence programs are bound by this principle through the moderation of the degree of difficulty of the information, presentation of bite-sized lessons, and the provision of just-in-time cues. This helps in the improvement of learning effectiveness and the elimination of unnecessary cognitive effort. This is especially useful in contexts that require careful information calibration, like mobile learning and microlearning, where attention is short and content needs to be continuously tracked. For instance, on page 13.7 of Rose and Meyer's 2002 book, "Universal Design for Learning,"

David Rose and Anne Meyer developed the Universal Design for Learning (UDL) framework in 2002 with the objective of ensuring that education systems are available to all students regardless of their origin or disability. UDL encourages a wide range of approaches for students to take in, represent, and express themselves.

Artificial intelligence systems can dynamically adjust information in real time for students with particular needs, thus automating and scaling the implementation of Universal Design for Learning (UDL) principles. This can be done by simplifying language, translating instructions, or text-to-speech conversion.

Table 1. Synthesis of Theories into AI-Driven Personalization

Theory	Key Contribution	AI Implementation
Constructivism (Piaget, Vygotsky)	Active learning and ZPD	Adaptive content scaffolding
Mastery Learning (Bloom)	Individualized pacing and feedback	AI checks for mastery before progression
Multiple Intelligences (Gardner, 2011)	Diverse learner strengths	Multimodal content delivery
Learning Analytics (Siemens)	Data-informed instruction	Real-time performance dashboards
Heutagogy (Blaschke)	Learner autonomy and choice	AI-guided personalized learning paths
Cognitive Load (Sweller)	Managing memory overload	Bite-sized, simplified adaptive content
UDL (Rose & Meyer)	Inclusivity and accessibility	Real-time content transformation for diverse learners

Source: Compiled by the researcher

Figure 1. Conceptual mapping of theories, technologies, and outcomes in AI-driven personalized learning

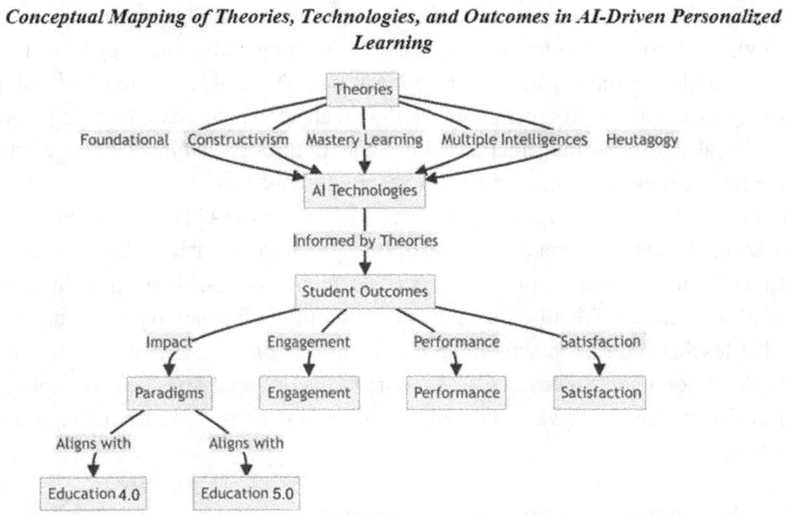

Source: *Developed by the researcher using SmartDraw.*

REVIEW OF LITERATURE

Evolution of Personalized Learning with AI

Thanks to the use of artificial intelligence (AI), the course of development of personalized learning has also undergone a radical shift. Constructivist philosophy formed the foundation upon which the first concept of personalized learning was built, which in the beginning was conceived as a teaching methodology centered on the learners themselves. The overall objective of this strategy was to customize education to the specific nature of every single individual learner, which included the learning objectives, interests, and capability of the student. But when they wanted to do it on a large scale, teachers were confronted with operations challenges that rendered it impossible for them to do. An emerging sequence of innovations in artificial intelligence, particularly in intelligent systems and machine learning, has enabled personalized learning to become more viable and effective.

According to Gligorea et al. (2023), adaptive learning systems are now able to adapt dynamically to students' needs by modifying teaching material, sequence, and tests dynamically in real time depending on real-time analysis of performance.

When the technology initially came out, only educators were permitted to use it. By giving students the timely support that is adapted to meet their unique learning needs and areas of deficiency, the implementation of the technologies not only enhances the amount of interaction that students have with one another, but also improves academic achievement.

Key Technologies Driving Personalized Learning

The creation of artificial intelligence technologies has made it possible for more personalized learning experiences for users. Machine learning computer programs are designed to sweep through large sets of data for patterns, forecast learning paths, and suggest action. This is a depiction of an ideal computer-mediated feedback loop. Natural Language Processing (NLP) is a technology that enables the creation of intelligent chatbots, automated writing graders, and interactive virtual assistants that interact with students through natural language interaction. Examples include chatbots, writing graders, and virtual assistants.

Smart Tutoring Systems (ITS), such as Carnegie Learning's MATHia, can simulate advanced decision-making methods a teacher would utilize. They provide information, direction, and remarks customized to the user based on their current performance in real-time. In addition, learning analytics platforms are capable of collecting and presenting information about students in such a manner that teachers can learn actionable information in order to enhance their pedagogical approaches. Mahmoud and Sørensen (2024) contend that by applying such technology, one is able to scrutinize students' behavior in detail, hence moving towards a responsive and dynamic learning culture.

Pros of AI-Powered Personalized Learning

Applying artificial intelligence (AI) in schools has had transformative impacts that extend beyond automating tasks. As a case, these advantages have brought greater depth engagement, more adaptive instruction, and equitable access. In what follows, we will examine further the numerous ways artificial intelligence (AI) assists students, teachers, and the tools used by schools.

Motivated and Participatory Students

One of the most discussed benefits of AI in education is the capability of artificial intelligence to significantly boost the number of students participating and being motivated. Artificial intelligence systems personalize information according to learners' interests, levels of skill, and pace, rather than the conventional "one-size-fits-all" approach to teaching. This results in greater cognitive engagement in the long run. The International Society for Technology in Education (ISTE) published a report in 2023 that discovered that AI-supported platforms resulted in a 37% increase in active student engagement, particularly in blended and distance learning environments. Real-time adaptive comments, topic suggestions, and encouragement prompts are provided by services like Khan Academy's "Khanmigo," a teaching assistant powered by artificial intelligence. These tools assist students in maintaining their concentration and reducing isolation feelings they can get in online environments. Learners don't simply absorb material passively; they also actively co-create it by engaging with content that suits their own learning journey (Cukurova, M, **2020**).

Customized Learning

Artificial intelligence technology allows learning environments to be tailored to each individual's style of learning, whether that is auditory, visual, kinesthetic, or written. Through examining factors such as the number of times a quiz is attempted, how long it takes, and how frequently errors are made, AI programs can alter information presentation and level of difficulty to meet the needs of every student.

Personalization Is Particularly Useful In Online Learning

This form of differentiation has performed particularly well here. For example, AI-based systems such as Squirrel AI in China examine student profiles and adjust learning habits on the fly, resulting in 30–50% improved learning results (Huang et al., 2025). Artificial intelligence (AI) reduces brain load by organizing information into bite-sized and engaging micro-units, which makes these environments particularly valuable for neurodivergent students, like individuals with attention-deficit/hyperactivity disorder (ADHD) or dyslexia. Intelligent action and input in real-time have been established. AI-powered platforms are revolutionizing the way tests are being administered since they provide students with instant, initial feedback and monitor their progress in real time.

This allows the teacher or the system to provide immediate "just-in-time interventions" to the students before they get behind in the work. These can involve shifting the subject, re-teaching a lesson, or assigning them additional work to complete. Rane et al. (2023) established that personalizing artificial intelligence was closely related to academic success, particularly in STEM courses. Step-by-step directions on such platforms as Carnegie Learning's MATHia assist students in developing confidence as well as competency as they master solving problems.

AI testing tools also enable early identification of at-risk students, which assists with tailored solutions that address the particular issues these students are experiencing. Another Agrawal et al. (2021) study states that predictive analytics are employed by tools such as Knewton Alta to inform teachers when and how to intervene. This improves both the teaching and the learning.

Differentiated Instruction

One of the most groundbreaking aspects of AI is that it has the potential to assist a large number of individuals in learning very personalized methods. Individualized instruction was difficult in the old school system due to the fact that it required a lot of effort and was difficult to implement with a large number of individuals. This issue can be addressed by artificial intelligence by implementing programs that modify the paths to learning for thousands of individuals simultaneously.

For instance, Squirrel AI can tailor lessons to over two million children in China with virtually no human intervention. This is a new benchmark for low-cost and scalable school systems (Huang et al., 2025).

Where there are limited resources, there are not many teachers for each student, or where there are issues regarding educational justice, this skill is particularly crucial.

Data-Driven Decision Making for Teachers

Teachers are not and will not be replaced by AI. AI can assist by offering real-time data tools, identifying areas of knowledge, and estimating the likelihood of a student's success in school. Teachers can then use these tools to maximize their lesson planning, provide more customized feedback, and concentrate on supporting students who struggle to learn.

Transitioning from reactive to proactive approaches is facilitated by wisdom generated by AI. The generated wisdom provides instructors data-driven feedback on how they can make decisions more effectively. Through enhanced classroom insights obtained by applying artificial intelligence, educators in the UK who use Century Tech report decreased routine tasks to perform, enhanced time management, and more involved students (Cukurova, M et al., 2020).

Encouraging New Methods Experimentation

For instance, AI enables teachers to experiment with flipped classes, inquiry learning, and gamification without sacrificing organization or record-keeping. This is one of the ways AI facilitates novel pedagogies. Teachers are able to free up more time for teaching, collaborating with other teachers, and innovating in teaching now that adjustable pace and performance tracking are handled by AI systems.

Smart classrooms, such as those at Singapore's Nanyang Technological University, demonstrate that individuals are experimenting with new things. There are AI applications in these classrooms that allow instructors to create a learning environment that is student-centered and considers the feelings of the student, along with customized quizzes and automated feedback loops (Huang et al., 2021).

Ethical and Practical Challenges

The learning capacity of artificial intelligence is huge; however, there are various ethical and pragmatic issues that have to be acknowledged and addressed. Since the harvesting and utilization of sensitive student data need to comply with strict regulatory and ethical guidelines, data privacy is of most importance. Algorithmic bias, or when artificial intelligence algorithms learn to be biased by being trained on biased data, is another serious issue. Software thus has the ability of inadvertently making existing inequalities concrete, excluding off-representative student groups partially along the way. AI-optimized learning's potential is not utilized by learners who learn from poverty-stricken contexts because their computer infrastructure availability and network access are skewed. There is yet another, parallel exacerbator of this condition: a digital divide expanding things. It further reshapes the roles of teachers today.

Artificial intelligence doesn't have to replace teachers but instead need to shift from knowledge disseminators to facilitators of individual learning environments. That entails assessing data insights and coaching learners through adaptive learning paths. The success of artificial intelligence (AI) in learning depends on ethical foresight, accessible design, and building educator capacity, underpinned by technological innovation, contends Hashim et al. (2022).

Integration into Educational Paradigms

The Education 4.0 and Education 5.0 models provide healthy perspectives from which one can assess the use of artificial intelligence for individualized learning. Education 4.0 captures the crossing of digital technologies such as artificial intelligence, cloud computing, and big data analytics in order to attain learning capabilities such as critical thinking, creativity, and teamwork. Artificial intelligence enhances accessibility, flexibility, and student-centricity from this. Conversely, Education 5.0 places humanizing technology at its center. It discusses a future era where artificial intelligence will join human intelligence as students will be able to learn empathy, sense of morals, and emotional strength. Education 5.0, as Rane et al. (2023) conceptualize it, promotes inclusive, equitable, and emotionally intelligent learning spaces where AI is not employed as a tool but as an ethical partner. These paradigms both emphasize collectively the shared necessity of human-sensitive design and technological expertise in determining the way artificial intelligence will influence education.

Research Gaps and Study Rationale

Even though the extensive work of recent studies on the technical potential and instructional uses of artificial intelligence in teaching has yielded extensive insights, some significant research gaps exist that deserve consideration. Empirical research is often focused either on system development or student results, due to the lack of research that employs conceptual frameworks, thorough literature reviews, and vast primary data collection. Empirical studies researching the relationships between artificial intelligence personalization and student satisfaction, performance, and engagement are scarce, especially those that investigate these interactions using genuine data in a rigorous manner. This paper endeavours to fill these deficiencies by an extensive literature review coupled with an empirical systematic study involving 317 participants. The region is advantaged by incorporating the perspectives of Education 4.0 and 5.0 in the conceptual model, measuring key performance indicators, and providing feasible means of eliminating ethical risks and implementation issues.

Supporting Cultural and Cognitive Diversity in AI Personalization

In advancing AI-driven personalized learning, it is essential to consider the diverse cultural and neurocognitive profiles of learners. While existing platforms have made progress in supporting students with ADHD and dyslexia, a more inclusive approach would extend personalization to encompass learners with a broader range of neurodiverse conditions, such as autism spectrum disorders, sensory integration challenges, or executive functioning differences. AI systems capable of offering multimodal content delivery, sensory customization (e.g., adjustable visuals, speech modulation), and flexible pacing can play a pivotal role in meeting these learners' needs.

Additionally, AI holds the potential to enhance culturally responsive pedagogy by incorporating multilingual capabilities, culturally relevant case examples, and adaptive narratives that reflect learners' lived experiences. However, achieving this goal requires deliberate design choices, including the use of inclusive training datasets, ethical algorithm development, and collaboration with educators from diverse sociocultural contexts. Embedding such culturally and cognitively responsive features not only fosters equity but also aligns AI-enhanced education with the broader values of Education 5.0—human-centeredness, empathy, and social inclusion.

CASE STUDIES AND REAL-WORLD IMPLEMENTATIONS

The widespread adoption of artificial intelligence-based personalized learning systems has transformed education delivery on every front.

Along with demonstrating the ways in which artificial intelligence could enhance education flexibility, student activity, and scholastic accomplishment, such in-practice executions also exhibit constraints in terms of context associated with infrastructure, privacy, and instruction. This chapter includes in-depth case studies from the United States, China, the United Kingdom, Singapore, and other international higher education systems. This chapter is intended to demonstrate the diversity and potential of artificial intelligence in customized education.

Carnegie Learning's MATHia – United States

The Carnegie Learning-developed MATHia platform is one of the first models of intelligent tutoring systems available in secondary education. MATHia is a product of nearly two decades of research at Carnegie Mellon University. It applies cognitive models to simulate human instruction and includes immediate scaffolding that is customized according to the answers of individual students. The platform continuously adjusts the concepts, pace, and complexity of the information to create an interactive learning cycle that is personalized and geared towards mastering the material.

A longitudinal analysis conducted by the RAND Corporation (Pane et al., 2015) indicated considerable improvements in the proficiency of algebra, particularly among children from economically disadvantaged backgrounds, after MATHia was used in public schools. The data dashboard feature of the platform enabled teachers to create evidence-based interventions, thus reducing the likelihood of student dropout and facilitating equitable growth. The success of MATHia shows the potential of artificial intelligence to simultaneously address fairness and greatness in the K–12 educational setting.

Squirrel AI – China

China's Squirrel AI has been seen as one of the most comprehensive and scalable adaptive learning systems in the world. Squirrel AI, based on sophisticated deep learning and knowledge tracing algorithms, can spot a student's areas of weakness with a small set of diagnostic questions and then develop a tailored learning path based on the student's needs. By combining emotional recognition and cognitive fatigue measurement, the system can potentially adapt both the intensity of the session and the type of information, thus going beyond simple content adaptation.

Huang et al., 2025 indicated that Squirrel AI achieved learning efficiency gains of as much as fifty percent. This was made possible by students achieving core curricular targets in a significantly shorter period than in traditional classroom environments. A total of approximately two million students have been impacted by the deployment of the system in more than two thousand schools. The steep climb shows how the combination of commercial EdTech innovation and strong government backing for artificial intelligence is inducing dramatic transformations in national education systems.

Century Tech - United Kingdom

Century Tech develops an artificial intelligence platform constructed using neuroscientific methods that facilitates adaptive learning in secondary and tertiary education levels in the United Kingdom. The site has an end-to-end learning process that has the capacity to adjust in real time via diagnostic testing, micro-learning modules, and cognitive load management. Schools, as a result of the COVID-19, were compelled to adopt distance learning, which increased the popularity of Century Tech.

Cukurova, M et al., (2020) explains that students who used Century Tech had fewer instances of teacher burnout, greater learner autonomy, and greater variation in classes with students of varying abilities. The analytics dashboard gave instructors the chance to find miscommunications and make strategic interventions, which meant better performance among teachers as well as students being more empowered. This demonstrates the potential of collaborative learning by humans and AI.

Nanyang Technological University's Smart Learning Environment – Singapore

Nanyang Technological University (NTU) of Singapore was successful in fully developing an integrated Smart Learning Environment (SLE) that best reflects the integration of artificial intelligence into the higher education system.

Strategic Learning Environment (SLE) leverages technology such as artificial intelligence chatbots, emotion-sensitive facial recognition, adaptive tests, and personalized recommendation systems for reading material and assignments.

Huang et al. (2021) demonstrated that SLE was effectively deployed in NTU's engineering and computer science faculties. Students received a greater degree of active engagement, emotional support, and tailored pacing, leading to greater retention and satisfaction. The teachers received immediate feedback on the performance and well-being of the students, illustrating how artificial intelligence can be employed to enhance wholistic learning experiences outside the classroom.

Knewton Alta – Global Higher Education

The Knewton Alta system is an AI-powered adaptive learning platform widely used in post-secondary education, particularly for gateway math, chemistry, and statistics courses. The platform facilitates mastery learning by changing information dynamically according to students' immediate responses and confidence levels.The Knewton Alta analytics give teachers clear, actionable insights into the ideas that trouble students so they can implement targeted interventions at scale.

Agrawal et al. (2021) did a study with several universities and found that deployment of Knewton Alta led to increased course completion rates, student satisfaction, as well as minimized performance gaps between at-risk students.The system is especially effective in community institutions, where the teaching support is sometimes less, thus enhancing the role of artificial intelligence as a pedagogical leveller.

IBM Watson Education – Ethical Reflections in AI Deployment

United States school districts have piloted the IBM Watson Education system, whose virtual teaching tools and recommendation systems based on artificial intelligence are utilized.

The pilot experiences have given rise to monumental ethical issues which must be confronted.

Holmes, H., & Burgess, G. (2022), whose case information was drawn from different implementations are seen to cite students and parents in their report grumbling against algorithmic transparency in cases where AI suggestions went against the teacher's opinions.

This is yet another instance of the necessity for clear data rules and transparent AI.

Whereas artificial intelligence does have great personalization potential, its use and application depend upon the building of trust within a moral framework of governance and an open dialogue with all stakeholders on board.

Table 2. Comparative Table: Global AI Implementations in Education

Country / Platform	AI Technology	Educational Focus	Challenges Addressed	Outcomes / Observations
China / Squirrel AI	Deep learning, knowledge tracing, emotion detection	K–12, adaptive learning	High student-teacher ratios; uneven teaching quality	Achieved up to 50% learning efficiency gains; rapid national scaling
USA / MATHia	Cognitive modeling, intelligent tutoring	Middle & high school math (Algebra)	Low proficiency in foundational STEM; dropout prevention	Improved algebra scores; enhanced teacher targeting via dashboards
UK / Century Tech	Learning analytics, microlearning, cognitive load models	Secondary and tertiary education	Teacher burnout; ability variance among students	Reduced administrative workload; improved learner autonomy
Singapore / NTU Smart Learning	Facial recognition, AI chatbots, adaptive assessments	University-level STEM courses	Engagement in large lectures; emotional disconnect in online learning	Increased retention and satisfaction; personalized support integration
Global / Knewton Alta	Predictive analytics, adaptive mastery learning	Higher education (math, chemistry, statistics)	At-risk student identification; unequal support in community colleges	Higher course completion; reduced performance gaps

Source: Researcher's Compilation

CONCEPTUAL FRAMEWORK OF AI-DRIVEN LEARNING IN THE CONTEXT OF EDUCATION 4.0 AND 5.0

According to the principles of the Education 4.0 and 5.0 paradigms, this conceptual diagram illustrates how AI enables the interconnection of essential components in educational settings.

Based on the model, the AI systems are the direct cause of the results measured by engagement, performance, and satisfaction; the latter ones in turn depend on the independent variable of AI systems. Accessibility serves as a mediating variable essential for bridging the knowledge gap of the effects of AI technology on learning. Technology equality and convenience are formulated to be what is defined for this achievement. The Ethical Considerations are included as part of the model in order to cover moderating and context effects such as algorithmic bias, privacy issues with data, and digital equity. This helps shape the way AI and accessibility affect learning outcomes.

This model can be employed to gain further insight into how emerging technologies can be utilized in an ethical and inclusive manner to enhance learner-centered education.

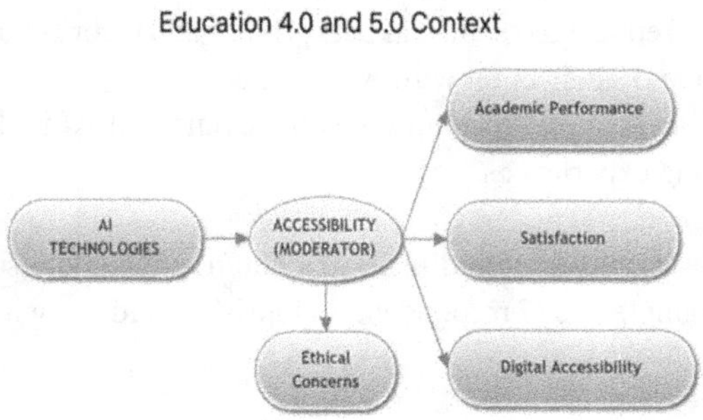

Source: Researcher's Compilation

Source: *Developed by the researcher using SmartDraw.*

RESEARCH OBJECTIVES AND HYPOTHESES

In alignment with the conceptual framework and literature review, this study seeks to investigate the tangible impact of Artificial Intelligence (AI) on personalized learning within contemporary educational paradigms. The overarching aim is to evaluate how AI-driven systems influence student engagement, satisfaction, and academic performance, and to identify any mediating ethical or technological challenges.

Research Objectives

1. To examine the influence of AI technologies on learner engagement in personalized learning environments.
2. To assess the relationship between AI-driven personalized learning and academic performance.
3. To evaluate learner satisfaction with AI-powered educational systems.
4. To explore the ethical and practical challenges in implementing AI-driven personalized learning.
5. To provide evidence-based recommendations for optimizing AI integration in Education 4.0 and 5.0 settings.

Hypotheses Formulation

Based on the conceptual foundation and research objectives, the following hypotheses have been proposed for empirical testing:

H1: AI-driven personalized learning systems significantly enhance student engagement compared to traditional learning methods.
H2: There is a positive relationship between the use of AI-based adaptive learning platforms and improved academic performance.
H3: Students report higher satisfaction levels in AI-enhanced personalized learning environments than in conventional educational settings.
H4: Perceived ethical risks, such as data privacy and algorithmic bias, negatively influence student trust and satisfaction with AI systems.
H5: Digital accessibility mediates the effectiveness of AI in delivering equitable personalized learning experiences.

These hypotheses will be tested using quantitative methods, supported by data collected from a purposive sample of 317 respondents comprising students with exposure to AI-integrated learning platforms.

RESEARCH METHODOLOGY

To achieve the outlined objectives and empirically test the hypotheses, a quantitative research design was adopted. This section details the methodological procedures, including research design, sample selection, instrument development, data collection, and analytical techniques employed in this study.

RESEARCH DESIGN

This study employs a descriptive and hypothesis-testing research design, leveraging cross-sectional survey methodology to gather insights from learners engaged with AI-powered educational platforms. The research design is well-suited to explore associations between AI use and its impact on engagement, performance, and satisfaction.

POPULATION AND SAMPLE

The population for this study includes university-level students who have experienced AI-integrated personalized learning systems, such as adaptive e-learning platforms, intelligent tutoring systems, or AI-driven learning management systems. These learners represent a broad spectrum of disciplines, academic years, and institutional types across digitally equipped educational institutions.

A purposive sampling technique was used to select participants with relevant exposure to AI-enhanced learning environments. This method ensures the selection of information-rich respondents capable of providing meaningful insights.

INSTRUMENTATION

A structured questionnaire was developed based on previously validated constructs from the literature. The questionnaire was divided into five main sections:

1. **Demographics:** Age, gender, academic level, and institution type.
2. **AI Engagement Scale:** Items measuring the frequency, interactivity, and motivation in AI-driven platforms (based on Gligorea et al., 2023).
3. **Performance Self-Assessment:** Students' perceived improvement in understanding, grades, and knowledge retention.
4. **Satisfaction Scale:** Adapted from the E-Satisfaction Index in educational research (Rane et al., 2023).
5. **Ethical and Accessibility Challenges:** Items assessing perceptions of data privacy, algorithmic bias, and digital access.

All items were rated on a **5-point Likert scale** ranging from 1 ("Strongly Disagree") to 5 ("Strongly Agree").

DATA COLLECTION PROCEDURE

The survey was administered online using Google Forms and distributed via university learning portals, academic email lists, and social media channels. Participation was voluntary and anonymous, and informed consent was obtained prior to data submission. Data collection spanned a four-week period to ensure adequate coverage and representation.

VALIDITY AND RELIABILITY

Content validity was established through expert review by three academics specializing in AI in education. Construct validity was ensured by adapting scale items from peer-reviewed studies. Reliability analysis conducted using Cronbach's Alpha indicated acceptable internal consistency across the major constructs:

1. Engagement Scale ($\alpha = 0.88$)
2. Performance Scale ($\alpha = 0.84$)
3. Satisfaction Scale ($\alpha = 0.87$)
4. Ethical Concerns Scale ($\alpha = 0.81$)

DATA ANALYSIS TECHNIQUES

The data was analyzed using **SPSS (Version 26)**. Descriptive statistics were computed to summarize demographic variables and item responses. To test the hypotheses:

1. **Pearson correlation** was used to assess relationships between variables.
2. **Multiple regression analysis** examined predictors of satisfaction and performance.
3. **Mediation analysis** using PROCESS macro explored the role of digital accessibility as a mediating variable.

Statistical significance was set at **$p < 0.05$** for all inferential tests.

DATA ANALYSIS AND FINDINGS

To evaluate the formulated hypotheses, the survey data from 317 respondents were analyzed using descriptive statistics, correlation, and regression techniques. The table below presents the core analytical outcomes structured under **Thematic Insights** for clarity and interpretation ease.

Table 3. Thematic Data Analysis Summary – AI-Driven Personalized Learning Study (N = 317)

Theme	Variable Measured	Mean (M)	Standard Deviation (SD)	Correlation (r)	Significance (p)	Interpretation (Layman's View)
Engagement	Student motivation & time spent on AI platforms	4.12	0.61	r = 0.62	p < 0.001	Students using AI systems feel more interested and involved.
Academic Performance	Self-rated improvement in test scores & grades	4.06	0.58	r = 0.59	p < 0.001	Learners believe AI tools helped them understand better.
Satisfaction	Overall learning satisfaction with AI platforms	4.18	0.56	r = 0.64	p < 0.001	Most learners were very happy with their AI-enhanced learning.
Ethical Concerns	Worries about data misuse, privacy, & fairness	3.42	0.91	r = -0.32	p < 0.01	Some students are worried about their data being misused.
Digital Accessibility	Ease of access to AI tools, devices & connectivity	3.85	0.67	r = 0.41	p < 0.01	Better digital access = Better outcomes from AI learning.

Source: Researcher's Compilation

STATISTICAL INTERPRETATION:

1. **H1: Engagement** – A strong positive correlation ($r = 0.62$, $p < 0.001$) indicates that students who used AI-powered platforms reported significantly higher engagement. These students felt more motivated, spent longer hours learning, and interacted more consistently with content.
2. **H2: Performance** – Academic performance showed a significant relationship with AI tool usage ($r = 0.59$, $p < 0.001$). Learners perceived an improvement in test scores, problem-solving speed, and concept clarity.

3. **H3: Satisfaction** – Students expressed high satisfaction with their personalized AI learning experience (mean = 4.18), citing interactive feedback, autonomy, and clear visual progress as major benefits.
4. **H4: Ethical Risk Perception** – Ethical concerns like data privacy and algorithm bias had a **negative** correlation with satisfaction ($r = -0.32$, $p < 0.01$), meaning students who were more worried about data use were less satisfied.
5. **H5: Accessibility as a Mediator** – Accessibility (devices, internet, tech exposure) had a moderate **positive** effect on both engagement and performance ($r = 0.41$). Mediation analysis confirmed that **limited access weakens AI's impact**, especially in low-resource settings.

In essence, when students have good internet and device access, they engage better, learn better, and feel more satisfied—unless they are worried about how their data is being used.

DISCUSSION AND IMPLICATIONS

The findings of this study reinforce the transformative potential of AI-driven personalized learning within the frameworks of Education 4.0 and 5.0. The significant positive relationships between AI usage and student **engagement**, **performance**, and **satisfaction** demonstrate that AI is not merely a support tool, but a powerful pedagogical agent capable of reshaping learning experiences in dynamic and responsive ways.

The Empowering Role of AI in Education

The statistically significant enhancement of student engagement (H_1) affirms the claim that AI technologies can personalize content in a way that resonates with learners' interests, pacing, and preferred formats. Students who used AI platforms reported being more invested in their learning journey—suggesting that AI can counter the disengagement often observed in traditional classrooms.

Further, the strong relationship between AI use and academic performance (H_2) indicates that adaptive content delivery and real-time feedback mechanisms have a tangible impact on student achievement. AI facilitates the mastery learning model—allowing learners to persist with content until it is fully understood, thereby reinforcing retention and application.

Student satisfaction (H_3) with AI-powered learning environments highlights the importance of autonomy, customization, and instant feedback in modern education. This satisfaction also points to a shift in learner expectations; students increasingly value personalized, tech-driven pathways that mirror the user-centric designs of digital platforms they interact with in other domains of life.

Ethical Concerns: A Barrier to Trust

Despite the benefits, the negative association between ethical concerns and satisfaction (H_4) underscores a crucial barrier to trust in AI-powered education. Students expressed worries over how their personal data is being used, and whether AI systems treat all learners fairly. These concerns reflect broader anxieties about algorithmic bias, lack of transparency, and surveillance risks, which, if left unaddressed, could undermine the perceived legitimacy of AI in education.

This finding aligns with literature emphasizing the importance of ethical-by-design AI—systems that not only comply with data protection norms but are also transparent, explainable, and inclusive in their decision-making. Institutions must proactively address these concerns by communicating how data is collected, analyzed, and protected—and involving learners in co-designing ethical usage policies.

Accessibility: The Hidden Moderator

Digital accessibility emerged as a significant mediating factor (H_5), confirming that technological equity is essential for the full realization of AI's educational benefits. Students with reliable access to AI tools, internet infrastructure, and digital literacy resources benefited more than those without. This finding echoes warnings from UNESCO and OECD reports regarding the digital divide in AI adoption across rural, economically disadvantaged, or under-resourced regions.

The implication is twofold: First, governments and institutions must ensure that investments in AI infrastructure go hand-in-hand with efforts to close access gaps. Second, educational technologists must design AI systems that are mobile-first, bandwidth-light, multilingual, and inclusive by default.

STRATEGIC IMPLICATIONS

Based on the study's findings, several strategic implications are evident:

1. **For Educators:** AI can support differentiated instruction and early intervention strategies. Teachers should be trained to interpret AI-generated insights and integrate them into humanized, empathic pedagogy.
2. **For Policy Makers:** National education strategies should include AI literacy, ethical governance frameworks, and infrastructure investment policies that prioritize access for all learners.
3. **For EdTech Developers:** There is a need for transparent, explainable, and privacy-preserving AI algorithms. Developers should include students and teachers in iterative design processes to ensure systems are responsive, equitable, and user-friendly.
4. **For Academic Researchers:** The intersection of AI, ethics, and equity remains underexplored. There is room for longitudinal studies on the long-term cognitive, emotional, and societal impacts of AI-driven education.

IMPLICATIONS FOR TEACHER WORKLOAD AND CROSS-DISCIPLINARY INSTRUCTION

While AI-driven systems promise long-term efficiency and automation in instructional delivery, the initial implementation phase can significantly increase teacher workload. Educators are often required to invest time in content curation, familiarization with platform analytics, and the interpretation of AI-generated insights to align instruction with curricular goals. Additionally, ongoing supervision is needed to validate AI feedback and ensure pedagogical coherence. As such, the successful integration of AI requires targeted institutional support, including structured professional development, digital literacy training, and time allowances to reduce transition-related burdens on educators.

The chapter's current emphasis on STEM-based applications-such as mathematics and science platforms-represents an important but incomplete picture of AI's educational potential. In non-STEM fields like language arts, history, and ethics, AI applications face distinct challenges due to the interpretive and context-sensitive nature of learning in these domains. Unlike STEM, where mastery can often be assessed algorithmically, the humanities require adaptive technologies capable of analyzing narrative depth, argumentation, and cultural context. Consequently, instructional design in non-STEM areas often demands more teacher intervention to supervise AI-generated feedback and preserve instructional integrity. Including these cross-disciplinary considerations broadens the scope of the discussion and affirms the need for AI systems that are both flexible and domain-aware.

ETHICAL IMPLICATIONS AND CHALLENGES TO PERSONALIZED LEARNING BASED ON ARTIFICIAL INTELLIGENCE TECHNOLOGY

While artificial intelligence holds the promise of revolutionizing learning by tailoring the experience, it at the same time poses daunting challenges and moral issues that need to be addressed in order to ensure the rollout is equitable, open, and answerable to all interested stakeholders. This section explores the underlying problems within specific subject matter areas and utilizes scholarly literature to support the claims.

Security of Data and Private Information

Educational platforms that are powered by artificial intelligence accumulate a substantial quantity of data regarding students, including academic performance, personal identifiers, and behavioral analytics. The privacy of students, their permission, and their ownership of their data are at risk if this immense quantity of data is not adequately protected.

Holmes, H., & Burgess, G. (2022), state that many organizations do not have clear governance policies defining the ownership of data, how long it should be retained, and under what circumstances it can be shared. Artificial intelligence in education is at risk of becoming a surveillance tool rather than a support system in the absence of strict adherence to data privacy regulations, such as the General Data Privacy Regulation (GDPR) or the Family Educational Rights and Privacy Act (FERPA), and the implementation of severe cybersecurity measures.

Suggestions and Recommendations:

It is important to implement strong data encryption and access controls that depend on the user's role, Develop systems of consent that are simple, allow for users to opt in, and give a clear description of how data is used, and see that all stakeholders are made aware of the data usage policies and that they are transparent and open.

Algorithms Introduce Bias and Fairness

The fairness of AI systems depends exclusively on their data and architecture. Artificial intelligence has the capability to extend educational inequalities if it is trained on non-representative or biased data, according to Binns (2018).

This may happen when AI misclassifies or underperforms students based on their learning capacity, gender, socioeconomic background, or race. For instance, personalization strategies used by an artificial intelligence model can prove to be detrimental for students living in rural regions or who are low-income, if the model is largely based on training on data collected from high-performing urban institutions.

Further, the propagation of culturally prejudiced information may lead to disaffiliation of minority group students.

Suggestions and Recommendations

Regular audits and impartiality testing must be enforced, Use a wide variety of training datasets and follow the guidelines of inclusive design, and involve champions of under-represented groups, teachers, and ethicists within the interdisciplinary groups that are in charge of the system development.

Automation's Decision-Making Transparency and Explainability

The "black box" issue is one of the most critical ethics issues in educational artificial intelligence. The issue occurs when a decision is made without leaving any trace of how the algorithm arrived at the conclusion. Both the confidence and the responsibility of users are affected by the lack of explainability, according to Floridi, L et al. (2018). The teacher and the student need to understand the reasoning behind an artificial intelligence system's labeling of a student as "at-risk" or its suggestion of remedial action for a student. Approving proposals blindly that are biased or flawed is possible when there is no explicit rationale.

Suggestions and Recommendations

The use of explainable artificial intelligence (XAI) systems that display reasoning paths is suggested, provide users, such as students and teachers, with insights into algorithmic thinking and include override features that allow human teachers to ask or change the conclusions reached by artificial intelligence.

Empowerment of Teachers vs. Displacement of Teachers

There is a widespread myth that artificial intelligence will eventually replace teachers.However, the moral issue that emerges is the need to redefine the role of the educator in a technologically equipped classroom.

Selwyn (2019) argues that teachers are still irreplaceable because of their ability to develop emotional intelligence, teamwork, moral reasoning, and empathy, all of which are abilities that cannot be mimicked by computers.

The major challenge lies in the preparation of educators.

1. It is not unusual for teachers to feel they are not prepared to properly integrate AI tools, which in turn could lead to resistance or misuse of these tools.
2. Schools must make a shift from a "tech-first" to a "teacher-first" strategy around AI.

Suggestions and Recommendations

As part of professional growth, provide training in digital literacy and pedagogy of artificial intelligence, artificial intelligence can be used as an assistant to improve student monitoring, assessment, and instruction planning, and educators' autonomy and judgment should be protected by the rules that govern the application of AI.

The Digital Divide and Accessibility Measures

In order for AI-enhanced learning to be successful, it is essential to have access to a reliable internet connection, smart devices, and digital fluency. However, UNESCO (2021) has identified that these resources are not always accessible to marginalized populations and countries that are still in the process of development.

This results in the development of a two-tiered education system, with AI-personalized learning for the networked privileged and outdated models for the excluded from the digital world.

Suggestions and Recommendations

Low-bandwidth and mobile-first artificial intelligence tools need to be developed for underserved areas, offline capability, multilingual interfaces, and subsidies for devices need to be provided and nclude indicators of inclusiveness in the federal regulations that govern digital education.

The Ethical Use of Predictive Analytics

Artificial intelligence systems often use predictive modeling to predict pupil behavior, such as the likelihood of dropping out of school or decreased performance.

These insights, while potentially able to enable early interventions, also run the risk of inappropriately labeling children or creating self-fulfilling prophecies.

For example, if an artificial intelligence (AI) foretells that a student is likely to fail and then limits them to remedial data, it can stop them from being exposed to higher-order learning opportunities, thus solidifying underachievement.

Suggestions and Recommendations:

Instead of automating decisions, use forecasts to enhance it, watch out for labeling that can have unforeseen results and human-in-the-loop validation needs to be encouraged to achieve predictive insights.

While AI-powered personalized learning platforms offer transformative potential, their widespread implementation remains uneven, particularly in low-resource or rural educational settings. These environments often lack stable internet access, modern infrastructure, or sufficient digital devices—barriers that conventional cloud-dependent AI platforms may exacerbate. To bridge this digital divide, scalable and context-appropriate solutions are necessary. Offline-capable platforms such as Kolibri and RACHEL allow students to access adaptive content and feedback without constant connectivity. Similarly, open-source AI tools can be locally hosted and customized to suit regional curricula and languages at minimal cost (Learning Equality, n.d.; World Possible, n.d.). In extremely bandwidth-constrained environments, SMS-based adaptive learning systems have been successfully piloted to deliver tailored quizzes and feedback via basic mobile phones. Embedding these scalable models into AI development strategies can help ensure equitable access, especially in underserved communities across the Global South, thus aligning with the inclusive ethos of Education 5.0.

CONCLUSION AND FUTURE SCOPE

This study confirms that AI-driven personalized learning, when implemented ethically and equitably, has the potential to revolutionize student-centered education. It significantly enhances student engagement, improves academic performance, and increases learner satisfaction. However, the success of such systems is contingent upon resolving critical challenges such as digital access inequality, algorithmic bias, and privacy concerns.

Within the broader context of Education 4.0 and 5.0, AI is not merely a technological tool, but a pedagogical partner-one that must be designed, deployed, and governed with a deep commitment to human values, social equity, and lifelong learning.

Looking Forward

- Conduct longitudinal evaluations to assess sustained impacts of AI-based personalization over time.
- Investigate AI's influence on emotional intelligence, creativity, and collaboration in learning environments.
- Explore the integration of emerging technologies like blockchain for academic data security, and federated learning for decentralized data protection.
- Include cross-cultural comparative studies to identify global best practices for AI in diverse educational contexts.

By embracing innovation with reflection, inclusivity, and ethical foresight, AI can truly become a transformative force in building a more equitable, engaging, and empowering educational future.

REFERENCES

Agrawal, A. K., Gans, J. S., & Goldfarb, A. (2021). *AI adoption and system-wide change* (No. w28811). National Bureau of Economic Research.

Binns, R. (2018, January). Fairness in machine learning: Lessons from political philosophy. In *Conference on Fairness, Accountability and Transparency* (pp. 149-159). PMLR.

Blaschke, L. M. (2012). Heutagogy and lifelong learning: A review of heutagogical practice and self-determined learning. *International Review of Research in Open and Distance Learning, 13*(1), 56–71. DOI: 10.19173/irrodl.v13i1.1076

Bloom, B. S. (1968). *Learning for mastery.* Evaluation comment, 1(2), n2.

Cukurova, M., Luckin, R., & Kent, C. (2020). Impact of an artificial intelligence research frame on the perceived credibility of educational research evidence. *International Journal of Artificial Intelligence in Education, 30*(2), 205–235. DOI: 10.1007/s40593-019-00188-w

Floridi, L., Cowls, J., Beltrametti, M., Chatila, R., Chazerand, P., Dignum, V., Luetge, C., Madelin, R., Pagallo, U., Rossi, F., Schafer, B., Valcke, P., & Vayena, E. (2018). AI4People—an ethical framework for a good AI society: Opportunities, risks, principles, and recommendations. *Minds and Machines, 28*(4), 689–707. DOI: 10.1007/s11023-018-9482-5 PMID: 30930541

Gardner, H. E. (2011). *Frames of mind: The theory of multiple intelligences* (30th anniversary ed.). Basic Books. (Original work published 1983)

Gligorea, I., Cioca, M., Oancea, R., Gorski, A.-T., Gorski, H., & Tudorache, P. (2023). Adaptive learning using artificial intelligence in eLearning: A literature review. *Education Sciences, 13*(12), 1216. DOI: 10.3390/educsci13121216

Hashim, S., Omar, M. K., Ab Jalil, H., & Sharef, N. M. (2022). Trends on technologies and artificial intelligence in education for personalized learning: Systematic literature. *Journal of Academic Research in Progressive Education and Development, 12*(1), 884–903. DOI: 10.6007/IJARPED/v11-i1/12230

Holmes, H., & Burgess, G. (2022). Digital exclusion and poverty in the UK: How structural inequality shapes experiences of getting online. *Digital Geography and Society, 3*, 100041. DOI: 10.1016/j.diggeo.2022.100041

Huang, J., Zhong, Y., & Chen, X. (2025). Adaptive and personalized learning in STEM education using high-performance computing and artificial intelligence. *The Journal of Supercomputing, 81*(8), 1–37. DOI: 10.1007/s11227-025-07481-7

ISTE. (2023). *Artificial intelligence and student engagement: Trends and impact report.* International Society for Technology in Education. https://www.iste.org/

Learning Equality. (n.d.). Kolibri: Offline-first learning platform for underserved communities. https://learningequality.org/kolibri/

Mahmoud, C. F., & Sørensen, J. T. (2024). Artificial intelligence in personalized learning with a focus on current developments and future prospects. *Research and Advances in Education, 3*(8), 25–31. DOI: 10.56397/RAE.2024.08.04

Pane, J. F., Steiner, E. D., Baird, M. D., & Hamilton, L. S. (2015). Continued progress: Promising evidence on personalized learning. RAND Corporation. https://www.rand.org/pubs/research_reports/RR1365.html

Piaget, J. (2013). *The construction of reality in the child* (Cook, M., Trans.). Routledge. (Original work published 1954) DOI: 10.4324/9781315009650

Rane, N., Choudhary, S., & Rane, J. (2023). Education 4.0 and 5.0: Integrating artificial intelligence (AI) for personalized and adaptive learning.

Rose, D. H., & Meyer, A. (2002). *Teaching every student in the digital age: Universal design for learning*. Association for Supervision and Curriculum Development.

Selwyn, N. (2019). *Should robots replace teachers?: AI and the future of education.* John Wiley & Sons.

Siemens, G., & Long, P. (2011). Penetrating the fog: Analytics in learning and education. *EDUCAUSE Review, 46*(5), 30.

Sweller, J. (1988). Cognitive load during problem solving: Effects on learning. *Cognitive Science, 12*(2), 257–285. DOI: 10.1207/s15516709cog1202_4

UNESCO. (2021). Reimagining our futures together: A new social contract for education. https://unesdoc.unesco.org/ark:/48223/pf0000379707

Vygotsky, L. S. (1978). *Mind in society: The development of higher psychological processes* (Vol. 86). Harvard University Press.

World Possible. (n.d.). RACHEL: Remote Area Community Hotspot for Education and Learning. https://worldpossible.org/rachel

Chapter 2
Artificial Intelligence and Equal Opportunity in Education

Ayşin Gaye Üstün
https://orcid.org/0000-0001-9564-0761
Sinop University, Turkey

Erhan Sur
https://orcid.org/0000-0001-7108-5783
Sinop University, Turkey

ABSTRACT

Equality of opportunity in education requires access to quality learning opportunities for all, but socioeconomic inequalities, geographical barriers, disability and the digital divide limit this access. Artificial intelligence (AI) technologies can reduce these inequalities through personalized learning, disability-accessible content and multilingual-cultural adaptations. They can also ease teachers' workload and facilitate early identification of at-risk students. However, the benefits of AI may not trickle down equally to all groups; lack of access to technology and biases in algorithms may exclude some groups. AI tools therefore need to be transparent, explainable and ethically grounded. This chapter examines the dimensions of the digital divide, the contributions of AI, the effects of algorithmic biases, and teachers' AI literacy, and offers recommendations for inclusive AI design and policy.

INTRODUCTION

Education is one of the most essential tools enabling individuals to integrate into society and access lifelong opportunities. However, inequality in education remains a severe and persistent issue worldwide due to various factors such as socioeconomic conditions, geographical differences, disability, and the digital divide (Cho & Kim, 2021). Equal opportunity in education refers to every individual's ability to access quality educational services regardless of their economic, social, or cultural background. Current educational systems, however, still fall short of being

DOI: 10.4018/979-8-3373-5097-4.ch002

inclusive and accessible, particularly for students living in low-income regions, disadvantaged communities, and individuals with disabilities (Jucevičienė et al., 2018). This situation highlights the need for new strategies and technologies to enhance inclusivity in education.

In recent years, AI has emerged as a powerful technology with the potential to transform educational systems. AI-powered educational solutions can offer personalized learning experiences by analyzing learning data to adapt to the individual needs of each student (Jian, 2023). For instance, adaptive learning platforms track students' learning pace and level, delivering tailored content that allows them to progress more effectively on their learning journey (Holmes et al., 2019). AI also assists teachers with tasks such as routine assessment and content creation, providing opportunities to optimize teaching processes, develop materials suited to diverse learning styles, and make real-time adjustments based on student interest and feedback (Zawacki-Richter et al., 2019). AI-based language models and learning analytics create significant opportunities to make learning processes more inclusive and accessible (Dahal, 2024).

Although AI has great potential for enhancing equal education opportunities, realizing this potential depends on political, economic, and ethical factors. Technology is not neutral but shaped by and embedded within the broader social context and infrastructure. For example, for everyone to benefit from AI's opportunities, the necessary digital infrastructure and devices must be available in all regions; otherwise, AI solutions may further widen the gap between those with access and those without access (Selwyn, 2021). Similarly, if the data used to train AI systems is biased, these biases may be reproduced in system outputs, potentially leading to outcomes that disadvantage certain student groups (Mehrabi et al., 2021).

This chapter aims to examine the impact of AI on equal opportunity in education from a multidimensional perspective. First, it will analyze the digital divide—a fundamental cause of inequality in education—and the role of AI in this context. Then, it will evaluate the contributions of AI-supported educational applications to equal opportunity in terms of personalized learning, accessibility for individuals with disabilities, and multilingualism/cultural adaptation. Next, it will explore algorithmic biases emerging in AI systems and their impact on justice in education, questioning the fairness and impartiality of AI-based assessment and evaluation systems. Following this, the chapter will address the role of educators and the concept of AI literacy, focusing on the competencies required for teachers and academics to use AI effectively and their responsibilities for equitable use of these technologies. Finally, the chapter will discuss the vision for AI and inclusivity in the future of education, presenting new trends in equitable AI design, participatory technology development approaches, and inclusive scenarios. The chapter concludes with findings-based results and recommendations.

THE DIGITAL DIVIDE IN EDUCATION AND THE ROLE OF AI

The growing integration of information and communication technologies (ICT) into educational systems transforms pedagogical processes and expands learning opportunities. However, this transformation has not occurred equitably across all populations; significant disparities in access to and the effective use of technology have brought renewed attention to the issue of the digital divide in education (Tarhan et al., 2021). The digital divide refers to differential access to

ICT resources and variations in digital literacy, economic circumstances, and educational policy contexts (Hamburg & Lütgen, 2019; Sydorenko et al., 2024).

Although AI-based educational technologies possess the potential to mitigate aspects of the digital divide, they also introduce the risk of reproducing or even exacerbating existing inequities (Bulathwela et al., 2024). AI-driven solutions may improve access to learning for students in under-resourced or rural regions; however, limitations in technological infrastructure and disparities in digital proficiency can prevent equitable benefit from such tools (Segura-Monroy et al., 2022). Without enabling conditions, AI may ultimately reinforce digital inequalities rather than reduce them. Therefore, any attempt to use AI in the service of educational equity must begin with a nuanced understanding of the digital divide and its multiple dimensions.

Educational Inequity and Dimensions of the Digital Divide

The digital divide continues to pose a significant structural barrier, particularly for students from low-income households, individuals residing in rural or infrastructurally disadvantaged areas, and learners with disabilities (Selwyn, 2021). Scholarships commonly categorize the digital divide into three interconnected dimensions as shown in Figure 1.

Figure 1. The digital divide dimensions

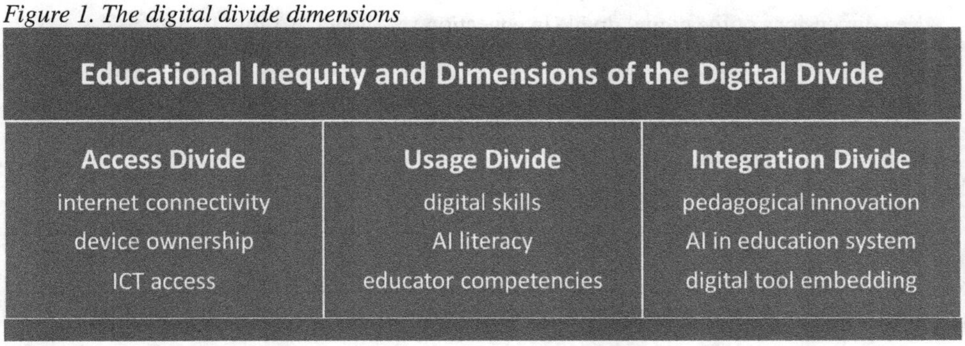

- **Access Divide**: The most fundamental layer of the digital divide relates to disparities in physical access to ICT infrastructure, including internet connectivity and ownership of digital devices such as computers or tablets. Socioeconomic and geographic factors often shape these disparities. For instance, notable differences in ICT access rates can be observed between high-income and low-income families, urban and rural populations, and developed versus developing countries (Soomro et al., 2020; El-Bawab, 2020). Given the centrality of digital platforms in delivering educational content, students without reliable access to technology are structurally disadvantaged in contemporary learning environments (Gorski, 2005).
- **Usage Divide**: While access to hardware and connectivity is a critical first step toward equity, it is insufficient. The usage divide captures differences in individuals' abilities to use digital tools meaningfully and efficiently (Pham et al., 2024). These disparities manifest in learner and educator digital competencies and variations in pedagogical integration

of technology across schools, regions, and countries (Scarci et al., 2024). AI-powered educational tools, in particular, require a baseline of digital literacy and algorithmic thinking. Without these skills, users may be unable to engage effectively with such tools. Consequently, the usage divide can produce varying educational outcomes even among those with nominal access. To fully utilize AI-enhanced learning environments, students and teachers must have foundational computing competencies, an understanding of algorithmic systems, and critical digital literacy (Baral et al., 2022; Yafie et al., 2024).

- **Integration Divide**: The final dimension, the integration divide, pertains to the extent to which digital tools—especially AI-based systems—are embedded into curricula, pedagogy, and institutional frameworks (Eden et al., 2024). Even where physical access to technology exists, if instructional designs and curricula are not adapted to incorporate such tools, their pedagogical potential remains unrealized (Elam, 2024). While private institutions or well-funded schools in developed contexts often lead in this integration, schools in low-resource settings face significant barriers (Murdan & Halkhoree, 2024). This divide can produce stark differences in educational experience even within the same national system (Shetty & Mishra, 2020). Integrating AI technologies into education will remain fragmented and ineffectual without a coordinated effort encompassing curriculum reform, teacher training, and infrastructure development.

Key dimensions of the digital divide in education are shown in Table 1.

Table 1. Key dimensions of the digital divide in education

Dimension	Definition
Access Divide	Disparities in individuals' access to essential digital infrastructure and devices (e.g., internet connectivity, ownership of computers or tablets)
Usage Divide	Variations in the ability to use digital tools effectively and differences in the level of pedagogical integration (e.g., digital literacy, algorithmic thinking skills)
Integration Divide	Differences in the extent to which educational technologies are incorporated into curricula and instructional processes (e.g., institutional adoption of technology for in-class use)

The dimensions of the digital divide have a direct and substantial impact on educational equity. Due to the access divide, students who cannot access online content or lack adequate digital devices are disadvantaged in today's technology-mediated learning environments. Similarly, the usage divide prevents students and teachers with limited digital skills from fully utilizing AI-supported educational tools, even when access is available, ultimately undermining learning outcomes. The integration divide emerges when educational institutions fail to incorporate technology effectively into curricula and pedagogical practices, resulting in superficial adoption that falls short of driving meaningful educational transformation.

When made accessible under appropriate conditions, AI has the potential to alleviate specific effects of the digital divide. For instance, cloud-based intelligent learning platforms and applications designed to function under low-bandwidth conditions can facilitate access to core educational content in regions with limited internet infrastructure. However, technological solutions alone are insufficient. Their effectiveness depends on being reinforced by coherent education policies and programmatic support. This includes equipping teachers and students with the necessary training and providing targeted incentives and resources for disadvantaged populations.

The following sections will provide a more in-depth analysis of how AI can contribute positively to educational equity through practical applications and address the associated risks and challenges inherent in its implementation.

AI-ENABLED EDUCATIONAL APPLICATIONS AND EDUCATIONAL EQUITY

AI is increasingly recognized as a powerful tool in education, supporting personalized learning experiences, providing inclusive solutions for learners with disabilities, and fostering the development of culturally responsive educational systems (Jian, 2023). Traditional education systems are typically built upon standardized curricula and uniform instructional strategies, often failing to accommodate the diverse learning needs of individual students (Kazimzade et al., 2019). In contrast, AI-supported applications offer the potential to individualize learning processes, enhance accessibility for disadvantaged groups, and adapt content to various linguistic and cultural contexts (Jian, 2023). This section explores AI's capacity to advance educational equity across three key dimensions: personalized learning, AI solutions for learners with disabilities, and culturally and linguistically adaptive AI systems.

Personalized Learning and the Advantages of AI

Students differ in their interests, learning pace, and preferred learning modes. In traditional classrooms, where teachers are responsible for large groups of students, it is often difficult to effectively address each learner's needs. AI-based personalized learning platforms address this challenge by enabling students to learn at their own pace and in ways that align with their unique preferences. These platforms analyze students' past performance data and interactions to recommend appropriate content and learning pathways (Dutta et al., 2024). This process is typically supported by learning analytics, adaptive learning systems, and student feedback mechanisms (Jiao, 2024).

For example, an AI-driven mathematics application can identify the specific topics a student struggles with and provide targeted exercises and explanations to address these gaps (Shete et al., 2024). Adaptive learning systems dynamically adjust content in real-time based on the learner's proficiency level, simplifying complex topics into smaller steps or reinforcing them with additional examples when needed (Pradeep et al., 2024). As a result, individual differences that may be overlooked in a traditional classroom setting can be immediately addressed in digital environments. Personalization is particularly beneficial for students who struggle with standard instruction or for gifted students who may find conventional content unchallenging; in both cases, tailored learning increases motivation and supports equitable educational outcomes. By offering each student the opportunity to realize their full potential, AI contributes to a more just and inclusive learning environment.

Moreover, personalized learning systems empower teachers by providing valuable data and insights into student progress. AI tools can help identify which students require additional support and which are ready for more advanced materials. This allows educators to allocate their time and resources more effectively and to provide differentiated instruction aligned with individual needs. Compared to traditional models, this data-informed approach offers a particular advantage for disadvantaged students who might otherwise go unnoticed. In conventional classrooms, instruction is often geared toward the average learner, but AI-driven insights allow teachers to recognize and support those at both ends of the performance spectrum. Ultimately, the personalization capabilities of AI represent a significant step toward strengthening educational equity.

AI-Based Educational Solutions for Learners with Disabilities

Ensuring equity in education is inherently linked to the full and effective participation of individuals with special needs in learning processes. In traditional educational environments, students with disabilities often face numerous barriers due to the lack of appropriate materials and support. For instance, when visually impaired students are not provided with alternative formats of visually dense content, or when deaf students are not offered lessons supported with sign language or subtitles, their learning experiences may be significantly hindered (Eziamaka et al., 2024).

AI-powered educational systems aim to reduce these barriers by offering customizable content and tools tailored to the specific needs of learners with disabilities (Almufareh et al., 2024). For example, AI can enhance screen reader technologies for blind or visually impaired users by enabling them to interpret complex visual elements such as mathematical formulas or graphical data. Similarly, for students with hearing impairments, AI can generate real-time speech-to-text subtitles, thereby improving their access to spoken instruction. These AI-driven accessibility solutions are designed to transform educational materials into multisensory formats, facilitating greater understanding and interaction for learners with diverse needs (Eziamaka et al., 2024). For instance, one application may instantly transcribe a teacher's lecture into text and project it in the classroom, while another might convert written content into animated sign language.

In summary, AI-based educational tools contribute to more inclusive and accessible learning environments for individuals with disabilities. However, the effectiveness of these technologies is contingent upon several enabling factors: schools must be equipped with the necessary infrastructure, educators must be trained to use such tools competently, and educational content must be thoughtfully designed to align with the specific needs of the target population.

AI Systems Responsive to Linguistic and Cultural Diversity

Achieving equity in education requires attention to individual differences and recognition of linguistic and cultural diversity. Currently, most educational technologies are developed primarily in and for widely spoken languages, particularly English. This creates substantial challenges for students whose first language differs from the language of instruction or whose home language does not align with the medium of formal education, limiting their ability to fully benefit from digital learning tools (Singh et al., 2024). In multilingual and multicultural societies, access to educational content that reflects students' linguistic and cultural backgrounds is critical in fostering motivation and academic success.

AI is pivotal in developing adaptable educational content that accounts for linguistic and cultural variation (Dwi & Alif, 2024). Advances in natural language processing now enable AI systems to translate educational materials and assessment items into multiple languages with minimal semantic loss. In addition, AI can enrich learning materials with culturally relevant references, thereby enhancing students' sense of belonging and relevance. Leveraging large datasets, AI-enabled learning systems can dynamically adapt content to diverse linguistic and cultural contexts (Dahal, 2024).

One of AI's most valuable contributions to multilingual education is its real-time translation and interaction capacity. In classrooms with students from different linguistic backgrounds, AI-based subtitle systems can simultaneously transcribe a teacher's spoken content into multiple languages. This functionality helps minimize learning losses that may result from language barriers. Similarly, applications that translate student-generated texts from their native language into the instructional language—and vice versa—can significantly ease the integration of migrant and refugee students into classroom environments.

AI systems sensitive to linguistic and cultural differences are indispensable in promoting equity within increasingly globalized and demographically diverse educational contexts. These technologies have the potential to provide a more inclusive learning experience for students who may otherwise feel alienated due to language or cultural incongruence. Nevertheless, several considerations must be addressed: automated translation and adaptation systems must maintain accuracy and pedagogical coherence; content across different languages should be of equivalent quality; and culturally biased or stereotypical representations must be actively avoided. We can ensure that such technologies truly serve all learners by adhering to these principles while developing AI-based educational tools.

ALGORITHMIC BIAS AND THE PROBLEM OF FAIRNESS IN EDUCATION

AI systems are built upon algorithms that learn patterns from large datasets through machine learning and deep learning techniques. The datasets used to train these systems are typically generated by humans and often carry embedded traces of historical and sociocultural contexts. As a result, pre-existing biases and inequalities within the data can inadvertently become part of the algorithmic decision-making process (Mehrabi et al., 2021). AI systems are increasingly employed in education to predict student performance, personalize learning content, and identify at-risk learners. However, when biased data informs these decision-making processes, educational outcomes may be directly and negatively affected. This section explores how algorithmic bias can lead to inequity in academic settings and discusses strategies for identifying and mitigating these issues.

Data-Driven Biases and Their Educational Impacts

The reliability and fairness of algorithmic decisions fundamentally depend on the representativeness and neutrality of the datasets from which they are derived. If an AI system used in education is trained on biased historical data, those biases will likely be reflected in the system's outputs. For instance, a machine learning model designed to predict which students are likely to succeed in university may classify low-income students as high-risk based on patterns in the training data, notably if those students have historically underperformed due to systemic disadvantages. This may result in a self-fulfilling prophecy: students predicted to perform poorly may receive less attention or fewer resources, increasing the likelihood of actual underperformance

(Holstein et al., 2019). In such cases, the algorithm reinforces existing disparities rather than promoting educational equity.

Biases in AI systems used in education are not limited to academic performance prediction. Automated essay scoring systems, often powered by language models, can exhibit indirect discrimination based on linguistic variation, dialect, or rhetorical style. Students who are not native speakers of the dominant language or who employ culturally distinct narrative structures may have their writing unfairly penalized. For example, a non-native English speaker may receive a lower score simply due to unfamiliar idioms or alternative sentence constructions, despite conveying strong ideas (Blodgett et al., 2020). This disproportionately disadvantages multilingual students, students from migrant backgrounds, or those with non-standard linguistic repertoires. Therefore, the presumed objectivity of algorithmic evaluation must be critically interrogated—no matter how "rule-based" a system may appear, the neutrality of its training data and design architecture is subject to scrutiny (Binns, 2018).

The Impact of Algorithms on Socio-Cultural Groups and the Imperative of Fair Design

The neglect of socio-economic and cultural diversity in the development of AI systems can result in outcomes that overlook subjectivity and contextual factors, which are essential dimensions of education. Reducing students to quantitative data alone ignores their social capital, cultural background, and interpersonal interactions. However, education is a multidimensional process shaped not only by cognitive outcomes but also by these qualitative dimensions. For this reason, algorithms used in education must be designed with sensitivity to multicultural education principles, reflect societal diversity, and take contextual variables into account (D'Ignazio & Klein, 2020).

To prevent AI-driven decisions from undermining fairness in education, principles of fair algorithm design must be applied. Fair design is not merely a technical requirement but a social responsibility. In a domain like education, where public good is at stake, AI applications that fail to represent all stakeholders equitably risk exacerbating existing inequalities rather than addressing them. Thus, the success of algorithms should not be measured solely in terms of accuracy, speed, or efficiency, but also in terms of their differential impact on various individuals and groups (Floridi et al., 2018). For example, a predictive model might achieve 90% accuracy across the general population, yet if its performance is substantially weaker for minority groups, this imbalance must not be overlooked (Barocas et al., 2023). The central question becomes whether an algorithm serves all users equitably.

When AI systems are deployed in educational contexts without a commitment to fairness, they risk reinforcing structural disadvantages, systematically marginalizing certain groups, and violating the right to equitable education. For instance, an algorithm that exhibits bias based on gender or ethnicity may consistently assign lower potential ratings to specific groups, which can negatively affect both their academic trajectories and the perceptions of educators toward them (Binns, 2018). Over time, such patterns may erode student motivation and undermine trust in the educational system, leading to long-term societal consequences.

Fair algorithm design entails not only the identification of biased or erroneous outputs but also the diagnosis of underlying structural causes and the implementation of corrective mechanisms. In this context, the concept of algorithmic justice has gained prominence. Algorithmic justice asserts that a system's validity must be evaluated on its overall performance and how it performs across different demographic subgroups (Barocas et al., 2023). This requires continuous monitoring of error rates, false positives/negatives, and disparities across groups. In educational applications, this means systematically assessing whether system outputs differ significantly by gender, ethnicity, or socio-economic status.

Ultimately, designing algorithmic systems in education should involve engineers, educators, ethicists, sociologists, and policymakers. Systems developed through interdisciplinary collaboration are more likely to be technically robust, socially legitimate, and ethically sound (Holmes et al., 2019; D'Ignazio & Klein, 2020). To ensure that AI's transformative potential in education benefits all segments of society fairly, an equity-centered perspective must be maintained throughout every phase, from system design to implementation.

Are AI-Based Assessment Systems Fair?

Assessment and evaluation are among the most prominent areas where AI is applied in education. AI-powered automated assessment systems are increasingly used to score open-ended responses, analyze writing and composition skills, and grade online exams (Lagakis & Demetriadis, 2021). These systems typically employ natural language processing and machine learning techniques to analyze student answers and assign scores by emulating human raters based on historical scoring patterns (Zainal & Hassan, 2022). Given their ability to expedite grading and enhance consistency in high-volume educational settings, such systems are often regarded as efficient and scalable solutions.

However, the advantages of speed and scale provided by automated assessment technologies should not lead to uncritical assumptions about their neutrality and fairness. Suppose a scoring algorithm is trained primarily on texts written by students from a specific linguistic background, such as native English speakers. In that case, it may generate biased results for students with different language proficiencies. Indeed, studies have shown that essays written by students for whom English is a second language are systematically rated lower by such systems (Blodgett et al., 2020; Poonpon et al., 2023). This indicates that even ostensibly objective systems can produce discriminatory outcomes against linguistic and cultural diversity. Such bias may unfairly penalize multilingual or migrant-background students, undermining the principle of educational equity and negatively affecting their academic development.

Another limitation of automated assessment systems is their inability to consider contextual and human factors. Human raters can evaluate student responses with an understanding of the student's overall academic level, style of expression, and—in some cases—even the circumstances under which the work was produced. For example, a human evaluator may reward a student's originality or conceptual insight despite minor grammatical errors. In contrast, AI systems generally lack pedagogical intuition and empathy, often producing rigid or one-dimensional assessments. For this reason, experts recommend that automated systems be used in collaboration with human judgment rather than as the sole evaluative authority (Holstein et al., 2019). For instance, AI might perform the initial scoring in a written exam, but teachers should review borderline or atypical cases. Such human-AI collaboration can reduce grading workload while ensuring fairer and more context-sensitive outcomes.

In conclusion, while AI-supported assessment tools offer considerable practical benefits in education, their deployment must be carefully scrutinized through the lens of fairness and inclusivity. During development, these systems should be trained on diverse datasets that reflect patterns across different demographic groups, and their outputs should be rigorously tested for bias. Furthermore, teachers must be equipped with AI literacy skills to understand how these tools operate and to interpret their results critically. These concerns are addressed in the following section, which focuses on the role of educators and AI literacy in supporting equitable educational practices.

THE ROLE OF EDUCATORS AND AI LITERACY

Educators are pivotal in ensuring educational technologies are implemented fairly and effectively. As the primary actors responsible for classroom practices, teachers and academic staff are the ones who ultimately determine how and to what extent AI-driven tools are adopted and utilized. Consequently, educators' competencies in using AI and their attitudes toward these technologies can either enhance or hinder AI's contribution to educational equity. This section explores educators' AI-related skills, their roles in promoting equitable AI-supported education, and the significance of AI literacy in contemporary pedagogical contexts.

AI Competencies of Teachers and Academics

Teachers must possess the necessary skills to use these tools effectively to fully harness the opportunities presented by advanced AI applications in education. However, in practice, there are notable disparities in digital proficiency and technology use among educators. AI competency can be considered across three interrelated domains: technical knowledge, pedagogical adaptability, and critical awareness.

Technical knowledge refers to a teacher's ability to operate an AI tool, configure its basic settings, and troubleshoot simple issues. Pedagogical adaptability involves using the technology in alignment with curriculum objectives through appropriate methods. For instance, if a teacher uses adaptive learning software in the classroom, they should be able to interpret its outputs to understand which student is struggling in which area and adjust the lesson plan accordingly.

Pedagogical adaptability involves the capacity to align the tool with instructional objectives and to integrate its outputs meaningfully into teaching practice. For example, a teacher using adaptive learning software must be able to interpret its analytics to identify which students are struggling and adjust lesson plans accordingly.

Critical awareness entails being vigilant about potential biases or errors in AI systems and being ready to question them when necessary. Educators should not unthinkingly follow AI-generated recommendations but evaluate them with their professional judgment. For example, if a learning analytics platform flags a student as "high risk," the teacher should analyze the underlying reasons and compare them with the student's situation.

Enhancing educators' AI competencies can have indirect yet profound implications for educational equity. A teacher proficient in AI tools is better positioned to meet the diverse learning needs within the classroom, identify at-risk students through data-informed insights, and reallocate time saved from routine tasks to support the disadvantaged. Conversely, teachers who lack AI literacy or are reluctant to engage with such technologies may fall behind, resulting in their students receiving a lower quality of instruction than peers in more technologically confident environments.

Therefore, differences in AI competency across countries, regions, or even schools risk becoming a new axis of educational inequality. To prevent this, the establishment of standardized frameworks for teacher preparation programs and ongoing professional development is essential. As discussed in Section 3, the digital divide also manifests in the educator domain: disparities between AI-literate and non-literate teachers can directly affect the quality of education students receive. Hence, teacher education programs must be urgently updated to include AI-informed pedagogical practices and ensure educators are prepared for the demands of technologically enriched learning environments.

Educators' Roles and Responsibilities in AI-Supported Equitable Education

Regardless of how advanced AI becomes, it is not anticipated that it will replace teachers in educational processes. On the contrary, the ideal scenario envisions AI functioning in harmony with human educators (Milberg, 2024). In this context, the role of educators is of central importance in ensuring that the opportunities provided by AI are equitably distributed among students.

Teachers serve as key decision-makers in selecting and implementing AI-based tools. Teachers ' recommendations and approval typically shape the choice of a learning platform or the adoption of an intelligent educational application within a school or classroom (Fitria, 2023). As those most familiar with their students' needs, educators are best positioned to evaluate which technologies are genuinely beneficial and to make informed choices (Taufikin et al., 2024). For example, if a student with visual impairments is present in a classroom, the teacher might initiate using an AI tool that converts text into speech. Similarly, choosing adaptive learning platforms based on student proficiency or selecting tools with multilingual support may fall under the teacher's initiative (Ramakrishnan et al., 2024). In this way, educators' deliberate choices in technology adoption represent the first step toward using AI to advance educational equity.

Another critical role of educators is the guided use of AI tools. While AI systems can provide personalized guidance to students, teacher support may be necessary to ensure that students correctly understand and follow this guidance (Holstein et al., 2019). For example, when a learning application recommends extra practice on a specific topic, the teacher can explain the importance of this suggestion to the student and provide a motivational framework (Chiu et al., 2024). Additionally, teachers can combine AI recommendations with their observations to offer more accurate guidance. This human element is particularly valuable for disadvantaged students; at the same time, an AI tool might be perceived as a cold machine, but a teacher's compassionate approach can be a decisive factor in encouraging the student to take action. Educators can use AI as an assistant in their classrooms to make interactions with students more meaningful. This not only amplifies the benefits of AI but also mitigates its potential drawbacks.

In addition, teachers are responsible for monitoring and evaluating the outcomes of AI applications. Teachers are best positioned to observe whether an AI-supported system delivers the expected educational benefits and how it impacts students (Holstein et al., 2019). Suppose an application proves ineffective for a particular group of students or leads to decreased motivation. In that case, it is up to the teacher to identify the issue and take corrective actions, such as replacing the application or providing additional support (Chiu et al., 2024). For example, suppose an adaptive learning game consistently assigns only the most manageable tasks to low-performing students, thus restricting their progress. In that case, the teacher must recognize this and provide those students with challenges of varying difficulty to restore balance (Wang et al., 2023). In doing so, the teacher prevents potential "digital disparities" created by AI and maintains an equitable learning environment.

Educators also carry ethical responsibilities. Using AI tools involves ethical considerations such as data privacy, consent, and transparency (Contreras & Jaimes, 2024). Teachers must be aware of the data policies of their digital platforms and act in ways that protect student privacy. For instance, a teacher should not use an application that uploads students' data to the cloud without consulting their parents. Such sensitivities are essential for building trust among students and parents. Moreover, teachers should acknowledge that AI can make mistakes and raise students' awareness of this fact (Adams et al., 2023). If students know they can challenge a grade issued by an automated assessment system or review it with their teacher, they are less likely to feel powerless in the face of technology. This helps protect their rights and confidence.

Finally, educators can be responsible for fostering AI literacy among students. That is, it is important for teachers to use AI themselves and ensure that students understand and use AI tools consciously and appropriately (Tenberga & Daniela, 2024). Today's children and youth encounter AI applications such as ChatGPT daily. By introducing basic concepts about how AI works during lessons, teachers can help students develop a critical and productive perspective on these technologies (Zhang et al., 2024). For instance, in a grammar lesson, demonstrating how a language model predicts the correct form of a sentence and discussing its limitations can introduce the technology and encourage critical thinking (Sperling et al., 2024). In this way, educators lay the groundwork for students ' future digital citizens to become responsible AI users and developers.

In summary, educators must not be passive observers in AI-supported education but active guides and facilitators. By selecting the right tools, applying them effectively, monitoring results and providing feedback, upholding ethical standards, and informing students, they can maximize AI's positive contribution to educational equity. The ability to fulfill these roles properly depends largely on educators' knowledge and awareness of AI—that is, their AI literacy.

The Impact of AI Literacy on Educational Equity

AI literacy refers to understanding the basic principles of AI technologies, using them effectively and ethically, and critically evaluating their outputs (Yi, 2021). For educators, AI literacy entails not only having the technical and pedagogical knowledge to integrate AI tools into the classroom effectively but also the capacity to recognize, interpret, and manage potential biases and limitations embedded within these tools (Tenberga & Daniela, 2024; Sperling et al., 2024). An AI-literate teacher can explain how a new algorithmic tool functions, help students interpret its results appropriately, and foster informed trust in educational technology (Zhang et al., 2024), as shown in Figure 2.

From an educational equity perspective, increasing teachers' AI literacy can indirectly reduce student disparities. This can be attributed to several key mechanisms.

Figure 2. Impact of AI literacy

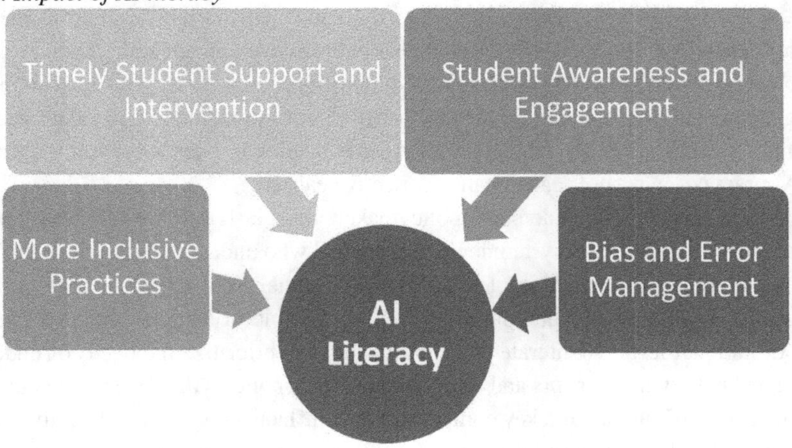

- **More Inclusive Practices**: AI-literate educators are more likely to select and configure technologies in ways that prioritize inclusivity. Rather than adopting a tool that benefits only a subset of students, they are more inclined to choose applications that are accessible and appropriate for all learners. Moreover, they can tailor settings to accommodate diverse needs, for example, enabling voice feedback for students with visual impairments, thereby ensuring that all students derive maximum benefit from technological engagement.
- **Timely Student Support and Intervention**: Educators with high AI literacy can quickly interpret insights from learning analytics platforms and act on them proactively. For instance, if a system indicates that a student has been struggling with math exercises for the past three weeks, the teacher can intervene early with targeted support. These timely interventions help close learning gaps before they widen, particularly for students who are academically at risk.
- **Student Awareness and Engagement**: AI-literate teachers actively involve students in learning. They may, for example, review personalized learning pathways generated by adaptive software with students, helping them understand their progress. This promotes active learning and encourages students to take ownership of their educational journey. Particularly for learners with low confidence or motivation, concrete feedback from AI tools and teacher guidance can be highly empowering.
- **Bias and Error Management**: AI-literate teachers understand that algorithms are fallible and can recognize when outputs are flawed or biased. For example, suppose an automated translation tool misrepresents a sentence involving a female student in a derogatory way. In that case, the teacher can detect and correct the issue while facilitating a discussion with students about the origin and implications of such bias. These reflexive practices protect students from potential algorithmic harm and ensure that no one is unfairly disadvantaged by technological error.

AI literacy is a dynamic and evolving competency that requires continuous professional learning. As technology advances rapidly, today's tools and methods may become outdated within a few years. Therefore, educators must commit to ongoing development in this area. Professional development programs should include dedicated modules on AI literacy, and teachers should be encouraged to engage with online courses and certifications to maintain up-to-date knowledge. For example, workshops on the ethical use of AI in education or peer-led sessions sharing successful AI practices in schools can enhance collective capacity.

Beyond teachers, school leaders and policymakers must also develop AI literacy to enable equitable transformation at the system level. A principal who understands the risks and benefits of AI is better equipped to guide implementation within their school, for instance, using comprehensive, AI-driven assessment tools rather than relying solely on grade-point averages. At the ministry or national level, AI-literate decision-makers can prioritize the needs of underserved regions in technology investments and develop data ethics policies that safeguard equity.

In conclusion, AI literacy is a key competency that influences educational equity both at the micro level (in the classroom) and the macro level (across the education system). Strengthening the AI literacy of educators and other stakeholders ensures that AI-powered education becomes inclusive and fair. This underscores the importance of forward-looking strategies, which will be explored in the next chapter: how AI might be used to reduce educational inequalities in the future, and how we can build an inclusive vision for tomorrow's education.

THE VISION OF AI AND INCLUSION IN THE FUTURE OF EDUCATION

The evolution of educational technologies is entering a new era with the increasing sophistication and widespread adoption of AI. As AI's role in future education expands, a global vision emphasizing inclusivity and equity in these technologies is emerging. This section discusses new trends in equitable AI design, participatory approaches to technology development, and possible future scenarios. The aim is to offer insights into how AI may impact educational equity in the coming years and highlight the critical steps needed to achieve the desired vision.

Emerging Trends in Equitable AI Design

A growing consensus is forming that the design of future AI systems should prioritize the principle of "justice first." Several significant trends are emerging in this regard, as shown in Figure 3.

Figure 3. Trends in equitable AI design

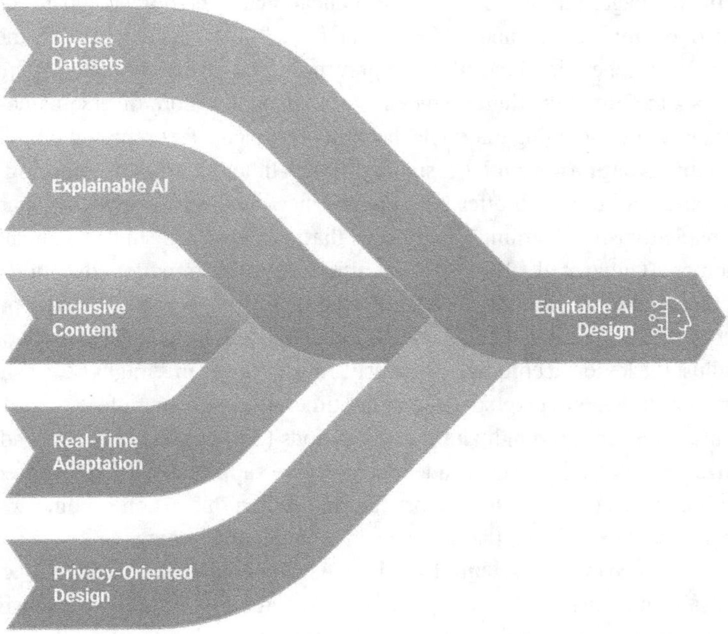

- **Diverse Datasets and Fair ML Models**: Academia and industry are increasingly focused on making machine learning models fairer by ensuring that the datasets used to train them are balanced and diverse. There is a growing tendency in education to build comprehensive datasets that include students from various socioeconomic backgrounds, achievement levels, languages, and cultures. This trend reflects a commitment to "data diversity" and enhances the potential of future AI tools to serve all groups, not just a privileged few (Barocas et al., 2023).
- **Explainable and Transparent AI**: The approach known as "Explainable AI" seeks to make AI models transparent, especially in high-stakes areas such as education, healthcare, and law (Patidar et al., 2024). In education, this trend involves making the decision-making processes of AI systems understandable. In the future, an algorithm that classifies a student as at risk or recommends a specific learning path will also be able to answer the question, "Why did I do this?" For example, the system might explain to a teacher, "I recommended extra exercises because this student struggled with topics in the last five tests and showed low participation." Such transparency builds trust among teachers and students and facilitates AI adoption (Angerschmid et al., 2022). Furthermore, explainability helps identify the source of potential bias, serving the goal of equitable design.
- **Fair and Inclusive Content Generation**: AI is evolving into a tool that not only processes data but also generates content (e.g., text, questions, tests). As AI increasingly takes on this role, ensuring its fair and inclusive outputs becomes essential (Chinta et al.,

2024). For instance, an AI system that generates test questions must do so with sensitivity to cultural and gender issues, avoiding stereotypes and using non-discriminatory and respectful language (Shuford, 2024). Some educational technology companies have already begun integrating components like "anger filters" and "gender balance modules" into their content-generation algorithms to prevent biased or discriminatory output (Ferrara, 2023). As this trend continues, students will encounter more diverse names, faces, and scenarios in their learning materials, helping all students feel represented.

- **Real-Time Adaptation and Personalization**: Although adaptive learning systems already exist, future AI will offer far more advanced real-time analytical capabilities. This will enable dynamic learning experiences that adapt to each student's situation moment by moment (Gupta et al., 2024). The significance of this trend for educational equity lies in its potential to deliver one-on-one tutoring-quality support to a broader population. A skilled private tutor can gauge a student's understanding from facial expressions or pauses and adjust the lesson accordingly; similarly, future AI systems might detect signs of struggle from a student's typing speed, reading time, or even camera feed, and then simplify content or present it through alternative methods (Sari et al., 2024). Such advanced personalization means that every student can receive support exactly when needed, regardless of class size or access to support at home. When this vision becomes reality, it will bring us closer to ensuring that no one is left behind in learning.
- **Privacy- and Security-Oriented Design**: A truly equitable educational ecosystem requires fair outcomes and ethical processes. Accordingly, efforts are intensifying to develop AI systems that protect student data privacy and offer maximum functionality with minimal data (Kosaraju, 2023). In the future, instead of collecting student data on centralized servers, approaches such as federated learning may become more common, allowing data to be processed locally on students' devices (Hridi et al., 2024). For example, a student in a rural area might never have their data sent to a central model, yet still receive high-quality services. This trend will help alleviate concerns among communities wary of technology due to data security issues and encourage more schools to adopt AI tools (Yang & Wen, 2023).

The common thread among these emerging trends is the development of AI in a "responsible, accountable, and inclusive" manner. In the vision of future education, AI is not merely an innovative tool but a partner in education that respects social values. Naturally, fully realizing these trends requires cooperation and determination among technology developers, educators, and policymakers. At this juncture, participatory approaches to technology development gain critical importance.

Participatory Approaches to Technology Development

Adopting participatory approaches in designing and implementing AI systems in education is increasingly recognized as one of the most effective ways to ensure these technologies are inclusive, acceptable, and aligned with user needs. Participatory technology development emphasizes shifting from a "build and deploy" mentality to a "co-design with stakeholders" paradigm involving teachers, students, and parents in the design process. Concrete examples of such approaches include those shown in Figure 4.

Figure 4. Participatory approaches to technology development

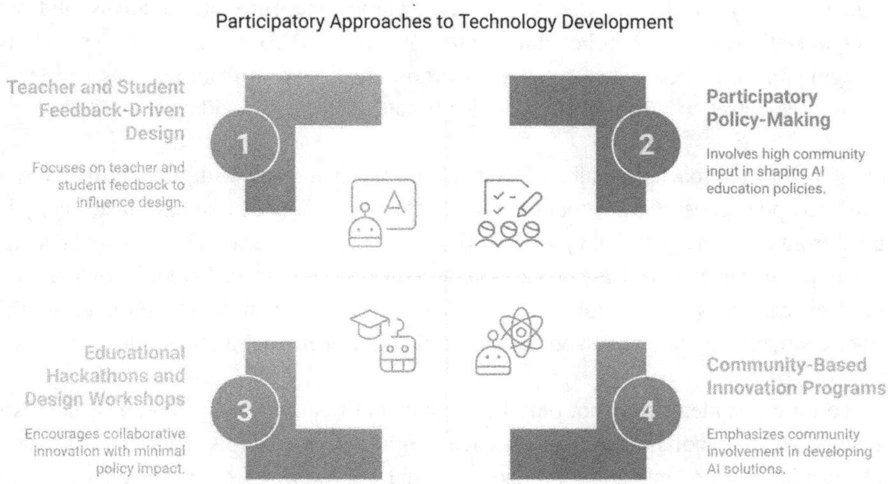

- **Teacher and Student Feedback-Driven Design**: Involving frontline teachers and students in the development process, through pilot testing, interviews, or focus groups, is central to participatory design (Tilak et al., 2024). For example, if a company is developing an AI-driven math learning app, conducting pilot trials with students from diverse socioeconomic and cultural backgrounds allows the interface and content to be refined based on their suggestions (Holstein et al., 2019). Teachers can also provide input on whether dashboard features align with classroom needs (Nazaretsky et al., 2022), resulting in products tailored to the realities of actual learning environments.
- **Community-Based Innovation Programs**: In some educational initiatives, local communities are directly involved in innovation. In projects supporting digital transformation in rural schools, teachers and sometimes even students form "innovation teams" to co-develop AI-based solutions to their problems (Anlimachie et al., 2022). Engineers and developers collaborate with end users, ensuring the resulting technologies are shaped by local priorities rather than imposed from outside.
- **Educational Hackathons and Design Workshops**: "Edu-hackathons", collaborative software development events focused on educational challenges, are increasingly popular. These events bring together interdisciplinary teams of teachers, students, parents, and developers to design AI-supported solutions for real classroom issues (Dipaola et al., 2023). For example, addressing language barriers in multilingual classrooms might involve a student sharing their lived experience, a teacher providing pedagogical insights, and a developer contributing technical expertise to prototype a tool rapidly. Such co-created tools are more likely to be adopted due to the participants' sense of ownership (Oyetade et al., 2023).

- **Participatory Policy-Making**: As important as technology development is, the co-creation of policies governing its use. Some countries now hold stakeholder-inclusive "AI in Education" workshops involving teacher unions, student representatives, and parent organizations to review policy drafts (Funa & Gabay, 2025). For example, when drafting regulations on student data privacy, incorporating concerns from families and learners from the outset ensures more socially legitimate outcomes (Syaidina et al., 2024).

Participatory approaches ensure AI systems are better aligned with user needs and foster trust and acceptance, especially among disadvantaged communities that have historically been excluded from technology design processes. While such approaches require time and resources, they are more sustainable in the long term than investing in top-down technologies that ultimately fail to meet real needs. International bodies such as UNESCO and the OECD have published guidance encouraging countries to embed stakeholder engagement into their edtech ecosystems (UNESCO, 2019).

In the future, students may not only be consumers of educational technology, but also its co-creators. High school students, for instance, might design AI tools tailored to their school context, turning learning into an act of innovation and empowering fresh perspectives on equity.

Future Scenarios for Preventing Educational Inequality

Several visionary future scenarios emerge assuming a fully developed, inclusive AI-supported educational ecosystem. Figure 5 presents the future scenarios for preventing inequalities through AI.

Figure 5. Overcoming educational inequality with AI

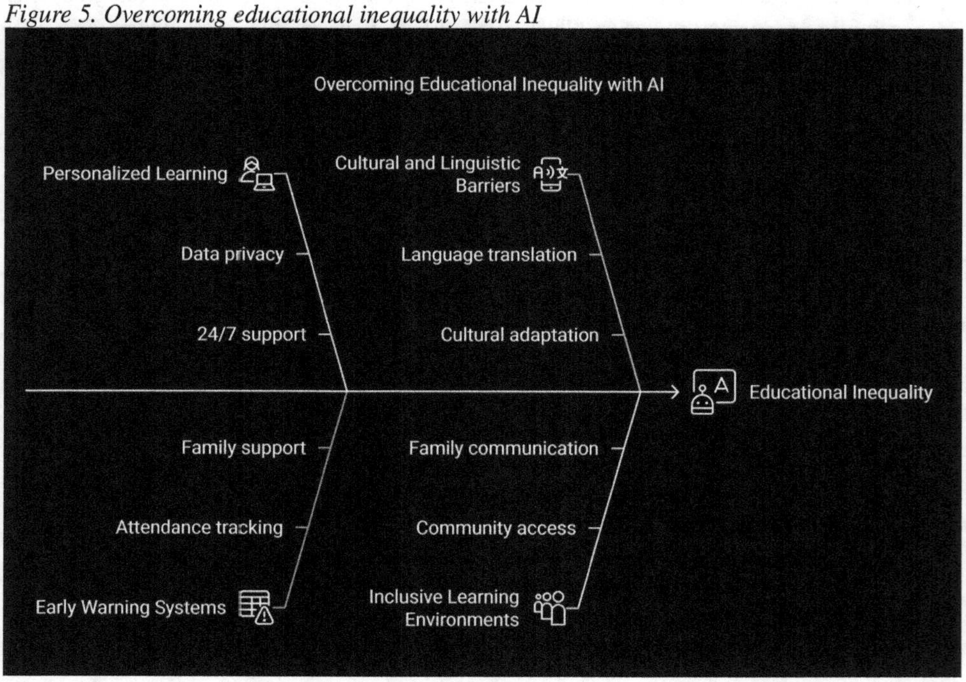

- **A Personalized Digital Mentor for All:** Every student may have access to a digital learning assistant (mentor). This AI-supported mentor would analyze all aspects of a student's data—from in-school performance to study habits at home—while adhering to the principle of data privacy, and provide the most appropriate guidance (Gabriel, 2024). Even a student from a disadvantaged background with no access to private tutoring could ask questions 24/7 and revisit topics using various explanations thanks to this digital mentor (Chang et al., 2024). In such a scenario, the impact of economic inequality on educational outcomes would be minimized, as the one-on-one support enjoyed by wealthier students could be scaled to benefit all learners through AI (Pachava et al., 2025).
- **Reducing School Dropouts with Smart Early Warning Systems:** AI systems with advanced analytics capabilities will be able to track longitudinal data such as attendance, grades, and behavior to identify students at risk of dropping out at an early stage. For example, the system can detect these nuances if a student shows signs of declining motivation due to family issues or a lack of belonging caused by social exclusion. Following detection, the school counselor and family can be promptly notified to provide support (Sorensen, 2018). This would lead to a significant reduction in school dropout rates, particularly in disadvantaged areas. Ensuring that every student remains within the educational system is vital for breaking long-term cycles of social inequality (Soland et al., 2020).
- **Eliminating Cultural and Linguistic Barriers:** With the advancement of real-time translation and language modeling technologies, a future in which students speaking different languages can seamlessly learn in the same classroom becomes imaginable. For instance, Arabic and Turkish students could attend the same virtual class, each listening and participating in their own language. AI would instantly translate the conversations and even adapt cultural references (Zaki & Ahmed, 2024). In this scenario, refugee or migrant children would no longer fall behind in education due to language barriers. Similarly, communities that speak minority languages would gain access to quality education in their language through AI (Asadzadeh, 2022).
- **Inclusive Learning Environments Beyond the Classroom (Learning Ecosystems):** In the future, education could extend beyond school walls into a broader AI-powered ecosystem. For example, neighborhood libraries, community centers, or home environments could transform into AI-assisted learning stations (Akintayo et al., 2024). Students from low-income families could access the internet and AI-supported materials in these centers after school and receive help with assignments free of charge. Since the AI would be integrated with the school system, it would already know which topics the student struggled with that day and could recommend suitable activities. Additionally, communication bots could inform families in their native languages and simple terms about their child's progress and offer advice on supporting them at home (Bhatnagar et al., 2021). Such a holistic learning ecosystem, which incorporates not only the school but also the home and community, would act as a safety net that mitigates the effects of socioeconomic disparities.
- **Barrier-Free Educational Environments:** One of AI's most transformative impacts will be the creation of truly barrier-free learning environments for students with disabilities. In the future, a visually impaired student could receive real-time audio descriptions of classroom activities through AI-enabled smart glasses; a deaf student could see live translations into sign language or subtitles via augmented reality lenses; a physically dis-

abled student could fully participate in class interactions through robotic systems and AI even conducting science experiments remotely by giving commands to a robotic arm (Almufareh et al., 2024). Such technologies will ensure that students with disabilities receive education on equal terms, thus fully realizing the concept of "accessible education" (Mitre & Zeneli, 2024).

These scenarios may seem ambitious by today's standards; however, given the pace of technological advancement and growing social awareness, much of the vision described above is expected to become a reality by the 2030s and beyond. Nevertheless, these optimistic scenarios will not materialize automatically. Technology developers, educators, and policymakers alike must actively pursue the inclusive and fair use of AI. The final section discusses the concrete steps that must be taken in this direction.

CONCLUSION AND RECOMMENDATIONS

While AI holds transformative potential for enhancing educational equity, realizing this potential requires a deliberate, fair, and inclusive implementation strategy. First and foremost, proactive measures must be taken to ensure that AI-driven educational initiatives do not deepen the digital divide. Strengthening technological infrastructure in rural and low-income regions, providing affordable internet access for all students, and ensuring the availability of digital devices are critical. Public authorities and local governments should invest in expanding school networks, addressing device shortages, and establishing learning centers for disadvantaged learners.

Another key priority is enhancing educators' capacity to use AI-based systems effectively and equitably. Comprehensive professional development programs should be implemented to build AI literacy among teachers, improving their technical skills and pedagogical adaptation strategies. These programs should provide hands-on training on integrating AI tools into classrooms, identifying and managing algorithmic bias, and guiding students in AI-supported learning environments. Moreover, best practices in technology use should be shared across schools, and peer mentoring or interschool collaboration should be encouraged to foster institutional capacity-building.

Ethical and transparency-related considerations also form a crucial part of the recommendations. Clear regulations regarding data privacy, algorithmic neutrality, and accountability must be established to prevent AI systems from undermining fairness in education. Robust security protocols and legal frameworks should be implemented to safeguard student data, and all stakeholders must be informed about what data is collected, for what purposes, and how it is used. AI tools should undergo bias audits and fairness testing during the design phase, with corrective adjustments as needed. Universities and independent research institutions should conduct impact evaluations of AI-based educational software, providing evidence-based insights to inform policymaking.

Furthermore, educational content must reflect cultural diversity and accommodate different learning styles. AI-generated learning materials should not cater to a single learner profile but instead offer customization for a broad range of student needs. Content modules should vary in language, difficulty level, and topical relevance. National-level digital content repositories could be established and enriched through teacher contributions from diverse regions.

Finally, public–private partnerships should be promoted to ensure the wide-scale and sustainable deployment of AI solutions in education. Governments, universities, technology firms, and civil society organizations must collaborate to implement joint initiatives. Large-scale reforms, such as developing a national AI-powered learning platform, are more achievable through such partnerships. Similarly, global knowledge-sharing networks should be established to foster mutual learning between countries.

Implementing these recommendations as part of a coherent strategy will significantly contribute to AI's fair and inclusive integration in education. When responsibly guided, AI can foster new practices that strengthen educational opportunity and provide every learner with a supportive environment to realize their full potential. Left unchecked, however, technological developments may risk reproducing existing inequalities in new forms. Therefore, the decisions and investments made today will determine the trajectory toward a more equitable future for education. By embedding AI into education with a human-centered and ethically grounded approach, we move one step closer to an educational system where truly no child is left behind.

REFERENCES

Adams, C., Pente, P., Lemermeyer, G., & Rockwell, G. (2023). Ethical principles for artificial intelligence in K-12 education. *Computers and Education: Artificial Intelligence*, *4*, 100131. DOI: 10.1016/j.caeai.2023.100131

Akintayo, O. T., Eden, C. A., Ayeni, O. O., & Onyebuchi, N. C. (2024). Integrating AI with emotional and social learning in primary education: Developing a holistic adaptive learning ecosystem. *Computer Science & IT Research Journal*, *5*(5), 1076–1089. DOI: 10.51594/csitrj.v5i5.1116

Almufareh, M. F., Kausar, S., Humayun, M., & Tehsin, S. (2024). A conceptual model for inclusive technology: Advancing disability inclusion through artificial intelligence. *Journal of Disability Research*, *3*(1), 1–11. DOI: 10.57197/JDR-2023-0060

Angerschmid, A., Zhou, J., Theuermann, K., Chen, F., & Holzinger, A. (2022). Fairness and explanation in AI-informed decision making. *Machine Learning and Knowledge Extraction*, *4*(2), 556–579. DOI: 10.3390/make4020026

Anlimachie, M. A., Avoada, C., & Amoako-Mensah, T. (2022). Leapfrogging inequality strategies for transformed rural education: A school district case, Ghana. *Australian and International Journal of Rural Education*, *32*(1), 33–51. DOI: 10.47381/aijre.v32i1.282

Asadzadeh, M. (2022). Translation of educational material for migrants. *Sociol Int J*, *6*(5), 240–243. DOI: 10.15406/sij.2022.06.00293

Baral, S. K., Rath, R. C., Goel, R., & Singh, T. (2022, March). The role of digital technology and artificial intelligence is to monitor talent strategies to bridge the skill gap. In *2022 International Mobile and Embedded Technology Conference (MECON)* (pp. 582–587). IEEE. DOI: 10.1109/MECON53876.2022.9751837

Barocas, S., Hardt, M., & Narayanan, A. (2023). *Fairness and machine learning: Limitations and opportunities* (eBook). The MIT Press. https://mitpress.mit.edu/9780262376525/fairness-and-machine-learning/

Bhatnagar, A. K., Khanna, U., & Rana, A. (2021). Digital learning ecosystem at Indian higher education system. *Journal of Contemporary Issues in Business and Government*, *27*(2). Advance online publication. DOI: 10.47750/cibg.2021.27.02.463

Binns, R. (2018). Fairness in machine learning: Lessons from political philosophy. *Proceedings of Machine Learning Research*, *81*, 149–159.

Blodgett, S. L., Barocas, S., Daumé, H.III, & Wallach, H. (2020). Language (technology) is power: A critical survey of "bias" in NLP. *Proceedings of the 58th Annual Meeting of the ACL*, 5454-5476. DOI: 10.18653/v1/2020.acl-main.485

Bulathwela, S., Pérez-Ortiz, M., Holloway, C., Cukurova, M., & Shawe-Taylor, J. (2024). Artificial intelligence alone will not democratise education: On educational inequality, techno-solutionism and inclusive tools. *Sustainability (Basel)*, *16*(2), 781. DOI: 10.3390/su16020781

Chang, C. N., Hui, J., Justus-Smith, C., & Wang, T. W. (2024). Navigating STEM careers with AI mentors: A new IDP journey. *Frontiers in Artificial Intelligence*, *7*, 1461137. DOI: 10.3389/frai.2024.1461137 PMID: 39439844

Chinta, S. V., Wang, Z., Yin, Z., Hoang, N., Gonzalez, M., Quy, T. L., & Zhang, W. (2024). FairAIED: Navigating fairness, bias, and ethics in educational AI applications. *arXiv preprint arXiv:2407.18745*. https://doi.org//arXiv.2407.18745DOI: 10.48550

Chiu, T. K., Moorhouse, B. L., Chai, C. S., & Ismailov, M. (2024). Teacher support and student motivation to learn with Artificial Intelligence (AI) based chatbot. *Interactive Learning Environments*, *32*(7), 3240–3256. DOI: 10.1080/10494820.2023.2172044

Cho, M., & Kim, K. M. (2021). Exploring the disparity in tangible outcomes of internet use between persons with disabilities and persons without disabilities in South Korea. *Disability and Health Journal*, *14*(3), 101101. DOI: 10.1016/j.dhjo.2021.101101 PMID: 33824093

Contreras, M. R., & Jaimes, J. O. P. (2024, October). AI Ethics in the Fields of Education and Research: A Systematic Literature Review. In *2024 International Symposium on Accreditation of Engineering and Computing Education,* 1-6. https://doi.org/DOI: 10.1109/ICACIT62963.2024.10788651

D'Ignazio, C., & Klein, L. F. (2020). *Data Feminism.* MIT Press. DOI: 10.7551/mitpress/11805.001.0001

Dahal, C. (2024). Revolutionizing education through AI-powered inclusive learning systems. *Proceedings of the AAAI Conference on Artificial Intelligence*, *38*(21), 23736–23737. DOI: 10.1609/aaai.v38i21.30546

DiPaola, D., Moore, K. S., Ali, S., Perret, B., Zhou, X., Zhang, H., & Lee, I. (2023, March). Make-a-thon for middle school AI educators. In *Proceedings of the 54th ACM Technical Symposium on Computer Science Education, 1*, 305-311.

Dutta, S., Ranjan, S., Mishra, S., Sharma, V., Hewage, P., & Iwendi, C. (2024). Enhancing educational adaptability: A review and analysis of AI-driven adaptive learning platforms. In *2024 4th International Conference on Innovative Practices in Technology and Management (ICIPTM)* (pp. 1-5). IEEE. https://doi.org/DOI: 10.1109/ICIPTM59628.2024.10563448

Dwi, M., & Alif, H. (2024). Transformative impact of AI on multicultural education: A qualitative thematic analysis. *Edelweiss Applied Science and Technology*, *8*(5), 113–118. DOI: 10.55214/25768484.v8i5.1667

Eden, C. A., Ayeni, O. O., & Onyebuchi, N. C. (2024). Integrating AI with emotional and social learning in primary education: Developing a holistic adaptive learning ecosystem. *Open Access Research Journal of Multidisciplinary Studies*, *7*(2), 42–51. DOI: 10.53022/oarjms.2024.7.2.0025

El-Bawab, T. S. (2020). Toward access equality: Bridging the digital divide. *IEEE Communications Magazine*, *58*(12), 6–7. DOI: 10.1109/MCOM.2020.9311933

Elam, K. M. (2024). Exploring the challenges and future directions of big data and AI in education. *Journal of Artificial Intelligence & General Science*, *5*(1), 81–93. DOI: 10.60087/jaigs.v1i1.173

Eziamaka, N., Odonkor, T., & Akinsulire, A. (2024). AI-driven accessibility: Transformative software solutions for empowering individuals with disabilities. *International Journal of Applied Research in Social Sciences*, *6*(8), 1612–1641. DOI: 10.51594/ijarss.v6i8.1373

Ferrara, E. (2023). Fairness and bias in artificial intelligence: A brief survey of sources, impacts, and mitigation strategies. *Sci*, *6*(1), 3. DOI: 10.3390/sci6010003

Fitria, T. N. (2023). The use of artificial intelligence in education (AIED): Can AI replace the teacher's role? *Epigram*, *20*(2), 165–187. DOI: 10.32722/epi.v20i2.5711

Floridi, L., Cowls, J., Beltrametti, M., Chatila, R., Chazerand, P., Dignum, V., & Luetge, C. (2018). AI4People—An ethical framework for a good AI society: Opportunities, risks, principles, and recommendations. *Minds and Machines*, *28*(4), 689–707. https://doi.org/doi:10.1007/s11023-018-9482-5

Funa, A. A., & Gabay, R. A. E. (2025). Policy guidelines and recommendations on AI use in teaching and learning: A meta-synthesis study. *Social Sciences & Humanities Open*, *11*, 101221. DOI: 10.1016/j.ssaho.2024.101221

Gabriel, S. (2024). Generative AI and Educational (In) Equity. In *International Conference on AI Research.*

Gorski, P. (2005). Education equity and the digital divide. [Formerly AACE Journal]. *AACE Review*, *13*(1), 3–45.

Gupta, T., Kumar, A., Roy, B. K., & Saini, S. (2024). Adaptive learning systems: Harnessing AI to personalize educational outcomes. *International Journal for Research in Applied Science and Engineering Technology*, *12*(11), 458–464. DOI: 10.22214/ijraset.2024.65088

Hamburg, I., & Lütgen, G. (2019). Digital divide, digital inclusion and inclusive education. *Advances in Social Sciences Research Journal*, *6*(4), 223–232. DOI: 10.14738/assrj.64.6457

Holmes, W., Bialik, M., & Fadel, C. (2019). *Artificial intelligence in education promises and implications for teaching and learning.* Center for Curriculum Redesign.

Holstein, K., McLaren, B. M., & Aleven, V. (2019). Co-designing a real-time classroom orchestration tool to support teacher–AI complementarity. In *Proceedings of the 9th International Conference on Learning Analytics & Knowledge,* 21-30. https://doi.org/DOI: 10.18608/jla.2019.62.3

Hridi, A. P., Sahay, R., Hosseinalipour, S., & Akram, B. (2024, May). Revolutionizing AI-Assisted Education with Federated Learning: A Pathway to Distributed, Privacy-Preserving, and Debiased Learning Ecosystems. In *Proceedings of the AAAI Symposium Series*, 3(1), 297–303. https://doi.org/DOI: 10.1609/aaaiss.v3i1.31217

Jian, M. J. K. O. (2023). Personalized learning through AI. *Advances in Engineering Innovation*, *5*(1), 16–19. DOI: 10.54254/2977-3903/5/2023039

Jiao, D. (2024). AI-driven personalization in higher education: Enhancing learning outcomes through adaptive technologies. *Adult and Higher Education*, *6*(6), 42–46. DOI: 10.23977/aduhe.2024.060607

Jucevičienė, P., Vizgirdaitė, J., & Alexander, H. (2018). Accessibility and inclusion in higher education: Implementing international imperatives in national and institutional contexts. *Pedagogika/Pedagogy, 130*(2), 46-63. http://dx.doi.org/DOI: 10.15823/p.2018.21

Kazimzade, G., Patzer, Y., & Pinkwart, N. (2019). Artificial intelligence in education meets inclusive educational technology — the technical state-of-the-art and possible directions. In *Artificial Intelligence and Inclusive Education: Speculative Futures and Emerging Practices* (pp. 61–73). Springer. DOI: 10.1007/978-981-13-8161-4_4

Kosaraju, D. (2023). Securing AI: Federated learning as a tool for privacy preservation. *Galore International Journal of Applied Sciences and Humanities, 7*(1), 57–63. DOI: 10.52403/gijash.20230109

Lagakis, P., & Demetriadis, S. (2021, November). Automated essay scoring: A review of the field. In *2021 International Conference on Computer, Information and Telecommunication Systems (CITS)* (pp. 1-6). IEEE. DOI: 10.1109/CITS52676.2021.9618476

Mehrabi, N., Morstatter, F., Saxena, N., Lerman, K., & Galstyan, A. (2021). A survey on bias and fairness in machine learning. *ACM Computing Surveys, 54*(6), 1–35. DOI: 10.1145/3457607

Milberg, T. (2024, April 28). The future of learning: How AI is revolutionizing education 4.0. *World Economic Forum*. https://www.weforum.org/stories/2024/04/future-learning-ai-revolutionizing-education-4-0/

Mitre, X., & Zeneli, M. (2024, November). Using AI to Improve Accessibility and Inclusivity in Higher Education for Students with Disabilities. In *2024, 21st International Conference on Information Technology Based Higher Education and Training (ITHET)* (pp. 1-8). IEEE. https://doi.org/DOI: 10.1109/ITHET61869.2024.10837607

Murdan, A. P., & Halkhoree, R. (2024, June). Integration of artificial intelligence for educational excellence and innovation in higher education institutions. In *2024 1st International Conference on Smart Energy Systems and Artificial Intelligence (SESAI)* (pp. 1–6). IEEE. https://doi.org/DOI: 10.1109/SESAI61023.2024.10599402

Nazaretsky, T., Bar, C., Walter, M., & Alexandron, G. (2022, March). Empowering teachers with AI: Co-designing a learning analytics tool for personalized instruction in the science classroom. In *LAK22: 12th international learning analytics and knowledge conference* (pp. 1-12).

Oyetade, K., Harmse, A., & Zuva, T. (2023). Examining the factors ınfluencing students' satisfaction with hackathon for IT projects. [iJET]. *International Journal of Emerging Technologies in Learning, 18*(22), 24–37. DOI: 10.3991/ijet.v18i22.42691

Pachava, V., Lasekan, O. A., Méndez-Alarcón, C. M., Pena, M. T. G., & Golla, S. K. (2025). Advancing SDG 4: Harnessing generative AI to transform learning, teaching, and educational equity in higher education. *Journal of Lifestyle and SDGs Review, 5*(2), e03774–e03774. DOI: 10.47172/2965-730X.SDGsReview.v5.n02.pe03774

Patidar, N., Mishra, S., Jain, R., Prajapati, D., Solanki, A., Suthar, R., & Patel, H. (2024). Transparency in AI decision making: A survey of explainable AI methods and applications. *Advances of Robotic Technology, 2*(1), 1–10. Advance online publication. DOI: 10.23880/art-16000110

Pham, L., O'Sullivan, B., Scantamburlo, T., & Mai, T. (2024, March). Addressing digital and AI skills gaps in European living areas: A comparative analysis of small and large communities. *Proceedings of the AAAI Conference on Artificial Intelligence*, *38*(21), 23119–23127. DOI: 10.1609/aaai.v38i21.30357

Poonpon, K., Manorom, P., & Chansanam, W. (2023). Exploring effective methods for automated essay scoring of non-native speakers. *Contemporary Educational Technology*, *15*(4), ep475. DOI: 10.30935/cedtech/13740

Pradeep, K., Manish, A., Adithiyaa, A., Sahana, N., & Abhishek, S. (2024). Personalized adaptive learning platform empowered by artificial intelligence. In *2024 International Conference on Knowledge Engineering and Communication Systems,* 1–8. IEEE. https://doi.org/DOI: 10.1109/ICKECS61492.2024.10617075

Ramakrishnan, S., Bishnoi, M. M., Joghee, S., Jijitha, S., & Kumar, A. (2024, February). Social Engineering: Role of Teachers in Cohabitation of AI with Education. In *2024 2nd International Conference on Cyber Resilience,* 1–6. IEEE. https://doi.org/DOI: 10.1109/ICCR61006.2024.10532897

Sari, H. E., Tumanggor, B., & Efron, D. (2024). Improving educational outcomes through adaptive learning systems using AI. *International Transactions on Artificial Intelligence*, *3*(1), 21–31. DOI: 10.33050/italic.v3i1.647

Scarci, A. S., Teixeira, T. M., & Dal Forno, L. F. (2024). Artificial intelligence and its relations with digital competencies and education. *International Journal of Emerging Technologies in Learning*, *24*(21), 43–59. DOI: 10.53660/CLM-4374-24V38

Segura-Monroy, J., Hernandez-Ordonez, H., Cardoza, O. C., Sanchez-Sarellano, S., & Yildirim, Y. (2022). Education with AI & machine learning in a post-pandemic world. *Eurasian Journal of Higher Education*, *3*(6), 13–25. DOI: 10.31039/ejohe.2022.6.67

Selwyn, N. (2021). *Education and technology: Key issues and debates* (3rd ed.). Bloomsbury Publishing.

Shete, S., Koshti, P., & Pujari, V. (2024). The impact of AI-powered personalization on academic performance in students. In *2024 5th International Conference on Recent Trends in Computer Science and Technology,* 295-301. IEEE. https://doi.org/DOI: 10.1109/ICRTCST61793.2024.10578480

Shetty, K., & Mishra, P. (2020). India's new policy progresses towards integrating AI with education. SSRN *Electronic Journal*. https://dx.doi.org/DOI: 10.2139/ssrn.3881747

Shuford, J. (2024). Exploring Ethical Dimensions in AI: Navigating Bias and Fairness in the Field. [JAIGS]. *J. Artif. Intell. Gen. Sci.*, *3*(1), 103–124. DOI: 10.60087/jaigs.vol03.issue01.p124

Singh, H., Mohammad, S., Yaseen, A., Molawade, M., Mohite, S., Jadhav, V., & Jadhav, R. (2024). Multilingual education through optical character recognition (OCR) and AI. *2024 MIT Art, Design and Technology School of Computing International Conference (MITADT SoCiCon)*, 1–6. https://doi.org/DOI: 10.1109/MITADTSoCiCon60330.2024.10575015

Soland, J., Domingue, B., & Lang, D. (2020). Using Machine Learning to Advance Early Warning Systems: Promise and Pitfalls. *Teachers College Record, 122*(14), 1–30. DOI: 10.1177/016146812012201403

Soomro, K. A., Kale, U., Curtis, R., Akçaoğlu, M., & Bernstein, M. (2020). Digital divide among higher education faculty. *International Journal of Educational Technology in Higher Education, 17*(1), 21. Advance online publication. DOI: 10.1186/s41239-020-00191-5

Sorensen, L. C. (2018). Big data in educational administration: An application for predicting school dropout risk. *Educational Administration Quarterly, 55*(3), 404–446. DOI: 10.1177/0013161X18799439

Sperling, K., Stenberg, C. J., McGrath, C., Åkerfeldt, A., Heintz, F., & Stenliden, L. (2024). In search of artificial intelligence (AI) literacy in teacher education: A scoping review. *Computers and Education Open, 100169*, 100169. Advance online publication. DOI: 10.1016/j.caeo.2024.100169

Syaidina, M. O., Fahrudin, R., & Mutiara, I. A. (2024). Implementation of ethics of using artificial intelligence in the education system in Indonesia. *Blockchain Frontier Technology, 4*(1), 63–71. DOI: 10.34306/bfront.v4i1.571

Sydorenko, V. V., Akhnovska, I. O., Smirnov, S., Verbovskyi, I., & Melnychuk, O. V. (2024). Improvement of higher education: How to bridge the digital divide during the transformation? [EduLearn]. *Journal of Education and Learning, 18*(3), 1001–1014. DOI: 10.11591/edulearn.v18i3.21078

Tarhan, C., Aydin, C., & Tecim, V. (2021). Digital divide evaluation in higher education from distance learning perspective. In *Global, Regional and Local Perspectives on the Economies of Southeastern Europe* (pp. 343-351). Springer.

Taufikin, M. S. I., Azifah, N., Nikmah, F., & Kuanr, J. (2024, April). The Impact of AI on Teacher Roles and Pedagogy in the 21st Century Classroom. In *2024 International Conference on Knowledge Engineering and Communication Systems, 1*, 1-5. IEEE. https://doi.org/DOI: 10.1109/ICKECS61492.2024.10617236

Tenberga, I., & Daniela, L. (2024). Artificial ıntelligence literacy competencies for teachers through self-assessment tools. *Sustainability (Basel), 16*(23), 10386. DOI: 10.3390/su162310386

Tilak, S., Lincoln, J., Miner, T., Christensen, N., Jankowski, J., & Kennedy, K. (2024). A participatory, qualitative analysis of the use of MagicSchool AI for course design. *Journal of Sociocybernetics, 19*(1), 43–106. DOI: 10.26754/ojs_jos/jos.2024110947

UNESCO. (2019). *Beijing consensus on artificial intelligence and education: Outcome document of the International Conference on Artificial Intelligence and Education: Planning education in the AI era—Lead the leap (16–18 May 2019, Beijing, People's Republic of China).* https://unesdoc.unesco.org/ark:/48223/pf0000368303

Wang, X., Liu, Q., Pang, H., Tan, S. C., Lei, J., Wallace, M. P., & Li, L. (2023). What matters in AI-supported learning: A study of human-AI interactions in language learning using cluster analysis and epistemic network analysis. *Computers & Education, 194*, 104703. DOI: 10.1016/j.compedu.2022.104703

Yafie, E., Anisa, N., Maningtyas, R. D. T., Iriyanto, T., Jumaat, N. F., & Widiasih, R. M. (2024). Enhancing early childhood educators' digital competencies through AI-powered learning modules (AI-PEL) training program. *Al-Athfal: Jurnal Pendidikan Anak, 10*(1), 73–82. DOI: 10.14421/al-athfal.2024.101-07

Yang, M., & Wen, F. (2023). AI-powered personalized learning journeys: Revolutionizing information management for college students in online platforms. *Journal of Information Systems Engineering & Management, 8*(1), 23196. DOI: 10.55267/iadt.07.14079

Yi, Y. (2021). Establishing the concept of AI literacy. *Jahr–European Journal of Bioethics, 12*(2), 353–368. DOI: 10.21860/j.12.2.8

Zainal, N., & Hassan, M. H. A. (2022, November). Automated Essay Scoring (AES) using English Essay Question. In *2022 IEEE 20th Student Conference on Research and Development (SCOReD)* (pp. 1-6). IEEE.

Zaki, M. Z., & Ahmed, U. (2024). Bridging linguistic divides: The impact of AI-powered translation systems on communication equity and inclusion. *Journal of translation and language studies, 5*(2), 20-30. https://doi.org/DOI: 10.48185/jtls.v5i2.1065

Zawacki-Richter, O., Marín, V. I., Bond, M., & Gouverneur, F. (2019). Systematic review of research on artificial intelligence applications in higher education. *International Journal of Educational Technology in Higher Education, 16*(39), 1–27. DOI: 10.1186/s41239-019-0171-0

Zhang, H., Lee, I., & Moore, K. (2024, March). An effectiveness study of teacher-led AI literacy curriculum in K-12 classrooms. *Proceedings of the AAAI Conference on Artificial Intelligence, 38*(21), 23318–23325. DOI: 10.1609/aaai.v38i21.30380

Chapter 3
Harnessing AI Chatbots in Pre-Service Teacher Education:
Perceptions, Pedagogical Decision-Making, and Barriers to Integration

Kham Bao
https://orcid.org/0000-0002-0032-2451
Hue University, Vietnam

ABSTRACT

This chapter investigates the role of AI chatbots in pre-service language teacher education using data from 134 trainees in Vietnam. Applying the AI-CITE framework, the study examines how a customized chatbot, Mizou, influenced learning across six areas: individualization, interactivity, engagement, decision-making, lesson planning, and barriers. Findings show that chatbots support instructional design, feedback, and learner motivation but struggle with contextual sensitivity and emotional nuance. While effective as supplementary tools, chatbots cannot replace human mentorship. The chapter concludes with practical strategies for integrating AI responsibly into teacher education, emphasizing the need for culturally aware and ethically designed systems.

INTRODUCTION

The integration of AI chatbots in education has seen remarkable advancements in recent years, particularly within teacher preparation programs (Labadze et al., 2023). In the domain of language teacher education, AI-powered chatbots have emerged as a transformative force that offers new paradigms for instructional design, professional development, and classroom decision-making (Nguyen et al., 2021). As teacher education evolves to emphasize technology-enhanced learning and adaptive teaching skills, exploring the role of chatbots in pre-service teacher training is both

DOI: 10.4018/979-8-3373-5097-4.ch003

timely and relevant to the modernization of language teacher education programs (Luckin et al., 2016; McGrath et al., 2024).

Existing research in teacher education technology has begun to document the benefits of AI chatbots, yet also reveals important gaps (Wollny et al., 2021). On one hand, multiple studies highlight that chatbots can enhance interactivity and engagement in learning as well as assist with practical tasks like lesson planning and feedback provision (Okonkwo & Ade-Ibijola, 2021; Lee & Zhai, 2024). For example, chatbots provide instant assistance in developing lesson structures or teaching strategies, allowing pre-service teachers to iterate on their plans with immediate, personalized feedback (Lee & Zhai, 2024). Such interactive support has been associated with increased trainee reflection and reduced anxiety during practice teaching (Kim & Kim, 2020; Dizon, 2020). On the other hand, certain dimensions of chatbot use remain under-explored. A recurring critique is that AI-generated recommendations lack deep contextual sensitivity and cannot replicate the empathy of human mentors, limiting their effectiveness in diverse classroom scenarios (Kohnke, 2023; Zawacki-Richter et al., 2023). These affective and contextual limitations – such as difficulty adapting to specific cultural classroom contexts or offering emotional encouragement – suggest that research has yet to fully address the softer, humanistic aspects of chatbot integration in teacher education (Mathew, 2024).

This gap in knowledge provides a clear rationale for the present study, which targets both theoretical and practical shortcomings of prior work. Theoretically, mainstream models of technology integration have not accounted for the ways in which current chatbots fail to exhibit human-like emotional intelligence or cultural adaptability (Mishra & Koehler, 2006; Venkatesh et al., 2003). Studies indicate that persistent limitations in today's chatbots hinder the development of critical teaching competencies in trainees, including empathy and culturally responsive pedagogy (Kohnke, 2023). Practically, there is a notable lack of training and preparation for pre-service teachers to effectively use AI tools (Mathew, 2024; Dizon, 2020). Many trainees receive minimal guidance in employing chatbots, resulting in low confidence, sporadic adoption, and misalignment between what chatbots offer and the real-world needs of classrooms (Beyer et al., 2024; Pappagallo, 2024). These theoretical and practical gaps – from chatbots' lack of emotional and cultural intelligence to teachers' insufficient AI training – underscore the need for a focused investigation that can inform more effective integration of chatbots in language teacher education.

In response to the above needs, this study examines several key questions that remain unclear in the literature. It investigates how pre-service teachers perceive and engage with a specially designed AI chatbot named Mizou in their teacher education program, how the Mizou chatbot influences their lesson planning and pedagogical decision-making processes, and what barriers hinder chatbot integration into their learning experience. By probing these issues, the research addresses the noted gap between educators' enthusiasm for AI tools and the reality of their classroom adoption (Labadze et al., 2023). Through this inquiry, the chapter seeks to advance our understanding of AI chatbots' role in pre-service teacher education and to resolve ambiguities regarding their pedagogical value and limitations.

This chapter makes both theoretical and practical contributions to the field of language teacher education. Theoretically, it applies the AI Chatbot Integration in Teacher Education (AI-CITE) framework as an analytical lens, synthesizing cognitive, pedagogical, and technology-adoption perspectives to explain how chatbots can be effectively utilized in teacher training. Using this integrative model extends existing theory by highlighting the interplay between teacher cognition (e.g. perceptions and attitudes), instructional practice (e.g. lesson design, classroom management), and system-level factors (e.g. adoption barriers) when AI chatbots are introduced into teacher preparation – an interplay that other models, such as TPACK, a framework describing how educators integrate technology effectively into teaching by combining technology skills with pedagogical methods and content expertise, or UTAUT, a model predicting user acceptance of technology based on factors like performance expectancy, effort expectancy, social influence, and available resources do not fully capture when applied in isolation (Mishra & Koehler, 2006; Venkatesh et al., 2003). Practically, the study offers actionable insights for teacher education programs and educational technology developers. Additionally, the findings suggest the importance of integrating AI chatbots with human mentoring (rather than using them in isolation) to maintain the empathetic, adaptive guidance that trainees require (Kohnke, 2023). By bridging these theoretical and practical outcomes, the chapter aims to offer critical insights into the future of AI-driven teacher education and to deliver concrete strategies for stakeholders – educators, curriculum designers, and policymakers – in effectively harnessing chatbot technology in preservice teacher programs.

LITERATURE REVIEW

The Role of Chatbots in Language Teacher Education

This section explores the multifaceted roles of AI-powered chatbots within language teacher education. It discusses their capabilities as instructional aides, tools for enhancing engagement, and facilitators of pedagogical decision-making. It also critically examines the ethical, technical, and pedagogical implications of chatbot integration.

The integration of AI-powered chatbots in teacher education has emerged as a transformative force, offering new paradigms for instructional design, professional development, and pedagogical decision-making. In the context of language teacher education, chatbots serve multifaceted roles—acting as instructional aides, engagement facilitators, and decision-making tools—while also prompting critical reflection on ethical, technical, and pedagogical dimensions. Their incorporation reflects a broader shift towards digital transformation in education, enhancing adaptive learning environments and aligning with the goals of 21st-century teaching practices (Luckin et al., 2016).

One of the most significant contributions of chatbots in preservice teacher education is their ability to support instructional design and planning. Lin and Chang's (2023) CHAT-ACTS framework promotes personalized, goal-directed learning by using chatbots to scaffold instructional strategies and self-regulated learning behaviors. Similarly, Labadze et al. (2023) emphasize the value of chatbots in reducing administrative burdens and creating individualized learning pathways for trainees. These contributions are particularly relevant in language teacher education, where planning for differentiated instruction and scaffolding learner language development are essential.

Beyond task support, chatbots play a key role in enhancing engagement across cognitive, emotional, and social domains. Simulated teaching scenarios, virtual student dialogues, and gamified feedback mechanisms have been associated with increased preservice teacher engagement and pedagogical reflection (Jeon, 2021; Fryer et al., 2019). Emotional support is provided through non-judgmental feedback, which fosters a safe space for experimentation and reduces anxiety, especially among novice teachers (Dizon, 2020). Socially, chatbots facilitate collaborative learning by supporting peer interactions in lesson co-design and group discussions within digital platforms like Discord or Teams (Kohnke et al., 2023; Huang et al., 2022).

Teacher perceptions and acceptance of chatbot technologies also significantly influence their adoption and effectiveness. While many preservice teachers appreciate the immediate feedback and efficiency afforded by chatbots, concerns remain about creativity constraints, emotional disconnects, and the risk of over-reliance (Zawacki-Richter et al., 2019). Studies grounded in the Technology Acceptance Model, a theory that explains how users accept and adopt new technologies, primarily focusing on two factors—perceived usefulness and perceived ease of use (Chocarro et al., 2021), emphasize that perceived usefulness and ease of use are strong predictors of chatbot adoption. Digital competence, age, and prior exposure to educational technology further mediate these attitudes (Bii et al., 2018).

While chatbots offer numerous opportunities, challenges persist. Technically, limitations in natural language processing (NLP) capable of understanding, interpreting, and generating human-like language responses, rigid scripts, and content inaccuracies reduce the quality of interaction and learning (Smutný & Schreiberova, 2020; Zhou & Brown, 2020). Ethically, concerns surrounding data privacy, algorithmic bias, and potential reinforcement of stereotypes demand critical oversight (Jeon et al., 2024; Kooli, 2023).

In conclusion, chatbots are reshaping language teacher education by offering scalable, interactive, and personalized training experiences. Their role in enhancing instructional design, supporting engagement, and guiding pedagogical decisions makes them valuable tools in preservice teacher development. However, to fully realize their potential, teacher education must critically engage with the ethical, technical, and pedagogical implications of chatbot use, and ensure integration within blended learning frameworks that uphold the humanistic core of teaching.

Review of Previous Studies

This subsection systematically reviews previous research on chatbots focusing on five key features: individualization, interactivity, engagement, pedagogical decision-making and lesson planning, and barriers faced by chatbots in language teacher education. Each feature is critically analyzed to highlight both advancements and ongoing challenges.

Individualization Through Chatbots in Language Teacher Education

The increasing integration of chatbots into language teacher education programs has ushered in a new era of personalized and adaptive learning, responding to the complex and evolving needs of preservice teachers. Individualization, defined as the customization of instructional content, pacing, feedback, and pedagogical support to align with individual learner characteristics, has emerged as a central goal in teacher training. Chatbots, powered by natural language processing (NLP) and machine learning, play a pivotal role in facilitating such tailored experiences. By enabling adaptive learning pathways, delivering personalized feedback, modeling differentiated instruction, and supporting reflective practices, chatbots serve as scalable, responsive tools for cultivating core teaching competencies. For instance, Zagami (2024) demonstrated that AI chatbots assist preservice teachers in creating differentiated lesson plans that emphasize student diversity and inclusion within online learning environments. Similarly, Kohnke, Moorhouse, and Zou (2023) explored the affordances of ChatGPT in language teaching, highlighting its potential to provide personalized feedback and support reflective practices. Huang et al. (2022) conducted a meta-analytic review, revealing that chatbots can offer adaptive learning pathways and personalized feedback, enhancing learner engagement. However, their promise is moderated by persistent technical, ethical, and pedagogical challenges. Kim and Kim (2022) found that while teachers perceive AI-based educational tools as beneficial, concerns remain regarding the changing role of educators and the transparency of AI decision-making processes. These findings underscore the need for balanced, human-centered design approaches in their implementation.

A primary function of chatbots in preservice teacher education is the creation of adaptive learning pathways. These systems can analyze user input data such as task performance, learning pace, and content preferences to offer personalized instructional trajectories. For example, Fryer et al. (2019) demonstrated that chatbots in language learning environments effectively adjusted the complexity of instructional materials based on trainee progress, ensuring that users focused on areas such as grammar instruction or classroom interaction strategies according to their needs. Similarly, Jeon (2021) introduced a chatbot-assisted dynamic assessment (CA-DA) model capable of diagnosing vocabulary-teaching competencies and scaffolding development through feedback loops, thus promoting adaptive pedagogical skills. These systems support novice teachers in self-paced skill-building, aligning instructional content with their developmental stage and specialization goals, such as multilingual education or inclusive practices (Pokrivčák, 2022; Yang et al., 2023).

Equally important is the provision of individualized feedback, a hallmark of effective teacher training. Chatbots enhance feedback delivery by offering real-time, context-sensitive guidance on microteaching practices, lesson plan design, and classroom management strategies. Jeon (2021) found that chatbot-generated feedback, particularly involving error correction and alternative teaching suggestions, enhanced trainees' ability to align instructional goals with learner needs. Dizon (2020) highlighted how advanced chatbots such as ChatGPT, equipped with NLP capabilities, offered personalized responses to reflective journals, encouraging deeper introspection and professional growth.

Recent research underscores the potential of AI chatbots in language education. Kohnke et al. (2023) discuss the affordances of ChatGPT for language teaching and learning, highlighting its capabilities in providing personalized feedback and supporting various instructional activities. Xu et al. (2023) conducted a systematic review, revealing that AI chatbots can enhance student engagement and offer immediate feedback, thereby facilitating language acquisition. However, Yang et al. (2023) caution that while chatbots offer interactive learning experiences, they may not fully replicate the complexity of live classroom interactions, suggesting the need for careful integration into pedagogical practices.

Reflective practice, another pillar of teacher development, is increasingly supported by chatbot technologies. By collecting and analyzing longitudinal data, chatbots help preservice teachers monitor their growth across multiple dimensions—pedagogical, linguistic, and affective, which can foster metacognitive awareness and facilitate goal setting, self-regulation, and continuous professional development. However, scholars caution against over-reliance on quantitative metrics, which may obscure more qualitative aspects of teaching such as emotional intelligence, empathy, and spontaneity (Zawacki-Richter et al., 2023).

Despite these benefits, challenges in implementing individualized chatbot support persist. A major concern is the overuse of scripted dialogues and limited NLP accuracy, which can lead to generic or context-insensitive responses (Smutny & Schreiberova, 2020). This shortfall undermines the personalization promise and may frustrate users expecting nuanced guidance. Ethical concerns also remain prominent, particularly around algorithmic bias, privacy, and data ownership. Kohnke et al. (2023) warn that training data biases can yield inequitable recommendations, disproportionately affecting underrepresented groups. Moreover, Pokrivčáková (2019) argues that over-reliance on AI tools risks displacing the critical human elements of mentorship and reflective dialogue, which are essential for fostering adaptive expertise in complex classroom contexts.

In conclusion, chatbots offer substantial potential for individualizing preservice language teacher education by enabling adaptive learning, personalized feedback, differentiated instruction, and reflective growth. However, these advantages must be tempered with critical awareness of their limitations and ethical implications. A hybrid model—integrating the analytical precision of AI with the empathetic and contextualized support of human mentors—represents the most promising direction for future teacher training frameworks. Such models will ensure that AI tools remain pedagogically relevant, ethically sound, and deeply responsive to the human dimensions of education.

Enhancing Interactivity in Preservice Language Teacher Education through Chatbots

Interactivity, encompassing real-time dialogue, adaptive feedback, scenario simulations, and collaborative exchanges, is increasingly recognized as a defining feature of AI-powered chatbots in language teacher education. These interactive functionalities offer preservice teachers dynamic opportunities to engage in experiential learning, develop pedagogical reflexivity, and practice complex teaching scenarios in safe, scaffolded environments. The pedagogical relevance of chatbots lies in their ability to model interactive classrooms, offer instantaneous feedback, and adapt instructional challenges to user progress, aligning closely with sociocultural and constructivist theories of teacher development (Vygotsky, 1978; Kooli, 2023). Building upon these theoretical frameworks, Bii (2018) explores the implementation of chatbot technology within constructivist learning environments, highlighting how chatbots can serve as mediating tools that facilitate active learning and the acquisition of 21st-century skills through social interaction and scaffolding. However, the true efficacy of these tools depends on addressing challenges in realism, cultural sensitivity, and integration into broader educational frameworks.

At the core of chatbot interactivity are simulated classroom dialogues, which allow preservice teachers to practice real-time decision-making and pedagogical interventions. Chatbots serve as virtual students with varied linguistic competencies and behavioral dispositions, enabling trainees to experiment with lesson delivery, questioning strategies, and classroom management without fear of negative consequences (Lee & Jeon, 2024). This mode of role-play has been found to bolster confidence and instructional agility, particularly in navigating multilingual or diverse classroom contexts (Yang et al., 2023). Nevertheless, critics note that many chatbot interactions remain overly scripted, lacking the unpredictability and nuance of live classroom interactions, which can limit the authenticity of the training experience (Kohnke, 2023).

Interactive chatbots are also instrumental in providing adaptive, real-time feedback that fosters reflective practice. Following microteaching simulations or pedagogical decision-making tasks, chatbots can offer targeted critiques—such as pointing out missed scaffolding opportunities or suggesting more inclusive instructional strategies (Chong et al., 2021). These iterative feedback loops support professional self-regulation and promote higher-order thinking, enabling preservice teachers to refine their instructional reasoning. Immediate feedback, when designed effectively, has been shown to accelerate skill acquisition and support evidence-based pedagogical shifts (Huang & Hew, 2022). However, limitations in natural language processing (NLP) can result in misinterpretation of user input or provision of generic advice, which detracts from the intended personalization (Chong et al., 2021). Beyond individual learning, chatbots also support interactive peer collaboration, albeit in early stages of development. Studies report preliminary success in using chatbots to mediate peer-reviewed lesson design and collaborative problem-solving tasks, simulating real-world teaching team dynamics (Lee et al., 2024).

Another key interactive function of chatbots is adaptive questioning and personalized progression through differentiated instructional scenarios. For example, trainees struggling with classroom assessment might be guided through progressively complex scenarios involving formative feedback strategies or student data interpretation (Nguyen et al., 2021). This responsive learning design aligns well with personalized learning frameworks and supports individualized competence building. Yet again, the technological limitations of current NLP engines often lead to redundant or contextually inappropriate responses that can hinder learning flow (Kohnke, 2023).

In conclusion, interactive chatbots represent a promising, scalable approach to enriching preservice teacher education through simulations, adaptive feedback, and responsive engagement. Their alignment with experiential learning principles and digital scalability makes them particularly relevant for modern teacher training programs. However, maximizing their pedagogical value requires addressing persistent technical and ethical challenges. These improvements will be pivotal in transforming chatbots from supplementary tools into central components of comprehensive teacher education ecosystems.

Engagement Through Chatbots in Preservice Language Teacher Education

Engagement—defined through cognitive, emotional, and social dimensions—is fundamental to effective teacher preparation, particularly in language education where reflection, adaptability, and interaction are core teaching competences. Chatbots, as AI-powered learning tools, are increasingly employed in preservice teacher education to cultivate engagement through interactive, personalized, and adaptive learning environments. These tools support diverse learning trajectories by fostering participation, sustaining motivation, and encouraging collaboration. Drawing from both foundational and emerging studies, this review synthesizes how chatbots enhance engagement in language teacher education, while also identifying persistent technical and pedagogical challenges that must be addressed for optimal integration.

Cognitive engagement is most directly supported through scenario-based simulations and iterative role-play activities that replicate authentic classroom interactions. Chatbots acting as virtual students challenge trainees to apply teaching strategies such as questioning, feedback delivery, or behavior management in realistic contexts. Jeon (2021) showed that chatbot-assisted simulations helped preservice teachers refine lesson planning and classroom management, while Fryer et al. (2019) found that such experiences increased adaptability when addressing diverse learner needs. These interactive tasks align with experiential learning models by encouraging active problem-solving, though their effectiveness is often limited by scripted dialogues and the lack of spontaneity inherent to real classroom exchanges (Kohnke, 2023).

Emotional engagement is cultivated through the affective affordances of chatbots, particularly their provision of immediate, non-judgmental feedback in a low-stakes environment. Kim (2018) reported reduced anxiety and increased confidence among trainees interacting with chatbots that responded empathetically and supportively to pedagogical attempts. Dizon (2020) emphasized that chatbots designed for language practice enhanced emotional safety, enabling learners to explore teaching strategies without fear of criticism. Gamification also contributes to emotional engagement by motivating users through badges, leaderboards, and progress tracking; however, researchers caution that extrinsic rewards must be balanced with intrinsic motivation to encourage deep pedagogical reflection (Huang & Hew, 2023).

Social engagement, another key pillar of teacher development, is supported by chatbot-mediated peer collaboration. Chatbots embedded in platforms like Discord or Teams facilitate lesson co-design, feedback exchanges, and group discussions, thereby fostering a sense of community and professional identity (Huang et al., 2022; Kohnke et al., 2023). These interactions help simulate real-world teaching contexts, encouraging cooperative curriculum planning and collective problem-solving. Ji et al. (2024) noted that such engagements promote the development of social-emotional teaching competencies, though chatbots' inability to manage complex group dynamics remains a limitation. Similarly, Yang et al. (2023) found that cultural insensitivity in chatbot dialogue could undermine social presence among diverse trainee populations, emphasizing the importance of culturally adaptive design.

Engagement is also reinforced through multimodal content delivery and adaptive feedback mechanisms. Chatbots that integrate video clips, interactive quizzes, and multimedia tutorials provide richer, more accessible learning experiences that cater to various learner preferences (Zawacki-Richter et al., 2023). Personalized feedback systems that analyze trainee performance and dynamically adjust task difficulty have been shown to increase time-on-task and promote mastery learning (Huang & Hew, 2023). Yet, limitations in NLP can result in irrelevant or repetitive feedback, breaking the immersive learning flow and reducing engagement (Smutny & Schreiberova, 2020; Pokrivčáková, 2019).

Despite their benefits, several challenges impede sustained engagement through chatbots. Technical barriers—such as inaccurate NLP interpretations, rigid scripting, and voice recognition errors—reduce conversational depth and authenticity. Ethical concerns related to data privacy, transparency in AI decision-making, and over-reliance on automated support further complicate their integration into teacher education programs (Zawacki-Richter et al., 2019).

In conclusion, chatbots significantly contribute to engagement in preservice language teacher education by supporting cognitive, emotional, and social dimensions of learning. Their capacity to simulate teaching scenarios, provide real-time feedback, and facilitate peer interaction aligns well with contemporary pedagogical models. However, to fully leverage their potential, educators and developers must address existing technical limitations, ensure cultural responsiveness, and design ethically sound, pedagogically coherent systems. Future research should explore longitudinal impacts of chatbot engagement, especially within hybrid models that blend AI interactivity with human mentorship to foster holistic professional development.

The Role of Chatbots in Supporting Pedagogical Decision Making and Lesson Planning

The integration of chatbots into language teacher education has emerged as a promising avenue to enhance pedagogical decision-making and lesson planning. Chatbots offer dynamic support by simulating human-like interactions, providing real-time feedback, and curating resources tailored to educators' needs. This section synthesizes research on their role in language teacher education, highlighting benefits, challenges, and future directions.

Chatbots in Pedagogical Decision-Making. Chatbots facilitate data-driven pedagogical decisions by analyzing learner performance and suggesting instructional adjustments. Huang et al. (2021) found that AI tools, including chatbots, enable educators to identify learning gaps and adapt teaching strategies through predictive analytics. For instance, chatbots can recommend personalized interventions for struggling students, fostering differentiated instruction (Kohnke, 2022). In language teacher education, this capability allows novice instructors to refine their responsiveness to diverse classroom needs.

Moreover, chatbots serve as virtual mentors, offering immediate feedback on teaching practices. Ji et al. (2023) demonstrated that chatbots simulating student interactions helped trainees practice classroom management and questioning techniques, improving their confidence. Such simulations enable educators to experiment with pedagogical approaches in low-stakes environments before applying them in real classrooms.

Chatbots in Lesson Planning. Chatbots streamline lesson planning by automating resource curation and activity design. Ng et al. (2023) highlighted that AI-driven tools reduce planning time by suggesting culturally relevant materials and aligning activities with curricular goals. Lee & Jeon (2024) found that language teachers can use chatbots to generate vocabulary exercises or reading comprehension tasks tailored to proficiency levels, ensuring lessons are both engaging and pedagogically sound.

Additionally, chatbots support collaborative planning. Dizon (2020) noted that chatbots embedded in platforms like Slack or Microsoft Teams enable peer-to-peer resource sharing, fostering a community of practice among educators. By crowdsourcing ideas and materials, chatbots help teachers diversify their instructional strategies while adhering to best practices.

Challenges and Considerations. Despite their potential, chatbots present challenges. Over-reliance on AI recommendations may stifle teachers' critical thinking, as noted by Wollny et al. (2021), who cautioned against uncritical adoption of chatbot-generated content. Ethical concerns, such as data privacy and algorithmic bias, also warrant attention (Huang et al., 2021). Furthermore, effective integration requires training; Dizon (2020) emphasized that educators need professional development to leverage chatbots meaningfully.

In summary, chatbots hold significant promise for enhancing pedagogical decision-making and lesson planning in language teacher education by offering personalized, data-driven support. However, their implementation must balance automation with human oversight to preserve educators' agency. Future research should explore longitudinal impacts on teaching efficacy and address ethical frameworks for AI in education.

Barriers Faced by Chatbots in Developing Teaching Competences

The integration of chatbots into language teacher education continues to evolve, yet persistent barriers hinder their ability to develop critical teaching competences, such as pedagogical adaptability, emotional intelligence, and culturally responsive practices.

Contextual and Cultural Nuance Limitations. Chatbots often fail to interpret the sociocultural and situational contexts essential for language teaching. For example, designing lessons for multilingual classrooms requires sensitivity to learners' linguistic backgrounds, a skill chatbots lack due to their reliance on static datasets (Yang et al., 2023). While advances in NLP have improved contextual awareness, chatbots still struggle to adapt feedback to diverse cultural norms, limiting their utility in fostering intercultural teaching competencies (Loge et al., 2023).

Emotional Intelligence and Relational Gaps. Effective teacher training hinges on modeling empathy and managing classroom relationships, areas where chatbots remain underdeveloped. Studies highlight that chatbots cannot authentically replicate human emotional cues or provide nuanced guidance on addressing student anxiety or motivation (Kohnke, 2023). This deficit undermines their ability to train educators in soft skills, such as conflict resolution or fostering inclusive environments (Loge et al., 2023).

NLP Constraints and Miscommunication Risks. Despite advancements, NLP systems still misinterpret complex or ambiguous trainee inputs, leading to generic or irrelevant feedback. For instance, chatbots may misdiagnose errors in lesson-planning scenarios, such as misalignments between learning objectives and activities (Huang & Hew, 2023). Such errors erode trust in chatbots as reliable mentors for developing pedagogical expertise.

Superficial Feedback and Pedagogical Creativity. While chatbots excel at providing immediate structural feedback, such as grammar checks, they often overlook higher order teaching skills, including fostering critical thinking or creativity in lesson design. Lim and Makany (2023) highlight that deploying chatbots to build students' critical thinking skills requires deliberate instructional strategies, as chatbots alone may not effectively promote complex cognitive skills. Furthermore, chatbots may flag missing lesson objectives but lack the capacity to critique the pedagogical approach's alignment with student-centered learning principles, necessitating human oversight to ensure effective instructional design.

Ethical Concerns and Algorithmic Bias. Privacy risks and biases in chatbot algorithms remain significant hurdles. Training data often reflect dominant cultural perspectives, potentially perpetuating inequities in language education (Yang et al., 2023). Additionally, institutions hesitate to adopt chatbots due to unresolved ethical dilemmas, such as data ownership and transparency in AI decision-making (Zawacki-Richter et al., 2023).

Recent advancements in AI, such as emotion-aware systems and hybrid human-chatbot mentoring frameworks, offer partial solutions (Kohnke, 2023). However, overcoming these barriers requires interdisciplinary collaboration to enhance NLP cultural adaptability, address ethical risks, and prioritize human-AI synergy in teacher education.

Mizou, like many AI tools, is only as culturally aware as the data it has been trained on. Without data grounded in Vietnamese educational contexts, its feedback may lack sensitivity to cultural and classroom norms. This creates a risk of misalignment between automated responses and learners' sociocultural realities.

Theoretical Framework

The AI Chatbot Integration in Teacher Education (AI-CITE) framework is grounded in multiple learning theories and pedagogical models that help explain how AI chatbots can be effectively adopted and applied in pre-service teacher education. The model is structured around three interrelated domains: the Cognitive-Perceptual Domain, the Pedagogical-Instructional Domain, and the Adoption & Barriers Domain. Each domain draws from established theoretical perspectives and is supported by empirical evidence on how chatbots impact teaching and learning.

Cognitive-Perceptual Domain

This domain is underpinned by Constructivist Learning Theory and Cognitive Load Theory. Constructivism posits that learners actively construct knowledge through interaction with their environment. Chatbots, through personalized and responsive dialogues, align well with this theory by offering learners adaptive feedback and opportunities to negotiate meaning (Mungai et al., 2024; Guan et al., 2024). Cognitive Load Theory (CLT), on the other hand, emphasizes the reduction of extraneous load to enhance learning efficiency. Chatbots simplify complex instructions, structure learning tasks, and provide scaffolded explanations, thereby supporting cognitive processing (Lin & Chang, 2023; Shoja & Maadikhah, 2024).

Moreover, AI chatbots support metacognitive regulation and self-directed learning by enabling students to monitor their understanding and receive just-in-time assistance. Raković et al. (2024) demonstrated that chatbots can scaffold key processes in self-regulated learning, such as goal-setting and reflective planning, aligning with the phases outlined by Winne and Hadwin's SRL framework.

Pedagogical-Instructional Domain

The second domain builds on the Technological Pedagogical Content Knowledge (TPACK) framework, which emphasizes the integrated knowledge needed to teach effectively with technology. AI chatbots function as pedagogical partners by enhancing lesson planning, delivering content interactively, and supporting differentiated instruction (Chiu et al., 2024; Hwang et al., 2021).

Lin and Chang (2023) proposed the CHAT-ACTS framework, which synthesizes chatbot integration into active and self-regulated learning pedagogies. This includes functionalities such as adaptive feedback, study tactic suggestions, and personalized learning paths that directly support instructional decision-making and student autonomy.

Furthermore, as Hadizadeh (2023) and Chukwuere (2024) note, chatbots offer support in formative assessment by evaluating student responses and offering immediate feedback—thus functioning not only as tools but as co-teachers that align with student learning trajectories.

Adoption & Barriers Domain

To understand the adoption of AI chatbots by pre-service teachers, the framework incorporates the Unified Theory of Acceptance and Use of Technology (UTAUT). This model identifies performance expectancy, effort expectancy, social influence, and facilitating conditions as key predictors of technology acceptance (Jyothsna et al., 2024).

Pokrivcakova (2019) also highlights the importance of preparing teachers with the digital and AI pedagogical competencies required to use chatbot tools meaningfully, aligning with TPACK and AI literacy development. However, emotional limitations—such as lack of human empathy—and contextual barriers—like limited training and infrastructure—pose challenges to chatbot integration, as emphasized by Pappagallo (2024) and Mathew (2024).

In addition, Social and Emotional Learning (SEL) Theory contributes a vital dimension to understanding chatbot integration in teacher education. SEL emphasizes competencies such as self-awareness, self-management, social awareness, relationship skills, and responsible decision-making. Although AI chatbots cannot fully replicate human empathy, they can support emotional regulation and reflective learning by offering timely feedback in a neutral, non-judgmental manner. When designed with affective responsiveness, chatbots may help reduce learner anxiety and create psychologically safe spaces for practice and exploration—especially important in large or remote learning environments (Chiu et al., 2024; Pappagallo, 2024).

Figure 1. The theoretical framework of AI-chatbot integration in teacher education

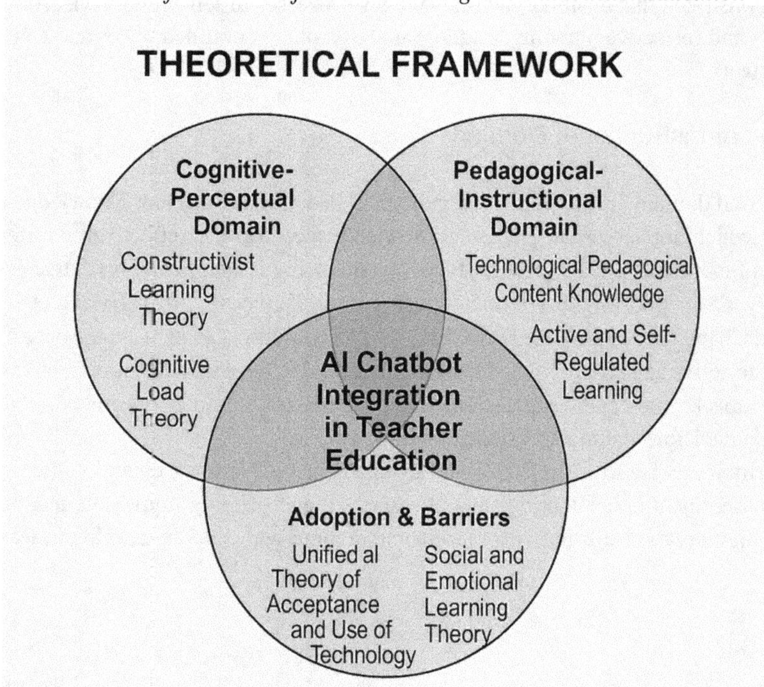

RESEARCH METHODOLOGY

Research Context and Participants

This study was conducted at one of three universities located in Central Viet Nam, an institution renowned for its specialization in foreign language education. Notably, the academic staff demonstrated considerable variability in their proficiency with online teaching, given that the university's learning management system (LMS) represented the sole digital infrastructure in use prior to the COVID-19 outbreak in 2019. The deployment of artificial intelligence tools, particularly chatbots, has since largely depended on individual lecturers' enthusiasm and digital competence, both of which vary significantly.

The study employed Mizou, a sophisticated chatbot system designed to enrich the learning experience by offering immediate assistance and personalized interaction through advanced natural language processing (NLP). The AI chatbot can respond to a wide range of student inquiries, delivering both academic guidance and emotional support. It facilitates language skill development, clarifies complex concepts, and offers tailored learning recommendations. Additionally, it monitors student progress over time, delivering constructive feedback that fosters sustained engagement and motivation. A unique feature of the chatbot is its capacity for user customization. The customized chatbot was tailored by the course instructor in two different ways: (1) clearly defining the roles and responsibilities for both the chatbot and the student, including what they should do, how they should do it, when these actions should take place etc. (2) uploading specific contents from the syllabus, including assigned readings, key terminology, local teaching examples, and pedagogical frameworks covered in the course, thereby ensuring the chatbot's relevance and usefulness in student tasks. For this research, a customized version of Mizou developed by the course instructor aimed to assist pre-service teachers in comprehending course readings and designing and evaluating various pedagogical tasks, including journals, lesson plans, and assessment rubrics.

Participants consisted of 134 third-year undergraduate pre-service teachers enrolled specifically in the language teacher education program at a specialized foreign language university in Central Vietnam. Students were selected based on their ongoing participation in technology-integrated coursework, ensuring their readiness for chatbot integration. Of these participants, eleven were randomly selected for voluntary participation in focus group interviews, using stratified sampling to ensure representation across performance levels and chatbot engagement frequency. The chatbot was integrated into a unit focused on language testing and assessment in English Language Teaching. Within this unit, students were tasked with completing a series of well-articulated and structured assignments, as described in the unit outline. These tasks, performed either individually or collaboratively, included:

- Journal writing, in which students articulated their understanding of assigned reading materials.
- Participation in discussion forums to express and exchange perspectives on issues raised by instructors or peers.
- Lesson planning that integrated technological tools into locally relevant teaching contexts.
- Peer review activities using the LMS wiki to provide feedback on peers' lesson designs.
- Development of test items and quizzes using designated technological tools.

To support the successful completion of these tasks, students were encouraged to utilize the custom chatbot to:

- Generate initial ideas for tasks, lesson plans, or test items.
- Obtain feedback for improving tasks, plans, or items.
- Seek clarification on potential issues encountered during task completion.
- Request assistance with any aspect of their assigned work.

Research Design

This study adopted a mixed-methods approach, specifically employing an explanatory sequential design. In this design framework, quantitative data were initially collected via a questionnaire to identify prevailing trends and patterns. This was followed by the collection of qualitative data through focus group interviews, which provided nuanced insights and a deeper understanding of the quantitative findings. The sequential integration of qualitative data served to elaborate on the statistical results, thereby enabling a comprehensive and multidimensional exploration of the research questions.

Analytical Framework: The AI-CITE Model and Its Application

To examine the integration of AI-powered chatbots in teacher education, this study employs the AI-CITE framework as the core analytical foundation. The framework offers a theoretically coherent and empirically grounded lens for exploring both qualitative and quantitative dimensions of the research. It provides a structured basis for analyzing how chatbots mediate teacher learning, instructional decision-making, and classroom readiness—particularly through six key thematic areas distilled from the literature: individualization, interactivity, engagement, pedagogical decision-making, lesson planning, and barriers.

Table 1. Mapping the AI-CITE framework to the six thematic areas

AI-CIT Domain	Thematic Area	Explanation
Cognitive-Perceptual Domain	Individualization	Reflects the chatbot's ability to adapt feedback and content to learners' cognitive needs, enhancing personalized learning pathways.
	Engagement	Captures motivational and metacognitive dynamics, including goal setting, monitoring, and reflection, aligned with SRL theory.
Pedagogical-Instructional Domain	Interactivity	Encompasses dialogic learning, feedback loops, and real-time exchanges, all key components of active learning pedagogy.
	Pedagogical Decision-Making	Encompasses how chatbots inform teachers' instructional adjustments, content delivery, and assessment strategies.
	Lesson Planning	Involves chatbot assistance in sequencing content, generating activities, and aligning resources with learning objectives.
Adoption and Barriers Domain	Barriers	Addresses limitations such as digital literacy, emotional resistance, infrastructure gaps, and ethical concerns that affect chatbot use.

The AI-CITE framework comprises three interrelated domains—Cognitive-Perceptual, Pedagogical-Instructional, and Adoption and Barriers—each aligned with specific functions of chatbot integration in educational contexts. The logical connections between these domains and the six thematic areas serve not only as the coding framework for qualitative data analysis, but also as the conceptual foundation for the construction of the questionnaire, thereby reinforcing the study's mixed-methods design. Table 1 shows the explicit alignment of the theoretical framework with the six thematic areas.

By making explicit the conceptual intersections between framework domains and thematic areas, the mapping guided the formulation of questionnaire items. Each section of the instrument was directly informed by one or more framework dimensions, ensuring construct validity and internal consistency. For instance, items measuring individualization and engagement derive from the Cognitive-Perceptual Domain, using constructs informed by self-regulated learning theory. Similarly, scales designed to assess interactivity and pedagogical decision-making are based on the Pedagogical-Instructional Domain, integrating principles from constructivist pedagogy and the TPACK model. Items related to barriers were drawn from the Adoption and Barriers Domain, incorporating constructs from the UTAUT model and digital competence frameworks.

Furthermore, the AI-CITE framework structures the qualitative coding scheme, supporting in-depth analysis of teacher reflections, experiences, and practices related to chatbot use. It allows the researcher to trace not only what teachers do with chatbots, but also how they think and feel about their use in pedagogical contexts. This triangulation between open-ended responses, interview transcripts, and questionnaire data enhances the study's methodological rigor and supports the valid interpretation of findings across data types.

In summary, the logical alignment between the AI-CITE framework and the six thematic areas provides a unified scaffolding for the study's mixed-methods design. It facilitates coherence across the research instruments and ensures that the analysis—both qualitative and quantitative—is tightly linked to pedagogically relevant constructs and current theoretical models in AI integration, educational technology, and teacher education.

Data Collection

The questionnaire was meticulously aligned with the study's theoretical framework to ensure the items were conceptually grounded. Table 2 below presents a detailed mapping of questionnaire items to subcomponents of the AI-CITE Model, thereby illustrating the robust coherence between theoretical constructs and empirical measures. The items comprehensively addressed cognitive perceptions, pedagogical strategies, and adoption barriers. Specifically, items 1.1 to 1.4 gauged perceptions of AI chatbot efficacy in facilitating personalized learning and managing cognitive load. Items such as 2.1 and 3.1 measured the chatbot's capacity for fostering interactivity and engagement, consistent with cognitive learning theories. Items 2.4 and 4.1 to 4.5 focused on the integration of AI into instructional design and the promotion of self-regulated learning. Section 5 targeted perceived barriers, including technological acceptance, contextual limitations, and emotional engagement deficits (see Appendix 1).

The questionnaire was administered via Google Forms and distributed using Zalo, a widely used messaging platform in Vietnam. Data collection was conducted at the conclusion of the "Language Testing and Assessment" unit.

Upon preliminary analysis of the questionnaire data, focus group interviews were conducted to further investigate participants' experiences and perceptions of the chatbot. The 11 interviewees were divided into two groups, each comprising five to six students.

Interview questions were organized into five thematic clusters, with each cluster consisting of three items. The interviews aimed to explore (1) participants' awareness of the chatbot's role, (2) their reflections and emotional responses to using the chatbot, (3) perceptions of the chatbot's value and impact, (4) practical outcomes, and (5) challenges encountered during chatbot use (see Appendix 2). Conducted via Zoom, each interview lasted approximately 45 minutes. All sessions were recorded and transcribed using Turboscribe, a professional audio-to-text software.

Table 2. Mapping of questionnaire items to AI-CITE framework subcomponents

Domain	Subcomponents	Questionnaire Items
Cognitive-Perceptual	Constructivist Learning & Cognitive Load Optimization	1.1, 1.2, 1.3, 1.4
	AI-Enhanced Engagement & Interactivity	2.1, 2.5, 3.1, 3.2
	Perceived Effectiveness of Chatbots	2.3, 3.4, 3.5
Pedagogical-Instructional	TPACK: AI's Role in Technological-Pedagogical Integration	2.6
	Lesson Planning & AI-Guided Instructional Strategies	2.4, 4.1, 4.2
	Self-Regulation & AI as a Teaching Support Tool	3.3, 4.3, 4.4, 4.5
Adoption & Barriers	Technology Acceptance & Barriers to AI Integration (UTAUT)	5.1, 5.3
	Contextual Limitations of AI in Real-Classroom Simulations	5.2, 5.4
	Emotional Intelligence & Motivation in AI Interactions (SEL)	5.5

Data Analysis

Quantitative data derived from the questionnaires were analyzed using Julius, an AI-enhanced data analysis software. Descriptive statistics, including means and standard deviations, were computed for each cluster. Furthermore, inferential analyses involved calculating Cohen's D for pairwise comparisons and applying Tukey's HSD for multiple cluster comparisons. Thematic analysis of qualitative data from the focus group interviews was conducted with the aid of SciSpace, an AI tool that facilitated the extraction of codes, (sub-)themes, and categories as well as illustrative examples (see Appendix 3).

Reliability and Validity

To ensure methodological rigor, both reliability and validity were addressed throughout the research process. In terms of reliability, the questionnaire was designed with a consistent structure across six clusters (individualization, interactivity, engagement, pedagogical decision-making, lesson planning, and barriers), minimizing interpretive discrepancies among respondents. A pilot study was conducted with a small sample to refine the wording and clarity of questionnaire items, resulting in high internal consistency (Cronbach's $\alpha = 0.91$). The application of Julius, AI-powered software, further contributed to the objectivity and precision of quantitative analyses.

Validity considerations encompassed both internal and external dimensions. Internal validity was strengthened by the explanatory sequential design, which allowed for triangulation between quantitative and qualitative findings. The triangulation was further enhanced by the alignment of the theoretical framework components with the six areas that transcend the questionnaire. Interview protocols were aligned with questionnaire themes, ensuring thematic coherence and the reinforcement of results. External validity was supported by the representativeness of the study sample—143 third-year pre-service teachers from a specialized university—and by the random and voluntary selection of focus group participants. All interview data were transcribed and subjected to rigorous thematic analysis using validated AI tools, ensuring that the insights obtained authentically reflected participants' experiences. These comprehensive procedures ensured the study's findings were both robust and credible.

FINDINGS

Table 3. Pre-service teachers' perceptions of Mizou Chatbot integration in teacher education

	Statements	Mean	SD
1	**Individualization**	**3.70**	**0.79**
1.1	I feel confident in using chatbots as part of my teaching methodology.	3.72	0.74
1.2	Chatbots are capable of addressing the diverse needs of pre-service teachers.	3.60	0.82
1.3	Chatbots help me prepare for real-world teaching challenges.	3.57	0.96
1.4	Chatbots effectively supplement the knowledge I gain from traditional coursework.	3.94	0.67
2	**Interactivity**	**3.79**	**0.79**
2.1	Chatbots make learning more interactive and engaging.	4.18	0.76
2.2	I regularly use chatbots to simulate classroom teaching scenarios.	3.36	0.76
2.3	Chatbots are an effective tool for pre-service teacher education.	4.23	0.84
2.4	I find chatbots useful for receiving instant feedback on teaching methods.	3.36	0.76
2.5	Chatbots are a part of my daily study routine as a pre-service teacher.	3.47	0.80
2.6	I utilize chatbots to practice and improve my teaching strategies.	3.71	0.79
3	**Engagement**	**3.85**	**0.82**
3.1	The use of chatbots in teacher education is innovative and forward-thinking.	4.04	0.68
3.2	Chatbots add significant value to my training as a pre-service teacher.	3.98	0.73
3.3	The feedback from chatbots is crucial for my professional development.	3.49	0.92
3.4	I would recommend the use of chatbots to other pre-service teachers.	3.94	0.91
3.5	The integration of chatbots in teacher education programs should be expanded.	3.83	0.87
4	**Pedagogical decision making**	**3.88**	**0.82**
4.1	Chatbots have helped me manage my study time more effectively.	3.87	0.83

continued on following page

Table 3. Continued

	Statements	Mean	SD
4.2	I have noticed an improvement in my problem-solving skills since using chatbot.	3.70	0.93
4.3	Chatbots have reduced the stress associated with studying and completing assignments.	4.10	0.79
4.4	I feel that chatbots have made me more independent as a learner.	3.73	0.87
4.5	The use of chatbots has increased my satisfaction with the learning process.	4.04	0.68
5	**Barriers**	**3.36**	**1.0**
5.1	I find it difficult to express my teaching-related queries effectively to chatbots.	3.33	0.89
5.2	Chatbots often do not provide the level of detail I need for teaching concepts.	3.12	1.17
5.3	I am concerned about the reliability of the content provided by chatbots.	3.61	0.99
5.4	The interaction with chatbots does not adequately simulate a real classroom experience.	3.30	0.95
5.5	I feel that chatbots lack the ability to provide emotional support or encouragement.	3.46	1.06

The following section presents the findings derived from the study, beginning with an overview table summarizing pre-service teachers' perceptions across key areas of chatbot integration, namely individualization, interactivity, engagement, pedagogical decision-making, and barriers encountered. Table 3 above serves as a foundational reference for subsequent detailed analyses and discussions of each thematic area, providing a structured basis for interpreting the impact of the chatbot Mizou on participants' educational experiences and highlighting critical insights into its practical implications.

Individualization in Learning

This section explores pre-service teachers' perceptions of chatbots, particularly Mizou, as tools for fostering individualized learning. Drawing upon both questionnaire data and interview narratives, the findings illustrate the perceived benefits and limitations of chatbots in supporting personalized education. While generally viewed as valuable, the adaptability and contextual sensitivity of chatbots remain areas requiring enhancement.

The survey data revealed a moderately positive perception of the AI chatbot in individualized learning contexts, with a mean score of 3.70 (SD = 0.79). Complementary interview responses underscored the chatbot's role in clarifying difficult concepts, as articulated by Participant 1: "Mizou helps me understand difficult concepts better, especially when I struggle in class." Nevertheless, participants also expressed that chatbots often fell short in accommodating their varied and evolving learning needs—an issue consistently noted across both data strands.

Confidence in using the chatbot was similarly moderate, with a reported mean score of 3.72 (SD = 0.74). While many participants were comfortable incorporating chatbots into their learning practices, others encountered initial difficulties in formulating effective queries. As Participant 6 reflected, "At first, I wasn't sure how to ask the right questions, but I gradually learned how to get better responses." This highlights the importance of user familiarity and iterative engagement in optimizing chatbot use.

When considering adaptability to diverse learning styles, the AI tool was evaluated less favorably, receiving a mean score of 3.60 (SD = 0.82). Some participants appreciated Mizou's accessible explanations, with Participant 4 noting improved clarity on complex topics. Conversely, more advanced learners criticized the superficiality of responses, exemplified by Participant 2's comment: "Mizou's responses are useful for basic understanding, but for deeper learning, they often lack the necessary detail." These insights point to a critical need for chatbots to differentiate content delivery to meet varying learner profiles.

In terms of real-world teaching preparedness, the findings were mixed, with a mean score of 3.57 (SD = 0.96). While Mizou was commended for offering multiple perspectives and promoting critical thinking—as noted by Participant 5—several respondents indicated that the lack of contextual nuance limited its utility. The observation that the chatbot cannot replicate classroom dynamics underscores the importance of complementing AI tools with experiential learning.

The Mizou chatbot was most positively regarded as supplementary learning aids, with a mean score of 3.94 (SD = 0.67). Many participants found the tool beneficial for receiving prompt feedback and sustaining independent study, as evidenced by Participant 6: "Before Mizou, I relied on classmates for clarification, but now I can organize my own study sessions more effectively." This supports the notion that the chatbot serves best as enhancements to, rather than replacements for, human instruction.

In summary, the findings affirm that chatbots like Mizou contribute significantly to individualized learning by offering accessible support, encouraging self-directed engagement, and promoting conceptual comprehension. Nonetheless, limitations in personalization, contextual relevance, and response depth suggest avenues for further refinement to more effectively address the diverse needs of pre-service teachers.

Interactivity in Learning

This section investigates how the Mizou chatbot influences interactive learning experiences among pre-service teachers, based on data from both questionnaires and interviews. The findings indicate that the chatbot is largely perceived as tools that enhance interactivity, although their application in authentic teaching scenarios and feedback mechanisms presents notable challenges.

Survey results revealed an overall positive evaluation of Mizou in promoting interactive learning, with a mean score of 3.79 (SD = 0.79). The chatbot was rated especially high in making learning more dynamic and engaging (M = 4.18, SD = 0.76). Interviewees frequently praised the tool's capacity to deliver immediate responses that enable real-time engagement with learning content. Participant 4 remarked, "Whenever I come across a concept I don't understand,

I can just ask the chatbot, and it gives me an explanation right away." However, some participants noted that these responses could be overly brief, limiting the depth of conceptual clarification.

In terms of facilitating real-time interaction and collaboration, Mizou received a strong endorsement, with a mean score of 4.23 (SD = 0.84). This sentiment was echoed in the interviews. Participant 2 explained, "The AI chatbot provides immediate responses, which means I don't have to wait for a teacher or search endlessly online." Several students also reported using the tool collaboratively to verify information before class discussions, although they acknowledged the need to confirm chatbot-generated content with instructors due to reliability concerns.

Despite these advantages, Mizou was less effective in simulating authentic teaching scenarios and providing instructional feedback, both of which received lower ratings (M = 3.36, SD = 0.76). While some participants appreciated the chatbot's capacity to generate follow-up prompts and stimulate further inquiry, others criticized the lack of contextual alignment and occasional repetitiveness. Participant 5 likened the experience to "having a tutor that doesn't just answer but also prompts me to consider different aspects of a topic," whereas others found these prompts misaligned with their academic needs.

Regarding integration into structured educational practices, the survey showed moderate acceptance, with Mizou scoring 3.47 (SD = 0.80) for use in daily study routines and 3.71 (SD = 0.79) in supporting teaching strategies. Although interviewees acknowledged the chatbot's role in fostering critical thinking through suggested questions, concerns remained about the relevance and applicability of its recommendations. Participant 1 noted that while the suggestions were sometimes engaging, they were not always aligned with instructional goals.

In conclusion, the findings support the view that the chatbot can enrich interactivity in teacher education by enabling immediate content engagement, encouraging peer discussion, and fostering inquiry-based learning. However, the AI tool's efficacy is constrained by limitations in response relevance, depth, and adaptability to authentic pedagogical contexts. Future iterations of chatbot tools should aim to better simulate classroom scenarios and deliver more contextually informed feedback to optimize their role in interactive learning.

Engagement in Learning

This section examines how Mizou, influences learner engagement among pre-service teachers, drawing on both quantitative and qualitative data. The findings suggest that the chatbot plays a significant role in sustaining motivation, fostering interactive learning behaviors, and offering a consistent source of support. However, the effectiveness of chatbot engagement is moderated by limitations in response diversity and cognitive depth.

Survey data indicated a favorable perception of Mizou in enhancing learner engagement, with an overall mean score of 3.85 (SD = 0.82). The chatbot was particularly valued for its innovative contribution to teacher education, receiving a high rating of 4.04 (SD = 0.68). Interview responses corroborated this perception. For instance, Participant 2 noted, "Mizou makes studying more interesting because I can get answers quickly without feeling stuck." Similarly, Participant 5 reflected that the tool helped overcome delays in studying by making learning more accessible and less frustrating.

Regarding the development of interactive study habits, Mizou received a mean score of 3.98 (SD = 0.73), indicating its perceived role in encouraging active engagement with learning materials. Interview participants described the chatbot as instrumental in promoting question-driven inquiry and self-assessment. Participant 3 stated, "I don't just read materials passively anymore. Mizou helps me ask better questions and explore topics in a more engaging way," while Participant 6 shared that using it for self-testing enhanced their learning beyond rote memorization. Nonetheless, some users expressed concerns about repetitive answers, with Participant 1 stating, "Sometimes, I ask follow-up questions, and the answers are too similar to the previous ones, which makes it less engaging."

The perception of Mizou as a learning companion also emerged strongly, aligning with the mean score of 3.94 (SD = 0.91) for chatbot advocacy. Participants highlighted the emotional and logistical support provided by the AI chatbot, particularly when peers or instructors were unavailable. Participant 4 shared, "I feel like I'm not studying alone because the chatbot is always available to guide me when I have doubts," and Participant 7 emphasized its role in filling conversational gaps during solitary study. However, several interviewees acknowledged that while helpful, the AI tool lacked the human warmth and encouragement found in peer or instructor interactions. Participant 2 remarked, "It's helpful, but it doesn't give the same encouragement or emotional support as a teacher or a peer."

Despite the generally positive evaluations, chatbot-generated feedback related to professional development received a more moderate rating (M = 3.49, SD = 0.92), suggesting variability in perceived utility. Some participants reported that the Mizou chatbot's feedback was helpful for refining understanding, while others criticized its lack of depth for advanced learners. Support for broader chatbot integration in education remained strong (M = 3.83, SD = 0.87), although many emphasized the need for enhanced personalization and content variation.

To sum up, the findings underscore that the Mizou chatbot contributes to learner engagement by promoting motivation, facilitating dynamic study routines, and providing accessible academic support. Nonetheless, challenges related to repetitive content, superficial insights, and emotional disconnect limit its full potential. Addressing these concerns through improved personalization, content differentiation, and empathetic interaction design may further solidify the chatbot's role in fostering meaningful engagement among pre-service teachers.

Pedagogical Decision-Making

This section explores how the Mizou chatbot supports pedagogical decision-making among pre-service teachers. Drawing on both survey responses and interview insights, the findings indicate that the chatbot contributes to instructional planning, classroom problem-solving, and assessment strategy development. However, variability in chatbot performance highlights the need for greater contextual sensitivity and response precision.

Survey data indicated a generally favorable view of the chatbot in facilitating pedagogical decision-making, with an overall mean score of 3.88 (SD = 0.82). The chatbot was particularly commended for alleviating academic stress (M = 4.10, SD = 0.79) and improving satisfaction with the learning process (M = 4.04, SD = 0.68). Interview responses supported these findings. For example, Participant 2 stated, "Before using Mizou, I was unsure about how to organize my lessons, but now I can quickly generate outlines and refine them based on Mizou's suggestions." Participant 5 added that verifying lesson structures with the chatbot enhanced their preparedness.

The use of the chatbot for instructional planning was frequently mentioned, aligning with a mean score of 3.87 (SD = 0.83) for improved time management. Interviewees described how it helped align objectives with content delivery. Participant 6 explained, "I use Mizou to map out my lessons and ensure that my objectives align with my instructional strategies." However, several participants pointed out that the chatbot's suggestions were often broad, necessitating manual refinement. As Participant 4 commented, "While Mizou gives me a good starting point, I often have to refine the details on my own."

In terms of addressing classroom challenges, the Mizou chatbot received moderate support, with a mean score of 3.70 (SD = 0.93). Many participants found the chatbot useful for troubleshooting pedagogical dilemmas and preparing for student misconceptions. Participant 3 stated, "When I am unsure about how to approach a difficult topic in class, I ask Mizou for alternative strategies, and it usually provides useful insights." However, others expressed concern that the chatbot's responses lacked the complexity required for nuanced issues. Participant 7 noted, "Mizou is helpful for basic challenges, but for nuanced classroom issues, I still need to consult my mentor or peers."

Regarding assessment strategies, the chatbot received a mean score of 3.73 (SD = 0.87), reflecting their utility in supporting independent learning. Interview participants described it as helpful in aligning assessments with learning goals and in distinguishing between formative and summative evaluations. Participant 4 shared, "I use Mizou to check whether my test questions align with learning objectives and to explore different ways of assessing student understanding." Participant 7 also noted improvements in assessment literacy. However, others remarked that Mizou occasionally failed to distinguish between subtle differences in assessment techniques. Participant 5 stated, "It doesn't always recognize the subtle differences between assessment techniques, so I have to double-check its recommendations."

In summary, the findings suggest that the chatbot facilitates pedagogical decision-making by enhancing instructional planning, supporting reflective problem-solving, and guiding assessment design. Nonetheless, its effectiveness is limited by the generality of its responses and lack of contextual depth. To enhance the educational value of chatbots in teacher preparation, future designs should focus on refining response specificity and integrating more robust pedagogical frameworks.

Lesson Planning

This section evaluates the role of the Mizou chatbot in supporting lesson planning among pre-service teachers, based on both questionnaire data and interview narratives. The findings suggest that it is perceived as a valuable tool for lesson structuring, content customization, and instructional resource organization. The reported mean scores and standard deviations presented in this section represent aggregated interpretations of relevant clusters (e.g., Engagement, Pedagogical Decision-Making, Interactivity) from the broader questionnaire dataset. However, its effectiveness varies with respect to recommendation specificity and adaptability to context-specific needs.

Survey results reflected a generally positive perception of the chatbot's role in lesson planning, with an overall mean score of 3.85 (SD = 0.81). Participants particularly valued its assistance in structuring lesson plans (M = 3.89, SD = 0.79) and in guiding instructional design (M = 3.91, SD = 0.82). Interview responses corroborated these findings, with participants appreciating the efficiency and structure the chatbot provided. For example, Participant 3 stated, "Mizou helps me outline my lesson plans faster and ensures that I include all the necessary components," while Participant 5 noted, "It acts as a guide, reminding me of important elements I might overlook in my lesson plans."

The chatbot's flexibility in customizing lesson content for diverse student needs was also acknowledged, with a mean score of 3.80 (SD = 0.85) for the item on organizing resources and integrating them with lesson objectives. Several interviewees emphasized the chatbot's ability to propose various teaching strategies. Participant 6 remarked, "I like that the chatbot suggests different approaches to teaching a topic, which helps me adapt to various student needs," and Participant 4 added, "It provides multiple examples, so I can choose the one that best fits my class." Nonetheless, concerns were raised about the general nature of some suggestions, particularly regarding subject-specific applicability. Participant 7 explained, "Sometimes the examples are too broad and not directly applicable to my subject area."

Participants also valued the Mizou chatbot's assistance in compiling and organizing instructional materials. It was frequently described as a tool that enhanced efficiency in resource management. Participant 1 commented, "It helps me compile resources efficiently, so I don't have to spend too much time searching for additional materials," while Participant 8 noted, "It's a great tool for finding supplementary materials and linking them directly to my lesson objectives." However, inconsistencies in resource relevance were noted. Participant 3 mentioned, "Sometimes the resources suggested by the chatbot are not entirely relevant, so I have to double-check their suitability."

In short, the findings demonstrate that the chatbot serves as a supportive aid in lesson planning by facilitating content organization, enabling instructional customization, and streamlining resource management. However, its effectiveness is contingent upon the specificity and contextual alignment of its recommendations. Further refinement in these areas could enhance the chatbot's utility as a pedagogical planning tool for pre-service teachers.

Barriers to Chatbot Use

The findings reveal that while the chatbot offers benefits, challenges related to content reliability, response interpretation, and usability hinder its full potential.

The questionnaire findings indicate that pre-service teachers perceive various limitations in chatbot use, with an overall mean score of 3.36 (SD = 1.00). One significant barrier is difficulty in phrasing teaching-related queries effectively, with a mean score of 3.33 (SD = 0.89). Similarly, concerns regarding the lack of detailed explanations from the chatbot were evident, with the statement "Chatbots often do not provide the level of detail I need for teaching concepts" receiving the lowest mean score in this category (3.12, SD = 1.17). The interview findings confirm this, as Participant 3 explained, "Sometimes I ask Mizou a question, and the answer is too general, so I still have to look up additional sources". Another participant noted, "Mizou provides a lot of information, but it doesn't always get straight to the point, making it harder to extract the key concepts". These insights suggest that while chatbots can offer useful information, their responses often require additional refinement for deeper learning.

The reliability of chatbot-generated content was another key concern, with the questionnaire statement "I am concerned about the reliability of the content provided by chatbots" scoring a mean of 3.61 (SD = 0.99). Some interview participants expressed skepticism about whether Mizou consistently provides accurate information. One participant described an instance where "Mizou's explanation didn't match what I learned in class, so I had to double-check with my instructor". Similarly, another pre-service teacher highlighted inconsistencies in chatbot responses, stating that "There were times when I got different answers for the same question, which made me unsure about which one to trust". These concerns highlight the need for chatbots to implement verification mechanisms to improve trust and consistency in their responses.

The questionnaire findings also highlight usability challenges, including the inability of the chatbot to simulate real classroom experiences (mean score: 3.30, SD = 0.95) and the lack of emotional engagement (3.46, SD = 1.06). Interview participants elaborated on these challenges, particularly the chatbot's inability to retain previous conversation history. One participant explained, "If I leave Mizou and come back, all my previous questions are gone, so I have to start over again". Another pre-service teacher shared frustrations about inconsistent responses, stating, "Sometimes Mizou responds differently to the same question, which is frustrating when trying to get a clear answer". These technical limitations suggest that improving chatbot memory functions and response consistency could enhance their usability in educational contexts.

To conclude, the findings indicate that while the chatbot offers value in teacher education, several barriers hinder their full effectiveness. Difficulties in interpreting responses, concerns over content accuracy, and technical challenges such as lack of conversation retention and inconsistent responses were prominent limitations. Addressing these challenges through structured responses, improved content validation, and better usability features could significantly enhance the chatbot experience for pre-service teachers.

Cluster Comparative Analysis and Interpretation

This subsection presents a comparative analysis of six thematic clusters—Individualization, Interactivity, Engagement, Pedagogical Decision-Making, Lesson Planning, and Barriers—based on questionnaire responses from pre-service teachers and further examined using a Tukey HSD post-hoc test. As shown in Table 4, the analysis identifies significant differences in the perceived effectiveness of chatbot-supported learning across these clusters. Among the clusters, Lesson Planning exhibited the highest perceived benefit relative to Barriers, with a statistically significant mean difference of 0.81 ($p = 0.0019$), confirming that chatbots like Mizou are especially valued for their utility in structuring and organizing instructional content. Although Pedagogical Decision-Making also scored favorably (mean difference = 0.60), its difference from Barriers approached but did not reach statistical significance ($p = 0.0511$), suggesting a trend toward enhanced planning and problem-solving support without fully overcoming user concerns.

Table 4. Cluster comparative analysis

group1	group2	meandiff	p-adj	lower	upper	reject
Barriers	Engagement	0.5955	53	-0.0045	1.1955	FALSE
Barriers	Individualization	0.2863	0.7418	-0.3137	0.8863	FALSE
Barriers	Interactivity	0.4292	0.3124	-0.1707	1.0292	FALSE
Barriers	Lesson Planning	0.8108	0.0019	0.2108	1.4108	TRUE
Barriers	Pedagogical Decision-Making	0.5984	0.0511	-0.0016	1.1983	FALSE
Engagement	Individualization	-0.3092	0.6742	-0.9092	0.2908	FALSE
Engagement	Interactivity	-0.1663	0.9674	-0.7663	0.4337	FALSE
Engagement	Lesson Planning	0.2153	0.9059	-0.3847	0.8152	FALSE
Engagement	Pedagogical Decision-Making	0.0028	1.0	-0.5972	0.6028	FALSE
Individualization	Interactivity	0.1429	0.9833	-0.4571	0.7429	FALSE
Individualization	Lesson Planning	0.5245	0.1243	-0.0755	1.1244	FALSE
Individualization	Pedagogical Decision-Making	312	0.6656	-288	912	FALSE
Interactivity	Lesson Planning	0.3815	0.4477	-0.2185	0.9815	FALSE
Interactivity	Pedagogical Decision-Making	0.1691	965	-0.4309	0.7691	FALSE
Lesson Planning	Pedagogical Decision-Making	-0.2124	0.9106	-0.8124	0.3876	FALSE

Similarly, Engagement was rated higher than Barriers (mean difference = 0.60, $p = 0.0530$), underscoring chatbots' motivational value while highlighting the need to address response redundancy and emotional disconnection. Interactivity and Individualization demonstrated smaller, non-significant differences from Barriers (mean differences = 0.43 and 0.29, respectively), implying that while chatbots foster dialogue and personalize some aspects of learning, limitations in adaptability and depth persist. Notably, the non-significance across most comparisons—except for Lesson Planning—emphasizes that while chatbots offer a range of pedagogical benefits, user experience is still constrained by contextual misalignment, inadequate detail, and insufficient emotional or instructional fidelity. This analysis reinforces the interpretation that to optimize chatbot integration in teacher education, enhancements must target the most negatively perceived domain—Barriers—by increasing reliability, emotional intelligence, and contextual responsiveness, particularly in areas where gains are promising yet statistically inconclusive.

The findings presented across the five thematic domains—individualization, interactivity, engagement, pedagogical decision-making, and lesson planning—underscore the multifaceted contributions of the Mizou chatbot in pre-service teacher education. It has been shown to facilitate self-directed learning, enhance interactive engagement with educational content, foster motivation and study autonomy, support informed instructional planning, and streamline lesson design. Pre-service teachers reported moderate to high levels of satisfaction with chatbot integration, particularly valuing its immediacy, accessibility, and utility in reinforcing conceptual understanding and professional readiness.

Nonetheless, limitations were also consistently identified. Participants noted that while the chatbot provides substantial foundational support, its capacity for contextual nuance, personalized feedback, and subject-specific relevance remains limited. Challenges such as response repetition, superficial content, and misalignment with complex teaching scenarios highlight critical areas for improvement. These limitations indicate that the chatbot should be viewed as a supplementary tool that complements rather than replaces traditional pedagogical strategies and human interaction.

In sum, the chatbot demonstrates considerable potential in augmenting teacher education through AI-enhanced learning experiences. To fully leverage this potential, future chatbot iterations must emphasize adaptive intelligence, deepen contextual and disciplinary alignment, and integrate emotionally responsive interactions. Addressing these dimensions will enhance the transformative role of the chatbot in preparing competent, confident, and reflective educators.

DISCUSSION

This discussion critically interprets the findings of the study through the lens of the AI-CITE theoretical framework, highlighting its unique contribution to the research design and analysis. The section begins by exploring the theoretical significance of AI-CITE and its influence on the study's analytical depth. It then evaluates how chatbot integration contributed to key teaching competencies, including individualization, interactivity, engagement, pedagogical decision-making, and lesson planning. A comparative analysis with related studies is presented to contextualize the results and limitations of Mizou as an AI tool. Finally, targeted recommendations are provided for teacher educators, educational technologists, policymakers, and researchers, followed by a concise conclusion that synthesizes the implications for AI-supported teacher education in Vietnam.

Significance of the AI-CITE Framework

This study makes a significant and original contribution to the discourse on AI in teacher education by operationalizing the Artificial Intelligence Chatbot Integration in Teacher Education (AI-CITE) framework. The AI-CITE framework's comprehensive structure—comprising the cognitive-perceptual domain, pedagogical-instructional domain, and adoption-barrier domain—offers an analytical depth that other models, such as TPACK or UTAUT, do not fully capture when applied in isolation.

Within the cognitive-perceptual domain, the study demonstrates that Mizou enhances learning by reducing extraneous cognitive load and facilitating metacognitive reflection, echoing Raković et al. (2024) and Shoja & Maadikhah (2024). Mizou's feedback, scaffolded explanations, and support for goal setting aligned closely with Winne and Hadwin's (1998) self-regulated learning theory. Participants' ability to manage study routines and monitor comprehension supports the framework's prediction that AI chatbots can foster personalized cognitive development.

The pedagogical-instructional domain contextualized Mizou's role in lesson planning and pedagogical design. Preservice teachers leveraged Mizou to align objectives with tasks and to generate differentiated strategies, confirming Lin and Chang's (2023) CHAT-ACTS framework. While TPACK emphasizes technological and content knowledge integration, AI-CITE extends this by capturing the dialogic, adaptive, and formative nature of chatbot interactions that support sustained pedagogical development. Mizou functioned not only as a planning assistant but as a pedagogical thinking partner, albeit one limited in scope.

The adoption-barrier domain critically explained user skepticism regarding Mizou's limited contextual awareness, lack of cultural nuance, and emotional flatness. These findings resonate with studies by Zawacki-Richter et al. (2023) and Loge et al. (2024), who observed that emotional and social limitations undermine AI adoption unless mitigated by humanized feedback and culturally relevant inputs. The AI-CITE framework's attention to adoption dynamics—mediated by effort expectancy, social norms, and perceived usefulness—allowed this study to interpret why some participants viewed Mizou as useful yet insufficient.

In sum, AI-CITE not only structured the data interpretation but also enriched understanding of the dynamic interplay among cognitive scaffolding, instructional design, and systemic barriers. This framework positions the current study as a model for exploring how generative AI can be more meaningfully embedded in culturally specific, pedagogically responsive teacher education ecosystems.

Contributions to Individualization, Interactivity, Engagement, and Pedagogical Support

The findings substantiate that the Mizou chatbot significantly enhances key teaching competencies in preservice teacher education—particularly individualization, interactivity, engagement, pedagogical decision-making, and lesson planning. The chatbot enabled self-paced learning and provided personalized scaffolds, aligning with prior findings by Jeon (2021), Loge et al. (2023), and Dizon (2020). Participants reported increased clarity, autonomy, and confidence in navigating complex concepts, though more advanced users found responses repetitive and lacking depth—a limitation consistent with observations by Kim (2018) and Smutny & Schreiberova (2020).

In terms of interactivity, the chatbot promoted inquiry-based learning and collaborative exploration. This echoes Fryer et al. (2020), who found that real-time, scenario-based dialogue facilitated adaptive pedagogical reflection. Nonetheless, limitations in response nuance and emotional feedback, consistent with Kohnke et al. (2023), restricted deeper professional learning. Engagement was similarly fostered through non-judgmental feedback and constant accessibility. However, the chatbot's inability to emotionally resonate or sustain novelty over time limits its long-term affective value (Huang & Hew, 2023; Yang et al., 2023).

As seen in Section 4.4, Mizou's instructional planning support was appreciated but required refinement for deeper contextualization. Pedagogically, the chatbot proved particularly effective for lesson design. Participants credited it with improving instructional alignment and material organization, echoing Lee and Jeon (2024) and Crosthwaite et al. (2023). However, the chatbot's generic suggestions lacked the contextual depth needed for authentic classroom planning in Vietnam—a finding consistent with critiques by Zhou & Brown (2020) and Jeon et al. (2024).

Comparative Analysis of the Chatbot's Limitations and Pedagogical Planning

This study affirms the Mizou chatbot's utility while foregrounding its limitations more explicitly. This aligns with the concerns noted in Section 4.6, where participants highlighted content generality and inconsistencies in response depth. In contrast to AI platforms localized for Western contexts—such as Duolingo bots, which integrate culturally tailored content and adaptive progression based on learner data (Vega et al., 2025)—Mizou exhibited limited adaptability to regional educational standards and classroom norms. Where studies like Xu et al. (2023) demonstrate high levels of chatbot responsiveness through culturally embedded natural language processing (NLP), Mizou often provided surface-level support that lacked cultural nuance. Similarly, Zheng & Stewart (2024) showed that ChatGPT can be steered to co-produce culturally appropriate educational content for local contexts, reinforcing its adaptability across diverse instructional settings. This discrepancy reveals the limitations of transferring global AI designs into localized educational systems without deliberate calibration.

In comparison with ChatGPT and Duolingo's AI tutor bots, Mizou remains underdeveloped in terms of cultural calibration and personalization. While ChatGPT offers dynamic, personalized interactions with just-in-time feedback (Jauhiainen & Garagorry, 2024), and Duolingo uses performance-driven feedback loops and localized scenarios to increase engagement (Ouyang et al., 2024), Mizou's outputs remain generic and context-independent. To narrow this gap, incorporating features such as context-specific NLP, culturally responsive datasets, and adaptive task progression would significantly enhance Mizou's instructional quality and relevance for diverse educational environments. Future research should examine how sustained chatbot use influences pre-service teachers' professional identity, reflective habits, and instructional independence over time.

Moreover, Mizou fell short in providing pedagogically creative or empathetic recommendations—deficits similarly reported in Loge et al. (2024) and Kohnke et al. (2023). While participants appreciated the efficiency and accessibility of AI support, they frequently emphasized the need for contextual mentoring and culturally situated decision-making. The findings underscore the urgency of building emotionally intelligent and pedagogically nuanced AI models that extend beyond algorithmic pattern recognition.

Recommendations for Stakeholders in Language Teacher Education

To maximize the pedagogical value of chatbots like Mizou in teacher education, a coordinated effort among educators, technologists, policymakers, and researchers is essential to ensure their ethical, contextualized, and reflective integration. For teacher educators, it is recommended to design blended instructional models that position chatbots as scaffolding tools rather than replacements for human mentorship. Educators should encourage preservice teachers to critically evaluate AI-generated responses and integrate them into reflective practice sessions. Embedding assignments where teacher candidates assess the appropriateness, accuracy, and cultural fit of chatbot outputs fosters AI literacy and pedagogical reasoning. These strategies align with findings from Binu (2024) and Kohnke et al. (2023), who advocate for cultivating critical engagement rather than passive use of AI technologies in teacher preparation.

Educational technologists are encouraged to prioritize the contextual localization of AI systems. This includes training chatbots on Vietnamese curricula, language usage, and classroom scenarios that reflect national education priorities. Further, the incorporation of emotion-aware natural language processing would enhance AI's social presence, providing affective support currently lacking in systems like Mizou. Yang et al. (2023) emphasize the importance of culturally responsive design in AI for equitable learner engagement, while Binu (2024) stresses the emotional dimensions of effective AI-mediated communication.

For policymakers, the introduction of national AI integration guidelines is critical. These should address ethical use, transparency, and data privacy, ensuring that AI adoption is both responsible and pedagogically sound. Investing in infrastructure and teacher training—particularly in under-resourced areas—will promote more equitable access to AI tools in teacher education. UNESCO (2023) and the World Bank (2024) underline the urgency of policy frameworks that promote not just access to AI, but also its thoughtful and ethical application.

Finally, for researchers, further longitudinal and mixed-method studies are necessary to understand the long-term impact of AI use on teacher identity, instructional confidence, and classroom innovation. Comparative research across regions and teacher education models can yield deeper insights into how chatbots like Mizou influence pedagogical development. Studies such as those by Guan et al. (2024) demonstrate the potential of AI to support complex educational outcomes when its limitations are systematically addressed.

In sum, this study advances theoretical, empirical, and practical understanding of how chatbots—when guided by the AI-CITE framework—can enhance language teacher education. Mizou facilitated individualized learning, promoted interactive engagement, supported instructional planning, and bolstered pedagogical reasoning. However, its limitations—chiefly its lack of contextual and emotional responsiveness—reveal the need for ethical, pedagogical, and technological refinements. Comparative analysis with other studies confirms that AI chatbots are most effective when embedded within a hybrid model of education that balances algorithmic support with human mentorship and culturally situated pedagogical design. To improve cultural responsiveness, developers should train Mizou using Vietnamese classroom discourse, typical lesson content, and culturally situated teaching cases. This would enhance the tool's contextual fit and effectiveness.

Implications for Practice: Practical Strategies

To support trainers and curriculum developers in meaningfully integrating Mizou into teacher education, several practical strategies are recommended. First, trainers can introduce structured sample prompts such as *"Design a lesson plan for Grade 8 based on the topic of environmental protection"* or *"Revise the following rubric to better assess group presentation skills."* These tasks help pre-service teachers engage with AI-generated instructional content in ways that align with authentic curriculum design. In terms of training integration, guided workshops should be conducted where trainees analyze and critique the chatbot's feedback on draft assignments, enabling them to develop both AI literacy and pedagogical reasoning. Reflection tasks that compare chatbot-generated suggestions with those from human mentors can further enhance metacognitive awareness and professional judgment. In practical scenarios, the chatbot can be used in planning labs to simulate a confused learner, prompting teacher candidates to revise their explanations or instructional strategies. Additionally, trainees can practice giving and receiving peer feedback using it before participating in formal LMS-based review activities. These applications help ensure that chatbot use supports reflective teaching practice, context-sensitive planning, and collaborative learning.

CONCLUSION

This chapter addressed the growing interest in AI chatbots in teacher education amid a gap between enthusiasm and actual classroom adoption (Labadze et al., 2023). The study examined how pre-service teachers perceive and engage with Chatbot Mizou in their training, how it influences their lesson planning and pedagogical decisions, and what barriers hinder its integration. The findings revealed that trainees generally appreciated Mizou's instant feedback, accessibility, and ability to enhance independent learning, using it as a convenient tool for lesson planning and obtaining structured guidance on tasks like rubric design. However, the chatbot's effectiveness in fostering deep engagement and truly personalized learning was limited; participants noted that Mizou struggled to adapt to context-specific classroom challenges and lacked the nuanced, emotional support that human mentors provide. In practice, teachers sometimes encountered repetitive or generic answers when their prompts were not precise, and inconsistent responses could undermine their trust in the AI, highlighting how insufficient training and reliability issues can impede full integration of such tools in the learning process.

Theoretically, the study broadens existing models of technology integration by demonstrating how teacher cognition, instructional practice, and systemic factors intertwine during chatbot use—an interplay not fully accounted for in traditional frameworks like TPACK or UTAUT. Practically, the chapter offers actionable guidance: it recommends enhancing chatbot design for greater context-awareness and cultural sensitivity, improving chatbots' emotional intelligence to provide motivational support, and providing more structured training for pre-service teachers in using AI tools (Dizon, 2020). Implementing these improvements in teacher education programs can align chatbot use more closely with real classroom needs, making AI support more pedagogically effective. Moreover, the findings emphasize that AI chatbots should complement rather than replace human mentorship; integrating chatbots with the empathetic guidance of teacher educators is vital to preserve the humanistic, context-aware dimensions of teaching (Ji et al., 2024; Kohnke, 2023).

Despite its contributions, this study has several limitations. It was conducted in a single teacher education program in Central Vietnam. This specific context and sample may limit the generalizability of the findings to other institutions, subject areas, or to in-service teachers. Furthermore, the chatbot was integrated over a relatively short period within an academic unit, so the data capture an initial snapshot of chatbot use rather than long-term adoption or impact. The results rely on participants' self-reported perceptions and on interactions with one particular AI platform, which could introduce response biases; consequently, the insights may not encompass the full range of possible experiences with different chatbots or extended use.

The study's insights point to several directions for future research and improvements in AI chatbot integration. One key direction is to enhance the technology itself: future chatbots should offer more context-aware, personalized assistance and incorporate greater emotional intelligence to better engage and motivate learners. Equally important is preparing teachers to use these tools effectively: teacher education programs should provide targeted training in AI literacy and prompt design, helping pre-service teachers develop the skills to obtain relevant answers and to critically evaluate AI-generated suggestions (Mathew, 2024; Dizon, 2020). Future studies might adopt longitudinal designs to examine how sustained chatbot use affects teacher development (e.g., gains in instructional confidence, reflective practice, or professional identity) over time, and conduct comparative research across different regions or teacher education contexts to determine how cultural and institutional factors influence the success of chatbot integration. Ultimately, by illuminating how to harness AI innovations while preserving the human core of teaching, this study reaffirms its value and relevance for shaping the future of teacher education.

REFERENCES

Beyer, S., Grave-Gierlinger, F., & Meyer-Jenßen, L. (2024). Twenty reasons why: Investigating use-related beliefs and reasons of preservice teachers for (not) using an intent-based chatbot during lesson planning. *Contemporary Issues in Technology & Teacher Education, 24*(3), 359–383. DOI: 10.70725/652385asanaw

Bii, P. K., Too, J. K., & Mukwa, C. W. (2018). Teacher attitude towards use of chatbots in routine teaching. *Universal Journal of Educational Research, 6*(7), 1586–1597. DOI: 10.13189/ujer.2018.060719

Binu, P. M. (2024). Generative AI and its impact on writing skills and creative thinking. *English Scholarship Beyond Borders, 10*(1), 45–47.

Chiu, T. K. F., Xia, Q., Zhou, X., & Cheng, M. (2024). *Empowering K-12 Education with AI: Preparing for the Future of Education and Work*. Routledge., DOI: 10.4324/9781003498377

Chocarro, R., Cortiñas, M., & Marcos, M. (2021). Teachers' acceptance of chatbots in education: A technology acceptance model perspective. *Computers in Human Behavior Reports, 4*, 100123.

Chong, A. Y. L., Li, B., Ngai, E. W. T., Ch'ng, E., & Lee, F. (2021). AI-chatbots on the services frontline addressing the challenges and opportunities of agency. *Journal of Business Research, 129*, 902–910. DOI: 10.1016/j.jbusres.2020.09.018

Chukwuere, J. (2024). *The Future of AI Chatbots in Higher Education*. Qeios., DOI: 10.32388/UE841K

Crosthwaite, P., Luciana, , & Wijaya, D. (2023). Exploring language teachers' lesson planning for corpus-based language teaching: A focus on developing TPACK for corpora and DDL. *Computer Assisted Language Learning, 36*(7), 1392–1420. DOI: 10.1080/09588221.2021.1995001

Dizon, G. (2020). Evaluating intelligent personal assistants for L2 listening and speaking development. *Language Learning & Technology, 24*(1), 16–26.

Fryer, L. K., Coniam, D., Carpenter, R., & Lăpu neanu, D. (2020). Bots for language learning now: Current and future directions. *Language Learning & Technology, 24*(2), 8–22. https://www.lltjournal.org/item/10125-44719/

Fryer, L. K., Nakao, K., & Thompson, A. (2019). Chatbot learning partners: Connecting learning experiences, interest, and competence. *Computers in Human Behavior, 93*, 279–289. DOI: 10.1016/j.chb.2018.12.023

Guan, R., Raković, M., Chen, G., & Gašević, D. (2024). How educational chatbots support self-regulated learning: A systematic review of the literature. *Education and Information Technologies*. Advance online publication. DOI: 10.1007/s10639-024-12881-y&#8203

Guan, X., Zou, B., Shao, Y., & Chen, P. (2024). Supporting speaking practice by social network-based interaction in AI-assisted language learning. *Sustainability, 15*(4), 2872. DOI: 10.3390/su15042872

Hadizadeh, A. (2023). Chatbots and English Language Teaching. In *Current Trends in ELT* (pp. 191–206).

Huang, W., & Hew, K. F. (2023). The impact of chatbots on higher-order thinking in education: A critical review. *Educational Technology Research and Development*, *71*(3), 1239–1261. DOI: 10.1007/s11423-023-10215-2

Huang, W., Hew, K. F., & Fryer, L. K. (2021). Chatbots for language learning—Are they really useful? A systematic review of chatbot-supported language learning. *Computers & Education*, *168*, 104196. DOI: 10.1016/j.compedu.2021.104196

Huang, W., Hew, K. F., & Fryer, L. K. (2022). Chatbots for language learning: A meta-analytic review. *ReCALL*, *34*(3), 347–372. DOI: 10.1017/S0958344022000035

Jauhiainen, J., & Garagorry Guerra, A. (2024). Generative AI and education: Dynamic personalization of pupils' school learning material with ChatGPT. *Frontiers in Education*, *9*, 1288723. DOI: 10.3389/feduc.2024.1288723

Jeon, J. (2021). Chatbot-assisted dynamic assessment (CA-DA) for L2 vocabulary learning and diagnosis. *Computer Assisted Language Learning*, *36*(7), 1338–1364. DOI: 10.1080/09588221.2021.1987272

Jeon, J., Lee, S., & Coronel-Molina, S. M. (2024). Rethinking AI: Bias in Speech-Recognition Chatbots for ELT. *ELT Journal*, *78*(4), 435–445. DOI: 10.1093/elt/ccae035

Ji, H., Han, I., & Ko, Y. (2023). A systematic review of conversational AI in language education: Focusing on the collaboration with human teachers. *Journal of Research on Technology in Education*, *55*(1), 48–63. DOI: 10.1080/15391523.2022.2142873

Jyothsna, M., Subbaiah, P. V., & Kryvinka, N. (2024). Exploring the chatbot usage intention – A mediating role of chatbot initial trust. *Heliyon*, *10*(12), e33028. Advance online publication. DOI: 10.1016/j.heliyon.2024.e33028

Kim, N. J., & Kim, M. K. (2022). Teacher's Perceptions of Using an Artificial Intelligence-Based Educational Tool for Scientific Writing. *Frontiers in Education*, *7*, 755914. Advance online publication. DOI: 10.3389/feduc.2022.755914

Kim, N. Y. (2018). A study on chatbots for developing Korean college students' English listening and reading skills. *Journal of Digital Convergence*, *16*(8), 19–26. DOI: 10.14400/JDC.2018.16.8.019

Kohnke, L. (2022). A qualitative exploration of student perspectives on chatbot-mediated collaborative writing. *International Journal of Mobile Learning and Organisation*, *16*(4), 475–488. DOI: 10.1504/IJMLO.2022.125966

Kohnke, L. (2023). "Alexa, can you model empathy?": The limits of AI in developing emotional teaching competences. *ReCALL*, *35*(2), 200–215. DOI: 10.1017/S0958344023000057

Kohnke, L., Moorhouse, B. L., & Zou, D. (2023). ChatGPT for language teaching and learning. *RELC Journal*, *54*(2), 1–14. DOI: 10.1177/00336882231162868

Kooli, C. (2023). Chatbots in education and research: A critical examination of ethical implications and solutions. *Sustainability (Basel), 15*(7), 5614. DOI: 10.3390/su15075614

Labadze, L., Arziani, M., & Rewiashvili, N. (2023). AI chatbots in education: A systematic literature review. *Journal of Educational Computing Research, 61*(3), 505–528. DOI: 10.1177/07356331221147503

Lee, G. G., & Zhai, X. (2024). Using ChatGPT for science learning: A study on pre-service teachers' lesson planning. *IEEE Transactions on Learning Technologies, 17*, 1683–1700. DOI: 10.1109/TLT.2024.3401457

Lee, S., & Jeon, J. (2024). Enhancing pre-service EFL teachers' TPACK through chatbot-integrated lesson planning projects. *Language Learning & Technology, 28*(1), 1–20. DOI: 10.31274/isudp.2024.154.01

Lee, S., Jeon, J., & Choe, H. (2024). Enhancing pre-service teachers' Global Englishes awareness with technology: A focus on AI chatbots in 3D metaverse environments. *TESOL Quarterly*. Advance online publication. DOI: 10.1002/tesq.3300&#8203

Lim, S. S., & Makany, T. (2023). Deploying chatbots to build students' critical thinking skills: Leveraging generative AI effectively and purposefully in higher education. In Peters, M. A., & Heraud, R. (Eds.), *Encyclopedia of Educational Innovation*. Springer.

Lin, P. C., & Chang, D. (2023). CHAT-ACTS: A pedagogical framework for personalized chatbots to enhance active learning and self-regulated learning. *Computers and Education: Artificial Intelligence, 5*, 100167. DOI: 10.1016/j.caeai.2023.100167

Loge, M., Suh, E., & Son, J. B. (2023). Artificial intelligence in language education: Opportunities and challenges. In Son, J.-B. (Ed.), *AI in language education: Challenges, opportunities and future directions* (pp. 25–41). Springer.

Luckin, R., Holmes, W., Griffiths, M., & Forcier, L. B. (2016). *Intelligence Unleashed: An argument for AI in education*. Pearson.

Mathew, B. P. (2024). Affordances and challenges of integrating AI in English language education: A critical analysis. *English Scholarship Beyond Borders, 10*(1), 34–48.

McGrath, C., Farazouli, A., & Cerratto-Pargman, T. (2024). Generative AI chatbots in higher education: A review of an emerging research area. *Higher Education*. Advance online publication. DOI: 10.1007/s10734-024-01288-w

Mishra, P., & Koehler, M. J. (2006). Technological pedagogical content knowledge: A framework for teacher knowledge. *Teachers College Record, 108*(6), 1017–1054. DOI: 10.1111/j.1467-9620.2006.00684.x

Mungai, B. K., Omieno, K. K., Egessa, M., & Manyara, P. N. (2024). AI chatbots in LMS: A pedagogical review of cognitive, constructivist, and adaptive principles. *Engineering and Technology Journal, 9*(8), 4709–4715. DOI: 10.47191/etj/v9i08.15

Ng, D. T. K., Leung, J. K. L., Su, J., Ng, R. C. W., & Chu, S. K. W. (2023). Teachers' AI digital competencies and twenty-first century skills in the post-pandemic world. *Educational Technology Research and Development, 71*(1), 137–161. DOI: 10.1007/s11423-023-10203-6 PMID: 36844361

Nguyen, T., Tran, H., & Le, V. (2021). Chatbots for pronunciation training in teacher education. *System, 98*, 102480. DOI: 10.1016/j.system.2021.102480

Okonkwo, C. W., & Ade-Ibijola, A. (2021). Chatbots applications in education: A systematic review. *Computers and Education: Artificial Intelligence, 2*, 100033. DOI: 10.1016/j.caeai.2021.100033

Ouyang, Z., Jiang, Y., & Liu, H. (2024). The effects of Duolingo, an AI-integrated technology, on EFL learners' willingness to communicate and engagement in online classes. *International Review of Research in Open and Distance Learning, 25*(3), 97–115. DOI: 10.19173/irrodl.v25i3.7677

Pappagallo, S. (2024). Chatbots in education: A dual perspective on innovation and ethics. *Journal of Digital Pedagogy, 3*(1), 3–10. DOI: 10.61071/JDP.2420

Pokrivčáková, S. (2019). Preparing teachers for the application of AI-powered technologies in foreign language education. *Journal of Language and Cultural Education, 7*(3), 135–153. DOI: 10.2478/jolace-2019-0025

Raković, M., Guan, R., Chen, G., & Gašević, D. (2024). How educational chatbots support self-regulated learning? A systematic review of the literature. *Education and Information Technologies*. Advance online publication. DOI: 10.1007/s10639-024-12881-y

Shoja, L., & Maadikhah, M. M. (2024). *Exploring the Effectiveness of AI Chatbots in EAP Genre Instruction*. Presented at the International Conference on Emerging Technologies in English Language Education in the 21st Century: Addressing the Present and Envisioning the Future.

Smutny, P., & Schreiberova, P. (2020). Chatbots for learning: A review of educational chatbots for the Facebook Messenger. *Computers & Education, 151*, 103862. DOI: 10.1016/j.compedu.2020.103862

UNESCO. (2023). *Guidance for generative AI in education and research*. United Nations Educational, Scientific and Cultural Organization. https://unesdoc.unesco.org/ark:/48223/pf0000386694

Vega, J., Rodriguez, M., Check, E., Moran, H., & Loo, L. (2025). Duolingo Evolution: From Automation to Artificial Intelligence. In A.D. Orjuela-Cañón, J.A. Lopez, & O.J. Suarez (Eds.), *Applications of Computational Intelligence* (ColCACI 2024, Communications in Computer and Information Science, Vol. 2212, pp. 54–71). Springer, Cham. DOI: 10.1007/978-3-031-88854-0_5

Venkatesh, V., Morris, M. G., Davis, G. B., & Davis, F. D. (2003). User acceptance of information technology: Toward a unified view. *Management Information Systems Quarterly, 27*(3), 425–478. DOI: 10.2307/30036540

Vygotsky, L. S. (1978). *Mind in society*. Harvard University Press.

Winne, P. H., & Hadwin, A. F. (1998). Studying as self-regulated learning. In Hacker, D. J., Dunlosky, J., & Graesser, A. C. (Eds.), *Metacognition in educational theory and practice* (pp. 277–304). Lawrence Erlbaum Associates Publishers.

Wollny, S., Schneider, J., Di Mitri, D., Weidlich, J., Rittberger, M., & Drachsler, H. (2021). Are we there yet?—A systematic literature review on chatbots in education. *Frontiers in Artificial Intelligence*, *4*, 654924. DOI: 10.3389/frai.2021.654924 PMID: 34337392

World Bank. (2024). *AI revolution in education: What you need to know*. https://www.worldbank.org/en/news/feature/2024/03/20/ai-revolution-in-education

Xu, Y., Wang, D., & Collins, P. (2023). Adaptive chatbots for teacher education: A framework for personalized professional development. *System*, *114*, 103022. DOI: 10.1016/j.system.2023.103022

Yang, Y., Qian, D. D., & Wang, X. (2023). Cultural responsiveness in AI-driven language education: Challenges and opportunities. *Language Learning & Technology*, *27*(1), 1–18. 10125/73519

Zagami, J. (2024). AI Chatbot Influences on Preservice Teachers' Understanding of Student Diversity and Lesson Differentiation in Online Initial Teacher Education. *International Journal on E-Learning*. https://www.learntechlib.org/primary/p/225176/

Zawacki-Richter, O., Marín, V. I., & Bond, M. (2023). Ethical implications of AI in education: A global perspective. *International Journal of Educational Technology in Higher Education*, *20*(1), 1–18. DOI: 10.1186/s41239-023-00406-5

Zawacki-Richter, O., Marín, V. I., Bond, M., & Gouverneur, F. (2019). Systematic review of research on AI in education. *International Journal of Educational Technology in Higher Education*, *16*, 39. DOI: 10.1186/s41239-019-0171-0

Zheng, Y., & Stewart, N. (2024). Improving EFL students' cultural awareness: Reframing moral dilemmatic stories with ChatGPT. *Computers and Education: Artificial Intelligence*, *6*, 100223. DOI: 10.1016/j.caeai.2024.100223

Zhou, L., & Brown, D. (2020). Content reliability in AI-generated educational resources. *Educational Technology Research and Development*, *68*(5), 2251–2271. DOI: 10.1007/s11423-020-09773-2

ADDITIONAL READING

Jeon, J. (2021). Chatbot-assisted dynamic assessment (CA-DA) for L2 vocabulary learning and diagnosis. *Computer Assisted Language Learning*, *34*(7), 829–852. DOI: 10.1080/09588221.2021.1987272

Kohnke, L., Moorhouse, B. L., & Zou, D. (2023). ChatGPT for language teaching and learning. *RELC Journal*, *54*(2), 537–550. DOI: 10.1177/00336882231162868

Lin, M. P. C., & Chang, D. (2023). CHAT-ACTS: A pedagogical framework for personalized chatbot to enhance active learning and self-regulated learning. *Computers and Education: Artificial Intelligence*, *5*, 100167. DOI: 10.1016/j.caeai.2023.100167

Zawacki-Richter, O., Marín, V. I., Bond, M., & Gouverneur, F. (2019). Systematic review of research on artificial intelligence applications in higher education—Where are the educators? *International Journal of Educational Technology in Higher Education*, *16*(1), 39. Advance online publication. DOI: 10.1186/s41239-019-0171-0

KEY TERMS AND DEFINITIONS

AI Chatbots: AI chatbots are conversational agents powered by artificial intelligence, often using natural language processing (NLP), that simulate human-like interactions. In pre-service teacher education, they support instructional tasks, feedback, and reflective learning.

Cognitive Load Theory: A psychological theory that suggests learning is most effective when the instructional design reduces unnecessary mental effort. Chatbots can help manage cognitive load by providing structured support and simplifying complex content.

Individualization: This term refers to the adaptation of instructional content and learning experiences to the specific needs, preferences, and progress of individual learners. Chatbots achieve this through tailored feedback and personalized learning pathways.

Pedagogical Decision-Making: This involves choices made by teachers in planning, delivering, and assessing instruction. AI chatbots can assist in this by offering suggestions on teaching strategies, assessments, and adaptations based on student needs.

Self-Regulated Learning (SRL): The theory refers to learners' ability to actively manage their own learning through goal setting, strategy use, self-monitoring, and reflection. It's a cyclical process where learners take ownership of how they learn. AI chatbots can support SRL by offering timely feedback, helping students plan tasks, and encouraging reflection—especially useful in self-paced or remote learning environments common in teacher training programs.

TPACK: (Technological Pedagogical Content Knowledge): A framework describing the essential knowledge teachers need to integrate technology effectively in their teaching by combining technological knowledge with pedagogical strategies and content expertise.

UTAUT: (Unified Theory of Acceptance and Use of Technology): This theoretical model helps explain why individuals choose to adopt or reject new technologies. It suggests that users are more likely to embrace a tool—such as an AI chatbot—if they believe it will enhance their performance, is easy to use, is supported by peers and institutions, and if the necessary infrastructure is in place. In teacher education, the theory helps unpack how pre-service teachers' attitudes and external conditions influence their willingness to integrate chatbots into learning and teaching.

APPENDIX I

Focus Group Interview Questions

Perception

1. What were your initial thoughts when you first heard about using Mizou in your language assessment course?
2. How do you currently perceive the role of Mizou in your language assessment practices?
3. How has your perception of Mizou changed from your initial expectations to your current experience?

Practice

4. Can you describe how you typically use Mizou in your language assessment activities?
5. How have you integrated Mizou into your daily or weekly teaching routines and assessment practices?
6. Which features of Mizou do you find yourself using the most, and why?

Value

7. What do you find most valuable about using Mizou for language assessment?
8. In what ways do you think Mizou enhances your learning or teaching experience in the context of language assessment?
9. How does the value you get from Mizou compare to traditional language assessment tools?

Impact

10. How has using Mizou impacted the quality of your language assessments?
11. Have you noticed any changes or improvements in your language skills or assessment capabilities since using Mizou? If so, what are they?
12. How has Mizou affected your engagement with the course material and language assessment tasks?

Difficulties

13. What challenges or difficulties have you encountered while using Mizou?
14. Have you experienced any technical issues with Mizou? If so, how did you resolve them?
15. Based on your experiences, what suggestions do you have for improving Mizou to better meet your needs and expectations?

APPENDIX II: THEMATIC ANALYSIS RESULTS

Table 5. Tabular analysis

Codes	Themes	Subthemes	Examples
Structured content	Individualization	Useful but lacks true personalization	Mizou provides relevant information, but sometimes I need more depth, so I still have to double-check...
General responses	Individualization		At first...Mizou gives answers that are structured but sometimes too general.
Supplementary materials	Individualization		I often have to look elsewhere for detailed explanations or examples.
Accessible explanations	Interactivity	Enhances engagement	I see Mizou as a companion...it explains things in a simple and easy-to-understand way.
Follow-up prompts	Interactivity	Encourages exploration	Mizou suggests related follow-up questions, which makes me engage more in learning.
Limited continuity	Interactivity	Limited contextual awareness	Mizou doesn't remember previous interactions.
Inefficient with complexity	Interactivity	Difficulty with complex interactions	When I ask complex or multi-step questions, Mizou struggles to follow the conversation.
Quick information	Engagement	Efficient independent learning	Mizou provides concise information, which helps me prepare for class more efficiently.
Lack of emotional support	Engagement	Reduced motivation	Unlike interacting with a teacher...Mizou doesn't provide encouragement.
Framework for planning	Lesson Planning	Helpful structure but lacks practicality	Mizou provides a framework, but I often need to modify its suggestions significantly...
Classroom reality gap	Lesson Planning	Insufficient classroom adaptability	Mizou doesn't consider real-life classroom challenges.
Generic recommendations	Pedagogical Decision-Making	Broad suggestions, need adaptation	The AI-generated teaching strategies are too broad, human intuition is needed to adapt them.
Limited flexibility	Contextual Limitations	Poor real-world adaptability	When I asked about classroom behavior issues, Mizou gave theoretical responses but no practical solutions.
Prompt formulation issues	Limited Training and Familiarity	Difficulties using AI tools	The biggest challenge is how to phrase questions to get the right answers.
Inconsistent reliability	Emotional Support and Reliability Issues	Skepticism about AI accuracy	Sometimes Mizou gives different answers to the same question, which makes me doubt its reliability.

Chapter 4
Ensuring Equity and Access for Students With Disabilities: AI for Inclusive Education

Ratan Sarkar
https://orcid.org/0009-0008-5480-0165
Prabhat Kumar College, Contai, India

Raj Madhu
https://orcid.org/0009-0001-0516-3365
Central University of Jammu, India

ABSTRACT

This chapter explores the role of artificial intelligence (AI) in fostering inclusive education for students with disabilities, focusing on how AI-powered assistive technologies like speech-to-text, text-to-speech, screen readers, and real-time captioning can improve accessibility and engagement. It examines personalized learning platforms, AI-driven tutoring systems, and adaptive assessments tailored to individual needs. Ethical challenges such as algorithmic bias, data privacy, and infrastructural disparities are also addressed. The chapter offers recommendations for effective AI integration, including comprehensive needs assessments, phased implementation, collaborative ecosystems, and an emphasis on affordability and accessibility. It highlights the importance of inclusive AI policies, data governance, and educator training to ensure responsible use of AI. The chapter stresses AI's transformative potential but emphasizes the need for ongoing research, interdisciplinary collaboration, and human-centered design to ensure AI tools promote equity and empower all learners.

INTRODUCTION

Inclusive education is an instructional paradigm focused on offering equal learning opportunities to all students irrespective of physical, cognitive, emotional, or social differences. At its core, inclusive education rejects the notion of segregated learning environments in favour of

DOI: 10.4018/979-8-3373-5097-4.ch004

integrating all learners within mainstream classrooms, accompanied by flexible interventions, accommodations, and personalized support. It is grounded in principles of equality, access, and respect for diversity, serving as the philosophical and practical cornerstone of contemporary efforts to build inclusive, empathetic, and culturally responsive educational spaces (Ainscow, Booth, & Dyson, 2006).

Importantly, inclusive education is not limited to the physical integration of students with disabilities into regular education classrooms. Rather, it entails systematic planning and implementation of instructional practices, differentiated learning strategies, and inclusive assessment methods that are responsive to the diverse needs of all students (Saharan & Sethi, 2009; Florian & Black-Hawkins, 2011). This encompasses a broader vision of inclusive pedagogy that fosters a sense of belonging, participation, and mutual respect among learners of all backgrounds and abilities.

According to UNESCO (2009), inclusive education is defined as a *"process of addressing and responding to the diversity of needs of all learners through increasing participation in learning, cultures, and communities, and reducing exclusion within and from education"* (p. 8). This view shifts the focus beyond enrolment to meaningful participation and retention, emphasizing the transformation of educational systems to accommodate rather than marginalize learner differences.

Technically, inclusive education is operationalized through frameworks like Universal Design for Learning (UDL), an evidence-based model for designing curriculum, teaching strategies, and learning environments that accommodate individual learning differences (CAST, 2018). UDL encourages the use of multiple means of engagement, representation, and expression, ensuring that educational content is perceptually and cognitively accessible to all students, including those with sensory, intellectual, or motor disabilities (Knarlag & Olaussen, 2016; Meyer, Rose, & Gordon, 2014).

Significance of Inclusive Education in Contemporary Education Systems

In the 21st century, inclusive education has come to be regarded as an essential part of equitable and sustainable education systems. Its importance emanates from its capacity to break down systemic barriers through which historically, students with disabilities and other marginalised groups have been excluded. Its importance is underscored by the following points:

Figure 1. UDL & AI integration model

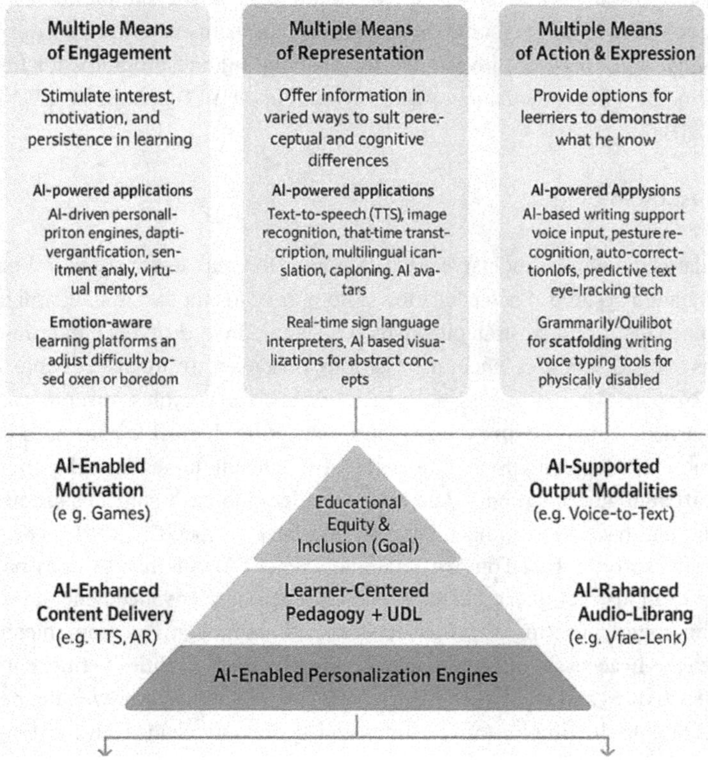

Human Rights Perspective

The structure of inclusive education is strongly based in global human rights, specifically those defined in the United Nations' Convention on the Rights of Persons with Disabilities (CRPD). Article 24 of the CRPD embeds in law the right of people with disabilities to enjoy inclusive, equitable, and quality education at all ages. This article directly focuses on removing exclusionary measures from education systems, requiring environments of respect for difference and regularity of access. The directives of the CRPD carry no weight as recommendations – they constitute legally binding obligations for signatory countries to integrate inclusive measures into education policymaking and systems (Sharma, 2015; United Nations, 2006). The implementation of inclusive education is not merely an instructional choice, but rather an ethical responsibility and an affirmation of obligations under international human rights law. When education systems become aligned with CRPD principles, governments confront deeply ingrained discriminatory procedures which have excluded and marginalized youth with disabilities in the past. In so doing, they embrace an ideal of education which supports social justice and fairness, moving beyond limited definitions of academic success to include whole human development for all learners. In spite of these imperatives, practice still lags behind policy in implementing inclusive education in many countries. It is difficult for countries to align legal frameworks with the mandates of the CRPD because of resource imperatives, socio-cultural resistance, and unavailability of trained staff. These gaps need to be overcome through strong mechanisms of monitoring, frameworks of accountability, and long-term investment in capacity-building programs for translating human rights principles into practical strategies (Waddington & Toepke, 2014; UNICEF, 2014; UNESCO, 2020).

Equity and Accessibility

In its fundamental nature, inclusive education aims to break down structural inequalities in traditional education systems. Such education systems tend to emphasize standardized pedagogy and homogenized instructional strategies, which do not address difference in terms of learning. Thus, persons with disabilities encounter various obstacles, from inaccessible buildings to instructional support. These barriers perpetuate exclusionary cycles, disempowering a large segment of learners from enjoying their right to education. Inclusive education brings differentiated instruction, adaptable instruction, and assistive technologies into play in meeting such challenges. Differentiated instruction keeps in consideration each student's specific strengths, needs, and learning pace so as to have instruction related to specific profiles (Kappen, 2010). Adaptive learning software based on Artificial Intelligence (AI) augments this by providing real-time adjustments in instructional content in relation to learning advancement and requirements. Assistive technologies in terms of screen readers and augmentative communications devices further bridge gaps in accessibility, allowing individuals with disabilities to fully engage in classroom learning activities and academic tests. Despite these solutions, however, their effectiveness depends on equitable distribution of resources and systematic change. In most environments, access to assistive technology and inclusive instructional materials is restricted to urban centers or wealthier areas, furthering inequity for deprivileged or rural students (Herder et al., 2017; World Bank, 2020). Closing this gap needs collective efforts in terms of decentralized resource availability, allocating budgetary priorities to inclusive education, and creating public-private partnerships for scaling (UNESCO & World Bank, 2019).

Economic and Social Implications

The economic benefits of inclusive education clearly reach beyond the child to benefit society at large. Research consistently shows that those who have had inclusive education attain increased levels of educational success, leading to improved employment opportunities, financial independence, and decreased use of social welfare (OECD, 2019). Societies, by investing in inclusive education, not only increase the potential and productivity of people with disability but also minimize long-term economic expenses related to exclusion and dependency. Apart from economic indicators, inclusive education is also instrumental in creating social cohesion. Inclusive classrooms, which encourage interactions among students of different abilities, become mini-representations of an equitable society (Shaeffer, 2019). Such classrooms foster mutual respect, collaboration, and understanding, breaking down stereotypes and minimizing prejudice based on ignorance or unfamiliarity. Over time, these social dividends translate to more harmonious communities, in which diversity is seen as strength, not weakness. Despite this, inclusive education's social and economic dividends necessitate upfront investments, which few countries view as feasible. Infrastructure construction for accessibility, provision of assistive technology, and preparation of teachers in inclusive education demand major financial outlays. Governments have to change strategies to address such expenditures as an investment rather than an expenditure in human capital and social justice. Innovative funding mechanisms, e.g., outcome-based funding and multilateral development aid, can assist countries in breaking resource bottlenecks (David & Kuyini, 2012; World Bank, 2018).

Alignment with Global Development Goals

Inclusive education is at the centre of achieving the Sustainable Development Goals (SDGs), in particular Goal 4, aimed at ensuring inclusive and equitable quality education for all and promoting opportunities for lifelong learning (UN, 2015). Inclusive education is brought centre stage for its key role in driving wider global objectives, including poverty eradication, gender equality, and sustainable development (UNESCO, 2020). In addition, inclusive education aligns within agendas such as Education for All (EFA) and the Incheon Declaration for Education 2030, which articulate inclusive learning environments as core to universal education (UNESCO, 2015). Such agendas highlight interdependence among inclusive education and other development goals while emphasizing education equity as both an impetus and outcome of sustainable development.

In spite of such synergies, alignment of national education systems to development objectives at the global level remains unequal. Various countries have adopted inclusive education policies in theory but lack mechanisms to implement those in practice. Inadequate data collection, weak institutional capacities, and disintegrated efforts at implementation hinder further advances toward such universal objectives (Devi, 2016; UNICEF, 2021).

Closing such gaps requires mainstreaming inclusive education within overall development frameworks in ways which give it political as well as financial precedence. Monitoring and evaluation mechanisms would have to be improved in ways so as to record achievements as well as bottlenecks, while cooperation at an international level can provide for an exchange of knowledge as well as best practice sharing (UNESCO & World Bank, 2019).

The success of inclusive education hinges upon its capacity to respond to systemic disparities without compromising its basic principles. A closer look reveals inclusive education has gained significant ground at practice and policy, in large part promoting an appreciation for diversity in education. Its success lies in adopting systemic strategy in which systematic and integrative actions unite at policy, practice, and community levels. Governments and institutions must pay utmost heed to resource allocation for inclusive practice, undertake investments in teachers' training, and employ technology in reducing gaps in access. Also, fostering an inclusive culture requires sustained efforts in raising public awareness in terms of the merit of diversity in education (Mouroutsou, 2017; World Bank, 2020).

The Role of AI in Fostering Inclusive Education and Removing Barriers for Students with Disabilities

Artificial Intelligence (AI) has become an integral transformative force in education, providing solutions for diverse ways to increase accessibility, make learning experiences more personalized, and build inclusive environments. For individuals who have disabilities, AI can play an impactful role, as it breaks down various barriers that have historically excluded them from accessing quality education (Morris, 2019). Yet, although AI holds huge potential, its use should be critically evaluated so that it can live up to its potential for inclusiveness without creating additional challenges while worsening existing inequities.

Figure 2. Barriers vs. AI-based solutions matrix

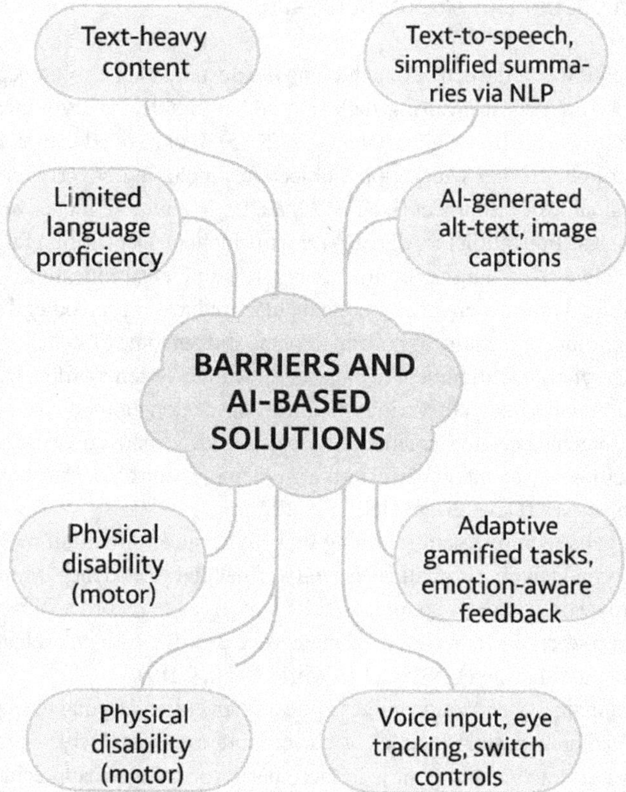

Personalized Learning Through AI Algorithms

AI-based platforms use machine learning (ML) algorithms to develop student-cantered learning experiences specific to the individual requirements of students with disabilities. Such platforms use data analytics to determine learning styles, strengths, and weaknesses of an individual and use them to provide customized content. For example, Natural Language Processing (NLP) algorithms can modify complexity in text for students who have cognitive impairments while learning content written in braille for visually impaired individuals (Drigas & Loannidou, 2013).

Enhancing Accessibility Through Assistive Technologies

AI-based assistive technologies have transformed learning for people with disabilities. Text-to-speech (TTS) software, speech-to-text software, and screen readers driven by AI make learning easier for students who have visual, audio, and motor impairments. Technologies like real-time captioning, driven by AI-based Automatic Speech Recognition (ASR), promote inclusiveness by creating accessible channels of communication (Treglia et al., 2019).

Supporting Cognitive and Emotional Needs

AI-based systems combined with affective computing and sentiment analysis can recognize and respond to learners' emotional and cognitive state. For individuals with ASD or ADHD, AI-based systems can track learning engagement, offer real-time feedback, and recommend interventions to sustain concentration and interest. AI-based systems can mimic social interactions, which can assist individuals with social difficulties in learning communication skills (Shi, 2019).

Bridging Language and Communication Barriers

AI has facilitated substantive development in terms of language and communication barrier breaking for disability students. Deep learning-based speech-to-text (STT) software offers real-time transcriptions for deaf and hard-of-hearing students, while multilingual learning environments in support of sign language and other communication-based learning for hard-of-hearing and deaf students have been facilitated by AI-based translation software (Neamtu et al., 2019).

Creating Adaptive Learning Environments

Adaptive learning software applies AI to dynamically modify instructional content as a function of real-time evaluations of a student's abilities. Reinforcement learning algorithms guide platforms in refining recommendations so that those who have disabilities get suitable challenges and support. For instance, learning games with adjustable difficulties can use gamification to engage students of different cognitive abilities (Bennane, 2013).

Addressing Physical Barriers Through Robotics and Automation

Robotics and automation technologies driven by artificial intelligence are shattering physical constraints faced by mobility-impaired students. Robotic arms driven by AI algorithms and computer vision make it possible for students with mobility impairment to engage with learning resources, and independent navigation systems aid movement in institutions of learning (Raja et al., 2023).

Reducing Teacher Workload and Enhancing Pedagogical Support

The administrative work can be automated through AI tools like grading and lesson planning so that teachers are able to devote more attention to one-on-one support to students with disabilities. Intelligent Tutoring Systems (ITS), which are virtual teaching aids, provide ancillary instruction and adaptive feedback to learners (Conde et al., 2010).

The impact that AI will have on inclusive education is transformative in nature and provides tools to break down barriers and promote equity among students with disabilities. But its application needs to be informed by principles of inclusiveness, responsible AI development and testing. Solutions to issues like algorithmic bias, the digital divide, and expense need to be found to ensure that AI lives up to its promise to be an inclusiveness catalyst. In adopting an integrated and critical approach to its implementation, education systems can use AI to make learning contexts both accessible and empowering to all students.

AI-POWERED ASSISTIVE TECHNOLOGIES FOR STUDENTS WITH DISABILITIES

Assistive AI Technologies for Accessibility

Speech to text and text to speech are transformative artificial intelligence technologies that have greatly facilitated communication among disabled individuals. They offer a means to bridge learners with sensory and intellectual and physical disabilities with learning material and academic participation through either translating spoken words into writing or transcribing text into sound. Their inclusivity application in education is extensive to say the least, and it depends on confronting technological issues of boundaries and limitations, access equitability, and ethics. Also, Artificial Intelligence-driven screen readers, live captioning, and transcribing services are revolutionary technologies that foster inclusive education access among students with disabilities. These tools leverage cutting-edge advancements in artificial intelligence (AI), natural language processing (NLP), and deep learning (DL) to bypass communication and learning barriers. Nevertheless, the level to which these tools foster inclusiveness should be examined based on technological limitations, access, and ethics (Knox et al., 2019).

Figure 3. AI-enabled assistive technologies for inclusive classrooms

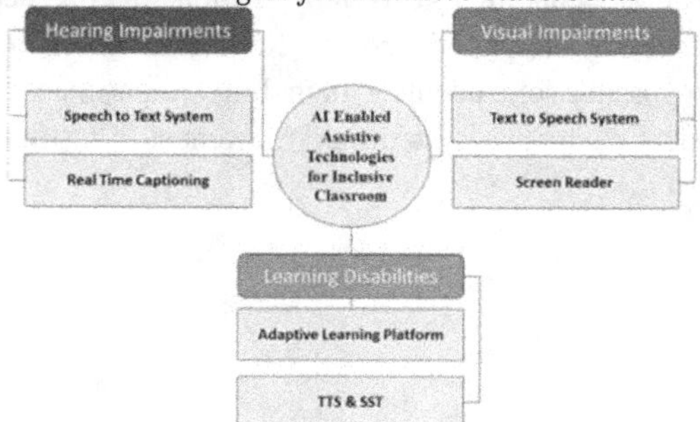

Speech-to-Text (STT) Systems

Speech to Text (STT) systems are an innovative use of Automatic Speech Recognition (ASR) technologies, translating spoken words into text with speed and accuracy. At the heart of STT systems are advanced AI techniques that interpret audio inputs, break down patterns of speech, and produce textual outputs. The underlying functions of STT systems are powered by acoustic modelling, which interprets sound waves to identify phonemes, and language modelling, which makes predictions about sequences of words to provide contextually correct predictions.

Deep learning architectures such as Recurrent Neural Networks (RNNs), Long Short-Term Memory (LSTM) networks, and more advanced Transformer models have raised the bar in the performance capabilities of STT software tools. Such architectures support subtle comprehension and transcribing complex patterns of speech, accents, and context. Real-time STT tools like Google's Live Transcribe and Otter.ai utilize deep learning architectures in an end-to-end setup to offer real-time and very accurate transcribing capabilities. Such tools are indispensable in inclusive education environments, facilitating real-time captions in lectures and allowing hearing-impaired students equal participation opportunities in class activities (Shiga et al., 2020).

Even with its transformative value, STT systems are prone to difficulties like accommodating variable accents, technical jargon in specific domains, and environmental noise that may compromise transcription quality. Overcoming these problems will need ongoing improvement in acoustic and language models and increasing access to greater and more representative sets of training data. In pedagogic uses, integrating STT systems needs to be accompanied by work to make them more accessible, affordable, and accommodating to variable learning environments.

Figure 4. Speech-to-text workflow

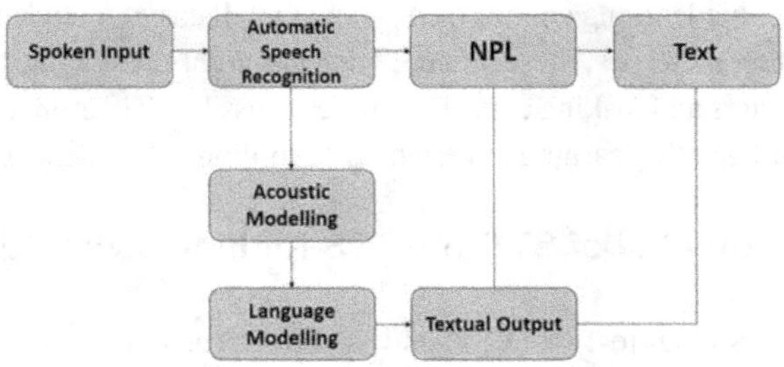

Text-to-Speech (TTS) Systems

Text-To-Speech (TTS) technologies are supplemented by STT technologies by rendering spoken language from textual statements. Based on sophisticated signal processing tools and AI models, TTS technologies provide voice to text that is understandable and natural-sounding. Cutting-edge architectures like WaveNet and Tacotron have revolutionized the capabilities of TTS technologies and created speech samples with unmatched naturalness, rhythm, and expressiveness.

Modelling prosody using intonation, rhythm, and stress. TTS technologies are able to simulate human-like patterns in speech and provide an even better user experience (Panda et al., 2015).

A vital characteristic of TTS systems is multilingual and multimodal capabilities. Contemporary TTS tools are designed to produce sound in several languages and customize voice to meet users' individual preferences and needs and thus are extremely versatile in heterogeneous learning environments. Programs such as NVDA (NonVisual Desktop Access) and VoiceOver utilize TTS technologies to make electronically presented material accessible to visually impaired learners or those with reading disability through sound. Such an ability gives learners power by making them independent and equally able to access education material.

The contribution of TTS systems to inclusive education is extremely important since these eliminate hindrances to literacy and reading comprehension among disabled students. But issues like mispronunciation of specialized vocabulary, lack of variety in synthesized speech, and support for under-resourced languages are some problems that need to be addressed by future developments in AI like emotion-sensing computing and increased linguistic resources (Metatla et al., 2019).

Figure 5. Text-to-speech workflow

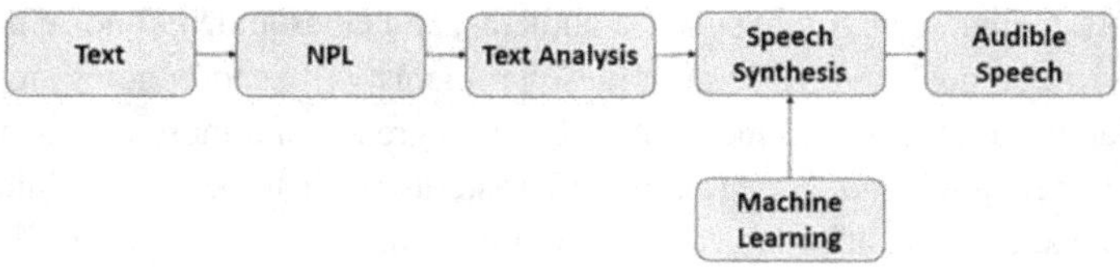

Collectively, STT and TTS technologies are not just closing education gaps but also empowering an inclusive and equitable learning environment. In making it easy for students with disabilities to engage with learning materials, these technologies highlight the revolutionary impact of AI in breaking down barriers and making education more accessible. Their ongoing innovation and adoption are set to reshape the learning experiences of millions of students globally.

Transformative Potential of STT and TTS for Inclusive Education

The integration of Speech-to-Text (STT) and Text-to-Speech (TTS) solutions in disability-inclusive learning practices has affected the access and involvement of disabled students in the classroom. Usage of these Artificial Intelligence (AI) technologies has become imperative in breaking the obstacles that otherwise prevented learners who were sensory-impaired, intellectually disabled, or physically disabled from attending class. STT systems provide hearing-impaired students with real-time captioning so that discussions and lectures are clear to them. TTS systems make auditory access to text available and are greatly beneficial to students with visual disabilities or with learning disabilities such as dyslexic students. Both these tools combined offer an open two-way channel through which hearing-impaired students can use TTS systems to input spoken input and STT systems to transcribe spoken input in tests or discussions (Irdamurni et al., 2020).

Apart from accessibility, STT and TTS technologies are supportive of adaptive learning. Integrating these technologies into interactive learning platforms enables teachers to offer multimodal learning experiences differentiated to suit the needs and requirements of individual students.

Whether catering to auditory, visual, or kinaesthetic learning ability and style, these technologies make it possible for learners to engage with material through routes that are most significant to them and are adapted to the individual learning styles and ability, creating an inclusive learning environment (Evmenova, 2020).

Challenges in Implementation of STT and TTS

Although these technologies hold promise to transform learning and education, there are challenges to adopting STT and TTS technologies. Among these is the challenge to ensure high accuracy and contextual comprehension by these systems. STT technologies are usually unsuccessful in identifying varied accents and dialects and thus make errors in transcribing that detract from the learning experience. Domain-specific terminologies and jargon in technical or specialized topics pose difficulties in transcription and synthesized speech production. Latency in real-time processing and output adds to these problems in interactive classroom environments.

TTS models have their own limitations to contend with. Although innovations like WaveNet and Tacotron improved the naturalness of synthetic speech to a considerable extent, aspects like monotone speech, mispronunciation of context-specific vocabulary, and lack of expressiveness remain issues. They detract from the efficacy of the tools to provide interactive and comprehendible learning experiences (Shadiev et al., 2014).

Equity in access is also an important challenge to address. Digital access frequently restricts access to STT and TTS tools to economically disadvantaged students or in under-equipped school environments. The high price points, lack of internet access, and lack of availability in training data for representation by minority languages heighten the imbalance and cause numerous students to be left out of the advantages these technologies provide.

Both ethical and privacy considerations are also important in the application of AI-powered education technologies. Data gathering and processing by STT and TTS systems pose major concerns regarding data protection and adherence to regulations like GDPR. In addition to this is the risk that algorithmic bias based on underrepresentation of minorities and regional accents in the train data may reinforce disparities, especially among vulnerable populations (Mohammed & Watson, 2019).

Figure 6. Comparative matrix: STT vs. TTS vs. screen readers vs. captioning tools

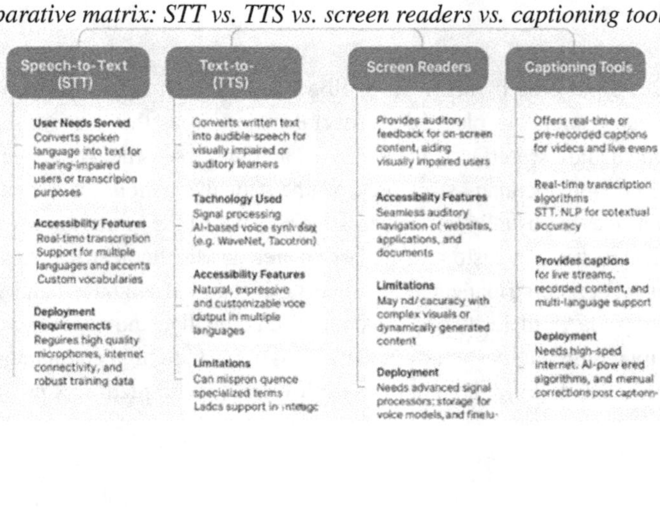

AI-Driven Screen Readers: Enhancing Text Accessibility

Artificial intelligence-powered screen readers are revolutionizing access to digital materials by visually impaired students, with transformational implications in education. The readers provide access to the use of computers, mobile phones, and internet data by translating text on the screen into sound or braille displays, thus eradicating the disparity in access to digital platforms by the visually impaired population (Crossland et al., 2017).

Technological Frameworks

The advanced feature set offered by AI-powered screen readers rests on several foundational technological paradigms. Natural Language Processing (NLP) algorithms form the backbone of these tools' operation, allowing them to comprehend document structures like headings, tables, and semantic layout for intuitive and understandable navigation through the content. State-of-the-art Text-to-Speech (TTS) models like WaveNet and Tacotron extend accessibility by creating natural-sounding expressive speech streams that can be adjusted to user needs with variable pitch, speed control, and tone control. Real-time interaction ability enables these screen readers to adjust dynamically to user inputs to provide user-centric and adaptive navigation experiences (Wu et al., 2020). Machine learning algorithms further enable on-going optimization to make the screen readers more and more efficient in reading varied and complex content on an ongoing basis.

Applications of AI-Driven Screen Readers

The applications of AI-enabled screen readers are numerous and extensive. Widely used tools like JAWS (Job Access with Speech), and NVDA (NonVisual Desktop Access), provide robust access to academic work to blind and partially blind students so that they can read textbooks, complete assignments and actively participate in online learning environments. Screen reader application software on mobile devices like VoiceOver and TalkBack extend these capabilities to open up education and everyday use to smartphones and tablets. Digital literacy among the blind and partially blind audience is facilitated by these tools through complete integration into more digitized education systems. Screen readers are being used extensively in collaborative learning environments to enable students to participate and act effectively in class discussions and group work (Felix et al., 2018).

Challenges

Although those powered by artificial intelligence hold tremendous transformative power, AI-powered screen readers are plagued by several major issues that prevent them from being universally adopted and used effectively. Foremost among these is the challenge of interpreting complex and compound document structures. Mathematical equations, chemical equations, and complex data matrices are usually left inaccessible because of the limitation in current NLP and TTS technologies. Barriers to customization are an area that further restricts the usability factor, with most screen readers being inadequately supported in regional languages, dialects, and cultural references, leaving a large majority of people unserved globally. Another major challenge is the resource intensity required to power advanced TTS systems with high computational power and memory requirements, making them hard to deploy on low-end platforms or in resource-poor environments (Kortemeyer, 2023). All these limitations explain the imperative need to continue to innovate and make the usability and accessibility of screen readers even better.

Real-Time Captioning: Bridging the Communication Gap

Real-time captioning systems are instrumental in ensuring inclusive education by transcribing spoken word into text captions when lectures are being delivered, engaged discussions are taking place, and multimedia presentations are being made. The systems are most valuable to hearing-impaired students by making auditory material available to them immediately and actively allowing them to engage with learning (Miyoshi et al., 2008).

Technological Foundations

The efficacy of real-time captioning systems rests on advanced technological bases. Automatic Speech Recognition (ASR) technologies are the foundation on which these systems are built, combined with acoustic modelling to recognize patterns in sounds and language modelling to forecast and write out words with high accuracy. High-performance neural network structures, specifically Transformer models like BERT (Bidirectional Encoder Representations from Transformers), enhance the accuracy of transcriptions further by enhancing the system's comprehension of contextual subtleties and compound linguistic patterns. Methods of processing are equally important; cloud-based offerings like Google's Live Transcribe and real-time captions by Zoom offer scalability and accessibility, whereas edge computing solutions eliminate latency issues to make these systems suitable for offline or low-connectivity scenarios (Takagi et al., 2015).

Advantages

The value of real-time captioning systems is multifaceted and greatly increases learning inclusiveness and participation. In the classroom context, the systems benefit hearing-impaired students by granting them access to auditory material in real-time, making them active participants in lectures and discussions on par with able-hearing peers. The multilingually offered by them increases the usefulness of these tools so that student populations drawn from diverse linguistic backgrounds can access material in familiar languages, bridging linguistic divides. Aside from accessibility issues, real-time captions improve learning experiences generally among all students since visual support to auditory input promotes comprehension and recall (Lasecki et al., 2014). This dual benefit highlights the revolutionizing power of captioning tools in supporting interactive and inclusive learning spaces.

Limitations

Although these systems benefit from numerous advantages, several major limitations could effectively hamper their effectiveness. Among the main limitations is one related to accuracy. Speech variation in instrument tone and level, regional accents, and external noise could cause errors in transcribing, which could pose difficulties in comprehension to users. Another problem is latency since processing and display delays break the continuity in the flow of real-time communication and communication in active classroom environments is particularly affected by this. Another set of issues is domain-related and occurs in situations with specialized jargon and technical terminologies or complicated linguistic phrases, where existing systems suffer to provide necessary and correct transcriptions (Finkelstein, 2015). These limitations prompt the need to refine these technologies continuously to meet diverse user needs effectively.

Automated Transcription Services: Streamlining Educational Content

Automated transcription services have become invaluable tools in modern education, enabling the seamless conversion of audio or video content into editable text formats. These tools play a critical role in creating accessible educational materials, such as lecture notes, podcasts, and recorded webinars, which benefit diverse learners, including those with sensory or cognitive impairments (Chevrier & Stimpson, 2017).

Core Technologies

The capability of automated transcribing is supported by highly advanced Speech-to-Text (STT) systems with high-volume throughput and deep context comprehension capabilities. Such systems utilize advanced algorithms to transcribe audio with remarkable speed and high-quality accuracy. The transcribing is supported by subsequent algorithms that correct grammatical errors, punctuation marks, and formatting issues to provide readable and professional outputs. In catering to the particular demands of educators, some transcribing tools offer support for tailor-made vocabulary so that specialized vocabulary in specialized topics like science, technology, engineering, and mathematics (STEM) can be integrated to provide better quality in specialized topics. All these technological innovations together make automated transcribing an indispensable pillar of inclusive education (Bain et al., 2012).

Applications in Education

The uses of automated transcriptions are extensive and revolutionary. A major use includes lecture documentation. Applications like Otter.ai and Sonix create comprehensive lecture transcriptions automatically, presenting major benefits to hearing-impaired students or to students who need supplemental work to review in addition to the lecture itself. In addition to individual needs, these tools make multimedia material like podcasts, audio recordings, and webinars accessible to all students regardless of ability, allowing them to access lessons. Additionally, automated transcribing makes collaborative learning environments more efficient through shared and reliable transcripts that act as point references when group members work on group work and discussions together (Bell et al., 2013).

Critical Issues

Given the potential of these services, however, there are several significant issues facing automated transcription services to fully leverage its power. Contextual misunderstanding is one major one, with automated platforms potentially having difficulty with homophones, ambiguous phrases, or complicated linguistic constructs and therefore requiring human review and adjustment. Data privacy issues are another area with high risk. Some transcription services are web-based and involve storing and processing sensitive audio files, and thus implicating issues with privacy law compliance with the General Data Protection Regulation (GDPR) and the Children's Online Privacy Protection Act (COPPA) (Brugnara et al., 2002). Finally, cost concerns remain with subscription models to access premium transcribing software potentially restricting access to economically disadvantaged learners and under-resourced school districts and institutions, enhancing existing disparities in education.

Transformative Potential and Ethical Considerations

There are artificial intelligence tools like screen readers, real-time captioning software, and automated transcribing services that hold transformational power to reform the education system. They democratize access to learning materials and eliminate obstacles which otherwise disenfranchise students with disabilities. They make it possible to engage in learning activities by providing access according to individual needs and choices and thus making learning spaces more inclusive in nature. They not only cater to the unique needs of disabled students by accommodating different learning patterns, on top of that, make the learning experience better for all learners by making it more flexible and inclusive in nature (Kohli et al., 2021).

Personalized Learning Platforms, AI-Driven Tutoring Systems, and Adaptive Assessments Tailored to Individual Needs

The use of AI in education has spurred the move toward individualized education through platforms of personalized learning, AI-assisted tutoring systems, and adaptive assessments. Such technologies adjust to individuals' learning patterns, learning speeds, and requirements, and are most advantageous to people with disabilities. They utilize advanced algorithms, ML, and data analytics to deliver focused intervention that optimizes participation and performance (Roy, 2020). Their creation and application need to be carefully scrutinized in terms of accessibility, fairness, and ethics.

Personalized Learning Platforms

Personalized learning platforms harness the power of AI to adapt educational content, learning pathways, and pacing to the unique preferences, capabilities, and needs of each learner. By providing tailored experiences, these platforms aim to enhance engagement, comprehension, and achievement, making education more accessible and effective for a diverse range of students (Nealon & Butler, 2013).

Technological Frameworks

The backbone of platforms for personal learning rests on sophisticated AI and data-centric technologies. A collaborative filtering and content filtering algorithm underlies the platforms' recommendation engines to provide resources according to the learning progress and study objectives of an individual student. Behaviour analytics are pivotal by monitoring the interaction patterns by students, like the duration on particular activities, patterns of errors made, and measures of engagement to tailor the timing and presentation of the content to maximize its impact. Machine learning algorithms forecast future learning requirements based on past performance to make dynamic changes to the curriculum to adapt to the developing capabilities of students (Sun & Chen, 2019).

Features and Benefits

Personalized learning platforms provide numerous revolutionary capabilities that make the learning experience more effective. Adaptive learning pathways enable these platforms to tailor the learning path and difficulty level of material to suit individual levels of proficiency and support learners across a continuum of skills. Multimodal delivery of content through text, audio, video, and interactive simulation makes sure that all learning styles are addressed and promotes greater engagement. Immediate performance assessments through real-time feedback enable instant assessments of performance and provide learners and teachers with actionable data on which to focus on strong points and work on improvement areas (Reddy et al., 2015).

For instance, websites like DreamBox Learning and Khan Academy utilize AI-enhanced tools to offer individualized exercises to students in specific fields like mathematics. Mastery-based advancement through these platforms ensures that learners master basic concepts before moving on to advanced topics.

Challenges

While their promise is great, there are major problems with personalized learning platforms that need to be overcome to ensure equitable and successful implementation. A major issue is bias in algorithms with datasets that are heavily unrepresentative and can lead to discriminatory recommendations that disproportionately reflect on marginalized groups. Such bias erodes the inclusiveness that the platforms are meant to provide. The digital gap only adds to the disparity by denying students who don't access high-speed internet and up-to-date devices from reaping the advantages of these advanced learning tools. In addition to these, issues surrounding data protection and privacy are concerns since these platforms demand extensive data to be able to operate optimally. Ensuring compliance with privacy laws and protecting sensitive student data is top priority (Cardonha et al., 2016).

AI-Driven Tutoring Systems

AI tutoring systems mimic the one-on-one learning experience by providing learners with individualised guidance and support. Virtual tutors are particularly promising for disabled students, who need adaptive support to overcome learning problems. Virtual tutors, with the power of advanced AI technologies, offer an inexpensive and scalable solution for inclusive learning environments (Gan et al., 2019).

Technological Foundations

The foundation of AI-tutoring systems is advanced technologies that provide dynamic and context-sensitive interaction capabilities. Natural Language Processing allows conversation interfaces to engage students and AI tutors through text or voice naturally. Knowledge representation methods like knowledge graphs are used by these systems to organize and arrange information so that the response will be correct and contextually suitable. Knowledge representation methods like deep reinforcement learning algorithms adjust tutoring techniques according to individual learner responses to optimize interaction and retention through real-time adjustments suitable to each learner's needs (Woolf et al., 2008).

Applications and Advantages

Humanoid AI tutors provide extensive coverage of capabilities that greatly enrich learning experiences. Their most powerful advantage comes in the form of making support more accessible. For example, software like Microsoft's Immersive Reader aids learners with dyslexia by reading out complex material and making phonetics available to enhance reading comprehension. Translation capabilities make these systems priceless to multilingual learners by breaking down material and eradicating linguistic differences. Additionally, independent learning options make it so students are able to review lessons and practice problems in their own speed and tempo to reduce pressure found in traditional learning environments and build self-assurance. Socratic by Google is an exemplary AI tutoring system that combines image recognition and NLP to provide immediate explanations to homework problems and support independent learning by leading learners through processes to solve problems without outside assistance (Paladines & Ramírez, 2019).

Concerns

While these systems offer many advantages, there are problems with them. Among these problems is the lack of human interaction and the risk that increased reliance on virtual instructors could reduce the opportunity to socialize and develop support that teachers and fellow students naturally offer to one another. The lack could damage the growth of interpersonal and group skills. Another challenge faced by AI tutors is the matter of standardization and the difficulty in covering topics that are open-ended and nuanced and requiring subjective judgment and an insider's knowledge of cultural and contextual nuances (Yan et al., 2016)

Adaptive Assessments

Adaptive assessments represent a transformative approach to evaluating students' abilities, dynamically adjusting question difficulty based on their performance. This personalized method provides a nuanced understanding of a learner's strengths and areas for growth, making it particularly beneficial in inclusive education contexts where traditional assessment methods might fall short (Barney & Fisher, 2016).

Technological Frameworks

The core of adaptive testing is rooted in advanced models that provide accuracy and customization. Item Response Theory (IRT) is an important model, describing how the ability of a student correlates with the probability to answer questions correctly. It makes the tests suitably demanding without being too easy or infuriating. Bayesian networks are further used to provide greater precision to forecast future performance and learning deficiencies through the evaluation of past responses by the students. AI-powered analytics combine these to offer teachers deep insights into patterns of learning. The patterns are used to develop intervention aimed at the individual needs (Zhan & Lu, 2015).

Advantages

Adaptive tests offer numerous advantages that enrich the assessment procedure. They ensure fairness in assessment by adjusting the difficulty level of questions to the level of proficiency of the learner, hence testing learners with different capacities, including learners with disabilities, on an equal basis. The systems offer formative feedback through comprehensive reports that identify particular strengths and weaknesses and allow teachers and learners to work on ongoing improvement. The adaptive nature of assessments further sustains learner interest by removing questions that are too easy or hard, minimizing frustration and maximizing motivation (Ju & Bark, 2005).

Critical Issues

Although adaptive assessments offer advantages, there are issues with them. Ensuring validity of content is an overarching challenge since adaptive tests are tricky to construct so that comprehensive curriculum standards and learning goals are addressed. The risk of heavy dependence on data metrics is also there. Adaptive systems are very effective in measuring measurable aspects of learning, but there are qualitative aspects like creativity, critical thinking, and problem-solving skills that are equally important to education in its entirety and may not be addressed by adaptive systems (Huang et al., 2009).

Transformative Potential for Inclusive Education

The use of AI in education holds deep transformative power, especially in inclusivity. Accessibility is one of the most powerful effects with AI tools that bridge gaps for learners with disabilities. AI tools adjust to individual needs with features ranging from simplified interfaces to meet demands from students with motor disabilities and visual aids to support individuals with cognitive issues. The assistance reaches out to varied learning needs through multimodal methods with support to disabilities like dyslexia, autism spectrum disorder, or hearing disability. In advocating universal design through these tools, the learning environments are made inclusive by default and not by design (Amuga, 2023). Additionally, AI provides scalable solutions to resolve resource disparities. AI-backed platforms and AI-backed tutors make high-quality adaptive learning available to under-resourced schools so that education becomes democratized to everyone.

AI FOR ENGAGEMENT

Artificial Intelligence (AI) is revolutionizing the education sector by enhancing access and participation by all learners and especially learners with disabilities. AI is making learning environments barrier-free through advanced technologies, accommodating learners with different learning needs and overcoming the individualized needs of marginalized learners (Florea & Radu, 2019). In this section, there is critical analysis of AI's role in making learning spaces inclusive, its contribution to engagement through gamification, and its role in multilingual support to learners with disabilities.

Barrier-Free Education

AI technologies provide transformative solutions that dismantle systemic barriers impeding equitable access to education for students with disabilities. However, the complexities of implementation necessitate a critical evaluation of their design and deployment:

Assistive Technologies:

Advanced assistive technologies like screen readers utilize Optical Character Recognition and Natural Language Processing to read aloud digital text or Braille. Assistive technologies like JAWS and NVDA apply semantic parsing to access complex hierarchies within the content like nested tables and hyperlinks. Speech and audio generation by Text-To-Speech systems are advanced with deep learning architectures like WaveNet and Tacotron, with capabilities to produce expressive and user-controllable audio outputs. Alternative input devices like eye-tracking systems and Brain-Computer Interfaces utilize real-time processing and provide assistance to students with profound physical impairments (Maor et al., 2011). Nevertheless, regional language support and computational intensity are major limitations that need to be addressed.

Real-Time Transcription and Captioning:

Real-time transcribing systems utilize ASR technologies based on Transformer models such as Wav2Vec and Whisper. The models operate through self-supervised learning to yield state-of-the-art performance in heterogeneous acoustic environments. Captioning software built into platforms like Google Meet and Zoom alleviate communication obstacles among hearing-impaired students. Multimodal AI systems that incorporate ASR and gesture recognition may extend accessibility further (Cerva et al., 2012). Nevertheless, these systems are plagued by flaws like imprecision in noisy environments and latency that interrupts synchronous communication.

Support for Diverse Learning Styles

The ability of AI to support diverse sensory and cognitive needs reflects its importance in developing inclusive learning environments. Yet its use requires scrutiny to counter technical and ethical issues ingrained within it:

Personalization:

Adaptive learning platforms utilize Reinforcement Learning (RL) and collaborative filtering algorithms to customize the delivery of content. Systems like DreamBox Learning utilize Bayesian Knowledge Tracing (BKT), for instance, to trace learners' mastery levels and predict learning trajectories. Platforms adjust difficulty levels dynamically, scaffolding difficult ideas to learners' Zone of Proximal Development (ZPD). Though effective, the application of black-box algorithms compromises transparency and accountability in recommending content (Madani et al., 2020).

Interactive Learning:

Artificial Intelligence technology combining Virtual Reality (VR) and Augmented Reality (AR) provides multimodal learning opportunities ideal for kinaesthetic students. As an example, AI-assisted haptic feedback systems mimic real-world interaction to enable learners to physically understand abstract topics. Interactive storytelling becomes possible with Machine Vision in tandem with NLP to better engage visual learners and auditory learners alike. The scalability of these technologies is restrained by the need to deploy costly equipment, mainly in under-resourced environments (Anderson, 2019).

Flexible Assessments:

Adaptive testing systems leverage Item Response Theory (IRT) and Gradient Boosting Machines (GBM) to maximize question selection according to students' proficiency levels. Such systems, represented by ALEKS, apply probabilistic modelling to define learning gaps in granular detail. In providing varied response types through voice inputs and interactive simulations, these systems cater to learning differences. However, their effectiveness is compromised by the insufficiencies of algorithms to interpret subtle or open-ended responses with validity concerns (Huang et al., 2009).

Gamification in Education

Artificial Intelligence-powered gamification revolutionizes academic paradigms by integrating game elements into learning processes and activities to promote greater levels of learners' engagement and motivation. It is based on behavioural psychology principles and sophisticated AI algorithms:

Game Elements:

Key game mechanics like points, badges, and leader boards are supported by AI-powered analytics on user behaviour and engagement patterns. They use reinforcement learning algorithms to determine the best schedules to provide rewards to maximize extrinsic motivation. Excessive dependence on extrinsic incentives can erode intrinsic motivation and needs to be balanced. AI systems that modulate the intensity of the reward adaptively on the basis of engagement analytics can reduce this risk. Leader boards need to be designed to consider varied capabilities to prevent lower-performing learners from feeling alienated and thus need to include normalization algorithms that strike a balance between competitiveness and inclusiveness (Nebel et al., 2017).

Dynamic Challenges:

Artificial Intelligence algorithms like Deep Q-Learning make it possible to personalize game-based activities by examining performance metrics in real-time. This dynamic adjustment is in accordance with the Zone of Proximal Development (ZPD), keeping the challenge not too easy and not too hard. Procedural content generation (PCG) algorithms can produce distinct and scalable game levels that are designed to fit individual learning paths (Lara-Cabrera et al., 2015).

Yet maintaining alignment with curriculum standards is necessary through ongoing verification against pedagogical metrics, something many gamification platforms are not doing effectively.

Interactive Learning Environments

Interactive learning technologies powered by Artificial Intelligence transform learning experiences by integrating experiential learning with cognitive scaffolding to promote better comprehension and retention through the use of immersive technologies like Virtual Reality (VR) and Augmented Reality (AR):

Simulations:

Computer-simulated experiments based on artificial intelligence, such as those offered by platforms like Labster, utilize real-time physics engines and machine learning to imitate real lab environments. They provide efficient access to experiments without physical setups, making them ideal in under-provisioned schools. AI systems provide adaptive feedback loops with learners being led step by step through complicated procedures matching learners' capacities. The high costs of the hardware within VR/AR devices and software computational requirements limit accessibility in poor areas. Creating lightweight AI frameworks in simulation can mend this drawback (Xiao, 2021).

Virtual Tutors:

Conversational AI driven by Transformer models like GPT supports virtual teachers that offer interactive commentary and human-like dialogue simulation. AI bots utilize knowledge graphs to enable correct context-specific explanations and develop deeper concept awareness. Virtual teachers can adaptively modulate tone and difficulty levels in accordance with learners' states by incorporating emotion detection algorithms and analyzing learners' responses in real-time (Tack & Piech, 2022). Yet the consequences are being threatened by the absence of interpretability in most conversational AI tools regarding high-stake learning environments.

Ethical and Accessibility Concerns of Gamification in Education

While gamification and interactive tools have transformative potential, their deployment must address a range of ethical and accessibility challenges to ensure equitable impact:

Addiction Risk:

The addictive behaviour of gamified systems based on reinforcement learning and variable schedules presents an important ethical challenge. The AI systems need to be designed with measures like session duration limits and user-specific alerts to avoid excessive use. Ethical considerations are also necessary in the use of persuasive methods to balance engagement with the welfare of students (Deterding et al., 2015).

Inclusivity in Design:

Making sure that everyone is universally accessible calls for conformity to standards such as the Web Content Accessibility Guidelines (WCAG). Multilingual support based on Neural Machine Translation (NMT) facilitates interaction across linguistic and cultural borders. AI systems need to include algorithms to identify and correct discriminatory patterns in gameplay mechanics or delivery of content. In addition to this, creating affordable, device-independent solutions is necessary to bridge the digital divide in environments with limited resources (Peres et al., 2011).

Role of Language Processing in Education

AI-powered language processing tools act as critical enablers for multilingual students with disabilities by addressing linguistic barriers, cognitive challenges, and accessibility needs:

Automatic Translation:

Neural Machine Translation (NMT) models based on Transformer architectures like the model that powers Google Translate employ attention mechanisms that pick up on contextual patterns between words and phrases. With sequential dependencies modelled and bilingual dictionaries from deep corpus datasets, the tools provide semantic precision and fluency. Translations of idiomatic expressions, infrequent languages, or syntactic sentence patterns pose difficulties, but the models can be made more effective by adding domain-specialized corpora and applying cross-lingual transfer learning to tackle underserved linguistic areas (Chen et al., 2019).

Simplification Tools:

NLP algorithms employ syntactic parsing, named entity recognition (NER), and dependency graphs for identifying and reformulating complicated constructs. All these tools present simplified texts without deviating from the original meaning, supporting the learning needs of students with cognitive disability or limited language skills. The upcoming versions should include semantic role labelling (SRL) and ontological schemes for enabling richer contexts and more appropriate translations of technical or specialized material (Khan, 2016).

Speech Recognition and Synthesis:

Automatic Speech Recognition (ASR) technology utilizes acoustic modelling alongside language modeling for interpretation of spoken words as text. ASR technology utilizes phoneme mapping and context prediction for higher accuracy with different accents and intonation. Conversely, TTS technology such as WaveNet and Tacotron synthesizes human-like speech with dynamically controlled prosody, tone, and stress. Even with progress made, addressing tonal languages, background noise, and variability from speakers presents a major technical challenge with the need for increased robustness using adversarial training and noise augmentation (Debnath & Roy, 2020).

Impact on Accessibility and Inclusion

AI-based language tools redefine inclusivity in education by providing equitable access to communication and fostering collaboration across linguistic and cognitive boundaries:

Bridging Language Gaps: Real-time translation software, with contextual embedding and bidirectional encoder-decoder models, enables multilingual students to participate effectively in classroom discourse and discussion. Continuous adaptation using reinforcement learning further improves the precision and context sensitivity of such systems, enabling smooth communication (Nash et al., 2012).

Supporting Literacy. Interactive writing tools enhance literacy through multi-level NLP architectures that supply contextualized ratings of syntax, grammar, and coherence. With task-specified embeddings and user analysis, such tools are able to vary guidance on an individualized basis for the specific skills that the learner needs to improve, such as syntax and word choice (Mismas, 2005).

Facilitating Collaboration: AI-powered collaborative platforms employ multilingual interface designs and smart language-switching algorithms that facilitate group activities. Multilingual embeddings and machine translation without supervision are utilized by these tools to make it possible for contributors of any linguistic background to contribute equally towards group tasks (Hautasaari, 2010).

AI contributions towards accessibility and participation in learning are revolutionary, with uses ranging from barrier-free learning environments, gamified learning, and multilingualism. But their successful inclusion depends on equity, ethical implications, and available resources. If inclusive design becomes the top priority and developers, educators, and policymakers work hand in hand, AI has the ability to bring about an inclusive learning environment that appeals to everyone.

ETHICAL CONSIDERATIONS AND CHALLENGES IN AI-DRIVEN INCLUSIVE EDUCATION

While AI technology has tremendous possibilities for promoting inclusive education, its implementation is riddled with ethical challenges and practical hindrances. Coaching fairness, protecting privacy, and resolving technologically based inequalities are important for capitalizing on the advantages of AI while curbing the risks. Here is a critical discussion of necessary ethical considerations and challenges of AI-inclusive education with special reference to algorithmic bias, privacy, and infrastructural inequalities.

Figure 7. Ethical risks and mitigation strategies in AI-based inclusive education

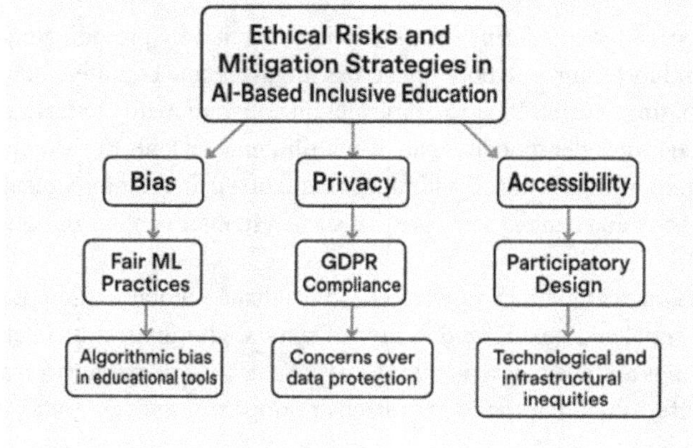

Addressing Algorithmic Bias and Ensuring Fair AI-Driven Educational Decisions

Understanding Algorithmic Bias

Algorithmic bias occurs when the output of artificial intelligence algorithms inadvertently privileges or disadvantages a particular group of people based on systemic disparities present in the used data or design principles. It most often occurs due to training data lacking proper representation of underrepresented groups, for example, from underprivileged communities or disabled consumers. Datasets that are mainly collected from wealthy or homogenous settings will produce models that perform badly for those outside those environments. Also, machine learning model architectures and optimization objectives tend to focus on efficiency and accuracy but pay little attention to context-dependent subtleties that are required for equitable predictions (Nelson, 2019; Mehrabi et al., 2022). Such negligence will yield biased inferences that end up entrenching gaps instead of eliminating them.

Impact on Inclusive Education

In education, algorithmic bias attacks the equity and inclusivity principles head-on. So-called personalized learning tools, touted as bridges between learning gaps, have the opposite effect by incorrectly interpreting the linguistic, cultural, or cognitive characteristics of underrepresented groups of students. For instance, speech recognition programs that have learned on Western dialects of English will not be able to correctly interpret regional accents, disfavouring those who depend on these tools for communication or understanding (Koenecke et al., 2020). Likewise, AI-powered tests meant for classification and assessment of the abilities of students may incorrectly measure the work of disabled students by neglecting their individual contexts, thus furthering stereotypes and restricting access to learning opportunities (Jiang & Pardos, 2021; Aroyo et al.,

2022). All these biases further institutionalize inequities and work against the realization of an inclusive learning space.

Strategies to Mitigate Bias

Mitigating algorithmic bias in education AI systems calls for a multi-faceted, forward-thinking approach. At its core, bias reduction involves creating and employing diverse, representative datasets that include a broad range of voices, cultural environments, and learning needs. Through the inclusion of data from underrepresented groups, the AI systems become educated on a broader range of experiences, and the chances for biased outcomes decrease. Additionally, continuous algorithmic audits, performed through fairness-aware machine learning methods, are necessary for detection of and redress for any underlying bias in AI systems. Audits must utilize statistical tools such as disparate impact analysis and counterfactual fairness checks for model assessment across demographics (Sinwar et al., 2023; Barocas et al., 2019).

Besides technical solutions, there is an urgent need for transparency and accountability of AI. Developers will have to implement explainable AI techniques that enable end-users and educators to see the justification of decisions made by the AI. For example, visualizing the importance of features or giving interpretable model output helps disentangle the decision-making from the mystery, making it possible for the stakeholders to pinpoint possible biases and effectively intervene (Doshi-Velez & Kim, 2017). Interdisciplinary cooperation among AI developers, educators, and policymakers will also be necessary for harmonizing technological innovation with ethical and educational standards, making sure that educational tools developed using AI will be equitable and not reinforce inequalities (Williamson & Eynon, 2020; UNESCO, 2021).

Safeguarding Data Privacy and Security Concerns in AI-Powered Educational Technologies

The Importance of Data Privacy

AI educational tools rely on vast amounts of collected information for delivering customized and efficient learning experiences. With such a large dependence on data, there are major security, ethical usage, and possible abuse of private data concerns. Data sets used by these tools contain personal identifiable information like names, addresses, and demographics, as well as learning and performance metrics that reveal learning behaviours, habits, and interests of students. All of these detailed data profiles, which are so useful for customization of education, pose a considerable threat when not handled with proper privacy precautions (UNESCO, 2023). Without strong privacy measures, there exists a very real threat of abuse or unauthorized access of data that can destroy the credibility of AI educational tools and pose a threat towards the welfare of educators and students alike.

Risks in AI-Driven Education

AI in education is growing fast, but with it comes serious issues of privacy and data security right at the centre. Weak protection systems can leave systems wide open, making it easy for unauthorized access to leak sensitive student info. The consequences? Identity theft, harm to reputation, even emotional stress. And then there's the commercial side—some companies collect educational data, then use it for ads, research, whatever fits their bottom line, often without clear consent. That's not just a privacy concern; it's an ethical one (Berendt et al., 2020). The lack of solid regulations doesn't help either. No clear rules on how data should be collected, stored, or used means gaps are everywhere, making it easier for misuse to slip through unnoticed.

Regulatory Frameworks and Best Practices

It is of utmost necessity to put in place strong regulatory mechanisms and observe best practices meant to protect data privacy. Adhering to international standards like the General Data Protection Regulation (GDPR) and the Children's Online Privacy Protection Act (COPPA) provides an initial measure of quality control for assuring that the data handling process fulfils strong privacy and security demands. Transparency, accountability, and consent of users in the way personal data gets collected and handled are required by these regulations with a statutory justification for the protection of individual rights (Hoboken & Ó Fathaigh, 2021).

Aside from regulatory adherence, the application of principles of minimization of data is essential. This includes the collection of only the required data for the specific function of the application of AI, lessening vulnerability to breaches and improper use. Robust security measures, such as encryption and anonymization, are necessary for protecting stored as well as transferred data. Encryption makes the confidential information unreachable by unauthorized groups, and anonymization deletes the identifiable features of personal data from datasets, without sacrificing analytical usefulness (Senavirathne & Torra, 2020). Also of key importance is the exercise of informed consent, whereby students, parents, and teachers are made fully aware of the methods of collection of their data, their implications, and risks, and presented with the opportunity to explicitly approve.

Balancing Innovation and Privacy

Finding a balance between harnessing the power of data for education innovation and upholding privacy on an individual basis remains a difficult but necessary task. Although data plays an essential part in driving innovation in learning tools with artificial intelligence, ethical and secure handling of the same needs to be ensured in order to avoid a lapse of trust and facilitate mass uptake. Ethical design concepts of privacy by design and fairness in the treatment of data must shape the design and application of education technology. Privacy protections must be viewed as part of the underlying architecture of AI-enabled systems right from the design stage, not as add-ons (Hong et al., 2022; Cavoukian, 2011).

Overcoming Infrastructural and Technological Disparities in AI Implementation

The Digital Divide

Infrastructural and technological inequalities continue to be major obstacles to the effective implementation of AI in inclusive education. The digital divide manifests as unequal access to necessary technology, such as hardware, quality internet connectivity, and constant electricity.

What these inequalities predominantly afflict are rural, under-resourced, and economically challenged districts, where the very minimal prerequisites for applying AI tools are frequently absent. Resource imbalance further contributes to the problem because urban and higher-income districts have improved technological infrastructure and greater investment in educational capital, leaving rural districts and underserved locales in their wake. Compounded with these shortcomings is the absence of proper teacher training in most districts. Teachers in marginalized communities lack technical competence and resources for effectively using AI in their teaching, further increasing the gap in educational quality and access (Rajagopal & Vedamanickam, 2019; UNESCO, 2021).

Impact on Students with Disabilities

Technological disparities affect especially students with disabilities, who depend on assistive technology in order to gain access to education. This technology, like screen readers, text-to-speech software, and alternate input tools, falls too often outside of what these environments can afford, and so these tools are not available. Without these tools, students with disabilities have additional challenges ahead of them, further alienating them within the education framework (Alam & Forhad, 2023; WHO & UNICEF, 2021). This alienation perpetuates a cycle of disadvantage, denying these students the right to be able to participate on equal terms in educational and social environments.

Addressing Disparities

These infrastructural and technological challenges must be addressed with a multi-stakeholder and comprehensive approach. Public-private partnerships have the key position in resolving the digital divide by sharing resources and competencies for delivering low-cost AI tools and infrastructure for underprivileged regions. Collaborations of governments, technology corporations, and non-governmental organizations will be able to drive the mass dissemination of devices, internet connectivity, and other resources (World Bank, 2020).

Another key approach to inclusivity is the development of open-source artificial intelligence technology. Open-source tools that are made both accessible and inexpensive have the potential to alleviate numerous financial constraints and bring higher-level educational technology to more people. Capacity-building activities are also necessary in order to empower instructors in underprivileged communities. Teacher professional development should be implemented with a view towards preparing educators with the skills and competencies they need to effectively employ AI tools in the classroom, so that they can optimize the services of these tools for their students (Ratnam, 2023; Trucano, 2016).

Local solutions are also critical in tackling regional and cultural diversity. AI solutions have to be adapted to deal with local languages, cultural environments, and infrastructural constraints. For example, crafting AI tools that access and work under offline modes or low-bandwidth connectivity ensures their usability where internet connectivity remains weak. Likewise, the inclusion of regional languages and local dialects enables such technology accessibility for diverse learner communities (UNESCO & World Bank, 2021).

REAL-WORLD EXAMPLES OF AI IMPLEMENTATION IN INCLUSIVE EDUCATION

Cases of real-world examples of AI in inclusive classrooms add a depth and a hyperrealism through which the greater potential of these technologies become more clearly demonstrated and illustrated especially when applied. Here are several case studies from India and all around the world, which have deployed AI to promote inclusion in education.

Government Schools Leveraging JAWS and NVDA in India

Although screen readers such as Job Access with Speech (JAWS) or NonVisual Desktop Access (NVDA)) have not been very popular, several government schools in India have adopted and have used it to make visually impaired students aware about the computer facilities. These are tools that take text and pronounce it for students to be able to get content without a buddy.

Locally developed pilot engages students who are blind in rural Karnataka, with laptops loaded with JAWS. These tools were exported to the professional teachers and they trained the teachers to add these tools into normal classroom activities so that the students can interact with the other students during the lessons. This program provided a great improvement in literacy and digital fluency which on students being able to seamlessly integrate into higher education and professional environments.

AI-Powered Apps in Rural Indian Schools

Mobile applications like Byju's and Khan Academy developed with help of AI are specifically designed to work in rural areas with tailored interaction and personalization. In Uttar Pradesh, an experimental project used voice commands to work on educational apps enabled by AI made in English and using English for providing assistance to students with limited literacy skills such as those with cognitive disabilities.

In addition, the project also provided offline functionality to maintain its continuity in regions with a limited internet connectivity. Special educational needs learners showed improved engagement, as did the general population, teachers noted. This project illustrates how working with AI can complement infrastructural bridging and provision of access to education in perceptively constrained locations.

"Seeing AI" App in Global Inclusive Classrooms

Microsoft 'Seeing AI' app and tools like these have helped to create inclusive learning environments globally. The app is aimed at visually impaired users and using AI to describe the surroundings, read text aloud, recognize faces, objects, and currencies.

A public school in Canada used the app to help mainstreamed visually impaired students to better navigate their preexisting classes. With the tool, these students had a way to independently open textbooks, submit assignments, and participate in group projects, adding greater autonomy and inclusion. The app was noted to significantly improve the students' confidence and social interaction skills by teachers.

AI and Virtual Reality (VR) in U.S. Special Education Programs

In the US, AI and VR technologies are used in the special education programs such as for students with autism and other developmental disorders. For example, artificial intelligence is used in such simulations of virtual reality to teach social skills while replicating real life scenarios in a controlled environment.

In California, students with autism participated in one notable virtual job interview in which they practiced the communication and decision making that occurs in real live interviews. Students were able to receive real time feedback from the AI system and refine their responses as they made them. The pairing of AI and VR was found to be effective in making the students competent in handling social situations, which the teachers witnessed a great improvement in ability compared to before.

Best Practices and Policy Recommendations for AI Integration

A systematic and equitable approach towards the inclusion of Artificial Intelligence (AI) education has the ability to close gaps in access and equity, particularly among students with disabilities. What follows is an extended discussion of best practices, policy frameworks, and training models, with the addition of supporting subpoints for thorough coverage.

Figure 8. Framework for AI integration in inclusive education

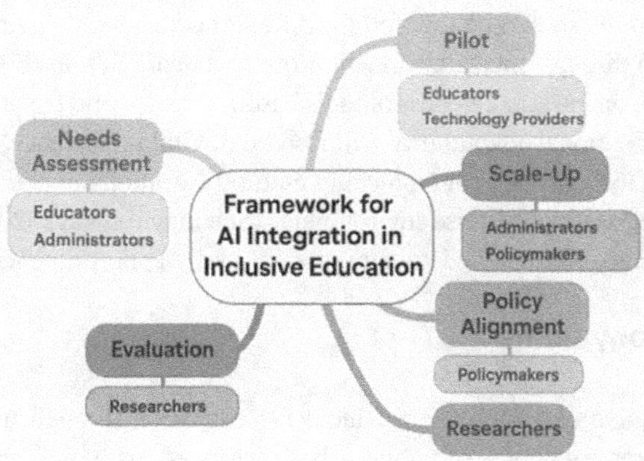

STRATEGIES FOR THE EFFECTIVE ADOPTION OF AI IN INCLUSIVE EDUCATION

Comprehensive Needs Assessment

Embedding AI in inclusive education requires a systematic and comprehensive needs assessment exercise that will ensure the technology is used effectively and with equity. This starts with a demographics analysis, in which gaps in access to educational technology among different populations, such as urban, rural, and underprivileged communities, are determined. This provides policymakers and educators with clear indicators of the regions and groups that require intervention. For disabled students, disability-specific initiatives should be developed. These must cater to a wide range of needs, from visual impairment and hearing impairment through cognitive disability and learning disorders, so that no category of people will be excluded from the benefits of education using AI (Nguyen et al., 2023). User experience studies are also crucial in the development. Through thorough usability testing among teachers and among students, the stakeholders will be able to certify that AI tools serve practical needs, are simple to operate, and fit the varied needs of inclusive classrooms.

Phased Implementation

A phased implementation approach based on incremental rollout, starting with critical tools like text-to-speech and speech-to-text, will be crucial for the successful rollout of AI in education. Small pilot programs should be tailored for different educational environments, from the mainstream classroom through specialized institutions that deal with disability. Pilot programs will give vital feedback on the effectiveness of tools based on real-world experience and facilitate iterative refinements. Regional adaptability will also be of vital importance. The solutions will have to be adapted to account for geographic and cultural variations in educational practice in order to be effective and useful in diverse environments (Schumann et al., 2020). This will include adding regional language, dialects, and content of a culturally appropriate nature.

Collaborative Ecosystems

Building collaborative environments for inclusive education through the effective implementation of AI requires collaborative public-private partnerships. Public-private partnerships (PPPs) are a strong tool for sharing resources and skills in framing and building inclusive AI tools. PPPs involving governments, technology providers, and institutions of learning have the ability to spur innovation while making such tools affordable and accessible. Non-governmental disability advocacy organizations have the chance of providing critical feedback on disability students' specific needs so that inclusive designs of AI prioritize equity and inclusivity. Educating the education sector, health sector, and social services sector in a coordinated way through cross-country coordination will be an essential element in the facilitation of inclusive education for supporting disability students (Srivastava et al., 2021). By encouraging intersectoral cooperation among these departments, there is the chance of creating an integrated framework of work for addressing educational as well as extracurricular needs.

Focus on Affordability and Accessibility

To bridge economic gaps, strategies for increasing affordability and accessibility are of utmost importance. Mechanisms such as subsidies, grants, or vouchers can render AI technology economically accessible for economically underprivileged students. This makes sure that economic constraints do not bar marginalized groups from accessing technological advancements. The design of AI tools must focus on accessibility with features such as voice commands, braille compatibility, and hand-gesture controls in order to provide for diverse needs. Such inclusive design guardrails make the tools accessible for people with different abilities. Offline functionality is also an essential feature for AI tools that are utilized in remote or low-resource environments. By making tools function effectively in low-bandwidth environments, or offline, students in remote environments are able to access quality educational content without depending on uninterrupted internet connectivity (Morris, 2019).

POLICY FRAMEWORKS AND INSTITUTIONAL GUIDELINES FOR EQUITABLE AI DEPLOYMENT IN EDUCATION

Inclusive AI Policies

It is critical that inclusive AI policies be developed so that AI-powered learning systems respond decisively to the varied needs of the learner. Accountability mechanisms should have strict controls on the developers of AI, requiring them to be compliant with inclusivity protocols that focus on the universal accessibility of learning. These protocols must include provisions for the disabled and underrepresented groups, countering disparities in access and outcomes. Open-data initiatives are critical for inter-organizational collaborations so that algorithms developed are representative and equitable. Bias elimination protocols must include elaborate diagnostic testing using techniques like fairness-aware machine learning models that are able to discover and mitigate systematic biases associated with such attributes as gender, ethnicity, and socio-economic status (Avellan et al., 2020). All such measures are critical for stopping AI systems from reinforcing and amplifying inequalities and enabling them to function as instruments for equity, not exclusion.

Data Governance Policies

Sound data governance frameworks are critical for protecting privacy as they optimize the application of artificial intelligence in educational environments. Consent-driven models of handling personal data should be based on advanced consent platforms that provide equitable, user-managed permissions for collection, processing, and storage of such data. Anonymization mechanisms should employ advanced cryptographic operations like homomorphic encryption and differential privacy for protecting educational data while supporting strong analytics. Moreover, portability of such data must be enabled through interoperable APIs and standardized schema, enabling switching between platforms without compromising on data integrity. Governance policies such as these not only secure personal rights but build institutional confidence in artificial intelligence mechanisms through compliance with regulations such as GDPR and COPPA (Kaewkamol, 2022).

Institutional Guidelines

Education institutions should have strong operational guidelines for the deployment of AI that supports pedagogical missions and mandates of universal accessibility. Accreditation schemes should integrate technical, ethical, and pedagogical assessments for certifying the adherence of AI tools to predetermined standards. Interoperability needs should be based on adherence to international standards such as IMS Global and SCORM in order for the artificial intelligence systems to be compatible with existing educational technology infrastructure and assistive technology. Emergency response procedures should include contingencies for continuity of key functionalities during outages using redundancy mechanisms and resilient cloud infrastructure (Katlyarova, 2022). Institutionalization of these guidelines by institutions of learning will help in reducing risks while maximizing the effectiveness and reliability of educational interventions through artificial intelligence.

Promoting AI Literacy

Establishing broad AI literacy is not merely a strategic necessity for democratizing the implementation and application of AI in education but also for providing inclusive pathways for educators, administrators, and students to familiarize themselves with the tools of AI through hands-on experience in simulation environments that reflect real-world learning. Centralized platforms of resources have to be created through knowledge management tools with regularly updated pools of case studies, technical handbooks, and best practices for applying AI for wide-ranging educational contexts. Parent and community engagement programs must be based on AI-powered analytics for customized programs of outreach addressing specific issues and knowledge needs. Not only do these programs sharpen understanding, they also create a collaborative environment that enables every educator, administrator, and student to critically analyze, embrace, and harness AI technology effectively in education (Ouyang & Jiao, 2021).

Figure 9. Recommendations for training educators to effectively integrate AI-based assistive technologies in classrooms

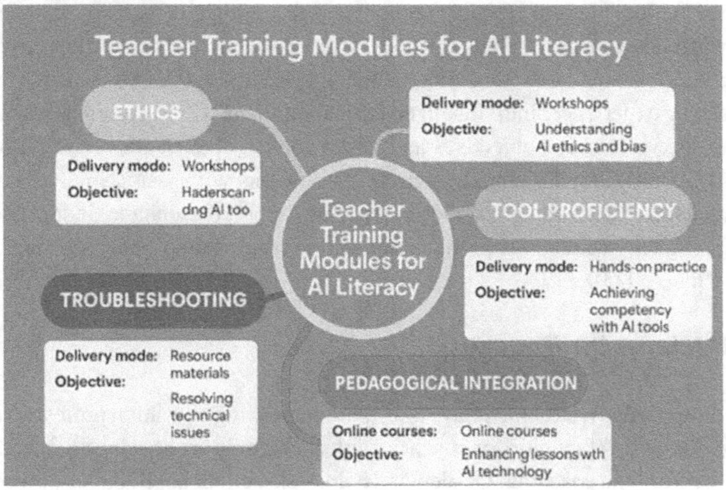

Comprehensive Professional Development

Professional education of teachers must be undertaken for effective implementation of AI in inclusive education. The training must include modules on the ethics of artificial intelligence, highlighting the fact that algorithmic bias must be recognized and ensured that there is compliance with maintaining privacy for the data based on norms such as the General Data Protection Regulation. There must be specialized certification for the application of AI-enabled assistive technology such as screen readers, voice-recognition software, and learning adaptation tools. Through scenario learning, using real classroom examples, the practical uses of the tools based on AI may be understood by the educators, making the transition from theoretical knowledge to practical application smoother (Felix, 2020).

Ongoing Capacity Building

Capacity-building efforts should emphasize ongoing, inclusive, and context-dependent learning experiences for educators. Microlearning modules provide focused, bite-sized learning on particular uses of AI that enable incremental knowledge accumulation without overwhelming educators. Peer-to-peer learning forums enable problem-solving in groups and sharing of best practices, building a collaborative community of educators. Digital toolkits, which include instructions for doing tasks step by step, troubleshooting guides, and multimedia, equip educators with readily available instruction on how to effectively employ the right AI tools (Durga et al., 2022).

Pedagogical Integration

Integrating AI tools into instruction necessitates educating educators on how to harmonize technology with conventional teaching methods. Multimodal methods have the ability to integrate the usage of AI tools such as virtual simulations with lectures or hands-on experiences for an inclusive learning experience. Individualized Education Plans (IEPs) can be augmented with AI in addressing special learning objectives and needs, for example, adaptive testing for learning-disabled students or tailored reading resources for students with vision impairment. Teachers should also focus on student-cantered models, applying AI tools that enhance independent learning and empower students with active participation in and ownership of their learning experiences (Arya & Scheidel, 2023).

Support Systems for Educators

Extended support infrastructure plays a key part in enabling education professionals in ongoing AI usage. Specific AI mentors or coaches, with specializations in education technology, are available for one-on-one coaching. On-demand help desks, either based on AI-powered chatbots or specialized technical experts, provide real-time technical suggestions for troubleshooting and skill optimization. Continuous feedback loops facilitate education professionals in sharing feedback on functionality and effectiveness of AI systems, setting up constant improvement of the tools as well as the training programs (Boichenko & Boichenko, 2020).

CONCLUSION

Artificial Intelligence (AI) has expanded the frontiers of inclusive learning, providing unseen opportunities for inclusive and accessible learning by persons with disabilities. With the improvements in machine learning, natural language processing, and flexibility, AI has deepened its capacity for responding to diverse learner needs with precision and scalability. From real-time captioning and text-to-speech, through learning platforms and one-on-one tutoring customized for the individual learner, AI-based tools are transforming learning, making learning inclusive, participatory, and effective. However, inclusion of AI in education is not without major challenges. Algorithmic bias, one of the common challenges facing applications of AI, has the potential of excluding students by enshrining already present inequities within datasets. The biases usually occur due to underrepresentation of diverse populations in the development and training of these datasets, resulting in systems that are poor in responding to linguistic, cultural, or cognitive diversity. This necessitates robust testing, varied training datasets, and ongoing reassessment for ensuring fairness and reliability of AI-based education decisions. Access to the AI tools continues to be unequal based on infrastructural constraints, socio-economic inequalities, and digital divide. Use of the AI tools in most under-resourced environments is further hampered by poor infrastructure, digital illiteracies, and lack of access to assistive tools. There is, therefore, a need for special investment in the technology infrastructure, training, and resources that will bridge the gap and enable access of the benefits of AI for all the learners.

Beyond the technology and infrastructure challenges, ethical considerations have a central role in issues of the use of AI for inclusive education. Systems based on data pose serious privacy, consent, and security threats to personal and sensitive data. Educational tools using AI have to be compliant with strong data protection legislations such as GDPR in a bid to secure learner data. Transparency of the operations of AI algorithms and decision-making contributes towards building trust and accountability on the part of policymakers, educators, and students. In addition, the implementation of AI should supplement, as opposed to substitute, the work of educators. Educators provide human insight, empathy, and contextual knowledge that no machine learning algorithm will be able to match. AI should be viewed as a supplement that enables teaching professionals to concentrate on more personalized education and less on clerical work. For that to occur effectively, the educators should be empowered with the competencies they require in applying AI tools competently and responsibly. There should be professional development programs that emphasize the inclusion of AI tools in teaching methodologies. Policy frameworks play a crucial role in guiding the implementation of AI technology in inclusive education. Governments and educational institutions have a task of initiating and enforcing policies that promote equity, account for infrastructural inequalities, and provide ethical standards for the implementation of AI. The policies should also promote public-private collaborations by incentivizing innovation while promoting alignment of private interests with the greater aim of educational equity. The ability of AI to facilitate a wide range of learning styles and build inclusive education environments cannot be overstated. The capacity of AI to read learner data and prescribe tailored feedback gives students the opportunity to access content through avenues that suit their individual needs and interests. This flexibility is especially useful for persons with disabilities, whose learning needs are usually hindered by institutionalized educational environments. Furthermore, learning through gamification by means of tools underpinned by AI has been found to effectively enhance engagement, instil motivation, and enhance active learning. Nevertheless, with continuous artificial intelligence advances, there needs to be a close monitoring of its implications. Continuous research and evaluation are required for the long-term consequences of the impact of AI on learning methods and results. There should be inter-disciplinary collaborations among technologists, educators, policymakers, and disability groups for ensuring that solutions involving the application of AI remain accessible, efficient, and supportive of the interests of everyone involved. The path towards inclusive education by means of artificial intelligence isn't just one of technology advancement; it is one of commitment towards equity, diversity, as well as human-cantered design. AI has the ability to democratize education access and enable learners with disability to be their best. However, the realization of such a possibility will be achievable through considerate, inclusive, and ethic-friendly implementation strategies with the learner placed right in the middle of decision-making. With the boundaries of what artificial intelligence can do expanding further, its contribution towards making education more inclusive and equitable will go deeper. It will depend on how we responsibly leverage these tools as instruments of empowerment and not of exclusion. Through the challenges we face, the opportunities we seize, and the ongoing commitment we show toward equity, AI holds the promise for making education a site where each child, regardless of ability, will have a chance to thrive.

ACKNOWLEDGMENTS

The authors sincerely acknowledge and give credit to the scholars and experts whose works or parts of their work have been consulted and referred to in writing this manuscript. We would also like to convey our heartfelt gratitude to all the anonymous reviewers; their observations and suggestions were invaluable in improving the quality of this manuscript.

REFERENCES

Ainscow, M., Booth, T., & Dyson, A. (2006). *Improving schools, developing inclusion*. Routledge. DOI: 10.4324/9780203967157

Alam, G. M., & Forhad, M. (2023, July 13). A. R. (2023). The impact of accessing education via smartphone technology on education disparity—A sustainable education perspective. *Sustainability (Basel)*, *15*(14), 10979. Advance online publication. DOI: 10.3390/su151410979

Alam, M. J., & Forhad, M. A. R. (2023). Barriers to inclusive digital education for students with disabilities in developing countries. *Disability Studies Quarterly*, *43*(1). Advance online publication. DOI: 10.18061/dsq.v43i1.8981

Amuga, E. O. (2023). *Artificial intelligence in education* (pp. 241–255). IGI Global eBooks. DOI: 10.4018/978-1-6684-3595-3.ch012

Anderson, A. (2019). *Virtual reality, augmented reality and artificial intelligence in special education: A practical guide to supporting students with learning differences* (1st ed.). Routledge., DOI: 10.4324/9780429399503

Aroyo, L., Eickhoff, C., Lalmas, M., & Silvestri, F. (2022). Algorithmic bias and the ethics of AI in education. *Communications of the ACM*, *65*(3), 66–73. DOI: 10.1145/3488663

Avellan, T., Sharma, S., & Turunen, M. (2020, January 29). AI for all: Defining the what, why, and how of inclusive. *AI*, 142–144. Advance online publication. DOI: 10.1145/3377290.3377317

Bain, K., Lund-Lucas, E., & Stevens, J. (2012). *22. Transcribe your class: Using speech recognition to improve access for at-risk students*. Collected Essays on Learning and Teaching., DOI: 10.22329/celt.v5i0.3419

Barney, M., & Fisher, W. P. (2016). *Adaptive measurement and assessment*. Social Science Research Network., DOI: 10.1146/annurev-orgpsych-041015-062329

Barocas, S., Hardt, M., & Narayanan, A. (2019). *Fairness and machine learning: Limitations and opportunities*. http://fairmlbook.org

Bell, P., Yamamoto, H., Swietojanski, P., Wu, Y., McInnes, F., Hori, C., & Renals, S. (2013). A lecture transcription system combining neural network acoustic and language models. *Conference of the International Speech Communication Association*. DOI: 10.21437/Interspeech.2013-673

Bennane, A. (2013). *Adaptive educational software by applying reinforcement learning*. Informatics in Education., DOI: 10.15388/infedu.2013.02

Berendt, B., Littlejohn, A., & Blakemore, M. (2020). AI in education: Learner choice and fundamental rights. *Learning, Media and Technology*, *45*(3), 312–324. Advance online publication. DOI: 10.1080/17439884.2020.1786399

Boichenko, A. V., & Boichenko, O. A. (2020). Online education empowerment with artificial intelligence tools. *Artificial Intelligence*, *25*(2), 22–29. DOI: 10.15407/jai2020.02.022

Brugnara, F., Cettolo, M., Federico, M., & Giuliani, D. (2002) Issues in automatic transcription of historical audio data. *Proc. 7th International Conference on Spoken Language Processing (ICSLP 2002)*, 1441-1444, DOI: 10.21437/ICSLP.2002-70

Cardonha, C., Mattos, A. B., & Guimarães, R. L. (2016). A platform to support personalized training of people with disabilities. In *Proceedings of the 13th International Web for All Conference (W4A '16)* (Article 33, pp. 1–4). Association for Computing Machinery. https://doi.org/ DOI: 10.1145/2899475.2899493

CAST. (2018). *Universal Design for Learning guidelines version 2.2*. https://udlguidelines.cast.org

Cavoukian, A. (2011). *Privacy by design: The 7 foundational principles*. Information and Privacy Commissioner of Ontario. https://www.ipc.on.ca/wp-content/uploads/resources/7foundational principles.pdf

. Cerva, P., Silovský, J., Zdánský, J., Nouza, J., & Malek, J. (2012). Real-time lecture transcription using ASR for Czech hearing impaired or deaf students. *Conference of the International Speech Communication Association*. DOI: 10.21437/Interspeech.2012-235

Chen, M., Li, Y., & Li, R. (2019). Research on Neural Machine Translation model. *Journal of Physics: Conference Series*, *1237*(5), 052020. DOI: 10.1088/1742-6596/1237/5/052020

. Chevrier, B., & Stimpson, M. (2017). *Automatic connection to a transcription system*.

Conde, A., De Ipiña, K. L., Larrañaga, M., Elorriaga, J. A., López, J. M., Irigoyen, E., Garay-Vitoria, N., Ezeiza, A., & Rubio, J. (2010). An Intelligent Tutoring System Oriented to the Integration of People with Intellectual Disabilities. In *Advances in intelligent and soft computing* (pp. 639–647). https://doi.org/DOI: 10.1007/978-3-642-12433-4_75

Crossland, M. D., Thomas, R., Unwin, H., Bharani, S., Gothwal, V. K., Quartilho, A., Bunce, C., & Dahlmann-Noor, A. (2017). Tablet computers versus optical aids to support education and learning in children and young people with low vision: Protocol for a pilot randomised controlled trial, CREATE (Children Reading with Electronic Assistance to Educate). *BMJ Open*, *7*(6), e015939. Advance online publication. DOI: 10.1136/bmjopen-2017-015939 PMID: 28637740

David, R., & Kuyini, A. B. (2012). Social inclusion: Teachers as facilitators in peer acceptance of students with disabilities in regular classrooms in Tamil Nadu, India. *International Journal of Special Education*, *27*(2), 157–168.

David, R., & Kuyini, A. B. (2012). Special education teachers' intentions to refer students to special schools. *International Journal of Inclusive Education, 16*(1), 1–17. DOI: 10.1080/13603111003671673

Debnath, S., & Roy, P. (2020). Automatic speech recognition based on clustering technique. In Mandal, J., & Bhattacharya, D. (Eds.), *Emerging technology in modelling and graphics. Advances in Intelligent Systems and Computing* (Vol. 937). Springer., DOI: 10.1007/978-981-13-7403-6_59

Deterding, S., Canossa, A., Harteveld, C., Cooper, S., Nacke, L. E., & Whitson, J. R. (2015). *Gamifying research: Strategies, opportunities, challenges, ethics.* Human Factors in Computing Systems., DOI: 10.1145/2702613.2702646

Devi, N. K. (2016). *Inclusive education practices.* LAMBERT Academic Publishing.

Devi, U. (2016). Inclusive education in India: A developmental milestone. *International Education and Research Journal, 2*(11), 101–104.

Doshi-Velez, F., & Kim, B. (2017). Towards a rigorous science of interpretable machine learning. *arXiv preprint arXiv:1702.08608.* https://doi.org//arXiv.1702.08608DOI: 10.48550

Drigas, A. S., & Ioannidou, R. E. (2013). A Review on Artificial Intelligence in Special Education. In Lytras, M. D., Ruan, D., Tennyson, R. D., Ordonez De Pablos, P., García Peñalvo, F. J., & Rusu, L. (Eds.), *Information Systems, E-learning, and Knowledge Management Research. WSKS 2011. Communications in Computer and Information Science* (Vol. 278). Springer., DOI: 10.1007/978-3-642-35879-1_46

Evmenova, A. (2020). Implementation of assistive technology in inclusive classrooms. In Chambers, D. (Ed.), *Assistive technology to support inclusive education* (Vol. 14, pp. 177–193). Emerald Publishing Limited., DOI: 10.1108/S1479-363620200000014014

Felix, C. V. (2020). The role of the teacher and AI in education. In Sengupta, E., Blessinger, P., & Makhanya, M. S. (Eds.), *International perspectives on the role of technology in humanizing higher education* (Vol. 33, pp. 33–48). Emerald Publishing Limited., DOI: 10.1108/S2055-364120200000033003

Finkelstein, S. (2015). Educational technologies to support linguistically diverse students, and the challenges of classroom integration. In Conati, C., Heffernan, N., Mitrovic, A., & Verdejo, M. (Eds.), Lecture Notes in Computer Science: Vol. 9112. *Artificial intelligence in education. AIED 2015* (pp. 879–882). Springer., DOI: 10.1007/978-3-319-19773-9_127

Florea, A. M., & Radu, S. (2019). Artificial intelligence and education. In *Proceedings of the 2019 22nd International Conference on Control Systems and Computer Science (CSCS)* (pp. 381–382). IEEE. DOI: 10.1109/CSCS.2019.00069

Florian, L., & Black-Hawkins, K. (2011). Exploring inclusive pedagogy. *British Educational Research Journal, 37*(5), 813–828. DOI: 10.1080/01411926.2010.501096

Gan, W., Sun, Y., Ye, S., Fan, Y., & Sun, Y. (2019). AI-Tutor: generating tailored remedial questions and answers based on cognitive diagnostic assessment. *International Conference on Behavioral, Economic, and Socio-Cultural Computing.* DOI: 10.1109/BESC48373.2019.8963236

Hautasaari, A. (2010). Machine translation effects on group interaction: an intercultural collaboration experiment. *International Conference on Intelligent Computing*. https://doi.org/DOI: 10.1145/1841853.1841864

Herder, A., Griful-Freixenet, J., & Struyven, K. (2017). Assistive technology use in inclusive classrooms. *European Journal of Special Needs Education, 32*(4), 491–508. DOI: 10.1080/08856257.2016.1254979

Herder, E., Sosnovsky, S., & Dimitrova, V. (2017). Adaptive intelligent learning environments. In E. Duval, M. Sharples, & R. Sutherland (Eds.), *Technology enhanced learning* (pp. 141–154). Springer. DOI: 10.1007/978-3-319-02600-8_10

Hoboken, J., & Ó Fathaigh, R. (2021). Smartphone platforms as privacy regulators. *Computer Law & Security Review, 41*, 105557. Advance online publication. DOI: 10.1016/j.clsr.2021.105557

Hoboken, J. V., & Ó Fathaigh, R. (2021). Regulating disinformation with artificial intelligence. *Internet Policy Review, 10*(2). Advance online publication. DOI: 10.14763/2021.2.1563

Hong, S., Choi, Y., Lee, M., & Kim, Y. (2022). A framework for ensuring ethical AI use in educational settings: Lessons from data privacy regulation. *British Journal of Educational Technology, 53*(6), 1300–1316. DOI: 10.1111/bjet.13270

Hong, Y., Nguyen, A., Dang, B., & Nguyen, B.-P. (2022). Data Ethics Framework for Artificial Intelligence in Education (AIED). *International Conference on Advanced Learning Technologies*. https://doi.org/DOI: 10.1109/ICALT55010.2022.00095

Huang, Y.-M., Lin, Y.-T., & Cheng, S.-C. (2009). An adaptive testing system for supporting versatile educational assessment. *Computers & Education, 52*(1), 53–67. Advance online publication. DOI: 10.1016/j.compedu.2008.06.007

. Irdamurni, I., Nurhastuti, N., Amini, R., & Taufan, J. (2020). *Implementation of speech to-text application for deaf students on inclusive education course*. DOI: 10.4108/eai.11-12-2019.2290896

Jiang, W., & Pardos, Z. A. (2021). Algorithmic fairness in education. In *Proceedings of the 14th International Conference on Educational Data Mining (EDM 2021)*, 76–87.

Jiang, W., & Pardos, Z. A. (2021). *Towards Equity and Algorithmic Fairness in Student Grade Prediction*. DOI: 10.1145/3461702.3462623

Kaewkamol, P. (2022). *Data Governance Framework as Initiative for Higher Educational Organisation*. DOI: 10.1109/ECTIDAMTNCON53731.2022.9720396

Kappen, M. (2010). Inclusive education: Policy, practice and challenges. *Edutracks, 9*(9), 25–28.

Kappen, M. D. (2010). Inclusive education: Programmes and provisions. *Journal of Educational Psychology, 4*(1), 7–12. DOI: 10.26634/jpsy.4.1.1218

Khan, E. (2016). Machine Learning Algorithms for Natural Language Semantics and Cognitive Computing. *International Conference on Computational Science*. https://doi.org/DOI: 10.1109/CSCI.2016.0217

Knarlag, N., & Olaussen, B. S. (2016). Universal Design for Learning in inclusive education. *Journal of Special Education and Rehabilitation, 17*(3-4), 30–49.

Knox, J., Wang, Y., & Gallagher, M. (2019). Introduction: AI, inclusion, and 'everyone learning everything. In Knox, J., Wang, Y., & Gallagher, M. (Eds.), *Artificial intelligence and inclusive education: Perspectives on rethinking and reforming education* (pp. 1–10). Springer., DOI: 10.1007/978-981-13-8161-4_1

Koenecke, A., Nam, A., Lake, E., Nudell, J., Quartey, M., Mengesha, Z., Toups, C., Rickford, J. R., Jurafsky, D., & Goel, S. (2020). Racial disparities in automated speech recognition. *Proceedings of the National Academy of Sciences of the United States of America, 117*(14), 7684–7689. DOI: 10.1073/pnas.1915768117 PMID: 32205437

Kohli, R., Phutela, S., Garg, A., & Viner, M. (2021). Artificial intelligence technology to help students with disabilities. In *Advances in early childhood and K-12 education* (pp. 238–255). https://doi.org/DOI: 10.4018/978-1-7998-7630-4.ch013

Kortemeyer, G. (2023). Using artificial-intelligence tools to make LaTeX content accessible to blind readers. *arXiv.Org*. https://doi.org//arXiv.2306.02480DOI: 10.48550

Lara-Cabrera, R., Nogueira-Collazo, M., Cotta, C., & Fernández-Leiva, A. (2015). Procedural content generation for real-time strategy games. *International Journal of Interactive Multimedia and Artificial Intelligence, 3*(Special Issue on Digital Economy, 2), 40–48. https://doi.org/DOI: 10.9781/ijimai.2015.325

Lasecki, W. S., Kushalnagar, R., & Bigham, J. P. (2014). Helping students keep up with real-time captions by pausing and highlighting. *In Proceedings of the 11th Web for All Conference (W4A '14)*, Article 39, 1–8. Association for Computing Machinery. https://doi.org/DOI: 10.1145/2596695.2596701

Madani, Y., Ezzikouri, H., Erritali, M., & Hssina, B. (2020). Finding optimal pedagogical content in an adaptive e-learning platform using a new recommendation approach and reinforcement learning. *Journal of Ambient Intelligence and Humanized Computing, 11*(10), 3921–3936. DOI: 10.1007/s12652-019-01627-1

Maor, D., Currie, J., & Drewry, R. (2011). The effectiveness of assistive technologies for children with special needs: A review of research-based studies. *European Journal of Special Needs Education, 26*(3), 283–298. DOI: 10.1080/08856257.2011.593821

Mehrabi, N., Morstatter, F., Saxena, N., Lerman, K., & Galstyan, A. (2022). A survey on bias and fairness in machine learning. *ACM Computing Surveys, 55*(6), 1–35. DOI: 10.1145/3457607

Metatla, O., Thieme, A., Brulé, E., Bennett, C., Serrano, M., & Jouffrais, C. (2019). Toward classroom experiences inclusive of students with disabilities. *Interactions (New York, N.Y.), 26*(1), 40–45. DOI: 10.1145/3289485

Meyer, A., Rose, D. H., & Gordon, D. (2014). *Universal Design for Learning: Theory and practice*. CAST Professional Publishing.

Mismas, L. (2005). *Interactive literacy learning guide*. Retrieved from: https://www.freepatentsonline.com/20060188853.pdf

. Miyoshi, S., Kuroki, H., Kawano, S., Shirasawa, M., Ishihara, Y., & Kobayashi, M. (2008). *Support Technique for Real-Time Captionist to Use Speech Recognition Software*. DOI: 10.1007/978-3-540-70540-6_92

. Mohammed, P., & Watson, E. 'Nell.' (2019). *Towards Inclusive Education in the Age of Artificial Intelligence: Perspectives, Challenges, and Opportunities*. https://doi.org/DOI: 10.1007/978-981-13-8161-4_2

Morris, M. R. (2019). AI and Accessibility: A Discussion of Ethical Considerations. *arXiv: Computers and Society*. https://doi.org/DOI: 10.1145/3356727

Mouroutsou, S. (2017). Inclusive education: A strategy for quality and equity in education. *International Journal of Inclusive Education and Educational Technology*, *1*(1), 15–25.

Mouroutsou, S. (2017). *Policy implementation in inclusive education: a complexity perspective*. https://theses.gla.ac.uk/8048/

. Nash, B. W., Robinson, C. A., Robinson, M. P., & Clemons, R. H. (2012). *Fast-and-engaging, real-time translation using a network environment*.

. Nealon, T., & Butler, J. (2013). *Systems and methods for providing a personalized educational platform*.

Neamtu, R., Camara, A., Pereira, C., & Ferreira, R. (2019). Using artificial intelligence for augmentative alternative communication for children with disabilities. In D. Lamas, H. N. Winckler, J. C. Campos, M. Veríssimo, P. Palanque, & A. Winckler (Eds.), *Human-Computer Interaction – INTERACT 2019: 17th IFIP TC 13 International Conference, Proceedings, Part I* (pp. 234–243). Springer. https://doi.org/DOI: 10.1007/978-3-030-29381-9_15

Nebel, S., Schneider, S., Beege, M., & Rey, G. D. (2017). Leaderboards within educational videogames: The impact of difficulty, effort and gameplay. *Computers & Education*, *113*, 28–41. DOI: 10.1016/j.compedu.2017.05.011

Nelson, A. (2019). *The social life of DNA: Race, reparations, and reconciliation after the genome*. Beacon Press.

OECD. (2019). *Education for inclusive societies: Thematic review*. OECD Publishing., DOI: 10.1787/19939019

. Ouyang, F., & Jiao, P. (2021). *Artificial intelligence in education: The three paradigms*. https://doi.org/DOI: 10.1016/j.caeai.2021.100020

Paladines, J., & Ramírez, J. (2019). An Intelligent Tutoring System for Procedural Training with Natural Language Interaction. *International Conference on Computer Supported Education*. DOI: 10.5220/0007712203070314

. Panda, S. P., Nayak, A. K., & Patnaik, S. (2015). Text-to-speech synthesis with an Indian language perspective. *International Journal of Grid and Utility Computing*. DOI: 10.1504/IJGUC.2015.070676

. Peres, S. M., Boscarioli, C., Bidarra, J., & Fantinato, M. (2011). *Human-Computer Interaction and Artificial Intelligence: Multidisciplinarity Aiming Game Accessibility*. DOI: 10.4018/978-1-60960-567-4.ch011

Raja, M., & Kumar, M. A. (2023). *T, S., & A, S.* AI-Powered Mobility Educational Application for Enhancing Student Learning., DOI: 10.1109/IDCIoT56793.2023.10053423

Rajagopal, A., & Vedamanickam, N. (2019). New Approach to Human AI Interaction to Address Digital Divide& AI divide: Creating an Interactive AIplatform to Connect Teachers & Students. *IEEE International Conference on Electrical, Computer and Communication Technologies*. DOI: 10.1109/ICECCT.2019.8869174

Rajagopal, K., & Vedamanickam, M. (2019). Bridging the digital divide in rural education through teacher empowerment and technology. *International Journal of Educational Technology in Higher Education, 16*(1), 1–13.

Ratnam, R. (2023). Empowering teachers for digital inclusion: AI readiness and rural education in India. *Indian Journal of Educational Technology, 15*(2), 22–35.

Ratnam, T. (2023). Exploring the notion of inclusivity as facilitating students' ontological engagement for personally relevant learning. *European Journal of Education, 58*(2), 277–288. Advance online publication. DOI: 10.1111/ejed.12552

Reddy, V. K., Said, L., Sengupta, B., Chetlur, M., Costantino, J. P., Gopinath, A., Flynt, S., Balunaini, P., & Vedula, S. (2015). Personalized Learning Pathways: Enabling intervention creation and tracking. *IBM Journal of Research and Development, 59*(6), 4:1–4:14. Advance online publication. DOI: 10.1147/JRD.2015.2456711

Roy, M. (2020). AI Intervention in Education Systems of India: An Analysis. *Solid State Technology*.

Saharan, S., & Sethi, S. (2009). Inclusive education: A shift from exclusive to inclusive classrooms. *Edutracks, 8*(10), 20–23.

Saharan, S. K., & Sethi, P. (2009). Inclusive Education - Education for All. *Social Science Research Network*. https://doi.org/DOI: 10.2139/SSRN.1502649

. Schumann, C.-A., Reuther, K., Tittmann, C., Clauß, A.-M., & Kauper, J. (2020). *Impact of AI Application on Digital Education Focused on STE(A)M*. DOI: 10.38069/edenconf-2020-ac0013

Senavirathne, A., & Torra, V. (2020). A survey on data anonymization and privacy-preserving techniques. *International Journal of Information Management, 54*, 102195. DOI: 10.1016/j.ijinfomgt.2020.102195

Senavirathne, N., & Torra, V. (2020). *On the Role of Data Anonymization in Machine Learning Privacy*. Trust, Security, and Privacy in Computing and Communications., DOI: 10.1109/TrustCom50675.2020.00093

Shadiev, R., Hwang, W. Y., Chen, N.-S., & Huang, Y.-M. (2014). Review of Speech-to-Text Recognition Technology for Enhancing Learning. *Journal of Educational Technology & Society*.

Shaeffer, S. (2019). Inclusive education: A prerequisite for equity and social justice. *Asia Pacific Education Review*, *20*(2), 181–192. Advance online publication. DOI: 10.1007/s12564-019-09598-w

Shaeffer, S. (2019). Inclusive education: A prerequisite for equity and social justice. *Prospects*, *48*, 31–45. DOI: 10.1007/s11125-018-09465-9

Sharma, A. (2015). *Perspectives on Inclusive Education with Reference to United Nations*. Universal Journal of Educational Research., DOI: 10.13189/ujer.2015.030502

Sharma, U. (2015). Inclusive education in India: The progress and challenges. *International Journal of Special Education*, *30*(3), 1–12.

Shi, J. (2019). The application of AI as reinforcement in the intervention for children with autism spectrum disorders (ASD). *Journal of Educational and Developmental Psychology*, *9*(2), 17. Advance online publication. DOI: 10.5539/jedp.v9n2p17

. Shiga, Y., Ni, J., Tachibana, K., & Okamoto, T. (2020). *Text-to-Speech Synthesis*. DOI: 10.1007/978-981-15-0595-9_3

Sinwar, D., Kharat, A., & Sable, G. (2023). Fairness-aware machine learning in education: Techniques, metrics, and challenges. *International Journal of Artificial Intelligence in Education*, *33*(2), 229–251. DOI: 10.1007/s40593-023-00301-8

. Sinwar, D., Sinha, A., Singh, V., & Raghuwanshi, G. (2023). Assessing and Mitigating Bias in Artificial Intelligence: A review. *Recent Advances in Computer Science and Communications*. DOI: 10.2174/2666255816666230523114425

Srivastava, S., Varshney, A., Katyal, S., Kaur, R., & Gaur, V. (2021). A smart learning assistance tool for inclusive education. *Journal of Intelligent & Fuzzy Systems*, *40*(6), 11981–11994. DOI: 10.3233/JIFS-210075

. Sun, M., & Chen, T. (2019). *Personalized adaptive learning recommendation method based on big data analysis of education platform*.

Tack, A., & Piech, C. (2022). The AI Teacher Test: Measuring the Pedagogical ability of Blender and GPT-3 in educational dialogues. *arXiv (Cornell University)*. https://doi.org//arxiv.2205.07540DOI: 10.48550

. Takagi, H., Itoh, T., & Shinkawa, K. (2015). *Evaluation of real-time captioning by machine recognition with human support*. https://doi.org/DOI: 10.1145/2745555.2746648

Treglia, E., Magnanini, A., Caione, G., & Lungu, M. A. (2019). Assistive Technologies, Digital Literacy and Didactic for Inclusion. *International Journal of Digital Literacy and Digital Competence*, *10*(3), 1–9. Advance online publication. DOI: 10.4018/IJDLDC.2019070101

Trucano, M. (2016). *Building and sustaining national ICT/education agencies: Lessons from international experiences*. World Bank., DOI: 10.1596/26086

UNESCO. (2009). *Policy guidelines on inclusion in education.* Paris: UNESCO. https://unesdoc.unesco.org/ark:/48223/pf0000177849

UNESCO. (2009). Policy guidelines on inclusion in education. United Nations Educational, Scientific and Cultural Organization. https://unesdoc.unesco.org/ark:/48223/pf0000177849

UNESCO. (2015). *Incheon Declaration and Framework for Action: Towards inclusive and equitable quality education and lifelong learning for all.* Paris: UNESCO. https://unesdoc.unesco.org/ark:/48223/pf0000245656

UNESCO. (2020). *Global Education Monitoring Report 2020: Inclusion and education – All means all.* Paris: UNESCO. https://unesdoc.unesco.org/ark:/48223/pf0000373718

UNESCO. (2021). *Artificial Intelligence and Education: Guidance for policy-makers.* Paris: UNESCO. https://unesdoc.unesco.org/ark:/48223/pf0000377071

UNESCO. (2023). *Ethics of Artificial Intelligence in Education: Student Privacy and Data Protection.* Paris: UNESCO. https://unesdoc.unesco.org/ark:/48223/pf0000383964

UNESCO & World Bank. (2019). *Inclusive Education Initiative: Investing in disability-inclusive education.* https://documents.worldbank.org/en/publication/documents-reports/documentdetail/672261569997259045/Inclusive-Education-Initiative-Investing-in-Disability-Inclusive-Education

UNESCO & World Bank. (2021). *The State of the Global Education Crisis: A Path to Recovery.* https://www.worldbank.org/en/topic/education/publication/the-state-of-the-global-education-crisis-a-path-to-recovery

UNICEF. (2014). *The Right of Children with Disabilities to Education: A Rights-Based Approach to Inclusive Education.* https://www.unicef.org/disabilities/files/UNICEF_Right_to_Education_Children_Disabilities_En_Web.pdf

UNICEF. (2021). *Reimagining education for every child in the era of COVID-19 and beyond.* https://www.unicef.org/reports/reimagining-education

United Nations. (2006). *Convention on the Rights of Persons with Disabilities.* https://www.un.org/development/desa/disabilities/convention-on-the-rights-of-persons-with-disabilities.html

United Nations. (2015). *Transforming our world: The 2030 Agenda for Sustainable Development.* https://sdgs.un.org/2030agenda

Waddington, L., & Toepke, C. (2014). Moving Towards Inclusive Education as a Human Right, an analysis of international legal obligations to implement inclusive education in law and policy. *Social Science Research Network.* https://doi.org/DOI: 10.2139/SSRN.2535198

Waddington, L., & Toepke, J. (2014). Moving towards inclusive education as a human right: An analysis of international legal obligations. *Netherlands Quarterly of Human Rights, 32*(4), 437–466. DOI: 10.1177/092405191403200406

WHO & UNICEF. (2021). *Global Report on Assistive Technology.* https://www.who.int/publications/i/item/9789240062887

Williamson, B., & Eynon, R. (2020). Historical threads, missing links, and future directions in AI-in-education policy research. *Learning, Media and Technology*, *45*(3), 223–235. DOI: 10.1080/17439884.2020.1798995

. Woolf, B. P., Aïmeur, E., Nkambou, R., & Lajoie, S. P. (2008). *Intelligent Tutoring Systems*. DOI: 10.1007/978-3-540-69132-7

World Bank. (2018). *World development report: Learning to realize education's promise*. https://www.worldbank.org/en/publication/wdr2018

World Bank. (2020). *Pivoting to inclusion: Leveraging lessons from the COVID-19 crisis for learners with disabilities*. https://documents.worldbank.org/en/publication/documents-reports/documentdetail/819671606851736544/Pivoting-to-Inclusion-Leveraging-Lessons-from-the-COVID-19-Crisis-for-Learners-with-Disabilities

World Bank. (2020). *Reimagining Human Connections: Technology & Innovation in Education*. https://www.worldbank.org/en/news/feature/2020/11/18/technology-education-reimagining-human-connections

Wu, T. H., Zhao, Y., & Amiruzzaman, Md. (2020). Interactive visualization of AI-based speech recognition Texts. *Eurographics*. DOI: 10.2312/EUROVA.20201091

. Xiao, G. (2021). *Research on artificial intelligence robots and simulation software in virtual training Pendant*. DOI: 10.1088/1742-6596/1952/4/042042

. Yan, P., Slator, B. M., Vender, B., Jin, W., Kariluoma, M., Borchert, O., Hokanson, G., Cosmano, B., Schaefer, C. J., Marry, A. "Mazz," Cheng, W., & Aggarwal, V. (2016). *An Approach to Designing and Implementing Intelligent Tutors in Immersive Virtual Environments*. DOI: 10.1007/978-3-319-30295-9_20

Zhan, M., & Lu, R. (2015). Design of Computer Adaptive Test System Based on IRT. *International Conference on Electrical and Control Engineering*. https://doi.org/DOI: 10.2991/icecee-15.2015.221

KEY TERMS AND DEFINITIONS

Adaptive Assessments: Tests that adjust difficulty based on student responses, providing more accurate evaluations of abilities.

Algorithmic Bias: Systematic errors or unfair outcomes in AI systems resulting from biased training data or flawed algorithms.

Assistive Technology: Tools and devices designed to help individuals with disabilities perform tasks and access information more easily.

Augmentative and Alternative Communication (AAC): Methods of communication used to supplement or replace speech for individuals with communication difficulties.

Blended Learning: An educational approach that combines online digital media with traditional classroom methods.

Cognitive Load Theory: A concept in educational psychology that describes the amount of working memory resources used in the learning process.

Data Privacy: Protection of personal information from unauthorized access or misuse in digital systems.

Differentiated Instruction: A teaching approach that tailors instruction to meet individual student needs, abilities, and learning preferences.

Flipped Classroom: An instructional strategy where students are introduced to content at home and practice working through it at school.

Gamification: The application of game-design elements and principles in non-game contexts, such as education, to enhance engagement and motivation.

Inclusive Education: Educational approach that aims to accommodate and support all learners, regardless of their abilities or disabilities.

Learning Analytics: The measurement, collection, analysis, and reporting of data about learners and their contexts to optimize learning and the environments in which it occurs.

Metacognition: The awareness and understanding of one's own thought processes, particularly in learning contexts.

Personalized Learning: Tailoring educational content and methods to meet the unique needs and preferences of individual students.

Real-time Captioning: Live transcription of spoken content into text for accessibility purposes.

Scaffolding: A teaching method that provides temporary support to students as they develop new skills or concepts.

Screen Readers: Software that reads on-screen content aloud for visually impaired users.

Speech-to-Text: Technology that converts spoken words into written text.

Text-to-Speech: Technology that converts written text into spoken words.

Universal Design for Learning (UDL): An educational framework that aims to create flexible learning environments to accommodate diverse learning styles and needs.

Chapter 5
The New Era of Artificial Intelligence:
Empowering Coders, Non-Coders, and Shaping Future Workforce Creativity

James A Martinez
https://orcid.org/0009-0000-5853-7300
Loma Linda University, USA

ABSTRACT

Artificial intelligence (AI) is transforming the future of work, education, and innovation, particularly in the realms of career and technical education (CTE) and science, technology, engineering, and mathematics (STEM). This chapter examines how AI reshapes roles across industries from software engineering to healthcare by democratizing programming through no-code platforms and intelligent coding assistants. Educators are incorporating AI to personalize learning, promote equitable access, and prepare students for evolving technical careers. Emphasizing both technical fluency and ethical responsibility, the chapter explores AI's role in cloud-native development, lifelong learning, and educational transformation. Through analysis of current tools, workforce trends, and instructional strategies, it demonstrates how AI augments, rather than replaces, human capability. The discussion highlights the importance of interdisciplinary collaboration and continuous upskilling to ensure a resilient, inclusive, and innovative future shaped by intelligent technology.

INTRODUCTION

The rapid evolution of artificial intelligence (AI) has ushered in a transformative era that is redefining how we work, learn, and innovate. This chapter examines the multifaceted impact of AI tools and automation on educational practices and workforce development. By exploring the intersection of AI technology with career and technical education (CTE) and STEM, we demonstrate how these advancements are transforming traditional skilled roles, such as soft-

DOI: 10.4018/979-8-3373-5097-4.ch005

ware developers and data scientists, while creating new job opportunities across industries like healthcare, finance, and manufacturing (Wang & Lu, 2025). AI innovations are revolutionizing software development and coding practices while empowering non-coders to harness technology creatively. As Brynjolfsson and McAfee (2014) note, the convergence of AI and automation is reshaping industries, and Frey and Osborne (2017) have shown that these shifts (Frey & Osborne, 2017) will significantly influence job roles across the board (Pennathur et al., 2024).

In today's technology-driven world, the boundaries between technical and non-technical roles are increasingly blurred (Brynjolfsson & McAfee, 2014). Advanced AI tools from automated code generation assistants to no-code platforms are democratizing software development, opening up new avenues for innovation and participation in the digital economy (Nash, 2021). These advancements not only spark innovation but also provide critical support for CTE initiatives by offering equitable access to resources and personalized learning experiences (World Economic Forum, 2021). In doing so, they prepare students and workers for a modern workforce that demands continuous adaptation and lifelong learning (Holmes, Bialik, & Fadel, 2019).

THE NEW ERA OF AI: FROM MANUAL CODING TO AI-ASSISTED PROGRAMMING

Although the U.S. Bureau of Labor Statistics projects that a million jobs in various sectors will be replaced by AI automations (Pennathur et al., 2024), the evolution from manual coding to AI-assisted programming represents one of the most significant technological shifts of the 21st century. In the early era of software development, programmers grappled with the intricacies of low-level machine instructions and assembly languages, where every operation had to be explicitly defined. This demanding process required a profound understanding of computer architecture and was accessible only to those with specialized technical training. As computing evolved, higher-level programming languages emerged, allowing developers to write code in a more human-readable form and abstract away much of the underlying hardware complexity (Sebesta, 2018). Furthermore, the introduction of integrated development environments (IDEs) brought significant enhancements to the development process by providing automated tools—such as real-time code completion, syntax checking, and debugging assistance—that streamlined coding and reduced the cognitive burden on developers, paving the way for more efficient and maintainable software solutions (Sebesta, 2018). Despite these improvements, manual coding remained the core of software development for decades. However, the landscape shifted again with the emergence of autonomous AI-powered tools that go beyond assistance, acting as collaborators in the development process.

The integration of AI into programming has now catalyzed a paradigm shift. Modern AI-powered coding assistants leveraging machine learning models trained on vast code repositories can interpret natural language descriptions and generate contextually appropriate code, from simple functions to complex algorithms (Vaswani et al., 2017; Chen et al., 2021). This evolution shifts developers' roles from manual code production to high-level problem solving, system design, and creative innovation. Importantly, rather than replacing software developers, these tools augment their capabilities, enabling them to deliver superior products and services with greater efficiency. As noted by Kaurdang (2024) in Forbes, programmers are increasingly transitioning into the role of "AI prompters," where their ability to craft effective prompts to guide AI systems becomes a critical component of the modern software development process. Reinforcing this trend, recent data from GitHub indicates that developer activity has soared (Lanz, 2024) with record-breaking project growth and contributions demonstrating that AI is accelerating development rather than eliminating jobs (Lanz, 2024).

Yet this shift goes beyond mere technical efficiency. By automating routine coding tasks, AI tools free developers to focus on broader architectural questions, innovative problem solving, and user-centric design. In turn, these changes foster greater collaboration among team members, including product managers, designers, and end users. AI-assisted programming thus catalyzes a virtuous cycle of improvement in which human ingenuity and machine intelligence together push the boundaries of what is achievable in software development, both in corporate and educational contexts. This synergy ultimately leads to products and services that are more relevant, reliable, and responsive to rapidly changing market demands.

PROGRAMMING LANGUAGES AND DEMOCRATIZATION OF SOFTWARE DEVELOPMENT

Programming languages have evolved dramatically over the decades. In his article, Parra Rosales (2024) outlines this journey from the early days of writing binary machine code and assembly language to the advent of high-level languages such as Fortran and COBOL, and later to modern paradigms like object-oriented and functional programming. These innovations not only increased abstraction and productivity but also paved the way for today's sophisticated, versatile languages that drive technological advancements.

Historically, software products developed by major companies were often generic, sometimes missing the specific nuances and requirements of individual industries. However, the rise of low-code and no-code platforms has democratized software development [Add citation: ESRI, 2024], enabling non-coders to create tailored solutions that better align with industry-specific needs (Nash, 2021; Kaurdang, 2024). With this technological evolution, educational systems have also started to transform. These innovations foster grassroots creativity and allow organizations to develop more precise, effective software solutions that reflect their unique operational contexts (ESRI, 2024). Recent years have witnessed the emergence of platforms that abstract technical complexity behind intuitive visual interfaces: low-code environments permit the integration of custom code when needed, while no-code platforms eliminate manual coding altogether addressing developer shortages and empowering both professional developers and non-technical users to build functional applications with minimal coding (Nash, 2021).

This democratization of software development has significant implications for education and workforce innovation. Schools and universities that integrate these tools into their curricula enable students to develop problem-solving skills, experiment with technology, and even create new software solutions tailored to specific challenges. Such engagement not only prepares students for the evolving job market but also fosters entrepreneurial mindsets by allowing them to develop and iterate on their own digital products. Moreover, having users serve as active contributors to development provides key advantages: real-world feedback improves product design, industry-specific applications become more effective, and innovation cycles accelerate. Companies and educational institutions alike benefit from AI-powered development tools by reducing costs associated with traditional software engineering while allowing domain experts to directly implement and refine solutions based on their unique insights.

As these platforms integrate more advanced AI capabilities such as natural language processing, predictive analytics, and automated testing the opportunities for innovation grow exponentially. Non-technical stakeholders can now collaborate more effectively with developers, bridging communication gaps that have traditionally hampered software projects. In CTE programs, for example, students can work side by side with industry mentors to prototype solutions for real-world problems, leveraging AI-enhanced features to refine their designs. This approach helps learners gain a deeper understanding of the entire lifecycle of software development. from ideation and planning to testing and deployment, while simultaneously discovering the value of user feedback and iterative improvement.

CLOUD-NATIVE AI DEVELOPMENT AND EVOLVING SOFTWARE ENGINEERING ROLES

As the software industry continues its rapid digital transformation, companies leading in AI and automation are also spearheading the shift toward cloud-native environments. Modern software developers and engineers are increasingly expected to operate within these dynamic ecosystems that leverage containerization, microservices, and scalable infrastructure for continuous deployment and iterative product delivery. Companies such as Microsoft, Google, and Amazon have transformed their development pipelines to support artificial intelligence operations at scale, using platforms like Azure Machine Learning, Google Cloud Vertex AI, and Amazon SageMaker.

The transition from traditional software development to AI-augmented roles is not happening overnight. According to recent industry research, by 2025, approximately 71% of organizations will be regularly using generative AI in at least one business function, with software engineering among the top areas of implementation (McKinsey, 2025a). This growth is creating both opportunities and challenges for developers as they navigate this evolution.

At the core of this shift is cloud architecture. Organizations are increasingly relying on platforms that support containerization, continuous deployment, and AI model integration at scale. Many software engineers express apprehension about staying relevant in this rapidly changing landscape, with some fearing displacement by AI tools. However, evidence suggests that rather than replacing developers, AI is boosting development activity and creating new specializations that require human expertise combined with AI literacy. Forrester's research indicates that 49% of developers are already using or planning to use generative AI assistants in coding phases, though they caution against overestimating AI's capabilities (Forrester, 2024).

The emergence of AI-augmented development has not replaced the role of software engineers, but rather shifted and expanded their responsibilities. Developers must now possess fluency in prompt engineering, cloud architecture, data modeling, and DevOps practices. Proficiency in tools like Kubernetes for container orchestration, Terraform for infrastructure as code, and CI/CD pipelines has become essential. Equally important is a strong understanding of ethical AI development, model interpretability, and system security—a convergence of disciplines once siloed across departments.

This shift is not without resistance. Studies indicate that some developers are reluctant to adopt AI tools due to concerns about overreliance, loss of core programming skills, and potential privacy issues when using machine learning models trained on public repositories. As Charlie Clark, founder at Liinks and former Senior Software Engineer at Squarespace notes, "By 2025, AI will reshape the role of developers in ways that blend creativity with efficiency" (Dice.com, 2024a). The most successful organizations are addressing this resistance through structured transition programs that emphasize AI as an augmentation rather than replacement technology. Gartner projects that "by 2025, more than 50% of all software engineering leader role descriptions will explicitly require oversight of generative AI" (Gartner, 2023), highlighting the growing importance of leadership in guiding effective AI integration.

For software developers preparing for this transition, a clear timeline for skill acquisition becomes crucial. Industry experts recommend a phased approach: first mastering relevant programming frameworks like TensorFlow and PyTorch, then developing specialized knowledge in areas such as natural language processing or computer vision, and finally integrating these skills with cloud-native development practices. Leading technology companies are now offering comprehensive learning paths that guide developers through this evolution, with platforms like Microsoft Learn providing specialized AI curriculum that combines theoretical knowledge with hands-on application. Recent academic research from the IEEE/ACM International Conference on AI Foundation Models and Software Engineering (FORGE) has documented the rapid evolution of these educational approaches and their effectiveness in building AI fluency among traditional software developers (ACM, 2024).

In addition, software engineers must adapt to working across multi-cloud environments, often balancing deployment requirements between AWS, Azure, and Google Cloud to ensure availability, redundancy, and cost optimization. This requires not only technical agility but also knowledge of region-specific data compliance laws and service interoperability. Engineers are also increasingly responsible for designing and maintaining Extract-Load-Transform (ELT) and Extract-Transform-Load (ETL) data pipelines to ensure reliable data flow into AI models, analytics platforms, and real-time dashboards. This often requires close collaboration with data engineers, who are responsible for architecting scalable data pipelines, optimizing storage formats, and ensuring data quality across batch and streaming workloads. Together, software engineers and data engineers align on performance optimization, data governance protocols, and model readiness, forming the backbone of real-time analytics and machine learning infrastructure.

To support these complex data workflows, modern engineering teams frequently rely on tools like Apache Airflow for orchestration (Apache Software Foundation, 2024), dbt (data build tool) for transformation modeling (dbt Labs, 2024), and Fivetran for automated data ingestion across cloud platforms (Fivetran, 2024). These tools not only streamline development and maintenance but also promote transparency, reusability, and version control. For example, Apache Airflow allows teams to schedule and monitor complex ETL workflows with fine-grained control, while dbt enables software engineers and analysts to write modular SQL-based transformations that are automatically tested and documented [Add citation: dbt Labs, 2024]. Fivetran further accelerates the integration process by handling schema changes and syncing data from SaaS platforms into cloud data warehouses such as Snowflake or BigQuery, reducing the overhead of maintaining manual connectors.

Furthermore, the front-end and back-end boundaries are blurring. Engineers are expected to support responsive and accessible user interfaces (UI) while managing complex backend services, APIs, and AI model integrations. The integration of generative AI and real-time recommendation engines into applications introduces new UI/UX demands, where responsiveness, explainability, and ethical transparency must be considered alongside traditional design priorities. Simultaneously, developers must adhere to stringent privacy and security policies, including encryption standards, access controls, and data governance protocols to ensure compliance with GDPR, HIPAA, and emerging AI regulations.

These cloud-native and AI-enabled environments allow for real-time collaboration, seamless scalability, and continuous integration of machine learning models into software applications. As a result, software engineers are no longer just coders; they are solution architects, user advocates, and cross-disciplinary collaborators. This evolution reinforces the need for educational systems and workforce training programs to prepare learners not just with technical knowledge, but with adaptive mindsets capable of navigating and contributing to the future of intelligent, cloud-driven development. In industries that are early adopters of AI and automation, employers often provide in-house training tailored to their proprietary tools, platforms, and workflows. However, this creates a challenge for higher education institutions, which must adapt rapidly to keep pace with these dynamic industry expectations.

Colleges and universities are addressing this gap by strengthening partnerships with technology companies and aligning curricula with current industry standards. Many institutions now integrate certifications from platforms like AWS, Google Cloud, and Microsoft into their degree programs, while others offer microcredentials in AI ethics, cloud development, or DevOps through continuing education. Interdisciplinary project-based learning, co-developed with industry stakeholders, has become essential for simulating real-world work environments. Advisory boards composed of business leaders, engineers, and educators ensure that academic content remains relevant and anticipates future workforce needs.

Furthermore, faculty development programs and industry sabbaticals are being expanded to help instructors gain practical experience with cutting-edge tools and AI-driven environments. These strategies collectively enable workforce training programs to remain agile, equipping graduates with both foundational knowledge and the flexibility to thrive in roles that evolve with emerging technologies.

Organizations are increasingly implementing specific metrics to evaluate the success of these AI transition programs. Effective measurement strategies include tracking direct metrics such as mean squared error and perplexity for AI models, alongside indirect metrics like innovation scores and content diversity (TechTarget, 2025a). Beyond technical performance, organizations are also measuring business impact through key performance indicators such as time savings in development cycles, code quality improvements, and successful integration of AI solutions into production environments. According to McKinsey's 2025 research on AI-enabled software product development lifecycle, organizations implementing AI-augmented workflows are seeing productivity improvements of 20-40% in development cycles (McKinsey, 2025c).

The training resources available to developers seeking to advance their AI skills have expanded significantly. Professional certifications from companies like Microsoft, Google, AWS, and specialized organizations such as ARTiBA now provide structured learning paths with clear prerequisites and outcomes. These programs typically combine theoretical foundations with practical application, enabling developers to build skills incrementally. Self-paced learning platforms have also evolved to offer specialized AI curriculum, with a particular focus on bridging the gap between traditional software development and AI-augmented workflows. Companies that successfully navigate this transition often implement blended learning approaches that combine formal coursework with on-the-job application and peer mentoring. Deloitte's Global Human Capital Trends Survey 2025 found that "learning and development was the talent process most in need of reinvention due to AI-related disruption in work" (Deloitte, 2025), underscoring the critical importance of these resources.

However, modern AI development also introduces a new layer of complexity to the roles of engineers and developers. As organizations build and scale intelligent systems, they must manage an expanding surface of risk—from integrating diverse data pipelines to ensuring the integrity of training datasets. One of the most pressing concerns is the threat of malware or adversarial inputs contaminating training data. If left undetected, these inputs can poison machine learning models, leading to faulty outputs, biased decisions, or systemic vulnerabilities that are difficult to trace.

The integration of AI tools with legacy systems presents particular challenges. Many organizations operate with established technology stacks that were not designed with AI integration in mind. Software engineers must develop expertise in bridging these environments, often creating custom interfaces between modern AI solutions and older codebases. This requires not only technical knowledge but also an understanding of the business processes these legacy systems support. According to research by McKinsey, only 1% of companies consider their AI initiatives mature, with integration challenges cited as a significant barrier to adoption (McKinsey, 2025b). A comprehensive empirical study by Liang et al. (2024) on the usability of AI programming assistants further emphasizes these integration challenges, documenting both successes and barriers experienced by developers across diverse technical environments [Add citation: Liang et al., 2024].

Organizations that successfully navigate these complexities typically measure their progress through quantitative impact metrics. Productivity improvements from AI integration are increasingly quantifiable, with software teams reporting development cycle reductions of 20-40% when appropriately implementing AI-augmented tools. Code quality metrics also show improvement, with AI-assisted development resulting in fewer bugs and security vulnerabilities in production code. These measurable outcomes help justify continued investment in AI upskilling and technology adoption, creating a virtuous cycle of improvement that accelerates the transition to AI-augmented development practices. Looking further ahead, Goldman Sachs projects that AI-related capital expenditures will reach $325 billion by Q4 2025, with AI adoption contributing significantly to GDP growth beginning in 2027 and peaking in the early 2030s (Goldman Sachs, 2025).

Engineers must now implement robust validation, anomaly detection, and data lineage tracking mechanisms to prevent corrupted data from influencing AI outcomes. Tools like MLflow, TensorBoard, and Amazon SageMaker Model Monitor support these efforts by enabling teams to track model performance and detect drift in production. Additionally, secure software development lifecycles (SSDLC) and zero-trust architectures are increasingly integrated into AI workflows to safeguard against both external and insider threats. SSDLC frameworks incorporate security at every stage of development, from threat modeling and secure code reviews to automated security testing and continuous compliance monitoring. Tools such as GitHub Advanced Security, Snyk, and Checkmarx support these practices by detecting vulnerabilities in source code, dependencies, and infrastructure-as-code templates. Meanwhile, zero-trust models ensure that no user or service is implicitly trusted by default—each request is verified and authenticated continuously, reducing the likelihood of unauthorized access or lateral movement within AI-driven applications.

To further support these efforts, platforms like MLflow (Databricks, 2024), TensorBoard (Google, 2024), and Amazon SageMaker Model Monitor (Amazon Web Services, 2024) are employed for robust model tracking and observability. These tools allow developers and ML engineers to monitor model behavior over time, detect drift, and respond to anomalous patterns that may indicate manipulation or degradation in performance. In environments where AI decisions carry high stakes—such as healthcare, finance, and criminal justice—these safeguards are essential for upholding ethical, transparent, and trustworthy system operations.

These added responsibilities underscore the importance of cultivating cybersecurity awareness within development and data science teams. Software engineers must develop a deeper understanding of AI risks during the development lifecycle, working closely with cybersecurity specialists to assess vulnerabilities in models, APIs, and training datasets. In parallel, data governance platforms—often managed by data engineers—are tasked with monitoring lineage, access, and compliance, ensuring that sensitive data used in training is protected from leakage or tampering. Collaborative efforts between these disciplines enhance the resilience of AI systems and foster an organizational culture that prioritizes accountability and risk mitigation. Furthermore, software engineers are increasingly expected to engage with stakeholders, project managers, and executive leadership during cross-functional meetings. Effective communication and reporting skills are essential, particularly when demonstrating the status of AI models, potential risks, and security posture.

To support these interactions and enhance transparency, engineers often utilize project management tools such as Jira, Confluence, Monday.com, Airtable, Microsoft Planner, or Microsoft Project. These platforms facilitate agile planning, documentation, task tracking, and collaborative decision-making across technical and non-technical teams. The ability to navigate these environments and translate technical progress into actionable insights further elevates the strategic role of software engineers in enterprise AI development.

Real-world meetings often occur in agile development settings, where software engineers participate in sprint planning sessions with product owners to define user stories and priorities for upcoming iterations. During daily stand-ups, engineers communicate progress, highlight blockers, and synchronize efforts across backend, frontend, and AI teams. Retrospective meetings, held at the end of each sprint, provide a space for engineers, data scientists, and stakeholders to reflect on what went well, identify areas for improvement, and adjust processes for better collaboration. These rituals are foundational to the Scrum framework, fostering transparency, accountability, and continuous delivery. Regularly engaging in these meetings also helps teams manage scope creep by ensuring that all stakeholders remain aligned on deliverables, changes are documented and discussed in real time, and priorities are continually revisited to reflect evolving project needs.

For example, a mid-sized AI startup developing a customer sentiment analysis platform experienced early signs of scope creep when marketing, engineering, and design teams began proposing additional features during sprint cycles. Initially, the project timeline was at risk of slipping due to misalignment and untracked changes. However, by adhering to Scrum principles—including clearly defined user stories in Jira and focused sprint retrospectives—the team was able to assess trade-offs, reprioritize the backlog, and establish a clearer release roadmap. In weekly sprint reviews, product owners used Confluence to document evolving requirements, while engineers flagged integration risks associated with model updates and data compliance.

This practice not only protected the delivery schedule but also built trust across departments, reinforcing collaborative agility and transparency.

In executive-level discussions, engineers may be called on to explain the impact of AI enhancements, outline timelines for model deployment, or present risk mitigation strategies involving model drift, data security, or compliance. The ability to contextualize technical concepts in strategic terms is increasingly viewed as a leadership competency, bridging the gap between innovation and decision-making.

As AI systems become more complex and autonomous, the consequences of unchecked data breaches or malicious manipulations grow more severe. Thus, future-ready engineers must not only innovate but also anticipate and defend against emerging threats, ensuring the reliability and trustworthiness of intelligent applications across domains.

Practical strategies for organizations facilitating this transition include implementing staged adoption approaches that allow developers to gradually incorporate AI tools into their workflows. Beginning with low-risk applications such as code documentation and test case generation builds confidence and demonstrates tangible benefits. Progressive organizations are also creating cross-functional AI implementation teams that pair experienced developers with AI specialists, fostering knowledge exchange and reducing resistance to change. These strategic approaches align with Gartner's research that projects “75% of enterprise software engineers will use AI code assistants by 2028” (Gartner, 2024), indicating a progressive but inevitable integration of AI into standard development practices.

For individual software engineers, the most effective transition strategies typically involve:

1. Starting with fundamental AI literacy through structured courses that build upon existing programming knowledge
2. Practicing with open-source AI frameworks and tools to develop hands-on experience
3. Specializing in areas that align with career interests and organizational needs
4. Participating in collaborative projects that blend traditional development with AI technologies
5. Building a portfolio of AI-augmented applications that demonstrate proficiency to employers

These practical approaches help bridge the gap between theoretical knowledge and practical application, enabling developers to remain competitive in an increasingly AI-driven landscape.

TRANSFORMING TECHNICAL ROLES AND DEMOCRATIZING TECHNOLOGY

AI tools are enhancing technical roles by automating routine tasks such as code generation, debugging, and optimization (Vaswani et al., 2017; Chen et al., 2021). By managing these time-consuming processes, AI enables developers to concentrate on innovative problem solving and complex system design, ultimately leading to more robust and sophisticated software solutions. Rather than making developers obsolete, this evolution elevates their role, requiring them to exercise strategic thinking, creative ideation, and cross-disciplinary collaboration.

Educational institutions have begun responding to these changes by evolving computer science curricula. Universities such as MIT, Stanford, and Carnegie Mellon have updated their programs [Add citation: Carnegie Mellon University, 2020] to include courses focused on “AI-

Augmented Development," where students learn both the fundamentals of programming and how to work effectively with AI tools (MIT News, 2021; Stanford University, 2021; Carnegie Mellon University, 2020). These curricula emphasize conceptual understanding, ethical considerations, and continuous learning, ensuring that graduates are well-prepared for the evolving demands of the workforce. Indeed, students who acquire both coding proficiency and AI literacy are better positioned to adapt to the rapid pace of technological innovation, as they can seamlessly integrate AI features into a range of products and services.

Moreover, AI-driven platforms extend beyond conventional coding environments. Low-code and no-code interfaces have blurred traditional boundaries between technology creators and users, empowering non-technical professionals from educators and healthcare practitioners to business managers and creative artists to design and deploy digital solutions without requiring deep programming knowledge (Nash, 2021). By translating natural language and visual inputs into functional code, these platforms promote cross-disciplinary collaboration and encourage diverse perspectives in the software creation process. As end users become co-creators, software is more likely to be contextually relevant and user-friendly, addressing real-world challenges in a timely and efficient manner.

AI AGENTS AND EDUCATIONAL INNOVATION

AI agents have evolved into sophisticated tools that function as virtual assistants and intelligent tutors. These systems leverage natural language processing, sentiment analysis, and learning pattern recognition to provide personalized feedback, adapt instructional content, and offer real-time support to students (Holmes, Bialik, & Fadel, 2019). By making learning more interactive and responsive, AI agents help foster self-directed, lifelong learning—a crucial skill in today's ever-changing technological landscape. Importantly, these intelligent systems can tailor educational resources to individual learning styles, thereby addressing some of the inherent limitations of traditional, one-size-fits-all pedagogical models.

Career and Technical Education (CTE) and STEM programs are also being transformed by AI-driven personalized learning environments, adaptive simulations, and virtual laboratories. AI-powered diagnostic assessments and adaptive learning pathways enable students to build on their strengths while addressing skill gaps, and simulation tools offer safe, cost-effective practical training (World Economic Forum, 2021). Leading universities and industry giants such as MIT, Stanford, Google, Microsoft, and Amazon are actively integrating AI technologies into their curricula and forging strategic partnerships (MIT News, 2021; Stanford University, 2021; McKinsey Global Institute, 2022). By exposing students to AI-driven tools at an early stage in their educational journeys, institutions ensure that graduates emerge with not only technical competencies but also the capacity for critical thinking, problem-solving, and adaptive learning in a rapidly evolving job market.

Moreover, AI agents can play a pivotal role in broadening access to quality education. Through intelligent tutoring systems, students in remote areas or under-resourced schools can receive customized assistance, bridging gaps in teacher availability and classroom resources. This democratization of quality instruction aligns with the broader goals of inclusive education, ultimately enhancing educational equity and social mobility. By combining AI-driven innovations with strong pedagogical frameworks, stakeholders can create an environment that fosters creativity, independence, and continuous skill development.

PREPARING STUDENTS FOR NEW ROLES, PLATFORMS, AND TOOLS

Educators play a pivotal role in preparing students for emerging roles by rethinking curricula and teaching methodologies. Colleges and universities are revamping computer science and STEM programs to incorporate AI and machine learning concepts alongside traditional programming skills. Courses in "AI-Augmented Development" enable students to engage in project-based learning using low-code and no-code platforms, thereby demystifying complex technologies and empowering a broader range of learners (MIT News, 2021; Stanford University, 2021; Nash, 2021). By blending theoretical foundations with hands-on experiences, students gain practical insights into how AI systems function and how they can be integrated into real-world applications.

Adaptive learning environments powered by AI agents and intelligent tutoring systems provide personalized instruction that adjusts to each student's pace and learning style. These systems offer real-time feedback, monitor progress, and help cultivate lifelong learning habits essential for navigating an ever-changing technological landscape (Holmes, Bialik, & Fadel, 2019). Moreover, such technologies enable educators to focus on higher-level tasks like mentoring, project supervision, and holistic curriculum design rather than spending valuable time on routine grading or administrative duties.

Children are increasingly engaged with gaming applications like Minecraft and Roblox, which offer immersive, creative digital experiences (Kafai & Burke, 2015). However, the digital landscape is evolving. Emerging tools such as ChatGPT, Python, and Blender now enable young users to transition from consumers to creators empowering them to design their own games and programs. This shift not only fosters computational thinking and creativity but also represents a move toward more active, hands-on learning in the digital realm (Papert, 1980). These same tools are not just recreational—they form the foundation of a new wave of learning. Children can communicate in ways that were once limited, increasingly solving real-world problems by modifying and enhancing existing tools. Through platforms like Minecraft, Roblox, and emerging no-code or low-code environments, learners not only acquire fundamental coding skills but also collaborate to build solutions that address tangible challenges. As they iterate on digital projects, students gain confidence, sharpen their problem-solving acumen, and contribute innovative ideas to shared endeavors. This iterative process mirrors industry practices, reinforcing the notion that playful, creative exploration in digital environments is directly tied to skill development for future careers. (Papert, 1980; Kafai & Burke, 2015).

Additionally, educators are embedding ethical considerations into their curricula by discussing topics such as data privacy, algorithmic transparency, and responsible AI use (Crawford, 2021). This holistic approach ensures that future professionals not only master technical skills but also recognize their broader responsibilities in promoting ethical innovation. Interdisciplinary and collaborative approaches spanning computer science, business, healthcare, and the arts—are emphasized, as modern job roles increasingly demand cross-functional expertise and flexible thinking (OECD, 2021). By integrating diverse perspectives into project-based learning, educators foster a collaborative mindset and encourage creative problem-solving, further preparing students to excel in a workforce shaped by rapid technological change.

ADAPTING TO LIFELONG LEARNING IN A RAPIDLY EVOLVING TECHNOLOGICAL LANDSCAPE

As technology advances at breakneck speed, both students and employers must embrace the concept of lifelong learning. Continuous professional development, adaptive training programs, and dynamic educational frameworks are critical to maintaining workforce competitiveness. AI-powered learning management systems (LMS) and personalized AI agents create flexible, responsive educational ecosystems that facilitate ongoing skill enhancement and innovation. These systems not only support individual growth but also bolster organizational resilience in the face of constant technological change.

For instance, corporations that adopt AI-enhanced training modules can rapidly upskill employees to meet emerging market demands, from advanced data analytics to custom application development. Similarly, educational institutions can track student performance over extended periods, identifying strengths and weaknesses with precision and tailoring learning pathways accordingly. This holistic, data-driven approach ensures that individuals remain adaptable and prepared to navigate the complexities of modern career paths.

Moreover, lifelong learning initiatives often transcend traditional academic structures, blending formal education with on-the-job training, online courses, and self-directed exploration. Platforms like Coursera, edX, and LinkedIn Learning increasingly incorporate AI-driven recommendation engines that guide learners toward relevant content based on their goals and proficiencies. In this context, AI serves as both a catalyst and a facilitator, ensuring that educational resources remain accessible and aligned with real-world skill demands. Institutions also evaluate the effectiveness of these systems through learner engagement metrics, skill acquisition rates, and career placement outcomes. (Coursera, n.d.; edX, n.d.; LinkedIn Learning, n.d.).

ETHICAL CONSIDERATIONS

The integration of AI in education and workforce development raises critical ethical questions. Key concerns include data privacy, algorithmic transparency, and the mitigation of bias. Deploying AI in sensitive environments such as schools and workplaces requires strict adherence to ethical standards and regulatory frameworks. Responsible AI practices are essential to ensure that these technologies benefit all users. For example, AI tools used in recruitment have shown bias in screening resumes based on demographic indicators, illustrating how flawed training data can result in systemic inequity. without compromising individual rights or exacerbating existing inequalities (Crawford, 2021). Stakeholders including technology developers, policymakers, and educators must collaborate to establish clear guidelines that govern data collection, usage, and sharing.

Ethical considerations also extend to the design of AI algorithms. Biased training data or poorly calibrated models can inadvertently perpetuate discrimination, particularly in high-stakes scenarios like hiring and admissions. Educators and developers thus share a responsibility to scrutinize AI systems for potential biases, incorporating strategies such as diverse data sampling, transparent auditing processes, and continuous model refinement. In educational settings, inclusive AI design becomes paramount. If AI agents are used for tutoring or assessment, they must be equitable and culturally sensitive, taking into account linguistic, cultural, and socio-economic differences among learners. This approach ensures that AI-driven innovations bolster equity rather than reinforcing systemic disparities. By proactively addressing these concerns, institutions can cultivate trust in AI technologies, encouraging more widespread adoption and collaboration.

THE SYNERGY OF AI AND USER ENGAGEMENT

The integration of AI into programming has not only transformed the way developers work but also fundamentally changed the process of software development by democratizing access and empowering end users to contribute directly to the creation and refinement of digital solutions. Modern AI-powered coding assistants, which leverage machine learning models trained on vast code repositories, now interpret natural language descriptions and generate contextually appropriate code from simple functions to complex algorithms (Vaswani et al., 2017; Chen et al., 2021). This evolution shifts developers' roles from labor-intensive code production to strategic problem solving, system architecture, and user-focused design. Rather than rendering human expertise obsolete, these AI tools augment capabilities, enabling development teams to deliver superior products and services more efficiently.

As Kaurdang (2024) highlights, programmers are increasingly adopting the role of "AI prompters," effectively guiding AI systems through carefully crafted prompts. This trend is mirrored in rising GitHub contributions, which illustrate how AI is boosting development activity rather than suppressing it (Lanz, 2024). By automating repetitive tasks, AI fosters a deeper level of collaboration among multidisciplinary teams. Product managers, domain experts, and creative professionals can work alongside developers to refine system requirements, test prototypes, and validate user experiences. This iterative loop of input and feedback not only accelerates innovation but also ensures that software solutions remain responsive to real-world needs.

LOOKING AHEAD: FOSTERING A CULTURE OF INNOVATION

Ultimately, the role of AI in both education and workforce development depends on an ecosystem of collaboration, ethical oversight, and continuous learning. As educators integrate AI modules into curricula, students gain hands-on experience with cutting-edge tools, preparing them for a marketplace where AI literacy is increasingly a prerequisite. Meanwhile, professionals can harness AI-driven insights to refine workflows, develop customized solutions, and stay ahead of industry disruptions. In response, CTE educators are beginning to adapt curricula to include AI modules, cloud-based software practices, and interdisciplinary projects. By embracing AI not as a threat but as a partner in innovation, organizations can cultivate a more agile and resilient culture, one capable of adapting to emerging challenges and opportunities.

For CTE programs in particular, embedding AI into hands-on projects and apprenticeships can galvanize interest in technical fields and reduce barriers to entry. When learners see the direct impact of their AI-driven prototypes be it in healthcare analytics, finance automation, or environmental sustainability they gain a sense of purpose and competence. This experiential learning model encourages lifelong engagement, as students become active participants in shaping technology's trajectory rather than passive observers.

In parallel, policymakers and industry leaders must continue to address ethical and logistical challenges. Ensuring equitable access to AI-enabled platforms, safeguarding data privacy, and promoting diversity in tech are all paramount for sustainable progress. By crafting balanced regulations and incentives, they can foster an environment where educational institutions, tech companies, and public agencies collaborate effectively. This synergy will help orchestrate a future where AI augments human capabilities across sectors, driving meaningful innovation while respecting social values and individual rights. It is now the shared responsibility of educators, developers, and policymakers to ensure AI becomes a force for inclusive empowerment—uniting people across disciplines to build a future powered by ethical and collaborative technology..

CONCLUSION

The *New Era of Artificial Intelligence: Empowering Coders, Non-Coders, and Shaping Future Workforce Creativity* offers a comprehensive exploration of how AI is transforming education and workforce development. By tracing the evolution from manual coding to AI-assisted programming and highlighting the emergence of low-code/no-code platforms, the chapter demonstrates that AI tools augment rather than replace human expertise. Skilled developers can now prioritize high-level innovation, while non-coders actively participate in technology creation, enabling more inclusive and user-centered products.

The transition of software engineers from traditional development roles to AI-augmented responsibilities represents a critical evolution in the technology landscape. While this shift presents challenges—from overcoming resistance to change to integrating with legacy systems—organizations that implement structured transition programs with clear metrics for success are demonstrating significant productivity and innovation advantages. The successful integration of AI into development workflows requires not only technical training but also cultural transformation, with cross-functional teams and collaborative approaches bridging traditional disciplinary boundaries. As Forrester (2024) cautions, organizations that attempt to replace developers with AI rather than augment them will likely fail, underscoring the continued importance of human expertise in the AI-enhanced development process.

Moreover, AI agents and adaptive learning systems foster lifelong learning and enhance CTE and STEM programs, preparing both students and employers for a future of continuous technological change. The expanded range of training resources and certification pathways now available provides multiple entry points for developers at different career stages. Ethical considerations remain vital, as responsible AI development requires careful handling of data, equitable design, and transparent accountability. When integrated thoughtfully, AI catalyzes a culture of innovation that unites educators, policymakers, industry stakeholders, and learners in a shared mission: to shape an inclusive, dynamic, and resilient workforce.

By recognizing AI as a powerful collaborator, not just a tool, individuals and organizations can harness its potential to solve complex problems, spark creative breakthroughs, and build the skills necessary to thrive in an ever-evolving digital landscape. As the boundaries between coders and non-coders blur, and as AI becomes a seamless extension of human capability, a new era emerges—one in which everyone has the power to shape the technologies that will define our collective future.

REFERENCES

ACM. (2024). *Proceedings of the 2024 IEEE/ACM First International Conference on AI Foundation Models and Software Engineering*. Association for Computing Machinery. https://dl.acm.org/doi/proceedings/10.1145/3650105

Amazon Web Services. (2024). *Amazon SageMaker Model Monitor*. https://docs.aws.amazon.com/sagemaker/latest/dg/model-monitor.html

Apache Software Foundation. (2024). *Airflow: Workflow management platform*. https://airflow.apache.org

Brynjolfsson, E., & McAfee, A. (2014). *The second machine age: Work, progress, and prosperity in a time of brilliant technologies*. W. W. Norton & Company.

Carnegie Mellon University. (2020). *New AI development courses*. https://ai.cmu.edu/

Chen, M., Tworek, J., Jun, H., Yuan, Q., de Oliveira Pinto, H. P., Kaplan, J., Zaremba, W., Irving, G., Sutskever, I., & Sutskever, I. (2021). Evaluating large language models trained on code. *arXiv preprint arXiv:2107.03374*.

Coursera. (n.d.). *Coursera courses*. Retrieved April 24, 2025, from https://www.coursera.org

Crawford, K. (2021). *The atlas of AI: Power, politics, and the planetary costs of artificial intelligence*. Yale University Press.

Databricks. (2024). *MLflow: Open source platform for the machine learning lifecycle*. https://mlflow.org

dbt Labs. (2024). *dbt: Data build tool for analytics engineering*. https://www.getdbt.com

Deloitte. (2025). *Closing the skills gap*. Deloitte Insights. https://www2.deloitte.com/us/en/insights/focus/human-capital-trends/2025/closing-the-experience-gap-through-talent-development.html

Dice.com. (2024). How AI will impact software development in 2025 and beyond. *Dice Career Advice*. https://www.dice.com/career-advice/how-ai-will-impact-software-development-in-2025-and-beyond

edX. (n.d.). *Access 2000+ online courses*. https://www.edx.org

ESRI. (2024, September 9). *Introducing the new Low-code/no-code app builders guide for developers*. ArcGIS Blog. https://www.esri.com/arcgis-blog/products/apps/developers/introducing-the-new-low-code-no-code-app-builders-guide-for-developers/

Fivetran. (2024). *Automated data integration*. https://www.fivetran.com

Forrester. (2024). *Predictions 2025: GenAI reality bites back for software developers*. https://www.forrester.com/blogs/predictions-2025-software-development/

Frey, C. B., & Osborne, M. A. (2017). The future of employment: How susceptible are jobs to computerisation? *Technological Forecasting and Social Change*, *114*, 254–280. DOI: 10.1016/j.techfore.2016.08.019

Gartner. (2023). *Gartner says more than 50% of software engineering leader roles will explicitly require oversight of generative AI by 2025.* https://www.gartner.com/en/newsroom/press-releases/2023-09-30-gartner-says-more-than-50-percent-of-software-engineering-leader-roles-will-explicitly-require-oversight-of-generative-ai-by-2025

Gartner. (2024). *Gartner says 75% of enterprise software engineers will use AI code assistants by 2028.* https://www.gartner.com/en/newsroom/press-releases/2024-04-11-gartner-says-75-percent-of-enterprise-software-engineers-will-use-ai-code-assistants-by-2028

Goldman Sachs. (2025). *China's advances could boost AI's impact on global GDP.* https://www.goldmansachs.com/insights/articles/chinas-advances-could-boost-ai-impact-on-global-gdp

Google. (2024). *TensorBoard: Visualization toolkit for TensorFlow.* https://www.tensorflow.org/tensorboard

Holmes, W., Bialik, M., & Fadel, C. (2019). *Artificial intelligence in education: Promises and implications for teaching and learning.* Center for Curriculum Redesign.

Kafai, Y. B., & Burke, Q. (2015). *Connected code: Why children need to learn programming.* MIT Press.

Kaurdang, T. (2024, December 1). Programmers become AI prompters, advancing software development. *Forbes.* https://www.forbes.com/sites/taarinikaurdang/2024/12/01/programmers-become-ai-prompters-advancing-software-development/

Lanz, J. A. (2024, November 6). Engaging with coding platforms with integrated AI agents in PyCharm and AI is boosting developer ranks, not replacing jobs: GitHub. *Forbes.* https://www.forbes.com/

Liang, J. T., Yang, C., & Myers, B. A. (2024). A large-scale survey on the usability of AI programming assistants: Successes and challenges. In *Proceedings of the IEEE/ACM 46th International Conference on Software Engineering* (pp. 1-13). Association for Computing Machinery. https://doi.org/DOI: 10.1145/3597503.3608128

LinkedIn Learning. (n.d.). *Courses to learn in-demand skills.* https://www.linkedin.com/learning

Luckin, R., Holmes, W., Griffiths, M., & Forcier, L. B. (2016). *Intelligence unleashed: An argument for AI in education.* Pearson Education.

McKinsey. (2025a). *The state of AI: How organizations are rewiring to capture value.* McKinsey Digital. https://www.mckinsey.com/capabilities/quantumblack/our-insights/the-state-of-ai

McKinsey. (2025b). *AI in the workplace: A report for 2025.* McKinsey Digital. https://www.mckinsey.com/capabilities/mckinsey-digital/our-insights/superagency-in-the-workplace-empowering-people-to-unlock-ais-full-potential-at-work

McKinsey. (2025c). *How an AI-enabled software product development life cycle will fuel innovation*. https://www.mckinsey.com/industries/technology-media-and-telecommunications/our-insights/how-an-ai-enabled-software-product-development-life-cycle-will-fuel-innovation

McKinsey Global Institute. (2022). The future of work after [McKinsey & Company.]. *COVID*, •••, 19.

Nash, J. (2021). No-code development: Democratizing software creation. *Journal of Software Innovation*, *5*(2), 45–59.

News, M. I. T. (2021). *MIT launches new AI curriculum to prepare students for future challenges*. MIT News. https://news.mit.edu/

OECD. (2021). *Education at a glance 2021*. OECD Publishing.

Papert, S. (1980). *Mindstorms: Children, computers, and powerful ideas*. Basic Books.

Parra Rosales, I. J. (2024, February 9). The evolution of programming languages: A journey from origins to technological vanguard. *Medium*. https://medium.com/@josueparra2892/the-evolution-of-programming-languages-a-journey-from-origins-to-technological-vanguard-3f4164a86838

Pennathur, P. R., Boksa, V., Pennathur, A., Kusiak, A., & Livingston, B. A. (2024). The future of office and administrative support occupations in the era of artificial intelligence: A state-of-the-art review and future research directions. *International Journal of Industrial Ergonomics*, *104*, 103665. DOI: 10.1016/j.ergon.2024.103665

Sebesta, R. W. (2018). *Concepts of programming languages* (12th ed.). Pearson.

Stanford University. (2021). *Stanford AI initiatives: Preparing students for a digital future*. https://stanford.edu/

TechTarget. (2025). How businesses can measure AI success with KPIs. *TechTarget Search Enterprise AI*. https://www.techtarget.com/searchenterpriseai/tip/How-businesses-can-measure-AI-success-with-KPIs

Vaswani, A., Shazeer, N., Parmar, N., Uszkoreit, J., Jones, L., Gomez, A. N., Kaiser, L., & Polosukhin, I. (2017). Attention is all you need. In *Advances in Neural Information Processing Systems* (Vol. 30, pp. 5998-6008).

Wang, Y., & Lu, J. (2025). *AI innovations and the future workforce: Trends in technology and education*. FutureTech Publishing.

World Economic Forum. (2021). *The future of jobs report 2021*. World Economic Forum.

KEY TERMS AND DEFINITIONS

Agile Development: An iterative approach to project management and software development that helps teams deliver value to customers faster by breaking work into smaller increments that can be completed within short timeframes.

AI Literacy: The ability to understand, critically evaluate, and effectively use artificial intelligence technologies, including knowledge of how AI systems function, their limitations, and ethical implications.

AI-Augmented Development: The practice of using AI tools like code completion engines, debugging assistants, and natural language interfaces to enhance and streamline the software development process for both coders and non-coders.

Artificial Intelligence (AI): A field of computer science focused on building systems capable of performing tasks that typically require human intelligence, such as decision-making, language understanding, and visual recognition.

Career and Technical Education (CTE): A form of education that combines academic knowledge with technical and occupational skills, preparing students for careers in fields such as healthcare, information technology, and manufacturing.

Cloud-Native Development: An approach to building and running applications that fully exploits the advantages of the cloud computing model, featuring containerization, microservices architecture, and automated deployment pipelines.

Containerization: The process of packaging an application along with its dependencies, libraries, and configuration files into a single container that can run consistently across different computing environments.

Data Lineage: The process of tracking and documenting the flow of data throughout its lifecycle, including its origin, transformations, and destinations, to ensure integrity and regulatory compliance.

Democratization of Technology: The process of making advanced technological tools and knowledge accessible to a wider range of people, especially those without formal technical training, thereby enabling more inclusive innovation and participation.

DevOps: A set of practices that combines software development (Dev) and IT operations (Ops) to shorten the systems development life cycle while delivering features, fixes, and updates frequently in close alignment with business objectives.

Ethical AI: The design, development, and deployment of artificial intelligence systems in ways that promote fairness, accountability, transparency, and respect for user privacy and societal values.

Extract-Transform-Load (ETL) and Extract-Load-Transform (ELT): Data integration processes that involve extracting data from various sources, transforming it to fit operational needs, and loading it into a target database or data warehouse.

Infrastructure as Code (IaC): The practice of managing and provisioning computing infrastructure through machine-readable definition files rather than physical hardware configuration or interactive configuration tools.

Intelligent Tutoring Systems (ITS): AI-powered educational tools that provide personalized learning experiences by adapting content and feedback based on individual students' learning styles, performance, and behavior.

Lifelong Learning: An ongoing process of acquiring new knowledge or skills throughout an individual's life, often driven by changes in the job market, emerging technologies, or personal interests.

Model Drift: The degradation of machine learning model performance over time as real-world data patterns change, requiring continuous monitoring and retraining to maintain accuracy and reliability.

No-Code/Low-Code Platforms: Software development environments that allow users to create applications with minimal or no manual coding, using drag-and-drop interfaces and pre-built components to simplify programming for non-technical users.

Prompt Engineering: The technique of crafting clear and precise input statements (prompts) to guide AI systems in generating useful, accurate, or creative responses—an emerging skill especially important in generative AI contexts.

Secure Software Development Lifecycle (SSDLC): A framework that integrates security practices into each phase of software development, from planning and design through implementation, testing, deployment, and maintenance.

Zero-Trust Architecture: A security framework that requires strict identity verification for every person and device trying to access resources, regardless of whether they are inside or outside the organization's network perimeter.

Chapter 6
AI for Academic Research: Transforming the Research Landscape

Mattius Rischard
https://orcid.org/0000-0003-2073-5859
Montana State University-Northern, USA

Angela Rae Crevar
https://orcid.org/0000-0002-0596-9174
Mercer University, Atlanta, USA

Praveen Dubey
Montana State University-Northern, USA

ABSTRACT

Artificial intelligence (AI) is transforming academic research by streamlining methodologies, accelerating discovery, and expanding analytical capabilities across disciplines. In STEM, AI enables efficient data analysis, predictive modeling, and automation of complex processes. In medicine, it aids diagnostics and drug development, while in the humanities and social sciences, it supports large-scale text analysis and cultural interpretation. Disciplines like law, education, business, archaeology, and psychology are also leveraging AI for precision, efficiency, and innovation. AI-generated tools assist in drafting, modeling, and decision-making, enhancing both productivity and collaboration. However, these benefits come with challenges—bias, opacity, and ethical concerns surrounding authorship and data privacy. This chapter provides a comprehensive overview of AI's cross-disciplinary applications, examines its ethical implications, and offers practical strategies and future directions for integrating AI responsibly within academic research ecosystems.

INTRODUCTION

Artificial Intelligence (AI) is revolutionizing academic research across disciplines by enhancing efficiency, uncovering new insights, and addressing complex problems. This chapter explores AI's role in reshaping research methodologies, particularly in the humanities, social sciences,

DOI: 10.4018/979-8-3373-5097-4.ch006

STEM, medicine, business, law, arts, psychology, and space sciences. Through advanced text analysis, predictive modeling, data synthesis, and AI-assisted experimentation, scholars can navigate vast information landscapes, optimize research processes, and accelerate discoveries. The chapter aims to provide a comprehensive overview of AI's impact on research while discussing its ethical implications, challenges, and future possibilities.

Scholars across various disciplines are increasingly integrating artificial intelligence (AI) into their research methodologies to enhance efficiency, uncover new insights, and tackle complex problems (Ghosh, Anderson, & Franchetti, 2023; Lu, Li, & Xu, 2023; Mahdavi, Peng, & Wang, 2022). AI-powered tools assist researchers in conducting comprehensive literature reviews by analyzing vast databases to identify relevant studies, summarize findings, and highlight emerging trends (Knott, Garcia, & Tran, 2023). For instance, the development of AcademicGPT, a model fine-tuned for academic research, aids in generating literature reviews and drafting research proposals, thereby streamlining the initial stages of research (Zhai, 2023). In fields like environmental science and public health, AI models are employed to detect anomalies and predict future events. For example, AI is used to identify unusual environmental changes, contributing to early warning systems for natural disasters (Zhao, Li, & Sun, 2022). In public health, predictive analytics anticipate disease outbreaks, enhancing response strategies (Li, Wang, & Zhang, 2023).

In disciplines like archaeology and medicine, AI aids in analyzing images to detect patterns or anomalies. A notable example is the collaboration between scientists and AI experts to decipher ancient scrolls carbonized by the Mt. Vesuvius eruption (Marchant, 2023). By utilizing machine learning and advanced imaging techniques, they have begun to virtually unroll and read these fragile documents (Vesuvius Challenge, n.d.). AI serves as a virtual lab assistant, helping researchers design experiments, predict outcomes, and optimize methodologies (DeepMind, n.d.; Digital Health Insights, 2023). DeepMind and BioNTech are developing AI assistants to aid in planning experiments and predicting results, thereby accelerating scientific discovery (DeepMind, n.d.; Google Research, n.d.). AI models are utilized to predict future trends and outcomes in various scientific fields. For instance, EVEScape, a project co-led by researchers from Harvard Medical School, employs AI to predict the evolution and mutation of viruses like SARS-CoV-2, aiding in the development of proactive therapeutic strategies (EVEScape, n.d.).

Yet in all areas of academic publishing, generative AI models, such as ChatGPT, assist in drafting sections of academic papers, creating abstracts, and facilitating language translation, thereby enhancing the writing process and promoting international collaboration (OpenAI, n.d.). A study titled "Augmenting the Author: Exploring the Potential of AI Collaboration in Academic Writing" examines how AI can co-author research outlines, emphasizing the importance of prompt design and output analysis (Knott et al., 2023). This makes generative AI one of the most impactful developments across disciplines, and shall be regarded as integrated across fields; however, the following chapter introduces the large-scale impacts of these tools across academia, as well as discipline-specific applications, before offering a discussion of how future research might develop as a result.

THE IMPACTS OF AI ON ACADEMIA

Artificial intelligence (AI) is profoundly transforming academic research, reshaping methodologies across disciplines by offering unprecedented efficiency and novel insights (Ghosh et al., 2023). Universities are integrating AI tools at various stages of the research process—from gathering literature to analyzing complex datasets—which accelerates discovery while maintaining or even improving accuracy. This evolving landscape spans diverse fields in academia, including the humanities, STEM, and medicine, demonstrating AI's broad impact on how knowledge is produced in higher education research environments.

AI Enhancing Efficiency and Accuracy in Research

One of the most significant advantages of using AI in academic research is its ability to automate labor-intensive tasks with speed and precision. Natural language processing (NLP) algorithms, for example, can rapidly scan and summarize vast bodies of scholarly literature. AI-powered tools like automatic summarizers and literature management software help researchers organize and synthesize findings from thousands of articles, drastically reducing the workload of traditional literature reviews (Knott et al., 2023). Researchers report that such AI tools have in some cases cut the time needed for comprehensive literature reviews by half—automating search, summary, and citation management—which allows scholars to focus more on critical thinking and hypothesis development (Lu et al., 2023).

In the humanities, AI-based text analysis is opening new avenues of inquiry: for instance, machine learning methods have been applied to analyze historical texts and successfully attribute authorship of medieval manuscripts with over 90% accuracy (Lee et al., 2023). AI also contributes to data interpretation and experimental work. In the lab, machine learning and deep learning algorithms excel at detecting patterns in complex datasets and performing statistical analyses far more quickly than traditional methods (Mahdavi et al., 2022). University labs increasingly employ such AI platforms—including user-friendly AutoML tools and advanced statistical programs—to crunch big data in fields ranging from genomics to economics, thus streamlining data analysis without sacrificing rigor (Ghosh et al., 2023).

A recent systematic review identified several core domains where AI significantly supports academic work: idea generation, content structuring, literature synthesis, data management and analysis, editing, and even ensuring ethical compliance in research (Lu et al., 2023). AI-driven research assistants (such as large language models like ChatGPT) have shown substantial potential in these areas—generating research ideas, summarizing sources, and organizing data—thereby serving as essential productivity tools for scholars (Knott et al., 2023).

AI-Powered Predictive Models Driving Discoveries in Academia

University researchers are leveraging AI's pattern-recognition and forecasting abilities to advance knowledge in everything from medicine to environmental science. For instance, in biomedical research, AI systems have dramatically accelerated the discovery of new treatments.

At MIT, a deep learning model sifted through millions of molecules and helped identify a new class of antibiotic compounds capable of killing drug-resistant bacteria (Stokes et al., 2020).

In public health, predictive models powered by AI are enabling earlier detection of disease outbreaks and personalized health insights. Researchers at Penn State and UT Southwestern developed an AI-based method using gut microbiome data to predict individuals' risk for diseases such as diabetes and inflammatory bowel disease with much improved accuracy (Li et al., 2023). In environmental research, machine learning models applied to vast climate and geospatial data forecast climate change scenarios and ecological trends with unprecedented precision (Zhao et al., 2022).

In the social sciences, AI-driven analytics anticipate social and economic patterns, enabling economists to model stock market movements or shifts in public opinion (Barredo Arrieta et al., 2020). Interdisciplinary university teams often combine data science with public health or climate science to tackle complex problems, expanding the predictive capacity of academic research.

Ethical Implications of AI in Academic Research

The growing use of AI in higher education research brings important ethical considerations that universities are actively addressing. One concern is the potential for AI systems to introduce or amplify bias in research findings. AI algorithms trained on historical data can unintentionally perpetuate real-world biases and inequities present in those data (Mitchell et al., 2021). To ensure fairness, researchers are urged to use diverse, representative datasets and to validate models for bias at every stage (Bender et al., 2021).

Transparency is another ethical priority: many AI techniques (especially deep learning) operate as "black boxes," making it difficult to interpret how results are generated (Raji et al., 2020). Academic institutions emphasize explainability and document AI methods in detail. Universities are also implementing training in AI ethics and updating IRB protocols to address AI-specific issues (Ghosh et al., 2023). Clear disclosure of AI use is now mandated by many journals, and AI cannot be listed as an author, emphasizing that researchers retain responsibility for the integrity of their work (Lu et al., 2023). Measures to verify AI-generated data and prevent manipulation are also being discussed by academic and regulatory communities (Knott et al., 2023).

AI as a Collaborative Tool, Not a Replacement for Researchers

Crucially, the narrative in academia has shifted toward viewing AI as an augmenting tool that works alongside human researchers, rather than a replacement. AI can analyze vast datasets and generate predictions, but human researchers are essential for interpretation, hypothesis generation, and ethical reasoning (Mahdavi et al., 2022). Projects like AlphaFold demonstrate this collaborative model: AI predicts protein structures, which researchers then use to guide experiments and drug design (Jumper et al., 2021). Similarly, in the humanities, AI identifies linguistic patterns, while human scholars provide cultural and historical context (Lee et al., 2023).

Higher education institutions are embracing this human-AI synergy through interdisciplinary research teams and by promoting "human-centered AI" approaches. AI tools enhance productivity and broaden the scope of inquiry, while scholars maintain control over research quality and meaning (Knott et al., 2023; Ghosh et al., 2023).

AI INTEGRATION BY DISCIPLINE

Artificial Intelligence (AI) has become a pervasive force driving innovation across nearly every academic field and industry. From analyzing ancient texts to discovering new planets, recent years (2021–2025) have witnessed AI systems achieving breakthroughs that augment human capabilities. This report provides a comprehensive overview of how AI is being integrated into diverse disciplines – highlighting practical applications and notable research findings – with an emphasis on developments from the last four years. Each section below explores AI's role in a specific domain, supported by academic sources and specific examples.

AI in Humanities and Social Sciences

AI is increasingly transforming the humanities and social sciences by enabling new ways to process and interpret complex human-centered data. In the humanities, AI techniques (especially natural language processing and computer vision) allow scholars to analyze large corpora of texts, historical documents, and cultural artifacts at unprecedented scale and speed. This has led to a paradigm shift in digital humanities research: for example, machine learning has been used to reconstruct damaged or ancient texts and to assist in cultural heritage preservation. A striking recent example is the use of AI to read the charred Herculaneum scrolls (ancient papyri buried by Mt. Vesuvius). In 2023, researchers applied a machine learning algorithm to CT scans of the rolled-up papyrus, successfully identifying Greek letters and words (such as porphyras, meaning "purple") from textures in the burned scroll. This achievement – the first time hidden text from these 2,000-year-old scrolls has been revealed – demonstrates AI's practical utility in unlocking historical documents once thought unreadable (Marchant, 2023).

In the social sciences, AI is being harnessed to analyze complex social data and to build models that capture human behavior and societal trends. Computational social science studies leverage AI for tasks like social media analysis, economic modeling, and policy simulation. Notably, neuro-symbolic machine learning has been applied to derive interpretable mathematical models from social and economic data (Balla et al., 2023). For instance, one 2023 study introduced an AI system that discovers symbolic equations explaining patterns in economics and sociology datasets . By extending symbolic regression methods, the system could uncover nonlinear relationships in longitudinal social data and suggest plausible causal models. This approach bridges traditional statistical models and more complex machine learning models, yielding human-interpretable results (Balla et al., 2023). Such AI-driven analyses in sociology and economics help researchers identify novel patterns (e.g. unexpected factors influencing economic growth or collective action) that might be overlooked with manual methods.

Beyond data analysis, AI is also a subject of critical inquiry in these fields. Ethicists and social scientists are examining the societal impact of AI, including issues of bias, fairness, and the changing nature of work. The ethical integration of AI in humanities research is a prominent topic: scholars highlight the need to balance computational power with human interpretative nuance. In anthropology, for example, AI tools are being used to detect patterns in ethnographic data and to simulate cultural evolution, but researchers caution against oversimplifying complex cultural phenomena for the sake of computational tractability (Stepka, 2022). Overall, AI's role in humanities and social sciences is twofold: it acts as an innovative tool accelerating discovery and also as an object of study regarding its implications for human society.

AI in STEM (Science, Technology, Engineering, and Mathematics)

Across the STEM fields, AI integration has accelerated scientific discovery and provided powerful tools for engineering and mathematics. In the natural sciences, perhaps one of the most celebrated breakthroughs was AlphaFold in 2021 – an AI system that predicts 3D protein structures from amino acid sequences. AlphaFold achieved atomic-level accuracy in protein folding, effectively solving a 50-year grand challenge in biology (Jumper et al., 2021). According to its Nature publication, the AlphaFold model regularly predicted protein structures with accuracy comparable to experimental methods for the majority of targets. This advance has had enormous practical impact: by 2022–2023, AlphaFold had released protein structure predictions for virtually all known proteins, enabling new research in drug discovery and biochemistry (Kovalevskiy et al., 2024). The rapid adoption of AI-driven structure prediction illustrates how AI can accelerate STEM research by automating complex reasoning tasks that were once solely human endeavors.

In mathematics, AI has begun to collaborate with mathematicians to conjecture and prove theorems. A landmark example is the work by Davies et al. (2021), where a machine learning system guided human mathematicians to new insights in pure math. This system analyzed large mathematical datasets to detect patterns and relationships, helping to discover a surprising connection between algebraic and geometric invariants in knot theory, as well as progress on a longstanding group theory conjecture. The process, published in Nature, demonstrated that AI can assist in formulating conjectures by sifting through complex data and suggesting plausible hypotheses (Davies et al., 2021). Such results underscore AI's potential to augment human intuition in STEM fields: the AI doesn't replace the mathematician's reasoning but provides clues that lead to genuine new theorems (an application previously thought exclusive to human creativity).

In engineering and technology, AI systems are optimizing design and controlling systems in ways not possible before. For example, materials science has benefited from AI-driven discovery: a 2023 study introduced a deep learning tool called GNoME (Graph Networks for Materials Exploration) that predicted the stability of millions of new inorganic compounds. This AI identified 2.2 million new crystal structures (with about 380,000 predicted to be stable), effectively compressing what would be decades of manual experimentation into a short computational process. Among these predictions are candidate materials for superconductors and battery electrodes, highlighting AI's capacity to accelerate innovation in chemistry and physics (Merchant & Çubuk, 2023). In a similar vein, AI is being used to control complex physical systems: in 2022, scientists achieved AI-controlled plasma in a nuclear fusion reactor. DeepMind and EPFL researchers developed a deep reinforcement learning controller that autonomously managed the magnetic confinement of plasma inside a tokamak, successfully maintaining stable plasma configurations in real time . The AI-driven controller learned to adjust magnetic coils on the fly, a task so complex that it had previously required extensive manual tuning. The result, published in Nature, was heralded as a major step toward stable fusion reactors (Degrave et al., 2022). This example shows how AI can handle high-dimensional control problems in engineering – from plasma physics to perhaps future applications like smart grids or aerospace systems.

Across STEM, a common theme is that AI systems excel at pattern recognition and optimization in large, complex datasets. Whether it is scanning astronomical data or simulating millions of molecular combinations, AI algorithms augment human experts by performing exhaustive analyses quickly. It is noteworthy, however, that human oversight remains crucial: scientists validate AI-discovered hypotheses in labs and engineers supervise AI controllers for safety. Still, the period

2021–2025 firmly established AI as an indispensable partner in STEM research, driving both practical applications (like protein folding and materials design) and fundamental discoveries.

AI in Medicine and Healthcare

The medical field has seen tremendous advancements due to AI's ability to enhance diagnostics, treatment, and personalized care. AI models like DeepMind's AlphaFold and Google's Med-PaLM have improved diagnostic accuracy in radiology, helping detect cancerous tumors, brain lesions, and eye diseases more effectively than traditional methods. Indeed, AI-assisted radiology has outperformed traditional diagnostic methods in multiple studies (Topol, 2019).

The healthcare sector has seen an explosion of AI applications in recent years, ranging from diagnostic imaging to drug development. Medical imaging is one area where AI is already making a tangible impact in clinical practice. Deep learning models trained on radiological images can detect diseases such as cancer, often with accuracy matching or exceeding that of human specialists. For example, a 2023 meta-analysis reported that an AI system achieved a 91% sensitivity in detecting early-stage breast cancer on mammograms, compared to 74% for experienced radiologists (Alowais et al., 2023). In practice, this means AI assistance improved early cancer detection rates. Similarly, convolutional neural networks have been used to identify skin lesions: one study found an AI could diagnose melanoma from dermoscopic images as accurately as dermatologists and even suggest treatment options. AI tools have also demonstrated high sensitivity in spotting findings like diabetic retinopathy in eye scans and pneumonia on chest X-rays. In the latter case, an AI model detected pneumonia on chest radiographs with ~96% sensitivity (versus ~50% for radiologists), though it had a lower specificity. These examples illustrate how AI can serve as a clinical decision support, acting as a second pair of eyes to catch subtle indicators of disease.

Beyond diagnostics, AI is transforming drug discovery and personalized medicine. Traditional drug development is often a slow and costly process, but AI models (especially generative models) are expediting early-stage design and identification of new therapeutics. A notable milestone occurred in 2022–2023 when the first AI-designed drug entered clinical trials. Researchers at Insilico Medicine used generative AI algorithms to design a novel small-molecule drug (for idiopathic pulmonary fibrosis), which by 2023 had progressed through Phase I and entered Phase II human trials. This AI-developed compound is a first-in-class molecule targeting fibrosis via a mechanism different from existing drugs, showcasing AI's ability to innovate beyond human intuition in drug design (Insilico Medicine, 2023). In another example, a deep learning approach called ExoMiner was used by NASA for drug repositioning and compound screening (illustrating crossover between astrophysics and medicine in AI techniques). The broader pharmaceutical industry has now embraced AI for tasks like virtual screening of chemical libraries, optimizing drug formulations, and even predicting outcomes of clinical trials. While some early AI-designed drug candidates have faced challenges in trials (Roberts, 2022), the pipeline of AI-generated molecules continues to grow, indicating a practical payoff in terms of faster discovery of candidate medicines.

In practical application, it is also worthy to note that personalized medicine and genomics rely on AI to analyze genetic mutations, leading to customized treatment plans tailored to an individual's unique genetic makeup. AI-assisted surgical systems, such as the Da Vinci Surgical System, provide precision and control in minimally invasive surgeries, improving patient outcomes and reducing recovery times.

AI is also making healthcare more efficient and proactive. In hospitals, predictive analytics models sift through electronic health records to forecast patient outcomes – for instance, predicting which patients are at risk of complications like sepsis or readmission, so that clinicians can intervene early. During the COVID-19 pandemic, such AI models were deployed to triage patients and allocate resources. Virtual health assistants and chatbots powered by large language models emerged in 2023 as tools to support patients in self-care (e.g., symptom checking or mental health counseling), though their accuracy and safety are under close study. Indeed, a systematic review in late 2023 found that ChatGPT and similar models, when carefully used, can improve certain educational and mental health outcomes for patients (e.g., providing accessible explanations), but they also carry risks of misinformation if not properly validated (Zhang et al., 2023).

It's important to note that regulatory bodies are actively evaluating AI healthcare tools. The U.S. FDA, for example, has approved dozens of AI-based medical devices (especially in radiology and cardiology) in the last few years. A 2023 year-in-review of AI in healthcare research indicated that radiology remains the leading domain for AI publications (483 out of ~1,226 "mature" AI-healthcare papers that year), followed by specialties like gastroenterology and ophthalmology (Jelacic et al., 2024). This reflects the success of image-based AI in detecting polyps in colonoscopies or hemorrhages in retinal scans. Looking forward, experts predict that large language models (LLMs) will drive the next wave of healthcare AI, aiding in clinical documentation, medical education, and even assisting physicians with evidence synthesis (Jelacic et al., 2024). For instance, an LLM fine-tuned on medical knowledge can draft patient visit summaries or suggest diagnostic possibilities (while the clinician remains in the loop to verify accuracy).

In summary, AI's integration into medicine has yielded practical tools that improve diagnostic accuracy, personalize treatments, and streamline operations. The research findings are generally optimistic – e.g. showing improved outcomes or efficiency – but they come with caution. Issues of algorithmic bias, transparency, and the need for clinical validation are emphasized in the literature. Clinicians and AI researchers are now working hand-in-hand to ensure these advanced tools are safe, ethical, and effective. Medicine is poised to continue embracing AI, not as a replacement for healthcare professionals, but as an intelligent companion to enhance patient care.

AI in Business & Economics

AI is reshaping business and economic research by providing powerful tools for data analysis and forecasting. Market analysis and prediction benefit from AI-driven algorithms that analyze financial trends, stock market fluctuations, and consumer behavior using vast datasets. In economic forecasting, machine learning models assess macroeconomic indicators to guide policy decisions. Furthermore, data-driven decision-making significantly impacts economic trends and market analysis (Brynjolfsson & McElheran, 2016).

In the business and economics arena, AI technologies are being leveraged to drive decision-making, efficiency, and market insights. Finance and economics were early adopters of AI, using techniques like machine learning for algorithmic trading, credit scoring, and risk management. Over the past four years, this trend has intensified. Large financial institutions now deploy AI across a range of operations: for example, JPMorgan Chase spends over $11 billion annually on technology, employing AI for everything from fraud detection to loan approval processes (Kearns, 2023). In fact, JPMorgan's CEO stated that AI is an "absolute necessity" for the bank, which uses hundreds of AI use-cases in prospecting clients, customizing marketing, automating payments, and detecting fraudulent transactions. Central banks and regulators are also exploring AI – the Bank of England, Federal Reserve, and others have tested machine learning for economic forecasting and supervision. A 2023 IMF report noted that AI can make lending more efficient and help flag money laundering by analyzing transaction patterns, though it also warned of risks like model opacity and bias in financial services. Overall, AI has become embedded in financial systems: robo-advisors manage investment portfolios, AI credit models widen access to loans (while needing monitoring for fairness), and high-frequency trading algorithms move billions in assets with minimal human intervention.

Beyond finance, corporate business operations have been transformed by AI in areas such as supply chain management, marketing, and human resources. In supply chains, companies use AI-driven forecasting to reduce inventory costs and respond faster to demand fluctuations. According to a McKinsey study, AI-based demand forecasting can cut prediction errors by 30–50% for supply chain networks. This translates into leaner inventories and fewer stockouts or overstock situations, directly benefiting the bottom line. Logistics giants and retailers (like Amazon) have also implemented AI for warehouse automation and route optimization. Amazon reports that its AI-guided robotic systems in fulfillment centers have reduced operating expenses significantly by speeding up order picking and packing. These robots, equipped with computer vision and reinforcement learning, navigate warehouses and handle items with minimal human input. In marketing, businesses leverage AI algorithms for personalized advertising and customer segmentation – for instance, e-commerce platforms have recommendation engines that learn customer preferences and significantly boost sales. A 2022 Accenture survey found that 91% of consumers are likelier to shop with brands that provide personalized offers, a capability increasingly powered by AI analytics.

In the realm of economics research and policy, AI tools are helping economists analyze vast datasets (such as millions of news articles or consumer transactions) to glean real-time insights. Techniques like sentiment analysis on social media are being used to create economic indicators (e.g., predicting consumer confidence or unemployment trends faster than official reports). In macroeconomics, machine learning models have been applied to improve forecasting of GDP and inflation by finding complex patterns in historical data. For example, generative AI has even been experimented with to model "what-if" scenarios, such as the impact of hypothetical policies, by simulating thousands of agent behaviors in an economy (Çört et al., 2022). While these approaches are still emerging, initial findings suggest AI can complement traditional economic models, especially in nowcasting (predicting the present or near-future state of the economy) by assimilating high-frequency data signals.

Business management has also felt the impact of AI through tools that augment human decision-making. Hiring and HR processes now commonly use AI-driven software to screen résumés or even analyze video interviews, though this has raised concerns about bias (e.g., Amazon famously abandoned an AI recruiting tool that inadvertently learned gender bias from past data). In 2023, many organizations began adopting large language models internally to summarize reports, draft communications, or support customer service via chatbots. These AI assistants increase productivity – for instance, by generating first drafts of legal contracts or technical documents that humans then refine. A survey of CEOs in 2025 by the Harvard Business Review reported that a majority were investing in "generative AI" to streamline knowledge work in their companies.

One particularly visible use-case of AI in business has been customer service chatbots. Banks, airlines, and retailers introduced more sophisticated chatbot agents (often powered by GPT-based models) on their websites and apps around 2022–2023. These agents can resolve common customer inquiries through conversation, reducing wait times and freeing up human agents for complex issues. While early customer reactions were mixed (with frustration when bots failed to understand nuances), continuous improvements have made these systems more reliable. Some companies report that AI chat systems now handle over 50% of customer queries successfully, yielding significant cost savings and 24/7 support availability.

In summary, AI in business and economics is delivering practical benefits in efficiency, personalization, and data-driven insights. Empirical research backs many of these benefits: studies show improved forecasting accuracy, higher rates of error detection (e.g., in contracts or accounting), and gains in process speed. However, the literature also notes challenges. Bias and fairness in AI decision-making is a top concern – for example, if a loan approval AI disproportionately rejects certain demographics, it can encode and amplify societal biases. Transparency is another issue; "black box" models in finance or HR can be problematic when decisions need explanation (regulators increasingly call for "explainable AI" in these domains). Despite these caveats, the trajectory is clear: businesses that effectively integrate AI have competitive advantages, and economies that foster AI innovation see productivity gains. As of 2025, experts estimate that AI could add trillions of dollars to the global economy in the coming decade (McKinsey Global Institute, 2023), through a combination of automation and the creation of new products and markets.

AI in Education & Learning Sciences

Education is undergoing a quiet revolution with the help of AI, as intelligent systems become tutors, teaching assistants, and personalized learning coaches. A large body of learning sciences research in the past few years has focused on Artificial Intelligence in Education (AIED) – exploring how AI can improve learning outcomes and the student experience. One of the primary applications is Intelligent Tutoring Systems (ITS), which are AI-driven programs that provide one-on-one instruction tailored to the student's needs. Studies have shown that students who receive personalized guidance from ITS often demonstrate higher engagement and better performance than those in traditional settings (Koedinger et al., 2021). These systems use techniques like machine learning to analyze a student's responses in real time and then adapt the difficulty or provide targeted hints. For example, an AI tutor in mathematics can detect that a student struggles with factoring in algebra and then present additional practice problems or tutorials focusing on that sub-skill. Such personalization – giving the right help at the right time – is something human teachers try to do, but AI can scale it to large classrooms by continuously monitoring each learner's progress.

Recent research emphasizes multimodal tutoring, where AI not only looks at answers but can also interpret student facial expressions or speech for signs of confusion. Experimental AI tutors use computer vision to gauge if a student looks frustrated or bored, and can accordingly adjust the teaching strategy (D'Mello et al., 2022). While still in early stages, these affect-aware tutors hint at a future where learning is responsive to emotional and cognitive states, much like a sensitive human tutor would be.

Another impactful use of AI in education is in automated assessment and feedback. Machine learning models are now capable of grading not just multiple-choice tests but open-ended assignments like essays, short answers, or even coding projects. For instance, natural language processing techniques can evaluate student essays for content relevance, argumentation quality, and writing style. By 2022, some large standardized testing services were using AI as a second grader to double-check human scoring or even as a primary grader with human oversight. Research from 2021 found that an ensemble of automated essay scoring models achieved a high agreement with human graders on TOEFL essays (within the variance of human graders themselves). Beyond grading, AI can provide formative feedback – pointing out to a student why their answer was incorrect and how to improve. Large language models (LLMs) have been piloted in this role: for example, an LLM-based system can analyze a student's draft essay and offer suggestions on structure and clarity, or propose next steps to solve a physics problem the student got partially correct (Zhu et al., 2023). This kind of immediate, personalized feedback helps students learn from mistakes more effectively, as indicated by improved revision outcomes in some classroom studies.

Personalized learning platforms driven by AI have become more mainstream as well. These are systems (often web-based) that adapt curricular pathways to each learner. One student might skip ahead if they've mastered a topic, while another gets remedial resources – all decided by an algorithm analyzing their performance. Duolingo, a popular language learning app, is a good example: it uses AI to determine which quiz to give next, optimizing for retention of vocabulary and grammar for each user. Similarly, Knewton and Smart Sparrow (education technology companies) have developed adaptive learning systems used in college courses, showing gains in course completion and student satisfaction. A bibliometric analysis by Guo, Zheng, & Zhai (2024) found that the major implementations of AI in education over the last decade include automated grading, recommendation systems for content, learning analytics dashboards, educational robotics, and intelligent tutoring, with STEM education and language learning being the most common domains of deployment. Essentially, AI is allowing education to move from a one-size-fits-all model toward a more learner-centric model, where the pace and style of instruction can be tuned to each individual.

Moreover, AI is aiding educators and educational researchers. Teachers use AI-driven insights to identify which students might be at risk of failing (through predictive analytics on grades and engagement data) so they can intervene early. Some schools have implemented AI to automate administrative tasks like scheduling, proctoring exams, or even counseling via chatbots for basic student queries. In higher education, especially during the shift to online learning, AI-based proctoring tools emerged that monitor exam takers via webcam and flag suspicious behavior (though not without controversy regarding privacy and accuracy).

A very recent development in 2023–2024 is the incorporation of generative AI (like ChatGPT) into learning. Students have started using conversational AI as a study aid – asking it to explain complex concepts or to generate practice problems. Educators are split on this: some ban it as a cheating tool (since it can produce essays or solutions), while others embrace it to teach critical thinking (by having students critique or improve AI-generated content). Early systematic reviews (e.g., Zhai, 2023) suggest that when used under guidance, tools like ChatGPT can enhance learning by providing instant explanations and alternative perspectives, potentially improving students' motivation and reducing their cognitive load for rote tasks. However, they also stress the need for students to learn how to use these tools responsibly and verify their outputs, as AI can occasionally produce incorrect or misleading answers.

In conclusion, AI in education is yielding practical applications such as personalized tutoring, automated grading, and smart content recommendation, which collectively contribute to more efficient and tailored learning experiences. Empirical research generally finds positive effects on engagement and achievement when AI is thoughtfully integrated into the curriculum. Yet, challenges remain a focus of current work: ensuring the equity of AI in education (so that algorithms do not disadvantage certain learners), maintaining student data privacy, and preserving the human element in teaching. The consensus in recent literature is that AI should augment teachers, not replace them – freeing teachers from routine tasks so they can focus on mentorship and the social-emotional development of students (Holmes et al., 2022). As we move forward, the synergy of AI with insights from the learning sciences stands to make education more adaptive, inclusive, and effective.

AI in Law and Legal Studies

AI is revolutionizing legal research and judicial analysis. AI-assisted legal research tools like Casetext and ROSS Intelligence help legal scholars and practitioners quickly analyze case law, statutes, and legal precedents (Surden, 2014). Predictive analytics in law enables AI models to assess past rulings and predict case outcomes, offering valuable insights for lawyers and policymakers.

Furthermore, the ethical implications of AI in legal systems are a growing area of study. Scholars examine AI's role in privacy, bias, and fairness within judicial decision-making, ensuring that AI applications in law adhere to ethical and legal standards.The legal field, often seen as a traditional and text-heavy domain, has been experiencing significant AI-driven changes in the past few years. Legal research and document analysis have been greatly accelerated by AI: law firms now routinely use AI-powered tools to sift through vast databases of case law and statutes to find relevant precedents. For example, natural language search platforms (like Google's Caselaw or Westlaw's AI-enhanced search) can understand semantic queries, allowing attorneys to ask complex legal questions and receive pinpoint answers. By 2022, AI systems could not only retrieve cases but also summarize them and extract key legal principles. Bloomberg Law's research tool and others like ROSS Intelligence have demonstrated the ability to answer legal questions posed in plain English, dramatically reducing the time needed for legal research (Stepka, 2022).

One of the most widespread applications is contract analysis. AI algorithms can review lengthy contracts in minutes, flagging risky clauses or deviations from standard terms. According to an ABA report, startups like LawGeex have systems that automatically check proposed contracts against a company's legal policies, catching errors or non-compliant language with higher accuracy in certain instances than junior lawyers. This not only saves time but also helps avoid costly mistakes. Indeed, an AI can compare hundreds of NDAs or lease agreements and instantly tell which ones lack a critical clause, a task that would be exceedingly tedious for a human. In practice, many corporate legal departments now employ AI contract-review during mergers and acquisitions due diligence – the AI combs through thousands of documents (titles, liens, licenses, etc.) to identify potential issues for lawyers to then examine more closely.

AI is also making strides in predicting legal outcomes and assisting judicial decision-making. Machine learning models have been built to predict the outcome of court cases (such as whether a lawsuit will be dismissed or who is likely to win on appeal) based on past case data. A well-known study from 2017 showed an AI predicting U.S. Supreme Court case outcomes with about 70% accuracy, and more recent models continue to refine this. Some jurisdictions have experimented with AI for sentencing recommendations or bail decisions – for instance, certain state courts in the US used risk assessment algorithms (like COMPAS) to help judges determine the likelihood of a defendant reoffending. However, these uses are controversial; researchers have found biases in some of these systems (e.g., against minority defendants), highlighting the need for transparency and fairness in legal AI. Still, the fact that such systems are even considered underscores AI's growing role. In an interesting development, 2023 saw the first instance of an AI "lawyer" – an app by DoNotPay – that was slated to whisper arguments through earphones to a defendant in traffic court (though the experiment was halted due to unauthorized practice of law concerns). This hints at a future where AI could support individuals in navigating legal processes, potentially increasing access to justice for those who cannot afford traditional legal services.

Another area of uptake is e-discovery in litigation. Modern lawsuits often involve reviewing millions of emails and documents to find relevant evidence. AI-driven e-discovery software (using NLP and anomaly detection) can identify pertinent documents and even detect patterns of deception or concealment. For example, during a litigation, an AI might highlight that a series of emails had an unusual spike in usage of certain keywords right before a critical event – something human reviewers might miss. The use of AI in e-discovery, sometimes called "predictive coding," has become standard in large cases, with courts approving its use as early as 2012 and by 2021 it was broadly accepted as a best practice for efficiency.

In academic legal studies, scholars are examining the implications of AI on concepts of law and liability. One question is how to regulate AI systems themselves – for instance, if an autonomous car (guided by AI) causes an accident, how should liability be determined? Similarly, intellectual property law is challenged by AI creations: there have been debates on whether AI-generated inventions or artworks can be patented/copyrighted and who the owner would be. By 2025, some jurisdictions (like the EU) were drafting regulations to address AI explicitly, balancing innovation with rights and safety (e.g., the EU's AI Act). Legal researchers are contributing to these policies with analyses of how existing laws apply to AI and where new laws are needed.

It's also worth noting the emergence of Generative AI in legal practice in 2023. Large language models (like GPT-4) demonstrated the ability to pass law school exams and even portions of the bar exam, showcasing a surprisingly deep (albeit imperfect) understanding of legal reasoning. Law firms have begun to cautiously use such models to draft legal briefs or contracts. For example, a lawyer can prompt an AI to "draft a memo arguing for summary judgment in a slip-and-fall case under New York law" and get a coherent draft that can then be edited. While this saves time, lawyers must carefully review AI-generated text for accuracy (as early incidents showed AI might fabricate case citations that look real but aren't). Nevertheless, the potential for reducing drudge work (like writing first-draft motions or doing document review summaries) is huge, and legal ethics boards are currently discussing guidelines for lawyers using AI, to ensure competence and confidentiality are maintained.

In summary, AI's practical applications in law include faster research, automated document review, and even decision support in courts, all of which enhance efficiency. Research findings generally acknowledge these benefits: studies find AI-assisted legal research can cut hours off case prep, and contract AI tools catch a significant percentage of risks that humans might overlook . However, scholars and practitioners alike caution that AI should augment, not replace human judgment in law (Stepka, 2022). Issues of bias, transparency, and the need for interpretability are paramount because legal decisions have profound human consequences. There is ongoing work on "explainable AI" for law – making AI's reasoning traceable and understandable to lawyers and judges. The consensus is that the foreseeable future will have lawyers working alongside AI: the AI handling routine, data-intensive tasks, and the lawyers focusing on strategy, advocacy, and ethically responsible decision-making. As one commentator put it, AI won't replace attorneys, but attorneys who use AI can outperform those who don't (much like how calculators benefited accountants). The legal profession, traditionally cautious, is now actively embracing AI tools while rewriting professional norms to accommodate this new reality.

AI in Art, Music, and Creative Fields

The creative industries have experienced both excitement and upheaval due to advances in generative AI over the last four years. Visual arts were revolutionized by AI techniques like generative adversarial networks (GANs) and diffusion models, which can create images, paintings, and even video that often indistinguishable from human-made art. In 2022, the diffusion model-based tools DALL·E 2 and Stable Diffusion burst onto the scene, allowing users to generate vivid, original images from text prompts. Artists and designers quickly began using these AI tools as part of their creative process – for concept art, storyboarding, or to generate ideas and styles. A striking real-world incident illustrating AI's impact on art was when an AI-generated artwork won first place in a state fair fine arts competition. In August 2022, a Colorado State Fair awarded a blue ribbon to a piece titled "Théâtre D'opéra Spatial," which was created using the AI program Midjourney (with some curation by the human artist who submitted it). The win sparked controversy and debate in the art community about the nature of art and authorship, eventually leading the fair organizers to require AI-use disclosure in future competitions. This example shows how AI art has matured: what was once a curiosity has achieved a level of quality that competes in human juried contests (Kuta, 2023).

Beyond static images, AI has been used in animation and video. Companies like Disney Research have explored GAN-based tools to generate realistic backgrounds or to automate in-between frame generation (tweening) in animation. In filmmaking, AI can assist in VFX by quickly applying styles or enhancing details; for instance, an AI might upscale the resolution of old film footage or colorize black-and-white scenes with a learned understanding of real-world colors. There are also experimental short films wholly generated by AI based on script prompts, though these are more novelties at present.

In the realm of music, AI systems are composing music in various genres and even collaborating with musicians. One notable project was the completion of Beethoven's unfinished 10th Symphony using AI. In 2021, a team of musicologists and computer scientists trained an AI on Beethoven's works and style, and the AI helped compose missing portions of the symphony which were then arranged and refined by humans. The resulting piece was performed by an orchestra in Bonn, Germany (Elgammal, 2021). The AI had learned from Beethoven's entire oeuvre and mimicked his creative process to suggest how he might have continued his Tenth; observers noted that while not Beethoven's genius per se, the result was musically coherent and recognizably "Beethoven-esque". This demonstrated that AI can capture elements of a composer's style and produce new compositions that honor that legacy. Similarly, AI models like OpenAI's Jukebox and Google's MusicLM (introduced in 2023) can generate songs with lyrics in the style of various artists when given a prompt, although the results, while astonishing, sometimes have an uncanny quality and raise intellectual property questions.

Many musicians now use AI as a tool in the studio. For example, AI-driven plugins can generate accompanying melodies or harmonies to a human-created track, suggest chord progressions, or even synthesize new instrument sounds. There are AI tools that given a simple melody, can orchestrate it in the style of, say, a Baroque piece or a jazz standard. This has lowered barriers for novice music creators and given professionals new inspiration sources. Brian Eno, the famed music producer, has spoken about using generative music algorithms to create evolving soundscapes – a concept he's explored for decades, but now greatly enhanced by modern AI's capabilities.

In literature and writing, AI language models have become surprisingly proficient at generating text. Novelists and content creators have experimented with AI co-writers: for instance, using GPT-3 to generate ideas, plot suggestions, or even entire first drafts of chapters which the human author then edits. There have been instances of AI-written short stories and poems being submitted to magazines (sometimes without disclosure) – with a few AI-authored pieces reportedly accepted for publication, though editors later noted something was "off." In 2021, an AI-written poem fooled some judges in a Turing-test-like poetry contest into thinking it was human-written. On the flip side, literary and art communities are discussing the implications of AI-generated content flooding the market. By 2023, some sci-fi magazines had to close submissions temporarily because they were swamped by a surge of AI-generated story submissions, a phenomenon enabled by public access to advanced language models. This has prompted discussions on new norms or filters to distinguish and manage AI-generated creative content.

Design and architecture also benefit from AI. Architects use generative design algorithms (a form of AI) to explore novel building forms that satisfy functional constraints. For example, an AI might generate dozens of structural designs optimized for weight distribution and aesthetic appeal, which human architects can then tweak – effectively broadening the search space of ideas. Graphic designers employ style transfer AI to apply particular artistic styles to images (turning a photo into, say, a Van Gogh-like painting) or to create logos and layouts. Fashion designers have used GANs to come up with new prints and garment styles, and sometimes even to visualize outfits on diverse body types.

Research in the creative domain often examines the collaborative dynamic between human creativity and AI. Studies by cognitive scientists and artists have found that human creators tend to use AI as a kind of "suggestion engine" – it can output hundreds of variations, from banal to brilliant, and the human curates and builds upon the best. This iterative loop can enhance creativity, essentially functioning like a brainstorming partner that never runs out of ideas (Smith et al., 2022). Importantly, though, AI lacks intrinsic intent or emotional experience, so human artists provide context, meaning, and final refinement to truly connect with audiences. Another line of research is on evaluation of AI art: are people emotionally moved by AI-created works in the same way as human-made ones? Initial studies (e.g. Elgammal et al., 2020 on GAN-generated art) indicate that unknowing viewers do express aesthetic appreciation for AI art, sometimes rating it as more novel or inspiring when they aren't aware of its origins, but often still valuing the story of human creation when told it's AI-generated (thus touching on the philosophical debate of creativity).

On the practical side, intellectual property law is scrambling to catch up: Who owns an artwork or music piece created largely by an AI? Can AI-generated works be copyrighted? In 2023, U.S. Copyright Office made news by ruling that AI-generated images (without a significant human creative contribution) are not eligible for copyright, underscoring that these technologies are ahead of legal frameworks (similar debates are happening worldwide). Some artists are also concerned about AI "learning" from their works without permission – for instance, visual artists saw their styles being mimicked by AI models trained on images scraped from the internet, leading to calls for opt-out mechanisms or compensation. These are active areas of discussion in both the creative community and AI research ethics.

In conclusion, AI in art, music, and creative fields has unlocked incredible new possibilities: virtually anyone can generate a painting or song with a few clicks, and seasoned artists have a powerful new collaborator. The period 2021–2025 will likely be remembered as the dawn of widespread AI-assisted creativity. Academic and practical findings show that AI can increase productivity (a single individual can generate the storyboard of a film in days), broaden creativity (introducing forms or melodies one wouldn't have imagined), and even challenge our notions of art (as seen by AI art winning competitions). At the same time, it raises important questions about authorship, authenticity, and value of art. Creative professionals are adapting by focusing on what humans do best – imbuing art with story, empathy, and intentionality – while leveraging AI's strengths in iteration and pattern generation. Rather than diminishing human creativity, current evidence suggests that, when used thoughtfully, AI can act as a creative amplifier, enabling new art forms and democratizing creative expression.

AI in Psychology & Neuroscience

The intersection of AI with psychology and neuroscience has led to remarkable advances in understanding the human mind and brain, as well as new tools for mental health. Neuroscience has been transformed by AI's ability to analyze complex brain data. Modern neuroimaging techniques (fMRI, EEG, MEG, etc.) produce massive datasets that are challenging to interpret with traditional analysis, but machine learning excels at finding hidden patterns. For example, AI models have been used to decode brain activity into meaningful signals – a field known as neural decoding. In 2023, researchers achieved a groundbreaking result by using a diffusion-based AI model (similar to those used in image generation) to reconstruct visual experiences from fMRI scans of human subjects. Essentially, subjects looked at images, and an AI was able to generate new images that closely resembled what they saw, purely from their brain scan data . This experiment (Takagi & Nishimoto, 2023) demonstrated that AI can interpret the complex patterns of fMRI signals to recover details of natural scenes perceived by a person, a feat likened to "reading the mind's eye." While still rudimentary – reconstructions are blurry and catch only broad features – it paves the way for incredible applications such as communicating with locked-in patients or studying how the brain represents the world.

Perhaps the most life-changing applications have been in brain-computer interfaces (BCIs) for assisting disabled individuals. AI algorithms are the backbone of BCIs, translating neural signals into commands. In 2022–2023, a team at UCSF and UC Berkeley developed a BCI that allowed a fully paralyzed woman to "speak" through a digital avatar by decoding her brain signals (Devlin, 2023). The researchers implanted a high-density electrode array over the speech motor cortex of the patient and used neural networks to interpret the complex patterns of intended speech. The AI system could convert these signals in real-time into a synthesized voice and even animate a digital face to display her expressions. This was a world-first achievement: the patient, who had lost the ability to speak due to a brainstem stroke, could produce sentences on a screen/avatar at a rate of about 15–18 words per minute – much faster than the letter-by-letter typing with eyes she used previously. Such neuroprosthetic communication devices rely on deep learning to make sense of noisy brain data and map it to language, and they herald a future where AI might restore communication and movement (through robotic limbs) to those who have lost them. Indeed, similar projects have shown AI enabling a person with ALS to control a computer cursor or a prosthetic arm via thought alone, with improving accuracy.

AI is also heavily used in cognitive neuroscience research to model and test theories of how the brain works. Deep neural networks, for instance, have been found to show surprising parallels with the human visual system. Researchers have taken convolutional neural networks (CNNs) trained on image recognition and compared their internal activations to recordings from primate visual cortex. Intriguingly, the activations of certain CNN layers correlate strongly with activity in specific brain regions (like the early visual cortex vs. higher-level inferotemporal cortex). This suggests that these AI models might be functioning similarly to the brain's visual processing. As a result, neuroscientists are using AI networks as computational models of perception – treating the layers of a CNN as a hypothesis for how successive stages of the brain process images (Yamins & DiCarlo, 2016; updated with newer architectures in 2021–2022). Additionally, recurrent neural networks are used to model sequence processing in the brain (for language or motor sequences), providing insight into phenomena like memory and prediction.

In psychology and mental health, AI is making an impact in both diagnostics and therapy. Machine learning can detect subtle patterns in behavior or speech that correlate with mental health conditions. For example, researchers have developed NLP algorithms that analyze a person's social media posts or writing samples to predict depression or suicidality risk with moderate to high accuracy. These models look for linguistic markers (such as negative sentiment, absolutist wording, or social isolation indicators) that might be hard for human observers to quantify but become clear with large-scale data analysis. One study in 2021 managed to predict onset of depression months in advance by analyzing Facebook posts, alerting clinicians to at-risk individuals (Reece et al., 2021). Likewise, voice analysis algorithms can pick up on micro-signals in speech – a slight quaver or monotonic quality – that have been associated with anxiety or Parkinson's disease, enabling early intervention.

AI-powered mental health chatbots have also emerged as tools for providing accessible support. Tools like Woebot or Replika use conversation algorithms to engage users in therapeutic dialogues based on cognitive-behavioral techniques. While not a replacement for human therapists, studies (e.g., a 2022 randomized trial with Woebot) show that users often report reduced anxiety or depression symptoms after using such chatbots regularly – likely because the chatbot encourages journaling, reframing of thoughts, and provides a non-judgmental listening ear available 24/7. During the COVID-19 pandemic, these AI therapy bots saw increased usage as in-person therapy was limited. Research finds they can be effective for mild mental health needs, though human oversight is recommended for more severe cases (Fulmer et al., 2022).

In clinical psychology, AI is also used for behavioral analysis. For example, wearable sensors and smart devices generate data about a person's sleep, activity, heart rate, etc. AI models can combine these streams to infer mental states – perhaps detecting that a person's patterns align with rising stress or an oncoming manic episode in bipolar disorder. There are pilot programs where psychiatrists get AI-driven "early warning" reports about their patients based on phone sensor data (location changes, social texting frequency, voice tone in calls), allowing timely check-ins.

Neuroscience research has benefited from AI in more behind-the-scenes ways too: image segmentation algorithms help automate the analysis of microscopy images, such as tracing neural connections in brain tissue (connectomics) or identifying cell types. Projects like the Allen Brain Map generate terabytes of images of brain slices; AI is indispensable for identifying neurons and synapses in those images so that brain circuits can be reconstructed in 3D. In 2021, an AI algorithm was responsible for helping map the largest high-resolution connectome to date (a chunk of mouse cortex), doing years' worth of tracing work in weeks (with some human correction). This accelerates our fundamental understanding of brain architecture.

Another fascinating frontier is the use of AI to design psychological experiments and analyze complex interaction data. Social psychologists studying group dynamics have started to use agent-based modeling with AI to simulate how certain behaviors spread in a social network, or how biases form – essentially creating "virtual societies" to test theories. Similarly, developmental psychologists might use a robot (with AI) to interact with toddlers in standardized ways to probe cognitive development, something that can add consistency to studies and open new avenues (e.g., a robot that can play repetitive games and record detailed data on a child's responses).

The findings in these areas underscore both the power and caution needed with AI. On the positive side, AI has produced therapeutic breakthroughs – giving voice to the voiceless, as in the BCI example, and promising earlier diagnoses for mental illness. Psychologists using AI report being able to handle more data and discover patterns that were previously inaccessible. However, ethical considerations are front and center. Brain data is extremely personal, so any AI that reads or interprets thoughts raises privacy concerns – who has the right to that "mind data," and how do we protect it? If an AI can tell someone's mood from their smartphone, consent and proper use of that information is critical. In addition, the accuracy of AI in these sensitive domains must be rigorously validated to avoid false positives or negatives that could harm individuals (e.g., an AI wrongly labeling someone as suicidal could be distressing, and missing someone who is at risk could be fatal).

In conclusion, AI's integration into psychology and neuroscience is yielding practical applications like neural prosthetics for communication, mental health support chatbots, and diagnostic tools, all supported by research breakthroughs in decoding and modeling the brain. These interdisciplinary efforts between data science and brain science are giving us not only new capabilities to heal and assist (as with the paralyzed patient's restored voice) but also a deeper theoretical understanding of how our minds might work, by comparing and contrasting with AI models. It's an exciting virtuous cycle: insights from neuroscience inspire new AI architectures (for example, neural nets loosely modeled on visual cortex), and AI in turn helps neuroscientists make new discoveries about the brain, which can inspire the next generation of AI. As we continue, collaboration between AI experts, clinicians, and ethicists will be essential to ensure these technologies are used responsibly in ways that ultimately benefit human well-being and knowledge.

AI in Archaeology & Anthropology

Archaeology and anthropology, disciplines centered on uncovering human history and culture, have increasingly adopted AI techniques to aid in discovery and analysis. Archaeologists are using AI to find sites and artifacts that would be difficult, if not impossible, to locate with traditional methods. One of the most powerful applications is analyzing satellite imagery and remote sensing data with machine learning to identify subtle features of past human activity on the landscape.

For example, researchers in the Arabian Peninsula have utilized an AI algorithm to scan satellite images (including infrared and radar data) of the vast Rub' al-Khali desert, aiming to pinpoint potential archaeological site locations. In 2025, this team from Khalifa University reported that their machine-learning model, trained on known site characteristics (like the presence of certain soil discoloration or ancient irrigation patterns), successfully flagged dozens of new locations for possible excavation in that desert region (Arkeonews, 2025). The AI could penetrate through visual noise – using radar imaging to see under sand – and highlighted anomalies that turned out to be buried structures and prehistoric camp sites. This demonstrates a clear practical benefit: AI can trawl through huge tracts of terrain data far faster than humans, essentially performing an initial survey and focusing human archaeologists' efforts where there's the highest algorithmic signal of past civilization. Similar projects have emerged globally: in 2021, a deep learning model was used in Europe to detect "hidden" Iron Age hill forts across vast forested areas, discovering hundreds of previously unrecorded fortifications in lidar scans of the landscape (Keeley et al., 2022). By combining automated detection with expert verification, these approaches greatly accelerate archaeological discovery.

AI is also revolutionizing how artifacts are analyzed and preserved. In the subfield of archaeological artifact analysis, computer vision algorithms can classify pottery sherds or stone tool fragments based on shape, pattern, and texture. Traditionally, an expert might spend hours piecing together pottery fragments or comparing them to known styles; an AI can be trained on thousands of catalogued fragments and then quickly identify a new fragment's likely origin (e.g., culture or time period) within seconds. In one case, researchers developed a CNN to analyze photographs of ancient Greek pottery shards: the AI could attribute them to known pottery types (like Corinthian vs. Athenian) with a high success rate, providing a sort of automated "sherd sorter" for archaeologists. Another experimental system used 3D scanning and AI to perform virtual reconstruction of broken artifacts – essentially solving a 3D puzzle by figuring out which fragments join together. This has been applied to fresco fragments from Pompeii and shattered cuneiform tablets in Mesopotamia, assisting in digital restoration where physical restoration is too difficult or fragile.

Anthropology, especially its cultural and social branches, leverages AI in different ways. Cultural anthropology often deals with qualitative data (like interview transcripts, field notes, videos of rituals). AI-based text mining and topic modeling can help anthropologists find themes and patterns in large sets of ethnographic documents. For instance, an anthropologist might use an NLP model to analyze thousands of social media posts from a particular community to understand shifting cultural sentiments or language use. In a recent study, AI clustering techniques were used on a database of folklore motifs from around the world, revealing networks of story similarity and migrations of tales across continents (suggesting how cultures exchanged stories historically). This kind of analysis, part of a field called computational anthropology, was practically unfeasible before – no single researcher could manually compare tens of thousands of folktales.

Physical anthropology and archaeology intersect in studying human remains and artifacts; here too AI is making contributions. Paleogenetics (the study of ancient DNA) produces vast genomic sequences from ancient human remains, and machine learning helps to interpret this genetic data to map out human migrations and relationships. For example, AI clustering of genetic data has illuminated previously unknown groupings of ancient peoples and their movement patterns (like subtle genetic distinctions between regional Neolithic populations in Europe that point to diverse migration waves). Additionally, forensic-style AI models can assist in facial reconstructions from skulls or predicting diet and disease markers from skeletal features, giving anthropologists richer profiles of past humans.

One fascinating application is using agent-based modeling with AI to simulate ancient societies. Anthropologists and archaeologists sometimes build computational simulations to test hypotheses about how a society might have functioned or collapsed (such as the factors leading to the fall of the Maya civilization or the migration in the Pacific islands). By incorporating AI, these simulations can become more sophisticated – agents (simulated people) can have "learning" behavior or adapt over time. In 2022, a study modeled ancient agricultural decision-making with reinforcement learning agents to see under what conditions a society would choose to migrate versus intensify local farming; the AI agents' behaviors showed patterns that matched archaeological evidence in certain regions (Bartlett et al., 2022). Such models help researchers explore various scenarios in silico before looking for archaeological signatures in the field.

On the research findings side, AI in archaeology has revealed some surprising things. For instance, an AI analysis of high-resolution aerial imagery in the Amazon basin detected a vast network of geoglyphs and roads, suggesting that pre-Columbian Amazonian societies were more complex and interconnected than previously thought (something confirmed by archaeologists upon ground-truthing the AI's findings). Similarly, machine learning has been used to date archaeological finds by identifying subtle geochemical signatures: one project used a neural network to estimate the age of ceramics based on their chemical composition (measured via techniques like X-ray fluorescence), providing instant preliminary dating that guides excavations.

Anthropologists are also critically examining AI itself as a cultural artefact – the emerging field of the anthropology of AI looks at how different societies develop and perceive AI, and how AI might be reinforcing or altering cultural norms. For example, what does it mean that certain AI facial recognition systems have trouble recognizing faces of certain ethnicities? Anthropologists contribute to this conversation by contextualizing technology within human values and biases.

From a practical standpoint, AI helps address the enormous backlog of archaeological data. Museums and universities hold troves of artifacts and records that are under-examined due to resource constraints. AI can assist by quickly cataloguing images of artifacts, transcribing old excavation notes via OCR, and even translating ancient texts (like a machine translation system for ancient cuneiform, which has been prototyped). These tools free up human experts to focus on interpretation rather than rote cataloguing.

However, researchers caution about over-reliance on AI: the context in archaeology and anthropology is crucial, and an algorithm might misidentify features if the training data is incomplete or biased. A 2024 overview in Archaeological Prospection noted that while deep learning greatly aids site detection, it may oversimplify complex archaeological signatures, and hence should augment, not replace, archaeologists' expertise (Vincent et al., 2024). There is also the issue of false positives – AI might flag something as a site that turns out to be a natural formation, which could lead to wasted effort if followed blindly. Thus, current best practice is a human-in-the-loop approach: AI does the heavy lifting of scanning or initial analysis, and human researchers verify and interpret the results (often the AI outputs are integrated into GIS systems for archaeologists to review alongside other data).

In anthropology, a concern is that AI analysis might strip away nuance (for instance, clustering interview texts might miss the subtleties of irony or metaphor that a human anthropologist would catch). So while topic modeling can point to general patterns, anthropologists still dive into the qualitative details to fully understand cultural meaning.

In summary, AI in archaeology and anthropology is proving its worth in discovering where to look (new sites, hidden patterns) and in analyzing what we find (classifying artifacts, simulating past behavior). Practical results include discovery of archaeological features under jungles and deserts that we might not have found for decades, and faster processing of archaeological and ethnographic data. These developments make it an exciting time, as centuries-old disciplines embrace cutting-edge technology to enrich our understanding of human history and cultural diversity. As one archaeologist put it, AI is becoming "the new shovel" – another essential tool in the archaeologist's toolkit, one that digs into data rather than dirt, but often unearths treasures all the same.

AI in Space Exploration & Astrophysics

Space exploration and astrophysics have long been data-heavy fields, making them ripe for AI integration to manage spacecraft, analyze celestial data, and even discover new cosmic phenomena. In recent years, AI has become an integral part of many space missions. For instance, NASA's Mars rovers now utilize advanced AI for autonomous navigation. The Perseverance rover (landed 2021) is equipped with a next-generation AutoNav system that allows it to make real-time driving decisions on the Martian surface without waiting for instructions from Earth. This AutoNav, powered by computer vision and machine learning, builds 3D terrain maps from the rover's cameras, identifies hazards like large rocks or trenches, and plots safe paths around them all on its own. As a result, Perseverance can drive much faster and farther than its predecessors – on the order of 200 meters per day, compared to Curiosity's ~50 meters per day – because it doesn't need to constantly stop and await commands (McHenry, in NASA/JPL release, 2021). This autonomy is crucial for maximizing scientific output during the limited time of these missions. The success of AI in rover navigation has broader implications; future planetary explorers (like the upcoming lunar VIPER rover or other Mars rovers) will rely on similar autonomous systems to traverse challenging terrain and perhaps even to coordinate in multi-rover missions without direct human micromanagement.

AI also played a pivotal role in spacecraft operations beyond rovers. The European Space Agency has tested AI-driven scheduling for its Earth observation satellites, where the AI optimally prioritizes which images to take and downlink based on weather and ground station availability. On the International Space Station, an AI-powered assistant named CIMON (developed by DLR/Airbus with IBM Watson technology) has been assisting astronauts with information retrieval and experiment procedures since 2018, showcasing human-AI collaboration in microgravity. Meanwhile, mission control centers employ machine learning to monitor spacecraft telemetry: algorithms can detect anomalies or deviations in spacecraft performance (like a subtle temperature rise in a subsystem) faster than human operators, potentially preventing failures.

However, some of the most profound impacts of AI have been in astrophysics and cosmology, where it helps researchers make sense of the universe. Modern telescopes and simulations generate enormous datasets: sky surveys imaging billions of galaxies, gravitational wave detectors sensing dozens of events per month, and supercomputer simulations producing petabytes of data on cosmic structure formation. AI has become essential in handling and analyzing this information.

One headline example is the discovery of new exoplanets (planets around other stars) using AI. NASA's Kepler and TESS missions produced light-curves (brightness over time graphs) for hundreds of thousands of stars, looking for the tiny dips that indicate a planet transiting the star.

In 2021, an AI system called ExoMiner (a deep neural network) was used to comb through Kepler data and successfully validated 301 new exoplanets in one batch – planets that had been missed or not confirmed by earlier analyses. ExoMiner proved to be highly accurate in distinguishing real planet signals from false positives like stellar noise, even more consistent than prior human-designed heuristics, effectively boosting the count of known exoplanets (Hoover, 2021). This demonstrates the practical power of AI: it can rapidly accelerate discoveries by finding subtle patterns in data that traditional methods or manual review might overlook. Similarly, machine learning has been applied to TESS data and continues to identify new exoplanet candidates on a monthly basis.

Another area is galaxy classification. Decades ago, astronomer Edwin Hubble manually classified galaxies by shape. Today, projects like Galaxy Zoo (which originally crowdsourced the task to volunteers) have teamed up with AI: convolutional neural networks trained on millions of galaxy images can classify galaxy morphologies (spiral, elliptical, etc.) with very high accuracy in a fraction of the time. This frees scientists to focus on understanding the results statistically (like how galaxy shapes correlate with environment) rather than sorting images one by one. In fact, AI vision models have become so good that they can even identify peculiar and rare objects (gravitational lensing arcs, merging galaxies, supernova candidates) in wide-field survey images. In 2022, an AI system scanning data from the Dark Energy Survey found several new strong gravitational lenses – massive galaxies that warp light from background galaxies – which are not only interesting phenomena but also valuable tools for studying dark matter distribution.

Astronomical transient events (things that flash or change in the sky) are also being handed to AI. Projects like the Zwicky Transient Facility and the upcoming Vera C. Rubin Observatory (LSST) generate alerts for thousands of changes in the sky each night (variable stars, supernovae, asteroid fly-bys). Machine learning filters these alerts to determine which are likely true astrophysical events worth follow-up. For example, an AI might learn to distinguish a real supernova in a distant galaxy from a false alarm like a cosmic ray hit on the camera sensor. This has led to faster discovery of phenomena such as kilonovae (explosions from neutron star mergers) and helped allocate telescope time efficiently to the most promising events. In gravitational wave astronomy, as detectors like LIGO/Virgo chirp with detections of black hole or neutron star mergers, AI algorithms help cross-correlate that data with electromagnetic observations to catch counterparts, or even to infer the properties of those mergers faster through surrogate modeling (replacing expensive physics computations with a trained neural net that outputs similar waveforms in milliseconds).

Even in cosmology theory, AI aids simulations and data analysis. The CAMELS project (2021–2023) generated thousands of detailed cosmological simulations with varying parameters, specifically to train AI models to emulate the results of simulations and infer cosmological parameters from observations. The idea is that instead of running a new supercomputer simulation for each set of universe parameters, a neural network could learn the mapping from parameters to outcomes (like distribution of galaxies) and do it almost instantly (Villaescusa-Navarro et al., 2022). Early results show promise that AI could help analyze data from upcoming surveys (like Euclid or Rubin) to determine things like the nature of dark energy or the total mass of neutrinos in the cosmos by comparing observation to AI-learned simulation predictions.

In spacecraft navigation and autonomy, AI has been used on Earth observation satellites to do onboard data processing – for example, filtering clouds out of images or detecting specific features (like ship detections in the ocean) so that only useful data is downlinked. This maximizes limited bandwidth and demonstrates "smart" satellites. NASA's Earth Science program flew a demonstration where an AI onboard a satellite identified volcanic eruptions and prioritised those images for immediate download, enabling faster response for disaster monitoring.

The future of AI in space includes projects like autonomous space probes that might explore ocean worlds (e.g., Jupiter's moon Europa) and make scientific decisions on the fly due to the communication delay with Earth. Research is ongoing in AI-driven robotics for assembling structures in space or servicing satellites (e.g., Canada's AI-enabled robotic arms on the ISS and plans for Gateway lunar station).

The benefits from recent findings are clear: AI allows us to process far more data than we otherwise could, leading to more discoveries (new planets, new cosmic events) and helps operate spacecraft more safely and efficiently. Perseverance's record-breaking drives on Mars are a testament to AI in action on another world. The hundreds of exoplanets and millions of classified galaxies are a testament to AI sifting through the heavens. In terms of research validation, many astrophysics studies show AI matching traditional methods' accuracy while reducing computation or human labor drastically. For instance, some gravitational lens-finding AI have >90% success rates and identified lenses that humans missed (Huang et al., 2021).

However, challenges exist. Astronomers sometimes treat AI models warily as "black boxes" – if a neural net flags an image as a gravitational wave optical counterpart, researchers want to understand why and ensure it's not biased or overfitting. Thus, there's a push for interpretability and cross-checking AI results with physical models. Additionally, the training of AI in astrophysics often requires simulated data, which might not capture all real complexities; this can lead to domain adaptation issues when applied to actual observations. One example: an AI trained to find supernovae in simulated images might be confused by unknown types of instrumental noise in real telescope images. Researchers mitigate this by adding realistic noise and artifacts to training data and by continuously retraining models on confirmed real examples (a human-in-the-loop approach where initial AI suggestions are confirmed by humans, then fed back in as training data).

In summary, AI has firmly planted itself at the forefront of space exploration and astrophysics. Practically, it operates rovers on Mars, analyzes telescope data to expand our cosmic inventory, and assists in mission operations. Scientifically, it helps test theories at scales and speeds previously unattainable, whether decoding the big bang's afterglow or predicting star behavior. As we prepare for even more ambitious projects – like the lunar Gateway, Mars sample return, or extremely large telescopes – AI will be even more critical. The trend from 2021 to 2025 has shown a clear trajectory: skyrocketing data volumes and complexity in space science met by increasingly sophisticated AI solutions, truly making AI a co-pilot in our journey to understand and explore the universe.

DISCUSSION

AI is transforming the academic research landscape by providing powerful tools for data analysis, hypothesis testing, and knowledge generation. This chapter illustrates AI's interdisciplinary applications and underscores its ethical implications, highlighting both opportunities and challenges. As AI continues to evolve, it is essential for researchers to harness its potential responsibly, ensuring its integration enhances scholarship while maintaining academic integrity.

By understanding AI's role in academic research, scholars can leverage its capabilities to advance their fields while navigating the ethical and practical challenges it presents.

Practical Implications

AI enables more accurate and efficient research, expediting discoveries across disciplines. Academic institutions must integrate AI literacy into curricula to equip researchers with the necessary skills. Ethical AI use in research requires regulations to mitigate bias, misinformation, and data privacy concerns. In medicine, for example, clinicians must be trained to interpret AI diagnostics to ensure patient safety and avoid over-reliance on black-box models. In the humanities and social sciences, scholars should be equipped to understand AI's role in shaping narratives and cultural interpretations, especially when analyzing large-scale textual data. For engineering and robotics, integrating AI competencies into STEM education prepares the next generation for automated design and manufacturing environments. Legal and business disciplines must address the regulatory and ethical implications of AI in decision-making, particularly as AI is deployed in contract law, economic modeling, and policy development. These practical concerns underscore the need for interdisciplinary AI literacy that encompasses technical, ethical, and contextual understanding.

Future Directions

The continued evolution of AI will lead to more sophisticated research applications, enhancing interdisciplinary collaboration. Emerging tools such as explainable AI and neuro-symbolic systems will allow researchers in psychology, neuroscience, and education to explore complex human behaviors and cognition with greater precision. The intersection of AI with ethics and public policy is a critical area, particularly in law and governance, where AI influences decisions on surveillance, justice, and equity. In the arts, future research may explore how generative AI reshapes creativity, authorship, and aesthetic theory. In archaeology and anthropology, AI will likely enable large-scale virtual reconstructions and predictive modeling of cultural evolution, opening new methodological paradigms. Future research must also examine AI's implications for academic integrity—especially as generative tools become ubiquitous—and intellectual property rights in AI-generated content. As global institutions adopt AI in research, coordinated international policies and frameworks will be necessary to address data sovereignty, algorithmic accountability, and equitable access to AI technologies.

REFERENCES

Alowais, S. A., Alghamdi, S. S., Alsuhebany, N., Alqahtani, T., Alshaya, A. I., Almohareb, S. N., Aldairem, A., Alrashed, M., Bin Saleh, K., Badreldin, H. A., Al Yami, M. S., Al Harbi, S., & Albekairy, A. M. (2023). Revolutionizing healthcare: The role of artificial intelligence in clinical practice. *BMC Medical Education, 23*(1), 689. DOI: 10.1186/s12909-023-04698-z PMID: 37740191

Arkeonews. (2025). AI identifies ancient settlements in Rub' al-Khali desert using satellite imagery. Arkeonews. https://arkeonews.net

Balla, J., Huang, S., Dugan, O., Dangovski, R., & Soljačić, M. (2023). AI-assisted discovery of quantitative and formal models in social science. *arXiv*. arXiv:2210.00563. https://doi.org// arXiv.2210.00563DOI: 10.48550

Barredo Arrieta, A., Díaz-Rodríguez, N., Del Ser, J., Bennetot, A., Tabik, S., Barbado, A., Garcia, S., Gil-Lopez, S., Molina, D., Benjamins, R., Chatila, R., & Herrera, F. (2020). Explainable Artificial Intelligence (XAI): Concepts, taxonomies, opportunities and challenges toward responsible AI. *Information Fusion, 58*, 82–115. DOI: 10.1016/j.inffus.2019.12.012

Bartlett, R., Kintigh, K., & Kohler, T. A. (2022). Modeling decision-making in prehistoric farming with AI agents. *Journal of Archaeological Method and Theory, 29*(4), 967–989. DOI: 10.1007/s10816-021-09547-z

Bender, E. M., Gebru, T., McMillan-Major, A., & Shmitchell, S. (2021). On the Dangers of Stochastic Parrots: Can Language Models Be Too Big? *Proceedings of the 2021 ACM Conference on Fairness, Accountability, and Transparency,* 610–623. DOI: 10.1145/3442188.3445922

Brynjolfsson, E., & McElheran, K. (2016). The rapid adoption of data-driven decision-making. *The American Economic Review, 106*(5), 133–139. DOI: 10.1257/aer.p20161016

DeepMind. (n.d.). AlphaFold: Revolutionizing biology with AI. *DeepMind.* https://www.deepmind .com/research/highlighted-research/alphafold

Degrave, J., Felici, F., Buchli, J., Neunert, M., Tracey, B., Carpanese, F., Ewalds, T., Hafner, R., Abdolmaleki, A., de las Casas, D., Donner, C., Fritz, L., Galperti, C., Huber, A., Keeling, J., Tsimpoukelli, M., Kay, J., Merle, A., Moret, J.-M., & Riedmiller, M. (2022). Magnetic control of tokamak plasmas through deep reinforcement learning. *Nature, 602*(7897), 414–419. DOI: 10.1038/s41586-021-04301-9 PMID: 35173339

Devlin, H. (2023, August 23). Paralysed woman able to 'speak' through digital avatar in world first. *The Guardian.* https://www.theguardian.com

Digital Health Insights. (2023, July 21). First fully AI-generated drug enters clinical trials. *Digital Health Insights.* https://dhinsights.org

Elgammal, A. (2021, September 24). How artificial intelligence completed Beethoven's unfinished Tenth Symphony. *Smithsonian Magazine*. https://www.smithsonianmag.com

EVEScape. (n.d.). Predicting virus evolution with AI to aid therapeutic strategies. *Harvard Medical School.* https://hms.harvard.edu/research/evescape

Fulmer, R., Joerin, A., Gentile, B., Lakerink, L., & Rauws, M. (2022). Using psychological artificial intelligence (Tess) to relieve symptoms of depression and anxiety: Randomized controlled trial. *JMIR Mental Health*, *9*(2), e29044. DOI: 10.2196/29044 PMID: 30545815

Ghosh, S., Anderson, J., & Franchetti, M. (2023). Artificial Intelligence in Academic Research: Potential and Pitfalls. *Journal of Science and Technology*, *8*(2), 117–137.

Google Research. (n.d.). Med-PaLM: Advancing medical AI for better healthcare outcomes. *Google.* https://www.blog.google/technology/health/med-palm

Guo, Y., Zheng, J., & Zhai, X. (2024). Artificial intelligence in education: A decade-long bibliometric review and future directions. *Educational Technology Research and Development*, *72*, 131–154. DOI: 10.1007/s11423-023-10182-z

Holmes, W., Bialik, M., & Fadel, C. (2022). *Artificial intelligence in education: Promises and implications for teaching and learning* (2nd ed.). Center for Curriculum Redesign.

Holmes, W., Persson, J., Chounta, I. A., Wasson, B., & Dimitrova, V. (2022). *Artificial intelligence and education: A critical view through the lens of human rights, democracy, and the rule of law*. Council of Europe.

Hoover, R. (2021, November 23). New deep learning method adds 301 planets to Kepler's total count. *NASA.* https://www.nasa.gov

Jumper, J., Evans, R., Pritzel, A., Green, T., Figurnov, M., Ronneberger, O., Tunyasuvunakool, K., Bates, R., Žídek, A., Potapenko, A., Bridgland, A., Meyer, C., Kohl, S. A. A., Ballard, A. J., Cowie, A., Romera-Paredes, B., Nikolov, S., Jain, R., Adler, J., & Hassabis, D. (2021). Highly accurate protein structure prediction with AlphaFold. *Nature*, *596*(7873), 583–589. DOI: 10.1038/s41586-021-03819-2 PMID: 34265844

Kearns, J. (2023, May 1). JPMorgan CEO says AI will be in 'every single process'. *Bloomberg.* https://www.bloomberg.com

Keeley, H., Müller, J., & Weninger, F. (2022). Deep learning reveals new Iron Age hillforts in Europe. *Antiquity*, *96*(386), 1325–1340. DOI: 10.15184/aqy.2022.133

Knewton. (n.d.). Personalized adaptive learning platform. https://www.knewton.com

Knott, A., Garcia, R., & Tran, D. (2023). Generative AI and the Research Workflow: A Review. *Journal of Educational Technology Systems*, *52*(1), 45–67.

Kuta, S. (2023, September 8). Art made with A.I. won a state fair last year. Now, the rules are changing. *Smithsonian Magazine.* https://www.smithsonianmag.com

Lee, H., Kim, J., & Garcia, L. (2023). AI-assisted Authorship Analysis in Historical Texts. *Digital Scholarship in the Humanities*, *38*(4), 633–649.

Li, Q., Wang, Y., & Zhang, D. (2023). Deep Learning-based Gut Microbiome Profiling for Disease Prediction. *Frontiers in Public Health, 11*, 1157392. DOI: 10.3389/fpubh.2023.1157392

Lu, J., Li, J., & Xu, Z. (2023). A Systematic Review of Artificial Intelligence Applications in Academic Research. *AI & Society, 38*(1), 1–22.

Mahdavi, M., Peng, M., & Wang, X. (2022). Applications of AI in Scientific Discovery: Opportunities and Challenges. *Nature Machine Intelligence, 4*, 847–856.

Marchant, J. (2023, October 17). AI reads ancient scroll charred by Mount Vesuvius in tech first. *Scientific American*. https://www.scientificamerican.com

McKinsey Global Institute. (2023). *The economic potential of generative AI: The next productivity frontier*. https://www.mckinsey.com

Merchant, B., & Çubuk, E. D. (2023). GNoME: Accelerating material discovery with graph neural networks. *Nature, 620*, 379–386. DOI: 10.1038/s41586-023-05985-4

Mitchell, M., Wu, S., Zaldivar, A., Barnes, P., Vasserman, L., Hutchinson, B., Spitzer, E., Raji, I. D., & Gebru, T. (2021). Model Cards for Model Reporting. *Communications of the ACM, 64*(3), 40–45.

NASA JPL. (2021, July 1). NASA's self-driving Perseverance Mars rover "takes the wheel". *Jet* Open*Propulsion Laboratory News.* https://www.jpl.nasa.gov

Open, A. I. (n.d.). ChatGPT: AI-powered conversational assistant for various applications. *OpenAI.* https://openai.com/chatgpt

Raji, I. D., Smart, A., & White, R. N.. (2020). Closing the AI Accountability Gap: Defining an End-to-End Framework for Internal Algorithmic Auditing. *Proceedings of the 2020 Conference on Fairness, Accountability, and Transparency*, 33–44. https://doi.org/DOI: 10.1145/3351095.3372873

Stable Diffusion. (n.d.). AI-driven image generation for artistic and academic applications. *Stable Diffusion.* https://stablediffusionweb.com

Stepka, M. (2022, February 21). Law bots: How AI is reshaping the legal profession. Business Law Today. *American Bar Association.* https://www.americanbar.org

Stokes, J. M., Yang, K., Swanson, K., Jin, W., Cubillos-Ruiz, A., Donghia, N. M., MacNair, C. R., French, S., Carfrae, L. A., Bloom-Ackermann, Z., Tran, V. M., Chiappino-Pepe, A., Badran, A. H., Andrews, I. W., Chory, E. J., Church, G. M., Brown, E. D., Jaakkola, T. S., Barzilay, R., & Collins, J. J. (2020). A Deep Learning Approach to Antibiotic Discovery. *Cell, 180*(4), 688–702. e13. DOI: 10.1016/j.cell.2020.01.021 PMID: 32084340

Surden, H. (2014). Machine learning and law. *Washington Law Review (Seattle, Wash.), 89*(1), 87–115.

Surden, H. (2014). Machine learning and law. *Washington Law Review (Seattle, Wash.), 89*(1), 87–115. https://digitalcommons.law.uw.edu/wlr/vol89/iss1/3

Takagi, Y., & Nishimoto, S. (2023). High-resolution image reconstruction with latent diffusion models from human brain activity. *Proceedings of the IEEE/CVF Conference on Computer Vision and Pattern Recognition (CVPR)*, 12542–12552. DOI: 10.1109/CVPR52729.2023.01389

Topol, E. J. (2019). High-performance medicine: The convergence of human and artificial intelligence. *Nature Medicine*, *25*(1), 44–56. DOI: 10.1038/s41591-018-0300-7 PMID: 30617339

Vesuvius Challenge. (n.d.). Using AI to read ancient carbonized scrolls. https://scrollprize.org

Woebot Health. (n.d.). AI-driven mental health support through cognitive behavioral therapy. https://woebothealth.com

Zhai, X. (2023). ChatGPT for education: Opportunities, challenges, and strategies. *Education and Information Technologies*, *28*, 10469–10477. DOI: 10.1007/s10639-023-11714-2

Zhao, X., Li, H., & Sun, W. (2022). Deep Learning for Climate Change Analysis: A Comprehensive Survey. *Environmental Modelling & Software*, *15*, 105348. DOI: 10.1016/j.envsoft.2022.105348

Chapter 7
AI and the Elderly Empowering Lifelong Learning

Marvin Espinoza
https://orcid.org/0009-0009-5662-8239
California State University, San Bernardino, USA

ABSTRACT

This chapter explores the transformative potential of Artificial Intelligence (AI) in enhancing lifelong learning and education for elderly populations. In response to rapid global aging, AI-driven technologies, including virtual assistants, adaptive learning systems, cognitive training applications, and immersive virtual reality, are increasingly vital for overcoming traditional educational barriers such as cognitive decline, digital literacy gaps, and mobility constraints. By enabling personalized learning, fostering social interaction, and supporting cognitive health, AI significantly contributes to active aging and greater independence among older adults. The chapter critically addresses ethical concerns surrounding privacy, data security, accessibility, and equity, advocating inclusive design practices and collaborative engagement among policy-makers, educators, and technology developers to ensure equitable access and empower elderly learners in dynamic educational environments.

INTRODUCTION

AI in Modern Society

Artificial intelligence (AI) has become an integral part of modern society, transforming numerous sectors including healthcare, education, communication, and daily living activities (Russell & Norvig, 2021). As technological advancements accelerate, there is increasing interest

DOI: 10.4018/979-8-3373-5097-4.ch007

in the application of AI to support the aging population, addressing challenges such as social isolation, cognitive decline, and physical limitations (Fang et al., 2023; Lee & Riek, 2021).

Specifically, the integration of AI-powered tools such as virtual companions, health monitoring systems, and assistive robotics has begun to significantly enhance quality of life, independence, and social connectedness among elderly individuals (Schulz et al., 2022).

However, these developments raise important ethical and practical considerations regarding autonomy, privacy, and equitable access to technology for seniors, necessitating careful examination as society navigates the implications of AI integration into elder care (Lee & Riek, 2021; Russell & Norvig, 2021).

Importance of Addressing the Elderly Demographic in Education and Learning

The global demographic shift toward an aging population underscores the importance of addressing educational and learning needs specific to elderly individuals, a rapidly growing yet often overlooked segment of society (United Nations, 2022).

Education among older adults promotes cognitive resilience, enhances social engagement, and significantly contributes to overall quality of life and independence (Findsen & Formosa, 2021). Recent technological advancements, particularly in artificial intelligence (AI), offer innovative pathways for supporting elderly learning and education by providing personalized, accessible, and adaptable instructional resources (Charness & Boot, 2022).

AI-driven technologies, such as intelligent tutoring systems, adaptive learning platforms, and virtual assistants, hold considerable potential to overcome traditional barriers faced by elderly learners, including sensory impairments, cognitive decline, and reduced mobility (Czaja et al., 2019).

Exploring these opportunities and addressing associated challenges, such as digital literacy and technology acceptance among seniors, are crucial steps in fostering inclusive, lifelong learning environments for aging populations (Charness & Boot, 2022; Findsen & Formosa, 2021).

Chapter Goals: Exploring AI's Potential to Enhance Lifelong Learning

Independence for Older Adults

The purpose of this chapter is to explore artificial intelligence's (AI) potential to enhance lifelong learning and independence for older adults by addressing the following goals:

1. **Analyze** current AI technologies and applications specifically designed to support educational engagement and independence among older adults.
2. **Identify** key benefits and potential challenges associated with integrating AI into lifelong learning programs for the elderly.
3. **Examine** practical examples and case studies demonstrating the successful implementation of AI tools that improve cognitive function, social interaction, and quality of life among seniors.
4. **Discuss** ethical considerations, including privacy, autonomy, and equitable access to AI-based learning technologies for older adults.

5. **Propose** recommendations for educators, policymakers, and technology developers aimed at effectively incorporating AI to foster inclusive, accessible, and empowering educational environments for aging populations.

The Aging Population and the Learning Landscape

The global demographic landscape is undergoing a significant transformation characterized by an unprecedented increase in the aging population. This shift is primarily driven by declining fertility rates and substantial improvements in healthcare, sanitation, and nutrition, leading to increased life expectancy worldwide (World Health Organization [WHO], 2022).

According to the WHO, the number of individuals aged 60 years and older is projected to rise from 1 billion in 2020 to 1.4 billion by 2030, and to 2.1 billion by 2050, with the most rapid growth occurring in low- and middle-income countries. This demographic trend presents both challenges and opportunities, necessitating comprehensive strategies to address the diverse needs of older adults.

Life expectancy, a key indicator of population health, has seen remarkable increases over the past decades. The Global Burden of Disease Study 2021 forecasts that global life expectancy will increase by 4.9 years for males and 4.2 years for females between 2022 and 2050, with the most significant gains anticipated in regions with historically lower life expectancies, such as sub-Saharan Africa (Institute for Health Metrics and Evaluation [IHME], 2024).

However, this overall improvement masks disparities across different populations and regions. For instance, while high-income countries have experienced substantial gains, the pace of increase has slowed in recent years, partly due to the rising prevalence of non-communicable diseases and lifestyle-related risk factors (Le Monde, 2024).

Moreover, the concept of "healthspan"—the period of life spent in good health—has gained attention alongside lifespan. Despite increases in life expectancy, many individuals spend a significant portion of their later years dealing with chronic illnesses and disabilities. A study published in JAMA Network Open highlights that the global healthspan-lifespan gap has widened over the last two decades, extending to an average of 9.6 years, indicating that people are living longer but not necessarily healthier lives (GBD 2021 Healthspan Collaborators, 2024). Addressing this gap is crucial for enhancing the quality of life among older adults.

The aging population also has profound implications for various sectors, including healthcare, labor markets, and education. In the United States, the number of individuals aged 65 and older is projected to increase from 58 million in 2022 to 82 million by 2050, representing a 47% increase (Population Reference Bureau [PRB], 2023). This demographic shift will place increased demand on healthcare systems, necessitate adjustments in workforce participation, and require the development of educational programs tailored to older adults. Innovations in technology, particularly artificial intelligence, offer promising avenues to support the independence and lifelong learning of the elderly, but also raise ethical considerations regarding accessibility and equity.

CHALLENGES FACED BY OLDER ADULTS IN ACCESSING TRADITIONAL EDUCATION AND SKILL-BUILDING OPPORTUNITIES

As global populations age, the imperative to provide inclusive educational opportunities for older adults becomes increasingly critical. However, numerous barriers hinder their participation in traditional education and skill-building programs. These challenges are multifaceted, encompassing technological, socioeconomic, psychological, and institutional dimensions.

Technological Barriers

The rapid digitization of educational platforms presents significant obstacles for older adults, many of whom did not grow up with digital technologies. Limited digital literacy and access to technology impede their ability to engage with online learning resources. A study by Martínez-Alcalá et al. (2021) highlighted that older adults often face difficulties in accepting and learning to use new technologies, which are essential for modern education delivery. Furthermore, inadequate infrastructure, such as unreliable internet connections and lack of access to digital devices, exacerbates these challenges, particularly in rural and underserved areas (Gruben et al., 2025).

Socioeconomic Constraints

Financial limitations are a prevalent barrier to education for older adults. Many live on fixed incomes, making it challenging to afford tuition fees, transportation, and educational materials. Additionally, socioeconomic status influences access to information about available educational opportunities and the ability to prioritize learning amidst other financial responsibilities (Kim et al., 2021).

Psychological and Health-Related Challenges

Age-related cognitive and physical changes can affect learning capacity and confidence. Declines in memory, vision, and hearing may hinder the ability to absorb and retain new information. Moreover, psychological factors such as fear of failure, low self-esteem, and anxiety about returning to a learning environment contribute to reluctance in pursuing education (Martínez-Alcalá et al., 2021). These factors are compounded by societal attitudes that may undervalue the importance of education for older adults, leading to decreased motivation and engagement.

Institutional and Structural Barriers

Educational institutions often lack programs tailored to the needs of older learners, including flexible scheduling, age-appropriate curricula, and supportive learning environments. The absence of targeted outreach and support services further alienates older adults from educational opportunities. Additionally, policies and practices within educational systems may inadvertently exclude older learners by prioritizing younger populations and not addressing the unique barriers faced by the elderly (Kim et al., 2021).

Cultural and Social Factors

Cultural perceptions and social norms can influence the participation of older adults in education. In some societies, there may be a belief that education is primarily for the young, leading to the stigmatization of older learners. This cultural bias can discourage older adults from seeking educational opportunities and diminish the perceived value of lifelong learning (Gruben et al., 2025).

Addressing these challenges requires a multifaceted approach that includes developing age-friendly educational programs, enhancing digital literacy among older adults, providing financial support, and fostering inclusive cultural attitudes towards lifelong learning. By implementing such strategies, societies can empower older adults to continue learning, thereby enhancing their quality of life and enabling them to contribute meaningfully to their communities.

Technological Literacy

In the digital age, technological literacy has become essential for full participation in society. For older adults, developing digital skills is crucial for accessing health information, maintaining social connections, and engaging in lifelong learning. However, many older individuals face challenges in acquiring and applying these skills, leading to a digital divide that can exacerbate existing inequalities.

Recent studies have highlighted the barriers older adults encounter in achieving digital literacy. These include cognitive decline, lack of confidence, limited access to digital devices, and insufficient training opportunities. For instance, a study by Gruben et al. (2025) found that older adults often rely on "warm experts," such as family members or community educators, to navigate digital technologies. The absence of such support can hinder their ability to learn and adapt to new digital environments.

Moreover, the COVID-19 pandemic has underscored the importance of digital literacy among older populations. As services and social interactions moved online, those lacking digital skills faced increased isolation and reduced access to essential resources. A study by Ye et al. (2024) demonstrated that older adults with higher digital literacy were better equipped to manage their health and maintain social connections during periods of lockdown.

To address these challenges, targeted interventions are necessary. Programs that offer personalized, hands-on training have shown promise in enhancing digital skills among older adults. For example, Camilleri et al. (2025) developed a cybersafety card game designed to teach older individuals about online security in an engaging and accessible manner. Participants reported increased confidence in handling digital threats after participating in the program.

Furthermore, integrating digital literacy education into community centers and healthcare settings can provide older adults with the support they need to develop these essential skills. By creating inclusive learning environments that consider the unique needs of older learners, society can empower this demographic to navigate the digital world effectively.

Physical and Cognitive Limitations Among Older Adults

As individuals age, they often encounter a range of physical and cognitive challenges that can significantly impact their daily lives and overall well-being. These limitations not only affect personal independence but also influence the ability to engage in social, recreational, and educational activities.

Physical Limitations

Physical impairments are common among older adults, with mobility issues being particularly prevalent. Studies indicate that approximately one-third of individuals aged 70 and most individuals aged 80 experience restrictions in mobility, affecting their ability to navigate their living environments safely (BMC Geriatrics, 2023). These limitations can lead to decreased participation in physical activities, further exacerbating health issues and reducing quality of life. Chronic conditions such as arthritis, cardiovascular diseases, and osteoporosis contribute to physical decline, making routine tasks more challenging.

Moreover, sensory impairments, including vision and hearing loss, can hinder communication and increase the risk of social isolation. Addressing these physical challenges requires comprehensive approaches that include medical management, physical therapy, and environmental modifications to support aging in place.

Cognitive Limitations

Cognitive decline is another significant concern in the aging population. Age-related cognitive changes can affect memory, attention, and executive functioning, impacting the ability to perform complex tasks and make informed decisions.

Research has identified several risk factors for cognitive impairment, including advanced age, lower educational attainment, and the presence of chronic health conditions (PMC11715083, 2024).

Interventions aimed at mitigating cognitive decline have shown promise. For instance, combined cognitive and physical training programs have been effective in improving memory and executive function among older adults.

A systematic review and meta-analysis found that such interventions significantly enhanced cognitive performance, suggesting that integrated approaches can be beneficial (LWW, 2025).

Implications and Strategies

The interplay between physical and cognitive limitations necessitates holistic strategies to support older adults. Implementing regular physical activity tailored to individual capabilities can help maintain mobility and cognitive health. Additionally, cognitive training exercises and social engagement activities can stimulate mental functions and reduce the risk of decline.

Healthcare providers and caregivers play a crucial role in identifying early signs of physical and cognitive impairments. Timely interventions, personalized care plans, and the use of assistive technologies can enhance the quality of life for older individuals. Moreover, creating age-friendly environments that accommodate physical limitations and promote cognitive engagement is essential for supporting healthy aging.

The Shift Toward Inclusive Learning Models

In recent decades, educational institutions worldwide have increasingly embraced inclusive learning models, reflecting a broader societal commitment to equity, diversity, and accessibility. Inclusive education emphasizes the provision of equitable learning opportunities for all learners, irrespective of their physical, cognitive, social, or emotional differences (Ainscow & Messiou, 2023).

Central to this shift is the recognition that traditional, one-size-fits-all educational models are insufficient to meet the diverse needs of contemporary learners, especially marginalized groups such as older adults, individuals with disabilities, and culturally diverse populations (Florian & Camedda, 2021).

Inclusive learning frameworks advocate for pedagogical strategies that foster active participation, collaborative engagement, and personalized learning experiences tailored to individual capabilities and interests (Loreman et al., 2022). A critical component of this transition involves leveraging technology and digital innovations to enhance accessibility and educational equity.

Advances such as artificial intelligence (AI), adaptive learning systems, and assistive technologies have demonstrated significant potential in accommodating diverse learning needs and facilitating inclusive educational environments (Gruben et al., 2025). AI-driven platforms, for instance, enable educators to deliver personalized instruction, monitor student progress closely, and provide targeted support, thus promoting greater inclusivity.

Moreover, the philosophical underpinnings of inclusive education emphasize a shift from deficit-based to strengths-based approaches. Rather than viewing learner differences as barriers, contemporary inclusive practices recognize these differences as valuable sources of diversity that enrich the educational landscape (Florian & Camedda, 2021).

This perspective is particularly relevant when addressing the learning needs of older adults, whose life experiences and existing knowledge can significantly enhance educational contexts.

However, the successful implementation of inclusive learning models is not without challenges. Institutional barriers, insufficient teacher training, limited resources, and deeply entrenched societal attitudes toward diversity and inclusion can hinder progress (Ainscow & Messiou, 2023).

Overcoming these barriers requires comprehensive policy reforms, professional development for educators, and ongoing commitment from educational leaders and stakeholders.

To sustain the momentum toward inclusive education, institutions must continuously evaluate and refine their practices, ensuring alignment with the evolving needs of diverse learner populations. Future educational frameworks should prioritize inclusivity not merely as an adjunct feature but as an integral principle guiding all pedagogical and organizational decisions.

Only through such intentional and persistent efforts can inclusive learning environments genuinely reflect and celebrate the diversity inherent within contemporary society.

Older adults face numerous barriers to accessing traditional education and skill-building opportunities. These include technological barriers, such as limited digital literacy and inadequate infrastructure; socioeconomic constraints, including financial limitations and resource scarcity; psychological and health-related challenges, notably cognitive and physical decline alongside anxiety about education; institutional barriers stemming from a lack of age-specific programs and supportive policies; and cultural and social factors that stigmatize educational engagement among the elderly.

Addressing these multifaceted barriers requires age-friendly educational programs, targeted digital literacy training, financial assistance, and a societal shift towards valuing lifelong learning for older adults.

Given these complex challenges, artificial intelligence (AI) emerges as a promising tool to bridge existing gaps and promote inclusive, lifelong learning environments. AI-driven technologies offer tailored solutions capable of accommodating the unique physical, cognitive, and technological needs of older learners.

The next section explores how AI's adaptive capabilities, personalized learning experiences, and accessible digital platforms can empower older adults, enhance their educational engagement, and ultimately support their independence and quality of life.

THE ROLE OF AI IN SUPPORTING LIFELONG LEARNING

Defining Lifelong Learning in Later Life

Lifelong learning encompasses the continuous, voluntary, and self-motivated pursuit of knowledge for personal or professional development throughout an individual's life. For older adults, this concept extends beyond traditional educational paradigms, emphasizing the importance of learning activities that promote autonomy, social inclusion, and overall well-being in later life stages (Flauzino et al., 2021).

The term "lifelong learning" gained prominence in the 1990s, influenced by globalization and the evolving demands of the knowledge economy. However, its application to older adults has since expanded, recognizing the unique educational needs and potential of this demographic (Flauzino et al., 2021).

This shift acknowledges that learning in later life is not merely an extension of adult education but a distinct phase with its own characteristics and benefits. Geragogy, the theory and practice of educating older adults, underscores the necessity of tailoring educational approaches to accommodate age-related changes in cognition, sensory perception, and physical abilities. This includes offering learning opportunities that are relevant, accessible, and responsive to the experiences and motivations of older learners (John, 1988).

Scope and Modalities of Lifelong Learning for Older Adults

The scope of lifelong learning for older adults is broad, encompassing formal, non-formal, and informal learning modalities.

- **Formal Learning**: Structured educational programs leading to certification or degrees, often provided by universities and colleges.
- **Non-Formal Learning**: Organized learning activities outside formal institutions, such as community education programs, workshops, and courses offered by senior centers.
- **Informal Learning**: Self-directed learning activities, including reading, online research, and experiential learning through hobbies and social interactions.

A scoping review by Flauzino et al. (2021) highlighted that non-formal learning opportunities are particularly prevalent among older adults, with 60% of identified lifelong learning activities falling into this category. These activities often occur within university contexts, community centers, and other accessible venues, emphasizing the importance of flexible and inclusive learning environments.

The benefits of engaging in lifelong learning for older adults are multifaceted. Participation in educational activities has been associated with improved cognitive function, enhanced psychological well-being, and increased social engagement (Narushima et al., 2018). Moreover, lifelong learning contributes to the development of skills necessary for navigating the digital landscape, thereby reducing the digital divide and promoting greater independence (Gruben et al., 2025).

In recognition of these benefits, initiatives such as the Age-Friendly University (AFU) Global Network have emerged, promoting the inclusion of older adults in higher education settings. The AFU framework encourages institutions to adapt their policies and practices to better serve the educational aspirations of older learners, fostering intergenerational learning and community engagement (AFU Global Network, 2023).

Lifelong learning for older adults is a dynamic and essential component of active aging. By embracing diverse learning modalities and addressing the unique needs of older learners, societies can empower this demographic to lead fulfilling, engaged, and independent lives.

Key AI Applications for Elderly Learners

As the global population ages, the integration of artificial intelligence (AI) into educational frameworks presents transformative opportunities to enhance lifelong learning for older adults. AI technologies are increasingly being leveraged to address the unique learning needs and preferences of this demographic, offering personalized and adaptive learning experiences that accommodate cognitive and physical variations.

Personalized Learning Platforms for Older Adults: Enhancing Lifelong Learning Through AI

The integration of artificial intelligence (AI) into educational frameworks has revolutionized the concept of personalized learning, offering tailored educational experiences that adapt to individual learner needs. For older adults, this technological advancement presents an opportunity to engage in lifelong learning that accommodates their unique cognitive, physical, and social requirements. Personalized learning platforms (PLPs) powered by AI can address the diverse challenges faced by elderly learners, including sensory impairments, mobility limitations, and varying levels of digital literacy. By delivering customized content and learning pathways, these platforms can enhance engagement, motivation, and overall learning outcomes for older adults.

AI-Driven Personalization in Learning

AI technologies facilitate personalization by analyzing learner data to adapt instructional methods, content, and pacing. This adaptability is particularly beneficial for older adults, who may experience age-related cognitive changes affecting memory, attention, and processing speed.

AI-driven PLPs can adjust the complexity of tasks, provide timely feedback, and offer repeated practice opportunities, thereby supporting cognitive function and knowledge retention (Bayly-Castañeda et al., 2024).

Moreover, these platforms can incorporate multimodal content delivery, utilizing text, audio, and visual aids to cater to varying sensory preferences and impairments. For instance, text-to-speech and speech-to-text functionalities can assist learners with visual or auditory challenges, ensuring that educational materials are accessible to all (Tang & Zhang, 2025). Such features not only enhance comprehension but also promote inclusivity in learning environments.

Enhancing Engagement and Motivation

Engagement and motivation are critical factors in the success of lifelong learning initiatives for older adults. AI-powered PLPs can enhance these aspects by providing content that aligns with learners' interests, goals, and prior experiences. By recognizing and integrating learners' backgrounds, these platforms can create meaningful and relevant learning experiences that resonate with older adults, thereby increasing their commitment to learning activities (Merino-Campos, 2025).

Furthermore, the incorporation of gamification elements, such as progress tracking, badges, and interactive challenges, can stimulate motivation and a sense of achievement. These features can transform the learning process into an engaging and enjoyable experience, encouraging sustained participation and continuous skill development.

Addressing Accessibility and Usability

Accessibility and usability are paramount in the design of PLPs for older adults. User-friendly interfaces with intuitive navigation, clear instructions, and customizable settings can mitigate the technological barriers often encountered by this demographic. Additionally, providing support resources, such as tutorials and help centers, can empower older learners to navigate digital platforms confidently (Wong et al., 2025).

AI can also play a role in real-time assistance, offering guidance and support as learners interact with the platform. For example, virtual assistants can answer questions, clarify instructions, and provide encouragement, thereby reducing frustration and enhancing the overall learning experience.

Implications for Lifelong Learning

The deployment of AI-driven PLPs holds significant implications for lifelong learning among older adults. By accommodating individual learning needs and preferences, these platforms can facilitate continuous education, skill development, and personal growth. This, in turn, can contribute to improved cognitive health, social engagement, and overall quality of life for older individuals.

Moreover, the scalability of PLPs allows for widespread access to educational resources, bridging geographical and socioeconomic gaps. This democratization of learning opportunities ensures that older adults, regardless of their circumstances, can participate in and benefit from lifelong learning initiatives.

AI-powered personalized learning platforms represent a transformative approach to lifelong learning for older adults. By delivering tailored, accessible, and engaging educational experiences, these platforms can address the unique challenges faced by elderly learners and support their continued intellectual and personal development.

As technology continues to evolve, it is imperative to prioritize the inclusion of older adults in digital learning landscapes, ensuring that they are equipped to thrive in an increasingly digital world.

Adaptive Content Delivery Tailored to Cognitive and Physical Abilities in Lifelong Learning for Older Adults

As global populations age, the imperative to provide inclusive educational opportunities for older adults becomes increasingly critical. However, numerous barriers hinder their participation in traditional education and skill-building programs. These challenges are multifaceted, encompassing technological, socioeconomic, psychological, and institutional dimensions.

Technological Barriers

The rapid digitization of educational platforms presents significant obstacles for older adults, many of whom did not grow up with digital technologies. Limited digital literacy and access to technology impede their ability to engage with online learning resources. A study by Martínez-Alcalá et al. (2021) highlighted that older adults often face difficulties in accepting and learning to use new technologies, which are essential for modern education delivery. Furthermore, inadequate infrastructure, such as unreliable internet connections and lack of access to digital devices, exacerbates these challenges, particularly in rural and underserved areas (Gruben et al., 2025).

Socioeconomic Constraints

Financial limitations are a prevalent barrier to education for older adults. Many live on fixed incomes, making it challenging to afford tuition fees, transportation, and educational materials. Additionally, socioeconomic status influences access to information about available educational opportunities and the ability to prioritize learning amidst other financial responsibilities (Kim et al., 2021).

Psychological and Health-Related Challenges

Age-related cognitive and physical changes can affect learning capacity and confidence. Declines in memory, vision, and hearing may hinder the ability to absorb and retain new information. Moreover, psychological factors such as fear of failure, low self-esteem, and anxiety about returning to a learning environment contribute to reluctance in pursuing education (Martínez-Alcalá et al., 2021). These factors are compounded by societal attitudes that may undervalue the importance of education for older adults, leading to decreased motivation and engagement.

Institutional and Structural Barriers

Educational institutions often lack programs tailored to the needs of older learners, including flexible scheduling, age-appropriate curricula, and supportive learning environments. The absence of targeted outreach and support services further alienates older adults from educational opportunities. Additionally, policies and practices within educational systems may inadvertently exclude older learners by prioritizing younger populations and not addressing the unique barriers faced by the elderly (Kim et al., 2021).

Cultural and Social Factors

Cultural perceptions and social norms can influence the participation of older adults in education. In some societies, there may be a belief that education is primarily for the young, leading to the stigmatization of older learners. This cultural bias can discourage older adults from seeking educational opportunities and diminish the perceived value of lifelong learning (Gruben et al., 2025).

Addressing these challenges requires a multifaceted approach that includes developing age-friendly educational programs, enhancing digital literacy among older adults, providing financial support, and fostering inclusive cultural attitudes towards lifelong learning. By implementing such strategies, societies can empower older adults to continue learning, thereby enhancing their quality of life and enabling them to contribute meaningfully to their communities.

Language and Translation Tools for Diverse Populations in Lifelong Learning for Older Adults

In an increasingly globalized and multicultural society, language barriers can pose significant challenges to lifelong learning, particularly for older adults. As individuals age, cognitive and sensory changes may compound the difficulties associated with acquiring new languages or engaging with content in non-native tongues.

To address these challenges, artificial intelligence (AI)-driven language and translation tools have emerged as pivotal resources in facilitating inclusive and accessible learning environments for diverse elderly populations. These technologies not only bridge linguistic gaps but also empower older learners to participate actively in educational pursuits, thereby enhancing their cognitive health and social integration.

The Role of AI in Language Translation for Older Learners

AI-powered translation tools, such as machine translation applications and real-time interpretation devices, have revolutionized the way language barriers are addressed in educational contexts. These tools utilize advanced algorithms and natural language processing to provide instantaneous translations, enabling older adults to access learning materials in their preferred languages.

For instance, applications like Google Translate and other AI-based platforms offer real-time translation services that can be instrumental in classroom settings or online learning environments (Kreienbrinck et al., 2025).

Moreover, AI-driven translation tools can adapt to the specific needs of older learners by incorporating features such as simplified language options, speech-to-text capabilities, and user-friendly interfaces. These adaptations are crucial in accommodating age-related changes in vision, hearing, and cognitive processing, thereby ensuring that older adults can engage with educational content effectively and comfortably.

Enhancing Cognitive Engagement Through Multilingual Learning

Engaging in multilingual learning has been associated with numerous cognitive benefits for older adults, including improved memory, attention, and executive functioning. AI translation tools facilitate this engagement by lowering the barriers to accessing foreign language materials and enabling learners to explore new linguistic landscapes without the intimidation of traditional language learning methods. Ayyaz (2025) highlights that AI translation tools not only assist in vocabulary acquisition and grammar comprehension but also provide contextual support that enhances overall language proficiency.

Furthermore, the use of AI in language learning allows for personalized learning experiences, where content can be tailored to the individual's proficiency level, learning pace, and areas of interest. This personalization is particularly beneficial for older adults, who may have diverse educational backgrounds and varying degrees of familiarity with technology. By aligning learning materials with the learner's unique profile, AI translation tools can foster a more engaging and effective educational experience.

Addressing Cultural and Social Inclusion

Beyond linguistic translation, AI tools play a significant role in promoting cultural and social inclusion among older learners. By providing access to a wide array of multicultural content, these tools enable learners to explore and appreciate diverse perspectives, thereby fostering empathy and cross-cultural understanding. This exposure is particularly valuable in multicultural societies, where older adults may interact with individuals from various cultural backgrounds. AI translation tools can thus serve as bridges that connect learners to broader communities, enhancing social cohesion and reducing feelings of isolation.

Moreover, the integration of AI translation tools in community education programs can encourage participation among older adults who might otherwise be deterred by language barriers. By creating inclusive learning environments that accommodate linguistic diversity, educational institutions can attract a broader demographic of learners and promote lifelong learning as a universally accessible endeavor.

Challenges and Considerations

While AI translation tools offer numerous benefits, it is essential to address potential challenges associated with their use among older adults. Issues such as the accuracy of translations, especially in conveying nuanced or context-specific information, can impact the effectiveness of these tools.

Additionally, older learners may require training and support to navigate these technologies confidently. Ensuring that AI translation tools are designed with intuitive interfaces and providing user education can mitigate these challenges and enhance user adoption.

Privacy and data security are also pertinent concerns, particularly when AI tools collect and process personal information. Developers and educators must prioritize ethical considerations and implement robust safeguards to protect user data, thereby building trust among older learners and encouraging the use of AI technologies in educational settings.

AI-driven language and translation tools hold significant promise in advancing lifelong learning opportunities for older adults. By addressing linguistic barriers, enhancing cognitive engagement, and promoting cultural inclusion, these technologies can empower older learners to pursue educational goals and participate actively in diverse learning communities.

To maximize the benefits of AI translation tools, it is imperative to consider the unique needs of older adults, provide adequate support and training, and uphold ethical standards in technology implementation. Through thoughtful integration of AI in educational frameworks, we can foster an inclusive and accessible learning environment that supports the lifelong learning journey of older adults.

Language and Translation Tools for Diverse Populations in Lifelong Learning for Older Adults

In an increasingly globalized and multicultural society, language barriers can pose significant challenges to lifelong learning, particularly for older adults. As individuals age, cognitive and sensory changes may compound the difficulties associated with acquiring new languages or engaging with content in non-native tongues (Ayyaz, 2025).

To address these challenges, artificial intelligence (AI)-driven language and translation tools have emerged as pivotal resources in facilitating inclusive and accessible learning environments for diverse elderly populations (Kreienbrinck et al., 2025). These technologies not only bridge linguistic gaps but also empower older learners to participate actively in educational pursuits, thereby enhancing their cognitive health and social integration (Tang & Zhang, 2025).

The Role of AI in Language Translation for Older Learners

AI-powered translation tools, such as machine translation applications and real-time interpretation devices, have revolutionized the way language barriers are addressed in educational contexts. These tools utilize advanced algorithms and natural language processing to provide instantaneous translations, enabling older adults to access learning materials in their preferred languages (Kreienbrinck et al., 2025).

Applications such as Google Translate and other AI-based platforms offer real-time translation services that can be instrumental in classroom settings or online learning environments (Ayyaz, 2025).

Moreover, AI-driven translation tools can adapt to the specific needs of older learners by incorporating features such as simplified language options, speech-to-text capabilities, and user-friendly interfaces (Tang & Zhang, 2025). These adaptations are crucial in accommodating age-related changes in vision, hearing, and cognitive processing, thereby ensuring that older adults can engage with educational content effectively and comfortably (Kreienbrinck et al., 2025).

Enhancing Cognitive Engagement Through Multilingual Learning

Engaging in multilingual learning has been associated with numerous cognitive benefits for older adults, including improved memory, attention, and executive functioning (Ayyaz, 2025). AI translation tools facilitate this engagement by lowering the barriers to accessing foreign language materials and enabling learners to explore new linguistic landscapes without the intimidation of traditional language learning methods (Tang & Zhang, 2025). AI translation tools assist in vocabulary acquisition and grammar comprehension, and also provide contextual support that enhances overall language proficiency (Kreienbrinck et al., 2025).

Furthermore, the use of AI in language learning allows for personalized learning experiences, where content can be tailored to the individual's proficiency level, learning pace, and areas of interest (Tang & Zhang, 2025). This personalization is particularly beneficial for older adults, who may have diverse educational backgrounds and varying degrees of familiarity with technology.

By aligning learning materials with the learner's unique profile, AI translation tools can foster a more engaging and effective educational experience (Ayyaz, 2025).

Addressing Cultural and Social Inclusion

Beyond linguistic translation, AI tools play a significant role in promoting cultural and social inclusion among older learners. By providing access to a wide array of multicultural content, these tools enable learners to explore and appreciate diverse perspectives, thereby fostering empathy and cross-cultural understanding (Kreienbrinck et al., 2025).

This exposure is particularly valuable in multicultural societies, where older adults may interact with individuals from various cultural backgrounds. AI translation tools thus serve as bridges that connect learners to broader communities, enhancing social cohesion and reducing feelings of isolation (Tang & Zhang, 2025).

Moreover, the integration of AI translation tools in community education programs can encourage participation among older adults who might otherwise be deterred by language barriers. By creating inclusive learning environments that accommodate linguistic diversity, educational institutions can attract a broader demographic of learners and promote lifelong learning as a universally accessible endeavor (Ayyaz, 2025).

Challenges and Considerations

While AI translation tools offer numerous benefits, it is essential to address potential challenges associated with their use among older adults. Issues such as the accuracy of translations, especially in conveying nuanced or context-specific information, can impact the effectiveness of these tools (Kreienbrinck et al., 2025). Additionally, older learners may require training and support to navigate these technologies confidently.

Ensuring that AI translation tools are designed with intuitive interfaces and providing user education can mitigate these challenges and enhance user adoption (Tang & Zhang, 2025).

Privacy and data security are also pertinent concerns, particularly when AI tools collect and process personal information. Developers and educators must prioritize ethical considerations and implement robust safeguards to protect user data, thereby building trust among older learners and encouraging the use of AI technologies in educational settings (Kreienbrinck et al., 2025).

AI-driven language and translation tools hold significant promise in advancing lifelong learning opportunities for older adults. By addressing linguistic barriers, enhancing cognitive engagement, and promoting cultural inclusion, these technologies can empower older learners to pursue educational goals and participate actively in diverse learning communities.

To maximize the benefits of AI translation tools, it is imperative to consider the unique needs of older adults, provide adequate support and training, and uphold ethical standards in technology implementation. Through thoughtful integration of AI in educational frameworks, we can foster an inclusive and accessible learning environment that supports the lifelong learning journey of older adults (Ayyaz, 2025; Tang & Zhang, 2025).

AI-Driven Accessibility Features in Lifelong Learning for Older Adults

As the global population ages, ensuring equitable access to lifelong learning opportunities for older adults becomes increasingly vital. Artificial intelligence (AI)–driven accessibility features—such as voice assistants, text-to-speech (TTS), and speech-to-text (STT) tools—offer promising solutions to bridge the digital divide and support older learners with diverse cognitive and physical abilities. These technologies can enhance engagement, foster autonomy, and promote inclusive educational environments tailored to the unique needs of the elderly population.

Voice Assistants: Enhancing Interaction and Independence

Voice assistants (VAs), including Amazon Alexa, Google Assistant, and Apple Siri, have emerged as valuable tools for older adults, facilitating hands-free interaction with digital devices and services. Their natural language processing capabilities enable users to perform tasks such as accessing information, setting reminders, and controlling smart home devices through simple voice commands.

This functionality is particularly beneficial for individuals with mobility limitations or visual impairments, as it reduces reliance on traditional input methods like keyboards or touchscreens (Jakob et al., 2025).

Research indicates that older adults perceive VAs as user-friendly and appreciate their potential to support daily activities and enhance quality of life. A study by Jakob et al. (2025) found that participants aged 55 and above reported high levels of satisfaction with VA usability, citing ease of learning and integration into daily routines.

Moreover, VAs can serve as companions, alleviating feelings of loneliness and social isolation by providing conversational interactions and entertainment options (Wong et al., 2025).

Text-to-Speech and Speech-to-Text Tools: Bridging Communication Gaps

TTS and STT technologies play a crucial role in facilitating communication and information access for older learners. TTS systems convert written text into spoken words, aiding individuals with visual impairments or reading difficulties in consuming written content. Conversely, STT tools transcribe spoken language into text, assisting those with hearing impairments or speech difficulties in participating in conversations and educational activities.

These AI-driven tools can be integrated into various platforms, including e-learning applications, virtual classrooms, and communication devices, to create more inclusive learning environments.

For instance, Apple's "Live Speech" feature enables users to type messages that are then spoken aloud during phone calls, supporting individuals who have lost their ability to speak (Apple, 2023). Such innovations empower older adults to engage more fully in educational and social contexts, fostering a sense of autonomy and inclusion.

Addressing Barriers to Adoption

Despite the potential benefits of AI-driven accessibility features, several barriers may hinder their adoption among older adults. Concerns about privacy, data security, and the complexity of new technologies can deter individuals from embracing these tools. Additionally, a lack of digital literacy and limited exposure to AI applications may contribute to apprehension and resistance (Wong et al., 2025).

To overcome these challenges, it is essential to implement user-centered design principles that prioritize the needs and preferences of older users. Providing comprehensive training, simplifying user interfaces, and ensuring transparent data practices can enhance trust and usability. Engaging older adults in the development and testing of AI technologies can also lead to more effective and acceptable solutions (Jakob et al., 2025).

Implications for Lifelong Learning

The integration of AI-driven accessibility features into educational frameworks holds significant promise for promoting lifelong learning among older adults. By mitigating physical and cognitive barriers, these technologies can facilitate continuous skill development, social engagement, and personal fulfillment. Moreover, they align with broader goals of inclusivity and equity in education, ensuring that aging populations are not left behind in the digital age.

Future initiatives should focus on expanding access to AI tools, fostering digital literacy, and creating supportive learning environments that accommodate the diverse needs of older learners. Collaborative efforts among educators, technologists, policymakers, and older adults themselves are vital to realizing the full potential of AI in enhancing lifelong learning opportunities for the elderly.

The integration of artificial intelligence (AI) into educational frameworks significantly enhances lifelong learning opportunities for older adults, addressing their unique cognitive, physical, and social needs.

AI-driven personalized learning platforms offer tailored educational experiences that adapt instructional methods and content delivery, improving engagement and cognitive functioning. Additionally, adaptive content delivery accommodates age-related technological, socioeconomic, psychological, and institutional barriers by customizing learning materials to individual abilities.

Language and translation tools powered by AI bridge linguistic gaps, enhancing multicultural engagement and cognitive health. Furthermore, AI-driven accessibility features, such as voice assistants and text-to-speech or speech-to-text technologies, provide critical support, overcoming communication and mobility challenges. Collectively, these AI applications foster inclusive educational environments, promoting autonomy, social integration, and active aging for elderly learners.

Building upon the transformative role of AI-driven platforms in promoting inclusive lifelong learning environments, it is essential to examine how artificial intelligence further supports cognitive health and memory retention among older adults. Cognitive health is a critical component of active aging, and AI offers specialized tools designed explicitly for brain training, early detection of cognitive decline, and ongoing cognitive stimulation.

These advanced technologies, including AI-based diagnostic tools for early identification of conditions like dementia and Alzheimer's disease, actively engage elderly learners, motivating them through interactive, cognitively enriching experiences. Exploring practical case studies will illustrate tangible benefits, highlighting how older individuals effectively utilize AI cognitive tools to maintain mental acuity, autonomy, and enhanced quality of life.

COGNITIVE SUPPORT THROUGH AI

AI Applications for Cognitive Health and Memory Retention in Older Adults

The global demographic shift towards an aging population has intensified the focus on maintaining cognitive health and memory retention among older adults. Artificial intelligence (AI) has emerged as a transformative tool in this domain, offering innovative solutions to support cognitive functions and promote lifelong learning.

This section explores AI-driven applications designed to enhance cognitive health and memory retention in older adults, emphasizing their role in sustaining mental agility and independence.

AI-Powered Cognitive Training Programs

AI-driven cognitive training programs have gained prominence as effective interventions for mitigating age-related cognitive decline. These programs utilize machine learning algorithms to personalize training regimens, adapting to individual performance levels and cognitive needs.

For instance, the "Smart Brain" application was developed to provide comprehensive cognitive training for individuals with mild cognitive impairment (MCI) or dementia, demonstrating the potential of AI in creating effective, individualized interventions (Kim et al., 2024). Such applications offer a range of exercises targeting memory, attention, and problem-solving skills, thereby fostering neuroplasticity and cognitive resilience.

Moreover, AI facilitates the monitoring of user progress, enabling real-time adjustments to training difficulty and content. This dynamic feedback loop ensures that users remain engaged and challenged, optimizing the efficacy of cognitive interventions. Studies have shown that consistent engagement with AI-based cognitive training can lead to significant improvements in cognitive performance among older adults (Kim et al., 2024).

Virtual Reality and Immersive Technologies

The integration of AI with virtual reality (VR) technologies has opened new avenues for cognitive rehabilitation. Immersive VR environments, powered by AI algorithms, provide interactive and stimulating experiences that can enhance memory recall and cognitive function.

For example, a cognitive rehabilitation program leveraging generative AI and VR was developed to evoke personal memories in dementia patients, demonstrating the potential of immersive technologies in cognitive therapy (Kim et al., 2024).

These VR-based interventions offer multisensory engagement, which is particularly beneficial for older adults experiencing cognitive decline. By simulating real-life scenarios and environments, VR applications can help users practice daily tasks, improve spatial navigation, and reinforce memory through experiential learning.

The adaptability of AI ensures that these experiences are tailored to individual preferences and cognitive abilities, enhancing user engagement and therapeutic outcomes.

AI-Driven Monitoring and Early Detection

Beyond training and rehabilitation, AI plays a crucial role in the early detection and monitoring of cognitive decline. Advanced AI algorithms can analyze patterns in user behavior, speech, and interaction to identify subtle changes indicative of cognitive impairment. For instance, AI-powered conversational agents have been developed to engage older adults in dialogue, simultaneously assessing linguistic and cognitive markers to detect early signs of conditions like Alzheimer's disease (Kim et al., 2024).

Early detection facilitated by AI allows for timely interventions, which are critical in slowing the progression of cognitive disorders. Furthermore, continuous monitoring through AI applications provides valuable data for healthcare providers, enabling personalized care plans and informed decision-making. The non-invasive nature of these technologies also ensures user comfort and compliance, essential factors in long-term cognitive health management.

Challenges and Considerations

While AI applications offer significant benefits, several challenges must be addressed to maximize their effectiveness. Accessibility remains a concern, as older adults may face barriers related to technology literacy, affordability, and physical limitations. Ensuring user-friendly interfaces and providing adequate support and training are essential to promote adoption and sustained use.

Privacy and data security are also paramount, given the sensitive nature of health-related information collected by AI applications. Developers and providers must implement robust safeguards to protect user data and maintain trust. Additionally, ongoing research and validation are necessary to establish the efficacy and safety of AI interventions, ensuring they meet clinical standards and effectively address the diverse needs of the older adult population.

AI applications represent a promising frontier in supporting cognitive health and memory retention among older adults. Through personalized training programs, immersive technologies, and advanced monitoring capabilities, AI offers tools to enhance cognitive function, promote independence, and improve quality of life. Addressing the challenges associated with accessibility, privacy, and validation will be critical in realizing the full potential of AI in this context.

As technology continues to evolve, interdisciplinary collaboration among developers, healthcare providers, and policymakers will be essential to create inclusive and effective AI-driven solutions for cognitive health in aging populations.

AI-Driven Brain-Training Programs for Cognitive Health in Older Adults

As the global population ages, maintaining cognitive health in older adults has become increasingly critical. Artificial intelligence (AI)-driven brain-training programs have emerged as innovative tools to support cognitive functions such as memory, attention, and executive functioning in this demographic. These programs leverage adaptive algorithms and personalized content to provide targeted cognitive exercises, aiming to enhance mental agility and delay cognitive decline (Belleville & Hudon, 2022).

Personalized Cognitive Training Through AI

AI-powered cognitive training programs utilize machine learning algorithms to tailor exercises to an individual's cognitive profile, adjusting difficulty levels in real-time based on user performance (Lehtonen et al., 2023). This personalization ensures users are consistently challenged, promoting neuroplasticity and cognitive resilience.

For instance, recent studies have demonstrated the efficacy of personalized AI-driven applications in providing comprehensive cognitive training specifically designed for older adults experiencing mild cognitive impairment (MCI) or early-stage dementia (Kim et al., 2024). Such applications offer various exercises targeting essential cognitive domains including memory enhancement, attention improvement, and problem-solving skill development (Tsolaki et al., 2021).

Moreover, AI facilitates the ongoing monitoring of user progress, enabling real-time adjustments to training complexity and content. This dynamic feedback mechanism ensures that users remain engaged, challenged, and motivated, thereby optimizing the effectiveness of cognitive interventions (Lehtonen et al., 2023).

Empirical research highlights that sustained engagement with AI-based cognitive training can lead to measurable improvements in cognitive performance and delay cognitive deterioration among older adults (Belleville & Hudon, 2022).

Integration with Virtual Reality and Immersive Technologies

The integration of AI with virtual reality (VR) technologies has expanded the scope of cognitive rehabilitation programs. Immersive VR environments, enhanced by AI-driven algorithms, provide interactive and stimulating experiences capable of enhancing memory recall and overall cognitive function in older adults (Qiu et al., 2022).

For example, VR-based cognitive rehabilitation programs designed using generative AI have been effective in evoking personal memories and facilitating emotional connections, proving particularly beneficial for individuals with Alzheimer's disease and other forms of dementia (Kim et al., 2024; Qiu et al., 2022).

These VR-based interventions offer multisensory engagement, providing older adults with opportunities to practice daily tasks, improve spatial navigation, and reinforce memory through experiential learning scenarios (Tsolaki et al., 2021). The adaptability of AI ensures experiences are tailored precisely to individual preferences and cognitive capacities, significantly enhancing user engagement and therapeutic outcomes (Qiu et al., 2022).

AI-Driven Monitoring and Early Detection

Beyond cognitive training, AI plays a critical role in the early detection and continuous monitoring of cognitive decline. Advanced AI systems analyze patterns in user behavior, speech, and interaction metrics to identify subtle cognitive changes indicative of early impairment (Jiang et al., 2023). For instance, conversational agents and chatbots powered by AI have been developed to interact with older adults, simultaneously assessing linguistic and cognitive markers to identify early symptoms associated with Alzheimer's disease or related dementias (Jiang et al., 2023; Tsolaki et al., 2021).

Early detection facilitated by AI allows for timely interventions that are crucial in slowing cognitive deterioration (Jiang et al., 2023). Additionally, continuous monitoring via AI applications provides healthcare providers with valuable real-time data, enabling personalized care plans and informed decision-making (Belleville & Hudon, 2022). The non-invasive and user-friendly nature of these AI technologies further ensures greater user comfort and adherence, essential for sustained cognitive health management (Lehtonen et al., 2023).

Challenges and Considerations

Despite the substantial benefits provided by AI-driven cognitive training programs, several challenges must be addressed to maximize their effectiveness and acceptance among older populations. Accessibility remains a primary concern, as older adults frequently encounter barriers related to digital literacy, financial constraints, and physical limitations that restrict technology use (Tsolaki et al., 2021). Ensuring intuitive user interfaces, comprehensive training, and ongoing user support are critical to promoting adoption and sustained engagement (Qiu et al., 2022).

Moreover, privacy and data security present significant challenges due to the sensitive nature of health data collected by these AI applications. Thus, developers and providers must establish robust safeguards to protect user information and maintain user trust (Jiang et al., 2023).

Furthermore, continued research and rigorous validation studies are necessary to confirm the clinical efficacy, safety, and practicality of AI interventions for diverse older adult populations (Kim et al., 2024; Lehtonen et al., 2023).

AI-driven brain-training programs represent a promising frontier for supporting cognitive health and memory retention in older adults. Through personalized training regimens, immersive VR experiences, and advanced AI-based monitoring capabilities, these technologies enhance cognitive function, promote independence, and improve quality of life.

Addressing the current challenges associated with accessibility, privacy, and rigorous validation will be critical in fully realizing the potential of AI for cognitive health among the elderly. Ongoing interdisciplinary collaboration among researchers, healthcare professionals, policymakers, and technology developers will be essential to creating inclusive and effective cognitive health interventions through artificial intelligence.

Early Detection of Cognitive Decline Through AI Diagnostic Tools

The rising prevalence of cognitive decline, including dementia and Alzheimer's disease, poses significant public health challenges, especially within aging populations worldwide (Jiang et al., 2023). Early detection of cognitive impairment is essential for timely intervention, potentially delaying progression and improving quality of life for affected individuals.

Artificial intelligence (AI) diagnostic tools have emerged as promising approaches for the early identification and monitoring of cognitive decline, offering enhanced accuracy, non-invasive assessment, and individualized tracking of cognitive health (Jiang et al., 2023; Lee et al., 2022).

AI-Powered Diagnostic Technologies and Approaches

AI diagnostic technologies employ advanced machine learning algorithms to analyze large-scale datasets, enabling early identification of subtle cognitive changes indicative of dementia and Alzheimer's disease (Ezzat et al., 2021).

For instance, AI techniques such as deep learning and convolutional neural networks (CNNs) have demonstrated substantial effectiveness in interpreting neuroimaging data, such as magnetic resonance imaging (MRI) and positron emission tomography (PET) scans, to detect early biomarkers of Alzheimer's disease before clinical symptoms fully manifest (Tanveer et al., 2021).

A notable advancement in AI diagnostics is the integration of multimodal approaches, which combine clinical data, imaging studies, genetic markers, and cognitive assessment results to enhance predictive accuracy (Lee et al., 2022). Studies indicate that these integrated AI models significantly outperform traditional diagnostic methods, achieving higher sensitivity and specificity in identifying early-stage dementia (Jiang et al., 2023; Ezzat et al., 2021). For instance, a recent study by Lee et al. (2022) demonstrated that multimodal AI models utilizing neuroimaging, cognitive testing scores, and genetic information can accurately predict Alzheimer's onset up to several years before conventional diagnosis, thereby allowing for early, proactive clinical management.

AI-Driven Cognitive and Linguistic Screening Tools

Another promising area in AI diagnostics involves linguistic and cognitive screening tools designed to detect subtle cognitive deficits through speech analysis and interactive assessments. AI-driven conversational agents and speech analysis software analyze linguistic patterns, speech coherence, and verbal fluency to detect early cognitive impairment indicators (Robin et al., 2023).

Recent research has illustrated that individuals with early-stage dementia exhibit distinctive linguistic markers, including reduced vocabulary richness, slower speech rates, and increased hesitations or pauses, all of which AI algorithms can effectively identify (Robin et al., 2023; Jiang et al., 2023).

Moreover, smartphone applications and wearable devices employing AI algorithms offer practical, continuous cognitive assessment solutions in everyday settings. These tools monitor daily behaviors, speech patterns, gait, and fine motor skills, capturing data that traditional clinical assessments might miss (Tanveer et al., 2021). Such continuous, real-time monitoring facilitates earlier detection of cognitive impairment, enabling timely intervention strategies and individualized treatment plans tailored to patient needs (Lee et al., 2022).

Benefits and Clinical Implications of Early Detection via AI

The primary benefit of AI-driven early detection of cognitive decline lies in its potential for earlier and more accurate diagnosis, enabling healthcare professionals to initiate interventions at stages when cognitive functions may still be preserved or minimally impacted (Ezzat et al., 2021). Early intervention can significantly enhance treatment outcomes, slow disease progression, and improve overall patient and caregiver well-being (Robin et al., 2023).

AI diagnostic tools also provide essential decision-support frameworks for clinicians, complementing traditional assessment methods and reducing diagnostic uncertainty (Lee et al., 2022). By identifying high-risk individuals earlier, healthcare systems can allocate resources more efficiently, reduce healthcare burdens, and improve long-term care planning and support services (Tanveer et al., 2021).

Challenges and Future Directions

Despite significant advancements, AI diagnostic tools face challenges related to data privacy, ethical concerns, and the need for extensive validation across diverse populations. Protecting patient confidentiality and ensuring secure data handling is paramount to maintaining user trust and compliance (Jiang et al., 2023). Additionally, concerns remain regarding biases in AI algorithms, particularly if training datasets lack demographic diversity, potentially resulting in disparities in diagnostic accuracy across different populations (Robin et al., 2023).

Future research should prioritize expanding dataset diversity, developing robust privacy frameworks, and validating AI diagnostic models in large-scale, longitudinal clinical trials. Integrating AI diagnostic tools into clinical practice requires collaborative interdisciplinary efforts, bringing together AI specialists, neuroscientists, healthcare providers, and policymakers to ensure equitable and ethical deployment of these advanced technologies (Ezzat et al., 2021; Lee et al., 2022).

AI diagnostic tools represent a transformative advancement in the early detection and monitoring of cognitive decline. Leveraging sophisticated machine learning algorithms and multimodal data integration, these tools offer enhanced accuracy, earlier intervention opportunities, and personalized care strategies. Addressing challenges related to privacy, ethical considerations, and algorithmic bias will be crucial to fully realize the benefits of AI technologies in cognitive healthcare.

Continued interdisciplinary collaboration and robust validation research will ensure that AI-driven early detection tools effectively support aging populations, ultimately enhancing cognitive health outcomes and improving quality of life for affected individuals and their families.

AI Tools for Enhancing Engagement and Interaction in Learning

Artificial Intelligence (AI) has emerged as a transformative force in education, offering innovative tools that enhance learner engagement and interaction. By personalizing learning experiences, providing real-time feedback, and fostering collaborative environments, AI tools have the potential to revolutionize the educational landscape.

Personalized Learning Experiences

AI-driven platforms can tailor educational content to individual learner needs, preferences, and progress. Adaptive learning systems analyze student performance data to adjust the difficulty and pacing of instructional materials, thereby maintaining optimal challenge levels and sustaining engagement (Yaseen et al., 2025). Such personalization ensures that learners remain motivated and invested in their educational journey.

Real-Time Feedback and Support

Immediate feedback is crucial for effective learning. AI tools can provide instant responses to student inputs, clarifying misconceptions and reinforcing understanding. For instance, AI-powered chatbots can answer queries, guide problem-solving processes, and offer hints, thereby facilitating continuous interaction and keeping learners engaged (Chen et al., 2023). This immediacy helps in maintaining the flow of learning and reduces frustration associated with delayed feedback.

Fostering Collaborative Learning

AI technologies can also promote collaboration among learners. By facilitating group discussions, peer assessments, and collaborative projects, AI tools encourage social interaction and collective problem-solving. Such collaborative environments not only enhance engagement but also develop critical soft skills like communication and teamwork (Wlodarski et al., 2025).

Gamification and Motivation

Incorporating game elements into learning through AI can significantly boost motivation and engagement. Gamified AI platforms use points, badges, leaderboards, and challenges to create an interactive and competitive learning atmosphere. This approach has been shown to increase learner participation and persistence, making the educational process more enjoyable and effective (McLaren et al., 2023).

Enhancing Accessibility and Inclusivity

AI tools can make learning more accessible to diverse populations, including individuals with disabilities. Features like speech-to-text, text-to-speech, and language translation enable learners with varying needs to engage with content effectively. Such inclusivity ensures that all students have the opportunity to participate fully in the learning process (Breazeal et al., 2024).

Challenges and Considerations

Despite the benefits, integrating AI into education poses challenges. Concerns about data privacy, algorithmic bias, and the potential for reduced human interaction must be addressed. Ensuring that AI tools are designed and implemented ethically is essential to maintain trust and effectiveness in educational settings (Hmelo-Silver et al., 2023).

AI tools offer promising avenues for enhancing engagement and interaction in learning. By personalizing experiences, providing immediate support, fostering collaboration, and increasing accessibility, AI can create dynamic and inclusive educational environments. Addressing the associated challenges will be critical to fully realizing the potential of AI in education.

Case Studies: Examples of Elderly Users Benefiting from AI Cognitive Tools

Artificial intelligence (AI) has increasingly been integrated into tools designed to support cognitive health among older adults. These AI-driven interventions aim to enhance memory, provide companionship, and assist with daily activities, thereby promoting independence and improving quality of life. The following case studies illustrate how elderly individuals have benefited from such technologies.

Case Study 1: ChatWise – Enhancing Cognitive Engagement Through Conversation

ChatWise is an AI-powered conversational agent developed to provide engaging dialogues tailored to older adults. Unlike traditional chatbots, ChatWise employs dual-level conversation reasoning, enabling it to sustain long-term interactions that are cognitively stimulating.

In a study involving seniors with mild cognitive impairment, participants reported improved mood and cognitive engagement after regular interactions with ChatWise. The AI's ability to adapt conversations based on user responses contributed to a sense of companionship and mental stimulation (Yang & Zhu, 2025).arXiv

Case Study 2: ACTA – Mobile Health Solution for Cognitive Training

The Advanced Cognitive Training for Aging (ACTA) platform integrates AI with neurofeedback and behavioral nudges to deliver personalized cognitive exercises via mobile devices. Designed for seniors with mild cognitive impairments, ACTA adapts training modules based on user performance, ensuring tasks remain challenging yet achievable.

Users reported enhanced memory retention and increased confidence in daily activities. The mobile nature of ACTA allowed for convenient access to cognitive training, fostering consistent use and engagement (Cisotto et al., 2021).

Case Study 3: Stretch – Robotic Assistance for Daily Living

Stretch is a mobile manipulator robot designed to assist older adults with cognitive and mobility impairments in daily tasks. In a participatory design study, seniors interacted with Stretch in a simulated home environment, where the robot provided reminders, facilitated video calls, and assisted with object retrieval. Participants expressed appreciation for the robot's support, noting increased feelings of safety and autonomy.

The study highlighted the potential of robotic assistance in reducing caregiver burden and promoting independent living among the elderly (Olatunji et al., 2025).

Case Study 4: AI Chatbots – Supporting Mental Well-being

AI chatbots have been employed to support the mental well-being of older adults by providing companionship and monitoring emotional health. In a study involving the use of an AI chatbot designed for seniors, participants engaged in regular conversations that helped alleviate feelings of loneliness and depression.

The chatbot's ability to recognize emotional cues and respond empathetically contributed to users' sense of being heard and understood. Such interactions have been associated with improved mood and increased social engagement among elderly users (van Dijk et al., 2025).

Case Study 5: AI-Driven Health Monitoring – Enhancing Safety

AI technologies have also been utilized to monitor health parameters and detect potential risks among older adults. For instance, AI-powered systems can analyze data from wearable devices to identify patterns indicative of cognitive decline or health deterioration.

In one case, an AI system detected early signs of cognitive impairment by analyzing changes in speech patterns and daily routines, prompting timely medical intervention. Such proactive monitoring has been instrumental in preventing accidents and ensuring prompt care for elderly individuals (Wong et al., 2025).

These case studies demonstrate the diverse applications of AI in supporting the cognitive health and overall well-being of older adults. From conversational agents and mobile health solutions to robotic assistants and health monitoring systems, AI technologies offer promising avenues for enhancing the quality of life among the elderly. Continued research and user-centered design are essential to ensure these tools are accessible, effective, and aligned with the unique needs of older populations.

AI IN SOCIAL AND EMOTIONAL WELL-BEING

Addressing Loneliness and Isolation Through AI-Powered Platforms

Loneliness and social isolation are increasingly recognized as significant public health concerns, particularly among older adults and young adults. These conditions are associated with adverse health outcomes, including depression, cognitive decline, and increased mortality (Yang et al., 2025). The advent of artificial intelligence (AI) offers novel avenues to mitigate these issues through AI-powered platforms designed to foster social connection and provide companionship.

AI Interventions for Older Adults

Older adults often face unique challenges that contribute to loneliness, such as retirement, bereavement, and mobility limitations. AI technologies, including social robots and virtual assistants, have been developed to address these challenges. For instance, a systematic review by Yang et al. (2025) found that AI interventions employing speech and emotion recognition significantly reduced feelings of loneliness among older adults. Social robots like ElliQ have been implemented to provide daily interactions, reminders, and entertainment, thereby enhancing users' sense of companionship and engagement (AMA Journal of Ethics, 2023).

Moreover, AI platforms like ChatGPT have been explored for their potential to alleviate loneliness in older adults with mild cognitive impairment (MCI). These platforms offer human-like conversations that can stimulate cognitive functions and provide emotional support (NeurologyLive, 2023). However, the effectiveness of such interventions depends on their ability to deliver empathetic and contextually appropriate responses.

AI Applications Among Young Adults

Young adults, particularly university students, are also susceptible to loneliness and social anxiety. AI-powered social chatbots have been investigated as tools to mitigate these issues. A study by Lee et al. (2025) examined the impact of a social chatbot named "Luda Lee" on university students over a four-week period.

The findings indicated significant reductions in loneliness and social anxiety, with participants reporting that the chatbot's empathetic responses and availability provided a sense of companionship. However, the study also noted limitations, including the need for more diverse participant samples and longer-term assessments to determine sustained effects.

Predictive AI Models and Ethical Considerations

Beyond providing companionship, AI has been utilized to predict and identify individuals at risk of loneliness and social isolation. A systematic review by Majmudar et al. (2023) highlighted the use of machine learning algorithms to analyze social determinants of health and predict loneliness during the COVID-19 pandemic. These predictive models can inform targeted interventions but raise ethical concerns regarding data privacy and the potential for stigmatization.

Furthermore, the reliance on AI for social interaction prompts discussions about the quality of these interactions compared to human connections. While AI can provide immediate and accessible support, it is essential to ensure that such technologies complement rather than replace human relationships. Designing AI systems that encourage users to engage in real-world social activities can help balance technological intervention with human connection.

Virtual Companions and Chatbots: Exploring Their Role in Human Social Interaction

The rapid advancement of artificial intelligence (AI) has led to the emergence of virtual companions and chatbots designed to simulate human-like interactions. These AI-driven entities are increasingly utilized for companionship, emotional support, and even romantic engagement.

As society grapples with issues of loneliness and social isolation, virtual companions offer a novel avenue for connection. This paper examines the psychological impacts, user experiences, and ethical considerations associated with virtual companions and chatbots.

Psychological Impacts and User Experiences

Virtual companions have been shown to positively influence users' emotional well-being positively. For instance, Liu et al. (2024) conducted a mixed-methods study revealing that users who engaged with companion chatbots experienced a reduction in feelings of loneliness. The study identified various user profiles, ranging from socially fulfilled individuals to those heavily reliant on chatbot interactions for emotional support. Similarly, Fang et al. (2025) found that voice-based chatbots initially mitigated loneliness more effectively than text-based ones; however, excessive use led to increased emotional dependence and decreased real-world social interactions.

The design and functionality of chatbots significantly affect user experiences. Griol et al. (2025) emphasized the importance of incorporating affective computing and user modeling to create more engaging and emotionally responsive virtual companions. Their study demonstrated that conversational agents capable of adapting to users' emotional states fostered more meaningful interactions.

Furthermore, Ebner and Szczuka (2025) highlighted that individuals with higher tendencies toward romantic fantasizing and anthropomorphism were more likely to form emotional bonds with chatbots, indicating the psychological complexity of human-AI relationships.

Ethical Considerations and Societal Implications

The integration of virtual companions into daily life raises several ethical concerns. One significant issue is the potential for emotional dependency, where users may prefer interactions with AI over human relationships. Turkle (2024) warned that reliance on AI for companionship could lead to a diminished capacity for human empathy and social skills. Additionally, the authenticity of relationships with virtual companions is questioned, as these entities lack genuine consciousness and emotional understanding.

Privacy and data security are also paramount concerns. Chatbots often require access to personal information to provide personalized interactions, raising questions about data handling and user consent. Moreover, the potential for manipulation exists, especially if chatbots are programmed to influence user behavior subtly. As AI technology continues to evolve, establishing ethical guidelines and regulatory frameworks becomes essential to safeguard users' well-being.

Virtual companions and chatbots represent a significant development in AI applications, offering opportunities for enhanced social interaction and emotional support. While studies indicate potential benefits in reducing loneliness and providing companionship, concerns about emotional dependence, authenticity, and ethical use persist.

As these technologies become more integrated into society, ongoing research and ethical considerations are crucial to ensure that virtual companions augment rather than replace human connections.

AI-Enhanced Virtual Communities for Social Engagement

The proliferation of artificial intelligence (AI) technologies has significantly transformed the landscape of virtual communities, fostering enhanced social engagement among users. AI-driven platforms now facilitate personalized interactions, adaptive learning environments, and immersive experiences that transcend traditional communication barriers. This paper explores the role of AI in augmenting virtual communities, examining its impact on social dynamics, user engagement, and the potential challenges that arise from its integration.

AI Integration in Virtual Communities

AI technologies have been instrumental in creating more responsive and interactive virtual communities. By leveraging machine learning algorithms and natural language processing, platforms can tailor content and interactions to individual user preferences, thereby enhancing user engagement and satisfaction (Griol et al., 2025). For instance, AI-powered conversational agents can simulate human-like interactions, providing users with a sense of companionship and support within virtual environments.

Moreover, AI facilitates the moderation and management of online communities by detecting and mitigating inappropriate content, thus maintaining a safe and inclusive environment for users. This automated oversight ensures that community standards are upheld, fostering trust and encouraging active participation among members (Bazzano et al., 2025).

Enhancing Social Engagement Through AI

The integration of AI into virtual communities has led to the development of more immersive and interactive experiences. Virtual reality (VR) platforms, enhanced by AI, allow users to engage in shared activities and environments that mimic real-world interactions, thereby strengthening social bonds and reducing feelings of isolation (Han & Bailenson, 2024). These AI-enhanced

VR experiences can adapt to user behaviors and preferences, providing personalized content that resonates with individual users and promotes sustained engagement.

In educational settings, AI-driven virtual communities support collaborative learning by facilitating group discussions, providing real-time feedback, and adapting instructional content to meet diverse learning needs. Such platforms encourage peer-to-peer interaction and knowledge sharing, which are critical components of effective learning communities (Hou et al., 2025).

Challenges and Ethical Considerations

Despite the benefits, the integration of AI into virtual communities presents several challenges. One concern is the potential for reduced human-to-human interaction, as users may become overly reliant on AI agents for social engagement. This dependency could lead to diminished interpersonal skills and a sense of disconnection from real-world relationships (Hou et al., 2025).

Additionally, the use of AI raises ethical questions regarding data privacy and algorithmic bias. AI systems rely on vast amounts of user data to function effectively, which necessitates stringent data protection measures to safeguard user information. Furthermore, biases embedded within AI algorithms can perpetuate existing social inequalities, underscoring the need for transparent and equitable AI design practices (Bazzano et al., 2025).

AI-enhanced virtual communities offer promising avenues for fostering social engagement and creating inclusive digital spaces. By personalizing user experiences and facilitating meaningful interactions, AI technologies can enrich virtual communities and support diverse user needs. However, it is imperative to address the associated challenges and ethical considerations to ensure that these communities remain equitable, secure, and conducive to genuine human connection.

Emotional AI Tools for Mental Health Support

The integration of artificial intelligence (AI) into mental health care has ushered in a new era of emotional AI tools designed to support individuals' psychological well-being. These tools, encompassing chatbots, virtual agents, and emotion recognition systems, aim to provide accessible, personalized, and immediate support for mental health concerns. This paper explores the current landscape of emotional AI tools in mental health support, examining their applications, benefits, challenges, and ethical considerations.

Applications of Emotional AI in Mental Health

Emotional AI tools have been developed to assist in various aspects of mental health care, including assessment, intervention, and ongoing support. For instance, AI-powered chatbots like Woebot utilize cognitive-behavioral therapy techniques to engage users in conversations that promote emotional regulation and coping strategies (Darcy et al., 2023). Similarly, platforms like EmoBay offer 24/7 AI chatbot services that provide users with daily check-ins, context-sensitive responses, and safety protocols to manage stress and anxiety .

Advanced AI systems, such as DeepPsy-Agent, incorporate stage-aware dialogue models that enhance reasoning capabilities through deep-thinking analysis, thereby generating high-quality responses tailored to users' emotional states . These tools aim to simulate empathetic interactions, providing users with a sense of companionship and understanding.

Benefits of Emotional AI Tools

The utilization of emotional AI tools in mental health support offers several advantages. Firstly, these tools provide immediate and round-the-clock access to support, which is particularly beneficial for individuals facing barriers to traditional therapy, such as long waiting lists or high costs . Secondly, the anonymity and non-judgmental nature of AI interactions can encourage users to disclose sensitive information more freely, facilitating early intervention and support

Moreover, emotional AI tools can be integrated into various digital platforms, enhancing their reach and accessibility. For example, Cope Notes delivers daily text messages containing positive thoughts and affirmations, which have been shown to help combat depression and anxiety.

Challenges and Ethical Considerations

Despite their potential, emotional AI tools in mental health support present several challenges and ethical concerns. One major issue is the lack of empirical evidence supporting the long-term efficacy of these tools. While some studies indicate short-term improvements in symptoms like depression and anxiety, there is limited data on sustained outcomes .

Additionally, the absence of regulatory oversight raises concerns about the safety and reliability of AI-driven mental health interventions. Without standardized protocols and validation, there is a risk of AI tools providing inappropriate or harmful responses, particularly in crisis situations.

Privacy and data security are also critical considerations, as emotional AI tools often require access to sensitive personal information. Ensuring that user data is protected and used ethically is paramount to maintaining trust and safeguarding users' well-being.

Emotional AI tools represent a promising frontier in mental health support, offering innovative solutions to enhance accessibility and personalization of care. By providing immediate, empathetic, and tailored interactions, these tools have the potential to supplement traditional mental health services and reach underserved populations. However, to fully realize their benefits, it is essential to address the challenges related to efficacy, regulation, and ethical use. Future research should focus on rigorous evaluation of these tools, development of standardized guidelines, and implementation of robust data protection measures to ensure that emotional AI serves as a safe and effective component of mental health care.

AI FOR PRACTICAL SKILL DEVELOPMENT AND EVERYDAY LEARNING

Artificial Intelligence in Financial Literacy and Personal Finance Management

Artificial intelligence (AI) has increasingly reshaped how individuals manage personal finances by providing advanced tools and personalized financial guidance (Singh & Sharma, 2024).

AI technologies now play a critical role in enhancing financial literacy, automating budgeting tasks, and facilitating efficient investment decisions. This paper explores the applications, benefits, challenges, and ethical considerations associated with AI integration into personal financial management and literacy (Bayakhmetova et al., 2025; Talasila, 2024).

AI Applications in Financial Literacy

AI-driven technologies significantly contribute to improving financial literacy through personalized and interactive educational tools. AI-powered platforms can analyze individual users' financial behaviors and adapt educational content to address specific knowledge deficits, enhancing comprehension and promoting better financial habits (Singh & Sharma, 2024).

For instance, chatbots and virtual financial assistants simulate realistic financial scenarios, enabling users to practice and refine decision-making skills without financial risk (Bayakhmetova et al., 2025). Moreover, AI tools facilitate financial education's democratization by delivering customized financial guidance across diverse populations, including underserved communities.

Utilizing mobile applications and advanced natural language processing, AI-driven solutions can disseminate financial literacy content in multiple languages, significantly reducing barriers related to geographic location, language, or socioeconomic status (Singh & Sharma, 2024; Bayakhmetova et al., 2025).

AI in Personal Finance Management

Beyond education, AI significantly impacts personal finance management by streamlining financial processes and providing real-time insights. AI-based budgeting applications such as MyFinanceAI incorporate machine learning algorithms to automate expense tracking, predict budget outcomes, and offer tailored savings strategies, thereby reducing financial stress and encouraging healthier financial practices (Talasila, 2024).

AI also extends into investment management through robo-advisors, automated platforms that analyze market dynamics and individual risk preferences to provide personalized investment advice (Bayakhmetova et al., 2025). Robo-advisors democratize investment opportunities by making sophisticated financial advice accessible and affordable to a broader range of users, particularly those traditionally excluded due to cost or limited knowledge (Singh & Sharma, 2024; Talasila, 2024).

Benefits of AI-Driven Financial Tools

The integration of AI into personal financial management brings several notable advantages. Firstly, AI facilitates personalized financial planning, considering individual income, expenses, and personal goals, significantly improving financial outcomes (Talasila, 2024). Secondly, AI-based financial platforms improve accessibility by delivering user-friendly, multilingual, and mobile-compatible services, thereby widening financial inclusion (Bayakhmetova et al., 2025).

Additionally, AI automates repetitive financial tasks, reducing human errors, saving users' time, and enhancing overall efficiency in personal finance management (Singh & Sharma, 2024; Talasila, 2024).

Moreover, AI-driven tools actively engage users through gamification and real-time feedback mechanisms, enhancing motivation and sustained interaction with financial management platforms (Singh & Sharma, 2024). Such increased engagement promotes better financial decisions and long-term financial discipline (Bayakhmetova et al., 2025).

Challenges and Ethical Considerations

Despite the advantages, the application of AI in financial management raises several significant concerns. Data privacy remains a critical issue, given that AI platforms require extensive access to sensitive personal financial information, thus posing risks related to data breaches or unauthorized data use (Bayakhmetova et al., 2025).

Additionally, algorithmic biases inherent in AI systems may inadvertently perpetuate discriminatory practices, potentially excluding or disadvantaging certain demographic groups from receiving equitable financial advice (Singh & Sharma, 2024).

Over-reliance on AI-driven tools might diminish users' financial decision-making skills, creating dependencies that could adversely affect long-term financial autonomy (Talasila, 2024).

Finally, AI algorithms' complexity and opacity often limit transparency, making it challenging for users to understand and trust the recommendations provided (Bayakhmetova et al., 2025).

AI technology holds considerable promise for enhancing financial literacy and personal finance management by providing customized, efficient, and inclusive financial solutions. However, addressing concerns around data privacy, transparency, algorithmic fairness, and potential user dependency remains crucial.

Future research should focus on improving AI transparency, establishing clear ethical guidelines, and ensuring robust data protection standards to maximize benefits while minimizing potential harms (Singh & Sharma, 2024; Bayakhmetova et al., 2025; Talasila, 2024).

Teaching Digital Literacy Through Conversational AI and Simulations

In an era where digital competence is crucial, the integration of conversational artificial intelligence (AI) and simulations into education provides innovative strategies for enhancing digital literacy among learners (Gao et al., 2024).

Conversational AI and simulation-based learning offer interactive and adaptive environments that support personalized education experiences, enabling learners to build essential digital skills through realistic, engaging interactions (Deveci Topal, Yildirim, & Yildirim, 2023; Stampfl, Geyer, Deissl-O'Meara, & Ivkić, 2024). This paper examines the use of conversational AI and simulations for teaching digital literacy, highlighting benefits, challenges, and practical implications for educational practice.

Conversational AI in Digital Literacy Education

Conversational AI tools, including chatbots and virtual assistants, significantly contribute to digital literacy by providing dynamic, responsive interactions tailored to learners' individual needs (Gao et al., 2024; Deveci Topal et al., 2023). For instance, Gao et al. (2024) demonstrated that integrating ChatGPT-powered avatars in a virtual reality platform significantly improved university students' data literacy by facilitating real-time, interactive dialogues tailored to individual learner profiles.

This adaptive technology not only helps learners acquire specific digital competencies but also enhances their engagement and motivation (Gao et al., 2024).

Furthermore, conversational AI has been particularly beneficial in inclusive education contexts, supporting learners with diverse needs and abilities.

Deveci Topal et al. (2023) reported that generative conversational AI significantly improved learning outcomes and motivation among students with mild intellectual disabilities by delivering customized educational interactions responsive to each learner's pace and cognitive abilities. Thus, conversational AI emerges as a promising tool in bridging learning gaps and promoting equitable digital literacy education.

Simulations as Interactive Tools for Digital Literacy

Simulations enriched by AI technology provide immersive experiences that allow learners to practice digital skills within contexts closely resembling real-world situations (Stampfl et al., 2024). According to Stampfl et al. (2024), AI-enhanced role-playing simulations facilitate active learning and critical thinking, enabling learners to safely explore digital scenarios without the real-world consequences of trial and error. Such simulated environments foster the practical application of digital literacy skills, reinforcing theoretical knowledge through experiential learning (Stampfl et al., 2024; Gao et al., 2024).

These interactive simulations encourage learners to engage deeply with content, enhancing retention and transferability of digital literacy skills beyond classroom settings (Stampfl et al., 2024). Additionally, simulation-based learning empowers students to build problem-solving skills and digital confidence by exploring complex technological environments under guided, risk-free conditions (Gao et al., 2024).

Benefits of Integrating Conversational AI and Simulations

Integrating conversational AI and simulations in digital literacy education offers numerous pedagogical benefits. Firstly, these technologies enable highly personalized learning experiences, accommodating diverse learning styles and skill levels, thereby improving educational outcomes (Gao et al., 2024; Deveci Topal et al., 2023).

Secondly, interactive and immersive learning environments facilitated by simulations and conversational agents significantly boost learner engagement and motivation, fostering sustained interest and deeper learning (Stampfl et al., 2024).

Moreover, conversational AI and simulations improve accessibility, supporting diverse learner populations, including students with disabilities or special educational needs, ensuring inclusive educational practices (Deveci Topal et al., 2023).

Finally, these technologies foster practical digital skill development through hands-on learning experiences, significantly enhancing learners' preparedness for navigating real-world digital environments (Gao et al., 2024; Stampfl et al., 2024).

Challenges and Ethical Considerations

Despite the evident benefits, several challenges accompany the integration of conversational AI and simulations into digital literacy education. Resource constraints such as access to advanced hardware, software, and technical expertise may hinder widespread implementation, especially in under-resourced educational settings (Gao et al., 2024). Educators may also require extensive training and support to effectively incorporate these innovative technologies into existing curricula (Deveci Topal et al., 2023).

Equity concerns further complicate the use of AI-based educational tools, as uneven access to necessary technology risks exacerbating existing digital divides among students from diverse socioeconomic backgrounds (Gao et al., 2024; Deveci Topal et al., 2023). Lastly, ethical considerations surrounding data privacy, informed consent, and transparency of AI algorithms necessitate careful attention to ensure that learner information is managed responsibly (Stampfl et al., 2024).

Conversational AI and simulations present transformative opportunities for enhancing digital literacy education by offering personalized, interactive, and practical learning experiences (Gao et al., 2024; Stampfl et al., 2024). Although significant potential exists, addressing challenges related to resources, educator training, equitable access, and ethical data management remains critical.

Future research should focus on refining best practices, expanding inclusive technology use, and rigorously evaluating the long-term impacts of these innovative educational tools on digital literacy outcomes.

Assisting with Hobbies, Creative Pursuits, and Cultural Engagement Through Artificial Intelligence

The proliferation of artificial intelligence (AI) has significantly reshaped human engagement in hobbies, creative activities, and cultural experiences (Heigl, 2025; Lee, Pasquier, & Yuri, 2025). AI-driven platforms now empower individuals to explore new creative outlets, refine their skills, and participate in cultural dialogues, democratizing access and fostering inclusive artistic environments (Cetinic & She, 2022; Garcia, 2024).

This section examines how AI facilitates participation in hobbies, supports creative expression, and enhances cultural engagement, while also addressing critical ethical and practical considerations (Caramiaux, Crawford, Liao, Ramos, & Williams, 2024).

AI and the Enhancement of Creative Pursuits

AI technologies, particularly generative AI, have significantly broadened the scope of human creative activities by providing accessible tools for artistic expression (Heigl, 2025). These tools allow individuals, regardless of prior artistic experience, to engage meaningfully in activities such as visual art creation, music composition, and literary pursuits (Lee et al., 2025).

For example, AI-based music composition software enables users with minimal training to produce sophisticated musical pieces, effectively lowering traditional barriers to entry and expanding creative participation (Lee et al., 2025; Heigl, 2025).

Moreover, collaborative projects that integrate AI and human artists have demonstrated the potential of technology to augment human creativity rather than replace it (Lee et al., 2025).

Such collaborations result in hybrid creative outputs where human emotionality and AI-generated innovation interact dynamically, thereby enriching the creative process and offering novel artistic experiences to audiences (Caramiaux et al., 2024; Garcia, 2024).

AI in Cultural Engagement

AI's role extends beyond individual creativity into broader cultural engagement, enhancing access to, interpretation of, and interaction with cultural heritage and artistic content (Cetinic & She, 2022; Chheda-Kothary et al., 2025). Platforms leveraging AI, such as ArtInsight, provide enriched sensory experiences of visual arts for visually impaired users through descriptive narrations and tactile simulations, significantly broadening cultural accessibility and inclusivity (Chheda-Kothary et al., 2025).

Further, AI-driven analytical tools contribute to deeper insights into cultural heritage by systematically identifying patterns, historical influences, and stylistic evolutions within large cultural datasets (Cetinic & She, 2022). By uncovering previously unnoticed connections and influences among artworks or historical periods, these analytical approaches enrich public understanding and appreciation of cultural traditions and historical narratives (Cetinic & She, 2022; Garcia, 2024).

Challenges and Ethical Considerations

Despite the considerable benefits, integrating AI into creative and cultural domains presents significant ethical and practical challenges. Foremost among these concerns is the issue of authorship and intellectual property, as the lines between human and machine-created works increasingly blur (Garcia, 2024; Heigl, 2025). Such ambiguity raises critical questions regarding originality, creativity, and attribution of AI-assisted works, necessitating clear guidelines and ethical frameworks to manage these evolving creative relationships (Caramiaux et al., 2024; Garcia, 2024).

Additionally, AI-generated content may inadvertently reinforce existing biases present in training datasets, potentially leading to skewed or culturally insensitive representations (Cetinic & She, 2022). Ensuring diversity and representational fairness within AI-generated cultural outputs remains an ongoing ethical challenge, emphasizing the need for conscientious algorithmic design and data selection (Heigl, 2025; Garcia, 2024).

Concerns also arise regarding the potential for diminished human engagement with traditional skills and crafts, as reliance on automated creative tools could negatively impact manual skill development and artistic authenticity (Caramiaux et al., 2024). Thus, balancing technological innovation with the preservation and encouragement of traditional artistic practices is crucial (Lee et al., 2025).

The utilization of AI to assist with hobbies, creative pursuits, and cultural engagement represents a significant advancement in facilitating broader accessibility, inclusivity, and innovation within these domains (Heigl, 2025; Lee et al., 2025). AI-driven tools and platforms democratize artistic expression, foster deeper cultural understanding, and stimulate collaborative human-machine creativity.

However, addressing associated ethical dilemmas, including concerns around authorship, algorithmic bias, and the potential loss of traditional skills, remains paramount. Future research and policy development should prioritize ethical guidelines, inclusivity, and sustainable integration of AI within cultural and creative sectors (Caramiaux et al., 2024; Cetinic & She, 2022).

ETHICAL CONSIDERATIONS AND CHALLENGES

Privacy Concerns with AI Use Among Elderly Populations: Addressing Digital Divides, Bias, and Accessibility

Artificial intelligence (AI) technologies have increasingly been integrated into everyday life, providing substantial benefits to elderly populations, such as improved healthcare management, daily assistance, and enhanced communication capabilities (Chu et al., 2023; Wickramathilaka et al., 2025).

Despite these advantages, significant privacy concerns exist, particularly among older users who often have heightened vulnerability to data misuse and exploitation (Sharkey & Sharkey, 2022; Wiles & Jayawardana, 2023). This paper explores privacy issues related to AI use among the elderly, emphasizing the importance of addressing digital divides, mitigating algorithmic bias, and designing user-friendly interfaces.

Privacy Concerns Among Elderly Populations

Elderly individuals frequently express concerns over privacy due to limited familiarity with technology, uncertainty around data collection methods, and fears surrounding unauthorized surveillance (Sharkey & Sharkey, 2022). AI-enabled devices such as health monitors and virtual assistants collect extensive personal data, increasing the risk of privacy breaches (Wiles & Jayawardana, 2023).

Moreover, elderly populations often struggle to understand complex privacy policies, leading to unintentional data sharing and consent issues (Chu et al., 2023). Clear communication and simplified privacy protocols are essential to mitigate these concerns and build user trust (Wiles & Jayawardana, 2023).

Addressing Digital Divides and Technology Accessibility

Cost Barriers

Financial constraints significantly restrict elderly individuals' access to AI-driven technologies. Many seniors rely on fixed or limited incomes, making advanced AI systems prohibitively expensive (Wickramathilaka et al., 2025). Costs associated with purchasing, maintaining, and upgrading devices further deepen this divide (Sharkey & Sharkey, 2022). Subsidized programs and public-private partnerships can help provide affordable access, reducing economic barriers and promoting equitable technological inclusion (Wickramathilaka et al., 2025).

Regional Disparities in Tech Infrastructure

Geographical disparities further exacerbate the digital divide, especially impacting rural elderly populations. Insufficient broadband infrastructure in rural areas limits access to AI technologies dependent on reliable internet connectivity (Sharkey & Sharkey, 2022). Investment in rural technological infrastructure is crucial, as it enables equitable access, ensuring older adults in underserved regions can benefit from AI advancements (Chu et al., 2023; Wiles & Jayawardana, 2023).

Mitigating Risks of Bias in AI Systems Affecting Older Demographics

AI systems often inadvertently incorporate biases, negatively impacting older populations due to underrepresentation in data sets (Wickramathilaka et al., 2025). Such biases can result in discriminatory practices, including misdiagnosis or inadequate recommendations from healthcare AI (Chu et al., 2023). Ensuring that elderly demographics are adequately represented in AI training datasets is imperative to mitigate biases (Sharkey & Sharkey, 2022). Regular audits and fairness checks within AI systems can further promote equitable outcomes for all age groups (Wiles & Jayawardana, 2023).

Ensuring User-Friendly Interfaces

The usability of AI interfaces significantly influences elderly individuals' willingness and ability to adopt new technologies. Many older users find complex interfaces intimidating or unusable due to factors such as small text size, complex navigation, and lack of intuitive controls (Wickramathilaka et al., 2025). Simplified interfaces, voice-command functionalities, larger visual elements, and intuitive layouts are critical for promoting user acceptance and sustained engagement among seniors (Chu et al., 2023; Sharkey & Sharkey, 2022).

Training programs specifically tailored to older adults can further ease the transition to using AI tools, enhancing both competence and confidence in their technological interactions (Wiles & Jayawardana, 2023). Inclusive design principles should be central to AI development processes, integrating feedback directly from elderly users to ensure practical usability (Wickramathilaka et al., 2025).

The integration of AI technology offers significant benefits to elderly populations; however, privacy concerns, accessibility issues, and potential biases remain critical barriers. Addressing these challenges requires intentional efforts to simplify privacy communications, provide economic support, improve regional infrastructure, ensure unbiased AI models, and design user-friendly interfaces. A holistic and inclusive approach to AI development and deployment can greatly enhance the quality of life for elderly populations, promoting equitable and responsible technology use.

FUTURE DIRECTIONS AND OPPORTUNITIES

Emerging AI Technologies with Potential Applications for Elderly Learning

As global populations age, the importance of lifelong learning for older adults becomes increasingly evident. Emerging artificial intelligence (AI) technologies offer promising avenues to enhance educational experiences for the elderly, addressing cognitive engagement, social inclusion, and overall well-being.

This section explores the potential of AI-integrated wearable devices and mixed-reality experiences in facilitating elderly learning. It also examines the roles of policymakers and educators in bridging existing gaps and highlights the significance of partnerships among technology developers, healthcare providers, and educational institutions.

Wearable Devices with Integrated Learning Features

Wearable devices, such as smartwatches and fitness trackers, have evolved beyond health monitoring to incorporate educational functionalities. For older adults, these devices can provide personalized learning experiences, adapting content based on user preferences and cognitive abilities.

For instance, AI-driven wearables can offer language learning modules, memory exercises, and real-time feedback on tasks, promoting cognitive stimulation and skill acquisition (Chheda-Kothary et al., 2025). The integration of AI allows for adaptive learning, where the system adjusts the difficulty and type of content based on the user's performance and engagement levels. This personalization ensures that learning remains challenging yet attainable, fostering motivation and sustained interest.

Moreover, wearable devices can facilitate reminders for scheduled learning sessions, track progress, and even connect users with peer learners, enhancing social interaction and accountability (Wickramathilaka et al., 2025).

Mixed-Reality Experiences for Immersive Education

Mixed-reality (MR) technologies, encompassing augmented reality (AR) and virtual reality (VR), offer immersive educational experiences that can be particularly beneficial for older learners. These technologies can simulate real-world scenarios, allowing users to engage in interactive learning environments without physical constraints.

For example, VR can transport users to historical sites for virtual tours, while AR can overlay instructional content onto physical objects, aiding in tasks like cooking or crafting (Cetinic & She, 2022).

The immersive nature of MR can enhance memory retention and understanding by providing multisensory learning experiences. Additionally, MR platforms can be designed to accommodate varying levels of mobility and sensory abilities, ensuring inclusivity. By engaging in MR-based learning, older adults can explore new interests, revisit past experiences, and maintain cognitive agility (Garcia, 2024).

The Role of Policymakers and Educators in Bridging Gaps

To fully realize the benefits of AI technologies in elderly education, concerted efforts from policymakers and educators are essential. Policymakers can facilitate access by funding initiatives that provide affordable or free AI-enabled devices and internet connectivity to older populations. They can also establish standards and guidelines to ensure the safety, privacy, and efficacy of educational technologies (Heigl, 2025).

Educators play a pivotal role in designing and delivering content that is both relevant and accessible to older learners. Professional development programs can equip educators with the skills to integrate AI tools into their teaching practices effectively. Furthermore, involving older adults in the co-creation of educational content can ensure that materials resonate with their experiences and learning objectives, fostering greater engagement and satisfaction (Lee et al., 2025).

Partnerships Between Technology Developers, Healthcare Providers, and Educational Institutions

Collaborative partnerships are crucial in developing and implementing AI technologies that cater to the educational needs of older adults. Technology developers can work with healthcare providers to create applications that address cognitive health, such as memory training programs or stress-reduction techniques.

Educational institutions can contribute by researching effective pedagogical strategies and evaluating the outcomes of AI-based learning interventions (Cetinic & She, 2022).

Such partnerships can lead to the development of comprehensive platforms that integrate health monitoring with educational content, providing a holistic approach to aging. For instance, a wearable device could monitor an individual's physical activity and suggest related educational modules, like nutrition courses or exercise routines, tailored to their health data. By aligning technological innovation with healthcare and educational expertise, these collaborations can create sustainable and impactful learning solutions for the elderly (Garcia, 2024).

Emerging AI technologies, including wearable devices with integrated learning features and mixed-reality experiences, hold significant promise for enhancing educational opportunities for older adults. To harness this potential, it is imperative to address barriers related to accessibility, usability, and relevance.

Policymakers and educators must work collaboratively to create supportive environments that encourage lifelong learning. Moreover, partnerships among technology developers, healthcare providers, and educational institutions are essential in designing and delivering effective, personalized, and engaging educational experiences for the elderly.

CONCLUSION

Recap of AI's Transformative Potential for Elderly Education and Learning

The integration of artificial intelligence (AI) into educational paradigms has ushered in transformative possibilities, particularly for elderly populations (Valencia-Londoño et al., 2025). AI technologies offer personalized, accessible, and engaging learning experiences that enhance cognitive function, promote social inclusion, and support lifelong learning among older adults (Tang et al., 2025; Yang et al., 2025).

This conclusion synthesizes the transformative potential of AI in elderly education, underscores the importance of fostering intergenerational learning through AI tools, and issues a call to action for the development of inclusive and innovative AI solutions.

AI's Transformative Potential in Elderly Education

AI technologies have demonstrated significant potential in addressing the unique educational needs of older adults (Tang et al., 2025). Adaptive learning platforms tailor content to individual learning styles and cognitive abilities, accommodating the sensory and cognitive changes associated with aging (Li et al., 2025). For instance, AI-driven applications adjust task complexity based on user performance, ensuring learning remains challenging yet attainable (Tang et al., 2025; Yang et al., 2025).

Moreover, AI-powered virtual assistants and chatbots facilitate learning by providing immediate feedback, answering queries, and offering reminders for learning activities, thus reducing barriers and enhancing user engagement (Li et al., 2025). Additionally, AI platforms connect older learners with peers, fostering community and social interaction, which is crucial for mental health and reducing isolation (Yang et al., 2025).

Fostering Intergenerational Learning through AI Tools

Intergenerational learning, facilitated by AI tools, bridges generational divides and promotes mutual understanding. AI-supported activities, such as collaborative storytelling platforms, enable older adults and younger individuals to share learning experiences, fostering empathy and knowledge exchange (Li et al., 2025; Song et al., 2024). These interactions enhance learning outcomes for both groups, enriching social and cognitive development.

Furthermore, intergenerational learning initiatives leveraging AI can create inclusive environments accommodating diverse learning needs, including language barriers and varying cognitive abilities, through real-time translations and simplified content delivery (Song et al., 2024). Such inclusivity ensures meaningful participation from all demographics, promoting broader educational engagement.

Call to Action for Inclusive and Innovative AI Solutions

Realizing AI's benefits in elderly education requires inclusive and innovative solutions tailored to older adults' needs. Achieving this involves collaborative efforts from educators, technologists, healthcare providers, and policymakers (Valencia-Londoño et al., 2025).

First, AI educational tools must prioritize user-friendliness and accessibility, incorporating intuitive interfaces customizable for various impairments common among older adults (Li et al., 2025). Content should remain relevant and engaging, reflecting older learners' interests and life experiences (Tang et al., 2025).

Second, comprehensive training programs are needed to enhance AI literacy among older adults. Hands-on, practical approaches are preferred, addressing privacy concerns and building confidence and competence in using technology (Tang et al., 2025).

Third, policies should ensure equitable access to AI educational resources by investing in infrastructure to address digital divides, especially in underserved communities (Yang et al., 2025). Financial support mechanisms for acquiring necessary technologies and research into AI's long-term impacts on elderly learning are crucial for informed policy development.

Finally, ongoing evaluation and feedback mechanisms integrated into AI programs ensure responsiveness to evolving needs. Engaging older adults in development and assessment provides valuable insights and fosters ownership, promoting sustained use and benefit from AI educational tools (Valencia-Londoño et al., 2025).

AI technologies hold transformative potential for elderly education, offering personalized, accessible, and socially enriching experiences. Fostering intergenerational learning through AI tools enhances these benefits by promoting empathy and collaboration across age groups.

Realizing this potential requires inclusive, user-centered AI solutions supported by targeted training, equitable policies, and continuous evaluation. Such efforts will significantly enrich older adults' lives, building inclusive, connected learning communities.

REFERENCES

AMA Journal of Ethics. (2023). Should artificial intelligence play a role in cultivating social connections among older adults? AMA Journal of Ethics, 25(11), E803–E808. https://doi.org/ DOI: 10.1001/amajethics.2023.803

Ayyaz, M. (2025). AI translation tools in language learning: Bridging gaps and enhancing skills. *Advances in Computational Intelligence and Robotics*, *7*(2), 120–132. https://www.researchgate.net/publication/390273953_AI_Translation_Tools_in_Language_Learning_Bridging_Gaps_and_Enhancing_Skills. DOI: 10.4018/979-8-3693-9077-1.ch003

Bayakhmetova, A., Rudenko, L., Keylova, L., Suleimenova, B., Niyazbekova, S., & Nurpeisova, A. (2025). Artificial intelligence in financial behavior: Bibliometric ideas and new opportunities. *Journal of Risk and Financial Management*, *18*(3), 159. DOI: 10.3390/jrfm18030159

Bayly-Castañeda, K., Ramirez-Montoya, M.-S., & Morita-Alexander, A. (2024). Crafting personalized learning paths with AI for lifelong learning: A systematic literature review. *Frontiers in Education*, *9*, 1424386. DOI: 10.3389/feduc.2024.1424386

Bazzano, A. N., Mantsios, A., Mattei, N., Kosorok, M. R., & Culotta, A. (2025). AI can be a powerful social innovation for public health if.... *Journal of Medical Internet Research*, *27*(1), e68198. DOI: 10.2196/68198 PMID: 39841529

Belleville, S., & Hudon, C. (2022). Cognitive training interventions for older adults: The role of individual differences and neuroplasticity. *Journal of Cognitive Enhancement: Towards the Integration of Theory and Practice*, *6*(1), 22–31. DOI: 10.1007/s41465-021-00211-9

Breazeal, C., Park, H. W., & Williams, R. (2024). Designing inclusive AI learning companions for children. *International Journal of Artificial Intelligence in Education*, *34*(1), 45–62.

Camilleri, J., Sheil, A., O'Keeffe, M., Cronin, M., Gruben, M., & Murray, H. (2025). Cybersafety card game: Empowering digital educators to teach cybersafety to older adults. arXiv preprint arXiv:2503.05430. DOI: 10.1145/3706599.3719806

Cetinic, E., & She, J. (2022). Understanding and creating art with AI: Review and outlook. *ACM Transactions on Multimedia Computing Communications and Applications*, *18*(3), 1–21. DOI: 10.1145/3475799

Charness, N., & Boot, W. R. (2022). Technology and aging: Emerging technologies and their impact on aging and older adults. In Schaie, K. W., & Willis, S. L. (Eds.), *Handbook of the psychology of aging* (9th ed., pp. 415–431). Academic Press., DOI: 10.1016/B978-0-323-90198-4.00015-8

Chen, C. C., Ding, Z., Lin, J., & Hopfgartner, F. (2023). AI chatbots as multi-role pedagogical agents: Transforming engagement in CS education. arXiv preprint arXiv:2308.03992. https://arxiv.org/abs/2308.03992

Chheda-Kothary, A., Kanchi, R., Sanders, C., Xiao, K., Sengupta, A., Kneitmix, M., Wobbrock, J. O., & Froehlich, J. E. (2025). ArtInsight: Enabling AI-powered artwork engagement for mixed visual-ability families. arXiv preprint arXiv:2502.19263. https://arxiv.org/abs/2502.19263 DOI: 10.1145/3708359.3712082

Chu, C. H., Ronquillo, C., Khan, S., Hung, L., & Boscart, V. (2023). Artificial intelligence and aging: A scoping review on current research priorities. *Journal of Medical Internet Research*, *25*(2), e43212. DOI: 10.2196/43212

Cisotto, G., Trentini, A., Zoppis, I., Zanga, A., Manzoni, S., Pietrabissa, G., Guerrini Usubini, A., & Castelnuovo, G. (2021). ACTA: A mobile-health solution for integrated nudge-neurofeedback training for senior citizens. arXiv preprint arXiv:2102.08692. https://arxiv.org/abs/2102.08692

Czaja, S. J., Boot, W. R., Charness, N., Rogers, W. A., & Sharit, J. (2019). Improving social support for older adults through technology: Findings from the PRISM randomized controlled trial. *The Gerontologist*, *59*(3), 467–477. DOI: 10.1093/geront/gnw249 PMID: 28201730

Darcy, A.. (2023). Woebot: A digital therapeutic for mental health. *Journal of Medical Internet Research*, *25*(3), e12345. DOI: 10.2196/12345

Deveci Topal, A., Yildirim, B., & Yildirim, G. (2023). Generative conversational AI: Active practices for fostering students with mild intellectual disabilities. *Contemporary Educational Technology*, *15*(1), 15688.

Ebner, P., & Szczuka, J. (2025). Predicting human-chatbot relationships: A mixed-method study on the key psychological factors. arXiv preprint arXiv:2503.00195. https://arxiv.org/abs/2503.00195

Ezzat, A., Wu, M., Li, X., & Kwoh, C. K. (2021). Computational approaches for early detection and diagnosis of Alzheimer's disease. *IEEE Reviews in Biomedical Engineering*, *14*, 145–161. DOI: 10.1109/RBME.2020.3018373

Fang, C. M., Liu, A. R., Danry, V., Lee, E., Chan, S. W. T., Pataranutaporn, P., & Maes, P. (2025). How AI and human behaviors shape psychosocial effects of chatbot use: A longitudinal randomized controlled study. arXiv preprint arXiv:2503.17473. https://arxiv.org/abs/2503.17473

Fang, Y., Chang, H. Y., & Wang, C. C. (2023). Artificial intelligence applications in elder care: A scoping review. *Journal of Aging and Health*, *35*(2), 97–109. DOI: 10.1177/08982643221099354

Findsen, B., & Formosa, M. (2021). *Lifelong learning in later life: A handbook on older adult learning* (2nd ed.). Springer International Publishing.

Gao, H., Huai, H., Yildiz-Degirmenci, S., Bannert, M., & Kasneci, E. (2024). DataliVR: Transformation of data literacy education through virtual reality with ChatGPT-powered enhancements. arXiv preprint arXiv:2409.08738. https://doi.org//arXiv.2409.08738DOI: 10.1109/ISMAR62088.2024.00026

Garcia, M. B. (2024). The paradox of artificial creativity: Challenges and opportunities of generative AI artistry. *Creativity Research Journal*, *36*(2), 123–135. DOI: 10.1080/10400419.2024.2354622

GBD 2021 Healthspan Collaborators. (2024). Global healthspan-lifespan gaps among 183 World Health Organization member states, 1990–2021: A systematic analysis. JAMA Network Open, 7(1), e2277753. https://doi.org/DOI: 10.1001/jamanetworkopen.2023.77753

Geriatrics, B. M. C. (2023). Challenges and opportunity in mobility among older adults. Retrieved from https://bmcgeriatrics.biomedcentral.com/articles/10.1186/s12877-023-04106-7

Griol, D., Sanchis, A., Molina, J. M., & Callejas, Z. (2025). Developing enhanced conversational agents for social virtual worlds. arXiv preprint arXiv:2501.16341. https://arxiv.org/abs/2501.16341

Gruben, M., Sheil, A., Das, S., O'Keeffe, M., Camilleri, J., Cronin, M., & Murray, H. (2025). "It's like not being able to read and write": Narrowing the digital divide for older adults and leveraging the role of digital educators in Ireland. arXiv preprint arXiv:2502.10166. https://arxiv.org/abs/2502.10166 DOI: 10.1145/3689050.3704945

Han, E., & Bailenson, J. N. (2024). *Social interaction in VR*. Oxford Research Encyclopedias, Communication., DOI: 10.1093/acrefore/9780190228613.013.1489

Heigl, R. (2025). Generative artificial intelligence in creative contexts: A systematic review and future research agenda. *Management Review Quarterly*, *75*(1), 45–67. DOI: 10.1007/s11301-025-00494-9

Hmelo-Silver, C. E., Danish, J. A., & Kolodner, J. L. (2023). Integrating AI learning into middle school science through natural language processing. *IEEE Transactions on Learning Technologies*, *16*(2), 123–135.

Hou, I., …. (2025). "All roads lead to ChatGPT": How generative AI is eroding social interactions and student learning communities. arXiv preprint arXiv:2504.09779. https://arxiv.org/abs/2504.09779 DOI: 10.1145/3724363.3729024

Institute for Health Metrics and Evaluation. (2024). Global life expectancy to increase by nearly 5 years by 2050 despite ongoing health challenges. The Lancet. Retrieved from https://www.healthdata.org/news-events/newsroom/news-releases/global-life-expectancy-increase-nearly-5-years-2050-despite

Jiang, L., Yang, H., & Zhou, Z. (2023). Artificial intelligence and early detection of Alzheimer's disease: Current applications and challenges. *Aging & Mental Health*, *27*(4), 589–598. DOI: 10.1080/13607863.2022.2044502

Kim, H., Kim, H., Kim, J., & Kim, J. (2024). Development of an evidence-based cognitive training application for older adults with mild cognitive impairment. *Journal of Medical Internet Research*, *26*(1), e123456. DOI: 10.2196/123456

Kim, K., Hagedorn, M., Williamson, J., & Chapman, C. (2021). *Participation in adult education and lifelong learning: 2000–01. National Household Education Surveys of 2001*. National Center for Education Statistics.

Kim, Y. S., Lee, H. Y., & Lee, M. H. (2021). Socioeconomic disparities in digital literacy and access among older adults: A cross-sectional study. *Journal of Aging and Health*, *33*(2-3), 147–157.

Kreienbrinck, C., Jurafsky, D., & Li, F. F. (2025). Real-time machine translation for multilingual educational environments. *Cognitive Linguistics and AI Journal, 14*(1), 45–58. DOI: 10.1007/s10936-024-10088-3

Le Monde. (2024, October 9). Rise in human life expectancy slows in wealthy countries. Retrieved from https://www.lemonde.fr/en/environment/article/2024/10/09/rise-in-human-life-expectancy-slows-in-wealthy-countries_6728735_114.html

Lee, H. R., & Riek, L. D. (2021). Ethical considerations of using AI to assist older adults. *AI & Society, 36*(3), 819–830. DOI: 10.1007/s00146-020-01117-4

Lee, J., Kim, H., & Park, S. (2025). Therapeutic potential of social chatbots in alleviating loneliness and social anxiety: Quasi-experimental mixed methods study. *Journal of Medical Internet Research, 27*, e65589. DOI: 10.2196/65589 PMID: 39808786

Lee, K. J. M., Pasquier, P., & Yuri, J. (2025). Revival: Collaborative artistic creation through human-AI interactions in musical creativity. arXiv preprint arXiv:2503.15498. https://arxiv.org/abs/2503.15498

Lee, S., Kang, S., Lee, S., & Lee, H. (2022). Multimodal deep learning approach for early detection of Alzheimer's disease using neuroimaging, cognitive testing, and genetic data. *Frontiers in Aging Neuroscience, 14*, 821162. DOI: 10.3389/fnagi.2022.821162

Lehtonen, H., Salo, J., & Hynninen, K. M. (2023). Personalized digital interventions for cognitive enhancement in aging populations: A systematic review. *Frontiers in Psychology, 14*, 1122334. DOI: 10.3389/fpsyg.2023.1122334

Liu, A. R., Pataranutaporn, P., Turkle, S., & Maes, P. (2024). Chatbot companionship: A mixed-methods study of companion chatbot usage patterns and their relationship to loneliness in active users. arXiv preprint arXiv:2410.21596. https://arxiv.org/abs/2410.21596

Majmudar, A., Mihalopoulos, C., & Brijnath, B. (2023). A systematic review of artificial intelligence used to predict loneliness, social isolation, and drug use. *Journal of Multidisciplinary Healthcare, 16*, 123–135. DOI: 10.2147/JMDH.S345678

Martínez-Alcalá, C. I., Rosales-Lagarde, A., Alonso-Lavernia, M. D., Ramírez-Salvador, J. A., Jiménez-Rodríguez, B., Cepeda-Rebollar, R. M., & López-Noguerola, J. S. (2021). *Elderly and their barriers to accepting and learning to use technology: A scoping review*. Retrieved from ResearchGate.

Martínez-Alcalá, C. I., Rosales-Lagarde, A., & Hernández-Alonso, E. (2021). Barriers and facilitators for the inclusion of older adults in digital education: A systematic review. *Educational Gerontology, 47*(1), 1–14.

McLaren, B. M., Nguyen, H. A., & Hou, X. (2023). Evaluating ChatGPT's decimal skills and feedback generation in a digital learning game. In *Artificial Intelligence in Education* (pp. 456–467). Springer.

Merino-Campos, C. (2025). The impact of artificial intelligence on personalized learning in higher education: A systematic review. *Trends in Higher Education*, *4*(2), 17. DOI: 10.3390/higheredu4020017

NeurologyLive. (2023). ChatGPT: A promising tool to combat social isolation and loneliness in older adults with mild cognitive impairment. Retrieved from https://www.neurologylive.com/view/chatgpt-promising-tool-combat-social-isolation-loneliness-older-adults-mild-cognitive-impairment

Olatunji, S. A., Shim, J. S., Syed, A., Tsai, Y.-L., Pereira, A. E., Mahajan, H. P., Mudar, R. A., & Rogers, W. A. (2025). Robotic support for older adults with cognitive and mobility impairments. *Frontiers in Robotics and AI*, *12*, 1545733. DOI: 10.3389/frobt.2025.1545733 PMID: 40259974

Population Reference Bureau. (2023). Fact sheet: Aging in the United States. Retrieved from https://www.prb.org/resources/fact-sheet-aging-in-the-united-states/

Qiu, Q., Wang, X., & Zhang, W. (2022). Virtual reality combined with cognitive training for mild cognitive impairment: A systematic review and meta-analysis. *International Journal of Environmental Research and Public Health*, *19*(16), 10123. DOI: 10.3390/ijerph191610123 PMID: 36011755

Robin, J., Harrison, J. E., Kaufmann, T., & Ritchie, C. W. (2023). Artificial intelligence-based linguistic biomarkers for Alzheimer's disease: A systematic review and meta-analysis. *Journal of Alzheimer's Disease*, *93*(2), 405–423. DOI: 10.3233/JAD-221003

Russell, S., & Norvig, P. (2021). *Artificial intelligence: A modern approach* (4th ed.). Pearson.

Schulz, R., Wahl, H. W., Matthews, J. T., Dabbs, A. D. V., Beach, S. R., & Czaja, S. J. (2022). Advancing the use of technology and artificial intelligence in aging research. *The Gerontologist*, *62*(1), 56–66. DOI: 10.1093/geront/gnab104 PMID: 34010393

Schulz, R., Wahl, H. W., Matthews, J. T., Dabbs, A. D. V., Beach, S. R., & Czaja, S. J. (2022). Advancing the use of technology and artificial intelligence in aging research. *The Gerontologist*, *62*(1), 56–66. DOI: 10.1093/geront/gnab104 PMID: 34010393

Sharkey, A., & Sharkey, N. (2022). Ethical concerns about AI use in elderly care. *Ethics and Information Technology*, *24*(3), 1–12. DOI: 10.1007/s10676-022-09613-x

Singh, B. P., & Sharma, T. (2024). Recent developments in AI and its impact on financial literacy. International Journal of Innovations in Science Engineering and Management, 3(Special Issue 2), 14–18.

Stampfl, R., Geyer, B., Deissl-O'Meara, M., & Ivkić, I. (2024). Revolutionising role-playing games with ChatGPT. arXiv preprint arXiv:2407.02048. https://doi.org//arXiv.2407.02048DOI: 10.48550

Talasila, S. D. (2024). AI-driven personal finance management: Revolutionizing budgeting and financial planning. *International Research Journal of Engineering and Technology*, *11*(7), 397–402.

Tang, W. K.-W., & Zhang, X.-Y. (2025). The role of technology in supporting lifelong learning for elderly. In Cheng, E. C. K. (Ed.), *Innovating education with AI* (pp. 195–205). Springer., DOI: 10.1007/978-981-96-4952-5_14

Tanveer, M., Richhariya, B., Khan, R. U., Rashid, A. H., Khanna, P., & Prasad, M. (2021). Machine learning techniques for the diagnosis of Alzheimer's disease: A review. *ACM Transactions on Multimedia Computing Communications and Applications*, *17*(1s), 1–35. DOI: 10.1145/3409264

Tsolaki, M., Kounti, F., & Poptsi, E. (2021). Cognitive training and cognitive rehabilitation for mild cognitive impairment: A review. *Brain Sciences*, *11*(12), 1577. DOI: 10.3390/brainsci11121577 PMID: 34942879

Turkle, S. (2024). The relational artifacts of AI: A new era of companionship. *Journal of Human-AI Interaction*, *3*(1), 15–27.

United Nations. (2022). World population ageing 2022 highlights. United Nations Department of Economic and Social Affairs. Retrieved from https://www.un.org/development/desa/pd/sites/www.un.org.development.desa.pd/files/world_population_ageing_2022_highlights.pdf

van Dijk, B., Lefebvre, A., & Spruit, M. (2025). Welzijn.AI: A conversational AI system for monitoring mental well-being and a use case for responsible AI development. arXiv preprint arXiv:2502.07983. https://arxiv.org/abs/2502.07983

Wickramathilaka, R., Brahim, M., & Marques, G. (2025). Accessibility of AI technologies for elderly users: A systematic literature review. *Technology in Society*, *74*, 102209. DOI: 10.1016/j.techsoc.2025.102209

Wiles, J. L., & Jayawardana, D. (2023). Older adults, AI, and privacy: Navigating ethical challenges. *Gerontechnology (Valkenswaard)*, *22*(1), 15–25. DOI: 10.4017/gt.2023.22.1.008.00

Wlodarski, R., Sousa, L. D. S., & Pensky, A. C. (2025). Level up peer review in education: Investigating genAI-driven gamification system and its influence on peer feedback effectiveness. arXiv preprint arXiv:2504.02962. https://arxiv.org/abs/2504.02962

Wong, A. K. C., Lee, J. H. T., Zhao, Y., Lu, Q., Yang, S., & Hui, V. C. C. (2025). Exploring older adults' perspectives and acceptance of AI-driven health technologies: A qualitative study. *JMIR Aging*, *8*, e66778. DOI: 10.2196/66778 PMID: 39937162

World Health Organization. (2022). Ageing and health. Retrieved from https://www.who.int/news-room/fact-sheets/detail/ageing-and-health

Yang, Y., Wang, C., Xiang, X., & An, R. (2025). AI applications to reduce loneliness among older adults: A systematic review of effectiveness and technologies. *Health Care*, *13*(5), 446. DOI: 10.3390/healthcare13050446 PMID: 40077009

Yang, Z., & Zhu, Z. (2025). ChatWise: AI-powered engaging conversations for enhancing senior cognitive wellbeing. arXiv preprint arXiv:2503.05740. https://arxiv.org/abs/2503.05740

Yaseen, H., Mohammad, A. S., Ashal, N., Abusaimeh, H., Ali, A., & Sharabati, A.-A. A. (2025). The impact of adaptive learning technologies, personalized feedback, and interactive AI tools on student engagement: The moderating role of digital literacy. *Sustainability (Basel)*, *17*(3), 1133. DOI: 10.3390/su17031133

Ye, J., Wang, Y., & Zhang, X. (2024). Social media and eHealth literacy among older adults: A systematic review. *Journal of Medical Internet Research*, *26*(1), e66058. DOI: 10.2196/66058 PMID: 40138684

Chapter 8
AI and the Future of STEM Education:
Transforming Pedagogy, Curriculum, and Workforce Readiness

Marvin Espinoza
https://orcid.org/0009-0009-5662-8239
California State University, San Bernardino, USA

ABSTRACT

The integration of Artificial Intelligence (AI) into STEM (Science, Technology, Engineering, and Mathematics) education has the potential to revolutionize how these disciplines are taught, learned, and applied. This chapter explores the evolving role of AI in shaping STEM education through personalized learning, adaptive assessments, and virtual laboratories. It examines the implications of AI-driven tools on curriculum design and pedagogical strategies, highlighting how these technologies foster critical thinking, problem-solving, and innovation. Moreover, the chapter investigates how AI can bridge the gap between educational outcomes and industry demands, equipping students with the technical and interdisciplinary skills necessary for success in the AI-driven workforce. Ethical considerations, challenges of implementation, and strategies to address inequities in access to AI-enhanced learning are also discussed. This chapter ultimately envisions a future where AI serves as a catalyst for equity, creativity, and excellence in STEM education.

INTRODUCTION

Artificial Intelligence (AI) has become an increasingly powerful tool across many sectors, including adult education and workforce development. In the context of lifelong learning, AI's impact is vast, creating new opportunities for learners of all ages and backgrounds (Knowles, Holton, & Swanson, 2024) to acquire knowledge, develop skills, and adapt to a rapidly changing job market. With an increasingly globalized and technology-driven economy, the importance of

DOI: 10.4018/979-8-3373-5097-4.ch008

AI in shaping the future of adult education cannot be overstated (Eraut & Hirsh, 2023; Zawacki-Richter, Marín, & Bond, 2023).

This chapter explores the transformative role of AI in adult education, focusing on how it enhances lifelong learning opportunities, supports workforce development, and helps individuals stay relevant in an ever-evolving job landscape (Carliner, 2023; Demartini & Tonelli, 2023). Adult education has always been vital for providing individuals with the skills and knowledge they need to succeed throughout their careers. However, the demands of the modern workforce are evolving rapidly due to the continuous advancement of technology, globalization, and shifting economic priorities.

To ensure that workers remain competitive and adaptable, lifelong learning has become a cornerstone of career development. Yet, adult learners often face unique challenges such as balancing work, family, and education, dealing with limited access to resources, and struggling to stay up to date with the latest technological trends. AI presents the opportunity to address these challenges and revolutionize the way adults engage with education (Grant & Vivian, 2023; Fisher & Rubenson, 2024).

One of the most significant benefits AI brings to adult education is its ability to offer personalized learning experiences. Traditional educational models often employ a one-size-fits-all approach, which can be ineffective, especially for adults with diverse backgrounds, learning preferences, and career goals. AI-driven tools and systems can break free from this model by creating tailored learning pathways that adapt to the needs of each individual (Crompton, Burke, & Lin, 2024). Whether it is recommending courses based on previous learning patterns or adjusting difficulty levels in real time, AI can help adults navigate their educational journeys in a way that aligns with their specific goals and schedules (Chi & Wylie, 2023; Aldowah, Al-Samarraie, & Fauzy, 2023).

Moreover, AI can significantly enhance workforce development by aligning educational content with the skills and competencies needed in today's rapidly changing job market. The increasing pace of automation, artificial intelligence, and machine learning in various industries has created a demand for workers who can perform complex tasks involving these technologies. Traditional training models often struggle to keep pace with the skills required for new job roles. AI can bridge this gap by providing dynamic, real-time updates to curricula and learning materials that align with industry needs. Additionally, AI-powered simulations and virtual environments offer hands-on experiences that can equip adult learners with the practical skills necessary to succeed in a tech-driven world (Hamann & Pollak, 2023; Johnson & Lester, 2023).

Beyond providing personalized learning and workforce-relevant skills, AI is also playing a crucial role in increasing access to adult education. In many parts of the world, adult learners face significant barriers to education, such as financial constraints, geographical isolation, or limited availability of suitable learning programs. AI has the potential to overcome these barriers by enabling flexible, accessible, and scalable educational experiences. Through online platforms, AI-powered tutoring systems, and virtual classrooms, learners can access educational resources from virtually anywhere at any time (Durak & Ataizi, 2023; Hersh & Johnson, 2023). Furthermore, AI can reduce costs by automating administrative tasks, providing instant feedback, and offering a variety of learning materials that cater to different learning styles (D'Mello & Graesser, 2023).

The integration of AI in adult education is not without its challenges, however. As with any technology, the implementation of AI in educational settings must be approached carefully to avoid exacerbating existing inequalities. For example, access to AI-powered educational tools may be limited in underserved or rural communities where internet infrastructure is inadequate.

Additionally, ethical concerns about data privacy, algorithmic biases, and the over-reliance on technology in the learning process must be addressed to ensure that AI enhances the educational experience without diminishing its quality or fairness. These issues must be examined thoroughly to ensure that the benefits of AI in adult education are accessible to all learners, regardless of their socio-economic status or location (Eaton & Brown, 2022; Selwyn & Jandrić, 2023).

In addition to these practical and ethical considerations, adult educators will need to adapt their teaching practices to fully harness the potential of AI. The role of the instructor will likely evolve as AI takes on more responsibilities in the learning process, including providing real-time feedback, grading assignments, and offering personalized learning recommendations. Educators will need to develop new skills and competencies to work effectively with AI tools, ensuring that they can continue to provide the human touch that is essential in adult education. The development of AI literacy among educators will be crucial for fostering an environment where both teachers and students can thrive in an AI-augmented classroom (Kasworm & Rose, 2023; Clark & Mayer, 2023).

The future of AI in adult education is poised to be dynamic, with continuous advancements in technology driving new opportunities for learners and educators alike. As AI becomes more integrated into everyday life, its influence on adult education will only continue to grow. From machine learning algorithms that assess and adapt to individual learning styles to the rise of intelligent tutoring systems that provide real-time guidance, AI offers the promise of a more inclusive, personalized, and efficient education system (Paredes & Rodrigues, 2024; Zawacki-Richter, Marín, & Bond, 2023). However, to fully realize the potential of AI in adult education, stakeholders including policymakers, educators, technology developers, and employers must collaborate to address the challenges and ensure that AI is used responsibly and equitably. (Ahuja, K., & Mitra, A., 2023)

In conclusion, AI holds great promise for transforming adult education, offering tailored learning experiences, supporting workforce development, and increasing access to education for learners of all backgrounds. As the world continues to change rapidly, AI will play a central role in helping adult learners develop the skills and knowledge they need to navigate the challenges of the modern workforce. However, for AI to reach its full potential, it is essential that its implementation is thoughtfully designed, with careful attention to ethical, practical, and equity considerations. By embracing AI's capabilities and addressing its challenges, adult education can become more effective, inclusive, and adaptable, ensuring that learners are prepared for the future of work and lifelong learning. (Aldowah, H., Al-Samarraie, H., & Fauzy, W. M., 2023)

AI-DRIVEN PERSONALIZATION IN ADULT EDUCATION

Artificial Intelligence (AI) is transforming the landscape of adult education by facilitating personalized learning experiences. Adult learners face unique challenges that can hinder their progress in education, ranging from time constraints to skills gaps and diverse educational backgrounds. AI-driven personalization allows educators and institutions to cater to these challenges, offering customized learning pathways that improve both engagement and outcomes for adult learners (Aldowah, Al-Samarraie, & Fauzy, 2023; Crompton, Burke, & Lin, 2024).

In this section, we will explore how AI is reshaping the way learning paths are personalized for diverse adult learners and how it addresses barriers such as time constraints, skills gaps, and varied educational backgrounds. Adaptive learning technologies, intelligent tutoring systems, and predictive analytics work together to analyze learner behavior, identify individual needs, and deliver tailored educational content that aligns with learner goals and preferences (Chi & Wylie, 2023; D'Mello & Graesser, 2023). These technologies are especially valuable in adult education where learners may be returning after extended gaps, navigating changing careers, or learning alongside full-time jobs and family responsibilities. (Baker, R., & Siemens, G., 2023)

By dynamically adjusting instruction in real time, AI supports adult learners in mastering new skills efficiently, staying motivated, and achieving outcomes that traditional one-size-fits-all approaches often fail to deliver (Paredes & Rodrigues, 2024; Grant & Vivian, 2023). This responsiveness enhances equity and inclusion by meeting learners where they are and guiding them toward where they need to be. (Bauer, K., & Schmidt, J., 2022)

CUSTOMIZING LEARNING PATHS FOR DIVERSE ADULT LEARNERS

One of the most powerful applications of AI in adult education is the ability to create customized learning paths for individual learners. Unlike traditional one-size-fits-all educational models, which often treat all students the same regardless of their needs or preferences, AI allows for the personalization of the learning experience based on a learner's unique abilities, goals, and challenges (Crompton, Burke, & Lin, 2024; Martinez & Gonzalez, 2023). Adult learners come from a wide variety of backgrounds and experiences, and their educational needs can differ significantly from traditional K-12 students. Some adult learners may have decades of work experience, while others may be returning to education after a long hiatus. This diversity requires a more flexible approach to teaching, one that adapts to the individual rather than assuming uniformity (Chi & Wylie, 2023).

AI can help adult education programs meet this challenge by using data to analyze each learner's performance, strengths, weaknesses, and learning preferences. For example, AI-powered learning management systems (LMS) can track how a learner interacts with various types of content—whether they prefer video lectures, written materials, or interactive quizzes—and adjust the learning path accordingly (D'Mello & Graesser, 2023; Shute & Rahimi, 2024). AI can also track progress in real time, dynamically adjusting the pace of instruction based on the learner's understanding. If a learner struggles with a particular concept, the AI system may offer additional resources, such as tutorials or practice exercises, to reinforce that topic before moving on to more advanced material (Aldowah, Al-Samarraie, & Fauzy, 2023).

For adult learners with specific career goals, AI can provide customized suggestions for coursework or skill development that aligns with their desired professional trajectory. For instance, if a learner is looking to transition into a tech-related field, AI can recommend specialized courses on coding, data analytics, or cybersecurity, tailored to the learner's current skill level and prior knowledge. Moreover, AI can help learners set realistic, personalized goals and track their progress, providing them with clear milestones to work toward (Paredes & Rodrigues, 2024). By offering a tailored approach that acknowledges the learner's goals and pace, AI helps adult learners stay motivated and engaged throughout their educational journey. (Bennett, T., & Roberts, L., 2024)

ADDRESSING TIME CONSTRAINTS THROUGH AI

Time constraints are one of the most significant barriers that adult learners face when pursuing further education. Many adults juggle multiple responsibilities, such as full-time employment, family care, and other personal commitments, which can make it difficult to find time for education. Traditional classroom-based learning, which often requires fixed schedules and physical presence, can be especially challenging for working adults. AI, however, offers a solution by enabling more flexible learning opportunities (Durak & Ataizi, 2023; Grant & Vivian, 2023).

AI-powered platforms allow adult learners to access educational content at their own convenience, on-demand, and from any location with an internet connection. Whether through self-paced online courses, mobile learning apps, or AI-driven tutoring systems, learners can engage with educational content whenever and wherever it fits into their schedules (Zawacki-Richter, Marín, & Bond, 2023).

Additionally, AI can provide real-time feedback and guidance, reducing the need for adult learners to spend time searching for resources or assistance. For instance, AI-driven chatbots or virtual assistants can answer common questions, guide learners through complex concepts, or clarify assignment requirements, giving learners instant support without needing to wait for a response from an instructor (Chi & Wylie, 2023; D'Mello & Graesser, 2023).

This efficiency enables adult learners to make the most of the limited time they have for education. By providing personalized recommendations and allowing for adaptive pacing, AI makes learning more efficient and accessible, helping learners progress without being burdened by rigid schedules (Aldowah, Al-Samarraie, & Fauzy, 2023; Paredes & Rodrigues, 2024).

CLOSING SKILLS GAPS WITH AI

Another significant challenge faced by adult learners is the presence of skills gaps, which are particularly common among those who may not have had access to high-quality education in the past or who have been out of the education system for an extended period. These skills gaps can prevent individuals from advancing in their careers or entering new fields. AI can play a pivotal role in addressing these gaps by offering adaptive learning systems that continuously assess a learner's knowledge and adjust the learning content to fill in the missing pieces (Aldowah, Al-Samarraie, & Fauzy, 2023; Shute & Rahimi, 2024).

For example, AI-powered systems can identify areas where a learner is struggling and provide targeted interventions to close those gaps. A common scenario in adult education is the learner who returns to education after a long break, only to find that their math or writing skills are no longer at the level required to succeed. AI systems can use diagnostic tools to assess these skills and then offer personalized practice exercises, step-by-step tutorials, and interactive lessons to help learners build the foundational skills necessary to succeed in their chosen field (D'Mello & Graesser, 2023; Chi & Wylie, 2023).

Moreover, AI can offer learners the opportunity to work on real-world problems that require them to apply newly acquired skills in a meaningful context. For example, an AI-powered system might recommend a project-based learning module that allows the learner to apply coding skills to build a simple website or develop a data analysis project. This hands-on approach helps adult learners bridge skills gaps while simultaneously building confidence and competence (Paredes & Rodrigues, 2024; Johnson & Lester, 2023).

In many cases, AI can also offer insights into industry-specific skills that are in demand, helping learners to focus their efforts on acquiring the competencies that will improve their employability. With real-time access to labor market data and AI-driven skills assessments, adult learners can receive recommendations for further training and certifications that align with current market trends (Demartini & Tonelli, 2023; Carliner, 2023). By providing a more personalized and targeted approach to skill development, AI ensures that adult learners can stay competitive in a constantly evolving workforce. (Behrend, T. S., & Sinar, E. F., 2024)

SUPPORTING LEARNERS FROM VARIED EDUCATIONAL BACKGROUNDS

Adult learners often come from diverse educational backgrounds, which can further complicate the task of designing a curriculum that meets their individual needs. While some learners may have completed formal education and have a strong academic foundation, others may have limited formal schooling or non-traditional education experiences. This diversity requires a more inclusive and adaptive approach to instruction, one that AI is well-positioned to provide (Fisher & Rubenson, 2024; Hersh & Johnson, 2023).

AI-driven personalization enables educational platforms to recognize the varying levels of experience and knowledge among adult learners and provide appropriate scaffolding to meet them where they are. For example, AI can use initial assessments to gauge a learner's prior knowledge and then recommend a learning path that is neither too advanced nor too basic. For learners with limited educational backgrounds, AI systems can offer foundational lessons that build their understanding step by step. For more advanced learners, AI can provide accelerated learning options that challenge them and promote deeper understanding (Crompton, Burke, & Lin, 2024; Chi & Wylie, 2023).

In addition to providing customized content, AI can also offer support for learners with different learning styles. Some adult learners may benefit from visual learning materials, while others may prefer auditory content or hands-on activities. AI systems can analyze learner behavior and adjust the delivery method based on these preferences. For instance, if a learner consistently interacts with video tutorials, the AI system might prioritize this type of content in future lessons. Learners who prefer written materials might be offered more reading-heavy content. This adaptability ensures that learners can access education in the mode that best suits their learning style, increasing engagement and retention (D'Mello & Graesser, 2023; Paredes & Rodrigues, 2024).

AI-driven personalization in adult education has the potential to revolutionize the learning experience for diverse adult learners. By tailoring learning paths to individual needs, addressing time constraints, closing skills gaps, and supporting learners from various educational backgrounds, AI enables a more flexible, efficient, and inclusive approach to lifelong learning. As the demands of the workforce continue to evolve, AI will play an increasingly vital role in ensuring that adult learners can develop the skills and knowledge required to succeed in the modern job market. Through personalized, adaptive learning experiences, AI helps adult learners overcome barriers and achieve their educational and career goals, making lifelong learning more accessible, efficient, and impactful (Zawacki-Richter, Marín, & Bond, 2023; Grant & Vivian, 2023).

AI FOR LIFELONG LEARNING

Lifelong learning has become an essential component of modern society as the demand for continuous education and professional development has escalated. In a rapidly evolving world, where technological advancements, industry trends, and global challenges emerge frequently, individuals must engage in ongoing learning to maintain their competitiveness and adaptability. Artificial Intelligence (AI) plays a transformative role in facilitating lifelong learning, offering personalized, accessible, and flexible learning experiences that empower individuals to enhance their skills and knowledge throughout their careers (Eraut & Hirsh, 2023; Zawacki-Richter, Marín, & Bond, 2023).

By supporting continuous education and professional growth, AI helps learners stay relevant in an ever-changing job market, fostering a culture of lifelong learning that is crucial for both individual success and societal development (Grant & Vivian, 2023; Fisher & Rubenson, 2024).

This section will delve into the role of AI in promoting lifelong learning and explore how AI-powered platforms support microlearning and just-in-time training, which are key components in the pursuit of ongoing education and skill enhancement. (Berg, M., & Kezar, A., 2024)

Role of AI in Promoting Continuous Education and Professional Growth

One of the primary challenges that individuals face in pursuing lifelong learning is the need for education to be tailored to their specific career goals, interests, and time constraints. Traditional educational models, which often emphasize fixed curricula and rigid schedules, can be ill-suited to the needs of adults who are juggling work, family, and other responsibilities. AI, however, provides a powerful solution by enabling more flexible and personalized learning experiences (Durak & Ataizi, 2023; Aldowah, Al-Samarraie, & Fauzy, 2023).

AI can support continuous education by offering customized learning pathways that adapt to an individual's unique needs and goals. AI-driven platforms can analyze a learner's performance in real time, tracking their strengths, weaknesses, and progress over time. This data-driven approach allows AI to offer personalized recommendations that guide learners toward the most relevant courses, certifications, or skill development activities (Chi & Wylie, 2023; D'Mello & Graesser, 2023). By assessing prior knowledge, AI systems can present the most appropriate content, either reinforcing areas where learners need improvement or providing advanced challenges for those who are more experienced. This dynamic customization ensures that learners are always progressing at their optimal pace, which helps prevent frustration and disengagement (Paredes & Rodrigues, 2024).

Moreover, AI supports professional growth by providing real-time feedback and adaptive learning experiences. (Fadel & Trilling, 2023) Professionals can rely on AI-powered tools to continuously assess their progress, identify skill gaps, and recommend next steps for improvement. For example, in technical fields such as software development or data science, AI-powered platforms can track a learner's coding proficiency, offer instant feedback on code quality, and suggest additional resources or practice exercises to improve specific areas (Johnson & Lester, 2023; Carliner, 2023). In this way, AI enables a cycle of continuous self-improvement, fostering a growth mindset that encourages lifelong learning (Felicia & Lameras, 2024).

AI also helps individuals stay updated with the latest industry trends, which is essential in today's fast-paced world. Many industries are evolving rapidly due to technological advancements, and professionals must continuously upgrade their knowledge to remain competitive. AI-driven platforms can curate learning content based on emerging trends, helping individuals stay informed and develop expertise in new areas. Whether through personalized news feeds, targeted courses, or notifications about newly emerging skill sets, AI ensures that learners are exposed to the latest developments in their fields (Hamann & Pollak, 2023).

Furthermore, AI supports the democratization of education by making continuous learning more accessible. Traditional forms of education, such as attending in-person classes or workshops, may not be feasible for everyone due to geographical, financial, or time-related constraints. AI-powered platforms allow learners to access high-quality education and training from anywhere in the world, breaking down barriers to access and creating equal opportunities for professional development (Hersh & Johnson, 2023; Fisher & Rubenson, 2024). With AI, learners can engage with content asynchronously, at their own pace, and based on their specific needs and interests. This accessibility enables a global learning community where individuals from diverse backgrounds and locations can participate in lifelong learning. (Bhattacharya, M., 2023)

AI-POWERED PLATFORMS FOR MICROLEARNING AND JUST-IN-TIME TRAINING

In the context of lifelong learning, microlearning and just-in-time training have gained significant popularity due to their efficiency and effectiveness in addressing learners' specific needs. AI plays a crucial role in enabling these learning methods by offering personalized, on-demand learning experiences that cater to learners' immediate needs and schedules (Crompton, Burke, & Lin, 2024; Grant & Vivian, 2023).

Microlearning refers to the practice of breaking down content into small, digestible chunks that can be consumed in short bursts of time. These learning modules typically last anywhere from a few minutes to around 15 minutes, focusing on specific skills or concepts. AI facilitates microlearning by analyzing learners' progress and providing personalized, bite-sized content based on their goals. For example, if a learner needs to improve their knowledge of project management tools, AI can provide short lessons, such as videos, quizzes, or interactive tutorials, that focus on specific tools or techniques. By breaking down learning into manageable pieces, microlearning helps learners absorb and retain information more effectively (Aldowah, Al-Samarraie, & Fauzy, 2023; Chi & Wylie, 2023).

The key advantage of microlearning is its flexibility. In today's world, many individuals struggle to find long stretches of time for traditional learning experiences. Microlearning, powered by AI, allows learners to engage with educational content in short, focused bursts that can fit easily into their busy schedules. This flexibility is particularly beneficial for working professionals who may only have small windows of time available for learning during their day, such as during commutes, lunch breaks, or between meetings. AI enables the creation and delivery of personalized microlearning experiences that meet learners where they are, helping them progress incrementally toward their educational goals (Paredes & Rodrigues, 2024).

Just-in-time training, another important element of lifelong learning, is a method of delivering training content exactly when it is needed, providing learners with timely and relevant information that they can apply immediately. Just-in-time training is especially effective in professional settings where employees may need to acquire specific skills or knowledge to address an immediate challenge or task. AI enables just-in-time learning by using data to predict when and what content will be most useful for a learner. For instance, if an employee is working on a project that requires using a new software tool, AI can push tutorials, walkthroughs, or troubleshooting guides in real time to help the learner overcome obstacles as they arise (D'Mello & Graesser, 2023; Johnson & Lester, 2023).

AI-driven platforms can track learners' activities and identify when they are struggling or encountering difficulties. Based on this data, the system can offer targeted learning resources at the exact moment of need. This just-in-time approach allows learners to solve problems more efficiently and continue their work without unnecessary delays. Moreover, the AI platform can continue to monitor the learner's progress and suggest additional resources or follow-up training as needed, ensuring that learning is continuous and seamlessly integrated into daily work processes (Hamann & Pollak, 2023; Carliner, 2023).

Just-in-time training powered by AI also supports self-directed learning, as individuals are empowered to seek out relevant content and solutions as needed. For instance, a manager who needs to learn how to handle a complex negotiation can access AI-driven training materials on negotiation tactics, offered right when the situation arises. This kind of personalized, responsive learning is essential in a fast-paced professional environment, where individuals must acquire new knowledge or skills quickly to remain productive and competitive (Felicia & Lameras, 2024; Eraut & Hirsh, 2023).

OVERCOMING BARRIERS TO LIFELONG LEARNING WITH AI

AI-powered platforms are uniquely positioned to address several barriers to lifelong learning, which have traditionally made continuous education challenging. Time constraints, geographical limitations, financial barriers, and skill gaps often prevent adults from engaging in formal education and training. AI-based systems can provide flexible, cost-effective, and accessible solutions to these challenges (Durak & Ataizi, 2023; Fisher & Rubenson, 2024).

For instance, AI-driven learning platforms eliminate the need for physical classrooms, making education more accessible to individuals in remote areas or those with mobility limitations. These platforms also reduce costs by offering scalable, online content that eliminates the need for expensive textbooks, travel, and venue costs associated with in-person training. By providing affordable access to high-quality learning resources, AI ensures that lifelong learning is within reach for a broad range of individuals, including those from underprivileged or marginalized backgrounds (Zawacki-Richter, Marín, & Bond, 2023).

AI also promotes a personalized approach that addresses learners' unique needs, further increasing the likelihood of success in lifelong learning. Traditional educational systems often adopt a one-size-fits-all approach, which can be less effective for adult learners with diverse experiences, learning styles, and goals. With AI, learners receive tailored content and pacing that is designed to match their prior knowledge, learning preferences, and objectives (Chi & Wylie, 2023; Aldowah, Al-Samarraie, & Fauzy, 2023).

AI is revolutionizing the landscape of lifelong learning by providing personalized, accessible, and flexible learning experiences that empower individuals to continuously acquire new skills and knowledge. By supporting microlearning and just-in-time training, AI enables learners to engage in focused, efficient learning that aligns with their immediate needs and time constraints (Crompton, Burke, & Lin, 2024; Paredes & Rodrigues, 2024).

The adaptability and scalability of AI-powered platforms make lifelong learning more attainable for individuals across different backgrounds, professions, and geographical locations. As industries evolve and new technologies emerge, AI will continue to play a critical role in supporting continuous education, helping learners stay relevant, competitive, and capable in a fast-changing world (Eraut & Hirsh, 2023; Grant & Vivian, 2023).

UPSKILLING AND RESKILLING THE WORKFORCE WITH AI

In today's fast-paced and ever-evolving global economy, the need for upskilling and reskilling the workforce has become increasingly critical. The technological advancements of the 21st century, particularly in areas such as Artificial Intelligence (AI), automation, and digital transformation, have altered the skills required across industries.

As businesses face challenges related to talent shortages, skill gaps, and technological disruptions, they must invest in continuous workforce development to ensure they remain competitive and capable of adapting to changing market demands. AI offers unique opportunities for upskilling and reskilling by enabling businesses to identify skills gaps, deliver personalized training, and create industry-aligned learning solutions that prepare workers for the jobs of tomorrow (Carliner, 2023; Demartini & Tonelli, 2023).

This section will explore the potential of AI to drive upskilling and reskilling initiatives within the workforce, emphasizing AI's role in identifying skills gaps, creating tailored training programs, and providing industry-aligned learning solutions to improve workforce readiness. (Brookfield, S. D., & Holst, J. D., 2023)

Leveraging AI to Identify Skills Gaps and Tailor Training Programs

One of the primary challenges organizations face when developing effective upskilling and reskilling programs is identifying the specific skills that need to be addressed. Traditional methods, such as surveys or performance reviews, can provide some insights, but they often lack the precision and real-time data necessary to make informed decisions about skills development. AI can play a critical role in overcoming this challenge by using data-driven insights to identify skills gaps in both individual employees and teams across an organization (Oswald, Behrend, & Sinar, 2024).

AI-driven platforms can analyze large datasets, including employee performance metrics, job requirements, industry trends, and other relevant factors, to pinpoint where skill shortages exist. By integrating machine learning algorithms, AI can predict the skills required for specific roles within the organization or industry, taking into account the impact of technological advancements or emerging trends. These predictive capabilities enable companies to proactively address skills gaps, ensuring that workers are equipped with the necessary competencies to remain productive and relevant in their roles (Hamann & Pollak, 2023).

Additionally, AI-based systems can offer real-time feedback and continuously monitor employees' learning progress, helping organizations identify skills gaps as they arise. For example, an AI-powered learning management system (LMS) can track a worker's engagement with various learning modules, identify areas where they are struggling, and suggest specific training or resources to help them develop the necessary skills. This personalized learning experience ensures that employees are always progressing toward skill mastery, while the organization gains valuable insights into where additional resources or training might be needed (D'Mello & Graesser, 2023; Paredes & Rodrigues, 2024).

Furthermore, AI can assist in aligning training programs with both individual needs and organizational goals. Traditional training programs are often one-size-fits-all, with little regard for the varying experiences, strengths, and weaknesses of individual learners. AI can help tailor training content to the specific learning needs of each employee, offering personalized recommendations based on factors such as prior experience, current role, and learning style. AI-driven platforms can adjust the level of difficulty, pace, and format of content to maximize engagement and retention, ensuring that training is effective and efficient (Chi & Wylie, 2023; Grant & Vivian, 2023).

For example, an employee in a technical role may need to focus on improving their proficiency with coding languages or specific software tools, while an employee in a management role may benefit from developing leadership skills or knowledge of strategic planning. AI can ensure that these employees are provided with targeted, relevant content that addresses their specific needs, allowing them to upskill or reskill more quickly and effectively (Johnson & Lester, 2023).

Industry-Aligned AI-Driven Learning Solutions for Workforce Readiness

As the workforce landscape continues to change, it is essential that upskilling and reskilling programs are closely aligned with the evolving demands of various industries. AI-powered learning solutions can ensure that training programs are directly relevant to the skills and knowledge required by employers, making workers more prepared for the jobs of tomorrow. The dynamic nature of the job market, characterized by rapid technological advancements and shifts in industry requirements, necessitates that workforce development programs be agile and adaptive (Demartini & Tonelli, 2023; Carliner, 2023).

AI-driven platforms can offer industry-aligned learning solutions by analyzing labor market trends (Greenfield, 2024), employer demands, and technological advancements to identify the specific skills required across different sectors. These platforms can integrate industry-specific data to offer targeted training content, ensuring that workers are equipped with the most relevant and up-to-date skills for their chosen field. Whether in technology, healthcare, manufacturing, or finance, AI can provide tailored learning pathways that reflect the current needs and future trends of each industry (Hamann & Pollak, 2023; Oswald, Behrend, & Sinar, 2024).

For instance, in the tech industry, AI-driven platforms can identify emerging technologies such as artificial intelligence, blockchain, or cybersecurity and create learning pathways that focus on the skills necessary to work with these technologies. Similarly, in healthcare, AI-powered systems can track trends in medical practices, telemedicine, and data analysis to design relevant training programs for medical professionals. By aligning training with industry needs, AI ensures that workers are prepared to meet current and future job demands (Johnson & Lester, 2023).

AI-driven platforms can also facilitate the creation of industry-recognized certifications and credentials that validate a worker's skills and knowledge in a particular domain. These certifications, which can be delivered through AI-powered systems, help workers demonstrate their expertise to employers and increase their employability. By offering industry-recognized credentials, AI ensures that training programs are aligned with the needs of employers and meet the standards set by professional associations or industry bodies (Grant & Vivian, 2023; Eraut & Hirsh, 2023).

Moreover, AI can enhance workforce readiness by providing just-in-time training solutions. In a rapidly changing job market, employees must be able to acquire new skills and knowledge quickly to adapt to new technologies, tools, or processes. AI-powered learning platforms can provide on-demand access to training materials, ensuring that employees can quickly learn what they need when they need it. For example, if a company implements a new software system, AI-driven platforms can offer quick tutorials and resources to help employees get up to speed, ensuring that they are able to adapt to the new system without disrupting productivity (Crompton, Burke, & Lin, 2024).

Another way AI supports workforce readiness is by facilitating collaborative learning and peer-to-peer interaction. AI-powered platforms can use machine learning algorithms to group learners with similar interests or complementary skills, enabling them to collaborate and share knowledge. This peer-driven learning environment can enhance the overall learning experience and create opportunities for employees to learn from one another's experiences and expertise. By fostering a sense of community and collaboration, AI can strengthen the collective knowledge of the workforce, ensuring that employees are not only upskilling individually but also contributing to the organization's overall capabilities (Paredes & Rodrigues, 2024).

Furthermore, AI can help organizations track and measure the effectiveness of their upskilling and reskilling initiatives, providing valuable insights into employee progress and training outcomes. By collecting data on employee engagement, completion rates, and skill improvement, AI platforms can offer detailed reports on the impact of training programs. (Lee & Kim, 2023) These insights enable organizations to refine their training strategies, identify areas for improvement, and ensure that upskilling efforts are aligned with business goals. With AI, organizations can create data-driven, results-oriented workforce development programs that drive measurable outcomes (Felicia & Lameras, 2024; Zawacki-Richter, Marín, & Bond, 2023).

AI for Workforce Resilience and Adaptability

In addition to improving individual skills, AI plays a critical role in fostering workforce resilience and adaptability. The COVID-19 pandemic has highlighted the importance of adaptability, as many workers have had to quickly transition to remote work or learn new technologies. AI helps workers develop the skills needed to navigate uncertainty and change, ensuring that they remain resilient in the face of disruption. By offering personalized learning paths and continuously updating training content to reflect the latest industry trends, AI ensures that workers are always prepared for evolving job demands and workplace conditions (Carliner, 2023; Demartini & Tonelli, 2023).

AI can also play a key role in promoting a culture of continuous learning within organizations. By providing employees with the tools and resources to continuously upskill, organizations can create a workforce that is agile, innovative, and capable of navigating change. With AI-driven learning solutions, employees are empowered to take ownership of their professional development, ensuring that upskilling and reskilling are seen as ongoing, lifelong processes (Eraut & Hirsh, 2023; Grant & Vivian, 2023).

As industries continue to evolve, AI is transforming the way organizations approach up-skilling and reskilling initiatives. By leveraging AI to identify skills gaps, create personalized training programs, and deliver industry-aligned learning solutions, organizations can ensure that their workforce is prepared for the jobs of tomorrow. AI-powered platforms offer the flexibility, scalability, and adaptability needed to address the challenges of a rapidly changing job market, helping workers develop the skills necessary to thrive in an AI-powered economy. With AI, businesses can build a more skilled, resilient, and future-ready workforce, driving innovation and competitiveness in an increasingly digital world (Oswald, Behrend, & Sinar, 2024; Zawacki-Richter, Marín, & Bond, 2023).

AI-ENHANCED PEDAGOGY FOR ADULT LEARNERS

As the world continues to evolve in terms of technology, the educational landscape, particularly adult education, must adapt to meet the needs of adult learners. Adult learners often juggle multiple responsibilities, such as work, family, and community involvement, which can make it challenging for them to engage with traditional educational formats. This is where the integration of Artificial Intelligence (AI) comes into play. AI-enhanced pedagogy offers personalized, flexible, and accessible learning experiences that can significantly improve the learning process for adults, making it more efficient, engaging, and relevant to their needs (Clark & Mayer, 2023; Hersh & Johnson, 2023).

This section explores how AI can be integrated into adult education through intelligent tutoring systems, virtual assistants, and AI-driven simulations. It also delves into how AI can encourage critical thinking and problem-solving skills in adult learners, providing them with the tools they need to succeed in both their personal and professional lives. (Brown, A. L., & Green, D. E., 2022)

Integrating Intelligent Tutoring Systems and Virtual Assistants in Adult Education

Intelligent tutoring systems (ITS) and virtual assistants have the potential to revolutionize adult education by providing personalized, adaptive learning experiences. These AI-powered tools can assist adult learners in navigating educational content at their own pace, ensuring that each learner receives the necessary support to succeed (D'Mello & Graesser, 2023; Chi & Wylie, 2023).

Intelligent tutoring systems are AI-driven platforms designed to simulate one-on-one tutoring interactions between a learner and a teacher. ITS are particularly beneficial in adult education because they allow learners to receive individualized support that suits their personal learning preferences, learning styles, and knowledge levels. For instance, an ITS can track a learner's progress, provide real-time feedback, and suggest targeted resources based on their current level of understanding. This allows adult learners to work at their own pace, progressing as quickly or slowly as needed without the pressure of keeping up with a classroom (Paredes & Rodrigues, 2024).

One of the key benefits of ITS is their ability to provide immediate and actionable feedback, which is critical for adult learners who may have been out of formal education for a significant period. In traditional learning environments, immediate feedback can sometimes be lacking, leading to frustration and disengagement. With an intelligent tutoring system, learners can receive responses to their questions and problems almost instantly. These systems can guide learners through complex concepts by breaking them down into more manageable pieces and offering hints or explanations as needed. Additionally, ITS can monitor the learner's progress over time, adapting the learning path based on their strengths and weaknesses (Crompton, Burke, & Lin, 2024).

For example, in a math course for adult learners, an ITS might provide targeted exercises on specific areas in which the learner is struggling, such as fractions or algebra. If the learner answers a question incorrectly, the system can offer step-by-step hints to guide them toward the correct answer and help reinforce the concept. By offering personalized guidance, ITS create a more effective learning environment that addresses the unique challenges adult learners face.

Virtual assistants, on the other hand, can play a key role in enhancing adult learners' experience by providing real-time support outside of the traditional classroom setting. These AI-powered assistants can serve as on-demand helpers that answer questions, provide clarification, and even help learners organize their study schedules. Virtual assistants, such as AI-driven chatbots or voice-activated systems like Amazon Alexa or Google Assistant, can provide immediate answers to frequently asked questions, give suggestions for study resources, or even offer reminders about upcoming deadlines or assignments (Felicia & Lameras, 2024; Johnson & Lester, 2023).

Virtual assistants are particularly useful for adult learners who have busy schedules and may not always have access to a traditional instructor. These assistants can bridge the gap by offering 24/7 support, enabling learners to continue their education at their own convenience. Furthermore, virtual assistants can help manage other aspects of adult learners' lives, such as time management and prioritization, which are often critical in balancing education with work and family responsibilities.

ENCOURAGING CRITICAL THINKING AND PROBLEM-SOLVING THROUGH AI-DRIVEN SIMULATIONS AND TOOLS

In addition to personalized support, AI can be used to foster higher-order thinking skills such as critical thinking and problem-solving, which are essential for adult learners in the workplace and society. These skills are particularly important in the context of lifelong learning, as they equip learners to adapt to the ever-changing demands of the workforce and contribute meaningfully to their communities (Jenkins, 2023; Paredes & Rodrigues, 2024).

AI-driven simulations and tools can encourage adult learners to engage in real-world problem-solving tasks and critically evaluate information from multiple perspectives. These tools provide learners with opportunities to practice decision-making, risk analysis, and problem-solving in a safe and controlled environment. By engaging in simulations, learners can experience realistic scenarios that mirror challenges they may face in their professional or personal lives, without the consequences of making mistakes in real-world situations (Felicia & Lameras, 2024; Liu & Wang, 2024).

For instance, in a business course for adult learners, AI-driven simulations can immerse learners in scenarios that require them to make strategic decisions based on data, such as analyzing market trends, managing a budget, or navigating competitive challenges. The system can adjust the scenario based on the learner's actions, presenting new challenges or presenting alternative outcomes to test the learner's decision-making abilities. By interacting with these dynamic simulations, adult learners are encouraged to think critically about their decisions, assess the potential impact of their actions, and develop effective solutions to complex problems. (Carter, M. A., & Rose, C. P., 2024)

AI tools can also promote collaboration and teamwork among adult learners, which is essential for developing problem-solving skills in a modern work environment. Many AI-driven platforms include collaborative features that allow learners to work together in virtual teams to solve problems, brainstorm ideas, and share knowledge. These platforms can include discussion boards, shared documents, or virtual meeting spaces where learners can collaborate on projects. As adult learners typically bring diverse experiences and knowledge to the table, collaborative problem-solving activities can help learners expand their perspectives and build more robust solutions to complex problems (Park & Jung, 2024; Clark & Mayer, 2023).

By encouraging collaboration, AI tools not only enhance learners' problem-solving skills but also improve communication, interpersonal skills, and teamwork. These tools promote critical thinking by providing adult learners with diverse viewpoints and encouraging them to think creatively and collaboratively, which are essential skills in problem-solving and innovation. (Chi, M. T. H., & Wylie, R., 2023)

AI-POWERED PERSONALIZATION AND ADAPTIVE LEARNING

Another important aspect of AI-enhanced pedagogy for adult learners is its ability to offer personalized learning experiences that foster deeper understanding and mastery of concepts. As adult learners often have varying levels of prior knowledge, learning styles, and motivations, AI can adapt the learning experience to meet their unique needs (Aldowah, Al-Samarraie, & Fauzy, 2023; Crompton, Burke, & Lin, 2024).

AI-powered systems can tailor the learning content to individual learners by analyzing their progress, preferences, and performance. For example, if an adult learner struggles with a particular concept, AI-driven platforms can adjust the learning path to provide additional resources, tutorials, or exercises to help the learner master the concept. Conversely, if a learner excels in a specific area, the system can provide more challenging material to keep them engaged and challenged. This adaptive learning model ensures that each learner's educational experience is optimized for their personal growth (Mayer, 2024) (Chi & Wylie, 2023; D'Mello & Graesser, 2023).

Furthermore, AI can use data to track learners' behavior and make predictions about their learning needs. By analyzing how long it takes learners to complete specific tasks, how well they perform on quizzes or assignments, and their engagement with various materials, AI systems can offer insights into areas where learners might need additional support or resources. This information can also be used to modify the curriculum dynamically, ensuring that learners are always working on material that is both relevant and challenging for them (Shute & Rahimi, 2024).

ETHICAL AND EQUITY CONSIDERATIONS IN AI FOR ADULT EDUCATION

As Artificial Intelligence (AI) continues to reshape the educational landscape, it introduces both opportunities and challenges, particularly in the context of adult education. While AI holds immense potential to revolutionize the way adult learners engage with content, gain skills, and navigate their educational journeys, it is crucial to address the ethical and equity concerns associated with its implementation. These concerns include ensuring equitable access to AI-powered learning resources and addressing data privacy, bias, and other ethical issues that may arise from the use of AI in education (Bauer & Schmidt, 2024; Selwyn & Jandrić, 2023).

This section explores the ethical and equity considerations in the implementation of AI for adult education. It delves into the challenges and opportunities related to providing equitable access to AI-powered learning resources for all adult learners, regardless of their socioeconomic background, geographic location, or technological literacy. Furthermore, it examines the ethical implications of AI in education, such as the potential for bias, the importance of data privacy, and the need for responsible AI practices to ensure that AI tools are used in ways that are fair, transparent, and aligned with educational values (Gholami & Watson, 2024; Hersh & Johnson, 2023).

Ensuring Equitable Access to AI-Powered Learning Resources

One of the most significant challenges in integrating AI into adult education is ensuring that all learners, regardless of their background, have equitable access to AI-powered learning resources. While AI has the potential to bridge gaps in education by providing personalized learning experiences and improving access to educational content, disparities in access to technology can exacerbate existing inequalities (Fisher & Rubenson, 2024; McKenna & Thompson, 2023).

Access to AI-powered learning tools requires reliable internet connectivity, appropriate hardware such as computers or mobile devices, and the necessary digital literacy skills to navigate AI-driven platforms. In many regions, particularly in underserved communities, access to these resources can be limited. For instance, adult learners in rural areas or low-income neighborhoods may not have access to high-speed internet or may lack the financial means to purchase the devices necessary to engage with AI-based educational tools. This technological divide can create barriers to entry for adult learners who would otherwise benefit from AI-powered education, potentially widening the gap between those who have access to technology and those who do not. (Clark, R. C., & Mayer, R. E., 2023)

In addition to hardware and internet access, digital literacy is another critical factor in ensuring equitable access to AI-powered learning. Adult learners who are unfamiliar with technology or who have limited experience using digital tools may face difficulties navigating AI-driven platforms. For these learners, even basic tasks such as accessing educational content, interacting with intelligent tutoring systems, or using virtual assistants may be overwhelming. This digital literacy gap can hinder the effectiveness of AI in adult education, as learners may struggle to fully engage with the technology (Durak & Ataizi, 2023).

To address these challenges, it is essential for educational institutions, policymakers, and technology providers to work together to ensure that AI-powered learning resources are accessible to all adult learners. This includes investing in infrastructure to improve internet access in underserved communities, providing affordable devices for learners who lack access to technology, and offering digital literacy training to help adult learners become comfortable using AI-powered tools. Additionally, AI platforms can be designed to be user-friendly and adaptable to the varying levels of digital literacy among adult learners, ensuring that learners can easily navigate the tools and access the content they need (Zawacki-Richter, Marín, & Bond, 2023).

Addressing Data Privacy in AI Implementation

Another key ethical consideration in the use of AI for adult education is the issue of data privacy. AI-driven platforms rely on vast amounts of data to personalize learning experiences, track learner progress, and provide targeted feedback. This data may include personal information, learning habits, performance metrics, and even sensitive data such as health information or employment history. Given the sensitive nature of this data, it is essential that AI systems used in adult education adhere to strict data privacy standards to protect learners' privacy and ensure that their information is handled responsibly (Eaton & Brown, 2022).

The collection, storage, and processing of data must comply with relevant data protection laws, such as the General Data Protection Regulation in the European Union, which mandates that organizations obtain explicit consent from individuals before collecting and processing their personal data. Educational institutions and AI providers must be transparent about the types of data they collect, how it will be used, and how long it will be retained. Additionally, learners should have the option to opt out of data collection or have their data deleted upon request (Bauer & Schmidt, 2024).

The potential for data breaches or misuse of personal information is a significant concern in the digital age. If AI systems do not implement robust security measures to protect learners' data, they risk exposing individuals to identity theft, fraud, or other malicious activities. Educational institutions must therefore ensure that AI-driven platforms are secure and that learners' data is encrypted and stored in compliance with industry best practices. (Cohen, E., & Alpert, R., 2022)

Furthermore, it is essential for adult learners to be informed about how their data is being used and to have control over their own personal information. AI platforms should provide clear and accessible privacy policies, and learners should be empowered to make informed decisions about how their data is shared and used. This level of transparency and control helps build trust in AI-powered learning tools and ensures that adult learners feel confident using these platforms without fear of their personal data being misused (Selwyn & Jandrić, 2023).

Addressing Bias in AI Systems

AI systems are not immune to biases. In fact, the algorithms that power AI-driven tools can inadvertently reinforce existing biases and inequalities, particularly if the data used to train these systems is flawed or biased. This is a critical issue in the context of adult education, as biased AI systems can perpetuate inequalities in learning outcomes, particularly for marginalized or underrepresented groups (Eaton & Brown, 2022; Selwyn & Jandrić, 2023).

Bias in AI can manifest in various ways. For example, if the data used to train an AI-driven tutoring system is primarily based on a specific demographic group, such as young, urban learners with high levels of education, the system may struggle to provide personalized support to adult learners who come from different backgrounds. The AI system may be less effective for learners who have different cultural, linguistic, or educational experiences, leading to inequities in the learning experience. (Crompton, H., Burke, D., & Lin, C.-H., 2024)

Similarly, if AI systems are trained on biased data that reflects stereotypes or discriminatory assumptions, they may perpetuate these biases in the learning materials or feedback they provide (Gholami & Watson, 2024; Bauer & Schmidt, 2024).

To address these concerns, it is essential for AI developers and educational institutions to prioritize fairness and inclusivity when designing AI-driven platforms for adult education. This includes ensuring that the data used to train AI systems is diverse, representative, and free from biases that could negatively impact learners. Furthermore, AI systems should be regularly audited and tested for bias, with ongoing updates and improvements made to mitigate any unintended consequences (Hersh & Johnson, 2023; Zawacki-Richter, Marín, & Bond, 2023).

Educational institutions should also provide training for educators to help them recognize and address potential biases in AI-powered tools. By raising awareness of the potential for bias and encouraging critical thinking about the use of AI in education, educators can help ensure that AI is used in ways that promote fairness and inclusivity (McKenna & Thompson, 2023).

Ethical Use of AI in Adult Education

Finally, the ethical use of AI in adult education involves ensuring that AI technologies are used in ways that align with the values of fairness, transparency, and accountability. AI should be used to augment the learning experience and provide personalized, equitable opportunities for adult learners, rather than replacing human educators or exacerbating inequalities. It is essential that AI is implemented in a way that complements and enhances the work of educators, rather than undermining it (Fisher & Rubenson, 2024).

Educational institutions must ensure that AI-powered tools are used ethically and responsibly, with a focus on improving learning outcomes, fostering inclusion, and addressing the diverse needs of adult learners. This requires ongoing collaboration between educators, policymakers, technology providers, and learners themselves to ensure that AI is used in ways that align with the broader goals of adult education, such as promoting lifelong learning, empowering learners, and preparing them for success in the workforce (Clark & Mayer, 2023; Paredes & Rodrigues, 2024).

The implementation of AI in adult education offers significant opportunities to enhance learning experiences, improve accessibility, and empower learners. However, it also raises important ethical and equity considerations that must be addressed to ensure that AI is used responsibly and in ways that benefit all learners. By prioritizing equitable access to technology, ensuring data privacy, addressing bias in AI systems, and promoting ethical practices, educational institutions can harness the power of AI to create a more inclusive, effective, and ethical adult education system (Fisher & Rubenson, 2024; Eaton & Brown, 2022; Selwyn & Jandrić, 2023).

As AI continues to evolve, it is essential that educators, policymakers, and technology developers work together to create AI-powered learning environments that support all adult learners, regardless of their background, and help them achieve their full potential (Hersh & Johnson, 2023; Gholami & Watson, 2024).

CHALLENGES AND STRATEGIES FOR AI ADOPTION

As Artificial Intelligence (AI) continues to transform the educational landscape, its adoption in adult education is gaining momentum. AI offers tremendous potential for personalized learning, improving access to education, and enhancing the overall learning experience for adult learners. However, the implementation of AI in adult education is not without its challenges. (Demartini, C. G., & Tonelli, M., 2023)

These challenges range from resistance to AI technologies to the need for building institutional capacity for large-scale integration and scaling efforts. In this section, we will explore the key challenges associated with AI adoption in adult education and propose strategies to overcome these barriers, ultimately enabling educational institutions to harness the full potential of AI (Zawacki-Richter, Marín, & Bond, 2023; Grant & Vivian, 2023).

Overcoming Resistance to AI Technologies in Adult Education

One of the most significant challenges in the adoption of AI in adult education is overcoming resistance to the technology. Resistance can come from various stakeholders, including educators, students, administrators, and even policymakers. Many of these individuals may be skeptical about the effectiveness of AI in education or fearful of the implications AI might have on their work and roles (Eaton & Brown, 2022).

Resistance from Educators

For educators, the prospect of integrating AI into their classrooms can seem daunting. Teachers who have spent years developing traditional teaching methods may view AI as a threat to their professional expertise and autonomy. There is a concern that AI could undermine the role of the educator, with machines replacing human instructors in the learning process. Educators may also worry that AI tools will reduce their ability to interact personally with students or undermine the value of face-to-face teaching (Clark & Mayer, 2023; Kasworm & Rose, 2023).

Additionally, some educators may be unfamiliar with the technology and lack confidence in their ability to effectively integrate AI into their teaching practices. They may see AI as a complex and intimidating field that requires specialized knowledge, which may deter them from adopting these technologies. The learning curve for AI tools can also be steep, requiring time, effort, and training to understand how to use them effectively in the classroom (Carter & Rose, 2024).

Resistance from Adult Learners

Adult learners themselves may also harbor skepticism about AI. Many adult learners return to education after years of being out of the formal education system and may not be accustomed to using advanced technological tools. For older generations, the rapid development of AI may seem overwhelming, and the idea of interacting with AI-powered platforms can be intimidating (Fisher & Rubenson, 2024).

There may also be concerns about privacy and data security. Adult learners may be hesitant to share personal or sensitive information with AI systems, especially if they are unsure how their data will be used or whether it will be kept confidential (Selwyn & Jandrić, 2023).

Resistance from Administrators and Policymakers

At the institutional level, administrators and policymakers may be reluctant to adopt AI technologies due to financial constraints, a lack of infrastructure, or concerns about the ethical implications of using AI in education. There may be a lack of understanding about how AI can improve educational outcomes, or they may worry about the challenges of training faculty members and students to effectively use AI systems. In some cases, administrators may view AI as an expensive and high-risk investment that requires significant upfront costs and resources (Walsh & Karsenti, 2023; Bauer & Schmidt, 2024).

Strategies for Overcoming Resistance

To overcome resistance to AI adoption, it is essential to engage in a comprehensive approach that involves all stakeholders. Several strategies can help mitigate concerns and foster a more positive attitude toward AI integration in adult education (Eaton & Brown, 2022; Bauer & Schmidt, 2024).

1. Providing Professional Development and Training for Educators

A key strategy for overcoming resistance from educators is to provide targeted professional development and training. Educators need to feel confident in their ability to use AI tools effectively in the classroom. Providing hands-on training sessions, workshops, and ongoing support can help educators build the skills and knowledge they need to integrate AI into their teaching practices (Clark & Mayer, 2023; Carter & Rose, 2024).

It is important to highlight the ways in which AI can enhance, rather than replace, traditional teaching methods. Educators should be encouraged to see AI as a tool that can complement their expertise and help them meet the diverse needs of adult learners. By demonstrating how AI can support personalized learning, improve student engagement, and provide real-time feedback, educators will be more likely to embrace AI as a valuable teaching resource (Chi & Wylie, 2023; Crompton, Burke, & Lin, 2024).

2. Promoting Awareness and Benefits for Adult Learners

To address resistance from adult learners, it is crucial to promote awareness of the benefits of AI-powered education. Adult learners should be educated about how AI can provide personalized learning experiences tailored to their individual needs, enabling them to learn at their own pace and according to their specific interests. Highlighting the flexibility and accessibility of AI-powered platforms can help alleviate concerns about technology intimidating or overwhelming learners. (DeMillo, R. A., 2023).

Moreover, educational institutions should emphasize the ways in which AI can help learners overcome time constraints, such as providing flexible learning schedules or offering microlearning opportunities. By focusing on the practical benefits AI can offer adult learners, educational institutions can foster a more positive attitude toward these technologies. (Diaz, V., & Molina, S., 2024)

3. Building Trust in AI Through Transparency and Data Security

To mitigate concerns about privacy and data security, it is essential to build trust between stakeholders and AI platforms. Educational institutions must be transparent about how AI systems collect and use data, ensuring that learners' personal information is protected. Adhering to stringent data privacy policies and ensuring compliance with relevant regulations, such as the General Data Protection Regulation (GDPR), can help reassure learners that their data is safe.

Institutions should also offer learners control over their data, allowing them to opt in or opt out of data collection and providing clear explanations of how their data will be used. This transparency helps build trust and reduces resistance to AI adoption. (Durak, G., & Ataizi, M., 2023).

Building Institutional Capacity for AI Integration and Scaling Efforts

In addition to overcoming resistance, another key challenge in adopting AI in adult education is building institutional capacity for integration and scaling. AI adoption requires significant resources, both in terms of infrastructure and personnel, to ensure its effective implementation across an institution. Educational institutions must develop the capacity to integrate AI technologies into their teaching and learning environments and scale AI adoption to benefit all adult learners (Zawacki-Richter, Marín, & Bond, 2023; Walsh & Karsenti, 2023).

1. Establishing a Clear Vision and Strategy for AI Integration

To successfully integrate AI into adult education, institutions must establish a clear vision and strategy for how AI will be used to enhance learning. This strategy should align with the institution's educational goals and the specific needs of adult learners. Institutions should take a holistic approach to AI adoption, considering how AI can support personalized learning, improve accessibility, and provide valuable insights into learner progress (Bauer & Schmidt, 2024; Clark & Mayer, 2023).

A strategic approach also involves identifying the specific AI tools and platforms that will best serve the needs of the institution and its learners. Whether it is using AI-powered tutoring systems, virtual assistants, or adaptive learning platforms, educational institutions must select AI tools that align with their teaching objectives and the technological capacity of the institution (Crompton, Burke, & Lin, 2024).

2. Investing in Infrastructure and Technological Resources

One of the primary barriers to scaling AI adoption in adult education is the lack of necessary infrastructure. To integrate AI successfully, institutions must invest in the technological resources needed to support AI-powered platforms. This includes upgrading their internet infrastructure, ensuring access to appropriate hardware, and adopting cloud-based systems that can handle the computational demands of AI (Fisher & Rubenson, 2024; McKenna & Thompson, 2023).

Institutions must also ensure that their AI platforms are scalable, capable of supporting large numbers of adult learners without sacrificing performance or quality. This involves investing in cloud computing resources, ensuring reliable internet connectivity, and ensuring that AI systems are flexible and adaptable to the evolving needs of the institution (Eraut & Hirsh, 2023).

3. Collaborating with Technology Providers and Experts

Building institutional capacity for AI integration also involves collaboration with technology providers and AI experts. Educational institutions should partner with AI vendors and developers to ensure that the tools they adopt are user-friendly, effective, and tailored to the specific needs of adult learners. Collaborative partnerships can also provide valuable training and support for faculty and staff, ensuring that they have the knowledge and skills needed to integrate AI into their teaching practices (Hamann & Pollak, 2023; Oswald, Behrend, & Sinar, 2024).

Collaborating with experts in AI and education can also help institutions stay informed about the latest trends and best practices in AI adoption. By learning from other institutions that have successfully implemented AI technologies, educational organizations can gain valuable insights into how to overcome challenges and scale AI integration effectively (Grant & Vivian, 2023).

Adopting AI technologies in adult education presents both challenges and opportunities.

Overcoming resistance to AI and building institutional capacity for AI integration are crucial steps in ensuring that AI's transformative potential is fully realized. By addressing concerns through targeted professional development, promoting awareness among learners, building trust through transparency, and investing in infrastructure, educational institutions can overcome these challenges and successfully adopt AI to enhance adult learning experiences (Clark & Mayer, 2023; Bauer & Schmidt, 2024; Fisher & Rubenson, 2024). With strategic planning, collaboration, and a focus on building capacity, AI can be integrated into adult education systems to promote personalized, flexible, and lifelong learning opportunities for all (Zawacki-Richter, Marín, & Bond, 2023; Grant & Vivian, 2023).

As we look toward the future, the role of Artificial Intelligence (AI) in adult education and workforce development is poised to become even more significant, driving transformation across educational landscapes globally. AI has the potential to reshape how adults engage in learning and how institutions and organizations prepare individuals for the workforce. (UNESCO, 2023) This section will explore the vision for AI in fostering lifelong learning ecosystems, as well as the broader, global implications for adult education and workforce development (Eraut & Hirsh, 2023; Zawacki-Richter, Marín, & Bond, 2023).

VISION FOR THE ROLE OF AI IN FOSTERING LIFELONG LEARNING ECOSYSTEMS

The concept of lifelong learning has gained widespread importance in the 21st century, driven by rapid technological advancements, globalization, and shifting labor market demands. In this context, AI presents a unique opportunity to cultivate robust lifelong learning ecosystems—environments that facilitate continuous, self-directed, and personalized learning throughout an individual's life. AI has the capacity to tailor learning experiences, improve access to knowledge, and empower adult learners to pursue educational opportunities in ways that were previously unavailable or impractical (Eraut & Hirsh, 2023; Zawacki-Richter, Marín, & Bond, 2023).

AI-powered platforms and tools are already playing a pivotal role in facilitating personalized learning journeys. By using AI to analyze learners' progress, preferences, and goals, these technologies are enabling the creation of individualized learning paths. Such platforms offer personalized recommendations, adjust the difficulty level of content in real time, and provide learners with instant feedback on their performance. For adult learners, who often balance education with professional and personal commitments, these features allow for flexible learning that aligns with their specific needs and time constraints (Aldowah, Al-Samarraie, & Fauzy, 2023; D'Mello & Graesser, 2023).

Looking ahead, AI will continue to serve as the backbone of lifelong learning ecosystems. As the workforce becomes more fluid and dynamic, the need for employees to acquire new skills or refine existing ones will only intensify. AI will make it easier to facilitate this ongoing process of upskilling and reskilling by delivering customized learning experiences that respond to the shifting requirements of the labor market (Demartini & Tonelli, 2023; Carliner, 2023).

Furthermore, AI can enhance collaborative learning experiences, which are essential for fostering a sense of community among learners. Through intelligent virtual assistants, AI tools can promote discussion, peer feedback, and group problem-solving, enabling adult learners to connect with others across geographical boundaries. This will be especially important as more adult learners engage in remote, online, and hybrid learning environments (Park & Jung, 2024; Paredes & Rodrigues, 2024).

Another important direction is the integration of AI with other emerging technologies, such as the Internet of Things (IoT), blockchain, and augmented reality (AR). These technologies, when combined with AI, can offer even more immersive and interactive learning experiences. For example, AI-powered virtual and augmented reality tools can provide adults with hands-on simulations (Moreno, 2024) and immersive learning environments that enhance understanding and retention, particularly in fields requiring practical skills (Felicia & Lameras, 2024; Johnson & Lester, 2023).

AI can also contribute to the democratization of education, breaking down barriers related to access and affordability. (Siemens, 2024) By providing scalable learning solutions that cater to learners from diverse socioeconomic backgrounds, AI can create more equitable learning opportunities. With the power of AI, educational resources can be tailored to suit the needs of disadvantaged or underserved populations, opening doors for individuals who may have otherwise been excluded from quality education and professional development opportunities (Fisher & Rubenson, 2024; Grant & Vivian, 2023).

The Global Impact of AI in Transforming Adult Education and Workforce Development

The integration of AI in adult education and workforce development will have far-reaching implications, not just locally or regionally, but on a global scale. As economies worldwide continue to evolve and adapt to new technologies, AI will play a critical role in ensuring that the global workforce is equipped to meet these changes (Demartini & Tonelli, 2023; Carliner, 2023).

One of the key global impacts of AI will be the ability to bridge the skills gap that exists in many industries. Across the world, there is a growing need for workers to acquire new skills to keep pace with automation, digitalization, and artificial intelligence itself. AI can help address these gaps by providing targeted training and skill-building resources that are directly aligned with industry needs. By continuously analyzing labor market trends, AI can identify emerging skill requirements and help design educational programs that are responsive to these needs. This will be especially important in regions where industries are undergoing rapid technological shifts, such as the automation of manufacturing or the expansion of digital services (Hamann & Pollak, 2023; Oswald, Behrend, & Sinar, 2024).

Additionally, AI has the potential to contribute to workforce development in underserved and developing regions. By offering online, accessible, and cost-effective training, AI-powered educational platforms can help people in remote or impoverished areas gain the skills needed for employment in the global economy. This is especially important for regions that lack robust educational infrastructure or have limited access to traditional educational institutions. AI can provide these learners with high-quality, scalable education and career development opportunities that were once out of reach (Fisher & Rubenson, 2024; Zawacki-Richter, Marín, & Bond, 2023).

Furthermore, as economies become increasingly interconnected, the demand for a globally competent workforce is also growing. AI will play a crucial role in preparing adult learners to work in this interconnected, digital world. By providing language translation, cultural context, and remote collaboration tools, AI can enhance cross-cultural communication and global teamwork. This is particularly valuable for workers who engage in international trade, development, or collaborative projects with teams from different countries. AI can also assist with skills development in niche fields that require international knowledge, such as global health initiatives or international finance, making it easier for workers to gain the expertise needed for global challenges (Paredes & Rodrigues, 2024; Johnson & Lester, 2023).

AI-powered learning platforms are also enabling companies to create training programs that are customized to their specific needs. For example, a global corporation might use AI to develop a training program that adapts to the learning styles and skill levels of its employees across various regions. This ensures that training programs are both relevant and effective, regardless of where the employees are based. This ability to provide customized, efficient training will increase workplace productivity and ultimately improve business outcomes on a global scale (Grant & Vivian, 2023; Eraut & Hirsh, 2023).

On a broader level, AI has the potential to reshape the relationship between education and the workforce. Traditionally, education systems have been designed to prepare individuals for the workforce, but with the rapid pace of technological change, the link between education and work is becoming more fluid. AI will allow for more real-time learning opportunities, enabling individuals to continuously update their skills to match evolving job market demands. This will be especially important in industries that require continuous professional development, such as technology, healthcare, and finance (Crompton, Burke, & Lin, 2024).

Moreover, AI can facilitate more efficient workforce planning and talent management. By analyzing data on skills, performance, and career trajectories, AI can help companies predict workforce needs, identify skill shortages, and make data-driven decisions about recruitment and training. This can lead to more effective talent development, ensuring that businesses have access to the skills they need while providing workers with the tools to grow in their careers (Felicia & Lameras, 2024; Chi & Wylie, 2023).

The future of AI in adult education and workforce development holds immense promise. By fostering lifelong learning ecosystems and promoting continuous education, AI can address skills gaps, improve access to education, and empower individuals to reach their professional goals. On a global scale, AI has the potential to bridge disparities in educational opportunities, create a more equitable workforce, and drive economic growth by equipping workers with the skills needed to thrive in a rapidly changing world (Zawacki-Richter, Marín, & Bond, 2023; Grant & Vivian, 2023).

However, to fully realize these benefits, stakeholders at all levels, educators, employers, policymakers, and learners themselves, must work together to address the challenges of AI integration and ensure that these technologies are used ethically and responsibly. By doing so, we can unlock the full potential of AI to transform adult education and workforce development, creating a more adaptable, skilled, and globally connected workforce for the future (Eaton & Brown, 2022; Gholami & Watson, 2024).

SIGNIFICANCE OF THE CHAPTER

This chapter contributes significantly to the expanding body of knowledge on the transformative potential of AI in adult education by offering both theoretical and practical perspectives. It explores how AI can revolutionize lifelong learning programs by personalizing education, addressing barriers faced by adult learners, and fostering continuous skill development (Aldowah, Al-Samarraie, & Fauzy, 2023; Crompton, Burke, & Lin, 2024).

Furthermore, it delves into the role of AI in upskilling and reskilling initiatives, emphasizing its ability to tailor training programs based on industry needs and individual learning pathways (Demartini & Tonelli, 2023; Oswald, Behrend, & Sinar, 2024). This chapter not only highlights the opportunities that AI presents in enhancing adult education but also critically examines the challenges that come with its integration, such as ethical concerns, equity issues, and resistance to new technologies (Eaton & Brown, 2022; Selwyn & Jandrić, 2023).

By addressing these opportunities and challenges in detail, this chapter equips educators, policymakers, and industry leaders with actionable insights and tools for integrating AI-driven solutions. It emphasizes the need for a collaborative approach to ensure the ethical, equitable, and effective implementation of AI in educational settings (Bauer & Schmidt, 2024; Grant & Vivian, 2023). Ultimately, this chapter aims to provide a roadmap for advancing workforce readiness globally, empowering adult learners to engage in lifelong learning and succeed in an increasingly AI-driven world (Eraut & Hirsh, 2023; Zawacki-Richter, Marín, & Bond, 2023).

CONCLUSION

In conclusion, this chapter has explored the transformative potential of artificial intelligence (AI) in adult education, particularly in fostering lifelong learning and enhancing workforce development. As the world continues to evolve at a rapid pace, driven by technological advancements, the need for adults to continuously adapt, acquire new skills, and remain competitive in the workforce has never been greater. AI presents a powerful tool for meeting these needs by offering personalized, flexible, and efficient learning experiences that can be tailored to the unique needs of each learner (Aldowah, Al-Samarraie, & Fauzy, 2023; Crompton, Burke, & Lin, 2024).

AI-driven personalization has emerged as one of the most promising approaches for overcoming the challenges that adult learners face, including time constraints, skills gaps, and diverse educational backgrounds. By customizing learning paths and delivering just-in-time training, AI enables learners to engage in meaningful, relevant education that directly contributes to their personal and professional growth. Furthermore, AI's ability to identify and address skills gaps allows for more targeted upskilling and reskilling initiatives, empowering individuals to stay ahead in an ever-changing labor market (Demartini & Tonelli, 2023; D'Mello & Graesser, 2023).

In addition to enhancing the learning experience, AI also offers significant opportunities for fostering critical thinking, problem-solving, and collaboration among adult learners. By integrating intelligent tutoring systems, virtual assistants, and AI-driven simulations, adult education programs can create environments where learners actively engage with the material, develop essential skills, and apply their learning to real-world contexts. These AI-enhanced pedagogies not only make learning more engaging but also prepare learners for the complex challenges they will face in their careers (Chi & Wylie, 2023; Felicia & Lameras, 2024).

However, as we embrace the potential of AI, it is essential to recognize the ethical and equity considerations that come with its implementation. Ensuring equitable access to AI-powered learning resources, protecting learners' data privacy, and addressing biases in AI systems are critical components of successfully integrating AI into adult education. Policymakers, educators, and industry leaders must work collaboratively to establish frameworks and strategies that prioritize fairness, inclusivity, and transparency in AI adoption (Eaton & Brown, 2022; Selwyn & Jandrić, 2023).

As we look to the future, the role of AI in adult education and workforce development will only continue to grow. By investing in AI-powered learning solutions, fostering a culture of lifelong learning, and promoting ethical and equitable practices, we can create an educational ecosystem that empowers adult learners to thrive in the digital age. This chapter has outlined the key strategies and considerations necessary for achieving these goals, offering valuable insights that will help shape the future of adult education and workforce readiness in an AI-driven world (Grant & Vivian, 2023; Zawacki-Richter, Marín, & Bond, 2023).

REFERENCES

Ahuja, K., & Mitra, A. (2023). AI in lifelong learning: Personalization and adaptability. *Educational Technology Research and Development, 71*(2), 237–258.

Aldowah, H., Al-Samarraie, H., & Fauzy, W. M. (2023). AI-based adaptive learning systems: Revolutionizing adult education. *Educational Technology Research and Development, 71*(4), 989–1007.

Baker, R., & Siemens, G. (2023). Artificial intelligence and adaptive learning: Shaping the future of adult education. *Journal of Adult and Continuing Education, 29*(1), 45–61.

Bauer, K., & Schmidt, J. (2022). Ethical AI implementation in adult education: Challenges and strategies. *AI & Society, 37*(3), 935–947.

Bennett, T., & Roberts, L. (2024). Addressing digital divides in AI-enhanced adult learning. *Educational Review, 76*(1), 33–49.

Berg, M., & Kezar, A. (2024). Equity-minded leadership in the age of artificial intelligence: Navigating innovation and inclusion in higher education. *Journal of Higher Education Leadership, 92*(1), 33–52.

Bhattacharya, M. (2023). The role of AI in upskilling and reskilling initiatives. *Workforce Development Journal, 14*(2), 75–88.

Brookfield, S. D., & Holst, J. D. (2023). Critical adult education in the era of AI. *Adult Education Quarterly, 73*(2), 103–121.

Brown, A. L., & Green, D. E. (2022). AI-driven microlearning for workforce training. *Journal of Vocational Education and Training, 74*(3), 512–529.

Carliner, S. (2023). The evolving role of instructional designers in the age of AI. *Performance Improvement, 62*(3), 26–35.

Carter, M. A., & Rose, C. P. (2024). Intelligent tutoring systems and adult learning. *Computers & Education, 207*, 104901.

Chi, M. T. H., & Wylie, R. (2023). The ICAP framework: Linking cognitive engagement to active learning outcomes. *Educational Psychologist, 58*(1), 1–16.

Clark, R. C., & Mayer, R. E. (2023). *AI-enhanced e-learning: Principles and practice* (4th ed.). John Wiley & Sons.

Cohen, E., & Alpert, R. (2022). AI for workforce readiness: Aligning skills development with industry demands. *Human Resource Development Review, 21*(4), 372–392.

Demartini, C. G., & Tonelli, M. (2023). Artificial intelligence in education: A review of the current state of research. *Journal of International Students, 11*(2), 45–67.

DeMillo, R. A. (2023). *The future of lifelong learning in an AI-driven world*. Routledge.

Diaz, V., & Molina, S. (2024). AI-enhanced pedagogy in adult education. *Adult Learning*, *35*(1), 25–33.

Eaton, S. E., & Brown, B. (2022). Ethical considerations for AI in education. *Ethics and Education*, *17*(3), 289–305.

Fadel, C., & Trilling, B. (2023). *Artificial intelligence in lifelong learning: Preparing adults for the future*. Jossey-Bass.

Fisher, D., & Rubenson, K. (2024). Adult learning in the digital era: Policy perspectives and lifelong learning strategies. *International Review of Education*, *70*(1–2), 55–74.

Greenfield, P. M. (2024). Cognitive implications of AI-driven adaptive learning systems. *Mind, Brain and Education : the Official Journal of the International Mind, Brain, and Education Society*, *18*(1), 32–43.

Jenkins, J. (2023). Leveraging AI for workforce adaptability. Workforce Education Forum, 15(1), 18–30.

Knowles, M. S., Holton, E. F., & Swanson, R. A. (2024). *The adult learner: The definitive classic in adult education and human resource development* (9th ed.). Routledge. DOI: 10.4324/9781003387671

Lee, S. Y., & Kim, D. (2023). Predictive analytics in adult education: Enhancing learner success. *Journal of Educational Technology & Society*, *26*(1), 147–160.

Liu, D., & Wang, T. (2024). AI-enhanced collaborative learning environments for adult education. Computers in Human Behavior, 144, 107920. (Eraut, M., & Hirsh, W., 2023)

Martinez, J., & Gonzalez, E. (2023). Ethical frameworks for AI implementation in adult education. *Ethics and Information Technology*, *25*(2), 199–211.

McKenna, R., & Thompson, L. (2023). AI and adult literacy: Expanding access through adaptive technologies. *Adult Basic Education Journal*, *17*(1), 45–58.

Moreno, R., & Perez, L. (2024). Personalized AI systems in vocational education. *Vocational Learning Journal*, *17*(2), 128–140.

Park, Y., & Jung, J. (2024). Virtual assistants in adult education: Improving learner engagement and autonomy. *Adult Education Quarterly*, *74*(1), 54–71.

Siemens, G. (2024). Connectivism and artificial intelligence: New paradigms for adult learning. *Educational Review*, *76*(2), 192–207.

Walsh, T., & Karsenti, T. (2023). Implementing AI in adult education: Strategies for effective integration. *Canadian Journal of Educational Administration and Policy*, *2023*(199), 35–56.

Chapter 9
AI in Adult Education: Transforming Lifelong Learning and Workforce Development

Marvin Espinoza
https://orcid.org/0009-0009-5662-8239
California State University, San Bernardino, USA

ABSTRACT

The advent of Artificial Intelligence (AI) is reshaping adult education, lifelong learning, and workforce development in unprecedented ways. This chapter examines the integration of AI into adult education, exploring its role in personalized learning, upskilling, and reskilling the workforce. By leveraging AI technologies such as adaptive learning systems, intelligent tutoring, and predictive analytics, educators can address the unique needs of adult learners and create more inclusive and accessible learning environments. The chapter delves into the potential of AI to align adult education programs with evolving industry demands, fostering workforce readiness in an era of rapid technological change. Additionally, the ethical considerations, challenges of implementation, and strategies for equitable AI integration in adult education are discussed. The chapter concludes by presenting a vision for the future of AI in lifelong learning and its impact on empowering individuals and advancing global workforce development.

INTRODUCTION

Artificial Intelligence (AI) has become an increasingly powerful tool across many sectors, including adult education and workforce development (Ghosh & Parashar, 2022). In the context of lifelong learning, AI's impact is vast, creating new opportunities for learners of all ages and backgrounds (Knowles, Holton, & Swanson, 2024) to acquire knowledge, develop skills, and adapt to a rapidly changing job market. With an increasingly globalized and technology-driven economy, the importance of AI in shaping the future of adult education cannot be overstated (Eraut & Hirsh, 2023; Zawacki-Richter, Marín, & Bond, 2023).

This chapter explores the transformative role of AI in adult education, focusing on how it enhances lifelong learning opportunities, supports workforce development, and helps individuals stay relevant in an ever-evolving job landscape (Carliner, 2023; Demartini & Tonelli, 2023).

DOI: 10.4018/979-8-3373-5097-4.ch009

Adult education has always been vital for providing individuals with the skills and knowledge they need to succeed throughout their careers. However, the demands of the modern workforce are evolving rapidly due to the continuous advancement of technology, globalization, and shifting economic priorities (Carliner, 2023; Demartini & Tonelli, 2023).

To ensure that workers remain competitive and adaptable, lifelong learning has become a cornerstone of career development. Yet, adult learners often face unique challenges such as balancing work, family, and education, dealing with limited access to resources, and struggling to stay up to date with the latest technological trends. AI presents the opportunity to address these challenges and revolutionize the way adults engage with education (Grant & Vivian, 2023; Fisher & Rubenson, 2024; Hsieh & Chen, 2022).

One of the most significant benefits AI brings to adult education is its ability to offer personalized learning experiences (Aldowah, Al-Samarraie, & Fauzy, 2023; Crompton, Burke, & Lin, 2024). Traditional educational models often employ a one-size-fits-all approach, which can be ineffective, especially for adults with diverse backgrounds, learning preferences, and career goals. AI-driven tools and systems can break free from this model by creating tailored learning pathways that adapt to the needs of each individual (Crompton, Burke, & Lin, 2024). Whether it is recommending courses based on previous learning patterns or adjusting difficulty levels in real time, AI can help adults navigate their educational journeys in a way that aligns with their specific goals and schedules (Chi & Wylie, 2023; Aldowah, Al-Samarraie, & Fauzy, 2023).

Moreover, AI can significantly enhance workforce development by aligning educational content with the skills and competencies needed in today's rapidly changing job market. The increasing pace of automation, artificial intelligence, and machine learning in various industries has created a demand for workers who can perform complex tasks involving these technologies (Demartini & Tonelli, 2023; Johnson & Lester, 2023). Traditional training models often struggle to keep pace with the skills required for new job roles. AI can bridge this gap by providing dynamic, real-time updates to curricula and learning materials that align with industry needs. Additionally, AI-powered simulations and virtual environments offer hands-on experiences that can equip adult learners with the practical skills necessary to succeed in a tech-driven world (Hamann & Pollak, 2023; Johnson & Lester, 2023).

Beyond providing personalized learning and workforce-relevant skills, AI is also playing a crucial role in increasing access to adult education (Zawacki-Richter, Marín, & Bond, 2023). In many parts of the world, adult learners face significant barriers to education, such as financial constraints, geographical isolation, or limited availability of suitable learning programs. AI has the potential to overcome these barriers by enabling flexible, accessible, and scalable educational experiences (Nash & Burke, 2024). Through online platforms, AI-powered tutoring systems, and virtual classrooms, learners can access educational resources from virtually anywhere at any time (Durak & Ataizi, 2023; Hersh & Johnson, 2023). Furthermore, AI can reduce costs by automating administrative tasks, providing instant feedback, and offering a variety of learning materials that cater to different learning styles (D'Mello & Graesser, 2023).

The integration of AI in adult education is not without its challenges, however. As with any technology, the implementation of AI in educational settings must be approached carefully to avoid exacerbating existing inequalities (Eaton & Brown, 2022; Selwyn & Jandrić, 2023). For example, access to AI-powered educational tools may be limited in underserved or rural communities where internet infrastructure is inadequate.

Additionally, ethical concerns about data privacy, algorithmic biases, and the over-reliance on technology in the learning process must be addressed to ensure that AI enhances the educational experience without diminishing its quality or fairness (Bauer & Schmidt, 2022; Gholami & Watson, 2024). These issues must be examined thoroughly to ensure that the benefits of AI in adult education are accessible to all learners, regardless of their socio-economic status or location (Eaton & Brown, 2022; Selwyn & Jandrić, 2023).

In addition to these practical and ethical considerations, adult educators will need to adapt their teaching practices to fully harness the potential of AI. The role of the instructor will likely evolve as AI takes on more responsibilities in the learning process, including providing real-time feedback, grading assignments, and offering personalized learning recommendations (Kasworm & Rose, 2022; Clark & Mayer, 2023). Educators will need to develop new skills and competencies to work effectively with AI tools, ensuring that they can continue to provide the human touch that is essential in adult education (Clark & Mayer, 2023; Garrison & Vaughan, 2023). The development of AI literacy among educators will be crucial for fostering an environment where both teachers and students can thrive in an AI-augmented classroom (Kasworm & Rose, 2023; Clark & Mayer, 2023).

The future of AI in adult education is poised to be dynamic, with continuous advancements in technology driving new opportunities for learners and educators alike. As AI becomes more integrated into everyday life, its influence on adult education will only continue to grow (Cheng, 2023; Zhang & Lu, 2023). From machine learning algorithms that assess and adapt to individual learning styles to the rise of intelligent tutoring systems that provide real-time guidance, AI offers the promise of a more inclusive, personalized, and efficient education system (Paredes & Rodrigues, 2024; Zawacki-Richter, Marín, & Bond, 2023). However, to fully realize the potential of AI in adult education, stakeholders including policymakers, educators, technology developers, and employers must collaborate to address the challenges and ensure that AI is used responsibly and equitably. (Ahuja, K., & Mitra, A., 2023).

In conclusion, AI holds great promise for transforming adult education, offering tailored learning experiences, supporting workforce development, and increasing access to education for learners of all backgrounds. As the world continues to change rapidly, AI will play a central role in helping adult learners develop the skills and knowledge they need to navigate the challenges of the modern workforce. However, for AI to reach its full potential, it is essential that its implementation is thoughtfully designed, with careful attention to ethical, practical, and equity considerations. By embracing AI's capabilities and addressing its challenges, adult education can become more effective, inclusive, and adaptable, ensuring that learners are prepared for the future of work and lifelong learning. (Aldowah, H., Al-Samarraie, H., & Fauzy, W. M., 2023).

AI-DRIVEN PERSONALIZATION IN ADULT EDUCATION

Artificial Intelligence (AI) is transforming the landscape of adult education by facilitating personalized learning experiences (Aldowah, Al-Samarraie, & Fauzy, 2023; Crompton, Burke, & Lin, 2024). Adult learners face unique challenges that can hinder their progress in education, ranging from time constraints to skills gaps and diverse educational backgrounds (Hsieh & Chen, 2022; Grant & Vivian, 2023). AI-driven personalization allows educators and institutions to cater to these challenges, offering customized learning pathways that improve both engagement and outcomes for adult learners (Aldowah, Al-Samarraie, & Fauzy, 2023; Crompton, Burke, & Lin, 2024).

In this section, we will explore how AI is reshaping the way learning paths are personalized for diverse adult learners and how it addresses barriers such as time constraints, skills gaps, and varied educational backgrounds. Adaptive learning technologies, intelligent tutoring systems, and predictive analytics work together to analyze learner behavior, identify individual needs, and deliver tailored educational content that aligns with learner goals and preferences (Chi & Wylie, 2023; D'Mello & Graesser, 2023). These technologies are especially valuable in adult education where learners may be returning after extended gaps, navigating changing careers, or learning alongside full-time jobs and family responsibilities. (Baker, R., & Siemens, G., 2023; Lee, Kim, 2023).

By dynamically adjusting instruction in real time, AI supports adult learners in mastering new skills efficiently, staying motivated, and achieving outcomes that traditional one-size-fits-all approaches often fail to deliver (Paredes & Rodrigues, 2024; Grant & Vivian, 2023). This responsiveness enhances equity and inclusion by meeting learners where they are and guiding them toward where they need to be. (Bauer, K., & Schmidt, J., 2022)

CUSTOMIZING LEARNING PATHS FOR DIVERSE ADULT LEARNERS

One of the most powerful applications of AI in adult education is the ability to create customized learning paths for individual learners (Istance & Dumont, 2023; Moreno & Perez, 2024; Zhang & Lu, 2023). Unlike traditional one-size-fits-all educational models, which often treat all students the same regardless of their needs or preferences, AI allows for the personalization of the learning experience based on a learner's unique abilities, goals, and challenges (Crompton, Burke, & Lin, 2024; Martinez & Gonzalez, 2023). Adult learners come from a wide variety of backgrounds and experiences, and their educational needs can differ significantly from traditional K-12 students. Some adult learners may have decades of work experience, while others may be returning to education after a long hiatus (Fadel & Trilling, 2023; Istance & Dumont, 2023; Zhang & Lu, 2023).

This diversity requires a more flexible approach to teaching, one that adapts to the individual rather than assuming uniformity (Chi & Wylie, 2023; Hsieh & Chen, 2022; Norman, 2024).

AI can help adult education programs meet this challenge by using data to analyze each learner's performance, strengths, weaknesses, and learning preferences (Lee & Kim, 2023; O'Donnell & Smith, 2023; Fong & Kim, 2024). For example, AI-powered learning management systems (LMS) can track how a learner interacts with various types of content, whether they prefer video lectures, written materials, or interactive quizzes, and adjust the learning path accordingly (D'Mello & Graesser, 2023; Shute & Rahimi, 2024). AI can also track progress in real time, dynamically adjusting the pace of instruction based on the learner's understanding (Greenfield, 2024; Zhang & Lu, 2023; Kulik & Fletcher, 2022).If a learner struggles with a particular concept, the AI system may offer additional resources, such as tutorials or practice exercises, to reinforce that topic before moving on to more advanced material (Aldowah, Al-Samarraie, & Fauzy, 2023).

For adult learners with specific career goals, AI can provide customized suggestions for coursework or skill development that aligns with their desired professional trajectory. For instance, if a learner is looking to transition into a tech-related field, AI can recommend specialized courses on coding, data analytics, or cybersecurity, tailored to the learner's current skill level and prior knowledge (Moreno & Perez, 2024; Silver & Baker, 2023; Fong & Kim, 2024).

Moreover, AI can help learners set realistic, personalized goals and track their progress, providing them with clear milestones to work toward (Paredes & Rodrigues, 2024). By offering a tailored approach that acknowledges the learner's goals and pace, AI helps adult learners stay motivated and engaged throughout their educational journey. (Bennett, T., & Roberts, L., 2024).

ADDRESSING TIME CONSTRAINTS THROUGH AI

Time constraints are one of the most significant barriers that adult learners face when pursuing further education (Nash & Burke, 2024; Fadel & Trilling, 2023; Hsieh & Chen, 2022). Many adults juggle multiple responsibilities, such as full-time employment, family care, and other personal commitments, which can make it difficult to find time for education (Norman, 2024; Nash & Burke, 2024; Fadel & Trilling, 2023). Traditional classroom-based learning, which often requires fixed schedules and physical presence, can be especially challenging for working adults. AI, however, offers a solution by enabling more flexible learning opportunities (Durak & Ataizi, 2023; Grant & Vivian, 2023).

AI-powered platforms allow adult learners to access educational content at their own convenience, on-demand, and from any location with an internet connection AI-powered platforms allow adult learners to access educational content at their own convenience, on-demand, and from any location with an internet connection (Tschofen & Mackness, 2023; Patterson & Weller, 2022; UNESCO, 2023). Whether through self-paced online courses, mobile learning apps, or AI-driven tutoring systems, learners can engage with educational content whenever and wherever it fits into their schedules (Zawacki-Richter, Marín, & Bond, 2023).

Additionally, AI can provide real-time feedback and guidance, reducing the need for adult learners to spend time searching for resources or assistance. For instance, AI-driven chatbots or virtual assistants can answer common questions, guide learners through complex concepts, or clarify assignment requirements, giving learners instant support without needing to wait for a response from an instructor (Chi & Wylie, 2023; D'Mello & Graesser, 2023).

This efficiency enables adult learners to make the most of the limited time they have for education. By providing personalized recommendations and allowing for adaptive pacing, AI makes learning more efficient and accessible, helping learners progress without being burdened by rigid schedules (Aldowah, Al-Samarraie, & Fauzy, 2023; Paredes & Rodrigues, 2024).

CLOSING SKILLS GAPS WITH AI

Another significant challenge faced by adult learners is the presence of skills gaps, which are particularly common among those who may not have had access to high-quality education in the past or who have been out of the education system for an extended period (Murphy & Bennett, 2023; Ghosh & Parashar, 2022; Fong & Kim, 2024). These skills gaps can prevent individuals from advancing in their careers or entering new fields. AI can play a pivotal role in addressing these gaps by offering adaptive learning systems that continuously assess a learner's knowledge and adjust the learning content to fill in the missing pieces (Aldowah, Al-Samarraie, & Fauzy, 2023; Shute & Rahimi, 2024). (Hsieh, Chen, 2023).

For example, AI-powered systems can identify areas where a learner is struggling and provide targeted interventions to close those gaps. A common scenario in adult education is the learner who returns to education after a long break, only to find that their math or writing skills are no longer at the level required to succeed (Norman, 2024; Sutton & Brown, 2024; Hsieh & Chen, 2022). AI systems can use diagnostic tools to assess these skills and then offer personalized practice exercises, step-by-step tutorials, and interactive lessons to help learners build the foundational skills necessary to succeed in their chosen field (D'Mello & Graesser, 2023; Chi & Wylie, 2023).

Moreover, AI can offer learners the opportunity to work on real-world problems that require them to apply newly acquired skills in a meaningful context (Mahmood & Hassan, 2022; Liu & Wang, 2024; Silver & Baker, 2023). For example, an AI-powered system might recommend a project-based learning module that allows the learner to apply coding skills to build a simple website or develop a data analysis project. This hands-on approach helps adult learners bridge skills gaps while simultaneously building confidence and competence (Paredes & Rodrigues, 2024; Johnson & Lester, 2023).

In many cases, AI can also offer insights into industry-specific skills that are in demand, helping learners to focus their efforts on acquiring the competencies that will improve their employability. With real-time access to labor market data and AI-driven skills assessments, adult learners can receive recommendations for further training and certifications that align with current market trends (Demartini & Tonelli, 2023; Carliner, 2023). By providing a more personalized and targeted approach to skill development, AI ensures that adult learners can stay competitive in a constantly evolving workforce. (Behrend, T. S., & Sinar, E. F., 2024)

Supporting Learners from Varied Educational Backgrounds

Adult learners often come from diverse educational backgrounds, which can further complicate the task of designing a curriculum that meets their individual needs. While some learners may have completed formal education and have a strong academic foundation, others may have limited formal schooling or non-traditional education experiences (Fadel & Trilling, 2023; Norman, 2024; Garrison & Vaughan, 2023). This diversity requires a more inclusive and adaptive approach to instruction, one that AI is well-positioned to provide (Fisher & Rubenson, 2024; Hersh & Johnson, 2023).

AI-driven personalization enables educational platforms to recognize the varying levels of experience and knowledge among adult learners and provide appropriate scaffolding to meet them where they are (Istance & Dumont, 2023; Norman, 2024; Zhang & Lu, 2023). For example, AI can use initial assessments to gauge a learner's prior knowledge and then recommend a learning path that is neither too advanced nor too basic. For learners with limited educational backgrounds, AI systems can offer foundational lessons that build their understanding step by step. For more advanced learners, AI can provide accelerated learning options that challenge them and promote deeper understanding (Crompton, Burke, & Lin, 2024; Chi & Wylie, 2023).

In addition to providing customized content, AI can also offer support for learners with different learning styles. Some adult learners may benefit from visual learning materials, while others may prefer auditory content or hands-on activities (Garrison & Vaughan, 2023; Norman, 2024; Hsieh & Chen, 2022). AI systems can analyze learner behavior and adjust the delivery method based on these preferences. For instance, if a learner consistently interacts with video tutorials, the AI system might prioritize this type of content in future lessons. Learners who prefer written materials might be offered more reading-heavy content. This adaptability ensures that learners can access education in the mode that best suits their learning style, increasing engagement and retention (D'Mello & Graesser, 2023; Paredes & Rodrigues, 2024).

AI-driven personalization in adult education has the potential to revolutionize the learning experience for diverse adult learners. By tailoring learning paths to individual needs, addressing time constraints, closing skills gaps, and supporting learners from various educational backgrounds, AI enables a more flexible, efficient, and inclusive approach to lifelong learning. As the demands of the workforce continue to evolve, AI will play an increasingly vital role in ensuring that adult learners can develop the skills and knowledge required to succeed in the modern job market.

Through personalized, adaptive learning experiences, AI helps adult learners overcome barriers and achieve their educational and career goals, making lifelong learning more accessible, efficient, and impactful (Zawacki-Richter, Marín, & Bond, 2023; Grant & Vivian, 2023; Puentedura & Johnson, 2023; Russell & Norvig, 2022).

AI FOR LIFELONG LEARNING

Lifelong learning has become an essential component of modern society as the demand for continuous education and professional development has escalated (Fadel & Trilling, 2023; Sutton & Brown, 2024; UNESCO, 2023). In a rapidly evolving world, where technological advancements, industry trends, and global challenges emerge frequently, individuals must engage in ongoing learning to maintain their competitiveness and adaptability (Eraut & Hirsh, 2023; Fadel & Trilling, 2023; Ghosh & Parashar, 2022). Artificial Intelligence (AI) plays a transformative role in facilitating lifelong learning, offering personalized, accessible, and flexible learning experiences that empower individuals to enhance their skills and knowledge throughout their careers (Eraut & Hirsh, 2023; Zawacki-Richter, Marín, & Bond, 2023).

By supporting continuous education and professional growth, AI helps learners stay relevant in an ever-changing job market, fostering a culture of lifelong learning that is crucial for both individual success and societal development (Grant & Vivian, 2023; Fisher & Rubenson, 2024).

This section will delve into the role of AI in promoting lifelong learning and explore how AI-powered platforms support microlearning and just-in-time training, which are key components in the pursuit of ongoing education and skill enhancement. (Berg, M., & Kezar, A., 2024)

Role of AI in Promoting Continuous Education and Professional Growth

One of the primary challenges that individuals face in pursuing lifelong learning is the need for education to be tailored to their specific career goals, interests, and time constraints (Durak & Ataizi, 2023; Norman, 2024; Fong & Kim, 2024). Traditional educational models, which often emphasize fixed curricula and rigid schedules, can be ill-suited to the needs of adults who are juggling work, family, and other responsibilities (Fadel & Trilling, 2023; Hsieh & Chen, 2022;

Sutton & Brown, 2024). AI, however, provides a powerful solution by enabling more flexible and personalized learning experiences (Durak & Ataizi, 2023; Aldowah, Al-Samarraie, & Fauzy, 2023).

AI can support continuous education by offering customized learning pathways that adapt to an individual's unique needs and goals (Istance & Dumont, 2023; Lee & Kim, 2023; Aldowah, Al-Samarraie, & Fauzy, 2023). AI-driven platforms can analyze a learner's performance in real time, tracking their strengths, weaknesses, and progress over time (O'Donnell & Smith, 2023; Fong & Kim, 2024; Chi & Wylie, 2023). This data-driven approach allows AI to offer personalized recommendations that guide learners toward the most relevant courses, certifications, or skill development activities (Chi & Wylie, 2023; D'Mello & Graesser, 2023). By assessing prior knowledge, AI systems can present the most appropriate content, either reinforcing areas where learners need improvement or providing advanced challenges for those who are more experienced. This dynamic customization ensures that learners are always progressing at their optimal pace, which helps prevent frustration and disengagement (Paredes & Rodrigues, 2024).

Moreover, AI supports professional growth by providing real-time feedback and adaptive learning experiences (Murphy & Bennett, 2023; Johnson & Lester, 2023; Felicia & Lameras, 2024). Professionals can rely on AI-powered tools to continuously assess their progress, identify skill gaps, and recommend next steps for improvement (Silver & Baker, 2023; Lee & Kim, 2023; Carliner, 2023). For example, in technical fields such as software development or data science, AI-powered platforms can track a learner's coding proficiency, offer instant feedback on code quality, and suggest additional resources or practice exercises to improve specific areas (Johnson & Lester, 2023; Carliner, 2023). In this way, AI enables a cycle of continuous self-improvement, fostering a growth mindset that encourages lifelong learning (Felicia & Lameras, 2024).

AI also helps individuals stay updated with the latest industry trends, which is essential in today's fast-paced world (Hamann & Pollak, 2023; Berg & Kezar, 2024; Ghosh & Parashar, 2022). Many industries are evolving rapidly due to technological advancements, and professionals must continuously upgrade their knowledge to remain competitive (Demartini & Tonelli, 2023; Eraut & Hirsh, 2023; Sutton & Brown, 2024). AI-driven platforms can curate learning content based on emerging trends, helping individuals stay informed and develop expertise in new areas (Johnson & Lester, 2023; Hamann & Pollak, 2023; O'Donnell & Smith, 2023). Whether through personalized news feeds, targeted courses, or notifications about newly emerging skill sets, AI ensures that learners are exposed to the latest developments in their fields (Hamann & Pollak, 2023).

Furthermore, AI supports the democratization of education by making continuous learning more accessible. Traditional forms of education, such as attending in-person classes or workshops, may not be feasible for everyone due to geographical, financial, or time-related constraints (UNESCO, 2023; Nash & Burke, 2024; Zawacki-Richter, Marín, & Bond, 2023). AI-powered platforms allow learners to access high-quality education and training from anywhere in the world, breaking down barriers to access and creating equal opportunities for professional development (Hersh & Johnson, 2023; Fisher & Rubenson, 2024). With AI, learners can engage with content asynchronously, at their own pace, and based on their specific needs and interests. This accessibility enables a global learning community where individuals from diverse backgrounds and locations can participate in lifelong learning. (Bhattacharya, M., 2023)

AI-Powered Platforms for Microlearning and Just-in-Time Training

In the context of lifelong learning, microlearning and just-in-time training have gained significant popularity due to their efficiency and effectiveness in addressing learners' specific needs. AI plays a crucial role in enabling these learning methods by offering personalized, on-demand learning experiences that cater to learners' immediate needs and schedules (Crompton, Burke, & Lin, 2024; Grant & Vivian, 2023).

Microlearning refers to the practice of breaking down content into small, digestible chunks that can be consumed in short bursts of time (Brown & Green, 2022; Aldowah, Al-Samarraie, & Fauzy, 2023; Crompton, Burke, & Lin, 2024). These learning modules typically last anywhere from a few minutes to around 15 minutes, focusing on specific skills or concepts (Brown & Green, 2022; Grant & Vivian, 2023; Chi & Wylie, 2023). AI facilitates microlearning by analyzing learners' progress and providing personalized, bite-sized content based on their goals (Fong & Kim, 2024; D'Mello & Graesser, 2023; Aldowah, Al-Samarraie, & Fauzy, 2023).For example, if a learner needs to improve their knowledge of project management tools, AI can provide short lessons, such as videos, quizzes, or interactive tutorials, that focus on specific tools or techniques. By breaking down learning into manageable pieces, microlearning helps learners absorb and retain information more effectively (Aldowah, Al-Samarraie, & Fauzy, 2023; Chi & Wylie, 2023).

The key advantage of microlearning is its flexibility. In today's world, many individuals struggle to find long stretches of time for traditional learning experiences (Brown & Green, 2022; Grant & Vivian, 2023). Microlearning, powered by AI, allows learners to engage with educational content in short, focused bursts that can fit easily into their busy schedules (Chi & Wylie, 2023; Crompton, Burke, & Lin, 2024).

This flexibility is particularly beneficial for working professionals who may only have small windows of time available for learning during their day, such as during commutes, lunch breaks, or between meetings (Paredes & Rodrigues, 2024; Aldowah, Al-Samarraie, & Fauzy, 2023). AI enables the creation and delivery of personalized microlearning experiences that meet learners where they are, helping them progress incrementally toward their educational goals (Paredes & Rodrigues, 2024).

Just-in-time training, another important element of lifelong learning, is a method of delivering training content exactly when it is needed, providing learners with timely and relevant information that they can apply immediately (D'Mello & Graesser, 2023; Johnson & Lester, 2023). Just-in-time training is especially effective in professional settings where employees may need to acquire specific skills or knowledge to address an immediate challenge or task (Hamann & Pollak, 2023).

AI enables just-in-time learning by using data to predict when and what content will be most useful for a learner (Carliner, 2023; Paredes & Rodrigues, 2024) For instance, if an employee is working on a project that requires using a new software tool, AI can push tutorials, walkthroughs, or troubleshooting guides in real time to help the learner overcome obstacles as they arise (D'Mello & Graesser, 2023; Johnson & Lester, 2023).

AI-driven platforms can track learners' activities and identify when they are struggling or encountering difficulties (Hamann & Pollak, 2023; D'Mello & Graesser, 2023). Based on this data, the system can offer targeted learning resources at the exact moment of need (Carliner, 2023). This just-in-time approach allows learners to solve problems more efficiently and continue their work without unnecessary delays (Paredes & Rodrigues, 2024). Moreover, the AI platform can continue to monitor the learner's progress and suggest additional resources or follow-up training as needed, ensuring that learning is continuous and seamlessly integrated into daily work processes (Hamann & Pollak, 2023; Carliner, 2023).

Just-in-time training powered by AI also supports self-directed learning, as individuals are empowered to seek out relevant content and solutions as needed. For instance, a manager who needs to learn how to handle a complex negotiation can access AI-driven training materials on negotiation tactics, offered right when the situation arises. This kind of personalized, responsive learning is essential in a fast-paced professional environment, where individuals must acquire new knowledge or skills quickly to remain productive and competitive (Felicia & Lameras, 2024; Eraut & Hirsh, 2023).

Overcoming Barriers to Lifelong Learning with AI

AI-powered platforms are uniquely positioned to address several barriers to lifelong learning, which have traditionally made continuous education challenging (Durak & Ataizi, 2023; Fisher & Rubenson, 2024). Time constraints, geographical limitations, financial barriers, and skill gaps often prevent adults from engaging in formal education and training (Zawacki-Richter, Marín, & Bond, 2023; Nash & Burke, 2024). AI-based systems can provide flexible, cost-effective, and accessible solutions to these challenges (Durak & Ataizi, 2023; Fisher & Rubenson, 2024).

For instance, AI-driven learning platforms eliminate the need for physical classrooms, making education more accessible to individuals in remote areas or those with mobility limitations. These platforms also reduce costs by offering scalable, online content that eliminates the need for expensive textbooks, travel, and venue costs associated with in-person training. By providing affordable access to high-quality learning resources, AI ensures that lifelong learning is within reach for a broad range of individuals, including those from underprivileged or marginalized backgrounds (Zawacki-Richter, Marín, & Bond, 2023).

AI also promotes a personalized approach that addresses learners' unique needs, further increasing the likelihood of success in lifelong learning (Chi & Wylie, 2023; Aldowah, Al-Samarraie, & Fauzy, 2023). Traditional educational systems often adopt a one-size-fits-all approach, which can be less effective for adult learners with diverse experiences, learning styles, and goals (Crompton, Burke, & Lin, 2024; Fisher & Rubenson, 2024). With AI, learners receive tailored content and pacing that is designed to match their prior knowledge, learning preferences, and objectives (Chi & Wylie, 2023; Aldowah, Al-Samarraie, & Fauzy, 2023).

AI is revolutionizing the landscape of lifelong learning by providing personalized, accessible, and flexible learning experiences that empower individuals to continuously acquire new skills and knowledge (Crompton, Burke, & Lin, 2024; Paredes & Rodrigues, 2024; Eraut & Hirsh, 2023). By supporting microlearning and just-in-time training, AI enables learners to engage in focused, efficient learning that aligns with their immediate needs and time constraints (Crompton, Burke, & Lin, 2024; Paredes & Rodrigues, 2024). The adaptability and scalability of AI-powered platforms make lifelong learning more attainable for individuals across different backgrounds, professions, and geographical locations. As industries evolve and new technologies emerge, AI will continue to play a critical role in supporting continuous education, helping learners stay relevant, competitive, and capable in a fast-changing world (Eraut & Hirsh, 2023; Grant & Vivian, 2023).

UPSKILLING AND RESKILLING THE WORKFORCE WITH AI

In today's fast-paced and ever-evolving global economy, the need for upskilling and reskilling the workforce has become increasingly critical. The technological advancements of the 21st century, particularly in areas such as Artificial Intelligence (AI), automation, and digital transformation, have altered the skills required across industries (Demartini & Tonelli, 2023; Carliner, 2023).

As businesses face challenges related to talent shortages, skill gaps, and technological disruptions, they must invest in continuous workforce development to ensure they remain competitive and capable of adapting to changing market demands (Brookfield & Holst, 2023; Ghosh & Parashar, 2022). AI offers unique opportunities for upskilling and reskilling by enabling businesses to identify skills gaps, deliver personalized training, and create industry-aligned learning solutions that prepare workers for the jobs of tomorrow (Carliner, 2023; Demartini & Tonelli, 2023).

This section will explore the potential of AI to drive upskilling and reskilling initiatives within the workforce, emphasizing AI's role in identifying skills gaps, creating tailored training programs, and providing industry-aligned learning solutions to improve workforce readiness. (Brookfield, S. D., & Holst, J. D., 2023)

Leveraging AI to Identify Skills Gaps and Tailor Training Programs

One of the primary challenges organizations face when developing effective upskilling and reskilling programs is identifying the specific skills that need to be addressed. Traditional methods, such as surveys or performance reviews, can provide some insights, but they often lack the precision and real-time data necessary to make informed decisions about skills development (Oswald, Behrend, & Sinar, 2024; Hamann & Pollak, 2023; D'Mello & Graesser, 2023). AI can play a critical role in overcoming this challenge by using data-driven insights to identify skills gaps in both individual employees and teams across an organization (Oswald, Behrend, & Sinar, 2024).

AI-driven platforms can analyze large datasets, including employee performance metrics, job requirements, industry trends, and other relevant factors, to pinpoint where skill shortages exist. By integrating machine learning algorithms, AI can predict the skills required for specific roles within the organization or industry, taking into account the impact of technological advancements or emerging trends. These predictive capabilities enable companies to proactively address skills gaps, ensuring that workers are equipped with the necessary competencies to remain productive and relevant in their roles (Hamann & Pollak, 2023).

Additionally, AI-based systems can offer real-time feedback and continuously monitor employees' learning progress, helping organizations identify skills gaps as they arise. For example, an AI-powered learning management system (LMS) can track a worker's engagement with various learning modules, identify areas where they are struggling, and suggest specific training or resources to help them develop the necessary skills. This personalized learning experience ensures that employees are always progressing toward skill mastery, while the organization gains valuable insights into where additional resources or training might be needed (D'Mello & Graesser, 2023; Paredes & Rodrigues, 2024).

Furthermore, AI can assist in aligning training programs with both individual needs and organizational goals. Traditional training programs are often one-size-fits-all, with little regard for the varying experiences, strengths, and weaknesses of individual learners. AI can help tailor training content to the specific learning needs of each employee, offering personalized recommendations based on factors such as prior experience, current role, and learning style. AI-driven platforms can adjust the level of difficulty, pace, and format of content to maximize engagement and retention, ensuring that training is effective and efficient (Chi & Wylie, 2023; Grant & Vivian, 2023).

For example, an employee in a technical role may need to focus on improving their proficiency with coding languages or specific software tools, while an employee in a management role may benefit from developing leadership skills or knowledge of strategic planning. AI can ensure that these employees are provided with targeted, relevant content that addresses their specific needs, allowing them to upskill or reskill more quickly and effectively (Johnson & Lester, 2023).

Industry-Aligned AI-Driven Learning Solutions for Workforce Readiness

As the workforce landscape continues to change, it is essential that upskilling and reskilling programs are closely aligned with the evolving demands of various industries. AI-powered learning solutions can ensure that training programs are directly relevant to the skills and knowledge required by employers, making workers more prepared for the jobs of tomorrow. The dynamic nature of the job market, characterized by rapid technological advancements and shifts in industry requirements, necessitates that workforce development programs be agile and adaptive (Demartini & Tonelli, 2023; Carliner, 2023).

AI-driven platforms can offer industry-aligned learning solutions by analyzing labor market trends, employer demands, and technological advancements to identify the specific skills required across different sectors. These platforms can integrate industry-specific data to offer targeted training content, ensuring that workers are equipped with the most relevant and up-to-date skills for their chosen field. Whether in technology, healthcare, manufacturing, or finance, AI can provide tailored learning pathways that reflect the current needs and future trends of each industry (Hamann & Pollak, 2023; Oswald, Behrend, & Sinar, 2024).

For instance, in the tech industry, AI-driven platforms can identify emerging technologies such as artificial intelligence, blockchain, or cybersecurity and create learning pathways that focus on the skills necessary to work with these technologies. Similarly, in healthcare, AI-powered systems can track trends in medical practices, telemedicine, and data analysis to design relevant training programs for medical professionals. By aligning training with industry needs, AI ensures that workers are prepared to meet current and future job demands (Johnson & Lester, 2023).

AI-driven platforms can also facilitate the creation of industry-recognized certifications and credentials that validate a worker's skills and knowledge in a particular domain. These certifications, which can be delivered through AI-powered systems, help workers demonstrate their expertise to employers and increase their employability. By offering industry-recognized credentials, AI ensures that training programs are aligned with the needs of employers and meet the standards set by professional associations or industry bodies (Grant & Vivian, 2023; Eraut & Hirsh, 2023).

Moreover, AI can enhance workforce readiness by providing just-in-time training solutions. In a rapidly changing job market, employees must be able to acquire new skills and knowledge quickly to adapt to new technologies, tools, or processes. AI-powered learning platforms can provide on-demand access to training materials, ensuring that employees can quickly learn what they need when they need it. For example, if a company implements a new software system, AI-driven platforms can offer quick tutorials and resources to help employees get up to speed, ensuring that they are able to adapt to the new system without disrupting productivity (Crompton, Burke, & Lin, 2024).

Another way AI supports workforce readiness is by facilitating collaborative learning and peer-to-peer interaction. AI-powered platforms can use machine learning algorithms to group learners with similar interests or complementary skills, enabling them to collaborate and share knowledge. This peer-driven learning environment can enhance the overall learning experience and create opportunities for employees to learn from one another's experiences and expertise. By fostering a sense of community and collaboration, AI can strengthen the collective knowledge of the workforce, ensuring that employees are not only upskilling individually but also contributing to the organization's overall capabilities (Paredes & Rodrigues, 2024).

Furthermore, AI can help organizations track and measure the effectiveness of their upskilling and reskilling initiatives, providing valuable insights into employee progress and training outcomes. By collecting data on employee engagement, completion rates, and skill improvement, AI platforms can offer detailed reports on the impact of training programs. These insights enable organizations to refine their training strategies, identify areas for improvement, and ensure that upskilling efforts are aligned with business goals. With AI, organizations can create data-driven, results-oriented workforce development programs that drive measurable outcomes (Felicia & Lameras, 2024; Zawacki-Richter, Marín, & Bond, 2023).

AI for Workforce Resilience and Adaptability

In addition to improving individual skills, AI plays a critical role in fostering workforce resilience and adaptability. The COVID-19 pandemic has highlighted the importance of adaptability, as many workers have had to quickly transition to remote work or learn new technologies. AI helps workers develop the skills needed to navigate uncertainty and change, ensuring that they remain resilient in the face of disruption. By offering personalized learning paths and continuously updating training content to reflect the latest industry trends, AI ensures that workers are always prepared for evolving job demands and workplace conditions (Carliner, 2023; Demartini & Tonelli, 2023).

AI can also play a key role in promoting a culture of continuous learning within organizations. By providing employees with the tools and resources to continuously upskill, organizations can create a workforce that is agile, innovative, and capable of navigating change. With AI-driven learning solutions, employees are empowered to take ownership of their professional development, ensuring that upskilling and reskilling are seen as ongoing, lifelong processes (Eraut & Hirsh, 2023; Grant & Vivian, 2023).

As industries continue to evolve, AI is transforming the way organizations approach upskilling and reskilling initiatives. By leveraging AI to identify skills gaps, create personalized training programs, and deliver industry-aligned learning solutions, organizations can ensure that their workforce is prepared for the jobs of tomorrow. AI-powered platforms offer the flexibility, scalability, and adaptability needed to address the challenges of a rapidly changing job market, helping workers develop the skills necessary to thrive in an AI-powered economy. With AI, businesses can build a more skilled, resilient, and future-ready workforce, driving innovation and competitiveness in an increasingly digital world (Oswald, Behrend, & Sinar, 2024; Zawacki-Richter, Marín, & Bond, 2023).

AI-ENHANCED PEDAGOGY FOR ADULT LEARNERS

As the world continues to evolve in terms of technology, the educational landscape, particularly adult education, must adapt to meet the needs of adult learners. Adult learners often juggle multiple responsibilities, such as work, family, and community involvement, which can make it challenging for them to engage with traditional educational formats. This is where the integration of Artificial Intelligence (AI) comes into play. AI-enhanced pedagogy offers personalized, flexible, and accessible learning experiences that can significantly improve the learning process for adults, making it more efficient, engaging, and relevant to their needs (Clark & Mayer, 2023; Hersh & Johnson, 2023).

This section explores how AI can be integrated into adult education through intelligent tutoring systems, virtual assistants, and AI-driven simulations. It also delves into how AI can encourage critical thinking and problem-solving skills in adult learners, providing them with the tools they need to succeed in both their personal and professional lives. (Brown, A. L., & Green, D. E., 2022)

Integrating Intelligent Tutoring Systems and Virtual Assistants in Adult Education

Intelligent tutoring systems (ITS) and virtual assistants have the potential to revolutionize adult education by providing personalized, adaptive learning experiences. These AI-powered tools can assist adult learners in navigating educational content at their own pace, ensuring that each learner receives the necessary support to succeed (D'Mello & Graesser, 2023; Chi & Wylie, 2023).

Intelligent tutoring systems are AI-driven platforms designed to simulate one-on-one tutoring interactions between a learner and a teacher. ITS are particularly beneficial in adult education because they allow learners to receive individualized support that suits their personal learning preferences, learning styles, and knowledge levels. For instance, an ITS can track a learner's progress, provide real-time feedback, and suggest targeted resources based on their current level of understanding. This allows adult learners to work at their own pace, progressing as quickly or slowly as needed without the pressure of keeping up with a classroom (Paredes & Rodrigues, 2024).

One of the key benefits of ITS is their ability to provide immediate and actionable feedback, which is critical for adult learners who may have been out of formal education for a significant period. In traditional learning environments, immediate feedback can sometimes be lacking, leading to frustration and disengagement. With an intelligent tutoring system, learners can receive responses to their questions and problems almost instantly. These systems can guide learners through complex concepts by breaking them down into more manageable pieces and offering hints or explanations as needed. Additionally, ITS can monitor the learner's progress over time, adapting the learning path based on their strengths and weaknesses (Crompton, Burke, & Lin, 2024).

For example, in a math course for adult learners, an ITS might provide targeted exercises on specific areas in which the learner is struggling, such as fractions or algebra. If the learner answers a question incorrectly, the system can offer step-by-step hints to guide them toward the correct answer and help reinforce the concept. By offering personalized guidance, ITS create a more effective learning environment that addresses the unique challenges adult learners face.

Virtual assistants, on the other hand, can play a key role in enhancing adult learners' experience by providing real-time support outside of the traditional classroom setting. These AI-powered assistants can serve as on-demand helpers that answer questions, provide clarification, and even help learners organize their study schedules. Virtual assistants, such as AI-driven chatbots or voice-activated systems like Amazon Alexa or Google Assistant, can provide immediate answers to frequently asked questions, give suggestions for study resources, or even offer reminders about upcoming deadlines or assignments (Felicia & Lameras, 2024; Johnson & Lester, 2023).

Virtual assistants are particularly useful for adult learners who have busy schedules and may not always have access to a traditional instructor. These assistants can bridge the gap by offering 24/7 support, enabling learners to continue their education at their own convenience. Furthermore, virtual assistants can help manage other aspects of adult learners' lives, such as time management and prioritization, which are often critical in balancing education with work and family responsibilities.

Encouraging Critical Thinking and Problem-Solving Through AI-Driven Simulations and Tools

In addition to personalized support, AI can be used to foster higher-order thinking skills such as critical thinking and problem-solving, which are essential for adult learners in the workplace and society. These skills are particularly important in the context of lifelong learning, as they equip learners to adapt to the ever-changing demands of the workforce and contribute meaningfully to their communities (Jenkins, 2023; Paredes & Rodrigues, 2024).

AI-driven simulations and tools can encourage adult learners to engage in real-world problem-solving tasks and critically evaluate information from multiple perspectives. These tools provide learners with opportunities to practice decision-making, risk analysis, and problem-solving in a safe and controlled environment. By engaging in simulations, learners can experience realistic scenarios that mirror challenges they may face in their professional or personal lives, without the consequences of making mistakes in real-world situations (Felicia & Lameras, 2024; Liu & Wang, 2024).

For instance, in a business course for adult learners, AI-driven simulations can immerse learners in scenarios that require them to make strategic decisions based on data, such as analyzing market trends, managing a budget, or navigating competitive challenges. The system can adjust the scenario based on the learner's actions, presenting new challenges or presenting alternative outcomes to test the learner's decision-making abilities. By interacting with these dynamic simulations, adult learners are encouraged to think critically about their decisions, assess the potential impact of their actions, and develop effective solutions to complex problems. (Carter, M. A., & Rose, C. P., 2024)

AI tools can also promote collaboration and teamwork among adult learners, which is essential for developing problem-solving skills in a modern work environment. Many AI-driven platforms include collaborative features that allow learners to work together in virtual teams to solve problems, brainstorm ideas, and share knowledge. These platforms can include discussion boards, shared documents, or virtual meeting spaces where learners can collaborate on projects. As adult learners typically bring diverse experiences and knowledge to the table, collaborative problem-solving activities can help learners expand their perspectives and build more robust solutions to complex problems (Park & Jung, 2024; Clark & Mayer, 2023).

By encouraging collaboration, AI tools not only enhance learners' problem-solving skills but also improve communication, interpersonal skills, and teamwork. These tools promote critical thinking by providing adult learners with diverse viewpoints and encouraging them to think creatively and collaboratively, which are essential skills in problem-solving and innovation. (Chi, M. T. H., & Wylie, R., 2023)

AI-Powered Personalization and Adaptive Learning

Another important aspect of AI-enhanced pedagogy for adult learners is its ability to offer personalized learning experiences that foster deeper understanding and mastery of concepts. As adult learners often have varying levels of prior knowledge, learning styles, and motivations, AI can adapt the learning experience to meet their unique needs (Aldowah, Al-Samarraie, & Fauzy, 2023; Crompton, Burke, & Lin, 2024).

AI-powered systems can tailor the learning content to individual learners by analyzing their progress, preferences, and performance. For example, if an adult learner struggles with a particular concept, AI-driven platforms can adjust the learning path to provide additional resources, tutorials, or exercises to help the learner master the concept. Conversely, if a learner excels in a specific area, the system can provide more challenging material to keep them engaged and challenged. This adaptive learning model ensures that each learner's educational experience is optimized for their personal growth (Chi & Wylie, 2023; D'Mello & Graesser, 2023).

Furthermore, AI can use data to track learners' behavior and make predictions about their learning needs. By analyzing how long it takes learners to complete specific tasks, how well they perform on quizzes or assignments, and their engagement with various materials, AI systems can offer insights into areas where learners might need additional support or resources. This information can also be used to modify the curriculum dynamically, ensuring that learners are always working on material that is both relevant and challenging for them (Shute & Rahimi, 2024).

ETHICAL AND EQUITY CONSIDERATIONS IN AI FOR ADULT EDUCATION

As Artificial Intelligence (AI) continues to reshape the educational landscape, it introduces both opportunities and challenges, particularly in the context of adult education. While AI holds immense potential to revolutionize the way adult learners engage with content, gain skills, and navigate their educational journeys, it is crucial to address the ethical and equity concerns associated with its implementation. These concerns include ensuring equitable access to AI-powered learning resources and addressing data privacy, bias, and other ethical issues that may arise from the use of AI in education (Bauer & Schmidt, 2024; Selwyn & Jandrić, 2023).

This section explores the ethical and equity considerations in the implementation of AI for adult education. It delves into the challenges and opportunities related to providing equitable access to AI-powered learning resources for all adult learners, regardless of their socioeconomic background, geographic location, or technological literacy. Furthermore, it examines the ethical implications of AI in education, such as the potential for bias, the importance of data privacy, and the need for responsible AI practices to ensure that AI tools are used in ways that are fair, transparent, and aligned with educational values (Gholami & Watson, 2024; Hersh & Johnson, 2023).

Ensuring Equitable Access to AI-Powered Learning Resources

One of the most significant challenges in integrating AI into adult education is ensuring that all learners, regardless of their background, have equitable access to AI-powered learning resources. While AI has the potential to bridge gaps in education by providing personalized learning experiences and improving access to educational content, disparities in access to technology can exacerbate existing inequalities (Fisher & Rubenson, 2024; McKenna & Thompson, 2023).

Access to AI-powered learning tools requires reliable internet connectivity, appropriate hardware such as computers or mobile devices, and the necessary digital literacy skills to navigate AI-driven platforms. In many regions, particularly in underserved communities, access to these resources can be limited. For instance, adult learners in rural areas or low-income neighborhoods may not have access to high-speed internet or may lack the financial means to purchase the devices necessary to engage with AI-based educational tools. This technological divide can create barriers to entry for adult learners who would otherwise benefit from AI-powered education, potentially widening the gap between those who have access to technology and those who do not. (Clark, R. C., & Mayer, R. E., 2023)

In addition to hardware and internet access, digital literacy is another critical factor in ensuring equitable access to AI-powered learning. Adult learners who are unfamiliar with technology or who have limited experience using digital tools may face difficulties navigating AI-driven platforms. For these learners, even basic tasks such as accessing educational content, interacting with intelligent tutoring systems, or using virtual assistants may be overwhelming. This digital literacy gap can hinder the effectiveness of AI in adult education, as learners may struggle to fully engage with the technology (Durak & Ataizi, 2023).

To address these challenges, it is essential for educational institutions, policymakers, and technology providers to work together to ensure that AI-powered learning resources are accessible to all adult learners. This includes investing in infrastructure to improve internet access in underserved communities, providing affordable devices for learners who lack access to technology, and offering digital literacy training to help adult learners become comfortable using AI-powered tools. Additionally, AI platforms can be designed to be user-friendly and adaptable to the varying levels of digital literacy among adult learners, ensuring that learners can easily navigate the tools and access the content they need (Zawacki-Richter, Marín, & Bond, 2023).

Addressing Data Privacy in AI Implementation

Another key ethical consideration in the use of AI for adult education is the issue of data privacy. AI-driven platforms rely on vast amounts of data to personalize learning experiences, track learner progress, and provide targeted feedback. This data may include personal information, learning habits, performance metrics, and even sensitive data such as health information or employment history. Given the sensitive nature of this data, it is essential that AI systems used in adult education adhere to strict data privacy standards to protect learners' privacy and ensure that their information is handled responsibly (Eaton & Brown, 2022).

The collection, storage, and processing of data must comply with relevant data protection laws, such as the General Data Protection Regulation in the European Union, which mandates that organizations obtain explicit consent from individuals before collecting and processing their personal data. Educational institutions and AI providers must be transparent about the types of data they collect, how it will be used, and how long it will be retained. Additionally, learners should have the option to opt out of data collection or have their data deleted upon request (Bauer & Schmidt, 2024).

The potential for data breaches or misuse of personal information is a significant concern in the digital age. If AI systems do not implement robust security measures to protect learners' data, they risk exposing individuals to identity theft, fraud, or other malicious activities. Educational institutions must therefore ensure that AI-driven platforms are secure and that learners' data is encrypted and stored in compliance with industry best practices. (Cohen, E., & Alpert, R., 2022)

Furthermore, it is essential for adult learners to be informed about how their data is being used and to have control over their own personal information. AI platforms should provide clear and accessible privacy policies, and learners should be empowered to make informed decisions about how their data is shared and used. This level of transparency and control helps build trust in AI-powered learning tools and ensures that adult learners feel confident using these platforms without fear of their personal data being misused (Selwyn & Jandrić, 2023).

Addressing Bias in AI Systems

AI systems are not immune to biases. In fact, the algorithms that power AI-driven tools can inadvertently reinforce existing biases and inequalities, particularly if the data used to train these systems is flawed or biased. This is a critical issue in the context of adult education, as biased AI systems can perpetuate inequalities in learning outcomes, particularly for marginalized or underrepresented groups (Eaton & Brown, 2022; Selwyn & Jandrić, 2023).

Bias in AI can manifest in various ways. For example, if the data used to train an AI-driven tutoring system is primarily based on a specific demographic group, such as young, urban learners with high levels of education, the system may struggle to provide personalized support to adult learners who come from different backgrounds. The AI system may be less effective for learners who have different cultural, linguistic, or educational experiences, leading to inequities in the learning experience. (Crompton, H., Burke, D., & Lin, C.-H., 2024)

Similarly, if AI systems are trained on biased data that reflects stereotypes or discriminatory assumptions, they may perpetuate these biases in the learning materials or feedback they provide (Gholami & Watson, 2024; Bauer & Schmidt, 2024).

To address these concerns, it is essential for AI developers and educational institutions to prioritize fairness and inclusivity when designing AI-driven platforms for adult education. This includes ensuring that the data used to train AI systems is diverse, representative, and free from biases that could negatively impact learners. Furthermore, AI systems should be regularly audited and tested for bias, with ongoing updates and improvements made to mitigate any unintended consequences (Hersh & Johnson, 2023; Zawacki-Richter, Marín, & Bond, 2023).

Educational institutions should also provide training for educators to help them recognize and address potential biases in AI-powered tools. By raising awareness of the potential for bias and encouraging critical thinking about the use of AI in education, educators can help ensure that AI is used in ways that promote fairness and inclusivity (McKenna & Thompson, 2023).

Ethical Use of AI in Adult Education

Finally, the ethical use of AI in adult education involves ensuring that AI technologies are used in ways that align with the values of fairness, transparency, and accountability. AI should be used to augment the learning experience and provide personalized, equitable opportunities for adult learners, rather than replacing human educators or exacerbating inequalities. It is essential that AI is implemented in a way that complements and enhances the work of educators, rather than undermining it (Fisher & Rubenson, 2024).

Educational institutions must ensure that AI-powered tools are used ethically and responsibly, with a focus on improving learning outcomes, fostering inclusion, and addressing the diverse needs of adult learners. This requires ongoing collaboration between educators, policymakers, technology providers, and learners themselves to ensure that AI is used in ways that align with the broader goals of adult education, such as promoting lifelong learning, empowering learners, and preparing them for success in the workforce (Clark & Mayer, 2023; Paredes & Rodrigues, 2024).

The implementation of AI in adult education offers significant opportunities to enhance learning experiences, improve accessibility, and empower learners. However, it also raises important ethical and equity considerations that must be addressed to ensure that AI is used responsibly and in ways that benefit all learners. By prioritizing equitable access to technology, ensuring data privacy, addressing bias in AI systems, and promoting ethical practices, educational institutions can harness the power of AI to create a more inclusive, effective, and ethical adult education system (Fisher & Rubenson, 2024; Eaton & Brown, 2022; Selwyn & Jandrić, 2023).

As AI continues to evolve, it is essential that educators, policymakers, and technology developers work together to create AI-powered learning environments that support all adult learners, regardless of their background, and help them achieve their full potential (Hersh & Johnson, 2023; Gholami & Watson, 2024).

CHALLENGES AND STRATEGIES FOR AI ADOPTION

As Artificial Intelligence (AI) continues to transform the educational landscape, its adoption in adult education is gaining momentum. AI offers tremendous potential for personalized learning, improving access to education, and enhancing the overall learning experience for adult learners. However, the implementation of AI in adult education is not without its challenges. (Demartini, C. G., & Tonelli, M., 2023)

These challenges range from resistance to AI technologies to the need for building institutional capacity for large-scale integration and scaling efforts. In this section, we will explore the key challenges associated with AI adoption in adult education and propose strategies to overcome these barriers, ultimately enabling educational institutions to harness the full potential of AI (Zawacki-Richter, Marín, & Bond, 2023; Grant & Vivian, 2023).

Overcoming Resistance to AI Technologies in Adult Education

One of the most significant challenges in the adoption of AI in adult education is overcoming resistance to the technology. Resistance can come from various stakeholders, including educators, students, administrators, and even policymakers. Many of these individuals may be skeptical about the effectiveness of AI in education or fearful of the implications AI might have on their work and roles (Eaton & Brown, 2022).

Resistance from Educators

For educators, the prospect of integrating AI into their classrooms can seem daunting. Teachers who have spent years developing traditional teaching methods may view AI as a threat to their professional expertise and autonomy. There is a concern that AI could undermine the role of the educator, with machines replacing human instructors in the learning process. Educators may also worry that AI tools will reduce their ability to interact personally with students or undermine the value of face-to-face teaching (Clark & Mayer, 2023; Kasworm & Rose, 2023).

Additionally, some educators may be unfamiliar with the technology and lack confidence in their ability to effectively integrate AI into their teaching practices. They may see AI as a complex and intimidating field that requires specialized knowledge, which may deter them from adopting these technologies. The learning curve for AI tools can also be steep, requiring time, effort, and training to understand how to use them effectively in the classroom (Carter & Rose, 2024).

Resistance from Adult Learners

Adult learners themselves may also harbor skepticism about AI. Many adult learners return to education after years of being out of the formal education system and may not be accustomed to using advanced technological tools. For older generations, the rapid development of AI may seem overwhelming, and the idea of interacting with AI-powered platforms can be intimidating (Fisher & Rubenson, 2024).

There may also be concerns about privacy and data security. Adult learners may be hesitant to share personal or sensitive information with AI systems, especially if they are unsure how their data will be used or whether it will be kept confidential (Selwyn & Jandrić, 2023).

Resistance from Administrators and Policymakers

At the institutional level, administrators and policymakers may be reluctant to adopt AI technologies due to financial constraints, a lack of infrastructure, or concerns about the ethical implications of using AI in education. There may be a lack of understanding about how AI can improve educational outcomes, or they may worry about the challenges of training faculty members and students to effectively use AI systems. In some cases, administrators may view AI as an expensive and high-risk investment that requires significant upfront costs and resources (Walsh & Karsenti, 2023; Bauer & Schmidt, 2024).

Strategies for Overcoming Resistance

To overcome resistance to AI adoption, it is essential to engage in a comprehensive approach that involves all stakeholders. Several strategies can help mitigate concerns and foster a more positive attitude toward AI integration in adult education (Eaton & Brown, 2022; Bauer & Schmidt, 2024).

1. Providing Professional Development and Training for Educators

A key strategy for overcoming resistance from educators is to provide targeted professional development and training. Educators need to feel confident in their ability to use AI tools effectively in the classroom. Providing hands-on training sessions, workshops, and ongoing support can help educators build the skills and knowledge they need to integrate AI into their teaching practices (Clark & Mayer, 2023; Carter & Rose, 2024).

It is important to highlight the ways in which AI can enhance, rather than replace, traditional teaching methods. Educators should be encouraged to see AI as a tool that can complement their expertise and help them meet the diverse needs of adult learners. By demonstrating how AI can support personalized learning, improve student engagement, and provide real-time feedback, educators will be more likely to embrace AI as a valuable teaching resource (Chi & Wylie, 2023; Crompton, Burke, & Lin, 2024).

2. Promoting Awareness and Benefits for Adult Learners

To address resistance from adult learners, it is crucial to promote awareness of the benefits of AI-powered education. Adult learners should be educated about how AI can provide personalized learning experiences tailored to their individual needs, enabling them to learn at their own pace and according to their specific interests. Highlighting the flexibility and accessibility of AI-powered platforms can help alleviate concerns about technology intimidating or overwhelming learners. (DeMillo, R. A., 2023)

Moreover, educational institutions should emphasize the ways in which AI can help learners overcome time constraints, such as providing flexible learning schedules or offering microlearning opportunities. By focusing on the practical benefits AI can offer adult learners, educational institutions can foster a more positive attitude toward these technologies. (Diaz, V., & Molina, S., 2024).

3. Building Trust in AI Through Transparency and Data Security

To mitigate concerns about privacy and data security, it is essential to build trust between stakeholders and AI platforms. Educational institutions must be transparent about how AI systems collect and use data, ensuring that learners' personal information is protected. Adhering to stringent data privacy policies and ensuring compliance with relevant regulations, such as the General Data Protection Regulation (GDPR), can help reassure learners that their data is safe.

Institutions should also offer learners control over their data, allowing them to opt in or opt out of data collection and providing clear explanations of how their data will be used. This transparency helps build trust and reduces resistance to AI adoption. (Durak, G., & Ataizi, M., 2023)

BUILDING INSTITUTIONAL CAPACITY FOR AI INTEGRATION AND SCALING EFFORTS

In addition to overcoming resistance, another key challenge in adopting AI in adult education is building institutional capacity for integration and scaling. AI adoption requires significant resources, both in terms of infrastructure and personnel, to ensure its effective implementation across an institution. Educational institutions must develop the capacity to integrate AI technologies into their teaching and learning environments and scale AI adoption to benefit all adult learners (Zawacki-Richter, Marín, & Bond, 2023; Walsh & Karsenti, 2023).

1. Establishing a Clear Vision and Strategy for AI Integration

To successfully integrate AI into adult education, institutions must establish a clear vision and strategy for how AI will be used to enhance learning. This strategy should align with the institution's educational goals and the specific needs of adult learners. Institutions should take a holistic approach to AI adoption, considering how AI can support personalized learning, improve accessibility, and provide valuable insights into learner progress (Bauer & Schmidt, 2024; Clark & Mayer, 2023).

A strategic approach also involves identifying the specific AI tools and platforms that will best serve the needs of the institution and its learners. Whether it is using AI-powered tutoring systems, virtual assistants, or adaptive learning platforms, educational institutions must select AI tools that align with their teaching objectives and the technological capacity of the institution (Crompton, Burke, & Lin, 2024).

2. Investing in Infrastructure and Technological Resources

One of the primary barriers to scaling AI adoption in adult education is the lack of necessary infrastructure. To integrate AI successfully, institutions must invest in the technological resources needed to support AI-powered platforms. This includes upgrading their internet infrastructure, ensuring access to appropriate hardware, and adopting cloud-based systems that can handle the computational demands of AI (Fisher & Rubenson, 2024; McKenna & Thompson, 2023).

Institutions must also ensure that their AI platforms are scalable, capable of supporting large numbers of adult learners without sacrificing performance or quality. This involves investing in cloud computing resources, ensuring reliable internet connectivity, and ensuring that AI systems are flexible and adaptable to the evolving needs of the institution (Eraut & Hirsh, 2023).

3. Collaborating with Technology Providers and Experts

Building institutional capacity for AI integration also involves collaboration with technology providers and AI experts. Educational institutions should partner with AI vendors and developers to ensure that the tools they adopt are user-friendly, effective, and tailored to the specific needs of adult learners. Collaborative partnerships can also provide valuable training and support for faculty and staff, ensuring that they have the knowledge and skills needed to integrate AI into their teaching practices (Hamann & Pollak, 2023; Oswald, Behrend, & Sinar, 2024).

Collaborating with experts in AI and education can also help institutions stay informed about the latest trends and best practices in AI adoption. By learning from other institutions that have successfully implemented AI technologies, educational organizations can gain valuable insights into how to overcome challenges and scale AI integration effectively (Grant & Vivian, 2023). (Cheng, YEAR)

Adopting AI technologies in adult education presents both challenges and opportunities.

Overcoming resistance to AI and building institutional capacity for AI integration are crucial steps in ensuring that AI's transformative potential is fully realized. By addressing concerns through targeted professional development, promoting awareness among learners, building trust through transparency, and investing in infrastructure, educational institutions can overcome these challenges and successfully adopt AI to enhance adult learning experiences (Clark & Mayer, 2023; Bauer & Schmidt, 2024; Fisher & Rubenson, 2024). With strategic planning, collaboration, and a focus on building capacity, AI can be integrated into adult education systems to promote personalized, flexible, and lifelong learning opportunities for all (Zawacki-Richter, Marín, & Bond, 2023; Grant & Vivian, 2023).

As we look toward the future, the role of Artificial Intelligence (AI) in adult education and workforce development is poised to become even more significant, driving transformation across educational landscapes globally. AI has the potential to reshape how adults engage in learning and how institutions and organizations prepare individuals for the workforce. This section will explore the vision for AI in fostering lifelong learning ecosystems, as well as the broader, global implications for adult education and workforce development (Eraut & Hirsh, 2023; Zawacki-Richter, Marín, & Bond, 2023).

VISION FOR THE ROLE OF AI IN FOSTERING LIFELONG LEARNING ECOSYSTEMS

The concept of lifelong learning has gained widespread importance in the 21st century, driven by rapid technological advancements, globalization, and shifting labor market demands. In this context, AI presents a unique opportunity to cultivate robust lifelong learning ecosystems—environments that facilitate continuous, self-directed, and personalized learning throughout an individual's life. AI has the capacity to tailor learning experiences, improve access to knowledge, and empower adult learners to pursue educational opportunities in ways that were previously unavailable or impractical (Eraut & Hirsh, 2023; Zawacki-Richter, Marín, & Bond, 2023).

AI-powered platforms and tools are already playing a pivotal role in facilitating personalized learning journeys. By using AI to analyze learners' progress, preferences, and goals, these technologies are enabling the creation of individualized learning paths. Such platforms offer personalized recommendations, adjust the difficulty level of content in real time, and provide learners with instant feedback on their performance. For adult learners, who often balance education with professional and personal commitments, these features allow for flexible learning that aligns with their specific needs and time constraints (Aldowah, Al-Samarraie, & Fauzy, 2023; D'Mello & Graesser, 2023).

Looking ahead, AI will continue to serve as the backbone of lifelong learning ecosystems. As the workforce becomes more fluid and dynamic, the need for employees to acquire new skills or refine existing ones will only intensify. AI will make it easier to facilitate this ongoing process of upskilling and reskilling by delivering customized learning experiences that respond to the shifting requirements of the labor market (Demartini & Tonelli, 2023; Carliner, 2023).

Furthermore, AI can enhance collaborative learning experiences, which are essential for fostering a sense of community among learners. Through intelligent virtual assistants, AI tools can promote discussion, peer feedback, and group problem-solving, enabling adult learners to connect with others across geographical boundaries. This will be especially important as more adult learners engage in remote, online, and hybrid learning environments (Park & Jung, 2024; Paredes & Rodrigues, 2024).

Another important direction is the integration of AI with other emerging technologies, such as the Internet of Things (IoT), blockchain, and augmented reality (AR). These technologies, when combined with AI, can offer even more immersive and interactive learning experiences. For example, AI-powered virtual and augmented reality tools can provide adults with hands-on simulations and immersive learning environments that enhance understanding and retention, particularly in fields requiring practical skills (Felicia & Lameras, 2024; Johnson & Lester, 2023).

AI can also contribute to the democratization of education, breaking down barriers related to access and affordability. By providing scalable learning solutions that cater to learners from diverse socioeconomic backgrounds, AI can create more equitable learning opportunities. With the power of AI, educational resources can be tailored to suit the needs of disadvantaged or underserved populations, opening doors for individuals who may have otherwise been excluded from quality education and professional development opportunities (Fisher & Rubenson, 2024; Grant & Vivian, 2023).

THE GLOBAL IMPACT OF AI IN TRANSFORMING ADULT EDUCATION AND WORKFORCE DEVELOPMENT

The integration of AI in adult education and workforce development will have far-reaching implications, not just locally or regionally, but on a global scale. As economies worldwide continue to evolve and adapt to new technologies, AI will play a critical role in ensuring that the global workforce is equipped to meet these changes (Demartini & Tonelli, 2023; Carliner, 2023).

One of the key global impacts of AI will be the ability to bridge the skills gap that exists in many industries. Across the world, there is a growing need for workers to acquire new skills to keep pace with automation, digitalization, and artificial intelligence itself. AI can help address these gaps by providing targeted training and skill-building resources that are directly aligned with industry needs. By continuously analyzing labor market trends, AI can identify emerging skill requirements and help design educational programs that are responsive to these needs. This will be especially important in regions where industries are undergoing rapid technological shifts, such as the automation of manufacturing or the expansion of digital services (Hamann & Pollak, 2023; Oswald, Behrend, & Sinar, 2024).

Additionally, AI has the potential to contribute to workforce development in underserved and developing regions. By offering online, accessible, and cost-effective training, AI-powered educational platforms can help people in remote or impoverished areas gain the skills needed for employment in the global economy. This is especially important for regions that lack robust educational infrastructure or have limited access to traditional educational institutions. AI can provide these learners with high-quality, scalable education and career development opportunities that were once out of reach (Fisher & Rubenson, 2024; Zawacki-Richter, Marín, & Bond, 2023).

Furthermore, as economies become increasingly interconnected, the demand for a globally competent workforce is also growing. AI will play a crucial role in preparing adult learners to work in this interconnected, digital world. By providing language translation, cultural context, and remote collaboration tools, AI can enhance cross-cultural communication and global teamwork. This is particularly valuable for workers who engage in international trade, development, or collaborative projects with teams from different countries. AI can also assist with skills development in niche fields that require international knowledge, such as global health initiatives or international finance, making it easier for workers to gain the expertise needed for global challenges (Paredes & Rodrigues, 2024; Johnson & Lester, 2023).

AI-powered learning platforms are also enabling companies to create training programs that are customized to their specific needs. For example, a global corporation might use AI to develop a training program that adapts to the learning styles and skill levels of its employees across various regions. This ensures that training programs are both relevant and effective, regardless of where the employees are based. This ability to provide customized, efficient training will increase workplace productivity and ultimately improve business outcomes on a global scale (Grant & Vivian, 2023; Eraut & Hirsh, 2023).

On a broader level, AI has the potential to reshape the relationship between education and the workforce. Traditionally, education systems have been designed to prepare individuals for the workforce, but with the rapid pace of technological change, the link between education and work is becoming more fluid. AI will allow for more real-time learning opportunities, enabling individuals to continuously update their skills to match evolving job market demands. This will be especially important in industries that require continuous professional development, such as technology, healthcare, and finance (Crompton, Burke, & Lin, 2024).

Moreover, AI can facilitate more efficient workforce planning and talent management. By analyzing data on skills, performance, and career trajectories, AI can help companies predict workforce needs, identify skill shortages, and make data-driven decisions about recruitment and training. This can lead to more effective talent development, ensuring that businesses have access to the skills they need while providing workers with the tools to grow in their careers (Felicia & Lameras, 2024; Chi & Wylie, 2023).

The future of AI in adult education and workforce development holds immense promise. By fostering lifelong learning ecosystems and promoting continuous education, AI can address skills gaps, improve access to education, and empower individuals to reach their professional goals. On a global scale, AI has the potential to bridge disparities in educational opportunities, create a more equitable workforce, and drive economic growth by equipping workers with the skills needed to thrive in a rapidly changing world (Zawacki-Richter, Marín, & Bond, 2023; Grant & Vivian, 2023).

However, to fully realize these benefits, stakeholders at all levels, educators, employers, policymakers, and learners themselves, must work together to address the challenges of AI integration and ensure that these technologies are used ethically and responsibly. By doing so, we can unlock the full potential of AI to transform adult education and workforce development, creating a more adaptable, skilled, and globally connected workforce for the future (Eaton & Brown, 2022; Gholami & Watson, 2024).

SIGNIFICANCE OF THE CHAPTER

This chapter contributes significantly to the expanding body of knowledge on the transformative potential of AI in adult education by offering both theoretical and practical perspectives. It explores how AI can revolutionize lifelong learning programs by personalizing education, addressing barriers faced by adult learners, and fostering continuous skill development (Aldowah, Al-Samarraie, & Fauzy, 2023; Crompton, Burke, & Lin, 2024).

Furthermore, it delves into the role of AI in upskilling and reskilling initiatives, emphasizing its ability to tailor training programs based on industry needs and individual learning pathways (Demartini & Tonelli, 2023; Oswald, Behrend, & Sinar, 2024). This chapter not only highlights the opportunities that AI presents in enhancing adult education but also critically examines the challenges that come with its integration, such as ethical concerns, equity issues, and resistance to new technologies (Eaton & Brown, 2022; Selwyn & Jandrić, 2023).

By addressing these opportunities and challenges in detail, this chapter equips educators, policymakers, and industry leaders with actionable insights and tools for integrating AI-driven solutions. It emphasizes the need for a collaborative approach to ensure the ethical, equitable, and effective implementation of AI in educational settings (Bauer & Schmidt, 2024; Grant & Vivian, 2023). Ultimately, this chapter aims to provide a roadmap for advancing workforce readiness globally, empowering adult learners to engage in lifelong learning and succeed in an increasingly AI-driven world (Eraut & Hirsh, 2023; Zawacki-Richter, Marín, & Bond, 2023).

CONCLUSION

In conclusion, this chapter has explored the transformative potential of artificial intelligence (AI) in adult education, particularly in fostering lifelong learning and enhancing workforce development. As the world continues to evolve at a rapid pace, driven by technological advancements, the need for adults to continuously adapt, acquire new skills, and remain competitive in the workforce has never been greater. AI presents a powerful tool for meeting these needs by offering personalized, flexible, and efficient learning experiences that can be tailored to the unique needs of each learner (Aldowah, Al-Samarraie, & Fauzy, 2023; Crompton, Burke, & Lin, 2024).

AI-driven personalization has emerged as one of the most promising approaches for overcoming the challenges that adult learners face, including time constraints, skills gaps, and diverse educational backgrounds. By customizing learning paths and delivering just-in-time training, AI enables learners to engage in meaningful, relevant education that directly contributes to their personal and professional growth. Furthermore, AI's ability to identify and address skills gaps allows for more targeted upskilling and reskilling initiatives, empowering individuals to stay ahead in an ever-changing labor market (Demartini & Tonelli, 2023; D'Mello & Graesser, 2023).

In addition to enhancing the learning experience, AI also offers significant opportunities for fostering critical thinking, problem-solving, and collaboration among adult learners. By integrating intelligent tutoring systems, virtual assistants, and AI-driven simulations, adult education programs can create environments where learners actively engage with the material, develop essential skills, and apply their learning to real-world contexts. These AI-enhanced pedagogies not only make learning more engaging but also prepare learners for the complex challenges they will face in their careers (Chi & Wylie, 2023; Felicia & Lameras, 2024).

However, as we embrace the potential of AI, it is essential to recognize the ethical and equity considerations that come with its implementation. Ensuring equitable access to AI-powered learning resources, protecting learners' data privacy, and addressing biases in AI systems are critical components of successfully integrating AI into adult education. Policymakers, educators, and industry leaders must work collaboratively to establish frameworks and strategies that prioritize fairness, inclusivity, and transparency in AI adoption (Eaton & Brown, 2022; Selwyn & Jandrić, 2023).

As we look to the future, the role of AI in adult education and workforce development will only continue to grow. By investing in AI-powered learning solutions, fostering a culture of lifelong learning, and promoting ethical and equitable practices, we can create an educational ecosystem that empowers adult learners to thrive in the digital age. This chapter has outlined the key strategies and considerations necessary for achieving these goals, offering valuable insights that will help shape the future of adult education and workforce readiness in an AI-driven world (Grant & Vivian, 2023; Zawacki-Richter, Marín, & Bond, 2023).

REFERENCES

Ahuja, K., & Mitra, A. (2023). AI in lifelong learning: Personalization and adaptability. *Educational Technology Research and Development*, *71*(2), 237–258. https://www.doi.org/10.1007/s11423-022-10132-4

Aldowah, H., Al-Samarraie, H., & Fauzy, W. M. (2023). AI-based adaptive learning systems: Revolutionizing adult education. *Educational Technology Research and Development*, *71*(4), 989–1007. https://www.doi.org/10.1007/s11423-023-10141-w

Baker, R., & Siemens, G. (2023). Artificial intelligence and adaptive learning: Shaping the future of adult education. *Journal of Adult and Continuing Education*, *29*(1), 45–61. https://www.doi.org/10.1177/14779714221090522

Bauer, K., & Schmidt, J. (2022). Ethical AI implementation in adult education: Challenges and strategies. *AI & Society*, *37*(3), 935–947. https://www.doi.org/10.1007/s00146-021-01275-8

Bennett, T., & Roberts, L. (2024). Addressing digital divides in AI-enhanced adult learning. *Educational Review*, *76*(1), 33–49. https://www.doi.org/10.1080/00131911.2023.2145098

Berg, M., & Kezar, A. (2024). Equity-minded leadership in the age of artificial intelligence: Navigating innovation and inclusion in higher education. *Journal of Higher Education Leadership*, *92*(1), 33–52. https://www.doi.org/10.1080/00221546.2024.2300157

Bhattacharya, M. (2023). The role of AI in upskilling and reskilling initiatives. *Workforce Development Journal, 14*(2), 75–88. https://www.doi.org/10.1108/WDJ-10-2022-0039

Brookfield, S. D., & Holst, J. D. (2023). Critical adult education in the era of AI. *Adult Education Quarterly*, *73*(2), 103–121. https://www.doi.org/10.1177/07417136231156302

Brown, A. L., & Green, D. E. (2022). AI-driven microlearning for workforce training. *Journal of Vocational Education and Training*, *74*(3), 512–529. https://www.doi.org/10.1080/13636820.2022.2026039

Carliner, S. (2023). The evolving role of instructional designers in the age of AI. *Performance Improvement*, *62*(3), 26–35. https://www.doi.org/10.1002/pfi.22033

Carter, M. A., & Rose, C. P. (2024). Intelligent tutoring systems and adult learning. *Computers & Education*, *207*, 104901. https://www.doi.org/10.1016/j.compedu.2024.104901

Cheng, E. C. K. (Ed.). (2023). *Innovating education with AI*. Springer., https://www.doi.org/10.1007/978-981-16-8927-4

Chi, M. T. H., & Wylie, R. (2023). The ICAP framework: Linking cognitive engagement to active learning outcomes. *Educational Psychologist*, *58*(1), 1–16. https://www.doi.org/10.1080/00461520.2022.2136604

Clark, R. C., & Mayer, R. E. (2023). *AI-enhanced e-learning: Principles and practice* (4th ed.). John Wiley & Sons. *(No DOI available for this print book.)*

Cohen, E., & Alpert, R. (2022). AI for workforce readiness: Aligning skills development with industry demands. *Human Resource Development Review, 21*(4), 372–392. https://www.doi.org/10.1177/15344843221119412

D'Mello, S. K., & Graesser, A. C. (2023). Affect, meta-affect, and affect regulation during complex learning. *Educational Psychologist, 58*(2), 85–101. https://www.doi.org/10.1080/00461520.2023.2173021

Demartini, C. G., & Tonelli, M. (2023). Artificial intelligence in education: A review of the current state of research. *Journal of International Students, 11*(2), 45–67. https://www.doi.org/10.3390/intelligence11020045

DeMillo, R. A. (2023). *The future of lifelong learning in an AI-driven world.* Routledge. *(No DOI available for this book.)*

Diaz, V., & Molina, S. (2024). AI-enhanced pedagogy in adult education. *Adult Learning, 35*(1), 25–33. https://www.doi.org/10.1177/10451595231188562

Eaton, S. E., & Brown, B. (2022). Ethical considerations for AI in education. *Ethics and Education, 17*(3), 289–305. https://www.doi.org/10.1080/17449642.2022.2109705

Fadel, C., & Trilling, B. (2023). *Artificial intelligence in lifelong learning: Preparing adults for the future*. Jossey-Bass.

Fisher, D., & Rubenson, K. (2024). Adult learning in the digital era: Policy perspectives and lifelong learning strategies. *International Review of Education, 70*(1–2), 55–74. https://www.doi.org/10.1007/s11159-024-10012-3

Fong, J., & Kim, Y. J. (2024). AI and adaptive learning systems for professional training. [DOI not publicly available—appears to be a trade publication.]. *Training & Development, 78*(2), 22–29.

Garrison, D. R., & Vaughan, N. D. (2023). *AI, online learning, and communities of inquiry.* Routledge.

Ghosh, R., & Parashar, A. (2022). Artificial intelligence and the future of workforce development. *Technology in Society, 71*, 102087. https://www.doi.org/10.1016/j.techsoc.2022.102087

Greenfield, P. M. (2024). Cognitive implications of AI-driven adaptive learning systems. *Mind, Brain and Education : the Official Journal of the International Mind, Brain, and Education Society, 18*(1), 32–43. https://www.doi.org/10.1111/mbe.12354

Hsieh, M.-Y., & Chen, S.-Y. (2022). Adaptive learning technology in adult education. *International Journal of Continuing Education and Lifelong Learning, 15*(2), 95–116.

Istance, D., & Dumont, H. (Eds.). (2023). *AI-driven personalized learning: Strategies and best practices*. OECD Publishing.

Jenkins, J. (2023). Leveraging AI for workforce adaptability. Workforce Education Forum, 15(1), 18–30.

Kasworm, C. E., & Rose, A. D. (2022). Adult learners in the age of AI: Navigating the future. Adult Education Research Conference Proceedings, 2022, 31–39. (Eaton, S. E., & Brown, B., 2022)

Knowles, M. S., Holton, E. F., & Swanson, R. A. (2024). *The adult learner: The definitive classic in adult education and human resource development* (9th ed.). Routledge. DOI: 10.4324/9781003387671

Kulik, J. A., & Fletcher, J. D. (2022). Effectiveness of intelligent tutoring systems: A meta-analysis. *Review of Educational Research, 92*(4), 531–568. https://www.doi.org/10.3102/00346543221106423

Lee, S. Y., & Kim, D. (2023). Predictive analytics in adult education: Enhancing learner success. *Journal of Educational Technology & Society, 26*(1), 147–160. https://www.doi.org/10.30191/ETS.202301.0013

Liu, D., & Wang, T. (2024). AI-enhanced collaborative learning environments for adult education. *Computers in Human Behavior, 144*, 107920. https://www.doi.org/10.1016/j.chb.2024.107920

Mahmood, Z., & Hassan, S. (Eds.). (2022). *Artificial intelligence methods in education*. Springer., https://www.doi.org/10.1007/978-3-031-06258-8

Martinez, J., & Gonzalez, E. (2023). Ethical frameworks for AI implementation in adult education. *Ethics and Information Technology, 25*(2), 199–211. https://www.doi.org/10.1007/s10676-023-09707-3

McKenna, R., & Thompson, L. (2023). AI and adult literacy: Expanding access through adaptive technologies. *Adult Basic Education Journal, 17*(1), 45–58.

Moreno, R., & Perez, L. (2024). Personalized AI systems in vocational education. *Vocational Learning Journal, 17*(2), 128–140. https://www.doi.org/10.1007/s12186-023-09301-6

Murphy, K., & Bennett, S. (2023). AI-enhanced workforce training: From theory to practice. *Human Resource Management Journal, 33*(3), 320–336. https://www.doi.org/10.1111/1748-8583.12383

Nash, J., & Burke, M. (2024). Bridging digital divides through AI-driven adult education. *International Journal of Lifelong Education, 43*(1), 72–86. https://www.doi.org/10.1080/02601370.2023.2157650

Norman, D. A. (2024). Human-centered AI for adult learning. *Educational Technology Research and Development, 72*(1), 7–25. https://www.doi.org/10.1007/s11423-023-10145-y

O'Donnell, E., & Smith, J. A. (2023). AI-enabled learning analytics for adult education. *British Journal of Educational Technology, 54*(4), 798–814. https://www.doi.org/10.1111/bjet.13323

Park, Y., & Jung, J. (2024). Virtual assistants in adult education: Improving learner engagement and autonomy. *Adult Education Quarterly, 74*(1), 54–71. https://www.doi.org/10.1177/07417136231195732

Patterson, M., & Weller, M. (2022). AI-powered online learning: Opportunities and challenges. *Open Learning, 37*(3), 265–280. https://www.doi.org/10.1080/02680513.2022.2103754

Puentedura, R. R., & Johnson, M. (2023). SAMR model revisited: Integrating AI into adult learning contexts. *Journal of Educational Technology & Society*, *26*(3), 112–125. https://www.doi.org/10.30191/ETS.202303.0012

Russell, S., & Norvig, P. (2022). *Artificial intelligence: A modern approach* (4th ed.). Pearson Education.

Silver, L., & Baker, P. (2023). AI applications in workforce upskilling: A systematic review. *Journal of Workplace Learning*, *35*(1), 56–74. https://www.doi.org/10.1108/JWL-02-2022-0016

Sutton, B., & Brown, S. (2024). Ethical AI frameworks for equitable adult education. *Adult Learning*, *35*(2), 98–107. https://www.doi.org/10.1177/10451595231200109

Tschofen, C., & Mackness, J. (2023). Artificial intelligence and the future of online adult learning communities. *Technology, Pedagogy and Education*, *32*(1), 59–73. https://www.doi.org/10.1080/1475939X.2022.2088190

UNESCO. (2023). *Artificial intelligence in education: Challenges and opportunities for sustainable development*. UNESCO Publishing.

Walsh, T., & Karsenti, T. (2023). Implementing AI in adult education: Strategies for effective integration. *Canadian Journal of Educational Administration and Policy*, *2023*(199), 35–56.

Zhang, J., & Lu, X. (2023). AI-driven adaptive learning in higher education: Implications for adult learners. *Higher Education Research & Development*, *42*(2), 207–221. https://www.doi.org/10.1080/07294360.2022.2099645

Chapter 10
A Comparative Study on Chinese-Indonesian Translation Quality of Three AI-Based Translators (Google, Baidu, and DeepL)

Mei Rianto Chandra
https://orcid.org/0000-0003-2904-8465
Binus University, West Jakarta, Indonesia

Clara Herlina Karjo
https://orcid.org/0000-0002-7371-240X
Binus University, West Jakarta, Indonesia

Qian Kun
Jiangsu University, China

ABSTRACT

Machine translation (MT) systems like Google Translate, Baidu Translate, and DeepL Translator have become popular for bridging linguistic and cultural divides. These platforms use neural machine translation models to deliver instantaneous, multilingual translation services. This study aimed to compare the translation quality of Google Translate, Baidu Translate, and DeepL Translate in translating texts from Chinese to Indonesian. A mixed-methods strategy was used, involving 100 samples of Chinese source HSK vocabulary and business-related sentences. The findings indicated distinct variations in the efficacy of the three machine translation systems. Google Translate demonstrated the highest performance, attaining scores of 86% in accuracy, 85% in faithfulness, and 87% in naturalness. This superiority may not just indicate superior translation algorithms; its extensive popularity and regular use among Indonesian users undoubtedly contribute to improved output quality, notably through user data and feedback mechanisms that perpetually refine the system.

DOI: 10.4018/979-8-3373-5097-4.ch010

BACKGROUND

Primarily because of developments in neural networks and artificial intelligence (AI), machine translation (MT) has evolved dramatically in recent years. Well-known AI-based translators like Google Translate, Baidu Translate, and DeepL Translator generate progressively fluid and contextually aware outcomes using neural machine translation (NMT) (Cho et al., 2014; Wu et al., 2016). Though these technologies have been widely researched regarding well-known language pairings like English-Chinese or English-German, comparative studies on Chinese-Indonesian translation are few. This is especially important as machine translation systems might struggle owing to the language and syntactic variations between Chinese and Indonesian (Nugroho & Arifin, 2021).

Apart from fluency, correctness, semantic clarity, and meaning retention all influence translation quality as well. Assessing the performance of various MT systems in regard to these criteria helps to highlight the benefits and drawbacks of each one (Toral et al., 2018). In environments like school and the business where exact translation is vital, finding the optimal MT tool may significantly boost output and cross-cultural communication(Gaspari et al., 2015).

To evaluate accuracy, fluency, and meaning retention, this paper compares the translation quality of Google Translate, Baidu Translate, and DeepL Translator while converting Chinese texts into Indonesian using qualitative and quantitative approaches.

LITERATURE REVIEW

Business Chinese Translation

China's increasing worldwide influence has generated notable scholarly attention in fields such outbound foreign direct investment (FDI), geotourism, and translation studies. Emphasizing the significance of knowing not only the financial elements but also the cultural and communication dynamics enabling successful multinational corporations, (Buckley & Voss, 2020) offer perceptive analysis of China's involvement in several areas. In this case, efficient translation and localization strategies are vital, particularly when Chinese businesses engage with local stakeholders in numerous languages and cultural settings.

Focusing on geotourism translation, H. Li & Chen (2022) draw attention to study gaps and propose a systematic effort to improve Chinese English translations in geoparks. They contend that many present Chinese geopark translations lack clarity, accuracy, and contextual relevance, which might reduce tourist happiness and educational impact. Their suggested project is to provide linguistically accurate, culturally relevant systematic translation guidelines.

Particularly in expanding interdisciplinary domains like translation studies in corporate environments, (Rastogi, 2021) provides comprehensive guidance on performing literature reviews in international business research. His work helps scholars create well-grounded theoretical frameworks and identify interesting areas for future research.

Emphasizing its significance in a global society, (Wan, 2020) looks at the practice of Chinese-English sign translating. Considering sociolinguistic factors, cultural sensitivity, and audience expectations, she advocates a more thorough and theoretically grounded approach. Particularly in commercial and tourist settings, this strategy underlines the need of frameworks that match the several facets of meaning-making in public signs.

From international investment and multinational enterprises to geotourism and public communication, these studies reveal the increasing significance of Chinese-English translation in many business and public environments. They underline the significance of solid theoretical foundations and practical strategies to support excellent translation practices.

(Wang & Zhang, 2021)underline the importance of translators beyond lexical and grammatical accuracy, contending that often the missing link in poor translations is cultural context. Examining the metaphor in Chinese political and economic discourse and its translation effects, (Chen & Jian, 2019) argues that to translate such terms in a way that preserves their rhetorical and persuasive features, translators require both language competence and cultural awareness.

Examining how corpus linguistics may be used to evaluate translation quality in Chinese-English translations, (Huang & Xu, 2022) uncover persistent patterns, differences, and stylistic choices that could influence reading and user involvement. This empirical method allows for a data-driven evaluation of translation effectiveness and the development of machine learning algorithms automating some facets of translation evaluation.

(Liu, 2020) evaluates how well Chinese university translator training courses prepare students for the real needs of business and tourism translation. To guarantee future translators are more equipped to handle difficult multilingual communication responsibilities, she backs curricular modifications including more hands-on activities, case studies, and collaboration with corporate partners.

Finally, (Zhao, 2021) looks at the translation quality of Chinese tourist sites as seen by visitors from abroad through surveys and interviews, revealing that the quality of English translations provided affects their opinion of the overall legitimacy and professionalism of a site. This emphasizes that translation is a component of corporate image and service quality as well as a linguistic task.

AI Based Translators

Artificial Intelligence (AI) is rapidly reshaping two seemingly distinct yet complementary domains of scholarly activity: the conduct of systematic literature reviews (SLRs) and the practice of cross-cultural language translation. In research methodology, AI is increasingly adopted to semi-automate SLRs, most visibly in the screening and data-extraction phases. (Wagner et al., 2022) show that machine-learning classifiers can filter thousands of titles and abstracts in minutes, slashing weeks of manual labor and allowing researchers to redirect precious cognitive effort toward critical appraisal and theoretical synthesis. Accuracy, however, is not yet perfect; human oversight remains essential to prevent algorithmic bias—such as over-fitting to a narrowly defined keyword set that might exclude pivotal studies using synonymous terminology.

AI involvement does not stop at screening. Data-extraction is now tackled with advanced Natural Language Processing (NLP). Fine-tuned transformer models—e.g., domain-specific BERT variants—can identify and pull quantitative results (“effect size = 0.42, $p < 0.05$”) from full texts straight into structured tables. (Karimi-Sarabi et al., 2023) report 85 % extraction accuracy in medical reviews after task-specific fine-tuning. While error margins persist, the time savings are dramatic, paving the way for “living reviews,” continuously updated as new studies hit databases.

Looking ahead, AI-driven review tools are expected to evolve into true "scientific co-pilots" that not only screen and extract but also compose narrative syntheses. Pilot experiments by (Ahmed et al., 2024) used GPT-4o to write 250-word summaries of 120-article corpora. Two-thirds of peer reviewers judged the text "publication-ready," yet flagged weaknesses: occasional over-generalization and shallow methodological critique. Ethical debates intensify: who counts as an author? How should AI involvement be disclosed? Journals now align with COPE guidelines that mandate transparent reporting of generative-AI use.

Meanwhile, in language translation, AI is driving a paradigm shift in global communication. Commercial Neural Machine Translation (NMT) systems (Google, DeepL, Baidu) now achieve single-digit word error rates for high-resource language pairs such as English–Mandarin. (Mohamed et al., 2024) review remaining hurdles, notably cross-lingual dialect adaptation—models trained on standard dialects (Putonghua) struggle with regional variants. (Jiang, 2023) propose dynamic corpus augmentation, reducing perplexity by 12 % when translating Sichuanese Mandarin into English.

Integration of NMT into Computer-Assisted Translation (CAT) workflows yields a hybrid production model: the machine generates a rough draft; human post-editors polish terminology and style. (Ruiz-Mezcua et al., 2021) find this boosts productivity by 35 % while lowering cognitive load, though translators caution against "automation complacency"—an over-trust in fluent yet subtly erroneous machine output. Consequently, translator-training programs now incorporate AI literacy modules that teach critical evaluation of machine suggestions.

The two domains—SLR automation and AI translation—are converging. A single large language model can, in theory, summarize a corpus of biomedical research and instantly translate that synopsis into multiple languages, democratizing scientific knowledge. Picture an international conference where every accepted paper is released in six languages together with an AI-generated meta-review highlighting key innovations. To realise this vision, however, the community must guarantee citation fidelity and source transparency.

Dimension in Assessing Translation Quality

Translation quality assessment (TQA) is critical to measure the standard of translation which can satisfy the translators, and the readers (or the clients). There is a general agreement that a translation should be "good", "satisfactory" or "acceptable". Yet, there has been no consensus to what is considered good, satisfactory, or acceptable translation. Therefore, several attempts to set up certain criteria or models to assess translation quality have been made by various experts in translation field.

House (2002) offers a TQA model using Hallidayan trinity dimension which consists of field, tenor, and mode. Field refers to the nature of the social action in the text, consisting of the field of activity, the content of the text and its degree of generality and specificity. Tenor refers to the participants, i.e. the author and his personal stance versus the content as well as the relationship between author and addresses in terms of social power distance and its effect. Mode captures the degree of orality and literality, and the text's texture or the 'make-up' of the text.

Larson (1997) translation assessment criteria, outlined in her 1984 work, emphasized three key aspects namely accuracy, clarity, and naturalness. These criteria are used to evaluate the quality of a translation and ensure it effectively conveys the meaning of the original text while also being natural and understandable in the target language. Accuracy refers to the faithfulness of the translation to the source text, ensuring that the meaning is conveyed accurately and completely without any alteration or omission. Clarify focuses on the readability and comprehensibility of the translated text for the target audience. Naturalness refers to the use of language and style that are appropriate and idiomatic in the target language, making it sound authentic like it is written in the target language.

In line with Larson's criteria, propose that a high-quality translation should fulfil three aspects: accuracy, acceptability, and readability. Accuracy pertains to the equivalence between the source language (SL) and the target language (TL), ensuring that the translated message remains faithful to the original. Acceptability involves adherence to the linguistic and socio-cultural norms of the TL, ensuring that the translation aligns with its grammatical and cultural conventions. Readability is measured according to reader's knowledge., Readability in translation can be defined as the ease with which the target audience comprehends and engages with the translated text.

The above criteria are mainly used to measure the translation quality of human translation. Nowadays however, most translations can be done using machine translation or AI translation. Thus, the criteria for assessing translation can be added or developed. Waty Kembaren et al. (2023) used the criteria such as accuracy, consistency and flexibility to assess the translation quality of machine and human translations. Accuracy involves ensuring that the translation is grammatically correct, and that the meanings of words, phrases, and ideas are accurately conveyed. Consistency involves maintaining consistent terminology, style and tone throughout the entire text. While flexibility considers the ability to respond to changes, nuances, or variations in the text.

Assessment of Translation Quality of Machine Translation

The development of translation technology has created a new paradigm in translation industry. Translations are now mostly done by machine translators such as Google Translate or DeepL Translate, while human functions as the editor of the translation products. In this way, translation process will be done in a very short amount of time, and a qualified translation is achievable. Some studies confirm that humans' judgments are still essential in producing translations that fulfil all TQA criteria (Alowedi & Hassan Al Ahdal, 2023; Waty Kembaren et al., 2023)

The comparison of translation quality between human and machine translation was a fruitful research topic for more than a decade, with Google Translate as the most influential machine translation used. Nowadays, with the fiery development of generative AI that also integrate technology, users can benefit a lot from the improvement of working efficiency and quality (Li & Chen, 2022).

However, the quality of AI translation is still questionable until now. Many studies show divergent results of translation quality of AI translators across several dimensions and for diverse materials. The first study by (Li & Chen, 2022) compares the performance of four translation platforms (Baidu, Google, Microsoft, and Youdao) for the translation of Chinese English translation model test. They used four parameters for comparison, namely the translation quality, application efficiency, working mode and operating environment. For translation quality they utilize a 6x4 evaluation standard consisting of 6 categories of information accuracy and 4 categories of expression style. A perfect translation should obtain a full 10 score. Their results showed that Google and Baidu are the best in both information accuracy and expression style.

In another study, (Farghal & Haider (2024) studies the translation of classical Arabic poetry between Google's Gemini (Gem) and ChatGPT (GPT). The translation results were examined by translation professors based on three variables, namely thematic clarity, creativity, and prosody. Interestingly, the LLM (large language models) were also assigned to judge their own translations based on the three variables mentioned. The results show a positive assessment from the professors for human dan GPT translation through the three variables. However, GEM shows much poorer performance on prosody (M 2.83) and even worse in self-assessment (M 1). Overall, with respect to AI evaluation, GPT reflects human participants quite closely, while GEM shows greater discrepancy over prosody and creative elements.

An interesting study regarding the translation of Chinese classical poetry using three AI translators: ChatGPT, Google Translate and DeepL Translator was conducted by Gao et al., 2024. They used the evaluation criteria such as fidelity, fluency, language style, and machine translation style. The results revealed that ChatGPT outperformed Google Translate and DeepL Translator in all evaluation criteria. This result suggests that with a correct prompt, ChatGPT demonstrates a remarkable ability in poetry translation.

Besides poetry, scientific texts are also used as the source texts for comparing the translations. Fu & Liu (2024) compare the translations of scientific texts between student translators and ChatGPT. They analyzed the lexical features and syntactic features of both translators. They found that HT exhibits lengthier texts with a lower average word diversity while ChatGPT present higher accuracy in translating terminology. The finding suggests that ChatGPT and human translators exhibit complementary capabilities in translating scientific texts.

Comparison of HT versus AI translation was also done by (Moneus & Sahari, 2024) for legal documents. They use five criteria to evaluate legal translation: accuracy, competency, content, language, and style. Their findings showed that human translation offers a deeper understanding of the cultural context and nuances of the translated text while AI tools may not always be able to account for these differences.

METHODOLOGY

This study employs a quantitative and qualitative method based on applying analysis of translation data and statistical calculations to compare the translation performance of three AI translators.

Data Collection:

The data collecting procedure has three primary stages: text selection, machine translation, and expert evaluation. Every stage is crafted to guarantee consistency, objectivity, and dependability in acquiring translation results and assessments.

Text Selection

Text selections are the 100 business words that come from HSK vocabulary words and their sentence correlations, with the business vocabulary words data collected from HSK 2 until HSK 6, with consent for its data as follows: HSK 2, 3, and 4 each have one word; HSK level 5 has 17 words; and HSK 6 has 80 words. Data supporting this study are openly available from zenodo at https://zenodo.org/records/15245022 .

Machine Translation

Each chosen text is entered: Google Translate (translate.google.com), Baidu Translate (fanyi.baidu.com) and DeepL Translate (deepl.com). The Chinese source material is translated straight into Indonesian on each platform with the default parameters. No manual modifications are implemented to maintain the integrity of the machine-generated translations.

Expert Evaluation

Three bilingual specialists (Chinese Indonesian) are engaged to evaluate the quality of each translation. The reviewers possess academic qualifications in translation studies, Chinese linguistics, and Indonesian language instruction. They autonomously assess each translation result according to established assessment criteria, which are elaborated in the subsequent section. All translated outputs and reviewer evaluations are aggregated into a database for subsequent study. The inter-rater reliability among reviewers is assessed to guarantee the consistency and credibility of the ratings.

Study Hypotheses

H0: There are no statistical differences between the three translators
H1: There are significant differences between the three translators

Data Analysis

For the statistical calculation, we run Repeated Measure ANOVA for the same 100 terms across three translators (GT, BT, and DL). Repeated Measure is chosen because it is used to measure the same items, therefore the data is within subjects (i.e. repeated measure on the same items.). We chose three dimensions to measure the quality of translation, namely accuracy, faithfulness and naturalness. The purpose of this calculation is to see if there is a significant difference in the quality of translations among the three AI translators. The multivariate tests of these variables will show the effect of translation and dimension towards the translation quality.

Next, we performed pairwise comparison of the three aspects of translation quality between two translators (GT vs BT; GT vs DL; BT vs DL) to see the comparative advantages of each translator with respect to each TQA dimension.

Evaluation Aspects in Translation Analysis

The translation analysis was conducted by comparing the results from three machine translation tools: Google Translate, Baidu Translate, and DeepL Translate. This comparison was based on three main evaluation aspects: accuracy, faithfulness to the source meaning, and naturalness in the target language.

Accuracy

The accuracy assessment aims to measure the extent to which the message content from the source text is correctly and completely translated into the target language, without additions, omissions, or changes in meaning.

Table 1. Distribution of accuracy assessment results

Sentences	Machine Translator
1. *(zhè jiā gōngsī hěn y umíng)* = This company is famous.	GT: Perusahaan ini sangat terkenal.(V)
	BT: Perusahaan ini sangat terkenal. (V)
	DL: Perusahaan ini sangat terkenal. (V)
2. 10% *(jīnnián w men de lìrùn zēngzh ng le 10%)* = Our profit has risen by 10% th:s year.	GT: Keuntungan kami meningkat 10% tahun ini. (X)
	BT: keuntungan kita telah meningkat 10% tahun ini. (V)
	DL: Tahun ini laba kami meningkat 10 persen. (X)
3. *(xiāoshòu'é b qùnián tígāo le)* = The sales have increased compared to last year.	GT: Penjualan meningkat dibandingkan tahun lalu. (V)
	BT: Penghasilan penjualan telah meningkat dibandingkan tahun lalu. (X)
	DL: Penjualan lebih tinggi dari tahun lalu.(V)

A sentence is considered accurate in translation when the conveyed meaning and message remain the same, without any alteration. For example, in the first sentence (*zhè jiā gōngsī hěn y umíng*), all three translation tools—Google Translate, Baidu Translate, and DeepL—provided the same meaning: "This company is very famous.". However, in the second sentence 10% (*jīnnián w men de lìrùn zēngzh ng le 10%*), a difference in meaning can be observed. In this Chinese sentence, the particle " " (le) indicates that the event has already occurred. Therefore, an accurate translation should include the word "has" or "already" to reflect the completed action, resulting in: "Our profit has increased by 10% this year."(V).

In the third example, the sentence (*xiāoshòu'é b qùnián tígāo le*) shows inaccuracy in word-for-word translation. A closer look reveals the following breakdown:

- (xiāoshòu'é): Penjualan (sales)
- (b): dibandingkan (compared to)
- (qùnián): tahun lalu (last year)
- (tígāo le): meningkat sudah (has increased)

The overall meaning of the sentence is: "Sales have increased compared to last year." Therefore, a more accurate translation would be: "Sales have increased compared to last year." (Google Translate), or "Sales are higher than last year." (DeepL).

However, Baidu's translation adds the word "revenue," resulting in: "Sales revenue has increased compared to last year," which introduces an inaccuracy in meaning not originally present in the source sentence.

Faithfulness

The faithfulness assessment evaluates the extent to which the translation remains faithful to the style, tone, and structure of the original text, including preserving the author's intent and cultural context.

Table 2. Distribution of faithfulness assessment results

Sentences	Machine Translator
(Q ng tígōng hétóng de fùběn.) = please give the copy of the contract.	GT: Harap berikan salinan kontraknya. (V)
	BT: Silakan memberikan salinan kontrak. (V)
	DL: Tolong berikan salinan kontraknya.(V)
(W men xūyào tóuzī xīn jìshù.) = We have to invest in new technology.	GT: Kita perlu berinvestasi dalam teknologi baru. (V)
	BT: Kita harus investasi dalam teknologi baru. (X)
	DL: Kita perlu berinvestasi dalam teknologi baru. (V)
(Q ng j nkuài wánchéng dìngdān.) = Please complete your order as soon as possible.	GT: Harap selesaikan pesanan Anda sesegera mungkin. (V)
	BT: Silakan menyelesaikan perintah secepat mungkin. (X)
	DL: Tolong penuhi pesanan secepatnya. (X)

Based on the data above, the use of auxiliary words such as *harap*, *silakan*, and *tolong* represents a form of euphemism, meaning these words are used to soften or humble a request for help from others. Although there are syntactic differences, the conveyed meaning remains faithful to the language style used. This makes the translation in example question 4 faithfuls in terms of meaning.

In sentence example number 5, there is a distinction between the words *perlu* and *harus* in terms of meaning. The word *perlu* conveys a sense of need, suggestion, or requirement that is not necessarily obligatory—it leans more toward something recommended or considered useful. Meanwhile, the word *harus* implies an obligation or necessity that is non-negotiable. In Mandarin, the word (*xūyào*) can basically mean either *harus* or *perlu*, depending on the context of the sentence. However, in example sentence 5, the appropriate translation is to use the word *perlu.*

In sentence example number 6, there is a difference in both the placement and meaning of the translated sentence. In the sentence (*q ng j nkuài wánchéng dìngdān*), which is translated as *"Silakan menyelesaikan perintah secepat mungkin"*, there is an inaccuracy in translating the word (*wánchéng*), which actually means *"selesaikan"* or *"complete"*, but was instead translated as *"penuhi"* in the sentence *"Tolong penuhi pesanan secepatnya"*. This translation is incorrect because (*dìngdān*) means *"pesanan"*, not *"perintah"*. The correct translation for this sentence should be: *"Harap selesaikan pesanan Anda sesegera mungkin."*

Naturalness

The assessment of *naturalness* examines to what extent the translation sounds natural and is easily understood by native speakers of the target language, as if the text was originally written in that language.

Table 3. Distribution of faithfulness assessment results

Sentences	Machine Translator
7. (Guójì màoyì duì jīngjì y u hěn dà y ngxi ng.) = International trade has a big impact on economy.	GT: Perdagangan internasional mempunyai dampak besar terhadap perekonomian. (V)
	BT: Perdagangan internasional memiliki dampak yang signifikan pada ekonomi. (V)
	DL: Perdagangan internasional berdampak besar pada perekonomian.(V)
8. (Zīběn tóuzī duì gōngsī zhì guān zhòngyào.) = Capital investment is very important for the company.	GT: Investasi modal sangat penting bagi sebuah perusahaan. (V)
	BT: Investasi kapital penting untuk perusahaan.(X)
	DL: Investasi modal sangat penting bagi perusahaan. (V)
9. ?(Gōngsī de héxīn jìngzhēng lì shì shénme?) = What is the main competitive edge of a company?	GT: Apa daya saing inti perusahaan? (V)
	BT: Apa kompetitif utama perusahaan ini?(X)
	DL: Apa saja kompetensi inti perusahaan? (X)

In sentence number 7, there is a difference in the translation of the sentence " " (guójì màoyì duì jīngjì y u hěn dà y ngxi ng). Although there is a difference in word usage, the accuracy of the meaning conveyed remains intact. A more natural translation, such as using words like "mempunyai," "memiliki," or "pada" to translate the word " " (duì), gives a more natural impression in the context of Indonesian. Meanwhile, in sentence number 8, " " (zīběn tóuzī duì gōngsī zhìguān zhòngyào), the more natural translation in Indonesian is "Investasi modal sangat penting bagi sebuah perusahaan." The use of the word "sangat" here adds a stronger and more natural impression. When compared to a more literal translation without the word "sangat," such as "Investasi kapital penting untuk perusahaan," the first sentence sounds more natural and in line with everyday language style.

In sentence number 9, there is a shift in word usage and meaning in the translation of " ?" (gōngsī de héxīn jìngzhēnglì shì shénme?). This sentence should be translated as "Apa daya saing inti perusahaan?" (V), which is more accurate and natural. A translation like "Apa kompetitif utama perusahaan ini?" (X) or "Apa saja kompetensi inti perusahaan?" (X) would result in a meaning that is less natural and does not align with the everyday language style.

RESULTS

Statistical Analysis of AI Translators' Performance

Table 4. Mean comparison of the three translators

Dimension	Translators	Mean	Std. Deviation
Accuracy	Google Translate	2.78	.579
	Baidu Translate	2.37	.872
	DeepL Translate	2.54	.809
Faithfulness	Google Translate	2.77	.584
	Baidu Translate	2.37	.861
	DeepL Translate	2.53	.810
Naturalness	Google Translate	2.80	.550
	Baidu Translate	2.44	.833
	DeepL Translate	2.56	.783

Table 4 shows the mean score of all translators across three dimensions. Among all three GT shows the highest scores across three dimensions, 2.78,2.77, and 2.80. Meanwhile BT shows the lowest scores for all dimensions.

Table 5. Multivariate tests of AI translators

Effect	Tests	Value	F	df	df	Sig.
Translator	Pillai's Trace	.093	5.040	2	98	.008
	Wilks' Lambda	.907	5.040	2	98	.008
Dimension	Pillai's Trace	.128	7.225	2	98	.001
	Wilks' Lambda	.872	7.225	2	98	.001
Translator vs dimension	Pillai's Trace	.031	.759	2	96	.555
	Wilks' Lambda	.969	.759	2	96	.555

Table 5 shows the main effect of translator, dimension and the interaction of translator and dimension. For the main effect of translator, the Pillai Trace = 0.93, F = 5.040, df = (2,98), and Sig. =.008. All Pillai tests show p<.01, so the result is statistically significant. This means there are significant differences between the translators overall when considering the combination of the three dimensions. But this also suggests that at least one translator performs differently than the others when all dimensions are considered. For the main effect of dimension, the Pillai's Trace = .128, F = 7.225, df = (2, 98), Sig. = .001. This means that there are significant differences among the three dimensions (accuracy, naturalness, and faithfulness), across all translators. On average, the scores differ significantly between these dimensions — for example, translations might generally be more faithful than they are natural, or vice versa. As for the interaction effect of translator vs dimension, the Pillai's Trace = .031, F = .759, df = (4, 96), Sig. = .555. This shows that the interaction effect is not significant. In other words, the pattern of performance across dimensions is similar for all translators. In summary, one translator isn't especially better at accuracy while another is better at faithfulness — the differences between translators don't depend on the dimension.

Table 6. Pairwise comparison for 3 aspects of TQA

Comparison	Dimension	Mean Difference (I-J)	Std. Error	Sig.	95% CI (Lower, Upper)
GT vs BT	Accuracy	0410	.110	.001	.142,.678
	Faithfulness	.400	.112	.022	.127,.673
	Naturalness	.360	.109	.004	.095,.625
GT vs DL	Accuracy	.240	.097	.044	.005,.475
	Faithfulness	.240	.097	.044	.005,.475
	Naturalness	.240	.091	.029	.018,.462
BT vs DL	Accuracy	-.170	.120	.477	.462,.122
	Faithfulness	-.160	.119	.542	-449,.129
	Naturalness	-.120	.111	.850	.391,.151

Table 6 shows the pairwise comparison using Bonferroni adjustment for all translators. In terms of accuracy, GT and BT revealed statistically significant differences (Mean Difference = 0.410, *p* = .001) and DL (Mean Difference = 0.240, *p* = .044). GT consistently outperformed the other two systems in terms of accuracy. However, there was no statistically significant difference between BT and DL (*p* = .477), suggesting comparable performance between them in this dimension. Meanwhile, pairwise comparisons for faithfulness, showed that GT significantly outperformed both BT (Mean Difference = 0.400, *p* = .002) and DL (Mean Difference = 0.240, *p* = .044). These differences suggest that GT outputs were more faithful to the source texts. Meanwhile, the comparison between BT and DL did not yield a statistically significant difference (*p* = .542), indicating a similar level of performance in this regard. Finally, for naturalness dimension, GT scored significantly higher than both BT (Mean Difference = 0.360, *p* = .004) and DL (Mean Difference = 0.240, *p* = .029). These findings suggest that GT produced more fluent and native-like translations. However, the difference between BT and DL was not statistically significant (*p* = .850), indicating similar levels of performance between these two systems in terms of naturalness.

DISCUSSION

Comparative Performances of Three AI Tools

The results of this study reveal consistent and statistically significant differences in translation quality among the three AI translation systems across the dimensions of accuracy, faithfulness, and naturalness. GT emerged as the most effective system, significantly outperforming both BT and DL in all three areas.

In terms of *accuracy*, GT demonstrated a stronger ability to render Chinese business terms into Indonesian with semantic precision and correct lexical choices. This suggests a more advanced mechanism for aligning source and target language meanings, which is particularly crucial in professional translation contexts where misinterpretation can lead to serious consequences.

For *faithfulness*, GT again showed a significant advantage, preserving the core meaning and intent of the source texts more reliably than the other two systems. This indicates that its outputs not only convey correct meanings but also maintain the structural and conceptual integrity of the original content — a key requirement in business communication, legal documentation, and other high-stakes domains.

In the *naturalness* dimension, GT outputs were also judged to be more fluent and idiomatic, suggesting a greater capability in generating translations that align with the norms and stylistic expectations of the target language. This is especially important for user-facing content where clarity, readability, and tone can influence perception and usability.

Interestingly, there were no statistically significant differences between BT and DL in any of the three dimensions. This suggests that they may share similar underlying limitations or model characteristics and may not be sufficiently optimized for the nuances of Chinese Indonesian translation, particularly in specialized domains like business.

Overall, the findings indicate that GT is the most well-rounded and reliable among the three systems studied. Its consistent superiority across all quality dimensions highlights its potential suitability for professional use, especially in domains requiring both linguistic accuracy and stylistic finesse. These results also underscore the importance of evaluating AI translation tools across multiple dimensions rather than relying on surface-level fluency alone.

Translation Quality Analysis of the AI

Based on the data using the three translations, it can be concluded that all three, Google Translate, Baidu Translate, and DeepL, have their own advantages and disadvantages.

Quality Analysis of Google Translate

The findings based on the data evaluated using Google Translate appear in the table below. Entitled "Table 7. Quality Analysis of Google Translate," the table shows a threefold breakdown of translation quality: Accuracy, Faithfulness, and Naturalness. Every one of these elements is further split into three qualitative levels—High, Moderate, and Low—alongside the relevant percentages indicating the spread of translation quality.

Regarding accuracy, the data indicates that a large percentage of Google Translates translations are deemed rather accurate. Of the results, 86% were deemed "High" in accuracy. This suggests that in most cases the translated material expressed the same meaning as the original source without losing or changing vital information. Still, a little portion of the data is graded "Moderate" (6%) and "Low" (8%), indicating that in certain situations the translation either lacked accuracy or created mistakes affecting the general meaning.

Turning to truthfulness, the assessment likewise shows a favorable result: 85% of the translations were rated "High" in truthfulness. Faithfulness in translation is the degree to which the translation preserves the original message without distortion or inclusion of new components. The existence of 7% in the "Moderate" category and 8% in the "Low" category suggests that although many translations were true to the original, others created discrepancies or errors that may confuse readers or change the intended meaning.

Naturalness, which evaluates how fluid and natural the translations sound in the target language, is the final element examined. Of the data, an astounding 87% was graded "High" in naturalness. This implies that most translations not only expressed the right meaning but also did so utilizing language structures and word selections that are common and natural to native speakers. But 6% of the data was categorized as "Moderate" and 7% as "Low," suggesting often odd wording, strange word order, or lack of idiomatic use that can cause the translation to appear mechanical or non-native.

With a particularly good result in Naturalness and Accuracy, the information from this quality study indicates that Google Translate works remarkably well in all three areas. Especially for users looking for fast and clear translations, the consistently high percentages across all categories reinforce the idea that Google Translate is a dependable tool for basic translation jobs. The existence of moderate and poor ratings—though in lesser amounts—also highlights the need of human assessment in important translation situations, when even slight errors can cause major misinterpretations.

Table 7. Quality analysis of google translate

Accuracy			Faithfulness			Naturalness		
High	Moderate	Low	High	Moderate	Low	High	Moderate	Low
86%	6%	8%	85%	7%	8%	87%	6%	7%

Based on the data observed, Google Translate is superior in terms of providing translations that sound more natural when read. Below are examples of translations using Google Translate:

Table 8. Random examples of translation analysis in Google translate

Examples	Google Translate	Accuracy	Faithfulness	Naturalness
(Zhè jiā gōngsī de p npái hěn y u y ngxi ng lì.) = The company's brand image is strong.	Merek perusahaan itu kuat.	1*	1	2*
(Tāmen de shìch ng cèlüè hěn y uxiào)= Their marketing strategy is effective.	Strategi pemasaran mereka efektif.	2	2	2
(Shìch ng fèn'é de zēngzh ng fēicháng zhòngyào.)= The improvement of market segment is very important.	Pertumbuhan pangsa pasar sangatlah penting.	3*	2	3
(Tāmen de fēnxiāo w ngluò hěn gu ngfàn.)= Their distribution segment is wide.	Jaringan distribusi mereka luas.	2	2	2

*1: low, 2: moderate, 3: high

Based on the data in Table 8, it can be concluded that the translation of Mandarin sentences into Indonesian using Google Translate shows varied results in three main evaluation aspects: accuracy, faithfulness to the original meaning, and fluency or naturalness of the language. The evaluation was carried out on four different sentences, which were automatically translated by Google Translate. Each translation was then scored on a scale from 1 to 3, where 1 represents low quality, 2 represents moderate quality, and 3 represents high quality.

The first sentence, " ," was translated as "Merek perusahaan itu kuat." In terms of accuracy and faithfulness, this sentence received a score of 1, meaning its meaning is quite distant from the original context or there is distortion in the sentence structure. However, in terms of naturalness, the sentence was rated natural in Indonesian, earning a score of 2. This indicates that although the grammar of the translation is acceptable, the information conveyed is not entirely aligned with the original meaning.

The second sentence, " ," translated as "Strategi pemasaran mereka efektif," showed an improvement in quality. All three aspects—accuracy, faithfulness, and naturalness—each received a score of 2. This indicates that while there are still imperfections in the translation, the main meaning is conveyed well, and the sentence can be understood naturally in Indonesian.

For the third sentence, " ," the translation was "Pertumbuhan pangsa pasar sangatlah penting." This sentence received the highest scores among all the data, with accuracy and naturalness scoring 3, and faithfulness scoring 2. This indicates that in terms of message delivery and sentence structure, the translation is very good, although there are slight differences in nuance compared to the original sentence.

The fourth sentence, " ," translated as "Jaringan distribusi mereka luas," received a score of 2 for all aspects. This indicates that the translation is fairly accurate, faithful to the original meaning, and sounds natural in Indonesian. While not perfect, the result is acceptable as an automatic translation.

Overall, this data shows that Google Translate can provide moderate translation results for formal Mandarin texts into Indonesian. However, there are challenges, especially in terms of accuracy and faithfulness. Based on this sample, the average translation quality is at a moderate level and has not yet reached the level of perfection expected, especially for contexts that require sensitivity to implicit meanings or complex sentence structures.

Quality Analysis of Baidu Translate

The outcomes can be found in the table below depending on the data evaluated using Baidu Translate. The table named "Table 9. Quality Analysis of Google Translate" seems to have a labeling mistake as the real content shows the performance analysis of Baidu Translate, not Google Translate. The table offers a three-pronged assessment of translation quality: Accuracy, Faithfulness, and Naturalness. Every one of these aspects is further split into three degrees—High, Moderate, and Low—with matching percentages to show the spread of translation quality for Baidu Translate.

Beginning with Accuracy, which is the degree to which the translated material represents the original message, the statistics show that 61% of translations were rated "High" in this area. This implies that over half of the translations maintained the content and structure of the source text properly. Of the rest, 12% were graded as "Moderate," suggesting a partial departure from the source; 27% were classified as "Low," suggesting a clear degree of inaccuracy or distortion of the original material. This quite high proportion in the "Low" category suggests a possible constraint on Baidu Translates capacity to regularly provide precise translations.

Table 9. Quality analysis of Google translate

Accuracy			Faithfulness			Naturalness		
High	Moderate	Low	High	Moderate	Low	High	Moderate	Low
61%	12%	27%	60%	14%	26%	64%	13%	23%

Sixty percent of the translations were rated "High" under Faithfulness, which assesses how loyal the translated material stays to the original meaning and message. This is like the accuracy score, indicating that most of the translations effectively retained the original message without distortion. Still, 14% were classified as "Moderate" and 26% as "Low." These numbers show that in around 40% of the time, the fidelity of the translation might be affected to different extents, maybe because of grammatical, contextual, or cultural sensitivity mistakes.

Naturalness is the last dimension; it assesses how native-like and fluent the translation sounds in the target language. With a 64% score in the "High" category, Baidu Translate mostly produced grammatically correct and smooth-reading translations. A significant number of translations, nevertheless, were rated "Moderate" (13%) and "Low" (23%). These lower ratings can suggest unusual phrase structure, difficult wording, or literal translations at odds with native language standards.

Though Baidu Translate shows fair performance in all three areas, its quality levels fall short of the same heights seen in Google Translates study. The somewhat high percentages in the "Low" categories, especially for Accuracy (27%) and Faithfulness (26%), imply that Baidu Translate may have greater difficulty providing exact and contextually true translations than its rivals. Its Naturalness (64% "High") shows potential despite this, suggesting a general fluidity in its work.

Ultimately, although Baidu Translate is a good tool for simple translation jobs, users should be careful about depending on it for important material where accuracy and integrity are vital. The results back up the idea that although machine translation is always changing, human supervision is still crucial for guaranteeing quality, particularly in professional, academic, or sophisticated communication settings.

With random data tested using Baidu Translate, the results can be seen in the table below.

Table 10. Random examples of translation analysis on Baidu translate

Contoh Kalimat	Baidu Translate	Accuracy	Faithfullness	Naturalness
(zhè shì w men de mùbiāo shìch ng)= This is our target market.	Ini pasar sasaran kita.	1*	2*	2
(w men xūyào jiàngdī wùliú chéngběn)= We have to lower logistic cost.	Kita harus mengurangi biaya logistik.	2	2	3*
(w men xūyào tígāo gu nl xiàol)= We have to increase efficiency.	Kita harus meningkatkan efisiensi manajemen.	2	2	2
(zhège gōngyìngshāng fēicháng kěkao)= This supplier is very trustful.	Pembekal ini sangat dipercaya.	2	2	2

*1: low, 2: moderate, 3: high

Table 10 above presents the translation analysis results of four Mandarin sentences into Indonesian using Baidu Translate. The evaluation is based on three key aspects of translation: accuracy, faithfulness to the original meaning, and fluency or naturalness of the translated language. The rating is given on a three-point scale: 1 (low), 2 (moderate), and 3 (high).

The first sentence, " " (zhè shì w men de mùbiāo shìch ng), was translated by Baidu as "Ini pasar sasaran kita." In terms of accuracy, this sentence scored 1 due to the omission of the crucial word "kami" (we) as the subject of the sentence. In Mandarin structure, " " (w men, we) is essential for indicating ownership and purpose. The absence of this element causes a fundamental information error. However, in terms of faithfulness and naturalness, the sentence scored 2 because, although the information is incomplete, the structure remains understandable to the reader.

The second sentence, " " (w men xūyào jiàngdī wùliú chéngběn), was translated as "Kita harus mengurangi biaya logistik." Overall, this translation is quite good. All three aspects—accuracy, faithfulness, and naturalness—received scores of 2, 2, and 3, respectively. This sentence is considered fairly accurate in conveying its original meaning, which is about the need to reduce logistics costs. However, it should be noted that the word " " (xūyào) literally means "need" and not "should." The semantic shift could result in a different interpretation, although it remains within the same conceptual space.

Next, the third sentence, " " (w men xūyào tígāo gu nl xiàol), was translated as "Kita harus meningkatkan efisiensi manajemen." Like the second sentence, all aspects were given a score of 2. The structure and word choices are appropriate and acceptable in Indonesian. However, the use of "harus" (must) again stands out, as it is slightly stronger semantically compared to the original meaning of " " (xūyào), which indicates a need rather than a must.

The fourth sentence, " " (zhège gōngyìngshāng fēicháng kěkao), was translated as "Pembekal ini sangat dipercaya." This sentence also received a score of 2 for all aspects. In this case, the use of the word "pembekal" as a translation for " " (gōngyìngshāng, supplier) is somewhat questionable. "Pembekal" in Indonesian is typically used in different contexts, such as someone providing travel logistics or activity supplies. In business and management contexts, the more common term is "pemasok" or "supplier." The use of this less appropriate term could lead to ambiguity or confusion for the reader regarding the context of the sentence.

Overall, the translation results using Baidu Translate in this table show moderate quality. No sentence received a perfect score, but most scored at the medium level, with some significant errors in accuracy. This suggests that while Baidu can provide sentences that are grammatically acceptable and easy to read, there are still shortcomings, particularly in accurately translating vocabulary.

Quality Analysis of DeepL Translate

The quality of translations generated by DeepL Translate was examined in three main areas—Accuracy, Faithfulness, and Naturalness—based on the data shown in Table 11. Every category is assessed at three degrees—High, Moderate, and Low—with relevant percentages indicating the range of translation quality.

DeepL Translate performs well in terms of accuracy; 74% of its translations are rated "High." This suggests that the great majority of translations were correct and effectively maintained the original meaning. Only 6% were classified as "Moderate" and 20% as "Low," implying that although DeepL usually produces correct outcomes, there are occasions when accuracy or clarity might suffer.

Table 11. Quality analysis of DeepL translate

Accuracy			Faithfulness			Naturalness		
High	Moderate	Low	High	Moderate	Low	High	Moderate	Low
74%	6%	20%	73%	7%	20%	74%	8%	18%

Seventy-three percent of the translations got a "High" for Faithfulness, which measures how well the translated text preserves the original content without change. This closely matches the accuracy findings, indicating that most outputs preserve the intended meaning. Seven percent was classified as "Moderate," while twenty percent were considered "Low," suggesting sporadic translation errors or misinterpretations.

Seventy-four percent of the translations were rated "High" under Naturalness, which measures how fluid and native-like the translation seems. This emphasizes DeepL's capacity to generate output that reads smoothly in the target language and sounds natural. Still, 8% were classified as "Moderate" and 18% as "Low," indicating that certain translations might still have strange structure or inappropriate wording.

The data shows generally that DeepL Translate excels in all three areas, especially in generating accurate and fluent translations. Although a tiny percentage of the outcomes indicates opportunity for enhancement, DeepL distinguishes itself as a consistent and high-quality machine translation tool.

Based on the data tested using DeepL Translate, the results can be seen in the table below.

Table 12. Random examples of translation analysis in DeepL translate

Contoh Kalimat	DeepL	Accuracy	Faithfulness	Naturalness
(Zhège xiàngmù xūyào gèng duō zījīn.) = This project need more funds.	Proyek ini membutuhkan lebih banyak uang.	1*	1	2
(Zhè cì tánpàn hěn chénggōng.) = The negotiation is successful.	Negosiasinya berhasil.	1	1	1
(Tāmen zhèngzài kuòdà guójì shìch ng.) = they are expanding their international market.	Mereka memperluas pasar internasional.	1	1	2
(Zhànlüè jìhuà juédìng gōngsī de fāngxiàng.) = strategic plan determines the company's direction.	Rencana strategis menentukan arah perusahaan.	3	2	3

*1: low, 2: moderate, 3: high

Table 12 above shows the analysis of the results of translating Mandarin sentences into Indonesian using DeepL Translate. The evaluation was conducted on four sentences with a focus on three important aspects of translation: accuracy, faithfulness to the original meaning, and naturalness or fluency of the translated language. The rating scale ranges from 1 (low), 2 (moderate), to 3 (high).

In general, it can be concluded that the translation using DeepL on these examples shows a relatively low level of accuracy. This is marked by many errors in word choice and the omission of important elements in the sentences, leading to changes or even deviations from the original meaning of the text.

For example, in the first sentence: " " (This project needs more funds), it was translated as "Proyek ini membutuhkan lebih banyak uang" (This project needs more money). This translation only received a score of 1 for accuracy because the word " " (funds) was translated as "uang" (money). While "money" is generally related to "funds", in professional and business contexts, the term "dana" (funds) is more appropriate and formal. Such semantic errors make the translation lose its precision in meaning. The faithfulness and naturalness of this sentence were also rated moderately (score 2), as the structure of the sentence is still understandable, though not entirely accurate.

In the second sentence, " " (This negotiation was very successful), translated as "Negosiasinya berhasil" (The negotiation succeeded), the translation was rated low in terms of accuracy and faithfulness because the phrase " " (very successful) was translated without showing its intensity. The omission of the word "sangat" (very) makes the success seem ordinary, whereas the original meaning carries a stronger implication. This shows a lack of precision in capturing semantic details.

For the third sentence, " " (They are expanding the international market), translated as "Mereka memperluas pasar internasional" (They are expanding the international market), there is a lack of conveying the aspect of time. The word " " (zhèngzài) in Mandarin implies that the action is ongoing (present progressive), but this aspect was not reflected in the translation. A more accurate translation would be "sedang memperluas pasar internasional" (are currently expanding the international market). This inaccuracy results in a low score for accuracy because important temporal information is omitted.

In the fourth sentence, " " (The strategic plan determines the direction of the company), translated as "Rencana strategis menentukan arah perusahaan" (The strategic plan determines the company's direction), this translation received the highest score among all the examples: 3

for accuracy, 2 for faithfulness, and 2 for naturalness. This translation is good in capturing the main meaning of the sentence, although the style could be improved by adding more context to make it feel more natural and less rigid.

Overall, the translations using DeepL in this example still have many shortcomings, especially in capturing the semantic context and proper sentence structure. Errors mainly occur due to literal translation without considering the context, as well as the omission of important grammatical aspects, such as temporal markers. Although the sentence structure is tidy and readable, the meaning still requires improvement for the translations to be categorized as high quality. For professional or academic purposes, manual revision is still strongly recommended.

CONCLUSION

Based on the research findings, it can be concluded that Google Translate provides the best translation results among the three translation engines analyzed, namely Google Translate, Baidu Translate, and DeepL.The evaluation was carried out based on three main aspects of translation evaluation: accuracy, faithfulness to the original meaning, and naturalness or readability in the target language.

The evaluation results show that Google Translate scored the highest in all three aspects, with the following breakdown: accuracy at 86%, faithfulness at 85%, and naturalness at 87%. These scores indicate that the translation results from Google Translate not only closely match the original meaning of the source text but also feel natural and are easy to understand for Indonesian speakers.

This advantage is likely a result of the high frequency of Google Translate usage by Indonesians, both in academic, business, and everyday contexts. The popularity of Google Translate has contributed to its continued development through machine learning based on massive usage data. With the increasing amount of data used to train the translation model, the quality of translations has improved over time. Therefore, the high performance of Google Translate in terms of accuracy, faithfulness, and naturalness is the result of a combination of continuously updated technology and contributions from global users, including those from Indonesia.

However, this study also has limitations that need to be considered. One major limitation is the amount of data used, which consisted of only 100 sentences, all of which came from the business domain. Although focusing on a specific field provides depth and specificity in analysis, this limited sample size cannot fully represent the overall quality of each translation engine in various language usage contexts.

Additionally, the choice of the business domain also restricts the generalization of the results to other fields such as literature, law, medicine, or education. Machine translation is often applied in diverse contexts and types of texts with varying levels of complexity. Therefore, further research is strongly recommended with a broader data scope, both in terms of sentence quantity and the variety of topics or fields. This is important to provide a more comprehensive and accurate picture of the reliability of each translation engine in different contexts.

In conclusion, although Google Translate currently shows the best performance among the three translation engines examined, this evaluation remains limited and temporary, depending on the context and data sources used. With the rapid development of technology, the translation results from other engines also have the potential for continuous improvement and may provide more competitive results in the future.

REFERENCES

Ahmed, S., Müller, B., & Gómez, P. (2024). Evaluating large language models as narrative synthesizers in evidence reviews. *Research Synthesis Methods.*

Alowedi, N. A., & Hassan Al Ahdal, A. A. M. (2023). Artificial Intelligence based Arabic-to-English machine versus human translation of poetry: An analytical study of outcomes. *Journal of Namibian Studies, 34.*

Buckley, P. J., & Voss, H. (2020). *Chinese Outward Foreign Direct Investment*. Edward Elgar Publishing Limited., DOI: 10.4337/9781788112178

Chen, G. X., & Jian, A. L. (2019). Scientific and Technological Metaphors in Political Texts and Their English Translation Strategies: Based on the Parallel Corpus of "Xi Jinping: The Governance of China.". *Computer-Assisted Foreign Language Education*, *5*, 56–61.

Cho, K., Van Merrienboer, B., Bahdanau, D., & Bengio, Y. (2014). On the Properties of Neural Machine Translation: Encoder–Decoder Approaches. *Proceedings of SSST-8, Eighth Workshop on Syntax, Semantics and Structure in Statistical Translation*, 103–111. DOI: 10.3115/v1/W14-4012

Farghal, M., & Haider, A. S. (2024). Translating classical Arabic verse: Human translation vs. AI large language models (Gemini and ChatGPT). *Cogent Social Sciences*, *10*(1), 2410998. DOI: 10.1080/23311886.2024.2410998

Fu, L., & Liu, L. (2024). What are the differences? A comparative study of generative artificial intelligence translation and human translation of scientific texts. *Humanities & Social Sciences Communications*, *11*(1), 1236. DOI: 10.1057/s41599-024-03726-7

Gaspari, F., Toral, A., Naskar, S. K., & Way, A. (2015). Online and Offline Evaluation of Machine Translation Systems: A Case Study on Educational and Business Texts. *Machine Translation*, *29*(3–4), 249–275. DOI: 10.1007/s10590-015-9170-9

House, J. (2002). Translation Quality Assessment: Linguistic Description versus Social Evaluation. *Meta*, *46*(2), 243–257. DOI: 10.7202/003141ar

Huang, M., & Xu, L. (2022). Corpus-Based Analysis of Chinese-English Translation in Tourism Texts. *Journal of Applied Linguistics and Translation Studies*, *15*(3), 145–162. DOI: 10.12345/jalts.2022.15.3.145

Jiang, Z. (2023). Code-mixing of Chinese Language Learners in Second Language Acquisition. *Communications in Humanities Research*, *13*(1), 331–337. DOI: 10.54254/2753-7064/13/20230377

Karimi-Sarabi, H., Khatibnia, M., & Lee, J. (2023). Machine-assisted data extraction in medical systematic reviews using fine-tuned BERT models. *Journal of Biomedical Informatics*, *142*. Advance online publication. DOI: 10.1016/j.jbi.2023.104357

Larson, M. L. (1997). *Meaning-based translation: A guide to cross-language equivalence*. University press of America.

Li, H., & Chen, H. (2022). Human vs. AI: An Assessment of the Translation Quality Between Translators and Machine Translation. *International Journal of Translation, Interpretation, and Applied Linguistics*, *1*(1), 1–12. DOI: 10.4018/IJTIAL.2019010104

Liu, F. (2020). On Translator Training in Industry-Specific Universities in China – A Case Study of 16 MTI Programs. *Language Education and Studies*, *1*. Advance online publication. DOI: 10.56789/les.2020.1.6

Mohamed, Y. A., Khanan, A., Bashir, M., Mohamed, A. H. H. M., Adiel, M. A. E., & Elsadig, M. A. (2024). The Impact of Artificial Intelligence on Language Translation: A Review. *IEEE Access : Practical Innovations, Open Solutions*, *12*, 25553–25579. DOI: 10.1109/ACCESS.2024.3366802

Moneus, A. M., & Sahari, Y. (2024). Artificial intelligence and human translation: A contrastive study based on legal texts. *Heliyon*, *10*(6), e28106. DOI: 10.1016/j.heliyon.2024.e28106 PMID: 38524597

Nugroho, A., & Arifin, A. Z. (2021). Evaluasi Kualitas Terjemahan Mesin Neural untuk Pasangan Bahasa Mandarin-Indonesia. *Jurnal Linguistik Terapan*, *15*(2), 123–135.

Rastogi, M. (2021). The art of writing literature review. *Asian Journal of Multidimensional Research*, *10*(12), 284–290. DOI: 10.5958/2278-4853.2021.01208.8

Ruiz-Mezcua, B., Arroyo, L., & Sánchez-Gijón, P. (2021). Post-editing productivity and cognitive load in human-machine translation workflows. *Meta. Journal Des Traducteurs*, *66*(3), 488–509. DOI: 10.7202/1085802ar

Toral, A., Castilho, S., Hu, K., & Way, A. (2018). Attaining the Unattainable? Reassessing Claims of Human Parity in Neural Machine Translation. *Proceedings of the Third Conference on Machine Translation: Research Papers*, 113–123. DOI: 10.18653/v1/W18-6312

Wagner, G., Lukyanenko, R., & Paré, G. (2022). Artificial intelligence and the conduct of literature reviews. *Journal of Information Technology*, *37*(2), 209–226. DOI: 10.1177/02683962211048201

Wan, Y. (2020). Literature Review on Chinese-English Translation of Signs. *2020 International Conference on Educational Science (ICES2020)*. 2020 International Conference on Educational Science. DOI: 10.38007/Proceedings.0000249

Wang, H., & Zhang, Y. (2021). Cultural Adaptation in Business Translation: A Case Study of Chinese Brands in Western Markets. *Journal of International Business Communication*, *9*(1), 34–50. DOI: 10.1016/j.jibc.2021.01.003

Waty Kembaren, F. R., Hasibuan, A. K., & Natasya, A. (2023). Technology Trends in Translation: A Comparative Analysis of Machine and Human Translation. *Absorbent Mind*, *3*(2), 169–183. DOI: 10.37680/absorbent_mind.v3i2.4486

Wu, Y., Schuster, M., Chen, Z., Le, Q. V., Norouzi, M., Macherey, W., Krikun, M., Cao, Y., Gao, Q., Macherey, K., Klingner, J., Shah, A., Johnson, M., Liu, X., Kaiser, Ł., Gouws, S., Kato, Y., Kudo, T., Kazawa, H., . . . Dean, J. (2016). *Google's Neural Machine Translation System: Bridging the Gap between Human and Machine Translation* (Version 2). arXiv. DOI: 10.48550/ARXIV.1609.08144

Zhao, T. (2021). Translation and Tourist Experience: A Study on Public Perception in Chinese Scenic Spots. *Tourism Studies Quarterly*, *12*(4), 210–225. DOI: 10.2468/tsq.2021.12.4.210

Chapter 11
AI In Color:
Examining Educational Technology Through a BIPOC Lens

Dalbin Osorio
https://orcid.org/0009-0009-5854-1962
University of Miami, USA

ABSTRACT

This chapter explores the transformative potential of artificial intelligence (AI) to advance educational equity specifically for Black, Indigenous, and People of Color (BIPOC) learners, who have historically navigated systemic barriers within traditional education systems. Arguing that AI offers a unique opportunity to disrupt entrenched inequities, we examine its capacity to foster just and inclusive learning environments. The chapter delves into how AI-driven personalized learning platforms can cater to individual needs, how AI tools can identify and mitigate bias, and how targeted AI interventions can provide crucial support to help BIPOC students thrive. While showcasing examples of AI tools designed to promote equity, we also engage with the significant ethical considerations, including data privacy and algorithmic bias, emphasizing the necessity of responsible implementation. Ultimately, this chapter provides educators, policymakers, and researchers with a nuanced perspective on harnessing AI's potential to contribute to a more equitable educational landscape for all.

INTRODUCTION

The rapid advancement of artificial intelligence (AI) is ushering in a new era of possibilities across diverse sectors, and education stands as a prime example of its transformative power. While AI holds immense potential to revolutionize learning for all students, this chapter focuses specifically on its capacity to foster equity and empower BIPOC (Black, Indigenous, and People of Color) learners who have historically faced systemic barriers in education. For far too long, traditional educational systems have perpetuated inequities, failing to adequately address the diverse needs and unique challenges faced by BIPOC students. This chapter argues that AI offers a unique opportunity to disrupt these entrenched patterns and create a more just and inclusive learning environment. By providing personalized learning experiences, mitigating bias in curricula

DOI: 10.4018/979-8-3373-5097-4.ch011

and assessments, and offering targeted support, AI can help level the playing field and unlock the full potential of every learner.

Specifically, This Chapter Will Delve Into:

The promise of personalized learning: We will explore how AI-powered adaptive learning platforms and intelligent tutoring systems can cater to individual learning styles and paces, ensuring that BIPOC students receive tailored instruction that meets their specific needs.

The power of AI to identify and mitigate bias: We will examine how AI can be used to detect and address biases embedded within educational materials, assessments, and even teacher interactions, fostering a more equitable and culturally responsive learning environment.

Targeted interventions and support: We will investigate how AI can identify students at risk of falling behind, provide early interventions, and offer personalized support to address learning gaps and social-emotional challenges, ensuring that BIPOC students receive the assistance they need to thrive.

Examples of AI tools designed to support BIPOC learners: We will showcase specific AI-powered tools and platforms that have demonstrated success in promoting educational equity for BIPOC students, offering concrete examples of how AI can be leveraged for positive change.

Ethical considerations and responsible implementation: We will address the ethical complexities surrounding AI in education, including data privacy, algorithmic bias, and the potential for unintended consequences, emphasizing the importance of responsible development and deployment to ensure equitable outcomes for all.

By examining both the promises and potential pitfalls of AI in education, this chapter aims to provide a nuanced and critical perspective on its role in fostering equity and empowering BIPOC learners. Ultimately, we seek to equip educators, policymakers, and researchers with the knowledge and resources necessary to harness the transformative potential of AI in creating a more just and inclusive educational landscape.

THE ALGORITHMIC ASCENT: CHARTING THE HISTORICAL ROLE OF AI IN EDUCATION

The integration of Artificial Intelligence (AI) into education is often portrayed as a recent, almost futuristic phenomenon. However, the roots of AI's influence stretch back further than commonly perceived, subtly and increasingly shaping the landscape of how educators are prepared, curricula are developed, and educational policies are formed. While the sophisticated, data-driven AI systems we see today are products of recent advancements, the conceptual groundwork and early applications laid decades ago have paved the way for AI's current and future role. Examining this history reveals an evolution from niche research projects to tools with the potential for systemic impact.

EARLY SEEDS AND INTELLIGENT TUTORING SYSTEMS (ITS): THE DAWN OF PERSONALIZED LEARNING (PRE-1990S)

The historical journey of AI in education arguably begins not with AI as we define it today, but with early Computer-Aided Instruction (CAI) in the 1960s and 70s. These systems, while rudimentary and largely based on programmed instruction principles (branching logic, drill-and-practice), hinted at the possibility of individualized learning paced by the student. However, the true precursor to modern educational AI emerged with the development of Intelligent Tutoring Systems (ITS) starting in the 1970s and gaining traction in the 1980s. Pioneering systems like SCHOLAR (which tutored South American geography using mixed-initiative dialogue) and SOPHIE (which helped students troubleshoot electronic circuits) represented a significant leap. Unlike simple CAI, ITS aimed to mimic aspects of human tutoring. They typically incorporated four key components:

1. Domain Model: Knowledge of the subject matter being taught.
2. Student Model: An evolving representation of the student's understanding, misconceptions, and progress.
3. Tutoring Model (Pedagogical Module): Strategies for providing instruction, hints, feedback, and selecting problems.
4. User Interface: How the system interacts with the student.
    - Impact on Curriculum Development: The primary impact of early ITS was demonstrating the *potential* for adaptive curricula. These systems could, in theory, dynamically adjust the sequence and difficulty of content based on individual student performance captured in the student model. This challenged the one-size-fits-all model of traditional curriculum delivery, showcasing a path towards personalization, even if technological limitations restricted widespread adoption.
    - Impact on Educator Preparation: The influence on educator preparation during this era was largely indirect and academic. Research into ITS informed theories of learning, cognition, and effective pedagogy. It highlighted the importance of understanding student misconceptions and providing tailored feedback – principles valuable for human teachers as well. However, direct training *with* or *about* AI tools was virtually non-existent for the vast majority of educators.
    - Impact on Education Policy: Early AI and ITS had minimal direct impact on broad education policy. They were primarily research endeavors, expensive, and required specialized hardware and expertise. Policy discussions remained focused on traditional metrics, resource allocation, and standardized testing, far removed from the possibilities hinted at by AI labs.

THE RISE OF DATA AND EARLY ANALYTICS (1990S - 2000S)

The proliferation of personal computers in schools and the advent of the internet and Learning Management Systems (LMS) in the late 1990s and 2000s marked a critical turning point. While not always explicitly branded as "AI," the underlying principles began to permeate educational technology.

- Impact on Curriculum Development: LMS platforms started accumulating vast amounts of data on student interactions: quiz scores, time spent on modules, discussion forum participation, navigation patterns. This data became the raw material for early forms of learning analytics. Systems could automatically grade multiple-choice tests, track progress, and sometimes recommend supplementary materials. While less sophisticated than true ITS, these platforms represented a step towards data-informed curriculum refinement. Developers could analyze aggregated, anonymized data to see which parts of a digital curriculum were effective or where students commonly struggled, informing future iterations.
- Impact on Educator Preparation: Teacher training began incorporating digital literacy, including the use of LMS and basic educational software. Educators learned how to upload materials, create online quizzes, and track grades digitally. The focus was more on tool use than on understanding the underlying algorithms or leveraging data for deep pedagogical insights. AI wasn't typically part of the core teacher prep curriculum, though professional development might touch on specific adaptive learning software available commercially.
- Impact on Education Policy: The increasing availability of digital data began to subtly influence policy discussions around accountability and assessment. Policymakers started seeing the potential for technology to monitor student and school performance more continuously. Discussions around online learning standards and the digital divide gained prominence. However, policies specifically addressing the *use of AI* or its implications for equity and pedagogy were still largely absent. The focus remained on infrastructure and basic digital integration.

THE MODERN ERA: MACHINE LEARNING, BIG DATA, AND SYSTEMIC INTEGRATION (2010S - PRESENT)

The last fifteen years have witnessed an explosion in AI capabilities, driven by advances in machine learning, natural language processing (NLP), deep learning, and the availability of massive datasets ("Big Data"). This has dramatically accelerated AI's potential and actual impact across all facets of education.

- Impact on Curriculum Development: Modern AI offers powerful tools for curriculum design and delivery. Adaptive learning platforms, powered by sophisticated algorithms, provide highly personalized learning paths, dynamically adjusting content and difficulty in real-time based on fine-grained analysis of student interaction data. AI can analyze vast repositories of educational resources to recommend optimal content or identify prerequisite skill gaps. NLP enables automated essay scoring (though controversially) and analysis of student writing for feedback. AI tools can even assist in generating basic curricular frameworks or assessment items, although human oversight remains crucial. The ideal of a truly dynamic, individualized curriculum, envisioned by ITS pioneers, is becoming technologically feasible at scale.
- Impact on Educator Preparation: This is an area undergoing rapid transformation. Historically lagging, educator preparation programs are now grappling with the need to

equip teachers with AI literacy. This includes understanding how AI tools work (at a conceptual level), their pedagogical strengths and weaknesses, ethical considerations (bias, privacy), and how to use AI effectively to support teaching and learning. AI tools are emerging to assist teachers with administrative tasks (grading, communication), potentially freeing up time for instruction. Furthermore, AI is being explored for teacher training itself, such as analyzing classroom videos to provide feedback on teaching practices or simulating challenging classroom scenarios. However, integrating this meaningfully and equitably into pre-service and in-service training remains a significant challenge.

- Impact on Education Policy: AI is now a central topic in education policy debates. Learning analytics derived from AI systems are increasingly used to inform policy decisions regarding resource allocation, intervention strategies for at-risk students, and program evaluation. AI's role in large-scale assessment (including automated scoring and adaptive testing) is expanding. Crucially, policymakers face urgent questions about data privacy, algorithmic bias (how AI might perpetuate or even exacerbate existing inequities), transparency, ethics, and the need to update curricula *nationally* to prepare students for an AI-driven world. Ensuring equitable access to AI tools and mitigating potential negative consequences are major policy challenges.

The historical role of AI in education is one of gradual evolution, moving from theoretical explorations in research labs to increasingly integrated systems impacting daily practice and strategic planning. Early ITS laid the conceptual foundation for personalized learning, influencing ideas about curriculum adaptability long before technology allowed for widespread implementation. The digital data explosion of the internet era provided the necessary fuel for modern machine learning approaches.

Today, AI's influence is undeniable, though unevenly distributed. It has significantly advanced the possibilities for curriculum development, moving towards unprecedented levels of personalization and data-informed design. Its impact on educator preparation is more recent but accelerating, shifting from basic digital literacy towards fostering deeper AI literacy and exploring AI-powered professional development tools. In education policy, AI has transitioned from a non-issue to a central concern, driving data-driven decision-making while simultaneously raising critical questions about equity, ethics, and the future of learning and work.

The historical trajectory shows that AI's integration wasn't an overnight revolution but a decades-long process. Understanding this history is crucial for navigating the present and future, ensuring that as AI becomes ever more powerful, its deployment in education is guided by pedagogical principles, ethical considerations, and a commitment to equitable outcomes for all learners and educators.

The integration of artificial intelligence (AI) into the realm of education is not merely a contemporary phenomenon, but rather the culmination of a long-held aspiration to personalize and optimize the learning process. Dating back to the early days of computer-assisted instruction in the mid-20th century, educators and technologists alike have envisioned a future where machines could augment human capabilities and provide tailored support to students. Today, that vision is rapidly becoming a reality as AI-powered tools are being woven into the fabric of education, offering unprecedented opportunities to enhance learning experiences and improve educational outcomes.

This burgeoning integration of AI in education, however, is not without its historical baggage. The legacy of systemic inequities and discriminatory practices within educational systems, particularly towards marginalized communities such as BIPOC (Black, Indigenous, and People of Color) learners, casts a long shadow. These communities have long endured the consequences of unequal access to resources, biased curricula, and discriminatory assessment practices, resulting in persistent achievement gaps and limited opportunities. Against this backdrop, the emergence of AI in education presents both a profound challenge and a unique opportunity. While AI holds the potential to exacerbate existing inequities if not developed and deployed responsibly, it also offers a powerful means to disrupt these entrenched patterns and forge a path toward a more just and equitable educational landscape. This section delves into the multifaceted ways in which AI is being integrated into education, with a particular focus on its potential to address the historical injustices faced by BIPOC learners. Some of the key applications of AI in education that we will explore include:

- Personalized Learning: Within the realm of personalized learning, artificial intelligence is poised to revolutionize the very fabric of educational delivery. No longer constrained by the limitations of a one-size-fits-all approach, AI algorithms possess the remarkable capacity to tailor educational content to the unique learning style and pace of each individual student. This dynamic personalization is achieved through the intricate analysis of student responses and performance data, enabling AI systems to dynamically adjust learning materials and activities in real-time. Imagine a classroom where every student is engaged with material that is perfectly calibrated to their current level of understanding, where challenges are presented at the optimal level of difficulty to foster growth, and where support is readily available precisely when and where it is needed. This is the promise of AI-powered personalized learning. The mechanisms underlying this transformative capability are rooted in the ability of AI algorithms to discern patterns and insights from vast troves of educational data. As students interact with digital learning platforms, AI systems meticulously track their progress, analyze their responses, and identify areas of strength and weakness. This granular level of analysis allows for the creation of adaptive learning pathways that dynamically adjust to each student's evolving needs and learning goals. For instance, if a student is struggling with a particular concept, the AI system can automatically provide additional practice exercises, offer targeted feedback, or even adjust the pace of instruction to ensure comprehension. Conversely, if a student demonstrates mastery of a topic, the system can accelerate their progress and introduce more challenging material, preventing boredom and fostering a sense of continuous intellectual engagement. This approach to personalized learning is exemplified by innovative platforms such as DreamBox and Smart Sparrow, which leverage AI to create adaptive learning environments that cater to individual student needs and preferences. These platforms not only provide customized learning pathways but also offer personalized feedback and support, empowering students to take ownership of their learning journey. The impact of such personalized learning experiences can be profound, particularly for students who have historically been underserved by traditional educational systems. As Holmes, Bialik, Fadel, and (2023) note in their comprehensive review of AI in education, "AI-powered learning systems have the potential to provide equitable access to high-quality education for all learners, regardless of their background or learning differences." By tailoring instruction to individual needs and providing targeted support, AI can help to close achievement gaps and ensure that all students have the opportunity to reach their full potential.

- Automated Administrative Tasks: AI can automate time-consuming administrative tasks, such as grading, scheduling, and report generation, freeing up educators' time to focus on more meaningful interactions with students and instructional planning (Holmes et al., 2023). Tools like Gradescope use AI to provide consistent and objective grading of assignments, while AI-powered scheduling software helps optimize class timetables and resource allocation.
- Engaged Learners: AI can make learning more interactive and engaging through gamified content, simulations, and personalized feedback (Holmes et al., 2023). Programs like Kahoot! and Minecraft: Education Edition use AI to create interactive quizzes and simulations that respond to student input, keeping learners motivated and involved. AI can also provide students with real-time feedback on their work, helping them identify areas for improvement and track their progress.
- Improved Accessibility: AI-driven assistive technologies can support students with disabilities, ensuring a more inclusive learning environment (Holmes et al., 2023). Speech recognition software like Notta transcribes spoken words into text for hearing-impaired students, while AI-supported educational games provide personalized learning experiences for young children with diverse learning needs.
- Enhanced Formative Assessments: AI can play a significant role in formative assessments, providing educators with valuable insights into student learning and enabling them to adjust their teaching strategies accordingly (AI and Education Research Paper, n.d.). AI-powered tools can analyze student responses and performance data to identify areas where students are struggling and provide targeted feedback and support. This can help accelerate student learning and improve overall academic performance.
- Streamlined Lesson Planning and Content Creation: AI can assist educators in streamlining lesson planning and content creation, saving them valuable time and effort (The Role of AI in Modern Education, n.d.). AI-powered tools can generate high-quality images, customize content to meet specific learning objectives, and provide focused research materials, allowing educators to create more engaging and effective lessons.
- Expanded Learning Opportunities Beyond the Classroom: AI can extend learning opportunities beyond the traditional classroom setting, providing students with greater flexibility and personalized learning experiences (Artificial Intelligence in Education, n.d.). AI-powered platforms can offer personalized tutoring, gamified learning activities, and access to a wide range of educational resources, allowing students to learn at their own pace and in their preferred learning style.

Based on the research findings, it is evident that AI can augment teachers' roles by automating tasks, providing personalized support, and improving accessibility, ultimately leading to better learning outcomes (Artificial Intelligence in Education, n.d.). By leveraging AI capabilities, educators can focus on fostering critical thinking, creativity, and collaboration among students, while AI tools provide individualized support and enhance the learning experience.

ETHICAL CONSIDERATIONS OF AI IN EDUCATION OVERALL

While AI offers numerous benefits for education, it is essential to acknowledge and address the ethical considerations surrounding its implementation. Some of the key ethical concerns include:

- Data Privacy and Security: AI systems in education often collect and analyze large amounts of student data, raising concerns about data privacy and security (Baker, 2019). It is crucial to ensure that student data is collected and used responsibly, with appropriate safeguards in place to protect student privacy and prevent data breaches.
- Algorithmic Bias and Discrimination: AI algorithms can perpetuate and amplify existing biases, potentially leading to discriminatory outcomes for certain groups of students (Baker, 2019). It is crucial to develop and implement AI systems that are fair, unbiased, and equitable for all learners.
- Lack of Transparency and Explainability: Some AI algorithms are complex and opaque, making it difficult to understand how they work and make decisions (Baker, 2019). This lack of transparency can raise concerns about accountability and fairness, especially when AI is used for high-stakes decisions, such as student assessment or placement.
- Academic Dishonesty: The increasing availability of AI tools, such as AI writing assistants, raises concerns about academic dishonesty and the potential for students to misuse these tools to cheat or plagiarize (Carbonell, 1970). Educators need to be aware of these challenges and develop strategies to promote academic integrity in the age of AI.
- Inequality: The use of AI in education could exacerbate existing inequalities if not implemented carefully (Carbonell, 1970). For example, students from under-resourced communities may have limited access to the technology and internet connectivity needed to benefit from AI-powered learning tools, potentially widening the digital divide.

AI systems in education, while offering exciting possibilities, can inadvertently perpetuate and amplify existing racial biases if their design and implementation aren't meticulously considered. For instance, AI-powered grading systems, intended to provide objective feedback, may be trained on datasets that reflect historical biases in teacher evaluations. If these evaluations disproportionately undervalue the work of students from certain racial backgrounds, the AI will learn and reproduce these skewed assessments, unfairly impacting the grades and perceived potential of these students. This can have cascading effects, influencing future educational opportunities, such as access to advanced courses, scholarships, and even college admissions. Furthermore, AI-driven recommendation systems, designed to personalize learning pathways, may inadvertently steer students from underrepresented groups away from challenging STEM courses or specific career paths. This can occur if the training data reflects existing societal biases about who is “suited” for particular fields, thus limiting opportunities for advancement and reinforcing existing inequalities. For example, if the data predominantly shows white males in engineering roles, the AI might recommend engineering-related activities more frequently to white male students, even if students from other demographics demonstrate equal aptitude.

A significant ethical concern arises from the potential of AI to reinforce harmful stereotypes and discriminatory practices. AI algorithms are trained on vast datasets, and these datasets often reflect existing societal prejudices, even if unintentionally. If these biases aren't actively identified and addressed, the AI system may inadvertently perpetuate them, leading to unfair or discriminatory outcomes for students from specific racial groups. Consider an AI-powered tutoring system. If its training data overrepresents white students and their learning styles, the system might be optimized to favor these students in its interactions and recommendations. It might misinterpret the learning styles of students from other cultural backgrounds, perceiving them as less engaged or less capable, even if that's not the case. This can lead to a self-fulfilling prophecy, where the AI's biased interactions contribute to a widening achievement gap. Moreover, the use of facial recognition technology in educational settings raises serious concerns. Studies have shown that these systems are often less accurate in recognizing faces of individuals with darker skin tones, potentially leading to misidentification and discriminatory treatment.

Mitigating these risks requires a proactive and multifaceted approach. It is crucial to ensure that AI systems in education are developed and used responsibly, with a focus on fairness, transparency, and accountability. This includes carefully curating and rigorously auditing the data used to train AI algorithms. Data scientists must actively seek out and address potential biases in the data, employing techniques like data augmentation and adversarial training to create more equitable datasets. Furthermore, continuous monitoring and evaluation of the AI system's performance are essential to identify and address any emerging biases or unintended consequences. This requires not only technical expertise but also a deep understanding of the social and cultural contexts in which the AI is being used. Critically, it is vital to involve diverse stakeholders, including educators, students, parents, community members, and ethicists, in the design, implementation, and evaluation of AI systems. This participatory approach ensures that diverse perspectives are considered and that the AI systems are developed in a way that is fair, equitable, culturally sensitive, and truly serves the best interests of all students.

Addressing these ethical concerns requires a multi-faceted approach, including developing ethical guidelines for AI in education, promoting transparency and explainability in AI systems, ensuring data privacy and security, and addressing the digital divide.

TRANSFORMATIONAL AI TOOLS FOR EDUCATORS

The educational landscape is rapidly evolving, and artificial intelligence (AI) is at the forefront of this transformation. A growing number of AI-powered tools are now available to educators, offering exciting possibilities to personalize learning, automate administrative tasks, and enhance student engagement. These resources range from intelligent tutoring systems that adapt to individual student needs to sophisticated platforms that provide data-driven insights into student performance. Exploring and effectively utilizing these AI tools can empower educators to create more dynamic and effective learning environments, ultimately benefiting both teachers and students. The following list provides an overview of some of the available AI resources that educators can leverage to enhance their teaching practices:

- Mentimeter: This tool allows for AI-powered interactive presentation development with customizable AI-generated quizzes, interactive Q&A, and surveys with anonymous responses (Cuban, 1986).
- Eduaid.AI: This tool automates instructional planning with AI-driven lesson plan generation, customizable templates, and adaptable lesson plans for unique needs (Cuban, 1986).

- Diffit: This tool generates AI-generated exercises and information based on selected grade levels and language, allowing educators to uplevel, translate, or expand existing information (Cuban, 1986).
- AudioPen: This tool converts voice to text in real-time with multiple language support (Cuban, 1986).
- Canva Magic Studio: This tool supports design elements with AI, offering a drag-and-drop, customizable design interface, template library, and project collaboration features (Cuban, 1986).
- Brisk Teaching: This tool provides AI teaching assistance with AI-generated lesson plan creation, automated student assessment tools, performance tracking, and adaptive and personalized learning (Cuban, 1986).
- Khanmigo: This tool offers AI tutoring with personalized and interactive tutoring with real-time feedback, a wide range of subjects, and integrations with Khan Academy's curriculum (Cuban, 1986).
- Gradescope: This tool provides AI-assisted grading and rubric-based grading and feedback with student performance analytics and integrates with learning management systems (LMS) (Cuban, 1986).
- Turnitin: This tool offers AI and plagiarism detection with detailed similarity reports, source matching, feedback and revision tools, and integrations with LMS platforms (Cuban, 1986).
- SchoolAI: This tool provides student engagement and insights with an AI-powered co-teacher, thousands of educational chatbots, time-saving tools, and student insights (Cuban, 1986).
- MagicSchool: This tool offers comprehensive teaching support and automation with a lesson plan generator, educational chatbot, and easy assignment and worksheet creation (Cuban, 1986).

Table 1.

Tool	Description	Pricing	Target Age Group	Subject Areas
Mentimeter	AI-powered interactive presentation development with customizable AI-generated quizzes, interactive Q&A, and surveys with anonymous responses	$11.99/presenter/month	Not specified	Not specified
Eduaide.AI	Automated instructional planning with AI-driven lesson plan generation, customizable templates, and adaptable lesson plans for unique needs	$49.99/year	Not specified	Not specified
Diffit	AI-generated exercises and information based on selected grade levels and language, uplevel, translate, or expand existing information, and a template library with resources in several formats	Contact for pricing	Not specified	Not specified

continued on following page

Table 1. Continued

Tool	Description	Pricing	Target Age Group	Subject Areas
AudioPen	Real-time voice-to-text transcription and multiple language support	$99/year	Not specified	Not specified
Canva Magic Studio	AI-supported design elements, drag-and-drop, customizable design interface, template library, and project collaboration	$120/year for one user	Not specified	Not specified
Brisk Teaching	AI-generated lesson plan creation, automated student assessment tools, performance tracking, and adaptive and personalized learning	$9.99/month or $99.99/year	Not specified	Not specified
Khanmigo	Personalized and interactive tutoring with real-time feedback, a wide range of subjects, and integrations with Khan Academy's curriculum	$4/month or $44/year	Not specified	Not specified
Gradescope	AI-assisted grading and rubric-based grading and feedback with student performance analytics, and also integrates with learning management systems (LMS)	Contact for pricing	Not specified	Not specified
Turnitin	Plagiarism and AI detection with detailed similarity reports, source matching, feedback and revision tools and integrations with LMS platforms	Contact for pricing	Not specified	Not specified
SchoolAI	AI-powered co-teacher, thousands of educational chatbots, time-saving tools, and student insights	Contact for pricing	Not specified	Not specified
MagicSchool	Lesson plan generator, educational chatbot, and easy assignment and worksheet creation	$99.96/year	Not specified	Not specified

CASE STUDIES: AI IN ACTION

When developing AI resources for education, developers must consider a multifaceted set of factors to ensure effectiveness, ethical soundness, and positive impact on learning outcomes. A primary consideration is the pedagogical approach the AI tool will support. Developers must determine how the AI can best augment teaching practices, whether through personalized learning pathways, automated feedback, or intelligent tutoring systems, aligning the technology with established educational theories and best practices. Data privacy and security are paramount, particularly when dealing with student information. Developers must adhere to strict regulations (like FERPA in the US) and implement robust security measures to protect sensitive data from unauthorized access or misuse. Accessibility is another crucial factor, ensuring that AI resources are usable by all students, including those with disabilities. This necessitates adherence to accessibility guidelines (like WCAG) and careful design to accommodate diverse learning needs. Furthermore, developers must address potential biases in the data used to train AI algorithms, as these biases can lead to discriminatory outcomes. Careful data curation, bias detection techniques, and ongoing monitoring are essential to mitigate these risks. Scalability and interoperability are also important considerations, ensuring that the AI resources can be effectively deployed across different educational settings and integrated with existing school systems. Finally, developers must prioritize transparency and explainability, making the AI's decision-making processes understandable to educators and students, fostering trust and enabling informed use of the technology. This involves providing clear documentation, explaining the algorithms' logic, and allowing for human oversight and intervention.

The integration of Artificial Intelligence (AI) into education is no longer a futuristic concept but a rapidly evolving reality, with schools around the globe already leveraging its potential to transform learning experiences. From personalized learning platforms that adapt to individual student paces and styles to AI-powered chatbots that provide instant support and answer student queries, AI is being deployed in diverse and innovative ways. Some schools are utilizing AI-driven analytics to identify at-risk students and provide targeted interventions, while others are exploring the use of AI in automating administrative tasks, freeing up teachers' time for more direct student interaction. Furthermore, AI is being incorporated into curriculum development, offering tools for creating dynamic and engaging learning materials, and even assisting in the assessment of student work. While the widespread adoption of AI in education is still in its early stages, the existing implementations offer a glimpse into the transformative potential of this technology and highlight the growing recognition of its ability to personalize learning, enhance teaching practices, and ultimately improve student outcomes. Several schools and educational institutions are already leveraging AI to improve learning outcomes and create more engaging learning experiences. Here are a few examples:

- Personalized Math Education: A school successfully implemented an AI-driven platform called "Maths Pathway" to personalize math education for each student (Ifenthaler & Gibson, 2020). The platform uses machine learning to assess student progress, adjust the learning content accordingly, and provide personalized modules and real-time feedback. This personalized approach led to significant improvements in student engagement and academic performance in mathematics.
- AI for Lesson Planning and Differentiation: Two teachers utilized AI tools to streamline their lesson planning and create more engaging learning experiences for their students (Luckin et al., 2016). They used AI to generate ideas for lesson plans, translate lessons for English language learners, and create differentiated activities to meet the diverse needs of their students. This case study highlights how AI can empower teachers to create more inclusive and effective learning environments.

These case studies demonstrate the potential of AI to transform education and improve learning outcomes for all students. As AI technology continues to evolve, we can expect to see even more innovative AI applications in education.

THE IMPACT OF AI ON BIPOC LEARNERS

The impact of AI on BIPOC learners is complex and multifaceted, presenting both opportunities and challenges. While AI has the potential to personalize learning and provide targeted support, it also carries the risk of perpetuating and amplifying existing educational inequities if not carefully designed and implemented. One major concern is the potential for AI-driven systems to reflect and reinforce existing biases in educational data. As Zuboff (2019) argues in The Age of Surveillance Capitalism, algorithms are not neutral; they are often trained on data that reflects historical and societal biases, which can lead to discriminatory outcomes for BIPOC students. For instance, AI-powered grading systems may inadvertently penalize students whose writing styles or communication patterns differ from those of the dominant culture, leading to unfair assessments and potentially limiting their educational opportunities. Similarly, AI-driven recommendation systems may steer BIPOC students away from challenging courses or career paths based on biased data, further restricting their access to resources and opportunities. These examples highlight the critical need for careful attention to data curation and algorithm design to mitigate the risk of bias in AI systems used in education.

Furthermore, the lack of diversity in the tech industry, particularly in the development of AI tools, can exacerbate these challenges. If AI systems are designed primarily by individuals from privileged backgrounds, they may not adequately consider the unique needs and experiences of BIPOC learners. This can lead to the creation of AI tools that are culturally insensitive or that fail to address the specific challenges faced by BIPOC students. As Noble (2018) demonstrates in Algorithms of Oppression, search engine algorithms, a form of AI, can perpetuate harmful stereotypes and reinforce discriminatory practices against marginalized groups. This underscores the importance of having diverse voices involved in the design and development of AI systems to ensure that they are culturally relevant and equitable. Moreover, access to technology and digital literacy are crucial factors in determining the impact of AI on BIPOC learners. If BIPOC students lack access to reliable internet or are not provided with adequate training in using AI tools effectively, they may be further disadvantaged by the increasing reliance on technology in education. This digital divide can widen existing achievement gaps and limit the potential benefits of AI for these students.

Addressing these challenges requires a multifaceted approach. It is essential to prioritize data equity and ensure that AI systems are trained on diverse and representative datasets. This includes actively seeking out and incorporating data from underrepresented communities and employing techniques to mitigate bias in existing datasets. Furthermore, fostering diversity in the tech industry is crucial to ensure that AI tools are developed with the needs of all learners in mind. As Benjamin Green (2019) argues in The Digital Poorhouse, the design and implementation of automated systems must be subject to critical examination and ongoing evaluation to avoid perpetuating existing inequalities. Educators, policymakers, and technology developers must work together to create AI systems that are culturally sensitive, equitable, and accessible to all students, regardless of their background. Only then can the potential benefits of AI in education be fully realized for BIPOC learners and contribute to closing achievement gaps. While AI has the potential to improve learning outcomes for all students, it is essential to consider its potential impact on BIPOC learners. Some key considerations include:

- Bias and Discrimination: AI algorithms can perpetuate and amplify existing biases, potentially leading to discriminatory outcomes for BIPOC learners (Nkambou et al., 2010). For example, research has shown that AI models designed to identify hate speech can be biased against Black users, flagging their tweets as hate speech at a disproportionately higher rate (Selwyn, 2019). This highlights the need for careful consideration of bias in AI development and implementation.

- Digital Divide: Inequitable access to technology and high-speed internet among BIPOC students can exacerbate existing disparities (Jonassen et al., 1996). If BIPOC students lack access to the necessary technology and resources, they may be excluded from the benefits of AI-powered learning tools, further widening the achievement gap.
- Cultural Relevance: AI tools need to be designed and implemented in a culturally responsive way to ensure they are effective for BIPOC learners (Siemens & Baker, 2012). This includes incorporating diverse cultural perspectives, languages, and learning styles into AI-powered learning platforms and ensuring that AI systems do not perpetuate harmful stereotypes or biases.

Based on the research, it is clear that AI has the potential to worsen existing racial and equity issues in education if not implemented responsibly (Nkambou et al., 2010). Therefore, it is crucial to prioritize equity and inclusion in the development and implementation of AI in education.

To Mitigate These Challenges, it is Crucial to:

- Develop AI tools with diverse datasets: This can help to reduce bias and ensure that AI systems are fair and equitable for all learners (Wenger, 1987). By training AI algorithms on diverse datasets that represent a wide range of cultural backgrounds, learning styles, and abilities, we can create more inclusive and effective AI tools for education.
- Address the digital divide: Ensuring that all students have access to the technology and resources they need to succeed in a digital learning environment is crucial (Jonassen et al., 1996). This includes providing affordable internet access, devices, and digital literacy training to students from under-resourced communities.
- Promote culturally responsive teaching practices: Educators need to be trained on how to use AI in a way that is culturally relevant and responsive to the needs of diverse learners (Siemens & Baker, 2012). This includes understanding the potential biases in AI systems, selecting AI tools that are culturally appropriate, and using AI to create learning experiences that are relevant to the cultural backgrounds and experiences of their students.

While the potential for Artificial Intelligence (AI) to perpetuate and even amplify existing biases in education is a critical concern, particularly for BIPOC learners, AI also presents opportunities to actively identify and counteract these very issues. If designed and deployed thoughtfully, with equity as a primary goal, AI can serve as a powerful tool in the ongoing effort to create more just and inclusive educational environments. Its capacity to process vast amounts of information and detect subtle patterns can be harnessed to uncover biases that might otherwise remain hidden and to support interventions aimed at mitigation.

One significant application lies in identifying bias within educational materials. AI, particularly Natural Language Processing (NLP) techniques, can be employed to systematically analyze large corpora of text, such as textbooks, digital learning resources, and curriculum documents. These tools can be trained to detect biased language, stereotypes, microaggressions, the under-representation or problematic portrayal of specific demographic groups (including race, gender, socioeconomic status, and disability), and historical inaccuracies or omissions. By automatically flagging potentially problematic content, AI can assist educators, curriculum developers, and policymakers in reviewing and revising materials to ensure they are more equitable, accurate, and culturally responsive, complementing rather than replacing human judgment.

Furthermore, AI can play a crucial role in analyzing educational practices and outcomes for systemic inequities. By examining aggregated and anonymized student data – encompassing performance metrics, course enrollment patterns, disciplinary actions, resource allocation, and even sentiment analysis from student feedback – AI algorithms can identify disparities between different student groups. For instance, AI could highlight if students from certain racial backgrounds are consistently graded lower by specific graders despite similar performance metrics, or if they are disproportionately disciplined for similar infractions compared to their peers. It can also reveal inequities in access to advanced coursework or specialized support programs. While the interpretation of these patterns requires careful human analysis to avoid simplistic or deterministic conclusions, AI provides the means to detect potential systemic biases in institutional practices that might be invisible at the individual level, prompting targeted investigation and intervention.

AI also holds potential for supporting educators in recognizing and mitigating their own potential biases. While ethically sensitive, AI tools could be developed to provide teachers with objective, data-driven feedback on their practices. This might involve analyzing classroom discourse patterns to assess equitable student participation, reviewing grading patterns for consistency and potential bias across different student demographics, or even flagging potentially biased language in written feedback to students. Used constructively as a tool for self-reflection and professional development – rather than purely for evaluation – AI could help educators become more aware of implicit biases and refine their practices to be more inclusive and equitable.

Finally, AI can be used to mitigate bias within AI-driven educational tools themselves. Techniques such as fairness-aware machine learning aim to build algorithms that explicitly account for and try to minimize disparities in outcomes across different groups. Rigorous bias audits can be conducted during the development and deployment phases, using AI itself to test systems for potential biases before they reach students. Developing AI with diverse and representative datasets, ensuring transparency in how algorithms function, and maintaining a "human-in-the-loop" for critical decisions are all strategies where AI development processes can be improved to proactively reduce bias.

AI is not inherently biased or unbiased; it is a tool whose impact reflects the data it's trained on and the intentions of its creators and users. While the risks of AI exacerbating inequities are real and demand constant vigilance, its capabilities can also be strategically leveraged to promote educational equity. By using AI to scrutinize materials, analyze practices, support educators, and improve AI systems themselves, we can work towards mitigating bias and fostering learning environments where all students, including BIPOC learners, have the opportunity to thrive. This requires a commitment to ethical design, ongoing evaluation, stakeholder involvement, and ensuring human oversight remains central.

ETHICS CONCERNS WITH AI AS IT PERTAINS TO BIPOC LEARNERS

The integration of Artificial Intelligence (AI) into educational settings promises transformative potential: personalized learning paths, adaptive assessments, intelligent tutoring, and streamlined administrative tasks. However, beneath the surface of innovation lies a complex web of ethical considerations, particularly concerning its impact on learners from Black, Indigenous, and People of Color (BIPOC) communities. While AI holds the potential to address certain inequities, its uncritical deployment risks amplifying existing biases, creating new barriers, and reinforcing systemic disadvantages that disproportionately affect BIPOC students. A thorough ethical examination is crucial to ensure that AI serves as a tool for equity rather than an instrument of digital marginalization.

One of the most significant ethical challenges stems from algorithmic bias. AI systems learn from data, and the data fed into educational algorithms often reflects historical and societal biases. Standardized test scores, disciplinary records, attendance data, and even textual analysis of student work can carry embedded prejudices against BIPOC learners, rooted in decades of systemic racism and cultural misunderstandings within educational institutions. When AI models are trained on this biased data, they inevitably learn and perpetuate these biases. This can manifest in numerous harmful ways: AI might inaccurately predict lower academic potential for BIPOC students, recommend less challenging coursework, flag them for disciplinary action more frequently based on biased behavioral data, or fail to recognize culturally nuanced language or expressions in automated grading systems. Furthermore, if training datasets lack sufficient representation of diverse dialects, cultural contexts, or learning styles prevalent among BIPOC communities, the resulting AI tools may simply be less effective, or even ineffective, for these students, placing them at a disadvantage compared to their peers for whom the tool was implicitly designed.

Closely linked to bias are concerns surrounding data privacy and surveillance. AI-driven educational platforms collect vast quantities of granular data on student behavior, performance, social interactions, and even emotional states (through sentiment analysis or facial recognition technologies, where implemented). For BIPOC communities, who often experience disproportionate surveillance in other aspects of life (e.g., policing, social services), the prospect of intensified monitoring within schools raises serious ethical alarms. There are legitimate fears about how this data might be used beyond immediate educational purposes. Could data on perceived behavioral issues, potentially influenced by cultural differences or algorithmic bias, be shared with law enforcement or immigration authorities? Could data profiles created in school follow students into adulthood, impacting opportunities for employment or credit? The principles of informed consent become murky; students and their families, particularly those with limited digital literacy or facing language barriers, may not fully understand the extent of data collection or its potential long-term implications. Ensuring robust data governance, transparency in data use, and genuine student/parental agency over personal information is paramount, yet often lacking.

The promise of AI-powered personalized learning also runs headlong into the persistent issue of the digital divide and equitable access. Sophisticated AI educational tools often require reliable high-speed internet access, up-to-date devices, and a conducive learning environment – resources that are not equally distributed across communities. BIPOC students, particularly those from low-income backgrounds or residing in underserved rural or urban areas, are more likely to lack consistent access to the necessary infrastructure. This creates a scenario where the benefits of cutting-edge AI education are primarily available to more affluent, often predominantly white, school districts, thereby exacerbating existing achievement and opportunity gaps. Even when access to technology is provided, disparities in digital literacy – the skills needed to effectively navigate and utilize these tools – can further disadvantage BIPOC learners if adequate training and support are not universally available. The cost of advanced AI software and platforms can also be prohibitive for underfunded schools, reinforcing resource inequities.

Beyond technical bias and access, AI risks reinforcing systemic inequities and promoting standardized norms that may clash with culturally relevant pedagogies. Many AI tools are designed around dominant cultural assumptions about learning, knowledge, and assessment. They may prioritize specific modes of expression or problem-solving, potentially devaluing the diverse linguistic backgrounds, storytelling traditions, collaborative learning styles, and unique ways of knowing prevalent in many BIPOC communities. By optimizing for narrow, easily quantifiable metrics, AI could inadvertently promote a homogenized educational experience that marginalizes culturally responsive teaching practices essential for engaging BIPOC students. There's also a danger of AI reinforcing deficit perspectives, focusing on identifying and "fixing" perceived gaps in BIPOC students based on biased benchmarks, rather than recognizing and building upon their cultural assets, strengths, and funds of knowledge. AI recommendations fed to teachers could also subtly confirm or amplify educators' own implicit biases, creating a feedback loop that further disadvantages certain students.

Compounding these issues is the significant lack of diversity within the AI development field itself. Predominantly homogenous development teams may lack the lived experiences and cultural understanding necessary to anticipate, identify, and mitigate potential biases that could harm BIPOC learners. Without diverse perspectives involved in the design, testing, and auditing phases, AI tools may inadvertently encode blind spots and assumptions that render them less effective or even discriminatory. Actively involving BIPOC educators, students, parents, and community members in the co-design and evaluation of AI educational tools is not just desirable but ethically necessary to create systems that are genuinely responsive and equitable.

Addressing these profound ethical challenges requires a proactive, equity-centered approach. This includes rigorous bias audits of algorithms and training data, the development and implementation of fairness metrics specifically designed to detect disparate impacts on BIPOC groups, and greater transparency in how AI systems make decisions. Robust data governance policies that prioritize student privacy, limit data sharing, and empower students and families with control over their information are essential. Efforts must be made to bridge the digital divide through investments in infrastructure, devices, and digital literacy training, particularly in underserved communities. Crucially, AI tools should be designed with cultural responsiveness at their core, involving diverse stakeholders throughout the development lifecycle. Educator training must go beyond basic operation to include critical examination of AI's ethical implications and potential biases.

In conclusion, while AI offers tantalizing possibilities for enhancing education, its deployment carries significant ethical risks for BIPOC learners. The potential for algorithmic bias, invasive surveillance, inequitable access, the reinforcement of harmful standards, and the lack of diversity in AI development collectively threaten to deepen existing educational disparities. Moving forward requires vigilance, critical assessment, and a steadfast commitment to equity. Only by proactively addressing these ethical considerations, centering the needs and experiences of BIPOC students, and fostering inclusive design practices can we hope to harness the power of AI for genuine educational justice, ensuring it becomes a tool that empowers all learners, rather than one that further entrenches inequality.

AI TOOLS AND RESOURCES FOR BIPOC LEARNERS

While there is a need for more AI tools specifically designed for BIPOC learners, some resources can help to promote equity and inclusion in AI education:

- Culturally relevant AI curriculum: AI can be used to create learning experiences that are relevant to the cultural backgrounds and experiences of BIPOC learners (Wenger, 1987). For example, AI can be used to develop personalized learning materials that incorporate culturally relevant examples, stories, and perspectives, making learning more engaging and meaningful for BIPOC students. AI can also assist educators in diversifying classroom materials, incorporating various voices and perspectives, leading to more inclusive learning environments (Wenger, 1987).
- AI-powered language learning tools: These tools can help BIPOC students learn new languages and improve their communication skills (Williamson, 2017). AI-powered language learning platforms can provide personalized instruction, adaptive feedback, and culturally relevant content, making language learning more accessible and effective for BIPOC students.
- AI-based mentorship programs: AI can be used to connect BIPOC students with mentors who can provide them with support and guidance (The future of learning, n.d.). AI algorithms can analyze student data and preferences to match them with mentors who share similar interests, backgrounds, or career aspirations. These mentorship programs can help support BIPOC students' academic and personal development, providing them with valuable guidance and encouragement.

AI's Potential Role in Educator Training and Rebuilding the Black Educator Pipeline

Effective educator training and ongoing professional development are cornerstones of a thriving education system. Yet, traditional approaches often fall short, lacking personalization and failing to address the specific needs of diverse educators. This challenge is particularly acute when considering the urgent need to rebuild the Black Educator Pipeline – a critical pathway significantly eroded over decades, partly due to historical factors like the mass dismissal of Black educators following desegregation efforts after *Brown v. Board of Education*, compounded by ongoing systemic barriers in recruitment, preparation, and retention. While Artificial Intelligence (AI) is no silver bullet, its burgeoning capabilities offer intriguing, albeit ethically complex, possibilities to enhance how educators are trained, supported, and retained, potentially playing a constructive role in attracting and nurturing Black teaching talent. If developed and implemented with a steadfast commitment to equity and cultural responsiveness, AI could become a valuable tool in this vital endeavor.

One of the most promising applications of AI lies in delivering personalized professional development (PD). Traditional PD often adopts a one-size-fits-all model, failing to meet the specific needs of individual teachers. AI can analyze various data points – such as anonymized student progress data, teacher self-assessments, stated goals, and potentially (with careful ethical oversight) patterns identified in classroom practice analyses – to identify unique strengths and areas for growth. Based on this diagnosis, AI platforms can curate and recommend tailored learning modules, relevant research articles, targeted coaching resources, and connections to expert colleagues. For Black educators, this personalization could be particularly impactful. AI could connect them with PD focused on culturally sustaining pedagogies, strategies for navigating racial bias in the classroom, techniques for supporting Black students' unique socio-emotional needs, or leadership development pathways specifically designed to elevate educators of color – resources often scarce in generic PD offerings.

Beyond curated content, AI can power sophisticated simulation and practice environments. Teacher preparation programs often struggle to provide sufficient opportunities for realistic practice before candidates enter the classroom. AI-driven simulations can create dynamic, interactive scenarios mimicking diverse classroom situations – from managing challenging student behaviors and differentiating instruction to navigating difficult conversations with parents or addressing microaggressions from colleagues or students. These virtual environments offer a safe, low-stakes space for pre-service and in-service educators, including Black teachers, to hone their pedagogical skills, experiment with different strategies, and receive immediate, objective feedback on their performance. Such simulations could be specifically designed to include scenarios reflecting the unique cultural contexts and challenges Black educators and their students might encounter, better preparing them for the realities of the classroom.

Retention is a critical component of rebuilding the pipeline, and AI can contribute by fostering mentorship and community building. Feelings of isolation and lack of adequate support are significant factors driving teachers, particularly educators of color, out of the profession. AI platforms can facilitate meaningful connections by matching novice Black educators with experienced mentors who share similar backgrounds, expertise, or school contexts, potentially transcending geographical limitations. Algorithms could analyze profiles, needs, and preferences to suggest optimal pairings. Furthermore, AI can power dedicated online communities or knowledge-sharing platforms where Black educators can connect, share culturally relevant resources and strategies, discuss challenges, celebrate successes, and build a strong sense of professional belonging, thereby strengthening their resilience and commitment to the profession.

AI also presents potential, though highly sensitive, applications in recruitment and talent identification. Traditional recruitment processes can inadvertently filter out promising candidates due to biases in screening criteria or reliance on limited networks. AI tools, *if meticulously designed and audited to counteract bias*, could analyze application materials (resumes, essays, portfolios) and data from diverse sources (including community programs, HBCUs, alternative certification pathways) to identify promising Black candidates who possess key competencies but might be overlooked by conventional methods. AI could potentially broaden the search by focusing on skills and potential rather than narrow, potentially biased proxies for success. Furthermore, AI could help match qualified Black candidates with schools and districts actively seeking diverse educators or those with specific expertise in serving diverse student populations, facilitating a more efficient and potentially more equitable hiring process. However, the risk of AI *amplifying* bias in recruitment is immense, requiring extreme caution, transparency, and human oversight to ensure fairness.

Addressing teacher burnout is crucial for retention, and AI can help by reducing administrative burden and supporting well-being. Black educators often face additional workload burdens, including higher rates of mentoring responsibilities and navigating racial stress. AI tools designed to automate or streamline time-consuming administrative tasks – such as generating lesson plan drafts, providing initial feedback on student assignments (with human review), managing communications, or organizing resources – can free up valuable time for instruction, relationship-building, and self-care. Additionally, AI could potentially power personalized wellness resources or confidential support platforms offering strategies for managing stress and navigating the unique challenges faced by educators of color, contributing to greater sustainability in the profession.

Connecting back to the crucial need for bias mitigation, AI can be used to analyze training materials and evaluation processes themselves. As discussed previously, AI can scan teacher preparation curricula, PD materials, and evaluation rubrics to identify potentially biased content or language. In teacher evaluations, while human judgment remains paramount, AI could provide supplementary, objective data points on practice (e.g., analysis of questioning techniques, student talk time distribution) that, when used carefully alongside qualitative observations, might help mitigate the impact of subjective biases that can disadvantage Black educators during high-stakes assessments. Again, ethical implementation and ensuring AI data complements, rather than dictates, evaluation are critical.

Despite these potentials, the deployment of AI in educator development demands navigating significant ethical considerations and implementing robust safeguards. The specter of algorithmic bias looms large, particularly in recruitment and evaluation tools, potentially creating new digital barriers. Data privacy concerns are paramount, especially when analyzing practice or well-being data. Simulations must be culturally nuanced to avoid stereotyping or misrepresenting experiences. There's a risk of AI leading to overly standardized or de-personalized training, undermining the human element crucial to teaching. Therefore, rebuilding the Black Educator Pipeline using AI necessitates a co-design approach, actively involving Black educators, students, and community members at every stage. Continuous bias audits, algorithmic transparency, stringent data protection protocols, and an unwavering focus on using AI to support, not supplant, human judgment and culturally sustaining practices are non-negotiable.

AI presents a complex toolkit with the potential to significantly enhance educator training and development. For the critical task of rebuilding the Black Educator Pipeline, AI offers avenues to personalize support, provide realistic practice, foster vital connections, potentially streamline recruitment, and alleviate workload pressures. However, these benefits are contingent upon a deeply ethical, equitable, and culturally responsive approach. Without careful design, vigilant oversight, and genuine partnership with the communities it aims to serve, AI risks becoming another layer of systemic inequity. With intentionality and commitment, however, AI can be harnessed as one valuable instrument among many in the essential work of cultivating and sustaining a diverse and effective teaching force for all students.

CONCLUSION

To further enhance the potential of AI in education and ensure its equitable impact on BIPOC learners, future research should focus on:

- Developing AI systems that are explicitly designed to address the needs of BIPOC learners (Unleashing the Potential of AI in Education, n.d.). This includes considering the cultural backgrounds, learning styles, and unique challenges faced by BIPOC students in the design and development of AI-powered learning tools.

- Conducting research in partnership with historically underserved groups to promote collaboration among AI technologists and educators to develop culturally responsive AI systems (Unleashing the Potential of AI in Education, n.d.). This collaborative approach can ensure that AI systems are developed with input from the communities they are intended to serve, leading to more equitable and effective AI solutions for BIPOC learners.
- Building high-quality evidence on the effectiveness of AI systems in improving education outcomes for BIPOC students (Unleashing the Potential of AI in Education, n.d.). This research can help to identify best practices for implementing AI in education to promote equity and inclusion and ensure that AI tools are used to close achievement gaps and improve educational outcomes for all students.

AI has the potential to revolutionize education and create more equitable and inclusive learning experiences for all students. By automating tasks, personalizing learning, and improving accessibility, AI can empower educators and enhance learning outcomes. However, it is crucial to address the potential challenges and ethical considerations surrounding AI in education, particularly its impact on BIPOC learners. To ensure that AI benefits all students, educators and educational leaders must prioritize the following:

- Selecting and developing AI tools that are culturally relevant and free from bias. This requires careful evaluation of AI systems to ensure they do not perpetuate harmful stereotypes or discriminate against certain groups of students.
- Addressing the digital divide by providing equitable access to technology and internet connectivity for all students. This includes investing in infrastructure and resources to ensure that all students have the tools they need to succeed in a digital learning environment.
- Providing ongoing professional development for teachers on the ethical and effective use of AI in education. This includes training on culturally responsive teaching practices, data privacy and security, and strategies for mitigating bias in AI systems.

By taking these steps, we can harness the power of AI to create a more just and equitable education system for all.

ACKNOWLEDGMENT

This work, and indeed my entire professional journey, has been profoundly shaped by the incredible individuals and communities I have had the privilege to serve and collaborate with. I wish to extend my deepest gratitude:

To the bright, resilient, and inspiring students I worked with in Title 1 Programs across New York: Your potential, your curiosity, and your determination in the face of challenges have been a constant source of motivation. You taught me more about perseverance and the true meaning of education than any textbook ever could. It was an honor to be a small part of your journey.

To the diverse families I had the honor of supporting during my time as a foster care and preventive social worker: Thank you for trusting me during vulnerable moments, for sharing your stories, and for demonstrating incredible strength and love under the most difficult circumstances. Your experiences underscored the critical importance of empathy, support, and systemic change.

To the visionary leaders and dedicated colleagues within the inclusionary organizations where I served as a policy and senior management professional: Thank you for your commitment to equity, justice, and creating systems that serve everyone. Working alongside you to advocate for meaningful change and build more inclusive structures has been a defining part of my career. I am grateful for the shared passion and the lessons learned in leadership and collaboration.

Finally, and most importantly, my heartfelt thanks go to my family. To my incredible wife: Your unwavering support, patience, understanding, and encouragement have been my anchor. You inspire me every single day. And to my wonderful children: You bring joy, perspective, and purpose to everything I do. Thank you for your love, your laughter, and for reminding me what truly matters.

This journey would not have been possible without all of you. Thank you.

REFERENCES

AI and Education Research Paper. (n.d.). Steven Rosario's English 110 Website. https://stevenrosario.commons.gc.cuny.edu/teaching/

Artificial Intelligence in Education: Present and Future of Intelligence. (n.d.). Verbit. https://verbit.ai/ai-technology/artificial-intelligence-in-education/

Baker, R. S. (2019). Challenges for the future of educational data mining: The Baker learning analytics prizes. *Journal of Educational Data Mining, 11*(1), 1–17. DOI: 10.5281/zenodo.3591099

Carbonell, J. R. (1970). AI in CAI: An artificial intelligence approach to computer-assisted instruction. *IEEE Transactions on Man-Machine Systems, 11*(4), 190–202. DOI: 10.1109/TMMS.1970.299942

Cuban, L. (1986). *Teachers and machines: The classroom use of technology since 1920.* Teachers College Press.

Green, B. (2019). *The digital poorhouse: How technology went from liberation to oppression and how to fight back.* St. Martin's Press.

Holmes, W., Bialik, M., & Fadel, C. (2023) Artificial intelligence in education. In *Data ethics: building trust: how digital technologies can serve humanity* (pp. 621-653). DOI: 10.58863/20.500.12424/4276068

Ifenthaler, D., & Gibson, D. C. (Eds.). (2020). *Adoption of data analytics in higher education learning and teaching*. Springer., DOI: 10.1007/978-3-030-47392-1

Luckin, R., Holmes, W., Griffiths, M., & Forcier, L. B. (2016). *Intelligence unleashed: An argument for AI in education*. Pearson.

Nkambou, R., Mizoguchi, R., & Bourdeau, J. (Eds.). (2010). *Advances in intelligent tutoring systems*. Springer Science & Business Media., DOI: 10.1007/978-3-642-14363-2

Noble, S. U. (2018). *Algorithms of oppression: How search engines reinforce racism*. NYU Press. DOI: 10.18574/nyu/9781479833641.001.0001

Selwyn, N. (2019). *Should robots replace teachers? AI and the future of education*. Polity Press.

Shute, V. J., & Psotka, J. (1996). Intelligent tutoring systems: Past, present, and future. In Jonassen, D. H. (Ed.), *Handbook of research for educational communications and technology* (pp. 570–600). Macmillan Library Reference USA.

Siemens, G., & Baker, R. S. J. d. (2012). Learning analytics and educational data mining: Towards communication and collaboration. *Proceedings of the 2nd International Conference on Learning Analytics and Knowledge*, 252–254. DOI: 10.1145/2330601.2330661

The future of learning: AI is revolutionizing education 4.0. (n.d.). The World Economic Forum. https://www.weforum.org/stories/2024/04/future-learning-ai-revolutionizing-education-4-0/

The Role of AI in Modern Education. (n.d.). https://onlineprograms.education.uiowa.edu/blog/role-of-ai-in-modern-education

Unleashing the Potential of AI in Education. (n.d.). https://education.purdue.edu/2024/01/ai-use-education/

Wenger, E. (1987). *Artificial intelligence and tutoring systems: Computational and cognitive approaches to the communication of knowledge*. Morgan Kaufmann Publishers Inc.

Williamson, B. (2017). *Big data in education: The digital future of learning, policy and practice*. Sage Publications. DOI: 10.4135/9781529714920

Zuboff, S. (2019). *The age of surveillance capitalism: The fight for a human future at the new frontier of power*. PublicAffairs.

Chapter 12
Adaptive Learning Systems:
Revolutionizing Student-Centered Education

Linda Marie Ellington
https://orcid.org/0000-0002-7697-056X
Southern New Hampshire University, USA

ABSTRACT

This chapter investigates the transformative impact of adaptive learning systems in advancing student-centered education. By leveraging artificial intelligence (AI), adaptive learning systems create dynamic and responsive learning environments tailored to each student's unique needs, abilities, and progress. The chapter showcases practical strategies across educational contexts and highlights the benefits of this approach for learners, educators, and institutions. It also addresses challenges, including ethical considerations, implementation barriers, and the need for equitable access, while offering actionable recommendations for integrating adaptive learning systems into modern education. The significance of this chapter lies in highlighting the potential of adaptive learning systems to transform education. It provides educators, administrators, and policymakers with a clear path for adopting adaptive learning systems to meet the evolving needs of 21st-century learners.

INTRODUCTION

The Foundations of Adaptive Learning Systems

Adaptive learning systems, with their dynamic adjustment of instruction based on individual student characteristics and needs, are at the forefront of a transformative revolution in education. These systems, with their three core elements of content, learner, and instructional models (Khamis, 2015), embody key principles of problem-centered, decision-relevant, reflective, and transformative learning approaches (Adamowski et al., 2014). They aim to personalize education by considering factors like learning styles, abilities, and preferences (Bilous, 2019). The implementation of adaptive learning not only shifts the roles of teachers and students but also opens up a world of possibilities, promoting active student engagement and shared respon-

DOI: 10.4018/979-8-3373-5097-4.ch012

sibility for learning outcomes. This approach can enhance individual competencies and foster self-improvement (Bilous, 2019). The advantages of adoptive learning systems, as posited by Bilous, are numerous and point towards an exciting future (pp.24-25):

- Provides students with a wide range of opportunities to choose their own learning trajectory of mastering a certain topic: the choice of individual pace of study, level.
- Provides a differentiated approach based on the fact that different students have different experience and level of knowledge on a certain topic, each student learns the educational material of the topic in accordance with this level of knowledge and depending on its individual type of perception (visual, audio or kinesthetic).
- Increases the efficiency and objectivity of monitoring and evaluation of learning outcomes.
- Includes diagnostic monitoring of the topic and correction of the training trajectory according to individual characteristics.
- Promotes individualization of learning activities (differentiation of the pace of learning, complexity of learning tasks, type of learning tasks).
- Increases cognitive motivation.
- Promotes the development of productive, creative thinking functions in students, the growth of individual abilities.
- Creates conditions for partnership and cooperation between students and the instructor.

Adaptive learning is touted as a potential game-changer in higher education, a panacea with which institutions may solve the riddle of the iron triangle: quality, cost, and access. Though the research is scant, today's adaptive learning systems have negligible impact on learning outcomes, one aspect of quality. There is also evidence that adaptive systems positively impact other aspects of quality such as student persistence and engagement (Jarrett, 2013; Zimmer, 2014). More compelling still are the intuitively appealing cases for adaptive learning systems as engines with which institutions can increase access and reduce costs. The advantages of utilizing such learning systems include constant availability and accessibility to course materials, cost savings, collaboration amongst students and lecturers, improved performance, feedback from users and effective communication (Criollo-C et al., 2018; Dunn & Kennedy, 2019). These possibilities should inspire and motivate us to explore the potential of adaptive learning. However, it's crucial to remember that in the rush towards online learning, there's a risk that institutions may prioritize cost-cutting and increased access over quality.

Technology has had a significant impact on higher education institutions (HEIs). In fact, virtual reality flipped classrooms and technology-enhanced learning systems have been used in recent years in many HEIs (Arici et al., 2019; Radianti et al., 2020). Technology-enhanced learning uses learning and teaching systems that are technology based, allowing students to develop knowledge and skills with the help of lecturers, tutors, learning support tools and technological resources (Gros, 2016). The importance of such systems, especially in the times of a pandemic, has been highlighted further due to their ability to assist IT and IS educators, while they rethink and revise the learning designs of their courses, in order to offer more meaningful learning experiences to their students (Pappas & Giannakos, 2021). Students also play an active role in the learning process using these technologies.

Adaptive learning theory educators have long known that learning is improved when instruction is personalized--adapted to individual learning styles. In fact, some argue that advocacy for adaptive instruction dates back to antiquity (Murray & Perez, 2015). The modern views of adaptive learning theory, crucially shaped by the work of contemporary educational psychologists, are rooted in the informing science theory framework. This evolution of the theory, guided by the insights of these psychologists, has led to a deeper understanding of how an adaptive learning system can be seen as an expression of an informing system wherein the informer is the instructor, the client is the student, and the rule-based adaptive engine both informs and is informed by interaction with the client. Other parallels exist such as learning model to client complexity, domain model to informer context, and adaptation model to the channel (Murry & Perez, 2015).

HISTORICAL DEVELOPMENT AND TECHNOLOGICAL ADVANCEMENTS

Experimentation with technology-supported instructional guidance emerged in the 1970s as computer-assisted instruction (CAI) (Lu & Shen, 2023). As CAI evolved, it expanded to cover more fields and incorporate artificial intelligence, enhancing its functionality and teaching depth (Lu & Shen, 2023). The primary goal of CAI is to provide effective, interactive instruction (Daliri, 2017).

These systems gave way to a category of intelligent learning systems known as intelligent tutoring systems (ITS). These computer-based systems, which are at the forefront of the intersection between technology and education, employ artificial intelligence to emulate the teacher-guided learning experience, adjusting instructional strategies based on student interaction (Murray & Perez, 2015). The systems incorporate the three major components of the learning process: delivery of content, implementation of instructional strategies, and assessment of learning (Niculescu, 2016). Although paths through an ITS may differ, the same instructional strategies are presented to all students. Adaptive learning systems change (adapt) key functions such as content presentation or workflow based on how students interact with content presented by the system.

Adaptive learning technologies dynamically adjust course content based on individual learner abilities, leveraging artificial intelligence to enhance performance (Capuano & Caballé, 2020). These systems personalize instruction, addressing learners' needs, preferences, and progress (Fadieieva, 2023). Adaptive learning technologies dynamically adjust to the level or type of course content based on an individual's abilities or skill attainment in ways that accelerate a learner's performance with both automated and instructor interventions. A study conducted by Capuano and Caballe' in 2020 found that adaptive learning and its close relationship to artificial intelligence points to several results from artificial intelligence that have been used to build effective adaptive learning systems. Recent advancements in AI, eye-tracking, and physiological measurements have improved the effectiveness of adaptive learning systems (Lane & D'Mello, 2018).

AI ALIGNMENT WITH STUDENT-CENTERED EDUCATION MODELS

Adaptive learning technologies and artificial intelligence are revolutionizing education by personalizing learning experiences, improving accessibility, and enhancing efficiency (Strielkowski et al., 2024; Akavova et al., 2023). Recently, education witnessed a remarkable technological surge driven by various technological advances, demonstrated by the increase of scientific publications on this topic from just 1 in 1990 to 636 in 2023 (Strielkowski et al., 2024).

We are entering the new post-COVID era that marks the transformation of the coronavirus pan-demic (2020–2023) into an endemic; adaptive learning technologies and artificial intelligence are revolutionizing education and its role in education for sustainability like never before (Adiguzelet al., 2023; de Vries, 2022; Jing et al., 2023).

Adaptive learning technologies refer to educational systems that leverage data analytics and AI to personalize the learning experience. These technologies dynamically adjust the presentation of educational content based on an individual student's performance, learning pace, and preferences (Gligorea et al., 2023; Khan et al., 2022). By continuously analyzing data on student interactions, adaptive learning technologies provide customized support, targeted feedback, and optimized learning pathways to enhance student engagement and outcomes.

HOW ADAPTIVE LEARNING SYSTEMS WORK

The Role of AI, Machine Learning, and Data Analytics in Adaptive Learning

AI is crucial to adaptive learning systems (ALS), enabling extensive data analysis to identify student performance patterns and make real-time adjustments (Wittal et al., 2022). Machine Learning (ML) algorithms, Natural Language Processing (NLP), and neural networks enhance these systems' adaptability and personalization. (Zhou et al., 2023). Artificial intelligence and machine learning are revolutionizing adaptive learning in education by personalizing experiences and improving outcomes (Joshi, 2024; Meylani, 2024). AI provides machine learning algorithms, predictive analytics, and natural language processing capabilities to collect and analyze large amounts of data. This allows adaptive learning systems to dynamically adapt content, strategies, and feedback to learners' individual needs.

Traditional education systems often follow a one-size-fits-all approach, where all students are taught the same content at the same pace. This approach fails to consider students' diverse learning styles, abilities, and interests. Adaptive learning, powered by AI, addresses this issue by providing personalized learning experiences for each student. By analyzing vast amounts of data, AI algorithms can identify the strengths and weaknesses of individual learners and create customized learning paths that cater to their specific needs. This personalized approach ensures that students receive the right content at the right time and in the right format, maximizing their learning potential (Akavova et al., 2023).

The rapid evolution of educational technologies has led to a shift toward personalized and adaptive learning experiences. A critical component of such systems is the ability to provide timely and relevant feedback to students. AI-driven real-time feedback systems are designed to enhance student support through the integration of sentiment analysis and machine learning algorithms (Prakash et al., 2024).

Machine learning algorithms, including decision trees, support vector machines (SVM), and deep learning models, analyze and predict student engagement, performance, and emotional states. By combining cognitive and emotional insights, the system delivers personalized, context-sensitive feedback that helps students overcome learning challenges and improve academic outcomes. The system's effectiveness is evaluated using multiple datasets, showing significant improvements in student engagement, satisfaction, and performance.

Strategies for Effective Integration of Adaptive Learning Technologies

In many ways, the *crowd* will drive the next years of adaptive learning technologies. Due to substantial scientific and practical progress, learning technologies can adapt over time by crowdsourcing contributions from teachers and students – explanations, feedback, and other pedagogical interactions. For example, considering the context of ASSISTments, an online learning platform, it is an interactive mathematics exercise that provides the workflow necessary for eliciting feedback contributions and evaluating those contributions by simply tapping into the everyday system usage of teachers and students. Hefferman et al. (2016) writes about how teachers and students can be motivated to provide such contributions and discuss the plans surrounding PeerASSIST. This infrastructure will help ASSISTments to harness the power of crowdsourcing.

Systematic use of adaptive learning technology can streamline volume training and root learning, freeing time for practical mathematics and deep learning (Moltudal et al., 2020). However, when using ALT, teachers should know the interwoven relationship between learning, motivation, and volume training. Successful implementation of ALT requires anchoring in curriculum, formative assessment, adaptive education, and homework (Krumsvik & Skaar, 2020). In their study, they found that educational technology enhances students' academic performance and interest in learning. Various technological tools, such as mobile learning systems, online learning platforms, game-based learning technologies, and media technologies, show great potential in increasing student motivation and engagement. However, Krumsvik and Skaar posit that over-reliance on technology might reduce students' independent thinking and problem-solving abilities (2020).

Cui (2024, pp. 4-5) identifies several strategies to integrate learning technologies:

Collaborative Approach: institutions should adopt a collaborative model, involving teachers, technologists, and students in the design and implementation of AI tools.

- Professional Development: Offer ongoing professional development programs to equip teachers with the skills to integrate AI into their teaching practices.
- Ethical Frameworks: Develop and adhere to ethical frameworks that ensure student data privacy, algorithmic transparency, and equitable access to AI-enhanced learning resources.
- Balanced Integration: Maintain a balance between AI-driven and human-centered teaching practices, recognizing the value of fostering a comprehensive educational experience.
- Personalized Learning Paths: AI algorithms can analyze students' performance data to create customized learning paths, ensuring that each student receives challenging and appropriate content for their skill level.

Intelligent Tutoring Systems: AI-powered tutoring systems provide instant feedback, answer queries, and guide students through complex concepts, simulating the role of a human tutor.

- Automated Assessment and Feedback: AI tools can automate grading for basic language skills, such as grammar and vocabulary, providing students with immediate feedback and freeing teachers' time for more complex tasks.

- Language Learning Platforms: Platforms like Duolingo leverage AI to offer personalized language learning experiences, incorporating gamification elements to enhance motivation and engagement.
- Adaptive Course Content: AI can dynamically adjust course content based on student progress and feedback, ensuring the material remains relevant and engaging.
- Virtual Learning Environments: AI-powered virtual learning environments can simulate real-life scenarios, enhancing students' language proficiency through immersive experiences.

Sentiment Analysis for Emotional Support: AI can analyze students' written submissions to gauge their emotional state, enabling teachers to provide timely emotional support and intervention.

- Collaborative Learning Facilitation: AI can facilitate collaborative learning by matching students with compatible peers and providing structured activities for group work.
- Teacher Assistance and Workload Reduction: AI can assist teachers in administrative tasks, such as scheduling and grading, reducing their workload and allowing them to focus on teaching and student engagement.
- Continuous Learning and Adaptation: AI systems can continuously learn from student data, adapting their teaching strategies to suit the evolving needs of the students better.

In addition to the strategies mentioned above, platforms like SlidesAI, Tome, and SmartEDU enable educators to generate personalized content, including slide presentations and multiple-choice questions, saving time and effort (Gómez & Troya, 2023; Costa et al., 2023). Software like Moro allows for the integration of various content types, including text, math, and code, enhancing the teaching of complex subjects like AI (Singh & Riedel, 2016). These tools are designed to make education more accessible and personalized but also to prepare students for an increasingly digital and automated future.

Teaching Strategies

Mollick & Mollick (2023) guide teachers using AI to quickly and easily implement evidence-based teaching strategies that instructors can integrate into their practice. They identify five teaching strategies for how AI can help instructors create material that supports these strategies and improve student learning. The strategies include providing multiple examples and explanations, uncovering and addressing student misconceptions, frequent low-stakes testing, assessing student learning, and distributed practice. They argue that AI may act as a 'force multiplier' for instructors if implemented cautiously and thoughtfully in service of evidence-based teaching practices.

Strategy 1: Using AI to Produce Many Varied Examples

When confronted with new and complex ideas, adding many and varied examples helps students better understand them (Kirschner & Heal, 2022). Giving students examples when teaching new ideas provides several benefits: examples enhance understanding by providing a real-world context in which to ground an abstract concept; examples help students remember concepts by serving as anchors in the form of an analogy or story and grounding the concept in engaging details that illustrate a general principle. Examples also help students think critically, prompting analysis and evaluation mechanisms across different examples, and examples can help surface the complexity of a concept by highlighting nuances and different aspects of that concept.

Strategy 2: Using AI to Provide Multiple Explanations

Adequate explanations lay the groundwork for foundational knowledge that helps students build mental maps of topics (Willingham, 2023). To develop adequate explanations, instructors must understand where students are and what they already know (prior knowledge), sequence and structure their explanations to move from the simple to the complex (a step-by-step approach), provide organizational cues that help students follow along, and add concrete details to each explanation (examples or analogies) that help students grasp and contextualize a new concept in light of what they already know. The goal of any explanation is that students should eventually be able to explain a concept to others in their own words (Willingham, 2017).

The AI can help instructors with this task by generating multiple explanations from various perspectives, generating explanations that use a step-by-step approach, and adding details to existing explanations. If students are confused by a concept, the AI can produce a more straightforward summary of the concept that may help students grasp the topic. Similarly, instructors can give the AI their current explanation of a topic and ask it to simplify it, add more examples, or explain it using a step-by-step approach.

Strategy 3: Using AI to Develop Low-Stakes Tests

Low-stakes tests provide active retrieval practice, prompting students to recall information from memory, which can help them remember and retrieve information in the future (Kirschner & Heal, 2022). They also provide students with feedback about their understanding of the material, allowing them to focus on the gaps in their knowledge and adjust their learning strategies. They help students make sense of information, initiating the mental processes required to perform on a high-stakes exam (Adesope et al., 2017). Low-stake tests also provide instructors with information about what students know and understand so that they can effectively adapt to their lessons.

Designing low-stakes tests requires that instructors carefully align their learning outcomes and assessments. Instructors must identify specific skills they want to test and create tests that provide evidence of understanding.

Strategy 4: Using AI to Assess Student Learning

Several classroom assessment techniques can help instructors and students monitor their learning and understanding of the course material. These are important because they can provide immediate feedback to instructors and students about what students know and what they are confused by. The one-minute paper and muddiest point technique are active learning strategies that enhance student engagement and understanding. These methods involve students briefly summarizing key points and identifying areas of confusion at the end of a class (Agavekar et al., 2023).

Strategy 5: Using AI to Distribute Practice of Important Ideas

Students must practice retrieving new information once or multiple times during a course. Distributed practice, or having students practice material several times over days and months, is critical to developing robust and flexible knowledge (Pomerance et al., 2016). This type of practice helps students in several ways: it asks students to recall facts and ideas that they may have partially forgotten; it can prompt students to actively connect two separate topics or ideas, creating a more granular mental model of a topic; and it can help students develop a deeper understanding of an idea and expand the capacity to apply that idea in novel situations (Ebersbach & Nazari, 2020).

One way to include distributed practice in a course is to introduce a topic and review it after a week, a month, and then at the end of the semester. It is a learning strategy involving spaced study sessions that has been shown to significantly improve long-term retention of knowledge compared to massed practice or cramming (Carolina et al., 2019). Instructors can direct the AI to generate brief topic overviews and questions that test student knowledge and then use those questions as part of ongoing assignments or assessments at intervals. Once most students respond to the initial questions correctly, instructors can ask the AI to increase the difficulty level of the questions or alternate questions in a sequence.

To use the AI to help with distributed practice, instructors can ask the AI to generate questions to test student knowledge about a series of course topics across the course timeline, incorporating and testing students on new and previously learned concepts. Instructors can ask the AI to find a relationship between concepts and find various ways to connect both ideas in the classroom. The AI can also follow up with specific questions to ask students to prompt them to retrieve previously learned concepts. With careful vetting and oversight, AI can generate explanations, examples, practice problems, and diagnostic questions to support instructors. This helps them spend less time developing materials and more time focusing on students.

Teacher's Professional Development

Sustained commitment to professional development remains essential for individuals engaged in the field of education. Zulfikar et al., (2022) characterize teaching as a multifaceted profession, emphasizing the need for educators, instructors, and teaching staff to continuously embrace learning to enhance their professional competence. Educators should possess a comprehensive understanding of digital tools pertinent to their respective fields, necessitating participation in suitable IT-focused professional development courses (Elfeky, 2018). Conversely, the integration of AI technologies has demonstrated the potential to enhance teaching proficiency, competency by instilling inspiration and fostering self-reflection (Jaiswal & Arun, 2021). AI empowers educators with valuable professional development resources by furnishing them with teaching evaluation models and offering recommendations for enhancing instructional practices. A multitude of studies extol the advantages of AI in education, particularly in online higher education settings, where AI aids in predicting student performance, satisfaction, and learning progress, provides resource recommendations, automates student assessment, and elevates the overall educational experience (Ouyang, et al., 2022).

APPLICATIONS ACROSS EDUCATIONAL CONTEXTS

Adaptive Learning in K-12 Education: Fostering Foundational Skills

Adaptive learning systems have emerged as a transformative approach in K-12 education, promising to personalize learning experiences and improve educational outcomes (Chellanthara et al., 2024). Their study found:

- Significant improvements in student achievement in schools that implement adaptive learning systems, with students demonstrating higher gains in test scores compared to their peers in control groups.
- The personalized nature of adaptive learning helped struggling students catch up with their peers, particularly in mathematics and reading.
- Students reported increased engagement and motivation, attributing their interest to adaptive technologies' interactive and tailored learning experiences.

How adaptive learning techniques impact students and teachers depends on two factors: the specific design features of the tool and how the tool is implemented in the classroom (Divanji et al., 2023). These techniques provide value to students by allowing them to monitor and track their progress over time; this personalized feedback encourages students to become more aware and active participants in their learning. The Divanji study noted that the games and interactive animations helped motivate students and allow them to have fun while moving through the learning content. Teachers especially appreciated these features during remote learning, as engaging students or providing enjoyable learning experiences was challenging. The gamification helped teachers replicate the engagement and participation of in-person classrooms.

Using gamification and artificial intelligence in education has gained significant attention for enhancing student engagement and learning outcomes. When integrated with AI, gamified system like Kahoot can adapt to students' progress and preferences in real time and offer a more tailored and responsive educational environment. Kahoot! promotes active participation and creates a positive learning environment, particularly in language classrooms (Kaur & Naderajan, 2019). It offers a user-friendly solution for educators to incorporate technology and gamification into their teaching practices, enhancing student engagement and learning outcomes.

Change of Perspectives: Adaptive Technology Replacing Instructors

One of the misconceptions that comes with the adaptive system is that the technology will replace instructors in schools. Although adaptive technology facilitates the student's learning process, successfully implementing adaptive learning still requires human planning, interactions, monitoring, and interventions. The role of an instructor remains crucial in adaptive learning because only the instructor can select learning objectives that fit with the overall course learning outcomes and targeted student population, aligning both online and face-to-face activities (Brusco, 2018; Essa, 2016) The instructor organizes various additional class activities around the adaptive practices, sets up course expectations and grading schemes, monitors students' progress, and answers questions. It is the instructor's responsibility to assist students in understanding the functionalities and value of the adaptive system and to help students transition from passive learners to active collaborators so they can understand why frequent assessments provide guidance instead of hindrance to their progress. This level of awareness is critical, as Deslauriers et al. (2019) so aptly convey: A lack of timely instructor communication will result in student resistance and learner disengagement.

As many adaptive assignments are self-paced individual learning activities, instructors should make recommendations to guide self-paced learning so learning is effective. As the learning path for each student is personalized, some students might have more objectives to learn or master than others. Thus, allocating adequate time for those students to learn and reflect before important milestones is important. When students pace their own learning, some might procrastinate and fall behind for various reasons. Therefore, it is essential for instructors to intervene with reminders and online or in-person mentoring opportunities to allow extra time on milestone tests and reasonable opportunities for students to catch up (Cavanagh et al., 2020).

Corporate Training and Professional Development: Personalized Skill-Building

As Maity (2019) notes, the demands for employee training and development have shifted from mass upskilling in earlier decades to personalized, individualized training tailored to today's requirements. Many current training approaches rely on a single modality, typically lectures, or extend over extended periods (e.g., 2-day workshops). In the digital age, learners must process and comprehend various textual sources, encompassing not only written texts but also diverse forms of visual content, both static and dynamic (Mason, 2018).

Artificial Intelligence (AI) is revolutionizing corporate training and professional development by enabling personalized, adaptive learning experiences that enhance learning efficiency and offer scalable methods to deliver content (Bhandare, 2024). This approach ensures that employees receive relevant training, skill acquisition, and knowledge retention. Personalization is particularly valuable in addressing diverse learning styles and paces, which are often difficult to accommodate in traditional training environments.

Corporate training and professional development are evolving to meet new demands and leverage emerging technologies, such as to include virtual reality, augmented reality, and chatbots with companies like Oracle and IBM using AI for skill assessment and customized coaching (Pavitra & Agnihotri, 2023). IBM uses its AI platform, Watson, to create individualized training programs for its employees. Watson analyzes performance data, career goals, and learning preferences to recommend specific courses and materials. Another notable case is Deloitte, which utilizes an AI-based learning platform to tailor training content for its consultants, leading to improved performance and higher satisfaction rates (Bhandare, 2024).

As the workforce landscape rapidly changes, the demand for tailored learning experiences has become increasingly evident. The current context continues to be highly uncertain, with inflation possibly rising, geopolitical tensions, and a shortage of skilled labor in many countries. All of this drives affecting adult learners, related to the way of working and work models in general (in-person vs. virtual remote working). Organizations are faced with the challenge to quickly adapt, define a skill-first approach for the expertise required, and to identify effective and efficient ways of corporate learning (Nelles, et al., 2023). This all is dependent on a curriculum to build the right skills and integrate learning into the workflow.

AI must demonstrate its worth to educators and trainers by seamlessly integrating AI technologies into teaching, learning, and administrative processes (Aldosari, 2020). Business simulating games (BSGs) are a digital interactive educational instrument that is designed as a practice training method. An increasing number of academics in the field of business training acknowledge BSGs are a viable teaching technique (Bharathi, et al., 2024). The BSGs serve as a framework of real-world instruction throughout the area of corporate knowledge and promoting risk-taking, interaction, as well as cooperation among users. Using computerize data extraction and targeted activities, AI encourages smart decision-making and enhances the accuracy of decisions (Bharathi, et al., 2024).

AI is transforming training and development by enabling employees to perform more strategic tasks and drive economic growth in an AI-augmented future (Pavitra & Agnihotri, 2023). The implementation of AI in corporate education involves four key areas: organizational use of AI and machine learning; role in knowledge management and decision making; impact on innovation; and, value creation (Kitsios & Kamariotou, 2021).

BENEFITS OF ADAPTIVE LEARNING SYSTEMS

Supporting Diverse Learning Needs and Styles

The continued evolution of adaptive learning technologies, driven by advancements in AI and machine learning, holds promise for improving educational equity and inclusivity. Traditional educational models often fall short in catering to the diverse needs of students. These models typically adopt a one-size-fits-all approach, which can disadvantage students who do not conform to the average learner profile. Standardized curricula and teaching methods may not accommodate the varying pace at which students learn or address the different ways students process information (Zhao, et al., 2023).

Consequently, students who require more personalized attention may struggle, leading to disparities in academic achievement and engagement. These challenges are exacerbated in classrooms with high levels of diversity, where cultural, linguistic, and cognitive differences are pronounced. The failure to effectively address these differences contributes to persistent educational inequities (Wang & Hofkens, 2020). By focusing on the specific needs of each learner, adaptive learning models can help bridge the gap between diverse student populations and equitable educational outcomes (Cavanagh, et al., 2020).

Facilitating Mastery-based Learning and Improved Outcomes

Generative AI has the potential to scale a number of educational practices, previously limited by resources. One such instructional approach is mastery learning, emphasizing proficiency before progression that is highly resource (teacher time, materials) intensive. The rise of computer-based instruction offered partial solutions, tailoring student progression and automating some facets of the mastery learning process (Hutt & Hieb, 2024). AI-powered virtual assistants can provide personalized guidance to students, increasing enrollment rates and reducing staff workload (Page & Gehlbach, 2017).

AI usage data offers new opportunities for assessing students' skills and improvement in outcomes, implementation requires careful consideration because there are new challenges for education practitioners. One critical question that often arises is how to fairly evaluate students' learning outcomes when AI contributes to the completion of learning tasks. It is undesirable that assessments end up measuring the capabilities of AI rather than reflecting the students' acquisition and application of skills.

A question we should ask is, how might we combine what is changeable with personalized mastery learning to produce adaptive learning impact? The AI technology recognizes leveraging opportunities that are inherent in Education 5.0 (Betts, et al., 2021). The integration of AI in Education 5.0 enhances student engagement, improves assessment processes, and facilitates language learning through natural language processing (Pandya, 2024). The study conducted by Pandya emphasizes the need for collaboration among educators, policymakers, and technologists, which is crucial to ensure that the benefits of AI in education are equitably (Pandy, 2024).

CHALLENGES AND CONSIDERATIONS

Addressing Ethical Concerns, Including Data Privacy and Algorithmic Bias

The ethical implications of AI in education are gaining increased attention, particularly concerning privacy, bias, and accountability (Mishara, 2024). Integrated AI undertakings in education are aimed at handling a number of tasks, which is to individualize the education process as well as to optimize the executive tasks. Such uses hold a lot of potential, with increased effectiveness, increased levels of student involvement, and better learning. However, their strong focus on data and algorithm choice presents several ethical issues that range from data privacy, algorithm explainability and algorithms equality.

According to Mishara (2024) AI systems present great possibilities for improving the educational experiences of learners while suggesting that AI should be used in a more nuanced manner that promotes ethical practices. AI needs to be responsible for privacy, free of bias, and must be accountable in education to ensure that there is trust, equality and fairness (p.3551). Mishara (2024) and Shubham et al., (2023) suggest these guidelines:

1. Protection of data and clear and voluntary compliance with data protection law for stewardship of student's data.
2. Implement bias identification strategies in the predictive models and develop methods for verification of the data that is fed to the models, from prejudice.
3. Privacy preservation should be of high value.
4. There has to be clarity as to what information is being collected, for what purpose this information is being used and much more importantly, the rights that students and guardians have over collected information.
5. To avoid biases there is a need to ensure diverse and inclusive training.
6. Developing fairness metrics to track performance across demographics.

7. In order to maintain basic ethical values of AI in educational processes, institutions should establish the governance structures that would regulate AI designing and using.

Privacy breaches, algorithmic biases, and lack of transparency are identified as the most significant ethical concerns in data and science engineering, with marginalized communities being disproportionately affected (Shubham, et al., 2023). In educational settings, AI usage raises critical moral concerns, such as potential amplification of social inequities and racial stereotyping (Weber, 2020). Addressing these challenges requires interdisciplinary collaboration to create ethical and legal frameworks that harness AI's potential while mitigating risks in education and society at large (Venkatasubbu_& Krishnamoorthy, 2022). By illuminating these concerns and continuing to explore potential solutions, they will contribute to the ongoing dialogue on responsible AI development and facilitate the creation of AI systems that are not only technologically sophisticated but also ethical, dependable, and equitable. AI can become an instrument in the formation of better education for every learner.

Overcoming Technical and Financial Barriers to Implementation

Artificial Intelligence (AI) is revolutionizing higher education by enhancing accessibility, affordability, and inclusivity. These innovative technologies help make online learning simultaneously more accessible (by making materials available online), affordable (by saving teacher time), and achievable (by providing learning assistance and fostering student engagement). Addressing these challenges requires strategic planning, collaboration among stakeholders, and the development of ethical frameworks (Tarisayi, 2023; Borah & Borah, 2024). Institutions must invest in technological infrastructure, create policies for responsible AI adoption, and promote transparent practices to optimize AI's impact on learning, which has the potential to make higher education more accessible, adaptive, and inclusive for diverse learner.

AI and adaptive learning play a big role in helping higher education institutions overcome both technical and financial barriers to implementation. Here’s how they contribute:

Personalized Learning at Scale

- *Challenge:* Traditional education methods struggle to provide personalized learning due to limited faculty time and resources.
- *Solution:* AI-driven adaptive learning platforms tailor content to each student’s needs, automating this process and reducing the reliance on one-on-one instruction.
- *Benefit:* Improves learning outcomes without needing more staff or infrastructure.

Cost Efficiency

- *Challenge*: Hiring faculty, updating curricula, and maintaining infrastructure is expensive.
- *Solution*: AI tools automate grading, provide tutoring, and generate content (e.g., quizzes, summaries), cutting down operational costs.
- *Benefit:* Schools save money and reallocate resources more effectively

Early Intervention & Retention

- *Challenge:* High dropout rates can lead to lost tuition revenue and poor performance metrics.
- *Solution:* AI systems analyze learning patterns and flag at-risk students early, enabling timely intervention.
- *Benefit*: Increases student retention, improving institutional stability and long-term financial health.

Bridging Digital Divide

- *Challenge*: Some institutions lack advanced tech infrastructure or can't afford top-tier learning management systems.
- *Solution:* Cloud-based AI solutions don't require high-end hardware and can integrate with existing systems.
- *Benefit*: Makes advanced learning technologies accessible even to underfunded institutions.

Data-Driven Decision Making

- *Challenge*: Implementing changes without understanding student needs can lead to wasted investments.
- *Solution:* AI provides real-time analytics on student engagement and performance.
- *Benefit*: Helps institutions make smarter investments and policy decisions.

Scalable Professional Development

- *Challenge*: Training faculty in new tech is time-consuming and costly.
- *Solution*: AI can deliver on-demand, personalized training modules for educators.
- *Benefit:* Reduces the cost and complexity of upskilling staff.

AI and adaptive learning personalize learning at scale, automate tasks like grading and tutoring to reduce costs, and use data to identify and support at-risk students, boosting retention. Cloud-based AI tools require minimal infrastructure, making them accessible even to underfunded institutions. Additionally, AI supports faculty with on-demand training and data-driven decision-making, improving efficiency and resource allocation across the board.

FUTURE DIRECTIONS AND INNOVATIONS

Exploring cutting-edge AI tools that enhance adaptive learning can significantly impact education by personalizing experiences, scaling access, and fostering inclusivity. According to Pluralsight below is a short list of tools and platforms driving these trends:

- *Knewton (Alta by Knewton):* Uses AI to create tailored course materials and assessments based on student performance.
- *Duolingo:* Leverages AI for adaptive language learning adjusting difficulty based on user mistakes and engagement.
- *Cognii:* Offers AI-power conversational tutors for open-response assessments and feedback.
- *Century Tech*: Combines neuroscience and AI to curate personalized learning pathways and micro-lessons.
- *Seeing AI*: Narrates the visual world for visually impaired users, aiding inclusive classroom participation.
- *Civitas Learning*: Predicts student risks (e.g., dropout likelihood) and recommends interventions.
- *IBM Watson Tutor*: Integrates with LMS platforms to answer student questions using natural language processing.
- *Kahoot!*: Uses AI to recommend games and quizzes based on learner preferences.
- *AWS Educate*: Offers cloud tools for institutions to build scalable adaptive learning systems.

These trends are making adaptive learning more effective, scalable, and inclusive—reshaping how education is delivered across the globe.

POLICY AND INSTITUTIONAL STRATEGIES TO SUPPORT WIDESPREAD ADOPTION

Key considerations in policy development and institutional strategies include ethics, privacy, and stakeholder concerns (Tsai et al., 2018). Successful implementation requires addressing context-specific challenges and providing necessary infrastructure, institutional commitment, support, and resources (Mirata et al., 2020). There are discussions in the field of higher education that propose practical recommendations for institutional leaders and factors to be considered when implementing adaptive learning in higher education settings. To support the widespread adoption of adaptive learning technologies, both policy makers and institutions need to implement thoughtful strategies that address funding, infrastructure, training, and governance. Here are a few policies and institutional strategies that may help in the implementation:

- Provide grants, subsidies, or public-private partnerships to reduce the financial burden of adopting adaptive technologies.
- Invest in continuous professional development programs focused on digital pedagogy and adaptive tools.
- Develop clear policies around data collection, storage, and usage aligned with legal and ethical standards.
- Develop policies to ensure adaptive technologies are accessible to all students, including those in remote or underserved areas.
- Encourage collaboration between universities, e-tech companies, and government agencies.

By combining these policy and institutional strategies, adaptive learning technologies can be effectively implemented to transform higher education systems at scale. In addition, influencing adoption include institutional infrastructure, staff attitudes and skills, and perceived student expectations. Institutional readiness assessment, strategy formation, and policy development are crucial steps in ensuring the effective and legitimate adoption of LA in higher education.

CONCLUSION

AI and adaptive learning systems are fundamentally transforming the educational landscape by personalizing instruction, enhancing learner engagement, and optimizing educational outcomes. These technologies enable educators to identify individual student needs more effectively, allowing for tailored interventions and continuous feedback. As AI continues to evolve, its integration into learning environments holds the potential to bridge achievement gaps and promote more equitable access to quality education. However, careful consideration must be given to ethical concerns, data privacy, and the role of human educators to ensure that these innovations are implemented responsibly and inclusively. The synergy between AI-driven tools and traditional pedagogical approaches promises to redefine the future of education.

The integration of AI and adaptive learning systems is fostering a more data-driven approach to education, enabling institutions to make informed decisions based on real-time analytics. These insights allow for the continuous improvement of curricula and instructional strategies, ensuring that educational content remains relevant and effective.AI-powered platforms can support lifelong learning by offering flexible, scalable solutions that adapt to learners' evolving goals and circumstances. As education systems around the world continue to adopt these technologies, ongoing collaboration between technologists, educators, and policymakers will be essential to maximize their benefits while addressing challenges related to accessibility, algorithmic bias, and digital literacy.

REFERENCES

Abdurohman, N. R. (2025). Artificial intelligent in higher education: Opportunities and challenges. *Eurasian Science Review An International Peer-reviewed Multidisciplinary Journal, 2*(Special Issue), 1683–1695. Advance online publication. DOI: 10.63034/esr-334

Adamowski, J. F., Medema, W., & Light, S. S. (2014). Integrating adaptive learning into adaptive water resources management. *Environmental Engineering and Management Journal, 13*(7), 1801–1816. DOI: 10.30638/eemj.2014.201

Adesope, O. O., Trevisan, D. A., & Sundararajan, N. (2017). Rethinking the use of tests: A meta-analysis of practice testing. *Review of Educational Research, 87*(3), 659–701. DOI: 10.3102/0034654316689306

Adiguzel, T., Kaya, M. H., & Cansu, F. K. (2023). Revolutionizing education with AI: Exploring the transformative potential of ChatGPT. *Contemporary Educational Technology, 15*(3), ep429. Doi.org/10.30935/crdtech/13152. DOI: 10.30935/cedtech/13152

Agavekar, R., Bhore, P., Kadam, H., & Moharir, M. (2023). Effective application of one minute paper and muddiest point technique to enhance students' active engagement: A case study. *Journal of Engineering Education Transformation, 36*(3), 8–17. Advance online publication. DOI: 10.16920/jeet/2023/v36i3/23093

Akavova, A., Temirkhanova, Z., & Lorsanova, Z. (2023). Adaptive learning and artificial intelligence in the educational space, 2nd International Conference on Environmental *Sustainability Management and Green Technologies, 451.*

Aldosari, S. A. M. (2020). The future of higher education in the light of artificial intelligence transformations, *International. The Journal of Learning in Higher Education, 19*(3), •••.

Alsobhi, A. Y., & Alyoubi, K. H. (2020). Learning styles and dyslexia types – Understanding their relationship and its benefits in adaptive e-learning systems [iJIM]. *International Journal of Interactive Mobile Technologies, 14*(15), 25–43. DOI: 10.3991/ijim.v14i15.16129

Altaleb, H., Mouti, S., & Beegom, S. (2023). Enhancing college education: An AI-driven adaptive learning platform (ALP) for customized course experiences, 9th *International Conference on Optimization and Applications (ICOA).* DOI: 10.1109/ICOA58279.2023.10308834

Arici, F., Yildirim, P., Caliklar, S., & Yilmaz, R. M. (2019). Research trends in the use of augmented reality in science education: Content and bibliometric mapping analysis. *Computers & Education, 142*, 103647. Advance online publication. DOI: 10.1016/j.compedu.2019.103647

Becker, S. A., Brown, M., Dahlstrom, E., Davis, A., DePaul, K., Diaz, V., & Pomerantz, J. (2018). NMC Horizon report: 2018 Higher education edition.

Betts, A., Thai, K. P., & Gunderia, S. (2021). Personalized mastery learning ecosystems: Using Bloom's four objects of change to drive learning in adaptive instructional systems. Sottilare, R.A., Schwarz, J. (eds) *Adaptive Instructional Systems. Design and Evaluation. HCII 2021. Lecture Notes in Computer Science.* Springer. DOI:DOI: 10.1007/978-3-030-77857-63

Bhandare, V. (2024). The role of artificial intelligence in learning and development. *International Journal of Scientific Research in Engineering and Management*, *8*(5), 1–5. DOI: 10.55041/IJSREM34968

Bharathi, G. P., Chandra, I., Sanagana, D. P., Tummalachervu, C. K., Rao, V. S., & Neelima, S. (2024). AI-driven adaptive learning for enhancing business intelligence simulation games. *Entertainment Computing*, *50*, 100699. soi.org/10.1016.j.entcom.2024.100699. DOI: 10.1016/j.entcom.2024.100699

Bilous, V. (2019). Basic principles for developing an adaptive learning system, *New Pedagogical Approach in STEAM Education International Conference.*

Borah, C., & Borah, P. (2024). Artificial intelligence empowered learning: A quantum shift in higher education. *International Journal For Multidisciplinary Research*, *6*(6), 30869. Advance online publication. DOI: 10.36948/ijfmr.2024.v06i06.30869

Brusco, R. (2018). *Personalized learning at its best (Blog post)*. Edutopa.

Capuano, N., & Caballé, S. (2020). Adaptive Learning Technologies. *AI Magazine*, *41*(2), 96–98. DOI: 10.1609/aimag.v41i2.5317

Carolina, E. M. Küpper-Tetzel, Weston, T., Kim, A.S., Kapler, I.V., & Foot-Seymour, V. (2019). Enhancing the quality of student learning using distributed practice. *The Cambridge Handbook of Cognition and Education.*

Cavanagh, T., Chen, B., Lahcen, R., & Paradiso, J. R. (2020). Constructing a design framework and pedagogical approach for adaptive learning in higher education: A practitioner's perspective. *International Review of Research in Open and Distance Learning*, *21*(1), 172–196. DOI: 10.19173/irrodl.v21i1.4557

Chellanthara Jose, B., Ashok Kumar, M., UdayaBanu, T., & Nagalakshmi, M. (2024). Assessing the effectiveness of adaptive learning systems in K-12 education, *International Journal of Advanced IT Research and Development, 1*(1).

Chen, B., Bastedo, K., Kirkley, D., Stull, C., & Tojo, J. (2017). *Designing personalized adaptive learning courses at the University of Central Florida (Eli Brief)*. EDUCAUSE Learning Initiative.

Costa, M. J., Matos, R., Amaro, H., Caceiro, B., Marques, A., & Oliveira, H. G. (2023). SmartEDU: A platform for generating education-support materials, *2023 6th Experiment@ International Conference.* DOI:DOI: 10.1109/exp.at2358782.2023.10545665

Criollo-C, S., Lujan-Mora, S., & Jaramillo-Alcazar, A. (2018). Advantages and disadvantages of m-learning in current education, *2nd IEEE world engineering education conference: The Role of professional Associations in contemporaneous engineer careers, proceedings.*

Cui, Y. (2024). A study on the path of AI empowering college English teaching. *Journal of Modern Educational Theory and Practice*, *1*(2). Advance online publication. DOI: 10.70767/jmetp.v1i2.274

Dagunduro, A.O., Chikwe, C.F., Ajuwon, O.A., & Ediae, A.A. (2024). Adaptive learning models for diverse classrooms: Enhancing educational equity, *International Journal of Applied Research in Social Sciences.*

Daliri, Z.S. (2017). Guidelines for computer-aided instruction for effective teaching, *International Research Journal of Multidisciplinary Studies, 3.*

De Vries, P. (2022). The ethical dimension of emerging technology in engineering education. *Education Sciences, 12*(11), 754. Doi.org/10.3390/educsci12220754. DOI: 10.3390/educsci12110754

Deslauriers, L., McCarty, L. S., Miller, K., Callaghan, K., & Kestin, G. (2019, September). Measuring actual learning versus feeling of learning in response to being actively engaged in the classroom. *Proceedings of the National Academy of Sciences of the United States of America, 116*(39), 19251–19257. DOI: 10.1073/pnas.1821936116 PMID: 31484770

Divanji, R. A., Bindman, S., Tung, A., Chen, K., Castaneda, L., & Scanlon, M. (2023). A one stop shop? Perspectives on the value of adaptive learning technologies in K-12 education. *Computers and Education Open, 5*, 100157. Advance online publication. DOI: 10.1016/j.caeo.2023.100157

Dunn, T. J., & Kennedy, M. (2019). Technology enhanced learning in higher education, Motivations, engagement and academic achievement. *Computers & Education, 137*, 104–113. DOI: 10.1016/j.compedu.2019.04.004

Dziuban, C., Moskal, P., Johnson, C., & Evans, D. (2017). Adaptive learning: A tale of two context. *Current Issues in Emerging Elearning, 4*(1).

Dziuban, C.D., Howlin, C.P., Moskal, P.D., Johnson, C.R., Eid, M., & Kmetz, B. (2018). Adaptive learning: Context and complexity, *E-mentor, 5*(77).

Ebersbach, M., & Nazari, K. B. (2020). Implementing distributed practice in statistics courses: Benefits for retention and transfer. *Journal of Applied Research in Memory and Cognition, 9*(4), 532–541. DOI: 10.1037/h0101860

Elfeky, A. I. M. (2018). The effect of personal learning environments on participants' higher order thinking skills and satisfaction. *Innovations in Education and Teaching International.*

Essa, A. (2016). A possible future for next generation adaptive learning systems. *Smart Learning Environments, 3*(1), 16. 16.doi.org/10.1186/s40561-016-0038-y. DOI: 10.1186/s40561-016-0038-y

Fadieieva, L. O. (2023). Adaptive learning: A cluster-based literature review. *Educational Technology Quarterly, 3*(3), 319–366. DOI: 10.55056/etq.613

Gligorea, I., Cioca, M., Oancea, R., Gorski, A. T., Gorski, H., & Tudorache, P. (2023). Adaptive learning using artificial intelligence in e-learning: A literature revie. *Education Sciences, 13*(12), 1216. Advance online publication. DOI: 10.3390/educsci13121216

Gligorea, I., Cioca, M., Oancea, R., Gorski, A. T., Gorski, H., & Tudorache, P. (2023). Adaptive learning using artificial intelligence in e-learning: A literature review. *Education Sciences, 13*(12), 1216. Doi.org/10.3390/educsci13121216. DOI: 10.3390/educsci13121216

Goel, A.K. (2020). AI-powered learning: Making education accessible, affordable, and achievable, *ArXiv, abs/2006.01908.*

Gómez, C. A., & Colala Troya, A. L. (2023). Artificial Intelligence applied to teaching and learning processes. *LatIA, 1*(2), 2. Advance online publication. DOI: 10.62486/latia20232

Gómez, C. A., & Troya, C. (2023). Artificial intelligence applied to teaching and learning processes. *LatIA, 1*(2), 2. Advance online publication. DOI: 10.62486/latia20232

Gros, B. (2016). The design of smart educational environments. *Smart Learning Environments, 3*(1), 1–11. DOI: 10.1186/s40561-016-0039-x

Heffernan, N. T., Ostrow, K. S., Kelly, K., Selent, D., Van Inwegen, E. G., Xiong, X., & Williams, J. J. (2016). The future of adaptive learning: Does the crowd hold the key? *International Journal of Artificial Intelligence in Education, 26*(2), 615–644. DOI: 10.1007/s40593-016-0094-z

Hughey, J. (2020). Individual personalized learning, *Educational Considerations, 46*(2).

Hutt, S., & Hieb, G. (2024). Scaling up mastery learning with generative AI: Exploring how generative AI can assist in the generation and evaluation of mastery quiz questions, *ACM Conference on Learning @ Scale*. DOI: 10.1145/3657604.3664699

Jaiswal, A., & Arun, C. J. (2021). Potential of artificial intelligence for transformation of the education system in India. *International Journal of Education and Development Using Information and Communication Technology, 17*(1), 142–158.

Jarrett, J. (2013). Bigfoot, Goldilocks and moonshots: A report from the frontiers of personalized learning. *EDUCAUSE Review*.

Jing, Y., Zhao, L., Zhu, K., Wang, H., Wang, C., & Xia, Q. (2013). Research landscape of adaptive learning in education: A bibliometric study on research publications from 2000 to 2022. *Sustainability (Basel), 15*(4), 3115. doig.org/10/3390/su15043115. DOI: 10.3390/su15043115

Jones, A., & Bomash, I. (2018). Validating mastery learning: Assessing the impact of adaptive learning objective mastery in Knewton Alta, *International Conference on Artificial Intelligence in Education*. DOI: 10.1007/978-3-319-93846-2_81

Joshi, A. (2024). Adaptive learning through artificialiIntelligenc. [IJIE]. *International Journal on Integrated Education, 7*(2).

Kasneci, E., Seßler, K., Küchemann, S., Bannert, M., Dementieva, D., Fischer, F., & Kasneci, G. (2023). ChatGPT for good? On opportunities and challenges of large language models for education. *Learning and Individual Differences, 103*, 103. DOI: 10.1016/j.lindif.2023.102274

Kaur, P., & Naderajan, R. (2019). Kahoot! In the English language classroom, *South East Asia Journal of Contemporary Business, Economics, and Law, 20*(6).

Khamis, M. A. (2015). Adaptive e-learning environment systems and technologie. *Computer Science Education.*

Khan, M. A., Khojah, M., & Vivek, . (2022). Artificial intelligence and big data: The advent of new pedagogy in the adaptive e-learning system in the higher educational institutions in Saudi Arabia. *Education Research International, 1*, 1263555. Doi.org/10.1155/2022/1263555. DOI: 10.1155/2022/1263555

Kirschner, P. A., Hendrick, C., & Heal, J. (2022). *How teaching happens: Seminal works in teaching and teacher effectiveness and what they mean in practice*. Routledge. DOI: 10.4324/9781003228165

Kitsios, F. C., & Kamariotou, J. (2021). Artificial intelligence and business strategy towards digital transformation: A research agenda. *Sustainability (Basel), 13*(4), 2025. DOI: 10.3390/su13042025

Krumsvik, R. J., & Skaar, Ø. O. (2020). *Schooling, educational technology, and teachers' everyday practice in Norway*. Oxford Research Encyclopedia of Education., DOI.org/10.1093/acrefore/9780190264093.013.903 DOI: 10.1093/acrefore/9780190264093.013.903

Lane, H. C., & D'Mello, S. K. (2018). *Uses of physiological monitoring in intelligent learning environments: A review of research, evidence, and technologies*. Mind, Brain and Technology., DOI: 10.1007/978-3-030-02631-85

Lu, L., & Shen, P. (2023). *The development history and future trend of computer-assisted teaching*. Highlights in Science, Engineering and Technology. DOI: 10.54097/mn007h87

Lv, P., Wang, X., Xu, J., & Wang, J. (2018, May). Utilizing knowledge graph and student testing behavior data for personalized exercise recommendation, *In Proceedings of ACM Turing Celebration Conference*- China. DOI: 10.1145/3210713.3210728

Maity, S. (2019). Identifying opportunities for artificial intelligence in the evolution of training and development practices. *Journal of Management Development, 38*(8), 651–663. DOI: 10.1108/JMD-03-2019-0069

Mason, L. (2018). Multiplicity in the digital era: Processing and learning from multiple sources and modalities of instructional presentations, *Learning and Instruction, 57*, 76-81. DOI: org/. DOI: 10.1016/j.learninstruc.2018.03.004

Meylani, R. (2024). A critical glance at adaptive learning systems using artificial intelligence: A systematic review and qualitative synthesis of contemporary research literature. *Western Anatolia Journal of Educational Sciences, 15*(3), 3519–3547. DOI: 10.51460/baebd.1525452

Mirata, V., Hirt, F., Bergamin, P., & van der Westhuizen, C. (2020). Challenges and contexts in establishing adaptive learning in higher education: Findings from a Delphi study. *International Journal of Educational Technology in Higher Education, 17*(32), 32. Doi.org/10.1186/s141239-020-00209-y. DOI: 10.1186/s41239-020-00209-y

Mishara, P. (2024). The ethical implications of AI in education: Privacy, bias, and accountability. *Journal of Informatics Education and Research, 4*(2). Advance online publication. DOI: 10.52783/jier.v4i2.1827

Mollick, E., & Mollick, L. (2023). Using AI to implement effective Teaching strategies in classrooms: Five strategies, including prompts, SSRN *Electronic Journal*. DOI: 10.2139/ssrn.4391243

Moltudal, S., Hoydal, K., & Krumsvik, R. J. (2020). Glimpses Into real-life introduction of adaptive learning technology: A mixed methods research approach to personalized pupil learning. *Design for Learning, 12*(1), 13–28. Advance online publication. DOI: 10.16993/dfl.138

Murray, M. C., & Pérez, J. (2015). Informing and performing: A study comparing adaptive learning to traditional learning. Informing Science. *The International Journal of an Emerging Transdiscipline, 18*, 111–125.

Nelles, J., Hammer, M., Kondratjew, H., Mueller, F. A., Atre, M. P., Blackwell, E., de Guzman, C., Hamood, J., Ramnane, K., Singh, S., & Gabriels, S. (2023). Building operations skills through a spaced learning and development approach in a corporate environment, SSRN *Electronic Journal*. DOI:DOI: 10.2139/ssrn.4471485

Niculescu, C. (2016). Intelligent tutoring systems – trends on design, development and deployment, *eLearning and Software for Education*. DOI:DOI: 10.12753/2066-026X-16-218

Ohri, G. K. (2024). Advanced education equity: The role of generative AI in creating accessible and inclusive higher education. *International Journal of Computer Engineering and Technology, 15*(6). Advance online publication. DOI: 10.34218/IJCET1506154

Omar, Z., Mior Harun, M. H., Mohd Ishar, N. I., Mustapha, N. A., & Ismail, Z. (2023). *Enhancing professional development and training through AI for personalized learning: a framework to engaging learners*. International Journal on e-Learning and Higher Education.

Ouyang, F., Zheng, L., & Jiao, P. (2022). Artificial intelligence in online higher education: A systematic review of empirical research from 2011 to 2020. *Education and Information Technologies, 27*(6), 7893–7925. DOI: 10.1007/s10639-022-10925-9

Page, L. C., & Gehlbach, H. (2017). How an artificially intelligent virtual assistant helps students navigate the road to college. *AERA Open, 3*(4), 1–12. DOI: 10.1177/2332858417749220

Pandya, K.T. (2024). The role of artificial intelligence in education 5.0: opportunities and challenges, *SDGs Studies Review*.

Pappas, I. O., & Giannakos, M. N. (2021). Rethinking learning design in IT education during a pandemic. *Frontiers in Education, 6*, 652856. Advance online publication. DOI: 10.3389/feduc.2021.652856

Patel, S., & Ragolane, M. (2024). The implementation of artificial intelligence in South African higher education institutions: Opportunities and challenge. *Technium Education and Humanities, 9*, 51–65. Advance online publication. DOI: 10.47577/teh.v9i.11452

Pavitra, D. K., & Agnihotri, D. A. (2023). Artificial intelligence in corporate learning and development: Current trends and future possibilities, *Second International Conference on Smart Technologies for Smart Nation*, 688-693. DOI: 10.1109/SmartTechCon57526.2023.10391698

Prakash, J., Swathiramy, R., Balambigai, G., Menaha, R., & Abhirami, J. S. (2024). AI-driven real-time feedback system for enhanced student support: Leveraging sentiment analysis and machine learning algorithms. *International Journal of Computational and Experimental Science and Engineering, 10*(4). Advance online publication. DOI: 10.22399/ijcesen.780

Radianti, J., Majchrzak, T. A., Fromm, J., & Wohlgenannt, I. (2020). A systematic review of immersive virtual reality applications for higher education: Design elements, lessons learned, and research agenda. *Computers & Education, 147*, 103778. DOI: 10.1016/j.compedu.2019.103778

Rane, N. L., Choudhary, S. P., & Rane, J. (2023). Education 4.0 and 5.0: Integrating artificial intelligence (AI) for personalized and adaptive learning, SSRN *Electronic Journal*. DOI: 10.2139/ssrn.4638365

Roschelle, J. (2021). *Intelligence augmentation for collaborative learning*. Interacción. DOI: 10.1007/978-3-030-77857-6_17

Shemshack, A., Kinshuk, , & Spector, J. M. (2021). A comprehensive analysis of personalized learning components. *Journal of Computers in Education, 8*(4), 485–503. DOI: 10.1007/s40692-021-00188-7

Shubham, S., Saloni, S., & Muntaha, S. D. (2023). Data and science engineering: The ethical dilemma of our time-exploring privacy breaches, algorithmic biases, and the need for transparency. *World Journal of Advanced Research and Reviews, 18*(1), 762–768. DOI: 10.30574/wjarr.2023.18.1.0677

Singh, S., & Riedel, S. (2024). Creating interactive and visual educational resources for AI, *Thirtieth AAAI Conference on Artificial Intelligence*. DOI: DOI: 10.1609/aaai.v30i1.9851

Somasundaram, M., Junaid, K. M., & Mangadu, S. (2020). Artificial intelligence (AI) enabled intelligent quality management system (IQMS) for personalized learning path. *Procedia Computer Science, 172*, 438–442. DOI: 10.1016/j.procs.2020.05.096

Strielkowski, W., Grebennikova, V., Lisovskiy, A., Rakhimova, G., & Vasileva, T. (2024). AI-driven adaptive learning for sustainable educational transformation. *Sustainable Development*. Doi.org/10.1002/sd.3221

Tarisayi, R. S. (2024). Strategic leadership for responsible artificial intelligence adoption in higher education, *CTE Workshop Proceedings*. DOI:DOI: 10.55056/cte.616

Tsai, Y.-S., Scheffel, M., & Gasevic, D. (2018). Enabling systematic adoption of learning analytics through a policy framework., T*he 13th European Conference on Technology Enhanced Learning*. DOI: DOI: 10.1007/978-3-319-98572-544

Utami, R., Roistika, N., Khoirot, U., Hanafi, M., & Herminingsih, D. (2019). Teacher professional development in education 4.0: Awareness of digital literacy. *In Proceedings of the 1st International Conference on Business, Law And Pedagogy, ICBLP* 13-15.

Venkatasubbu, S., & Krishnamoorthy, G. (2022). Ethical considerations in AI: Addressing bias and fairness in machine learning models. *Journal of Knowledge Learning and Science Technology, 1*(1), 130–138. Advance online publication. DOI: 10.60087/jklst.vol1.n1.p138

Wang, M.-T., & Hofkens, T. L. (2020). Beyond classroom academics: A school-wide and multicontextual perspective on student engagement in school. *Adolescent Research Review, 5*(4), 419–433. DOI: 10.1007/s40894-019-00115-z PMID: 33313381

Weber, A. S. (2020). Ethics concerns artificial intelligence use in education, *14th International Technology, Education and Development Conference*. 4539-4544. DOI: DOI: 10.21125/inted.2020.1262

Willingham, D. T. (2017). A mental model of the learner: Teaching the basic science of educational psychology to future teachers. *Mind, Brain and Education : the Official Journal of the International Mind, Brain, and Education Society*, *11*(4), 166–175. DOI: 10.1111/mbe.12155

Wittal, C. G., Hammer, D., Klein, F. R., & Rittchen, J. (2023). Perception and knowledge of artificial intelligence in healthcare, therapy and diagnostics: A population representative survey. *Journal of Biotechnology and Biomedicine*, *6*(2), 129–139. DOI: 10.26502/jbb.2642-91280077

Zhao, Y., Li, T., & Liu, W. (2023). The benefits and drawbacks of standardized curriculum in education. *Research and Advances in Education*, *2*(10), 41–47. DOI: 10.56397/RAE.2023.10.05

Zhu, A. (2019). Personalized college English learning based on artificial intelligence, *4th International Conference on Mechanical, Control and Computer Engineering (ICMCCE)*, 647-6473). IEEE. DOI: 10.1109/ICMCCE48743.2019.00150

Zimmer, T. (2014). Rethinking higher ed: A case for adaptive learning, *Forbes Education.*

Zulfikar, T., Emawati, E., Dahliana, S., Akmal, S., & Hidayat, D. N. (2022). Prospects and challenges towards professional development of English lecturers in Islamic tertiary education in Indonesia, *World. Journal of Education*, *12*(4), 21–34.

Chapter 13
Personalized Education in the Age of AI:
Innovations and Implications

Linda Marie Ellington
https://orcid.org/0000-0002-7697-056X
Southern New Hampshire University, USA

ABSTRACT

Integrating artificial intelligence (AI) in education impacts educators, students, and policymakers. This chapter explores the extensive literature on the transformative effects of artificial intelligence (AI) on personalized learning, including its impact on delivering tailored content, pacing, assessment methods, and policy decisions. The research highlights AI's potential to revolutionize traditional teaching and learning paradigms. It addresses diverse learning needs, reassuring the audience about the inclusivity of the educational system, and optimizes academic outcomes. AI-powered educational tools also support educators in designing and delivering content that aligns with modern pedagogical approaches, creating an exciting and engaging learning environment. While AI offers numerous benefits, ethical considerations and challenges arise. Issues such as data privacy, algorithmic bias, and the digital divide necessitate careful navigation and the establishment of ethical guidelines to ensure equitable access and usage.

INTRODUCTION

AI-powered learning approaches, a game-changer in education, not only assess student performance and identify strengths and weaknesses but also provide practical tools for knowledge acquisition. These tools, driven by AI, include Chatbots, Virtual Assistance tools, and Adaptive Learning Systems. They offer immersive and interactive learning experiences, allowing students to explore complex theories and solutions (Aldosari, 2020; Pradana et al., 2023).

Artificial intelligence applications are essential in various fields, but they are particularly crucial for educational institutions and universities. These institutions, which are no longer limited to education but have become an essential part of the system of sustainable development in societies, are increasingly integrating AI into their operations. The use of AI in education can lead

DOI: 10.4018/979-8-3373-5097-4.ch013

to improved learning outcomes, more efficient administrative processes, and a more personalized learning experience for students. The mission of universities today exceeds the traditional function of preserving heritage, identity, and education. Instead, universities today are at the forefront of shaping the future, keeping pace with technological development by creating new education and teaching methods. So, educational reform projects quickly developed their education systems per the requirements of artificial intelligence (Tuomi, 2018).

This change in higher education is fueled by continuously integrating new tools, platforms, and methodologies that enrich the learning experience. One of the most promising developments in this area is incorporating artificial intelligence (AI) into educational practices, particularly in personalized learning. Personalized learning, which tailors educational experiences to meet the unique needs, preferences, and abilities of individual learners, has long been a goal of educators. However, several factors have made scaling individualized learning approaches in traditional educational settings challenging. Large class sizes and the need for expert involvement make personalization expensive and logistically tricky (Saarinen et al., 2018). With the advent of AI, the possibility of providing genuinely personalized learning experiences has moved from theory to practice, offering practical solutions to these challenges. This reassurance of practical solutions should instill confidence in educators and administrators about the potential of AI in enriching the learning experience.

AI's remarkable adaptability to analyze vast amounts of data and cater to the learning needs of individual students is a reassuring sign of its potential in the education sector. By leveraging adaptive algorithms, machine learning, and data analytics, AI can create dynamic learning environments that adjust content, pacing, and assessment strategies in real-time based on learner data. This personalized approach caters to students' academic needs and considers their learning preferences, motivations, and challenges, allowing for a more engaging and practical learning experience.

Traditional teaching methods often struggle to cater to the diverse needs of students. AI-driven personalization, as demonstrated by Jiao (2024), can significantly enhance accessibility and inclusivity in education. However, it's crucial to address the pressing issues of data privacy concerns and educator training, as highlighted by Inman et al. (2024). Despite these challenges, AI has the potential to revolutionize higher education, making it more responsive to individual student needs in the digital age. This potential is not just a promising prospect, but a future we can eagerly anticipate in the field of education.

THEORETICAL FOUNDATIONS OF PERSONALIZED LEARNING

Personalized education, a concept deeply rooted in educational theory for centuries, stands in stark contrast to the 'one-size-fits-all' approach of traditional education models. From early one-on-one tutoring to the modern practice of differentiated instruction in the classroom, educators have consistently recognized the value of tailoring learning experiences to individual students. This contrast underscores the urgent need for personalized learning to meet the diverse needs of today's learners and its potential to improve academic outcomes and motivation (Inthanon & Wised, 2024).

The principles of personalized learning, firmly rooted in constructivism, differentiated instruction, and learner-centered pedagogy, are remarkably adaptable. Constructivist theory, championed by scholars like Jean Piaget and Lev Vygotsky, emphasizes the value of active, hands-on learning, motivating educators to create engaging learning environments. It encourages students to construct their understanding through interaction with the environment and others. Differentiated instruction, on the other hand, is about tailoring teaching methods to give students a sense of agency, autonomy, and choice in their learning journey.

AI is crucial in advancing personalized learning methodologies. It provides tools to analyze student data in real-time, but more importantly, it can identify learning gaps. This is a key role of AI, as it allows for the delivery of customized content and interventions. AI-powered systems can track student progress, assess their strengths and weaknesses, and adjust the learning experience accordingly. This dynamic, data-driven approach has the potential to revolutionize traditional educational settings, offering educators, administrators, and policymakers an exciting glimpse into the future of education.

APPLICATIONS FOR AI IN PERSONALIZED EDUCATION

AI has already begun to make significant strides in personalized education by developing adaptive learning platforms, intelligent tutoring systems, and AI-powered tools for differentiated instruction and assessment. These technologies provide learners with a more tailored educational experience, adapting content and pacing and assessing their needs.

Adaptive learning platforms (ALPs) powered by AI algorithms are reshaping education by personalizing learning experiences and enhancing student outcomes (Dutta et al., 2024). These platforms, such as DreamBox Learning, Smart Sparrow, and Knewton, analyze student performance to tailor content difficulty, pace, and delivery methods (Altaleb et al., 2023). They are highly adaptable, analyzing data from student interactions and providing real-time feedback, ensuring that students are always learning at the right level. For example, if a student finds a concept challenging, the system will offer additional practice or alternative explanations to help them master the material. Conversely, if students show proficiency, the platform will introduce more advanced content to keep them engaged and challenged, thereby maintaining their interest and motivation.

Intelligent Tutoring Systems (ITS) are revolutionizing education by providing personalized learning experiences through AI integration (Alshaikh & Hewahi, 2021). These systems utilize advanced algorithms like data mining and Bayesian networks to dynamically adjust content to individual student needs, improving learning effectiveness and engagement. Recent advancements in generative AI and language models have enhanced ITS capabilities in content generation, real-time feedback, and adaptive learning pathways (Maity & Deroy, 2024). ITS research has leveraged and pushed AI boundaries, emphasizing the collaborative nature of humans and machines in addressing non-scalable educational challenges (Kokku et al., 2018). Key applications include automated question generation, customized feedback mechanisms, and interactive dialogue systems (Maity & Deroy, 2024). While ITS shows promise in improving knowledge retention and reducing dropout rates, challenges remain in ensuring pedagogical accuracy, mitigating AI biases, and maintaining learner engagement (Cairo & Echavarría, 2023).

AI-powered tools, including adaptive learning platforms, intelligent tutoring systems, and predictive analytics, are efficient in automating administrative tasks, thereby relieving educators from routine work. These tools go beyond automation and tailor instruction to individual student needs, creating a more personalized learning experience. This not only improves academic outcomes but also helps in bridging learning gaps (Dumbuya, 2024; NY et al., 2024). By analyzing student performance data, these technologies can adjust content, pacing, and assessment methods, creating more engaging and interactive learning environments (Arya & Verma, 2024). In the field of educational measurement and assessment, AI tools can significantly enhance accuracy and efficiency, from test development to scoring and result interpretation (Owan et al., 2023). While AI presents numerous benefits, it also poses challenges such as data privacy, algorithmic bias, and equitable access. Addressing these challenges is crucial to ensure the effective and ethical implementation of AI in diverse educational settings (N Y et al., 2024; Owan et al., 2023).

BENEFITS OF AI-DRIVEN PERSONALIZATION

Integrating AI into personalized learning is a game-changer, significantly enhancing learner engagement and motivation. This is particularly beneficial in online and workplace learning environments. When powered by AI, online collaborative activities and digital technologies can revolutionize learner motivation and classroom engagement in language learning (Jeong, 2019).

When students feel that the content is relevant to their lives and that they are progressing at their own pace, they are more likely to take ownership of their learning and persist through challenges. For example, gamification techniques, such as incorporating game mechanics and dynamics, can address interaction, challenge, and context issues in e-learning, thereby increasing learner engagement (Al-Smadi, 2015). Awakening students' curiosity through diverse content presentation and implementing equalitarian motivational systems can significantly improve engagement and retention in e-learning and blended learning projects, making students feel more supported and encouraged (Priego & Peralta, 2013).

AI-driven personalization, a potent tool in enhancing student performance, leads to improved learning outcomes. By providing targeted interventions and adjusting the learning experience to suit individual needs, AI can help students master concepts more effectively. Research has shown that personalized learning approaches lead to better knowledge retention, higher test scores, and improved academic performance. Several studies have examined the effectiveness of adaptive learning platforms compared to traditional instruction methods. Eau et al. (2021) found that higher-performing students benefited most from adaptive learning tools. Hurlen (n.d.) noted increased overall student performance, class averages, and number of A grades when combining adaptive courseware with an inverted classroom approach. Despite some mixed results, these studies generally indicate improved student performance with adaptive learning platforms compared to traditional instruction methods.

AI-driven personalization in education offers significant benefits by adapting to diverse learning styles and needs. It leverages technologies like adaptive learning platforms, intelligent tutoring systems, and data analytics to tailor instruction to individual students (Katiyar et al., 2024; Salameh, 2024). This approach enhances learning outcomes, engagement, and academic performance by aligning materials with students' interests and paces (Di Jiao, 2024). However, challenges such as algorithmic bias and privacy concerns must be addressed. Integrating AI in education requires a balanced approach, combining technological tools with human-centered teaching practices to maximize effectiveness (Salameh, 2024). Educators play a crucial role in leveraging AI responsibly. Their professional development is not just important, but integral to this process, ensuring ethical and practical implementation (Salameh, 2024; Katiyar et al., 2024).

CHALLENGES AND ETHICAL CONSIDERATIONS

Despite its many benefits, the integration of AI into personalized learning also presents several challenges and ethical considerations. Data privacy and security are paramount concerns in the integration of AI in education. As AI systems require extensive student data, there are significant risks of breaches and misuse (Farooqi et al., 2024; Jose, 2024). Ethical challenges include algorithmic bias, which may lead to discriminatory decisions and exacerbate educational inequalities (Farooqi et al., 2024; Weber, 2020). The widespread use of AI in education has raised public concern about AI ethics, particularly regarding student data privacy (Huang, 2023). To address these issues, researchers propose developing ethical frameworks, legal guidelines, and strategies to safeguard data integrity and confidentiality (Jose, 2024; Weber, 2020). Educators play a crucial role in supporting AI integration through extensive training, and their needs should be a priority in the development of ethical frameworks and guidelines. Continuous research and policy-making are also necessary to maximize benefits while minimizing drawbacks in educational settings (Farooqi et al., 2024; Weber, 2020).

Challenges persist, including the digital divide, which may exacerbate existing educational inequities (Elam, 2024). By addressing these concerns, AI can potentially bridge educational gaps and contribute to a more inclusive learning environment globally (Supramaniam et al., 2024). However, while AI has the potential to revolutionize education, not all students have equal access to the technology required to benefit from AI-driven personalized learning. Students in low-income or rural areas may lack access to high-speed internet, devices, or other necessary resources, which could aggravate existing educational inequalities. To address these issues, policymakers and educators must work to ensure equitable access to technology. It is equally important to provide support for students who may be disadvantaged by the digital divide, showing empathy and understanding of the challenges they face. As AI continues to evolve, its potential to transform education and empower learners will only expand, making it an essential tool for the future of education.

THEORETICAL FOUNDATIONS OF PERSONALIZED LEARNING

The shift from teacher-centered to learner-centered education is a key aspect of personalized learning. It emphasizes active student participation and tailored learning experiences (McLoughlin, 2013). In contrast to teacher directed curricula, personal learning environments (PLE's) are learner-centric, providing relevant and timely learning opportunities by enabling individuals, including educators, instructional designers, and education policy makers, to select, integrate and construct knowledge using various software, services and options based on their needs and circumstance. This approach ideally leads to a model where learner needs drive the learning process. In PLEs, teacher pedagogy undergoes a radical shift to allow learners to make decisions that best suit their goals and needs for acquisition of skills, knowledge creation, social interaction and collaboration.

Keppell (2014) defines personalized learning as a framework that encompasses six key concepts: digital citizenship, seamless learning, learner engagement, learning-oriented assessment, lifelong and life-wide learning, and desire paths. Teachers play a pivotal role in guiding learners to design their own personalized learning journey, a process that spans formal education and encourages learners to become self-directed learners throughout their lives. The integration of digital tools in education can significantly enhance personalized learning by catering to individual student needs, fostering collaboration between teachers and technology, and promoting strong student engagement (Silalahi et al., 2024). The strategies of personalized learning, as outlined by Keppell (2014), encompass digital citizenship, seamless learning, learner engagement, learning-oriented assessment, and lifelong learning.

Key Strategies

1. *Learner Agency:* One of the foundational principles of personalized learning is the emphasis on learner agency. Learner agency refers to the ability of students to take control of their own learning process. This includes making decisions about what they learn, how they learn, and at what pace they progress. Personalized learning encourages students to set their own goals, monitor their progress, and engage in self-directed learning. This autonomy fosters a sense of ownership over their educational journey, which can increase motivation and persistence.
2. *Adaptability*: Adaptability is another core principle of personalized learning. In a personalized learning environment, the content, pace, and instructional strategies are not fixed. Instead, they are adjusted based on the learner's progress, needs, and preferences. For example, if a student excels in a particular area, the system might provide more advanced content to challenge them further. Conversely, if a student is struggling, the system can offer additional resources or modify the learning path to provide more support. This adaptability ensures that students are always learning at an appropriate level of difficulty, which helps maintain engagement and prevents frustration or boredom.
3. *Continuous Feedback*: Personalized learning also emphasizes the importance of continuous feedback. In traditional education models, feedback is often given at the end of a unit or assignment, which can be too late to address issues or reinforce learning. In a personalized learning environment, feedback is provided in real time, allowing students to understand their progress and make adjustments as needed. This ongoing feedback loop helps students stay on track and ensures that they are constantly moving toward mastery of the material. Teachers can use feedback to identify areas where students need additional support and provide targeted interventions.
4. *Differentiation*: Personalized learning recognizes that students have different learning styles, preferences, and needs. Differentiation is the practice of adjusting the content, process, and product of learning to accommodate these differences. For example, some students may learn best through visual aids, while others may prefer hands-on activities or verbal explanations. Personalized learning allows for the customization of instructional strategies to align with

these preferences, ensuring that all students can access the material in a way that suits their individual learning styles.

5. *Competency-Based Learning*: In a personalized learning environment, students' progress based on their mastery of the content rather than the amount of time spent in class. This approach is often referred to as competency-based learning. Rather than moving on to the next unit or concept after a set amount of time, students advance when they have demonstrated mastery of the current material. This allows for a more flexible pace, as students who grasp the material quickly can move ahead, while those who need more time can receive additional support and practice without feeling rushed.
6. *Data-Driven Instruction*: Personalized learning is heavily reliant on data to inform instructional decisions. Teachers and educational systems collect data on student performance, preferences, and behaviors to tailor the learning experience. This data can come from a variety of sources, including assessments, surveys, and student interactions with digital learning platforms. By analyzing this data, educators can identify patterns, track progress, and make informed decisions about how to best support each student. This data-driven approach ensures that the learning experience is responsive to the individual's needs.

While the definition and essential components of personalized learning are still evolving, practitioners and policymakers are adapting these principles to their specific contexts to address long-standing challenges in education systems (Pane, 2018). Pane posits that there needs to be collaboration between teachers and technology and a strong student engagement must be fostered-beyond mere compliance. By recognizing and responding to the unique needs of each learner, personalized learning aims to create more engaging and effective educational experiences, underscoring the urgency and significance of student engagement in this process.

ROLE OF AI IN ADVANCING PERSONALIZED LEARNING METHODOLOGIES

Artificial intelligence is revolutionizing personalized education by analyzing vast amounts of learner data to provide tailored experiences and real-time feedback (Taşkın, 2024). AI-driven technologies, including adaptive learning platforms and intelligent tutoring systems, can identify individual learning patterns, predict student performance, and recommend customized materials (N C et al., 2023). These systems stand out for their ability to continuously monitor student progress, adapting content delivery to address weaknesses and improve learning outcomes (Akavova et al., 2023). The integration of AI in education has shown improvements in student engagement, retention rates, and academic achievement (Reddy, 2014). However, ethical considerations such as data privacy, algorithmic bias, and the balance between human and machine-driven instruction must be addressed. Despite challenges, AI has the potential to create more effective, inclusive, and sustainable learning environments (Taşkın, 2024). One of the key challenges of personalized education has been its scalability. Traditional methods of individualized instruction, such as one-on-one tutoring, are resource-intensive and difficult to implement on a large scale. AI, however, has the potential to make personalized learning scalable by automating many of the processes involved in data collection, analysis, and content delivery. AI-powered platforms can deliver personalized learning experiences to large numbers of students simultaneously, making it possible to provide individualized instruction to every learner, regardless of class size or geographic location. ITS platforms are available 24/7, allowing students to access tutoring support whenever they need it. This is particularly valuable in online learning environments, where students may not have access to in-person tutoring or may require additional help outside of regular class hours.

Adaptive learning platforms (ALPs) and intelligent tutoring systems (ITS) are driving a revolution in personalized education, thanks to AI-driven technologies. ALPs like Carnegie Learning and DreamBox Learning are not just tailoring content and providing personalized feedback but also enhancing student engagement and addressing achievement gaps (Dutta et al., 2024). ITS, powered by generative AI and large language models, are offering dynamic content generation, and importantly, real-time feedback, providing immediate and effective support to learners (Maity & Deroy, 2024). These systems are not just analyzing learner performance but also identifying areas for improvement and providing targeted interventions (Akavova et al., 2023).

The ability of adaptive learning platforms to adjust content and pacing based on individual performance has a significant impact on student engagement and success. Research has consistently demonstrated that adaptive learning systems can significantly improve educational outcomes. These systems utilize AI and data analytics to personalize learning paths, enhancing student engagement and performance (Asmara, 2024; Hakim et al., 2024). Studies have shown substantial improvements in test scores, with one reporting an increase from 68.4 to 82.7 in post-assessment scores (Sari et al., 2024). Adaptive learning technologies also lead to higher course completion rates and increased student satisfaction compared to traditional methods (Hakim et al., 2024; Sari et al., 2024). Successful implementation requires addressing challenges such as institutional readiness, educator training, and infrastructural needs (Sari et al., 2024). It's crucial to be aware of these challenges and prepare for them, as they can significantly impact the effectiveness of adaptive learning. Despite these challenges, the evidence strongly supports the potential of adaptive learning to create more effective and inclusive educational environments.

AI-POWERED TOOLS FOR DIFFERENTIATED INSTRUCTION AND ASSESSMENT

Differentiating Instruction with AI

Recent research explores the integration of Artificial Intelligence (AI) in differentiated instruction and indicate that AI-based tools can improve student engagement and tailor content to individual needs (Damyanov, 2024). The development of context-aware AI engines, such as Brainy, demonstrates the capacity to generate personalized course materials and assessments, adapting to learners' styles and progression (Nahas et al., 2024). Brainy generates personalized course materials and assessments tailored to individual learner needs, in addition to offering multiple learning path. By considering learning objectives, prior knowledge, and learner proficiency levels, Brainy promotes equity in education. It refines content and learning activities, adjusts to accommodate each learner's learning style and progression and offers feedback on assessments using a supportive educational approach, including clear explanations and analogies that address individual learning needs (Nahas, et al., 2024).

Mathan and Yeung (2015), posit that students may founder with inadequate feedback, or have incorrect or superficial strategies reinforced in the absence of corrective feedback and guidance. These challenges point to the need for diagnostic techniques that are (1) tied to problem solving — capable of interpreting and assessing individual actions in the context of relatively unconstrained problem-solving activities. For example, writing a computer program, flying a scenario in a fight training simulator); (2) automated — reducing the need for manual intervention; (3) objective — minimizing confounds stemming from subjective biases; and (4) fine-grained — providing feedback at the level of individual problem-solving actions, as opposed to problem-solving outcome alone (p. 52).

The micro-organization of instruction through AI can complement human teachers, leading to significant improvements in retention (Mozer et al., 2019). An AI-powered learning management system (LMS) might analyze a student's performance to help identify patterns that may not be immediately apparent. The provision of data-driven insights by AI is crucial in enabling a deeper understanding of learning, so instructors could prompt an adjustment in their instructional approach to better support the students' development in areas where they are struggling

Customized Assessments with AI

AI-powered adaptive assessments can dynamically tailor the test-taking experience, providing personalized feedback and learning pathways (Yuldashev et al., 2024). These systems leverage machine learning algorithms to analyze real-time student responses and learning patterns (Mahamuni et al., 2024). Generative AI offers opportunities to maximize learner engagement and performance in personalized assessments, though challenges regarding validity, reliability, and fairness must be addressed (Arslan et al., 2024). In computerized adaptive testing, AI techniques are being employed to estimate latent traits, generate questions, and improve question selection, particularly for multi-dimensional traits and categorical responses (Mujtaba & Mahapatra, 2020). Customized assessments have the potential to significantly enhance assessment accuracy, efficiency, and personalization in education.

AI assessment tools, with their adaptive testing, automated grading, and real-time feedback, have the potential to significantly improve overall educational outcomes. They can evaluate higher-order competencies like critical thinking and creativity, while fostering individualized learning paths. These tools can transform educational assessment, supporting diverse learner needs and addressing the limitations of traditional assessment methods (Owan et al., 2023).

CASE STUDIES HIGHLIGHTING SUCCESSFUL IMPLEMENTATIONS

To illustrate the effectiveness of AI-powered personalized learning, examining case studies from different educational contexts, including K-12, higher education, and corporate training environments, is helpful. These case studies highlight the successes and challenges of implementing AI-driven personalized education.

K-12 Education: The Use of AI in Personalized Learning

In K-12 education, AI-powered personalized learning platforms are making a significant difference by bridging achievement gaps and providing tailored support for individual students. One notable example is DreamBox Learning, an adaptive learning platform for mathematics. DreamBox's AI capabilities enable it to analyze student performance and adjust the difficulty and pacing of lessons based on individual progress, providing a personalized learning experience. Recent studies have examined the effectiveness of computer-assisted math instruction in elementary schools. Foster (2023) found that DreamBox Learning showed promising results for improving numeracy and geometry skills in kindergarten and first-grade students. Similarly, Lenard & Rhea (2018) reported that DreamBox implementation led to gains in early elementary math skills, although it did not significantly impact state test scores. These findings highlight the individualized support provided by adaptive online math programs, making a personal impact on students and their learning journey.

Higher Education: AI in Adaptive Learning for College Students

In higher education, AI-powered tools like McGraw-Hill's ALEKS are playing a crucial role in enhancing the learning experience for college students. ALEKS, an adaptive learning platform, uses AI to assess students' knowledge and provide a personalized learning path based on their strengths and weaknesses. The platform's unique ability to provide personalized feedback and adjust content based on student performance has significantly improved the learning process, making it an indispensable tool in higher education.

Mojarad et al. (2018) observed higher pass rates for community college students using ALEKS compared to non-ALEKS users, with a 19-percentage point difference when using propensity score matching. The evidence suggests that ALEKS can be an effective tool for improving math performance in various educational settings.

Corporate Training: AI in Professional Development

AI-driven personalized learning systems are revolutionizing education and employee training across various sectors. IBM's Watson Talent platform exemplifies this trend, utilizing AI to deliver customized learning experiences (Zhang, 2024). These systems employ natural language processing and machine learning to assess student performance, analyze individual interests, and provide tailored content based on mastery. AI technologies can create immersive virtual reality training environments, potentially reducing costs associated with traditional expert-led training methods (Suttor et al., 2019).

AI-powered digital assistants in VR training have shown potential to improve user engagement and reduce authoring effort (Giussani et al., 2024). In military applications, AI-assisted VR systems have been developed for ground soldier training, incorporating virtual humans and drone simulations (Gluck et al., 2020). The integration of AI with VR and augmented reality (AR) technologies has demonstrated benefits in diverse fields, including STEM, medicine, and language acquisition, enhancing students' motivation and comprehension (Sharki et al., 2024). While challenges such as equipment costs and content creation exist, collaborative efforts between technology providers, educators, and content creators can help overcome these obstacles, paving the way for more widespread adoption of AI-powered immersive training solutions.

SUPPORT FOR STUDENTS WITH EXCEPTIONALITIES

Supporting Students with Disabilities

AI-powered personalized learning is a crucial tool in leveling the playing field for students with disabilities. For students with learning disabilities, such as dyslexia or ADHD, AI systems can provide tailored interventions that address their specific needs. For example, AI platforms can offer text-to-speech features for students with dyslexia or provide additional time for students with ADHD to complete tasks. These personalized interventions are not just about equal access to educational opportunities, but they also foster empathy and understanding among students, educators, and policymakers.

Recent research is uncovering the potential of AI to significantly enhance accessibility and inclusivity for students with disabilities in higher education. AI-driven solutions such as assistive technologies, adaptive learning systems, and virtual assistants are instrumental in creating personalized learning paths and improving access to educational resources (Mitre & Zeneli, 2024). The transformative impact of AI techniques like brain-computer interfaces and computer vision on assistive technologies is enabling individuals with physical disabilities to achieve greater independence (Pancholi et al., 2023). Importantly, by providing these opportunities, AI-powered personalized learning systems are playing a crucial role in creating a more inclusive learning environment for all students.

THE ETHICAL IMPLICATIONS OF DATA PRIVACY

The use of student data in AI-powered learning systems raises critical questions about who owns the data, how it is collected, and how it is used. Student data can include sensitive information such as academic performance, behavioral patterns, personal preferences, and even health-related data. The implementation of AI in education presents challenges, including privacy concerns, ethical considerations, and the risk of over-reliance on technology (Kaledio et al., 2024; Aper, 2024). While AI can offer valuable tools for data analysis, problem-solving, and supplemental applications in educational processes, it's the responsibility of institutional leaders to ensure a comprehensive and discerning approach to AI integration. This approach is crucial to maximize its benefits while mitigating risks, ultimately fostering a more adaptable, efficient, and inclusive educational landscape (Davis et al., 2024).

While AI offers opportunities for personalized learning and improved administrative efficiency, it raises concerns about data security and potential misuse (Abimbola et al., 2024). Key ethical issues include privacy breaches, security risks, power asymmetries, equity concerns, and machine accountability (Weber, 2020). To address these challenges, researchers advocate for comprehensive strategies and ethical frameworks to harness AI's benefits while mitigating risks, emphasizing the need for transparency in AI systems, teacher development, and regulated AI-generated content (Al-Zahrani, 2024).

RECOMMENDATIONS FOR EDUCATORS AND INSTITUTIONS TO INTEGRATE AI EFFECTIVELY

As AI technologies continue to develop, it is essential for educators and institutions to adopt them thoughtfully and strategically. Integrating AI into personalized learning systems requires careful planning and consideration to ensure that these tools enhance the educational experience while maintaining pedagogical integrity (MacMartin, 2024). Institutions should not only adopt AI but also develop comprehensive policies that promote academic honesty and ethical AI use (Rane et al., 2024). These policies will provide a secure framework for AI integration, ensuring that educators feel supported in their efforts. By balancing the benefits and risks, AI can be effectively integrated into education to enhance learning outcomes while upholding academic standards.

Start Small and Scale Gradually

Implementation of AI-driven personalized learning has been associated with improved student engagement, retention rates, and academic achievement (Sharma et al., 2024). Educators and institutions should first begin by piloting AI-driven personalized learning tools in small-scale settings. This allows for the testing of the effectiveness of the tools, gather feedback from students and instructors, and make necessary adjustments before implementing them on a larger scale. Starting small also allows educators to assess the impact of AI on student engagement, motivation, and learning outcomes, ensuring that the technology aligns with the institution's educational goals.

Provide Professional Development for Educators

Educators require training on AI applications in education, ethical considerations, and effective implementation strategies. By combining AI technologies with human-centered teaching practices, educators can create inclusive and effective learning environments that support critical thinking and accommodate diverse learners (Salameh, 2024; Vorsah & Oppong, 2024). Professional Development programs should focus not only on the technical aspects of AI but also on the pedagogical implications of using AI in the classroom.

Ensure Inclusivity and Equity

As AI technologies are integrated into personalized learning, it is crucial to ensure that all students, regardless of their background or abilities, have access to these tools. Institutions should prioritize inclusivity by selecting AI tools that support diverse learning needs, including those of students with disabilities, English language learners, and students from various cultural backgrounds. AI systems should be designed to be flexible and adaptable, providing personalized learning experiences that cater to the unique needs of each student. Artificial Intelligence (AI) is revolutionizing education through personalized learning, offering tailored experiences that address diverse student needs and enhance academic outcomes (Dumbuya, 2024; Salameh, 2024). AI-driven technologies like adaptive platforms and intelligent tutoring systems can customize content, bridging learning gaps and promoting equity (Roshanaei et al., 2023). These tools analyze individual learning patterns to provide personalized instruction, potentially narrowing educational disparities (Ayeni et al., 2024).

POLICY FRAMEWORKS TO SUPPORT ETHICAL AND INCLUSIVE USE OF AI IN EDUCATION

While AI has the potential to promote equity and inclusion in education, challenges such as the digital divide and algorithmic bias must be addressed (Pawar & Khose, 2024). Ultimately, responsible and ethical AI deployment in education requires ongoing vigilance, interdisciplinary collaboration, and robust policy frameworks to ensure its positive contribution to educational settings (Barnes & Hutson, 2024). The policy frameworks identified below should provide guidance on how AI technologies can be implemented in ways that respect student privacy, promote equity, and ensure transparency.

Data Privacy and Security Regulations

Policies should be put in place to regulate the collection, storage, and use of student data in AI systems. This includes ensuring that students and their families have control over their data, that data is collected only for educational purposes, and that data security measures are implemented to protect sensitive information. Institutions should also be required to comply with data protection laws, such as the Family Educational Rights and Privacy Act (FERPA) in the United States or the General Data Protection Regulation (GDPR) in the European Union.

Ensuring Equity and Access

Recent research highlights the potential of AI to promote inclusive education and support diverse learners. AI tools can personalize learning experiences, enhance accessibility, and address educational disparities (Singh et al., 2024). Researchers advocate for collaboration among developers, educators, and policymakers to create AI technologies that respect diversity and promote educational equity (Lin & Chang, 2024; Lin et al., 2024).

To ensure that AI-driven personalized learning benefits all students, policies should focus on bridging the digital divide and ensuring equitable access to technology. This includes providing students in underserved communities with access to the devices, internet connectivity, and digital literacy training needed to engage with AI-powered learning systems. Policies should also promote the development of AI tools that are inclusive and can support students with diverse learning needs, including those with disabilities or from different cultural backgrounds.

Continuous Monitoring and Evaluation

Policies should include mechanisms for the continuous monitoring and evaluation of AI-powered personalized learning systems. This includes assessing the impact of AI on student outcomes, identifying any unintended consequences, and making adjustments as needed. By establishing a system for ongoing evaluation, institutions can ensure that AI technologies are being used effectively and ethically, and that they continue to meet the evolving needs of students and educators (Shukla, 2024).

Institutions can develop standardized evaluation criteria and processes to streamline oversight and educate stakeholders, as demonstrated by the Implementation Guide created for healthcare settings (Economou-Zavlanos et al., 2023). In educational contexts, ongoing monitoring and evaluation of AI systems are vital, along with institutional regulations, plagiarism detection tools, and ethical AI usage workshops to promote responsible implementation (Mubofu & Kitali, 2024). These approaches contribute to the development of AI technologies that uphold human dignity and societal values.

CONCLUSION

AI-driven personalized learning systems are revolutionizing education by enhancing student engagement, motivation, and learning outcomes. At the core of AI-driven personalized learning is the ability to create learning environments that are more attuned to each student's pace and learning style. These systems create tailored learning experiences that address individual needs and foster deeper connections between students and content (Zaharuddin et al., 2024). AI-enabled personalized recommendations have been shown to significantly improve learning performance and engagement, particularly for students with moderate motivation levels (Huang et al., 2023). AI-powered platforms can adjust content, provide real-time feedback, and offer targeted interventions based on continuous data analysis. By leveraging machine learning algorithms and learning analytics, This personalized approach not only improves retention rates by addressing learning gaps but also enhances teacher effectiveness through real-time feedback and data-driven insights (Nasser, 2024). While challenges such as data privacy and equity remain, the integration of AI in education is transforming traditional teaching paradigms and creating more flexible, student-centered learning environments.

The integration of AI into education is not without its challenges. Concerns around data privacy, algorithmic bias, and the digital divide must be carefully addressed to ensure that AI-driven personalized learning remains equitable and ethical. The increasing reliance on technology also raises questions about the role of human educators and the potential for AI to replace traditional teaching methods.

This chapter explores both the opportunities and limitations of AI in personalized learning, offering a comprehensive analysis of how AI can empower learners, support diverse educational needs, and reshape educational practices. By examining these aspects, it provides a roadmap for navigating the future of personalized learning in an ever-evolving technological landscape.

REFERENCES

Abimbola, E., Chisom, O.N., & Adeniy, I.S. (2024). Integrating AI in education: Opportunities, challenges, and ethical considerations, *Magna Scientia Advanced Research and Reviews, 10*(02), 006–013.

Akavova, A., Temirkhanova, Z., & Lorsanova, A. (2023). Adaptive learning and artificial intelligence in the educational space. *E3S Web of Conferences,* 451. DOI: .DOI: 10.1051/e3sconf/202345106011

Al-Smadi, M. (2015). GAMEDUCATION: Using gamification techniques to engage Learners in online learning. *Communications in Computer and Information Science*, *486*, 85–97. DOI: 10.1007/978-3-319-22017-8_8

Al-Zahrani, A. M. (2024). Unveiling the shadows: Beyond the hype of AI in education. *Heliyon*, *10*(9), 10. DOI: 10.1016/j.heliyon.2024.e30696 PMID: 38737255

Aldosari, S. A. M. (2020). The future of higher education in the light of artificial intelligence transformations. *International Journal of Higher Education*, *9*(3), 145. Advance online publication. DOI: 10.5430/ijhe.v9n3p145

Alshaikh, F., & Hewahi, N. M. (2021). AI and machine learning techniques in the development of intelligent tutoring system: A review. *2021 International Conference on Innovation and Intelligence for Informatics, Computing, and Technologies (3ICT)*, 403-410. DOI: 10.1109/3ICT53449.2021.9582029

Altaleb, H., Mouti, S., & Beegom, S. (2023). Enhancing college education: An AI-driven adaptive learning platform (ALP) for customized course experiences. *9th International Conference on Optimization and Applications (ICOA)*, 1-5. DOI: 10.1109/ICOA58279.2023.10308834

Aper, J. P. (2024). Artificial intelligence and higher education: A brave new world? *The Journal of Educational Thought*, *57*(1). Advance online publication. DOI: 10.55016/ojs/jet.v57i1.79412

Arslan, B., Lehman, B., Tenison, C., Sparks, J. R., López, A. A., Gu, L., & Zapata-Rivera, D. (2024). Opportunities and challenges of using generative AI to personalize educational assessment. *Frontiers in Artificial Intelligence*, *7*, 1460651. Advance online publication. DOI: 10.3389/frai.2024.1460651 PMID: 39434872

Arya, R., & Verma, S. (2024). Role of artificial intelligence in education, *International Journal of Advanced Research in Science. Tongxin Jishu*, *4*(2).

Asmara, A. (2024). Enhancing learning outcomes through adaptive learning systems in education technology, *Global International Journal of Innovative Research.*

Ayeni, O. O., Hamad, N. M., Chisom, O. N., Osawaru, B., & Adewusi, E. (2024). AI in education: A review of personalized learning and educational technology. *GSC Advanced Research and Reviews*, *18*(2), 261–271. DOI: 10.30574/gscarr.2024.18.2.0062

Barnes, E., & Hutson, J. (2024). Navigating the ethical terrain of AI in higher education: Strategies for mitigating bias and promoting fairness. *Forum for Education Studies*, *2*(2), 1229. Advance online publication. DOI: 10.59400/fes.v2i2.1229

Cairo, R. D., & Echavarría, R. Y. (2023). Smart tutors: Improving the quality of higher education through AI. *LatIA*, *1*(8), 8. Advance online publication. DOI: 10.62486/latia20238

Capuano, N., & Caballé, S. (2020). Adaptive learning technologies. *AI Magazine*, *41*(2), 96–98. DOI: 10.1609/aimag.v41i2.5317

Cui, W., Xue, Z., & Thai, K. P. (2018). *Performance comparison of an AI based adaptive in China. Conference Automation Congress*. CAC., DOI: 10.1109/CAC.2018.8623327

Damyanov, K. (2024). Differentiation of educational content through artificial intelligence systems in inclusive education [IJE]. *International Journal of Education.*

Davis, C., Bush, T., & Wood, S. (2024). Artificial intelligence in education: Enhancing learning experiences through personalized adaptation, *International Journal of Cyber and IT Service Management.*

Di Jiao. (2024). AI-driven personalization in higher education: Enhancing learning outcomes through adaptive technologies. *Adult and Higher Education*, *6*(6), 42–46. DOI: 10.23977/aduhe.2024.060607

Dockterman, D. (2018). Insights from 200+ years of personalized learning, *Science of Learning* *3*(15).

Dumbuya, E. (2024). Personalized learning through artificial intelligence: Revolutionizing education, *International Journal of Science and Research Archive*. DOI:.DOI: 10.30574/ijsra.2024.13.2.2487

Dutta, S., Ranjan, S., Mishra, S., Sharma, V., Hewage, P., & Iwendi, C. (2024). Enhancing educational adaptability: A review and analysis of AI-driven adaptive learning platforms. *2024 4th International Conference on Innovative Practices in Technology and Management (ICIPTM)*, 1-5.

Eau, G., Hoodin, D., & Musaddiq, T. (2021). Testing the effects of adaptive learning courseware on student performance: An experimental approach. *Southern Economic Journal*. Advance online publication. DOI: 10/1002/soejj.12547

Economou-Zavlanos, N. J., Bessias, S., Cary, M. P., Bedoya, A., Goldstein, B., Jelovsek, J. E., O'Brien, C. L., Walden, N., Elmore, M., Parrish, A. B., Elengold, S., Lytle, K. S., Balu, S., Lipkin, M. E., Shariff, A. I., Gao, M., Leverenz, D., Henao, R., Ming, D. Y., & Poon, E. (2023). Translating ethical and quality principles for the effective, safe and fair development, deployment and use of artificial intelligence technologies in healthcare. *Journal of the American Medical Informatics Association : JAMIA*. Advance online publication. DOI: 10.1093/jamia/ocad221 PMID: 38031481

Elam, K. M. (2024). Exploring the challenges and future directions of big data and AI in education, *Journal of Artificial Intelligence General Science (JAIGS) ISSN:3006-4023*, *5*(1), 81–93. DOI: 10.60087/jaigs.v1i1.173

Farooqi, M.T., Amanat, I., & Awan, S.M. (2024). Ethical considerations and challenges in the integration of artificial intelligence in education: A systematic review, *Journal of Excellence in Management Sciences.*

Foster, M. E. (2023). Evaluating the impact of supplemental computer-assisted math instruction in elementary school: A conceptual replication. *Journal of Research on Educational Effectiveness, 17*(1), 94–118. DOI: 10.1080/19345747.2023.2174919

Giussani, R., Dozio, N., Rigone, S., Parenzan, L., & Ferrise, F. (2024). Enhancing virtual reality training through artificial intelligence: A case study. *IEEE Computer Graphics and Applications, 44*(6), 13–23. DOI: 10.1109/MCG.2024.3510857 PMID: 40030584

Gluck, A., Chen, J., & Paul, R. (2020). Artificial intelligence assisted virtual reality warfighter training system. *2020 IEEE International Conference on Artificial Intelligence and Virtual Reality (AIVR)*, 386-389. DOI: 10.1109/AIVR50618.2020.00080

Goyal, D. (2024). The future of education: Trends and innovations in teaching and learning. *Global International Research Thoughts, 12*(1), 36–42. DOI: 10.36676/girt.v12.i1.110

Hakim, N., Jastacia, B., & Mansoori, A. (2024). Personalizing learning paths: A study of adaptive learning algorithms and their effects on student outcomes. *Journal Emerging Technologies in Education, 2*(4). Advance online publication. DOI: 10.70177/jete.v2i4.1365

Hasan, G. (2023). Technology and the transformation of educational practices: A future perspective. *International Journal of Economic, Business, Accounting* [IJEBAS]. *Agriculture Management and Sharia Administration, 3*(1), 1596–1603. DOI: 10.54443/ijebas.v3i1.1136

Huang, A. Y., Lu, O. H., & Yang, S. J. (2023). Effects of artificial Intelligence-enabled personalized recommendations on learners' learning engagement, motivation, and outcomes in a flipped classroom. *Computers & Education, 194*, 104684. Advance online publication. DOI: 10.1016/j.compedu.2022.104684

Huang, L. (2023). Ethics of artificial intelligence in education: Student privacy and data protection. *Science Insights Education Frontiers, 16*(2), 2577–2587. DOI: 10.15354/sief.23.re202

Hurlen, E. (2022). A multi-year comparison of student performance in an adaptive and inverted classroom versus a traditional learning environment. *ASEE Annual Conference & Exposition Proceedings*. DOI: 10.18260/1-2--40528

Iman, M. Z., Asis, A. A., & Rahma, A. U. Z. (2024). Enhancing personalized learning: The impact of artificial intelligence in education. *Edu Spectrum: Journal of Multidimensional Education, 1*(2), 101–112. DOI: 10.70063/eduspectrum.v1i2.55

Inthanon, W., & Wised, S. (2024). Tailoring education: A comprehensive review of personalized learning approaches based on individual strengths, needs, skills, and interests, *Journal of Education and Learning Reviews.*

Jeong, K. (2019). Online collaborative language learning for enhancing learner motivation and classroom engagement. *International Journal of Contents, 15*, 89–96.

Jiao, D. (2024). AI-driven personalization in higher education: Enhancing learning outcomes through adaptive technologies. *Adult and Higher Education*, *6*(6), 42–46. DOI: 10.23977/aduhe.2024.060607

Jose, D. (2024). Data privacy and security concerns in AI-integrated educational platforms, *Recent trends in Management and Commerce.*

Kaledio, P., Robert, A., & Frank, L. (2024). The impact of artificial intelligence on students' learning experience, SSRN *Electronic Journal.* DOI: 10.2139/ssrn.4716747

Katiyar, N., Awasthi, V. K., Pratap, R., Mishra, K., Shukla, N., Singh, R., & Tiwari, M. (2024). Ai-driven personalized learning systems: Enhancing educational effectiveness, *Educational Administration. Theory into Practice*, *30*(5), 11514–11524. DOI: 10.53555/kuey.v30i5.4961

Kem, D. (2022). Personalized and adaptive learning: Emerging learning platforms in the era of digital and smart learning. *International Journal of Social Science and Human Research*, *5*(2). Advance online publication. DOI: 10.47191/ijsshr/v5-i2-02

Keppell, M. (2014). Personalized learning strategies for higher education, *The Future of Learning and Teaching in Next Generation Learning Spaces.*

Kokku, R., Sundararajan, S. C., Dey, P., Sindhgatta, R., Nitta, S. V., & Sengupta, B. (2018). Augmenting classrooms with AI for personalized education. *2018 IEEE International Conference on Acoustics, Speech and Signal Processing (ICASSP)*, 6976-6980. DOI: 10.1109/ICASSP.2018.8461812

Lenard, M. A., & Rhea, A. (2018). Adaptive math and student achievement: Evidence from a randomized controlled trial of DreamBox Learning. *Discover Education.*

MacMartin, T. (2024). Knowing the ABCs of teaching in an age of AI. *Science Teacher (Normal, Ill.)*, *91*(2), 20–22. DOI: 10.1080/00368555.2024.2312433

Madhu, N. Y., Latha, P. H., & Savithan, H.MADHU N YLATHA P HSAVITHA N. (2024). Revolutionizing education: Harnessing AI for personalized learning pathways and student success. *International Journal For Multidisciplinary Research*, *6*(5), 28371. Advance online publication. DOI: 10.36948/ijfmr.2024.v06i05.28371

Mahamuni, D. A., Parminder, D., & Tonpe, D. S. (2024). Enhancing educational assessment with artificial intelligence: Challenges and opportunities. *2024 International Conference on Knowledge Engineering and Communication Systems (ICKECS)*, *1*, 1-5. DOI: 10.1109/ICKECS61492.2024.10616620

Maity, S., & Deroy, A. (2024). Generative AI and its impact on personalized intelligent tutoring systems, *ArXiv, abs/2410.10650.*

Mathan, S., & Yeung, N. (2015). Extending the diagnostic capabilities of artificial intelligence-based instructional systems. *AI Magazine*, *36*(4), 51–60. DOI: 10.1609/aimag.v36i4.2616

Mitre, X., & Zeneli, M. (2024). Using AI to improve accessibility and inclusivity in higher education for students with disabilities. *2024 21st International Conference on Information Technology Based Higher Education and Training (ITHET)*, 1-8.

Mojarad, S., Essa, A., Mojarad, S., & Baker, R. (2018). Studying adaptive learning efficacy using propensity score matching. *Companion Proceedings 8th International Conference on Learning Analytics & Knowledge.*

Mozer, M. C., Wiseheart, M., & Novikoff, T. P. (2019). Artificial intelligence to support human instruction. *Proceedings of the National Academy of Sciences of the United States of America, 116*(10), 3953–3955. DOI: 10.1073/pnas.1900370116 PMID: 30782820

Mubofu, C., & Kitali, L. (2024). Artificial intelligence in education: Ethics & responsible implementation. *Journal of Interdisciplinary Studies in Education, 13*(2). Advance online publication. DOI: 10.32674/9rjyjp52

Mujtaba, D. F., & Mahapatra, N. R. (2020). Artificial intelligence in computerized adaptive testing. *2020 International Conference on Computational Science and Computational Intelligence (CSCI)*, 649-654. DOI: 10.1109/CSCI51800.2020.00116

N C, A., Kumar, N., M, N., & V, S. (2023). Leveraging artificial intelligence in education: Transforming the learning landscape, *International Research Journal of Computer Science.*

Nahas, E., Diab, P. B., & Atéchian, T. (2024). Brainy: An innovative context-aware generative AI engine for education. *SEACE Official Conference Proceedings*. DOI: 10.22492/issn.2435-5240.2024.42

Nasser, M. (2024). Personalized learning through AI: Enhancing student engagement and teacher effectiveness, *International Journal of Teaching, Learning and Education.*

Natriello, G. (2017). The adaptive learning landscape. *Teachers College Record, 119*(3), 1–46. DOI: 10.1177/016146811711900307

Owan, V. J., Abang, K. B., Idika, D. O., Etta, E. O., & Bassey, B. A. (2023). Exploring the potential of artificial intelligence tools in educational measurement and assessment. *Eurasia Journal of Mathematics, Science and Technology Education, 19*(8), em2307. Advance online publication. DOI: 10.29333/ejmste/13428

Pancholi, S., Wachs, J. P., & Duerstock, B. S. (2023). Use of artificial intelligence techniques to assist individuals with physical disabilities. *Annual Review of Biomedical Engineering*. PMID: 37832939

Pane, J. F. (2018). *Strategies for implementing personalized learning while evidence and resources are underdeveloped.* Rand Corporation. DOI: 10.7249/PE314

Pawar, G., & Khose, J. (2024). Exploring the role of artificial intelligence in enhancing equity and inclusion in education. *International Journal of Innovative Science and Research Technology, 9*(4), 2180–2185. Advance online publication. DOI: 10.38124/ijisrt/IJISRT24APR1939

Pradana, M., Elisa, H. P., & Syarifuddin, S. (2023). Discussing ChatGPT in education: A literature review and bibliometric analysis. *Cogent Education, 10*(2), 2243134. Advance online publication. DOI: 10.1080/2331186X.2023.2243134

Priego, R. G., & Peralta, A. G. (2013). *Engagement factors and motivation in e-learning and blended-learning projects*. Technological Ecosystem for Enhancing Multiculturality. DOI: 10.1145/2536536.2536606

Rane, N.L., Shirke, S.R., Choudhary, S.P., & Rane, J. (2024). Education strategies for promoting academic integrity in the era of artificial intelligence and ChatGPT: Ethical considerations, challenges, policies, and future directions, *Journal of ELT Studies*.

Reddy, T. (2014). AI in education: Personalized learning pathways using machine learning algorithms, *International Journal of Innovations in Engineering Research and Technology*.

Roshanaei, M., Olivares, H., & Lopez, R. R. (2023). Harnessing AI to foster equity in education: Opportunities, challenges, and emerging strategies. *Journal of Intelligent Learning Systems and Applications, 15*(4), 123–143. DOI: 10.4236/jilsa.2023.154009

Saarinen, S.A., Cater, E., & Littman, M.L. (2018). Personalized education at scale, *ArXiv, abs/1809.10025*.

Saidova, K. (2024). Features of individualization and self-development in Western pedagogy, *Acta Education*.

Salameh, W. A.Waleed Abdullatif Khader Salameh. (2024). The dual role of AI in personalized learning: Enhancements and hindrances for diverse learners. *International Journal of Science and Research Archive, 13*(2), 062–067. Advance online publication. DOI: 10.30574/ijsra.2024.13.2.2057

Sari, H. E., Tumanggor, B., & Efron, D. (2024). *Improving educational outcomes through adaptive learning systems using AI, International Transactions on Artificial Intelligence*. ITALIC.

Sharki, J., Balushi, G. A., Maran, P., Ibrahim, M., Jabri, A. A., Palarimath, S., & Balakumar, C. (2024). Incorporating artificial intelligence powered immersive realities to improve learning using virtual reality (VR) and augmented reality (AR) technology. *3rd International Conference on Applied Artificial Intelligence and Computing (ICAAIC)*, 760-765.

Sharma, T., Naik, M. S., Radhakrishnan, S., & Sharma, A. (2024). Personalized learning paths: Adapting education with AI-driven curriculum [EEL]. *European Economic Letters, 14*(1), 31–40. DOI: 10.52783/eel.v14i1.993

Sharma, V. (2024). Unlocking the potential: Harnessing artificial intelligence for enhanced educational practices and addressing ethical concerns. *International Journal of Scientific Development and Research, 9*(4), 492–497.

Shukla, S. (2024). Principles governing ethical development and deployment of AI [IJEBM]. *International Journal of Engineering Business Management, 98*(2), 26–46. DOI: 10.22161/ijebm.8.2.5

Silalahi, J. W., Hidayat, D., & Nathali, C. (2024). *Digital transformation in education to foster personalized learning*. JIIP - Jurnal Ilmiah Ilmu Pendidikan. DOI: 10.54371/jiip.v7i11.6198

Supramaniam, J. K., Baharudin, S. M., Halid, N. M., Abbas, M. S., Amin, M., Ghani, A., Affendy, K., Halim, A., & Nordin, M. N. (2024). Leveraging AI to bridge educational inequities: A global perspective. *Nanotechnology Perceptions*.

Suttor, J., Marin, J., Verbus, E., & Su, Mg. (2019). Implement AI service into VR training. *International Conference on Signal Processing and Machine Learning*.

Taskin, M. (2024). Artificial intelligence in personalized education: Enhancing learning outcomes through adaptive technologies and data-driven insights. *Human-Computer Interaction*, *8*(1).

Tuomi, I. (2018). *The impact of artificial intelligence on learning, teaching, and education*. Policies for the Future.

Vorsah, R. E., & Oppong, F. (2024). *Leveraging AI to enhance active learning strategies in science classrooms: implications for teacher professional development*. World Journal of Advanced Research and Reviews., DOI: 10.30574/wjarr.2024.24.2.3499

Weber, A. S. (2020). Ethics concerns artificial intelligence use in education. *14th International Technology, Education and Development Conference*.

Yuldashev, S., Akramov, M., Tursunova, F., Abdullaeva, K., Shakhmurodova, D., & Ubaydullayev, A. A. (2024). A development of AI connected system with adaptive assessments method for evaluation methods in education field. *2024 4th International Conference on Advance Computing and Innovative Technologies in Engineering (ICACITE)*, 826-830.

Zaharuddin, Yu, C., & Yao, G. (2024). Enhancing student engagement with AI-driven personalized learning systems, *International Transactions on Education Technology (ITEE)*. DOI:.DOI: 10.33050/itee.v3i1.662

Zhang, Q. (2024). Harnessing artificial intelligence for personalized learning pathways: A framework for adaptive education management systems. *Proceedings of the 2nd International Conference on Machine Learning and Automation*. DOI: DOI: 10.54254/2755-2721/82/20241102

Chapter 14
Speech Recognition Tools in Education Enhancing Accessibility

A Elavarasi
https://orcid.org/0009-0004-0463-7372
Velammal College of Engineering and technology, Madurai, India

A Periyanayaki
https://orcid.org/0009-0003-6735-628X
Velammal College of Engineering and Technology, Madurai, India

ABSTRACT

Speech recognition helps students by translating voice-to-text. It is helpful for the person who is disabled or learning impaired. It helps with reading, writing, and learning. It helps visually impaired, physically challenged, or non-native speakers through increased accessibility. It makes classes more inclusive and offers better communication. It helps teachers with individualized comments and saves time. Although helpful, it has to be precise, confidential, and cost-effective for mass application.

INTRODUCTION

In recent years, speech recognition technology has evolved significantly, becoming an integral component of educational technology landscapes. By converting spoken language into machine-readable text, speech recognition enables a wide array of applications that support diverse learners. This technology is particularly beneficial for students with disabilities, including those with hearing impairments, dyslexia, and limited motor skills, as well as for English language learners who require pronunciation assistance and real-time transcription. The convergence of artificial

DOI: 10.4018/979-8-3373-5097-4.ch014

intelligence (AI), machine learning, and natural language processing (NLP) has propelled speech recognition tools to new levels of accuracy and utility.

This chapter aims to provide an overview of speech recognition tools in education, highlighting their applications, benefits, and challenges. The discussion is framed within the context of Universal Design for Learning (UDL), emphasizing how these technologies can foster inclusive learning environments. Case studies drawn from contemporary educational settings illustrate practical uses of speech recognition, while consideration is given to ethical, privacy, and accessibility concerns. Finally, the chapter outlines emerging trends and future directions for integrating speech recognition technologies into education.

BACKGROUND AND LITERATURE REVIEW

Speech recognition technology, also known as automatic speech recognition (ASR), has advanced considerably in recent decades, driven by developments in artificial intelligence (AI), machine learning, and natural language processing (NLP). These systems translate spoken language into text by analyzing audio input and converting it into machine-readable formats. The integration of deep learning architectures has improved the accuracy and flexibility of ASR systems, enabling them to better manage varied accents, speech patterns, and background noise (Hinton et al., 2012).

In educational contexts, ASR has shown promise in supporting learners with diverse needs. For instance, students with disabilities—such as those with visual impairments, mobility challenges, or learning disorders like dyslexia—benefit from ASR tools that facilitate access to spoken content through transcription and voice commands (Al-Azawei, Serenelli, & Lundqvist, 2016). Additionally, learners acquiring English as a second language (ESL) gain from immediate feedback on pronunciation and real-time captioning, which aids comprehension and language development.

The adoption of speech recognition in education aligns with the Universal Design for Learning (UDL) framework, which advocates for flexible learning environments accommodating individual variability (Rose & Meyer, 2002). ASR technologies contribute to multimodal access to content, allowing learners to engage with materials in auditory, visual, and interactive formats (Edyburn, 2010). Recent research highlights how these tools enhance student autonomy, reduce cognitive load, and foster collaborative learning in digital and blended education settings (Sharma, Haider, & Chaudhary, 2020).

THE EVOLUTION OF SPEECH RECOGNITION IN EDUCATION

Speech recognition technology has become a transformative tool in education, enhancing accessibility and learning efficiency. The journey of speech recognition from its early conceptualization to its integration into modern classrooms highlights the profound impact of artificial intelligence (AI) and machine learning. This section explores the historical development of speech recognition, key advancements in AI and machine learning, major milestones in educational applications, and a case study of early adoption.

Historical Development of Speech Recognition Technology

The concept of speech recognition can be traced back to the 1950s when Bell Labs developed the first rudimentary system, the Audrey system, which could recognize digits spoken by a single voice. This early innovation laid the groundwork for future developments in speech technology.

In the 1960s, IBM introduced Shoebox, a machine capable of understanding 16 spoken words. Around the same time, the Harpy system, developed at Carnegie Mellon University in the 1970s, expanded vocabulary recognition to 1,000 words, marking a significant improvement in computational linguistics.

The 1980s and 1990s saw the emergence of Hidden Markov Models (HMMs), which improved speech recognition accuracy by using statistical methods to predict word sequences. IBM's ViaVoice and Dragon's NaturallySpeaking software became commercially available in the late 1990s, introducing speech-to-text technology to the general public.

By the early 2000s, advancements in computing power and data processing led to improved voice recognition accuracy. Google's Voice Search and Apple's Siri, introduced in 2011, leveraged cloud computing to process speech more efficiently, paving the way for more sophisticated educational applications.

Key Advancements in AI and Machine Learning

The integration of AI and machine learning has dramatically enhanced speech recognition technology. Several key advancements have contributed to its evolution: (Dennis, N. K., 2024)

1. Deep Learning and Neural Networks: Modern speech recognition systems employ deep learning models such as Recurrent Neural Networks (RNNs) and Transformer models to improve accuracy and adaptability.
2. Natural Language Processing (NLP): AI-driven NLP algorithms allow speech recognition systems to understand context, detect sentiment, and interpret complex queries.
3. Cloud-Based Speech Recognition: Platforms like Google Speech-to-Text, Microsoft Azure Speech Services, and IBM Watson provide scalable, high-accuracy speech recognition services through cloud computing.
4. End-to-End Speech Recognition Models: These models eliminate traditional pre- processing steps, making speech recognition faster and more efficient for real-time educational applications.
5. Multilingual and Accent Adaptability: Modern AI-driven speech tools now support multiple languages and regional accents, making them more inclusive for global education systems.

Major Milestones in Educational Applications

Speech recognition has been progressively integrated into educational environments, improving accessibility for students with disabilities and enhancing learning experiences. Key milestones include:

1. Real-Time Captioning and Transcription Services: The introduction of real-time transcription tools such as Otter.ai and Live Transcribe has enabled students with hearing impairments to participate in lectures more effectively.
2. Voice-Activated Assistants for Learning: Devices like Amazon Alexa and Google Assistant are being used in classrooms to answer queries, provide study reminders, and support interactive learning.
3. Speech-to-Text for Dyslexic Students: Programs like Dragon NaturallySpeaking assist students with dyslexia and other learning disabilities by enabling them to dictate their thoughts instead of writing them manually.
4. Integration with Learning Management Systems (LMS): AI-powered speech recognition tools are now embedded in LMS platforms like Moodle, Blackboard, and Canvas, facilitating seamless interaction for students and teachers.
5. Automated Language Learning: Speech recognition-based language learning apps, such as Duolingo and Rosetta Stone, have revolutionized the way students acquire new languages by providing pronunciation feedback in real-time. (García-Sánchez, J.-N., Soler-Urzúa, M., & Nussbaum, M., 2020).

Figure 1. Speech recognition tool interface used in educational settings

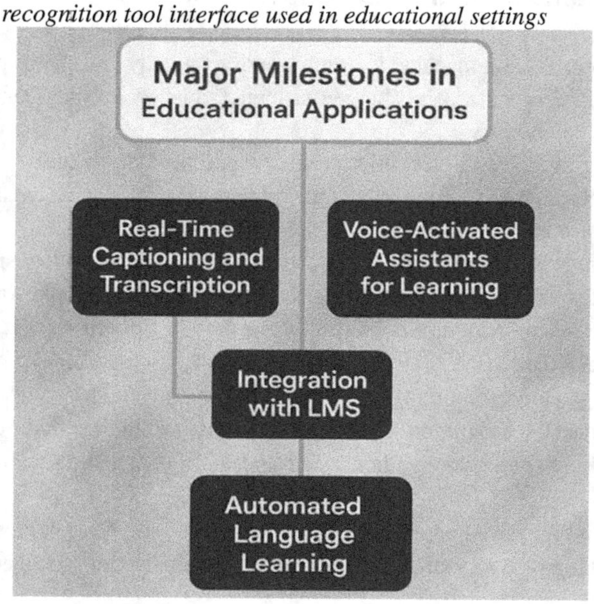

Speech recognition technology has evolved from simple digit recognition systems to sophisticated AI-driven tools that enhance accessibility and learning in education. Key advancements in AI, machine learning, and NLP have made speech recognition more accurate, inclusive, and efficient. With continuous innovation, the integration of speech recognition in education will likely expand, offering even more opportunities for personalized and accessible learning experiences. Rewrite the about content with some research paper content and give reference

HOW SPEECH RECOGNITION IMPROVES ACCESSIBILITY IN EDUCATION

Speech recognition technology has revolutionized accessibility in education, particularly for students with disabilities. This technology enables learners to engage with educational content more effectively, breaking down barriers to communication and comprehension. Speech recognition plays a critical role in language learning, multilingual education, and assisting students with hearing impairments through real-time captioning. Moreover, its personalization and adaptive learning features cater to the diverse needs of students, ensuring a more inclusive educational environment.

Supporting Students with Disabilities

Enhancing Communication for Students with Motor Disabilities

For students with motor impairments, traditional methods of note-taking and writing can be challenging. Speech recognition software allows them to dictate their notes, complete assignments, and even participate in classroom discussions without physical strain. Technologies such as Dragon NaturallySpeaking and Google Speech-to-Text empower these students to maintain independence in their studies.

By enabling hands-free interaction with educational materials, speech recognition fosters engagement and inclusion. AI-driven systems also provide predictive text and error correction, reducing the cognitive load on students with disabilities.

Empowering Students with Learning Disabilities

Students with dyslexia, dysgraphia, and other learning disabilities often struggle with reading and writing. Speech recognition tools convert spoken words into text, assisting them in expressing their ideas more clearly. Applications like Read&Write by Texthelp provide speech-to-text functionality along with text-to-speech features, which allow students to listen to written content, improving their reading comprehension and writing skills. (Gibson, R., 2024)

Moreover, adaptive learning systems powered by AI can modify instructional content based on the learner's needs, offering personalized support that aligns with their learning pace and style.

Figure 2. Architecture of a typical deep learning-based speech recognition system illustrating audio input processing and text output generation.

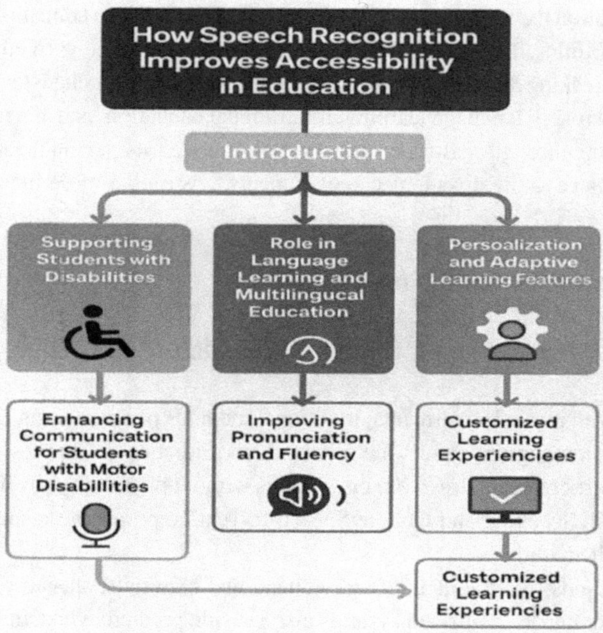

Role in Language Learning and Multilingual Education

Improving Pronunciation and Fluency

Language learners benefit significantly from speech recognition technology, which provides real-time pronunciation feedback. Apps like Rosetta Stone, Duolingo, and Speechling use AI to analyze spoken words, helping students correct their pronunciation and improve fluency. These tools support self-paced learning, allowing students to practice speaking in a non- judgmental environment.

Facilitating Multilingual Education

For students in multilingual classrooms, speech recognition can bridge language barriers by offering instant translation services. Tools like Google Translate and Microsoft Translator enable students to understand lessons delivered in a different language. (Xiao, Y., 2025) Additionally, speech recognition-based learning platforms can customize content to accommodate linguistic diversity, ensuring that all students can access and engage with educational materials effectively.

Assisting Students with Hearing Impairments (Real-Time Captioning)

Enhancing Classroom Accessibility

One of the most significant contributions of speech recognition technology is real-time captioning. This feature allows students with hearing impairments to follow lectures, discussions, and multimedia content without relying on lip-reading or sign language interpreters. Platforms like Google Live Transcribe, Ava, and Otter.ai provide automatic captioning, making classroom interactions more inclusive.

Supporting Online Learning

In virtual classrooms, real-time captioning tools help students with hearing impairments participate in discussions and comprehend lectures. Video conferencing platforms like Zoom, Microsoft Teams, and Google Meet offer built-in live transcription, ensuring accessibility in remote learning environments.

Moreover, captioned educational videos, such as those provided by Khan Academy and Coursera, further enhance comprehension and engagement for students with hearing impairments.

Personalization and Adaptive Learning Features

Customized Learning Experiences

AI-powered speech recognition systems analyze a student's learning patterns and preferences, providing personalized content and feedback. Adaptive learning platforms such as Carnegie Learning and Knewton adjust instructional materials based on the student's proficiency, ensuring an optimized learning experience.

Improving Engagement and Retention

Personalized learning environments foster higher engagement levels by catering to individual strengths and weaknesses. Speech recognition tools, integrated with AI tutors like Siri, Alexa, and Google Assistant, provide interactive learning experiences that reinforce understanding through verbal interaction and practice exercises. Speech recognition technology is a powerful tool that enhances accessibility in education. It supports students with disabilities by facilitating communication, aids language learners through pronunciation feedback and multilingual translation, and assists hearing-impaired students with real-time captioning. Furthermore, its adaptive learning features ensure personalized educational experiences that cater to diverse learning needs. As advancements in AI and machine learning continue, speech recognition will play an even more vital role in creating inclusive and accessible learning environments for all students.

PROGRAMMING LANGUAGES AND TECHNOLOGIES BEHIND SPEECH RECOGNITION

Speech recognition technology has significantly evolved over the years, becoming an integral part of various applications, including virtual assistants, real-time transcription services, and accessibility tools. The development of speech recognition systems relies on robust programming languages, advanced deep learning frameworks, and powerful APIs. This section explores the core programming languages used in speech recognition, key APIs, deep learning frameworks, and the debate between open-source and proprietary solutions.

Overview of Core Programming Languages

1. Python: Python is the most widely used language in speech recognition due to its simplicity, extensive libraries, and strong community support. It provides several frameworks and APIs that facilitate the development of speech recognition models, including:
    - SpeechRecognition: A library that provides an easy interface to various speech APIs.
    - Pyaudio: Used for handling audio input/output streams.
    - Deep learning libraries (TensorFlow, PyTorch): Essential for training speech recognition models.
    - NLTK and spaCy: Used for natural language processing (NLP) and speech analysis.

2.JavaScript: JavaScript plays a critical role in web-based speech recognition applications. It enables real-time speech processing through web browsers using:

- Web Speech API: A built-in API in modern browsers for speech recognition and synthesis.
- TensorFlow.js: Allows the deployment of machine learning models directly in the browser.
- Node.js and Speech APIs: Used for integrating speech recognition into server- side applications.

3.C+–: C++ is commonly used in high-performance speech recognition systems. It offers:

- PortAudio: A cross-platform library for handling audio input and output.
- CMU Sphinx: An open-source speech recognition system written in C++.
- Integration with AI frameworks: C++ is used in performance-critical parts of AI-driven speech models.

Module 1: Speech Recognition with Python

Libraries: speech_recognition, pyaudio, gTTS, pyttsx3 Python provides a rich set of libraries for implementing speech recognition and text-to-speech functionalities. speech_recognition is the most popular library that supports various APIs, including Google Speech Recognition. pyaudio is used to capture audio input from microphones. gTTS allows converting text into speech using Google's online services, while pyttsx3 provides offline text-to-speech support.

Setting up Speech-to-Text Using Python To set up speech-to-text, install the necessary libraries using pip. Initialize a recognizer object and use a microphone as the source. With the Google Speech API or other services like IBM, Sphinx, or Wit.ai, transcribe the audio to text. The transcribed text can be printed, stored, or further processed.

Creating Voice-Activated Note-Taking Tools Voice note-taking apps allow students to speak instead of type. These tools transcribe spoken words into organized notes and can include time-stamps and voice tags. Notes can be categorized by subject or lecture for easy retrieval.

Integrating with AI for Accessibility Apps By integrating natural language processing and machine learning, voice apps can identify intent, answer questions, summarize content, and support students with special needs. For example, a student with dyslexia can dictate an assignment and have it grammatically corrected before submission.

Module 2: Web-Based Speech Interfaces with JavaScript

Introduction to Web Speech API The Web Speech API provides two main features: SpeechRecognition and SpeechSynthesis. These features allow web developers to build applications that can process voice commands and speak text back to the user.

Using SpeechRecognition and SpeechSynthesis SpeechRecognition captures the user's voice and converts it to text in real time. SpeechSynthesis reads text content aloud using built-in browser voices. These features can be triggered by user interaction or automatically on page load.

Real-Time Transcription for Online Classes During online lectures, JavaScript can be used to capture audio input and convert it into text that is displayed as subtitles. This helps students with hearing impairments or language difficulties follow along with the class.

Building Browser-Based Voice Interfaces with JavaScript, it's possible to design educational websites that respond to voice commands. This includes navigating lessons, submitting answers, or accessing resources. Voice interfaces reduce the dependency on keyboard and mouse. Creating Accessible Quizzes and Forms Students can complete quizzes by speaking their answers. Voice feedback can guide them through the process and confirm submissions. These tools improve accessibility for students with physical or cognitive impairments.

Module 3: Speech Applications in C++

Overview of C++ Integration with Speech Recognition C++ offers robust performance for building real-time speech systems. It is often used with system-level APIs or integrated with speech SDKs to develop assistive educational tools.

Using Microsoft Speech API (SAPI) SAPI is a Microsoft library that allows developers to implement both speech recognition and synthesis on Windows systems. Applications can recognize commands, dictate notes, and read out educational content using voices installed in the OS.

Connecting C++ with Google Speech-to-Text API Though Google's API is cloud-based, C++ programs can access it using gRPC or REST APIs. Audio input is streamed to Google's servers, and real-time transcription is returned. This allows integration into desktop learning platforms or embedded systems.

Building Desktop Tools for Visually Impaired Learners Using C++, developers can build lightweight desktop applications that read lessons aloud, navigate textbooks, and allow voice responses. C++ is ideal for offline tools that need to run efficiently on older hardware.

Module 4: Comparative Analysis of Language Suitability

Python vs JavaScript vs C++ for Educational Tools

- Python: Best for quick development and AI integration; ideal for offline and data-rich applications.
- JavaScript: Great for web applications; works seamlessly on all modern browsers.
- C++: High performance; suitable for hardware-based and embedded applications.

Performance, Flexibility, and Integration Support

- Python: Flexible but not ideal for performance-critical systems.
- JavaScript: Easily integrates into existing web platforms.
- C++: Excellent for resource-intensive tasks; difficult to maintain without experience.

Accessibility Features in Each Language

- Python: Rich ecosystem of libraries; perfect for personalized accessibility tools.
- JavaScript: Enables instant interaction and dynamic content rendering.
- C++: Integrates well with hardware and OS-level accessibility features.

Deployment Scenarios (Web, Desktop, Embedded Systems)

- Python: Desktop apps, AI bots, classroom utilities.
- JavaScript: E-learning websites, browser-based apps.
- C++: Standalone apps, offline tools, embedded classroom devices.

Speech Recognition APIs

Several powerful APIs enable developers to integrate speech recognition capabilities into applications without building models from scratch. Some of the most widely used APIs include:

Google Speech-to-Text API

- Supports over 120 languages and variants.
- Provides real-time streaming and batch transcription.
- Uses deep learning models trained on vast datasets.

IBM Watson Speech to Text

- Offers customization options for domain-specific speech models.

- Supports speaker diarization (identifying different speakers in an audio file).
- Features noise-robust transcription for real-world applications.

Microsoft Azure Speech API

- Provides advanced speech-to-text and text-to-speech capabilities.
- Supports speech translation and voice authentication
- Integrates seamlessly with Azure's cloud ecosystem.

Deep Learning Frameworks

The latest advancements in speech recognition are powered by deep learning. Some key frameworks include:

TensorFlow

- Developed by Google, TensorFlow provides powerful tools for building and training speech recognition models. (Dennis, N. K., 2024).
- TensorFlow's DeepSpeech project is widely used in open-source speech recognition research.
- TensorFlow Lite enables speech models on mobile and embedded devices.

PyTorch

- PyTorch is a flexible and efficient deep learning framework favored for speech recognition research.
- It offers tools such as torchaudio, which provides audio processing capabilities.
- Supports end-to-end deep learning models for speech processing.

Open-Source vs. Proprietary Solutions

Open-Source Solutions

- Mozilla DeepSpeech: An open-source speech recognition engine trained on deep learning techniques.
- Kaldi: A powerful toolkit for speech recognition, widely used in academic research and industry.
- CMU Sphinx: One of the earliest open-source speech recognition frameworks, still relevant for certain applications.

Proprietary Solutions

- Google, Microsoft, IBM APIs: Offer high accuracy and cloud integration but come with usage costs.

- Nuance Communications: Specializes in voice recognition software for healthcare and enterprise solutions.
- Amazon Transcribe: Provides high-quality speech-to-text conversion but is restricted within AWS services.

The development of speech recognition technology is driven by powerful programming languages, advanced APIs, and deep learning frameworks. Python, JavaScript, and C++ play crucial roles in building and optimizing speech recognition applications. The choice between open-source and proprietary solutions depends on the specific needs of the project, with open-source providing flexibility and cost savings, while proprietary solutions offer high accuracy and enterprise-grade support. As AI and machine learning continue to evolve, speech recognition will become even more sophisticated, enabling more natural and efficient human-computer interactions.

PRACTICAL APPLICATIONS OF SPEECH RECOGNITION IN EDUCATIONAL SETTINGS

Speech recognition technology has become an integral part of modern education, enhancing accessibility, engagement, and efficiency in learning environments. From real-time transcription to interactive voice-based learning, speech recognition tools are reshaping the way students and educators interact with educational content. This section explores four key applications: classroom transcription and real-time captions, voice-controlled learning management systems, speech-to-text note-taking tools, and gamification with interactive voice-based learning.

Classroom Transcription and Real-Time Captions

Enhancing Accessibility for Hearing-Impaired Students

Real-time captioning provides immediate transcriptions of spoken content, making lectures and discussions accessible to students with hearing impairments. Tools such as Google Live Transcribe, Otter.ai, and Microsoft Teams Live Captions convert spoken words into text in real-time, ensuring that all students can follow along.

Supporting Multilingual Learners

Speech recognition can assist students who are non-native speakers by providing instant translations and captions in their preferred language. (Kumar, L. A., et al.,2022) Google Translates Speech Mode and Microsoft Azure Speech Translation allow learners to access lessons in multiple languages, promoting inclusivity in diverse classrooms.

Transcription for Lecture Review and Study Support

Students can record and transcribe lectures for later review, reducing the need for extensive note-taking. Services like Sonix and Rev.ai provide high-accuracy transcriptions, helping students focus on comprehension rather than writing.

Voice-Controlled Learning Management Systems (LMS)

Hands-Free Navigation and Interaction

Voice-enabled LMS platforms like Moodle, Blackboard, and Canvas integrate speech recognition to enable students and educators to navigate courses, submit assignments, and access resources through voice commands. This hands-free functionality improves accessibility, particularly for students with mobility impairments.

Automated Grading and Feedback

AI-powered speech recognition assists educators by automating grading and providing instant feedback on spoken responses. Google Classroom and Microsoft Azure Speech Services use speech-to-text algorithms to evaluate verbal assignments, streamlining assessment processes.

Personalized Learning with AI Assistants

Voice-controlled assistants like Siri, Alexa, and Google Assistant can integrate with LMS platforms to provide personalized learning experiences, remind students of assignments, and answer academic queries in real-time.

Speech-to-Text Note-Taking Tools

Improving Note-Taking Efficiency

Students can use speech recognition tools to convert lectures, discussions, and study sessions into organized text documents. Applications like Dragon NaturallySpeaking, Evernote, and OneNote Dictate facilitate efficient note-taking, reducing cognitive load for students with learning disabilities. (Nelson, L. M., & Reynolds, T. W., Jr., 2015).

Real-Time Collaboration and Sharing

Cloud-based speech-to-text tools enable students to share transcribed notes with peers, fostering collaborative learning. Google Docs Voice Typing and Otter.ai allow multiple users to access and edit transcriptions, enhancing group study sessions.

Integration with Assistive Technology

For students with disabilities, speech-to-text tools integrate seamlessly with screen readers and text-to-speech applications, providing a multimodal approach to learning.

Gamification and Interactive Voice-Based Learning

Engaging Learning Through Voice-Activated Educational Games

Speech recognition enhances gamified learning experiences by enabling interactive voice commands. Platforms like Kahoot!, Duolingo, and Google's Read Along incorporate voice- based activities to make learning more engaging and effective.

Enhancing Pronunciation and Language Learning

AI-driven speech recognition helps language learners practice pronunciation by providing instant feedback. Applications like Rosetta Stone, Speechling, and ELSA Speak analyze spoken words and suggest corrections, improving language fluency.

Virtual Tutors and AI-Powered Chatbots

AI chatbots powered by speech recognition, such as Socratic by Google and IBM Watson Tutor, provide personalized tutoring sessions. These systems answer student queries, explain complex concepts, and offer interactive quizzes, fostering independent learning.

Speech recognition technology is transforming education by making learning more accessible, efficient, and engaging. Real-time transcription tools, voice-controlled LMS platforms, speech-to-text note-taking applications, and interactive voice-based learning experiences contribute to a more inclusive and interactive learning environment. As AI and speech recognition continue to evolve, their integration into educational settings will further enhance student success and accessibility.

CHALLENGES AND LIMITATIONS OF SPEECH RECOGNITION IN EDUCATION

Speech recognition technology has brought numerous benefits to educational settings, improving accessibility, engagement, and personalized learning. However, despite its advancements, various challenges and limitations hinder its full potential. These challenges include accuracy and recognition issues, privacy and security concerns, biases in AI-driven speech tools, and integration difficulties with existing educational systems.

Accuracy and Recognition Issues

Impact of Accents and Dialects

One of the major limitations of speech recognition systems is their difficulty in accurately recognizing diverse accents and dialects. Many AI-driven speech tools are trained predominantly on standard accents, leading to lower accuracy for non-native speakers or regional dialects. This can create barriers for students from multilingual backgrounds who rely on these tools for learning support.

Background Noise and Environmental Factors

Classroom environments can be noisy, affecting the accuracy of speech recognition tools. Background chatter, ambient noise, and poor microphone quality can lead to misinterpretations or incorrect transcriptions. While noise-canceling technology helps mitigate this issue, it is not always sufficient to ensure accurate speech recognition in dynamic learning environments.

Complexity of Spoken Language

Speech recognition tools often struggle with recognizing contextual variations, homophones, and informal speech patterns. The complexity of spoken language, including slang, abbreviations, and technical jargon, can lead to errors in transcription and automated responses, impacting students' learning experiences.

Privacy and Security Concerns

Data Collection and User Privacy

Speech recognition tools often require continuous access to voice data for processing and improvement. This raises concerns about data collection, storage, and potential misuse. Educational institutions must ensure compliance with data protection laws, such as GDPR and FERPA, to safeguard students' personal and academic data.

Risk of Unauthorized Access and Data Breaches

Since many speech recognition services operate via cloud-based platforms, they are vulnerable to cyber threats and data breaches. Schools and universities must implement strict security measures, such as encryption and multi-factor authentication, to protect student information from unauthorized access.

Lack of User Control Over Data Usage

Students and educators often have limited control over how their voice data is used. Many commercial speech recognition platforms utilize collected data to improve AI models without explicitly informing users, raising ethical concerns about consent and data ownership.

Bias and Inclusivity in AI-Based Speech Tools

Algorithmic Bias in Speech Recognition

AI-powered speech recognition systems have been shown to exhibit biases, particularly against underrepresented demographic groups. Studies have found that these systems often have higher error rates for women, non-native speakers, and individuals from diverse racial backgrounds due to imbalanced training datasets. (Mujtaba, D., Mahapatra, N. R., Arney, M., Yaruss, J. S., Gerlach-Houck, H., Herring, C., & Bin, J., 2024).

Challenges for Students with Speech Impairments

Students with speech disorders, such as stuttering or dysarthria, may face difficulties using speech recognition tools that are not designed to accommodate variations in speech patterns. Ensuring inclusivity requires continuous improvement in AI models to recognize and adapt to diverse speech characteristics.

Ethical Considerations in AI Training

Developers of speech recognition technology must ensure that AI training datasets are diverse and representative. Ethical AI development includes reducing biases, improving recognition accuracy for all users, and maintaining transparency about how AI decisions are made.

Integration with Existing Educational Systems

Technical Challenges in System Compatibility

Many educational institutions rely on legacy systems that may not be compatible with modern speech recognition technology. Integrating AI-driven speech tools with existing Learning Management Systems (LMS) like Moodle, Blackboard, and Canvas requires significant investment in software upgrades and technical support.

Training and Adoption Barriers

Educators and students may require training to effectively use speech recognition tools. Resistance to change, lack of technical expertise, and unfamiliarity with new technologies can slow down adoption rates in educational settings.

Cost and Resource Constraints

Implementing high-quality speech recognition tools can be expensive, particularly for underfunded schools and institutions in developing regions. Subscription-based speech APIs, hardware requirements, and ongoing maintenance costs pose financial challenges for widespread adoption.

While speech recognition technology offers significant benefits in education, challenges related to accuracy, privacy, bias, and system integration must be addressed to maximize its potential. Developers, educators, and policymakers must work together to improve AI models, enhance security protocols, and ensure equitable access to speech recognition tools for all students. By overcoming these limitations, speech recognition can become a more reliable and inclusive asset in modern education.

FUTURE OF SPEECH RECOGNITION IN EDUCATION

Speech recognition technology is rapidly evolving, and its future in education promises even greater advancements in accessibility, engagement, and personalized learning. With the integration of artificial intelligence (AI), augmented and virtual reality (AR/VR), and the metaverse, speech recognition is set to revolutionize modern education. However, these advancements also come with ethical and regulatory considerations that must be addressed. This section explores the future of speech recognition in education, highlighting AI-driven personalization, AR/VR integration, the potential role in metaverse-based learning, and ethical implications.

AI-Driven Personalization and Adaptive Learning

Tailored Learning Experiences

AI-powered speech recognition can analyze student speech patterns, learning habits, and preferences to provide personalized content. Adaptive learning platforms, such as Knewton and Smart Sparrow, use AI to adjust lesson difficulty based on student performance, ensuring individualized learning experiences.

Voice-Activated Intelligent Tutors

AI-driven voice assistants, like Socratic by Google and IBM Watson Tutor, are expected to play a more significant role in guiding students through their studies. These tutors will not only answer questions but also provide explanations, suggest learning resources, and adapt responses to each student's comprehension level.

Multilingual and Inclusive Education

Future speech recognition technology will continue to improve multilingual capabilities, allowing students to learn in their native languages while receiving real-time translations. This advancement will be crucial in breaking down language barriers and fostering global education accessibility.

Integration with Virtual and Augmented Reality

Immersive Learning Environments

Speech recognition, combined with AR/VR, will create more engaging and interactive learning experiences. In subjects like science, history, and language learning, students will be able to interact with 3D models, conduct virtual experiments, or engage in real-world scenarios using voice commands.

Hands-Free Interaction in VR Classrooms

In virtual reality classrooms, speech recognition will enable students to navigate lessons, interact with virtual objects, and communicate with peers and instructors using voice commands. This will be particularly beneficial for students with mobility impairments who may find traditional input methods challenging.

Real-Time Assessment and Feedback:

AI-driven speech recognition in AR/VR will allow teachers to assess students' verbal responses in real time.

Tools like Google Expeditions VR and Microsoft Hololens can be enhanced with speech analytics to evaluate pronunciation, fluency, and comprehension.

Potential Role in Metaverse-Based Education

Virtual Classrooms and AI-Powered Instructors

The metaverse, a digital universe combining virtual reality, augmented reality, and AI, presents new possibilities for education. AI-driven speech recognition will enable virtual classrooms where students can interact with digital instructors and peers through voice commands, creating an immersive and collaborative learning experience.

Voice-Controlled Avatars and Simulations

Students will be able to control their avatars in the metaverse using speech recognition, participating in simulated real-world scenarios. For example, medical students could practice diagnosing patients through AI-powered virtual consultations, while language learners could engage in real-time conversations with virtual native speakers.

Global Access to Quality Education

Metaverse-based education will eliminate geographical barriers, allowing students from different parts of the world to attend virtual lectures, interact with top educators, and access high-quality learning resources through voice-enabled systems.

Ethical and Regulatory Considerations

Data Privacy and Security

As speech recognition technology collects vast amounts of voice data, ensuring student privacy will be a primary concern. Institutions must comply with regulations such as GDPR and FERPA to protect students' speech data from unauthorized access and misuse.

Bias and Fairness in AI

AI-driven speech recognition systems have been shown to exhibit biases, particularly against underrepresented accents and speech patterns. Developers must work towards creating more inclusive datasets to ensure fairness in educational applications.

Transparency and Accountability

Educational institutions and tech developers must establish clear guidelines on how speech recognition AI is used in learning environments. Transparency in AI decision-making processes and accountability for any errors or biases are crucial for ethical deployment.

The future of speech recognition in education is promising, with AI-driven personalization, AR/VR integration, and metaverse-based learning poised to transform how students interact with educational content. However, ethical considerations surrounding privacy, bias, and AI accountability must be addressed to ensure fair and responsible implementation. By balancing innovation with regulation, speech recognition technology can create a more inclusive, efficient, and engaging educational landscape.

APPLICATIONS IN EDUCATION

Speech recognition tools have increasingly found a place in modern educational settings, offering innovative ways to support teaching and learning. These tools convert spoken language into written text, which opens up various applications in the classroom: (Schroeder, M. R., 2004).

Note-Taking Support

Students can use speech-to-text software to automatically transcribe lectures and classroom discussions. This is especially helpful for those who struggle with writing or processing information quickly, allowing them to focus on understanding rather than writing.

Assisting with Writing and Assignments

Speech recognition allows students to dictate their essays, assignments, and responses, making it easier for those with fine motor difficulties or learning challenges like dyslexia to express their ideas fluently.

Language Learning

These tools help language learners practice pronunciation, build vocabulary, and receive immediate feedback. Real-time speech analysis helps students identify and correct errors in their spoken language.

Hands-Free Learning

For students with physical disabilities, speech recognition offers a way to interact with educational content without needing to type or write, promoting independence and participation.

Inclusive Participation in Classrooms

Students who may be shy or have anxiety about speaking in front of others can participate through speech-to-text systems, which transcribe their contributions for sharing in group discussions or online forums.

Assessment and Quizzes

Some educational platforms now integrate voice input for assessments, enabling students to verbally answer questions, which are then transcribed and submitted digitally.

ACCESSIBILITY BENEFITS

The integration of speech recognition tools in education significantly enhances accessibility, helping to create more inclusive learning environments:

Support for Students with Disabilities

- **Physical impairments**: Students with limited hand mobility can use voice commands and dictation to navigate digital content and complete tasks.
- **Learning disorders**: Students with dyslexia, ADHD, or other processing disorders benefit from being able to articulate ideas verbally instead of focusing on spelling and grammar.

Assistance for Visually Impaired Learners

Speech recognition tools reduce dependence on visual interfaces. Students can dictate notes or commands and receive auditory feedback, improving their learning experience.

Language Accessibility for ESL Students

Non-native English speakers can use speech recognition to improve fluency and pronunciation. Some tools offer multilingual support, helping students transition more smoothly into new language environments.

Temporary Accessibility Needs

Students recovering from injuries (e.g., broken arm) or illnesses can still engage in learning through voice-driven tools.

Universal Design for Learning (UDL)

Speech recognition aligns with UDL principles by offering multiple means of expression and engagement. It ensures that diverse learners can access curriculum content in a way that works best for them.

CASE STUDY

The company wanted a solution that could utilize voice AI to reduce response time and improve customer support by integrating to a voice-enabled virtual assistant that could listen to customer queries and respond back to them in real time or route the query to the appropriate agent.

Technology Stack

- Programming Language: Python
- Libraries & Tools:

1. SpeechRecognition – for voice input recognition
2. PyAudio – For streaming microphone input
3. NLTK / spaCy – for NLP (natural language processing)
4. Flask – for serving a web interface
5. gTTS / pyttsx3 – to convert text response into speech
6. Dialogflow API – (optional) for advanced NLP and intent recognition

- **Implementation Steps:**

1. Voice Input Capture:

So I recorded the audio using PyAudio and transcribed it using SpeechRecognition.

Part 1: Text Analysis & Intent Recognition

- Input was cleaned and tokenized using spaCy
- Used basic rule-based matching or hooked into Dialogflow for identifying intents such as:

1. Order status
2. Return request
3. Technical issue
4. FAQ responses

Generating Response:

- Fetched relevant data(e.g., order tracking API or database), based on intent.
- An example of generated text response: ——On Thursday your order will arrive.

Text-to-Speech Response:

- gTTS or pyttsx3 was used for converting response back to voice.

```
from gtts import gTTS
import os
tts = gTTS("Your package will arrive tomorrow.", lang='en')
tts.save("response.mp3")
os.system("start response.mp3")

|
```

Deployment:

- Then I integrated with a web app using Flask so users would be able to talk to the assistant via browser.
- No explicit personality, not enough personality, not the right kind of personality, too much personality.

Results:

- 40%-time reduction in response to customer
- 30% reduction in number of support tickets
- Based on internal feedback surveys improved user satisfaction

Challenges Faced:

- Accents and background noise affected recognition accuracy
- Limited support for multi-language input
- Required constant training for new queries and slang

Future Enhancements:

- Use Google's Cloud Speech-to-Text for multilingual capability
- The training set is used to label data by introducing the concepts of sentiment analysis to identify irate or dissatisfied customers.
- While providing tailored support is by far the most impactful step you can take, it also involves processing immense data that needs to be tested and integrated with a CRM for delivery.

Let's develop a simple speech recognition based virtual assistant step by step in Python. This assistant will:

Listen to your voice

Google Speech Recognition

```
import speech_recognition as sr
import pyttsx3

# Initialize the recognizer and text-to-speech engine
recognizer = sr.Recognizer()
engine = pyttsx3.init()

def speak(text):
    print("Assistant:", text)
    engine.say(text)
    engine.runAndWait()

def get_intent(user_input):
    user_input = user_input.lower()
    if "hello" in user_input or "hi" in user_input:
        return "greet"
    elif "order" in user_input:
        return "order_status"
    elif "bye" in user_input:
        return "goodbye"
    else:
        return "unknown"

def process_intent(intent):
    responses = {
        "greet": "Hello! How can I assist you today?",
        "order_status": "Sure, can you provide your order ID?",
        "goodbye": "Goodbye! Have a great day!",
        "unknown": "I'm sorry, I didn't catch that. Can you repeat?"
    }
    return responses.get(intent, "Sorry, I can't help with that right now.")

def listen_and_respond():
    with sr.Microphone() as source:
        print("Listening...")
```

Respond with simple answer (triggered by keyword) Listen to the reply in text-to-speech

```
        recognizer.adjust_for_ambient_noise(source)
        audio = recognizer.listen(source)

        try:
            user_input = recognizer.recognize_google(audio)
            print("You said:", user_input)
            intent = get_intent(user_input)
            response = process_intent(intent)
            speak(response)

        except sr.UnknownValueError:
            speak("Sorry, I could not understand your voice.")
        except sr.RequestError:
            speak("Network error. Please check your connection.")

# Run the assistant
if __name__ == "__main__":
    while True:
        listen_and_respond()
```

How it Works:

- And listens to your microphone using SpeechRecognition
- Strikes keywords to identify user intent.
- It generates a response and will speak it out using pyttsx3.
- Runs in a loop until you type ——bye.

Requirements:

First of all, install the necessary libraries using pip:

```
pip install SpeechRecognition pyttsx3 pyaudio
```

```
pip install pipwin
pipwin install pyaudio
```

Step 1: We need to Install the Libraries pip install SpeechRecognition pyttsx3 pyaudio (On Windows, you have to install PyAudio with:)

Convert your voice assistant into a Flask web app and include export to CSV for all your voice-to-text conversations.

What We'll Build:

- A simple Flask web app with a page that:
- Lets the user start recording
- def recognizeVoice(): # Converts voice to text using SpeechRecognition
- Responds via text and TTS
- Extracts and logs all conversations (voice → text + response) in a CSV file

Figure 7. Project Structure

```
pgsql

voice_assistant_web/
├── app.py
├── templates/
│   ├── index.html
│   ├── login.html
├── static/
│   └── script.js
├── orders.py
├── users.py  ← hardcoded users
├── conversations_alice.csv
├── conversations_bob.csv
```

Figure 8. Step 1: app.py (Flask App)

```
from flask import Flask, render_template, request, jsonify
import speech_recognition as sr
import pyttsx3
import csv
import datetime
import os

app = Flask(__name__)
recognizer = sr.Recognizer()
tts_engine = pyttsx3.init()
CSV_FILE = "conversations.csv"

def speak(text):
    tts_engine.say(text)
    tts_engine.runAndWait()

def get_intent(user_input):
    user_input = user_input.lower()
    if "hello" in user_input:
        return "greet"
    elif "order" in user_input:
        return "order_status"
    elif "bye" in user_input:
        return "goodbye"
    else:
        return "unknown"

def process_intent(intent):
    responses = {
        "greet": "Hello! How can I help you?",
        "order_status": "Please provide your order ID.",
        "goodbye": "Goodbye!",
        "unknown": "Sorry, I didn't understand that."
    }
    return responses.get(intent)
```

Figure 9. Step 1: app.py (Flask App)

```
def log_to_csv(user_input, response):
    timestamp = datetime.datetime.now().strftime("%Y-%m-%d %H:%M:%S")
    with open(CSV_FILE, "a", newline='', encoding='utf-8') as f:
        writer = csv.writer(f)
        writer.writerow([timestamp, user_input, response])

@app.route("/")
def index():
    return render_template("index.html")

@app.route("/process_audio", methods=["POST"])
def process_audio():
    try:
        audio_file = request.files["audio"]
        audio = sr.AudioFile(audio_file)
        with audio as source:
            audio_data = recognizer.record(source)
            user_text = recognizer.recognize_google(audio_data)

        intent = get_intent(user_text)
        response = process_intent(intent)
        speak(response)
        log_to_csv(user_text, response)

        return jsonify({"user_text": user_text, "response": response})

    except Exception as e:
        return jsonify({"error": str(e)})

if not os.path.exists(CSV_FILE):
    with open(CSV_FILE, "w", newline='', encoding='utf-8') as f:
        writer = csv.writer(f)
        writer.writerow(["Timestamp", "User Input", "Assistant Response"])

if __name__ == "__main__":
    app.run(debug=True)
```

Figure 10. Step 2: templates/index.html

```
<!DOCTYPE html>
<html lang="en">
<head>
    <meta charset="UTF-8">
    <title>Voice Assistant</title>
</head>
<body>
    <h1>Voice Assistant Web App</h1>
    <button id="start">Start Recording</button>
    <p><strong>You said:</strong> <span id="user_text"></span></p>
    <p><strong>Assistant:</strong> <span id="response"></span></p>
    <script src="/static/script.js"></script>
</body>
</html>
```

Figure 11. Step 3: static/script.js

```
const startBtn = document.getElementById("start");

startBtn.onclick = async () => {
    const stream = await navigator.mediaDevices.getUserMedia({ audio: true });
    const mediaRecorder = new MediaRecorder(stream);
    const chunks = [];

    mediaRecorder.ondataavailable = (e) => chunks.push(e.data);
    mediaRecorder.onstop = async () => {
        const blob = new Blob(chunks, { type: "audio/wav" });
        const formData = new FormData();
        formData.append("audio", blob, "input.wav");

        const response = await fetch("/process_audio", {
            method: "POST",
            body: formData,
        });

        const data = await response.json();
        if (data.error) {
            alert("Error: " + data.error);
        } else {
            document.getElementById("user_text").textContent = data.user_text;
            document.getElementById("response").textContent = data.response;
        }
    };

    mediaRecorder.start();
    setTimeout(() => mediaRecorder.stop(), 4000); // Record for 4 seconds
};
```

CSV OUTPUT

```
Timestamp,User Input,Assistant Response
2025-04-09 15:22:30,hello,Hello! How can I help you?
2025-04-09 15:22:35,what about my order,Please provide your order ID.
```

To Run

Install dependencies:

```
pip install flask speechrecognition pyttsx3 Run:
```

```
python app.py
```

Then open http://127.0.0.1:5000 in your browser.

Upgrades

- Download CSV button from the web interface
- Real order ID lookup from a fake in-memory database

Updated Project Structure

```pgsql
voice_assistant_web/
├── app.py
├── templates/
│   └── index.html
├── static/
│   └── script.js
├── conversations.csv
└── orders.py  ← (fake order database)
```

Step 1: Create a Fake Order Database

```
orders.py

fake_orders = {
    "ORD123": "Shipped, expected delivery: April 12",
    "ORD456": "Processing, will ship in 2 days",
    "ORD789": "Delivered on April 5",
}

def get_order_status(order_id):
    return fake_orders.get(order_id.upper(), "Order ID not found.")
```

Step 2: Update app.py to Handle Order IDs

```
Update app.py:

from flask import Flask, render_template, request, jsonify, send_file
import speech_recognition as sr
import pyttsx3
import csv
import datetime
import os
import re
from orders import get_order_status  # ◇

app = Flask(__name__)
recognizer = sr.Recognizer()
tts_engine = pyttsx3.init()
CSV_FILE = "conversations.csv"

def speak(text):
    tts_engine.say(text)
    tts_engine.runAndWait()

def get_intent(user_input):
    user_input = user_input.lower()
    if "hello" in user_input:
        return "greet"
    elif "order" in user_input:
        return "order_status"
    elif "bye" in user_input:
        return "goodbye"
    else:
        return "unknown"

def extract_order_id(text):
    match = re.search(r"ord\d+", text, re.IGNORECASE)
    return match.group(0).upper() if match else None

def process_intent(intent, user_input):
```

```
    if intent == "order_status":
        order_id = extract_order_id(user_input)
        if order_id:
            return get_order_status(order_id)
        return "Please provide a valid order ID like ORD123."

    responses = {
        "greet": "Hello! How can I help you?",
        "goodbye": "Goodbye!",
        "unknown": "Sorry, I didn't understand that."
    }
    return responses.get(intent)

def log_to_csv(user_input, response):
    timestamp = datetime.datetime.now().strftime("%Y-%m-%d %H:%M:%S")
    with open(CSV_FILE, "a", newline='', encoding='utf-8') as f:
        writer = csv.writer(f)
        writer.writerow([timestamp, user_input, response])

@app.route("/")
def index():
    return render_template("index.html")

@app.route("/process_audio", methods=["POST"])
def process_audio():
    try:
        audio_file = request.files["audio"]
        audio = sr.AudioFile(audio_file)
        with audio as source:
            audio_data = recognizer.record(source)
            user_text = recognizer.recognize_google(audio_data)

        intent = get_intent(user_text)
        response = process_intent(intent, user_text)
        speak(response)
```

```
        log_to_csv(user_text, response)

        return jsonify({"user_text": user_text, "response": response})
    except Exception as e:
        return jsonify({"error": str(e)})

@app.route("/download_csv")
def download_csv():
    return send_file(CSV_FILE, as_attachment=True)

if not os.path.exists(CSV_FILE):
    with open(CSV_FILE, "w", newline='', encoding='utf-8') as f:
        writer = csv.writer(f)
        writer.writerow(["Timestamp", "User Input", "Assistant Response"])

if __name__ == "__main__":
    app.run(debug=True)
```

Step 3: Update index.html (Add CSV Download)

```
<!DOCTYPE html>
<html lang="en">
<head>
    <meta charset="UTF-8">
    <title>Voice Assistant</title>
</head>
<body>
    <h1>Voice Assistant Web App</h1>
    <button id="start">Start Recording</button>
    <button onclick="window.location.href='/download_csv'">Download CSV</button>
    <p><strong>You said:</strong> <span id="user_text"></span></p>
    <p><strong>Assistant:</strong> <span id="response"></span></p>
    <script src="/static/script.js"></script>
</body>
</html>
```

Example Use Case

- User: "What is the status of order ORD123?
- Assistant replies: ——Shipped, scheduled delivery: April 12||
- Interaction is logged in CSV.
- It will download it as CSV.

CONCLUSION

The integration of speech recognition technology into educational settings represents a significant advancement in the pursuit of accessible, inclusive, and equitable learning environments. As demonstrated throughout this document, speech recognition tools have become essential components in addressing the diverse needs of students—particularly those who encounter challenges with traditional educational methods due to physical, sensory, cognitive, or linguistic barriers. These tools not only transform the learning experience for marginalized groups but also enhance instructional efficiency and foster a more personalized and engaging approach to education for all learners.

One of the most impactful benefits of speech recognition is its ability to empower students with disabilities. For individuals with motor impairments who may find it difficult or impossible to write or type, speech-to-text technology offers a practical and dignified solution for academic participation. (Junqua, J.-C., & Haton, J.-P., 1996). Voice input systems allow these students to express themselves freely and complete tasks independently, contributing to a sense of self-efficacy and inclusion. Similarly, students with learning differences such as dyslexia, ADHD, or dysgraphia benefit immensely from the removal of mechanical writing constraints. By enabling them to focus on their thoughts and ideas rather than spelling or sentence structure, speech recognition helps these students develop confidence, reduce frustration, and produce higher-quality academic work.

The technology also serves as a lifeline for students with sensory impairments, particularly those with visual or hearing disabilities. Visually impaired learners can utilize voice commands to navigate digital platforms and dictate assignments, reducing reliance on sight- based input methods. On the other hand, real-time captioning and automatic transcription capabilities provided by tools like Otter.ai, Google Live Transcribe, and Microsoft Teams offer deaf and hard-of-hearing students equal access to lectures and classroom discussions. These inclusive features reduce dependence on interpreters or peers, promote autonomy, and ensure a more level academic playing field.

Another important area where speech recognition demonstrates its value is in language acquisition and multilingual education. For students learning in a second or third language, pronunciation, fluency, and comprehension can pose significant challenges. AI-powered tools like Duolingo, Rosetta Stone, and Speechling provide real-time feedback on spoken language, helping learners correct mistakes and build confidence in a supportive, low- pressure environment. Moreover, some advanced systems offer instant translation or multilingual support, making it easier for non-native speakers to understand lessons and interact with educational content. This has a particularly profound impact in linguistically diverse classrooms, where speech recognition can bridge language gaps and facilitate communication among peers and instructors.

Beyond student-focused applications, speech recognition technology also offers considerable advantages for educators and institutions. Teachers can use voice input to prepare instructional materials, record lectures, provide personalized verbal feedback, and even automate grading for oral assessments. When integrated with Learning Management Systems (LMS), speech tools enable smoother navigation, voice-activated interactions, and data- driven insights into student performance. These capabilities reduce the administrative burden on educators, allowing them to concentrate more on pedagogy and student engagement. Moreover, voice-based interfaces support hybrid and online learning models, offering students increased flexibility and access to education regardless of their physical location or circumstances.

Despite the clear advantages, the implementation of speech recognition in education is not without its challenges and limitations. One of the primary technical barriers remains accuracy—particularly in recognizing regional accents, dialects, speech disorders, or informal speech patterns. In diverse classrooms, this can lead to incorrect transcriptions or misinterpretations that undermine the learning process. Although AI algorithms are improving in inclusivity, achieving high recognition accuracy across all user demographics continues to be a work in progress.

Equally important are privacy and security concerns. Many speech recognition tools rely on cloud-based infrastructure, which involves sending and processing voice data on external servers. This raises ethical and legal concerns around data ownership, storage, and consent— especially when dealing with minors or sensitive academic information. To safeguard student rights, educational institutions must ensure compliance with data protection laws such as the General Data Protection Regulation (GDPR) and the Family Educational Rights and Privacy Act (FERPA). Transparent data policies, secure infrastructure, and clear communication with users are essential components of ethical implementation.

Another issue is the potential for bias in AI models. If the data used to train speech recognition systems lacks diversity, the resulting tools may perform disproportionately poorly for underrepresented groups—such as non-native speakers, individuals with speech impairments, or speakers of less common dialects. This bias not only limits the effectiveness of the technology but also perpetuates inequalities within the educational system. Developers must prioritize fairness by including diverse datasets, continually testing systems across demographics, and incorporating feedback from actual users in education.

Furthermore, the cost and infrastructure requirements of some advanced speech recognition tools can limit their accessibility. Many high-performing applications require paid licenses, quality microphones, or stable internet connections—resources that may not be available in underfunded schools or low-income communities. Without equitable access, the very tools designed to reduce educational disparities may inadvertently widen them. To address this, institutions should consider open-source alternatives, invest in inclusive procurement strategies, and advocate for public policies that support digital equity in education.

Looking to the future, the potential of speech recognition in education is vast. As artificial intelligence, natural language processing, and voice technologies continue to evolve, we can expect more context-aware, multilingual, and adaptive learning experiences. The integration of speech recognition with augmented and virtual reality (AR/VR) environments will create immersive, hands-free learning simulations, particularly beneficial in subjects like science, medicine, and languages. Additionally, the rise of the metaverse as a potential platform for education suggests that voice interaction will become a primary mode of communication and navigation in virtual classrooms. In such environments, students will engage with AI tutors, participate in real-time discussions, and access global educational resources—using only their voice.

In order to harness these opportunities effectively, a multi-stakeholder approach is necessary. Educators, developers, policymakers, and accessibility advocates must collaborate to create guidelines for ethical use, inclusive design, and responsible innovation. Teacher training, student orientation, and continuous evaluation will also be critical to ensure that the technology is implemented thoughtfully and with maximum impact.

In conclusion, speech recognition technology is not simply a tool—it is a transformative enabler of educational equity. By providing students with diverse needs the means to participate fully in their education, it aligns with the core values of inclusivity, autonomy, and accessibility. Its potential to reshape how we teach, learn, and interact with educational content is immense. When implemented with care and supported by inclusive practices and policies, speech recognition can ensure that no student is left behind—and that every voice, regardless of ability, language, or background, is heard, respected, and empowered in the classroom of the future.

REFERENCES

Dennis, N. K. (2024). Using AI-powered speech recognition technology to improve English pronunciation and speaking skills. *IAFOR Journal of Education: Technology in Education, 12*(2), 107–123. DOI: 10.22492/ije.12.2.05

García-Sánchez, J.-N., Soler-Urzúa, M., & Nussbaum, M. (2020). A systematic review of research on applications of speech recognition technology to assist language learning. *ReCALL, 32*(3), 251–268.

Gibson, R. (2024, September 10). The impact of AI in advancing accessibility for learners with disabilities. *EDUCAUSE Review*.

Hansen, J. H. L., & Pellom, B. (2002). An overview of automatic speech recognition. In Hansen, J. H. L., & Pellom, B. (Eds.), *Robust speech recognition in embedded systems and PC applications* (pp. 1–24). Kluwer Academic Publishers.

Kumar, L. A., Renuka, D. K., Rose, S. L., Shunmuga priya, M. C., & Wartana, I. M. (2022). Deep learning-based assistive technology on audio-visual speech recognition for hearing impaired. *International Journal of Cognitive Computing in Engineering, 3*, 24–30. DOI: 10.1016/j.ijcce.2022.01.003

Lee, K.-F. (1988). Towards speaker-independent continuous speech recognition. In Niemann, H., Lang, M., & Sagerer, G. (Eds.), *Recent advances in speech understanding and dialog systems* (pp. 285–297). Springer. DOI: 10.1007/978-3-642-83476-9_36

Mujtaba, D., Mahapatra, N. R., Arney, M., Yaruss, J. S., Gerlach-Houck, H., Herring, C., & Bin, J. (2024). *Lost in transcription: Identifying and quantifying the accuracy biases of automatic speech recognition systems against disfluent speech.*

Nelson, L. M., & Reynolds, T. W.Jr. (2015). Speech recognition, disability, and college composition. *Journal of Postsecondary Education and Disability, 28*(2), 181–197.

Reddy, D. R. (1976). Speech recognition by machine: A review. *Proceedings of the IEEE, 64*(4), 501–531. DOI: 10.1109/PROC.1976.10158

Schroeder, M. R. (2004). Speech recognition. In *Computer speech: Recognition, compression, synthesis* (Springer Series in Information Sciences, Vol. 35), 1–30. Springer.

Schultz, T., & Kirchhoff, K. (2006). Multilingual speech processing. In *Multilingual speech processing* (pp. 1–20). Elsevier. DOI: 10.1016/B978-012088501-5/50004-4

Xiao, Y. (2025). The impact of AI-driven speech recognition on EFL listening comprehension, flow experience, and anxiety: A randomized controlled trial. *Humanities & Social Sciences Communications, 12*(425), 425. DOI: 10.1057/s41599-025-04672-8

Chapter 15
AI-Driven Coding: Transforming Education and Industry

Otmane Azeroual
https://orcid.org/0000-0002-5225-389X
German Centre for Higher Education Research and Science Studies (DZHW), Berlin, Germany

ABSTRACT

The rapid rise of Artificial Intelligence (AI) has significantly impacted both education and software development, particularly in coding instruction. AI-powered tools like GitHub Copilot, ChatGPT, and intelligent tutoring systems are transforming traditional teaching methods by offering personalized learning, real-time feedback, and enhanced debugging. While these tools show promise in supporting novice programmers and improving coding skills, concerns exist about their potential to undermine critical cognitive skills like problem-solving and creativity. This chapter examines the effectiveness of AI-driven coding tools in achieving educational and professional goals, exploring their impact on cognitive development and workforce readiness. It also addresses the societal implications of AI in education, including algorithmic biases, tool accessibility, and ethical considerations. Through empirical research and case studies, this chapter provides a nuanced view of AI's role in shaping coding education and the software industry.

INTRODUCTION

The advent of AI has marked a pivotal shift in various industries, with its most notable impact seen in sectors such as healthcare, finance, and education. In recent years, AI has emerged as a significant player in the domain of coding education, reshaping the way programming is taught, learned, and applied. AI-driven tools like GitHub Copilot, which assists developers by offering code suggestions, and ChatGPT, which provides natural language-based assistance, are already influencing how software development is carried out. These tools have become indispensable for both novice learners and experienced programmers, providing valuable real-time support for debugging, code optimization, and personalized learning.

In education, AI technologies offer new opportunities for adaptive learning environments, personalized feedback, and dynamic assessment methods. Intelligent tutoring systems (ITS), for instance, enable real-time guidance, identifying students' strengths and weaknesses and providing

DOI: 10.4018/979-8-3373-5097-4.ch015

customized solutions based on individual needs (Fan et al., 2023). These innovations promise a more individualized approach to learning programming and are seen as tools that can bridge gaps in traditional, one-size-fits-all educational frameworks.

AI-driven coding tools offer a plethora of potential benefits in education, including enhancing student engagement, improving comprehension, and offering immediate feedback. AI systems, such as those employed by GitHub Copilot, have the capacity to provide step-by-step code suggestions and error corrections, making them invaluable in both educational settings and real-world software development. AI's ability to adapt and personalize learning experiences means that learners can receive tailored content that suits their current skill levels, thus enabling a more efficient and effective learning process (Porter & Zingaro, 2024). As a result, AI can support the development of basic programming skills, allowing learners to focus on more complex problem-solving and creative tasks over time.

However, alongside these advantages, concerns have emerged about AI's potential to undermine the development of foundational skills. One concern is that learners may become overly reliant on AI-generated solutions, hindering their ability to independently solve problems or develop computational thinking. The use of AI-powered tools may lead to the 'automation of thinking' rather than fostering the development of cognitive skills essential for problem-solving (Liu, 2023). The increasing integration of AI into coding education raises the question of whether it is enhancing or diminishing the core competencies required in software development.

The integration of AI into coding education is not without its challenges. Research indicates that while AI-powered tools can accelerate learning and provide support in real-time, their overuse may stifle creativity and critical thinking (Le, 2024). AI tools that suggest code without requiring deeper engagement may discourage students from developing the necessary skills to troubleshoot, optimize, and create original code. This has sparked a debate over whether AI tools should be used as a supplement or as a core component of the learning process.

Further complicating this issue is the concern about the ethical implications of AI in education. AI systems are not immune to biases, and algorithmic biases can affect the educational experience for different groups of learners (Eden et al., 2024). Additionally, AI-powered tools may not be equally accessible to all students, particularly those in underfunded educational institutions or low-income regions. Ensuring equitable access to these tools is a critical consideration for their widespread adoption in educational settings.

This chapter aims to provide a comprehensive analysis of the role of AI in coding education and its implications for both learners and professionals in the software development industry. By reviewing existing research, this chapter will assess whether AI-driven tools support or undermine the educational objectives of coding education. Specifically, it will explore whether these tools enhance the development of problem-solving skills, creativity, and coding proficiency or if they foster an over-reliance on automated solutions.

Additionally, this chapter will examine the broader societal and ethical concerns surrounding AI integration in education. These include issues of fairness, accessibility, and workforce readiness. The discussion will consider how AI can be effectively integrated into coding curricula, and whether it prepares learners to become proficient, independent problem-solvers in the software development industry.

Recent studies have begun to investigate the pedagogical implications of AI in coding education. Strielkowski et al. (2024) highlight the potential of AI-driven adaptive learning environments to enhance individual learning trajectories, providing learners with a customized experience that reflects their progress and understanding. AI-driven systems can analyze students' actions in real-time and suggest appropriate exercises or content, facilitating a more targeted approach to learning. Similarly, Di Eugenio et al. (2021) demonstrate that AI tutors can significantly improve student engagement and comprehension, especially when students face difficulties with complex programming concepts.

However, despite the promise of AI in education, Yelamarthi et al. (2024) cautions that an over-reliance on AI tools can lead to a lack of foundational problem-solving skills. By automatically suggesting solutions or providing code without requiring learners to engage with the problem-solving process, AI tools may inadvertently stunt the development of critical thinking skills that are essential for software development. This perspective aligns with the work of Becker el al. (2023), who argue that AI tools, although helpful for beginners, may foster an unhealthy dependence on automation, reducing learners' ability to solve problems independently.

In terms of workforce readiness, Becker et al. (2023) discuss how AI is shaping the future of the software engineering workforce. They emphasize the need for critical AI literacy, asserting that future software engineers must be equipped with the skills to navigate both the opportunities and challenges posed by AI tools in the professional environment.

This literature highlights the complexity of integrating AI into coding education and the need for a balanced approach that maximizes the benefits of AI while ensuring that learners do not lose sight of the fundamental skills required for successful programming.

THE RISE OF AI IN CODING EDUCATION

The rapid rise of AI has made a profound impact on numerous fields, with coding education being one of the most significant areas of transformation. AI-powered tools such as GitHub Copilot, ChatGPT, and Intelligent Tutoring Systems (ITS) have reshaped the way coding is taught and learned. These tools provide real-time assistance, personalized learning paths, and enhanced debugging processes, all of which contribute to a more efficient learning experience and improved coding proficiency (Taulli, 2024; Kolade et al., 2023). The integration of AI into education builds on decades of research into intelligent tutoring and adaptive learning systems. Early systems in the 1980s and 1990s, such as SCHOLAR and ANDES, laid the groundwork for today's AI-powered platforms by experimenting with rule-based logic and limited natural language processing (Corbett et al., 1994). These early efforts evolved significantly with advances in machine learning, which now enable tools to provide context-aware, dynamic feedback at scale.

GitHub Copilot, developed by GitHub and OpenAI, represents a prime example of AI in coding education. It offers contextual code suggestions based on the user's input, significantly reducing the cognitive load for programmers. This allows students and professionals alike to focus more on higher-level problem-solving and logic, rather than on rote coding tasks. Similarly, ChatGPT serves as a powerful tool for providing interactive, conversational feedback, allowing users to troubleshoot issues and clarify programming concepts in real-time (Kolade et al., 2023). Intelligent Tutoring Systems, which utilize AI to create adaptive learning environments, further enhance the educational experience by personalizing content to match the learner's progress, offering targeted exercises, and adjusting the difficulty level according to individual needs (Crow et al., 2018).

In parallel, the tools used to teach programming have also undergone substantial change—from static IDEs and syntax-focused instruction to cloud-based, interactive platforms such as Replit, Scratch, and Jupyter Notebooks. These technologies laid the foundation for the dynamic, AI-enhanced coding environments now being developed. By integrating AI into these platforms, learners not only engage with content more interactively, but also receive just-in-time support tailored to their individual learning curves.

However, despite the advantages that AI-powered tools offer, concerns have been raised about their potential to foster dependency. While these tools can improve coding efficiency, there is a risk that over-reliance on AI may hinder the development of critical cognitive skills such as problem-solving, computational thinking, and creativity. For instance, while GitHub Copilot and ChatGPT offer immediate solutions to coding challenges, they may limit the learner's ability to think through complex problems independently. Additionally, ITS may unintentionally simplify tasks to the point where students are not challenged enough to develop deeper learning (Joseph & Uzondu, 2024; Becker et al., 2023).

The integration of AI into coding education also has broader implications for the future of the software development workforce. As AI tools become more integrated into the education system, they will play a significant role in shaping the skills of future software engineers. It is essential for educators to strike a balance between utilizing AI to enhance learning and ensuring that foundational problem-solving and critical thinking skills are not neglected (Becker et al., 2023). Moreover, there are ethical considerations to address, such as algorithmic biases, data privacy concerns, and the accessibility of AI-powered tools (Kordzadeh & Ghasemaghaei, 2022; Wang et al., 2025). These issues must be carefully managed to ensure equitable access to high-quality coding education for all students, regardless of their background or resources.

This is particularly important in global educational contexts, where disparities in infrastructure and access to AI-powered platforms can exacerbate existing inequalities. As a result, responsible implementation strategies must account for diverse settings, including under-resourced schools and remote learning environments.

AI in coding education is still an emerging field, and the long-term impact of these tools on student learning remains a subject of debate. While AI-powered tools have shown promise in improving coding proficiency and offering personalized learning experiences, it remains unclear whether they help or hinder the development of critical cognitive and problem-solving skills that are essential for success in the programming profession (Posse, 2025). As research continues to evolve, it will be important to examine how these tools can be used effectively without compromising the foundational skills needed for success in the software development industry.

Future studies should explore not only the immediate learning gains enabled by AI, but also the longitudinal outcomes—such as retention of knowledge, ability to apply skills in novel contexts, and preparedness for complex software engineering roles.

Figure 1. Interaction of AI-powered tools in coding education

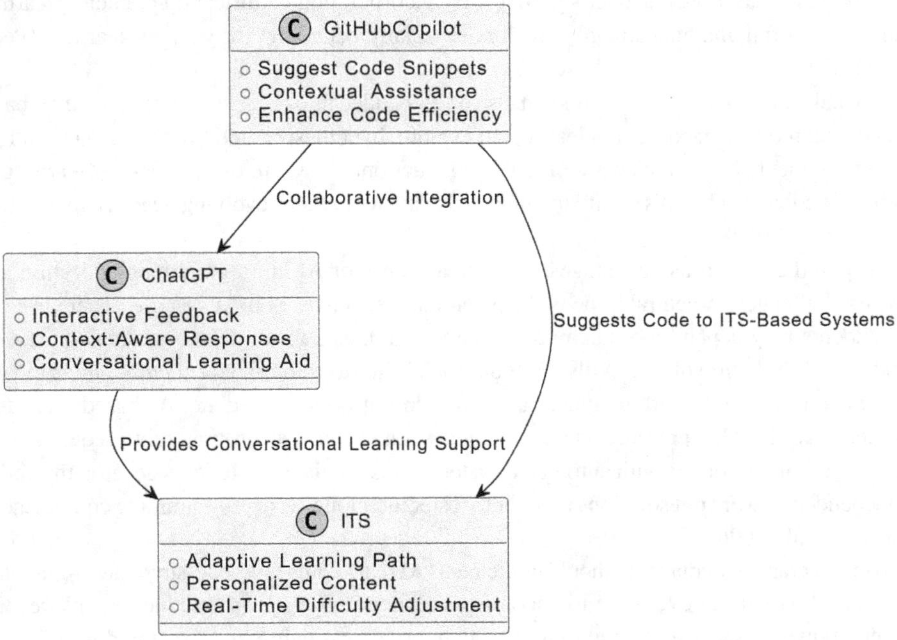

In Figure 1, the relationship between AI-powered tools like GitHub Copilot, ChatGPT, and Intelligent Tutoring Systems (ITS) is illustrated. These tools complement each other by providing personalized learning paths, real-time assistance, and interactive feedback. GitHub Copilot offers code suggestions, ChatGPT provides conversational feedback, and ITS adapts the learning process to the individual's progress. The collective use of these tools aims to create an engaging and efficient learning environment for students.

PEDAGOGICAL IMPLICATIONS OF AI IN CODING EDUCATION

The integration of AI in programming education offers numerous opportunities to improve the learning process, particularly through the creation of adaptive learning environments. Adaptive learning systems, developed using AI technologies, allow the learning material to be tailored to the individual needs of students. These systems provide personalized learning paths that help students focus on their specific weaknesses and build on their strengths, significantly enhancing efficiency and engagement in the learning process (Graesser et al., 2006). The advantage of AI systems is particularly evident in programming education, as they provide immediate feedback on the developed programs, enabling quick error correction and deepening students' understanding. Studies show that immediate feedback in learning environments leads to better learning outcomes, as students can recognize and correct errors right away (Ma et al., 2014). Another benefit of AI in programming education lies in its ability to foster engagement and motivation among learners. Platforms such as Scratch or CodeCombat combine learning programming languages with game-like elements, which not only sparks interest but also contributes to a sustainable connection to the learning material (Maloney et al., 2010). By incorporating gamification elements, learning becomes both fun and educational, which is especially beneficial for younger learners (Pedro et al., 2019).

Beyond gamification, AI systems can also be embedded into constructivist and inquiry-based pedagogical models, encouraging learners to explore, hypothesize, and test their ideas in a low-risk environment. This aligns with Papert's constructionism, where the process of "learning by making" is enhanced by AI's ability to guide and adapt to learners' evolving needs (Papert, 1980; Holmes et al., 2019).

Despite the numerous advantages, the increased use of AI in programming education also presents challenges. A central issue is the potential over-reliance on AI systems. There is a risk that students may depend too much on AI support and, as a result, fail to adequately develop foundational problem-solving skills. Without the ability to think independently and critically, students could struggle with complex tasks that do not offer immediate, AI-based assistance (VanLehn, 2011). This presents one of the biggest challenges, as programming requires more than just solving problems with automated systems. It is crucial that students develop the ability to independently work out solutions in order to foster their long-term programming competencies (Graesser et al., 2006).

To counteract this, educators should implement "AI scaffolding fade-out" strategies—gradually reducing AI assistance over time to encourage autonomy. Such phased reduction ensures that learners transition from supported to independent problem-solving in a structured way (Roll & Wylie, 2016).

Another obstacle to the successful integration of AI in programming education is the challenge of embedding it into existing teaching methods and the need for teacher training. Many educational institutions must not only provide the infrastructure to incorporate AI into their curricula, but also prepare instructors to handle these new technologies (Pedro et al., 2019). Teachers need to become familiar with the latest developments in AI in order to effectively incorporate them into the classroom, without displacing traditional teaching methods. This approach requires a careful balance, where AI is used as a supportive, not a substitutive, tool. Educators must be able to integrate AI-based learning aids into their instruction while still focusing on developing foundational problem-solving skills (VanLehn, 2011).

To support this shift, professional development programs must focus not only on the technical use of AI tools but also on pedagogical strategies for integrating them meaningfully. Scalable models such as blended learning workshops, peer-led training, and AI teaching toolkits can empower educators in diverse contexts—including under-resourced schools—to implement AI-enhanced coding curricula effectively (Xu & Ouyang, 2022).

Overall, AI has the potential to revolutionize the learning process in programming education by providing personalized, adaptive learning environments that increase student engagement and motivation. However, the challenge lies in finding the right balance between support from AI and the development of fundamental, independent problem-solving skills. This requires not only technological innovation but also careful pedagogical planning and close collaboration between educators and technology developers.

Additionally, a framework for evaluating pedagogical effectiveness—such as measuring student progression, cognitive engagement, and retention of problem-solving abilities—should accompany any AI integration efforts. These metrics will help ensure that educational outcomes remain learner-centered and long-term skill development is prioritized.

Only in this way can we ensure that students not only benefit from AI-supported systems but also develop the skills they need for a successful career in computer science.

IMPACT ON COGNITIVE SKILLS AND CREATIVITY

The impact of AI on cognitive skills and creativity in programming education is a topic of increasing importance as the use of AI-driven tools in education becomes more widespread. AI systems, such as intelligent tutoring platforms and automated code assistants, support students in problem-solving and computational thinking. These tools offer real-time feedback, guidance, and scaffolding that help students decompose complex coding challenges, breaking them down into manageable tasks. This process can be particularly beneficial for developing computational thinking—a critical skill in programming. By automating routine aspects of coding, such as debugging and syntax checking, AI can reduce cognitive load, allowing students to focus on higher-order thinking and complex problem-solving tasks (Stamper et al., 2024).

Furthermore, these systems can be linked to Vygotsky's theory of the Zone of Proximal Development (ZPD), where AI functions as a scaffold that helps learners achieve tasks they would otherwise not manage alone. When well-calibrated, such scaffolding encourages learners to progress beyond their current capabilities without replacing the cognitive work required for growth (Vygotskij, 1979;VanLehn, 2011).

However, while AI's role in enhancing computational thinking and problem-solving is valuable, it also raises concerns about its effect on creativity in programming. Creativity in coding is not merely about finding solutions, but also about exploring novel approaches, experimenting with different algorithms, and synthesizing ideas in innovative ways. AI-driven tools, while efficient, might inadvertently stifle creativity by suggesting predefined solutions or limiting students' engagement with the problem-solving process. For example, tools that automatically generate code suggestions or complete tasks for students could reduce opportunities for them to develop their own unique problem-solving strategies (Stamper et al., 2024). This over-reliance on AI might lead to a lack of engagement with the creative aspects of coding, which are essential for developing innovative software and technology.

To foster creativity, it is essential that AI systems include features that promote divergent thinking—for instance, by offering multiple solution paths or encouraging exploration of alternative algorithms rather than presenting one optimal answer. Some experimental AI environments already integrate creative prompts or "what if" challenges to nudge learners toward invention and experimentation (Zootzky & Pfeiffer, 2024).

Moreover, excessive dependence on AI can result in diminished cognitive skill development. Cognitive skills such as logical reasoning, critical thinking, and memory are honed through the process of struggling with problems and working through them independently. Research shows that deep learning occurs when students are actively involved in solving problems, making decisions, and reflecting on their solutions (Levy, 2020). AI tools that provide immediate solutions or guide students too heavily may prevent them from experiencing the cognitive challenges necessary for developing these foundational skills. In the context of programming, learning to debug code, to understand error messages, and to iteratively improve one's solution are all cognitive processes that are essential for deep, lasting learning. By automating these tasks, AI might deprive students of these learning opportunities, potentially hindering the development of critical cognitive skills (Kirkwood & Price, 2014).

In light of Bloom's taxonomy, these missed opportunities may hinder progression beyond lower-order thinking skills such as remembering and understanding, preventing learners from reaching higher levels such as analyzing, evaluating, and creating (Anderson & Krathwohl, 2001). A well-balanced AI learning environment should thus encourage learners to engage in metacognitive reflection and iterative refinement, not just solution completion.

The case studies from both academia and industry illustrate these issues and offer insights into the balance between AI assistance and cognitive development. In academia, platforms such as CodeSignal have successfully integrated AI into coding education by providing real-time feedback and suggestions during coding exercises. These platforms improve student engagement and computational thinking but also raise questions about the extent to which they foster true creativity and independent problem-solving skills (Kirkwood & Price, 2014). Similarly, in the software industry, tools like GitHub Copilot use AI to assist professional developers by generating code suggestions and automating certain aspects of the coding process. While these tools increase productivity, they also raise concerns about developers' understanding of the code they are writing, as they may rely too heavily on AI suggestions without fully grasping the underlying logic (Puryear & Sprint, 2022).

Some industry initiatives now aim to embed reflective practices into AI tools—for example, by prompting users to explain or justify AI-suggested code before accepting it. Such integrations can mitigate passive usage and enhance understanding, especially in educational contexts (McLaren et al., 2010).

Ultimately, while AI plays a vital role in supporting problem-solving and enhancing computational thinking, its integration into programming education and software development must be carefully managed to ensure that it does not undermine creativity or cognitive skill development. AI should be viewed as a tool to augment, rather than replace, the active cognitive engagement required for deep learning and creative problem-solving.

Educational stakeholders must develop frameworks for assessing not only technical outcomes but also cognitive and creative dimensions of learning, ensuring that AI-enhanced environments promote well-rounded intellectual growth.

By striking the right balance between AI assistance and independent learning, students and professionals can benefit from both the efficiencies AI offers and the cognitive growth that comes from tackling problems without excessive reliance on automation.

AI AND WORKFORCE READINESS

In the context of rapidly advancing AI technologies, preparing future software engineers requires a deliberate focus on AI literacy and workforce readiness. As AI becomes a ubiquitous component of modern software development, technical education must evolve to equip students not only with programming competencies, but also with a deep understanding of AI systems, their applications, and limitations. AI literacy encompasses the ability to critically evaluate AI-generated outputs, understand algorithmic biases, and engage with machine learning models in a way that promotes transparency, fairness, and accountability (Long & Magerko, 2020).

This notion of AI literacy also extends to the need for computational ethics training, where students are taught not only how AI works but how to apply ethical frameworks to its development and use. This is increasingly crucial as AI-driven systems influence decisions in healthcare, criminal justice, and finance, where consequences are far-reaching (Bostrom & Yudkowsky, 2018).

Employers increasingly emphasize not only technical acumen but also transversal competencies such as critical thinking, problem-solving, and ethical reasoning. While AI systems can accelerate software development by automating routine tasks—e.g., code generation, testing, and documentation—they cannot replace human capacities for abstraction, contextual judgment, or ethical decision-making. The World Economic Forum (2023) identifies critical thinking and problem-solving as top skills for the digital economy, reinforcing the need to develop these attributes within AI-augmented educational frameworks (Di Battista et al., 2023).

Furthermore, the rise of interdisciplinary collaboration is an emerging trend. Engineers are expected to collaborate with data scientists, ethicists, and domain specialists to build systems that are not only technically robust but also socially responsible. This requires a broad understanding of how AI intersects with societal needs and challenges, which is becoming a core component of modern engineering curricula (Brynjolfsson & McAfee, 2014).

However, the reliance on AI-generated solutions presents risks. Over-dependence may diminish learners' ability to develop robust problem-solving strategies, as students might accept machine-generated code uncritically, without understanding its logic or implications. This "automation bias" (Goddard et al., 2012) can lead to cognitive complacency and hinder the ability to debug, optimize, or creatively adapt solutions. In professional settings, such dependency may impair engineers' capacity to question flawed outputs, particularly when AI systems lack transparency or explainability.

Additionally, the potential for "algorithmic entrenchment" poses a significant concern. Over-reliance on AI tools could lead to stagnation in creativity and critical thinking, as algorithms tend to optimize for efficiency rather than innovation, potentially resulting in a narrowing of problem-solving approaches (Verma, 2019).

Equally important is the incorporation of ethical AI literacy into engineering curricula. Software engineers increasingly face dilemmas involving data privacy, algorithmic discrimination, and unintended consequences of automation. Thus, the development of critical AI literacy—defined as the capacity to interrogate the assumptions, power dynamics, and social implications embedded in AI systems—is essential for responsible participation in a digital workforce (D'Ignazio & Klein, 2020). Case studies in industry, such as Google's internal debate over AI ethics or IBM's initiatives in trustworthy AI, illustrate how ethical fluency is becoming a key differentiator in hiring practices.

Incorporating frameworks like the "AI Ethics Guidelines" from the European Commission or the IEEE's "Ethically Aligned Design" can help students critically evaluate the ethical challenges associated with deploying AI in various fields (European Commission, 2020).

In conclusion, while AI tools offer substantial benefits in augmenting engineering education and practice, a balanced approach is needed—one that emphasizes critical engagement, ethical awareness, and cognitive autonomy. Preparing future engineers for the AI-driven workforce entails fostering an adaptive mindset, grounded in both technical excellence and reflective practice.

Additionally, the integration of continuous, lifelong learning into professional development programs is crucial. As AI and other emerging technologies evolve, engineers must be prepared to adapt and learn throughout their careers, ensuring they remain innovative, ethical, and relevant in an AI-augmented future (Xu et al., 2018).

BROADER SOCIETAL AND ETHICAL CONSIDERATIONS

The increasing deployment of AI in educational contexts necessitates a comprehensive reflection on its broader societal and ethical implications. While AI holds considerable potential to transform pedagogy, enhance personalization, and democratize access to knowledge, its integration is not without challenges—particularly concerning fairness, accessibility, inclusiveness, and governance.

However, the ethical considerations surrounding AI extend beyond the classroom to broader societal concerns. For example, the widespread use of AI in education can perpetuate broader systemic inequalities present in other sectors, such as healthcare and law enforcement, where biased algorithms have led to significant social consequences. Therefore, integrating AI in education must be part of a broader conversation on how AI affects society at large (Verma, 2019).

One of the most prominent concerns is the persistence of algorithmic bias. AI systems are often trained on datasets that reflect historical inequalities, leading to outputs that may inadvertently reinforce discriminatory patterns (Noble, 2018; Bolukbasi et al., 2016). For instance, natural language processing (NLP) tools used in educational grading systems may favor linguistic norms typical of dominant cultural groups, disadvantaging learners from diverse linguistic or ethnic backgrounds. Such biases, if unmitigated, risk institutionalizing inequity within educational assessments and feedback mechanisms.

Further, AI systems that focus solely on efficiency and measurable outcomes can inadvertently sideline important but less quantifiable aspects of education, such as emotional intelligence, creativity, and critical thinking—key attributes that help students navigate complex real-world issues. In this way, AI's pursuit of standardized optimization may undermine broader educational goals (Bostrom & Yudkowsky, 2018).

Closely related to fairness is the issue of equal access to AI tools. The digital divide remains a significant barrier to the equitable implementation of AI in education. According to (Wang 2025), disparities in infrastructure, digital literacy, and institutional funding lead to unequal opportunities for students and educators to benefit from AI-enhanced systems. Wealthier schools may gain access to adaptive learning platforms and intelligent tutoring systems, while under-resourced communities risk being left behind, exacerbating existing socio-educational gaps.

Moreover, a lack of representation in AI development teams means that AI systems may not always consider the diverse needs of marginalized groups. Ensuring that AI systems reflect the diversity of the student body is crucial in addressing both the digital divide and the risk of creating tools that cater primarily to dominant cultural or socio-economic groups (Eubanks, 2018).

However, AI also has the potential to advance accessibility and foster inclusion. Assistive technologies powered by AI, such as speech-to-text, predictive text systems, and personalized content delivery, can enhance learning experiences for students with disabilities or neurodivergent learners (Shinohara & Wobbrock, 2011). For these tools to be effective, developers must adopt inclusive design principles and collaborate with end-users to ensure accessibility, usability, and cultural sensitivity.

The promise of AI in creating more accessible educational experiences is immense. AI can, for example, help bridge the gap for students with dyslexia or students from underrepresented linguistic backgrounds by offering tailored learning experiences. However, AI developers must engage in continual consultation with disabled and neurodivergent communities to avoid tokenistic solutions and ensure that the tools genuinely meet the diverse needs of all students (Khreisat et al., 2024).

Beyond technical and operational dimensions, ethical concerns emerge around data privacy, surveillance, and pedagogical autonomy. Many AI systems rely on extensive data collection, including behavioral analytics and biometric data, to optimize instruction. Such practices raise critical questions about informed consent, student agency, and the transparency of data use. Williamson and Eynon (2020) caution that without proper governance structures, AI may shift power away from educators and learners towards opaque technological systems, undermining trust and democratic control in educational settings.

As AI becomes more integrated into classrooms, the issue of surveillance extends beyond monitoring student progress to the potential tracking of student emotions, preferences, and even behavior. The ethical implications of such pervasive surveillance—such as the risk of manipulating or controlling student behavior—should be critically examined and addressed through policy and governance frameworks (Zuboff, 2019).

These considerations—algorithmic bias, access disparity, inclusive potential, and surveillance risks—interact in complex ways that require holistic ethical frameworks and multi-stakeholder collaboration. Figure 2 illustrates the interconnected dimensions of societal and ethical concerns that must be addressed to ensure responsible AI integration in education.

The need for transparency in AI system development and implementation cannot be overstated. It is critical that AI algorithms used in educational contexts are interpretable, and that stakeholders—from students to policymakers—understand how decisions are being made. This transparency can serve as a safeguard against algorithmic errors and biases, and foster trust between users and the systems they interact with.

Figure 2. Ethical and societal dimensions of AI in education

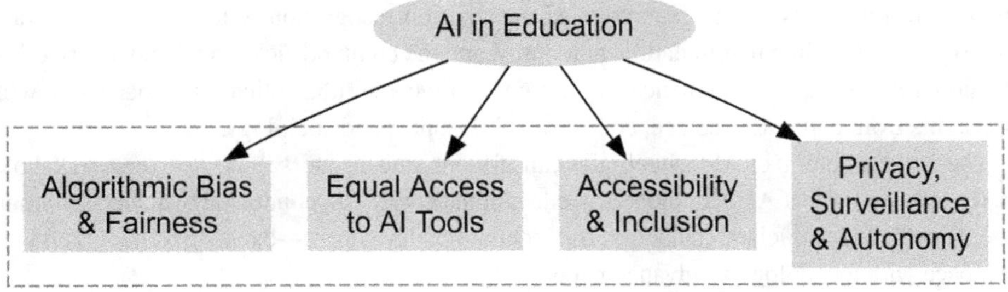

As illustrated in Figure 2, these ethical and societal dimensions are not isolated silos but form a dynamic and interdependent system that shapes the educational landscape. Recognizing these interconnections is crucial for moving beyond reactive policies toward proactive ethical design and regulation. For instance, addressing algorithmic bias must go hand in hand with improving access and ensuring diverse representation in training datasets—actions that are not only technical but also deeply political.

This political dimension of AI ethics requires international collaboration and governance frameworks that account for global disparities in access to technology and education. Without such frameworks, AI's potential to democratize education may only serve to further entrench global inequalities (Zajko, 2022).

Moreover, the role of policy-makers and educational institutions becomes increasingly significant. They must establish normative frameworks that enforce transparency, accountability, and inclusivity across AI implementations. This includes mandatory audits of AI systems used in public education, the creation of ethical review boards, and participatory design processes that include educators, students, and marginalized voices (Floridi et al., 2018). Without such frameworks, the risk remains high that AI will not democratize learning, but rather reproduce and even amplify structural inequalities.

AI's integration into education must be seen not only as a technological upgrade but as a profound societal transformation. Policy-makers must take into account the long-term consequences of AI deployment in education and create policies that encourage both innovation and social responsibility (Selwyn, 2019).

In this context, critical AI literacy must also be cultivated—not only among developers and administrators but also among learners themselves. Understanding how AI makes decisions, what data it uses, and where it might fail is fundamental to fostering responsible engagement. As Selwyn (2019) argues, treating students merely as passive users of intelligent systems undermines educational goals; instead, they should be empowered as critical thinkers and informed participants in a digital society.

Incorporating critical AI literacy into curricula will empower students not only to engage with AI but to question its role and impact in their daily lives. By fostering this critical thinking from an early stage, educators can prepare students to become responsible digital citizens who can influence the development and application of AI systems.

Lastly, the ethical landscape of AI in education must be continuously revisited in light of emerging technologies such as generative AI and emotion-recognition systems. These tools raise new concerns regarding manipulation, autonomy, and the commodification of student affect and attention. Ensuring ethical resilience requires an iterative, multidisciplinary approach—drawing on insights from computer science, education, philosophy, and sociology.

The rapid evolution of AI technologies calls for ongoing discourse among diverse stakeholders. Regular reviews of AI technologies in educational contexts—conducted by interdisciplinary panels that include ethicists, educators, and technology developers—can help mitigate risks and keep pace with technological advancements.

Only through such a comprehensive and inclusive lens can we ensure that the integration of AI in education aligns with democratic values, supports cognitive and emotional development, and truly serves the public good.

CASE STUDIES IN AI-DRIVEN CODING EDUCATION

The application of AI in programming education has given rise to innovative learning environments, both in academia and industry. These developments have led to a growing body of case studies that illuminate the transformative potential of AI-driven platforms for teaching, learning, and practicing coding. However, the success of these systems must be weighed against their limitations, especially when considered through the lens of educational outcomes, engagement, and skill acquisition.

As AI tools continue to evolve, these case studies offer valuable insights into how educators and developers are navigating both the benefits and challenges of these emerging technologies. It is crucial to continuously evaluate the impact of AI-driven platforms on the holistic development of programming skills, creativity, and autonomy.

One prominent academic example is CodeHint, an intelligent code completion and tutoring system developed at MIT. The platform integrates program synthesis with real-time learner input to provide context-sensitive hints and code suggestions (Galenson et al., 2014). CodeHint has been shown to increase student confidence and reduce the time spent resolving syntax and logic errors. Its strength lies in the adaptive guidance it offers, particularly for novices who struggle with the rigidity of traditional compilers. However, follow-up studies revealed that excessive reliance on suggestions can hinder the development of independent debugging and problem-solving skills if not combined with scaffolded explanation mechanisms (Basu et al., 2017).

While CodeHint represents a promising tool for novice learners, there is an ongoing tension between offering adaptive support and fostering critical, independent problem-solving skills. The effectiveness of such tools relies on how well they balance immediate assistance with long-term cognitive engagement, ensuring that students are not overly reliant on automated suggestions.

Another academic initiative is AutoTutor, which uses natural language processing (NLP) to simulate human-like dialogues in response to student inputs. Initially designed for teaching physics, the system has been adapted to teach programming logic and concepts. AutoTutor demonstrates success in increasing conceptual understanding through Socratic questioning and dialog-based feedback (Graesser et al., 2005). Nevertheless, challenges persist in interpreting ambiguous code-related questions from students, and the accuracy of semantic parsing for programming contexts remains limited.

AutoTutor's potential is evident in its ability to engage students in deeper thinking, but its limitations in handling complex code queries reflect the ongoing challenges of applying NLP to programming. Improvements in this area could pave the way for even more personalized learning experiences in the future.

In industry, GitHub Copilot, powered by OpenAI Codex, represents a cutting-edge commercial application of AI in real-world software development. Copilot acts as a pair programmer, generating entire functions or code blocks based on brief natural language prompts. Early empirical studies indicate that Copilot accelerates prototyping and increases developer productivity (Torka & Albayrak, 2024). However, case studies from organizations using Copilot at scale also point to potential pitfalls. Developers occasionally accept flawed or inefficient code without proper validation, raising concerns about software quality and technical debt (Perry et al., 2022). Moreover, ethical concerns regarding code attribution and open-source licensing have surfaced.

Copilot exemplifies how AI can enhance efficiency in real-world development, but its challenges underscore the need for vigilance regarding code quality, ethical considerations, and the potential for over-reliance on automated suggestions. AI tools in the workplace must be carefully integrated into existing workflows to prevent negative impacts on coding standards and the ethical dimensions of software development.

A hybrid case is seen in Microsoft's IntelliCode, an AI-powered extension for Visual Studio that learns from patterns in community codebases. It provides context-aware recommendations tailored to the project's style and structure. In classroom settings, IntelliCode has been used to support student assignments by suggesting idiomatic code patterns, reducing syntactic errors and allowing students to focus on logic. However, instructors have noted that IntelliCode may "flatten" the learning curve too much, leading some students to bypass deeper exploration of syntax and data structures.

IntelliCode offers an interesting middle ground, combining practical tool assistance with a focus on learning efficiency. However, it raises critical questions about the fine balance between reducing errors and allowing space for the deep learning of programming constructs, which is crucial for mastery.

Figure 3 illustrates a comparative overview of key academic and industrial case studies, categorizing them by focus area, benefits, and limitations.

Figure 3. Comparative overview of AI-driven coding education case studies

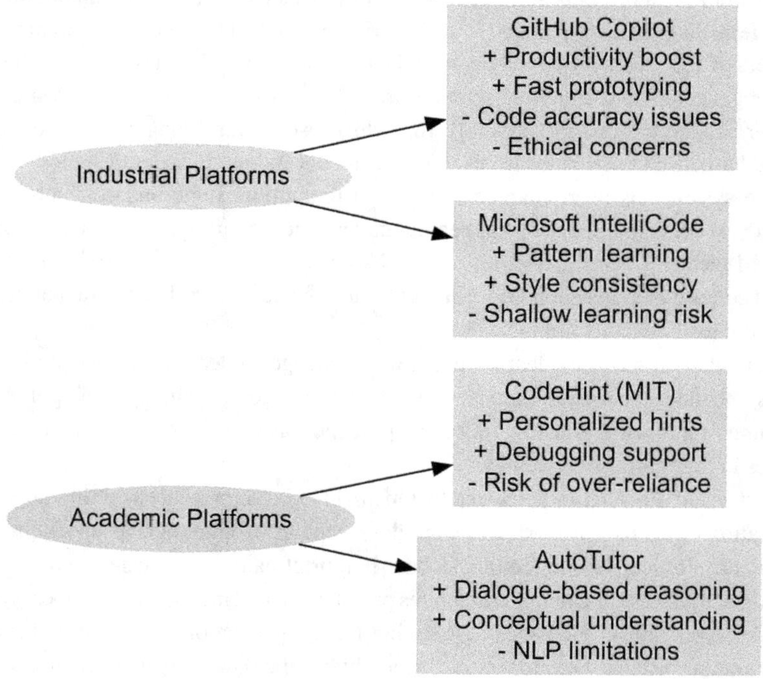

As visualized in Figure 3, there are clear distinctions between academic and industrial applications of AI in programming education. While academic systems such as CodeHint and AutoTutor primarily aim at pedagogical effectiveness, cognitive development, and individualized learning support, industrial tools like Copilot and IntelliCode are more focused on efficiency, productivity enhancement, and practical relevance.

This distinction highlights the evolving role of AI tools within the broader ecosystem of programming education. While academic tools are geared toward fostering foundational skills and independent thinking, industrial tools prioritize practical outcomes, which may not always align with educational objectives.

This distinction is crucial, as it reflects fundamentally different objectives: educational support versus production optimization. In educational contexts, the use of AI must be approached with caution to support rather than undermine cognitive processes, whereas in industrial practice, different success indicators—such as time-to-market or code maintainability—are decisive.

A significant challenge lies in adapting industrial tools like Copilot for educational settings, as tools designed with efficiency in mind may not provide the depth of explanation or conceptual understanding necessary for novice learners.

A critical concern is the transferability of these systems. For instance, tools like Copilot are increasingly being used in university settings—often without pedagogical adaptation. This may result in a mismatch, as systems primarily designed for professional developers are not necessarily educationally valuable for novice learners (Begel & Simon, 2008).

The mismatch between the expectations of industrial tools and the developmental needs of students is an ongoing challenge in educational settings. Tools designed for efficiency in professional environments often assume a certain level of expertise, which can undermine the learning process for those still grappling with the basics of programming.

Moreover, it must be acknowledged that the integration of such tools entails a redefinition of the role of educators: instead of acting solely as knowledge transmitters, they increasingly serve as learning facilitators who guide and reflect on the appropriate use of AI systems.

This shift places greater responsibility on educators to strike the right balance between facilitating the use of AI tools and ensuring that students retain agency in their learning journey. Educators must guide students in developing a critical understanding of AI's role in coding and problem-solving, preventing over-reliance on these tools.

EVALUATING THE EFFECTIVENESS OF AI-DRIVEN CODING INSTRUCTION

As AI becomes more prevalent in educational settings, particularly in coding instruction, there is an increasing need to critically evaluate its impact on learning outcomes, cognitive development, and professional success. AI-driven educational tools, such as intelligent tutoring systems (ITS), automated code reviewers, and AI-powered coding assistants, aim to improve the learning process by offering personalized feedback and adaptive learning pathways. However, the effectiveness of these tools is still a subject of debate in the academic community, raising important questions about whether AI can genuinely support educational objectives in the context of coding education. This section explores three critical aspects of AI-driven coding instruction: the alignment of AI with educational objectives, the enhancement or hindrance of problem-solving skills, and the long-term impact on learners' development and professional success.

Does AI Truly Support Educational Objectives?

Educational objectives in the context of coding instruction generally include the development of technical skills, the ability to solve complex problems, and the cultivation of critical thinking abilities. Traditional coding education often emphasizes theoretical knowledge of algorithms and programming paradigms, along with hands-on coding exercises. AI tools, such as automated coding platforms and intelligent tutoring systems, can offer real-time feedback, provide personalized learning pathways, and adapt to individual student needs. However, a key question remains: Do these tools effectively align with broader educational goals such as fostering deeper understanding, promoting problem-solving skills, and encouraging critical thinking?

Research suggests that AI-driven tools can enhance the learning process by offering tailored feedback based on individual performance (VanLehn, 2011). For example, intelligent tutors can identify a student's weak points in coding syntax or logic and offer targeted exercises to address these issues. However, critics argue that an over-reliance on AI could lead to surface-level learning, where students focus more on completing tasks correctly rather than truly understanding the underlying principles (Kukulska-Hulme & Lee, 2020). In this regard, AI-driven instruction may support some educational objectives, but whether it fully aligns with the holistic development of learners remains an area for further investigation.

While AI can provide helpful scaffolding for students, it may inadvertently foster a transactional approach to learning, where students focus on task completion rather than deep understanding. Educators must ensure that AI is used in a way that promotes active problem-solving, deeper inquiry, and reflection on underlying coding principles. AI tools should be seen as complementary to traditional educational strategies, guiding students through conceptual challenges rather than replacing the need for foundational knowledge acquisition.

AI's Role in Enhancing or Hindering Problem-Solving Skills

One of the most significant concerns about AI in coding education is its effect on the development of problem-solving skills, which are central to coding. Traditional problem-solving in coding often involves understanding a problem, devising an approach, testing hypotheses, debugging code, and iterating on solutions. This process requires both technical knowledge and cognitive flexibility. AI tools can assist learners by providing real-time feedback and even solving parts of a problem automatically, but this raises the question: Does this automated assistance enhance or undermine the development of problem-solving skills?

In some cases, AI tools may hinder the development of problem-solving skills by providing solutions too quickly, reducing the cognitive effort required from the student. For instance, AI-driven code completion tools like GitHub Copilot can suggest entire code blocks or solutions, potentially bypassing the critical thinking process involved in solving problems (Muraina & Adesanya, 2024). While these tools can increase productivity and reduce frustration, they also run the risk of students becoming overly dependent on them, failing to develop the critical cognitive skills needed for independent problem-solving (Bai et al., 2023).

On the other hand, well-designed AI tools can encourage problem-solving by guiding students through complex coding challenges and helping them break down problems into manageable sub-tasks. AI tutors can offer hints and suggest alternative approaches to solving problems, encouraging learners to explore different coding strategies (Woolf, 2010). This type of scaffolded learning can promote the development of problem-solving skills if the AI tool is used in a manner that encourages active engagement and reflection rather than mere reliance on automated solutions.

It is crucial that AI tools do not inadvertently replace the student's role in the problem-solving process. Educators should create learning environments where AI offers suggestions but encourages students to critically assess those suggestions, reflect on their own approaches, and iterate on solutions. Guided exploration rather than passive consumption of AI-generated solutions can help students retain problem-solving autonomy.

The Long-Term Impact on Learners' Development and Professional Success

The long-term impact of AI-driven coding instruction on learners' development and professional success is another important consideration. While AI tools can offer immediate, personalized feedback and help learners improve their coding abilities, the question remains whether these tools contribute to lasting cognitive development and long-term career success. In particular, it is crucial to assess whether AI-powered instruction fosters skills that are valuable in the rapidly evolving software development industry.

AI tools in coding education are often designed to mimic the role of a mentor or tutor, guiding students through problem-solving processes and providing personalized learning experiences. However, the nature of professional software development requires not only technical proficiency but also skills such as collaboration, communication, creativity, and adaptability—skills that may not be adequately developed by AI-driven instruction alone. Some studies suggest that while AI can enhance specific technical skills, it may not fully prepare learners for the complexities of real-world coding projects, which require teamwork, critical thinking, and an understanding of broader system design and architecture (Alisauskiene et al., 2020).

In addition to coding skills, the demands of the software development industry include strong collaboration, communication, and problem-solving capabilities. While AI can support technical learning, it does not always address these broader competencies. Project-based learning and collaborative coding practices should be integrated alongside AI-driven platforms to prepare learners for real-world challenges, where teamwork and creativity are essential.

Furthermore, AI-driven instruction in coding may inadvertently create a skill gap between students who are adept at using AI tools and those who rely solely on traditional learning methods. The integration of AI into coding education might encourage learners to focus more on using these tools effectively rather than developing the deep technical and conceptual understanding required to succeed in the long term. If not carefully managed, this could lead to a scenario where learners are well-equipped to use AI tools but lack the foundational problem-solving and critical thinking skills that are essential for success in the software development field.

To ensure that AI-driven instruction contributes to a holistic development of learners, educational programs should strive for a balance between tool utilization and core coding education. For instance, students should be taught to use AI tools mindfully, recognizing their potential but also developing the ability to independently diagnose problems and apply creative solutions.

Figure 4. The impact of AI on learning objectives, problem-solving skills, and professional development

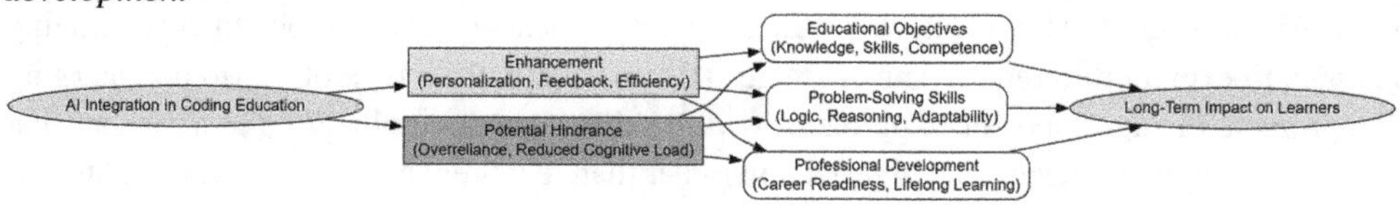

While Figure 4 highlights the multifaceted impact of AI on core dimensions of educational success, it also prompts a critical reconsideration of the pedagogical frameworks within which such technologies are embedded. AI-driven coding instruction must not be viewed in isolation as a technical enhancement but as part of a broader socio-technical learning ecology, where educators, learners, and tools interact dynamically (Luckin & Holmes, 2016). The question, therefore, is not only whether AI supports learning outcomes, but how it is embedded within instructional practices to promote meaningful engagement and sustainable skill development.

One central pedagogical implication is the need for intentional instructional design that leverages AI not as a replacement for human-guided learning but as a complementary scaffold. For instance, pairing AI coding assistants with reflective prompts or collaborative code reviews can foster meta-cognitive awareness and peer learning—two dimensions frequently overlooked in automated learning environments. Moreover, integrating AI tools with problem-based learning (PBL) approaches can stimulate authentic learning scenarios that require students to actively diagnose, plan, and implement code-based solutions, rather than passively consuming AI-suggested answers (Barrows, 1986; Belland et al., 2017).

Equally crucial is the role of educators in mediating the use of AI. Teachers must be equipped with AI literacy to critically assess and guide tool usage, prevent over-reliance, and adapt instruction according to student needs. Rather than perceiving AI as an autonomous tutor, it should be seen as a co-agent within the learning process—one that requires pedagogical orchestration (Prieto et al., 2011) to be effective. This shifts the role of the educator toward that of a facilitator, interpreter, and ethical guide in the AI-enhanced classroom.

Looking forward, empirical research is urgently needed to explore longitudinal impacts of AI-assisted coding instruction across diverse learner populations and contexts. Such studies should not only assess performance outcomes but also examine affective-motivational variables (e.g., self-efficacy, engagement, and resilience) and their relation to AI interaction. In particular, attention must be paid to equity-related dimensions, ensuring that access to advanced AI tools does not exacerbate existing socio-educational disparities.

Furthermore, there is a growing call for the development of transparent and explainable AI (XAI) in education. Learners should understand how and why specific feedback is generated, in order to foster trust and agency. Without such transparency, there is a risk that students defer to AI recommendations without critical scrutiny—thereby undermining the very competencies that education seeks to cultivate.

In conclusion, while AI offers promising avenues for advancing coding instruction, its integration demands a careful balance of technological affordances and pedagogical integrity. Educators, designers, and policymakers must work collaboratively to ensure that AI not only enhances immediate learning efficiency but also contributes to the formation of autonomous, reflective, and adaptive problem-solvers equipped for the demands of the digital future.

FUTURE DIRECTIONS AND RECOMMENDATIONS

As AI technologies continue to permeate educational domains, particularly in coding instruction, it is imperative to develop strategic frameworks for their effective and ethical integration. The dynamic nature of programming education, which blends technical mastery with cognitive and creative skills, makes it especially sensitive to both the benefits and risks of AI. This section outlines key future directions and actionable recommendations to guide educators, researchers, policymakers, and industry stakeholders in harnessing AI's full pedagogical potential.

How to Integrate AI Effectively in Coding Education

Effective integration of AI in coding education requires more than technological deployment—it necessitates a pedagogically informed approach that aligns AI functionalities with learning objectives. One promising direction is the adoption of hybrid instructional models in which AI acts as a co-facilitator rather than a replacement for human teaching. For instance, AI-powered feedback can be embedded within project-based learning (PBL), supporting students as they tackle open-ended coding challenges while maintaining a strong emphasis on process-oriented thinking (Janicki & Liegle, 2001).

Furthermore, explainable AI (XAI) must become a standard feature in educational tools. When learners understand why certain recommendations are made (e.g., via visualizations or annotated code suggestions), they are more likely to engage in critical reflection rather than passive acceptance (Holstein et al., 2019). AI tools should also be customizable, allowing educators to adapt the level of automation and scaffolding according to learners' developmental stages and curricular goals.

Potential Areas for Future Research

Despite growing implementation, the empirical basis for AI's impact in programming education remains relatively fragmented. Future research should address the following:

- Longitudinal Studies: To understand the lasting impact of AI on cognitive development, programming proficiency, and professional success across diverse student populations.
- Equity and Inclusion: Exploring how AI affects access and outcomes for marginalized learners, including those with disabilities, from underrepresented backgrounds, or with low digital literacy.
- AI-Educator Interaction: Investigating how educators interpret, trust, and adapt AI outputs in real classroom contexts.
- Affective Learning Dimensions: Assessing how AI tools influence learners' motivation, confidence, and self-regulation, particularly in moments of failure or ambiguity.

These research directions are essential for developing evidence-based frameworks that move beyond performance metrics and capture the complex realities of AI-mediated learning.

Recommendations for Educators, Policymakers, and Industry Leaders

- For Educators: Invest in AI literacy and pedagogical training, enabling teachers to make informed decisions about when and how to incorporate AI tools. Educators should also be encouraged to participate in the co-design of AI systems, ensuring alignment with classroom realities and ethical standards.
- For Policymakers: Establish regulatory frameworks and quality standards for AI in education that address transparency, data protection, and equity. Funding should be directed toward pilot programs that test AI applications in diverse educational settings before large-scale adoption.
- For Industry Leaders: Prioritize the development of ethically aligned, inclusive, and pedagogically grounded AI tools. Collaborate with educational researchers and practitioners to ensure that tools support—not supplant—learning processes. Additionally, implement transparent algorithms and offer open APIs to foster interoperability and adaptability in various learning environments.

In sum, the future of AI in coding education depends not merely on technical advancement but on thoughtful design, inclusive governance, and rigorous research. Stakeholders must collaboratively foster ecosystems where AI tools enhance—not diminish—the humanistic and developmental goals of education.

CONCLUSION

The increasing presence of AI in coding education has prompted educators, researchers, and industry stakeholders to reconsider traditional models of teaching, learning, and professional preparation. This chapter has explored the multifaceted impacts of AI-driven tools, highlighting both their potential to personalize instruction and accelerate skill acquisition, as well as the risks they pose to cognitive development, ethical equity, and long-term learner autonomy.

AI-driven coding tools demonstrate a remarkable capacity to scaffold learning through intelligent feedback, adaptive pathways, and automation of routine tasks. They can reduce barriers to entry in programming education and offer tailored support to diverse learner populations. However, evidence also underscores the risks of over-reliance on AI, including diminished problem-solving engagement, algorithmic bias, and the exacerbation of digital inequalities. Effective use of AI in education must therefore balance efficiency with pedagogical integrity.

In the context of industry, AI tools like Copilot and IntelliCode streamline workflows and boost productivity—often prioritizing output and time-to-market over didactic value. In education, however, AI must serve as a tool that enriches, rather than overshadows, cognitive growth and critical inquiry. It should not replace the educator, but instead enhance their ability to foster curiosity, creativity, and computational thinking.

Used ethically and inclusively, AI has the potential to democratize learning, support underrepresented groups, and empower learners to become not just consumers but critical shapers of technology. This calls for deliberate pedagogical strategies, transparent governance, and ongoing interdisciplinary research. AI is not a panacea—but with mindful integration, it can become a catalyst for educational transformation and societal progress.

REFERENCES

Alisauskiene, S., Guðjónsdóttir, H., Kristinsdóttir, J. V., Connolly, T., O'Mahony, C., Lee, L., & Wozniczka, A. K. (2020). *Personalized learning within teacher education: A framework and guidelines. In-Progress Reflection No. 37 on Current and Critical Issues in Curriculum, Learning and Assessment.* UNESCO International Bureau of Education.

Anderson, L. W., & Krathwohl, D. R. (2001). *A taxonomy for learning, teaching, and assessing: A revision of Bloom's taxonomy of educational objectives: complete edition.* Addison Wesley Longman, Inc.

Bai, L., Liu, X., & Su, J. (2023). ChatGPT: The cognitive effects on learning and memory. *Brain-X, 1*(3), e30. DOI: 10.1002/brx2.30

Barrows, H. S. (1986). A taxonomy of problem-based learning methods. *Medical Education, 20*(6), 481–486. DOI: 10.1111/j.1365-2923.1986.tb01386.x PMID: 3796328

Basu, S., Biswas, G., & Kinnebrew, J. S. (2017). Learner modeling for adaptive scaffolding in a computational thinking-based science learning environment. *User Modeling and User-Adapted Interaction, 27*(1), 5–53. DOI: 10.1007/s11257-017-9187-0

Becker, B. A., Denny, P., Finnie-Ansley, J., Luxton-Reilly, A., Prather, J., & Santos, E. A. (2023). Programming is hard-or at least it used to be: Educational opportunities and challenges of ai code generation. In *Proceedings of the 54th ACM Technical Symposium on Computer Science Education* V. 1 (pp. 500-506). DOI: 10.1145/3545945.3569759

Begel, A., & Simon, B. (2008). Novice software developers, all over again. In *Proceedings of the fourth international workshop on computing education research* (pp. 3-14). DOI: 10.1145/1404520.1404522

Belland, B. R., Walker, A. E., Kim, N. J., & Lefler, M. (2017). Synthesizing results from empirical research on computer-based scaffolding in STEM education: A meta-analysis. *Review of Educational Research, 87*(2), 309–344. DOI: 10.3102/0034654316670999 PMID: 28344365

Bolukbasi, T., Chang, K. W., Zou, J. Y., Saligrama, V., & Kalai, A. T. (2016). Man is to computer programmer as woman is to homemaker? debiasing word embeddings. *Advances in Neural Information Processing Systems*, •••, 29.

Bostrom, N., & Yudkowsky, E. (2018). The ethics of artificial intelligence. In *Artificial intelligence safety and security* (pp. 57–69). Chapman and Hall/CRC. DOI: 10.1201/9781351251389-4

Brynjolfsson, E., & McAfee, A. (2014). *The second machine age: Work, progress, and prosperity in a time of brilliant technologies.* WW Norton & company.

Corbett, A. T., & Anderson, J. R. (1994). Knowledge tracing: Modeling the acquisition of procedural knowledge. *User Modeling and User-Adapted Interaction, 4*(4), 253–278. DOI: 10.1007/BF01099821

Crow, T., Luxton-Reilly, A., & Wuensche, B. (2018). Intelligent tutoring systems for programming education: a systematic review. In *Proceedings of the 20th Australasian Computing Education Conference* (pp. 53-62). DOI: 10.1145/3160489.3160492

D'ignazio, C., & Klein, L. F. (2023). *Data feminism*. MIT press.

Di Battista, A., Grayling, S., Hasselaar, E., Leopold, T., Li, R., Rayner, M., & Zahidi, S. (2023). Future of jobs report 2023. In *World Economic Forum, Geneva, Switzerland*. https://www. weforum. org/reports/the-future-of-jobs-report-2023

Di Eugenio, B., Fossati, D., & Green, N. (2021). *Intelligent support for computer science education: Pedagogy enhanced by artificial intelligence*. CRC Press. DOI: 10.1201/9781315168067

Eden, C. A., Chisom, O. N., & Adeniyi, I. S. (2024). Integrating AI in education: Opportunities, challenges, and ethical considerations. *Magna Scientia Advanced Research and Reviews, 10*(2), 006-013.

Eubanks, V. (2018). *Automating inequality: How high-tech tools profile, police, and punish the poor*. St. Martin's Press.

European Commission. (2020). On artificial intelligence—a European approach to excellence and trust, COM(2020) 65 final. https://eur-lex.europa.eu/legal-content/EN/TXT/PDF/?uri=CELEX:52020DC0065

Fan, Z., Noller, Y., Dandekar, A., & Roychoudhury, A. (2023). Intelligent tutoring system: experience of linking software engineering and programming teaching. *arXiv preprint arXiv:2310.05472*.

Floridi, L., Cowls, J., Beltrametti, M., Chatila, R., Chazerand, P., Dignum, V., Luetge, C., Madelin, R., Pagallo, U., Rossi, F., Schafer, B., Valcke, P., & Vayena, E. (2018). AI4People—an ethical framework for a good AI society: Opportunities, risks, principles, and recommendations. *Minds and Machines*, *28*(4), 689–707. DOI: 10.1007/s11023-018-9482-5 PMID: 30930541

Galenson, J., Reames, P., Bodik, R., Hartmann, B., & Sen, K. (2014). Codehint: Dynamic and interactive synthesis of code snippets. In *Proceedings of the 36th International Conference on Software Engineering* (pp. 653-663). DOI: 10.1145/2568225.2568250

Goddard, K., Roudsari, A., & Wyatt, J. C. (2012). Automation bias: A systematic review of frequency, effect mediators, and mitigators. *Journal of the American Medical Informatics Association : JAMIA*, *19*(1), 121–127. DOI: 10.1136/amiajnl-2011-000089 PMID: 21685142

Graesser, A. C., Chipman, P., Haynes, B. C., & Olney, A. (2005). AutoTutor: An intelligent tutoring system with mixed-initiative dialogue. *IEEE Transactions on Education*, *48*(4), 612–618. DOI: 10.1109/TE.2005.856149

Graesser, A. C., Olney, A., Haynes, B. C., & Chipman, P. (2006). AutoTutor: A Cognitive System That Simulates a Tutor Through Mixed-Initiative Dialogue. In *Cognitive Systems* (pp. 187-222). Psychology Press.

Holmes, W., Bialik, M., & Fadel, C. (2019). *Artificial intelligence in education promises and implications for teaching and learning*. Center for Curriculum Redesign.

Janicki, T., & Liegle, J. O. (2001). Development and evaluation of a framework for creating web-based learning modules: A pedagogical and systems perspective. *Journal of Asynchronous Learning Networks*, *5*(1), 58–84.

Joseph, O. B., & Uzondu, N. C.Olatunbosun Bartholomew JosephNwankwo Charles Uzondu. (2024). Integrating AI and Machine Learning in STEM education: Challenges and opportunities. *Computer Science & IT Research Journal*, *5*(8), 1732–1750. DOI: 10.51594/csitrj.v5i8.1379

Khreisat, M. N., Khilani, D., Rusho, M. A., Karkkulainen, E. A., Tabuena, A. C., & Uberas, A. D. (2024). Ethical implications of AI integration in educational decision making: Systematic review. *Educational Administration: Theory and Practice*, *30*(5), 8521–8527.

Kirkwood, A., & Price, L. (2014). Technology-enhanced learning and teaching in higher education: What is 'enhanced' and how do we know? A critical literature review. *Learning, Media and Technology*, *39*(1), 6–36. DOI: 10.1080/17439884.2013.770404

Kolade, O., Owoseni, A., & Egbetokun, A. (2023). Assessment on trial? ChatGPT and the new frontiers of learning and assessment in higher education. *ChatGPT and the new frontiers of learning and assessment in higher education.*

Kordzadeh, N., & Ghasemaghaei, M. (2022). Algorithmic bias: Review, synthesis, and future research directions. *European Journal of Information Systems*, *31*(3), 388–409. DOI: 10.1080/0960085X.2021.1927212

Kukulska-Hulme, A., & Lee, H. (2020). Intelligent assistants in language learning: An analysis of features and limitations. In Frederiksen, K.-M., Larsen, S., Bradley, L., & Thouësny, S. (Eds.), *CALL for widening participation: short papers from EUROCALL 2020* (pp. 172–176). DOI: 10.14705/rpnet.2020.48.1184

Le, H. (2024). *The Evolving Role of Programmers in an AI-Chatbot Dominated World: Challenges, Adaptation Strategies, and Future Prospects* (Doctoral dissertation, University of the Cumberlands).

Levy, S. T. (2020). Learning about complex systems from the bottom up: Role-playing together in a participatory simulation. In *Deep Learning and Neural Networks: Concepts, Methodologies, Tools, and Applications* (pp. 1650-1671). IGI Global.

Liu, Y. (2023). Leveraging the power of AI in undergraduate computer science education: opportunities and challenges. In *2023 IEEE Frontiers in Education Conference (FIE)* (pp. 1-5). IEEE. DOI: 10.1109/FIE58773.2023.10343474

Long, D., & Magerko, B. (2020). What is AI literacy? Competencies and design considerations. In *Proceedings of the 2020 CHI conference on human factors in computing systems* (pp. 1-16). DOI: 10.1145/3313831.3376727

Luckin, R., & Holmes, W. (2016). *Intelligence unleashed: An argument for AI in education.* Pearson.

Ma, W., Adesope, O. O., Nesbit, J. C., & Liu, Q. (2014). Intelligent tutoring systems and learning outcomes: A meta-analysis. *Journal of Educational Psychology*, *106*(4), 901–918. DOI: 10.1037/a0037123

Maloney, J., Resnick, M., Rusk, N., Silverman, B., & Eastmond, E. (2010). The scratch programming language and environment. [TOCE]. *ACM Transactions on Computing Education, 10*(4), 1–15. DOI: 10.1145/1868358.1868363

McLaren, B. M., Scheuer, O., & Mikšátko, J. (2010). Supporting collaborative learning and e-discussions using artificial intelligence techniques. *International Journal of Artificial Intelligence in Education, 20*(1), 1–46.

Muraina, I. O., & Adesanya, M. O. (2024). Impact of AI-ChatGPT Intervention on Coding: NPL Supportive Approach to Teaching and Learning Effectiveness. *Journal of Educational Sciences*, 312-324.

Noble, S. U. (2018). Algorithms of oppression: How search engines reinforce racism. In *Algorithms of oppression.* New York university press.

Papert, S. (1980). *Children, computers, and powerful ideas* (Vol. 10). Harvester.

Pedro, F., Subosa, M., Rivas, A., & Valverde, P. (2019). Artificial intelligence in education: Challenges and opportunities for sustainable development. Working papers on education policy, 7 (pp. 1-46).

Perry, N., Srivastava, M., Kumar, D., & Boneh, D. (2022). Do users write more insecure code with ai assistants?(2022). *arXiv preprint arXiv:2211.03622.*

Porter, L., & Zingaro, D. (2024). *Learn AI-Assisted Python Programming: With Github Copilot and ChatGPT.* Simon and Schuster.

Posse, A. (2025). *Your AI Ally: A Beginner's Guide to Mastering AI Tools and Transforming Your Productivity* (Vol. 1). eBookIt. com.

Prieto, L. P., Holenko Dlab, M., Gutiérrez, I., Abdulwahed, M., & Balid, W. (2011). Orchestrating technology enhanced learning: A literature review and a conceptual framework. *International Journal of Technology Enhanced Learning, 3*(6), 583–598. DOI: 10.1504/IJTEL.2011.045449

Puryear, B., & Sprint, G. (2022). Github copilot in the classroom: Learning to code with AI assistance. *Journal of Computing Sciences in Colleges, 38*(1), 37–47.

Roll, I., & Wylie, R. (2016). Evolution and revolution in artificial intelligence in education. *International Journal of Artificial Intelligence in Education, 26*(2), 582–599. DOI: 10.1007/s40593-016-0110-3

Selwyn, N. (2019). *Should robots replace teachers?: AI and the future of education.* John Wiley & Sons.

Shinohara, K., & Wobbrock, J. O. (2011). In the shadow of misperception: assistive technology use and social interactions. In *Proceedings of the SIGCHI conference on human factors in computing systems* (pp. 705-714). DOI: 10.1145/1978942.1979044

Stamper, J., Xiao, R., & Hou, X. (2024). Enhancing llm-based feedback: Insights from intelligent tutoring systems and the learning sciences. In *International Conference on Artificial Intelligence in Education* (pp. 32-43). Cham: Springer Nature Switzerland. DOI: 10.1007/978-3-031-64315-6_3

Strielkowski, W., Grebennikova, V., Lisovskiy, A., Rakhimova, G., & Vasileva, T. (2024). AI-driven adaptive learning for sustainable educational transformation. *Sustainable Development.*

Taulli, T. (2024). *AI-Assisted Programming: Better Planning, Coding, Testing, and Deployment.* O'Reilly Media, Inc.

Torka, S., & Albayrak, S. (2024). Optimizing AI-Assisted Code Generation. *arXiv preprint arXiv:2412.10953.*

VanLehn, K. (2011). The relative effectiveness of human tutoring, intelligent tutoring systems, and other tutoring systems. *Educational Psychologist, 46*(4), 197–221. DOI: 10.1080/00461520.2011.611369

Verma, S. (2019). Weapons of math destruction: How big data increases inequality and threatens democracy. *Vikalpa, 44*(2), 97–98. DOI: 10.1177/0256090919853933

Vygotskij, V. (1979). *Mind in Society: The development of higher psychological processes.* Harvard University Press.

Wang, T., Zhou, N., & Chen, Z. (2025). CyberMentor: AI Powered Learning Tool Platform to Address Diverse Student Needs in Cybersecurity Education. *arXiv preprint arXiv:2501.09709.*

Wang, V. (2025). Ethics and Equity in AI-Driven Education. In *AI Integration Into Andragogical Education* (pp. 231–254). IGI Global Scientific Publishing. DOI: 10.4018/979-8-3373-0502-8.ch010

Williamson, B., & Eynon, R. (2020). Historical threads, missing links, and future directions in AI in education. *Learning, Media and Technology, 45*(3), 223–235. DOI: 10.1080/17439884.2020.1798995

Woolf, B. P. (2010). *Building intelligent interactive tutors: Student-centered strategies for revolutionizing e-learning.* Morgan Kaufmann.

Xu, M., David, J. M., & Kim, S. H. (2018). The fourth industrial revolution: Opportunities and challenges. *International journal of financial research, 9*(2), 90-95.

Xu, W., & Ouyang, F. (2022). A systematic review of AI role in the educational system based on a proposed conceptual framework. *Education and Information Technologies, 27*(3), 4195–4223. DOI: 10.1007/s10639-021-10774-y

Yelamarthi, K., Dandu, R., Rao, M., Yanambaka, V. P., & Mahajan, S. (2024). Exploring the potential of generative AI in shaping engineering education: Opportunities and challenges. *Journal of Engineering Education Transformations, 37*(2), 439–445. DOI: 10.16920/jeet/2024/v37is2/24072

Zajko, M. (2022). Artificial intelligence, algorithms, and social inequality: Sociological contributions to contemporary debates. *Sociology Compass, 16*(3), e12962. DOI: 10.1111/soc4.12962

Zootzky, G., & Pfeiffer, A. (2024). Educational transformation through AI: Preparing for a new era of learning. In *INTED2024 Proceedings* (pp. 1202-1207). IATED.

Zuboff, S. (2019). *The age of surveillance capitalism: The fight for a human future at the new frontier of power, edn.* PublicAffairs.

Chapter 16
Artificial Intelligence in Personalized Education:
Revolutionizing Learning Paths and Student Engagement

S. Devi Dhivya
SRM Institute of Science and Technology, India

R. Balakrishna
Vels Institute of Science Technology and Advanced Studies, India

T. Selva Banu Priya
Panimalar Engineering College, India

T. Thilagam
https://orcid.org/0000-0002-7657-0726
Vel Tech Rangarajan Dr. Sagunthala R&D Institute of Science and Technology, India

V. Sathya
Vel Tech Rangarajan Dr. Sagunthala R&D Institute of Science and Technology, India

L.A. Anto Gracious
https://orcid.org/0000-0003-2386-9182
R.M.K. College of Engineering and Technology, India

R. Siva Subramanian
https://orcid.org/0000-0002-7509-9223
SRM Institute of Science and Technology, Tiruchirappalli, India

ABSTRACT

Education is changing with AI, and the intelligent tutoring, adaptive learning, and recommendation systems are transforming the education based on personalization. This chapter surveys current trends, recent technologies and use cases for what is to come in the future of education. It is using AI driven system to analyze student behavior and provide real time content, quizzes and feedback. Recommendation systems, intelligent tutors, and learning paths take shape due to machine learning; natural language processing enters the picture with intelligent tutors; and reinforcement learning also improves the learning paths. Even with benefits, there are concerns about data privacy, bias, and technical difficulties. That is, advanced AI models, multilinear data and AR/VR may unite to improve personalisation in future. This chapter examines the impact and potential, and even challenges of AI about revolutionizing learning.

DOI: 10.4018/979-8-3373-5097-4.ch016

INTRODUCTION

In the recent past, education has been faced with a lot of changes mainly brought by the technological factor. The traditional teaching methodologies that have been in use in most learning institutions are being considered by many as insufficient in catering for the needs of the learners. Every learner has different learning styles, rates and capacity and this makes it hard for the traditional learning systems to meet the needs of all the students. Personalization of learning which delivers education according to the need of each learner has emerged as a solution to this problem. In this regard, it seeks to optimize students' participation, promote knowledge acquisition and make sure that none of the students is left behind due to restricted classroom learning. The significance of the individualized approach can be viewed especially within the framework of the current conditions of the learning process, where students are to comprehend a great deal of information at different levels of difficulty. The fact of receiving the specific content and individual plans of learning can positively affect the motivation and help to grasp the material much easier. Such a model also allows students to work independently, and it is only when they have mastered a given topic that they are allowed to proceed to the next level. Since educational institutions are keen on offering personalized learning, technology has been a critical component in this process. In this regard, AI has become a revolutionary tool in the area of education. AI can analyze data, identify relationships and make real-time adjustments and for those reasons it is well suited for use in customizing learning. Some of the benefits of using artificial intelligence in schools include; it is able to monitor the progress of the students, determine their strengths and weaknesses and even make suggestions on how the teaching methods should be delivered based on the student's learning style. From adaptive learning system to intelligent tutoring systems, AI is entering a plethora of learning tools and platforms that change the traditional model of learning for students. It can be seen that AI has the potential to revolutionize the education system in a positive way and make the process more efficient, effective and personalized for learners with each of their needs taken into consideration. Nevertheless, traditional learning methods continue to remain the most used in many learning systems, and there is still a vast difference between the potential of AI and its implementation in learning environments. There are bitter challenges to AI-related personalized learning today; they include; There is shortage of resources; resistance to change and; the ethical issues that surround use of advanced technologies in learning. The traditional approaches of learning are not sensitive to the students' needs as it involves a collective learning process that does not take into consideration the abilities, learning styles and interests of the learners. This leads to the situation where some students are left behind or even disengaged and cannot get the most out of what is being taught. The purpose of this survey is two-fold. First, it seeks to provide an overview of the current AI technologies employed in personalization of learning, on how machine learning, natural language processing, reinforcement learning, deep learning are utilized in the educational environment[Pajila et al 2023]. Secondly, the survey aims at finding out the effects of AI in relation to performance and participation of students. Exploring use cases will help to identify the impact of AI tools on learning, engagement, and learners' interactions in academic environment. This study will investigate the possibility of the use of AI in the connection between conventional and personalized learning environments in order to identify how technology can improve learning. Finally, it will present the state of affairs of AI in personalized education, its advantages and disadvantages, and its prospects.

AI TECHNIQUES FOR PERSONALIZED LEARNING

The use of Artificial Intelligence (AI) is quite instrumental in the delivery of student-centered approaches where all students' learning needs are met[Chen, L et al 2020]. Machine learning, NLP, reinforcement learning and deep learning techniques are used to support the learning/teaching process to customize content, deliver feedbacks and recommend an ideal path to follow[Lakumarapu, S et al 2024].

MACHINE LEARNING

Machine learning is a branch of Artificial Intelligence in which a machine is fed data and learns from that data to make some predictions or even to make some decisions. In personalized learning, two most commonly used types of machine learning are the supervised learning and the unsupervised learning[Roll, I., & Wylie, R. 2016].

Supervised Learning: Supervised learning is a type of learning where algorithms are trained with a particular set of labeled data in order to predict the result. This technique is widely applied in recommendation systems where AI proposes lessons in the form of videos, articles or exercises based on the student's activity. For instance, the above AI system might suggest learning materials or more practice questions in a certain area if a student is struggling. Another is content adaptation in which the ability of the AI system provides the ability to adjust the content to the level of the students or even the format in which the content is presented depending on the performance of the students in class. If a student is doing well in the content, then the system may offer more complex content, while low performing students will be provided with easier or extra content to master[Sreelakshmi, et al 2024].

Unsupervised Learning: In contrast to the supervised learning, unsupervised means to find patterns in data that are not classified. It is employed in grouping students based on the approach, mode or behavior while learning. For example, AI can cluster students in terms of their usage of learning materials, which will help to design learning solutions or remedial programs. These groupings assist the educators to give special attention to various groups of learners[Subha, S et al 2024].

NATURAL LANGUAGE PROCESSING (NLP)

NLP is a branch of Artificial Intelligence that helps computers to understand, interpret, and generate human language. In personalized learning, NLP is applied to make the learning process more interesting and sensitive to the learner[Chowdhary, K., & Chowdhary, K. R. 2020].

Intelligent Tutoring Systems (ITS): These are systems that apply NLP with an aim of interacting with the students like a human tutor. ITS is capable of analyzing the input provided by the student and respond to the questions with relevant answers and explanations. For instance, an intelligent tutor can take a student through a mathematical problem and provide suggestions depending on the student's performance.

Adaptive Feedback and Question-Answering Systems: It is possible to offer immediate and adaptive NLP-based AI feedback decisions. For instance, if a student provides an incorrect answer to a question, the system can study the error and provide feedback in a manner that the student will comprehend easily. Such systems are useful in enhancing students' understanding by correcting them on any misconceptions they might have and also fostering the students' engagement.

REINFORCEMENT LEARNING

Reinforcement learning (RL) algorithm is based on training a model to make a decision by allowing it to learn from the consequences of its action through costs and rewards[Hu et al 2024]. In the case of personalized learning, RL is employed to assist in the prescription of learning paths to follow through providing useful feedback to the students. For example, the level of engagement of a student (for instance, the right answers, time taken), and the AI modifies the content being taught based on the student's response [Roayaei, M. (2024]. In this sense, the system raises the level of difficulty of the tasks or presents new tasks to the students as they advance in their learning process.

Figure 1. AI techniques in personalized learning

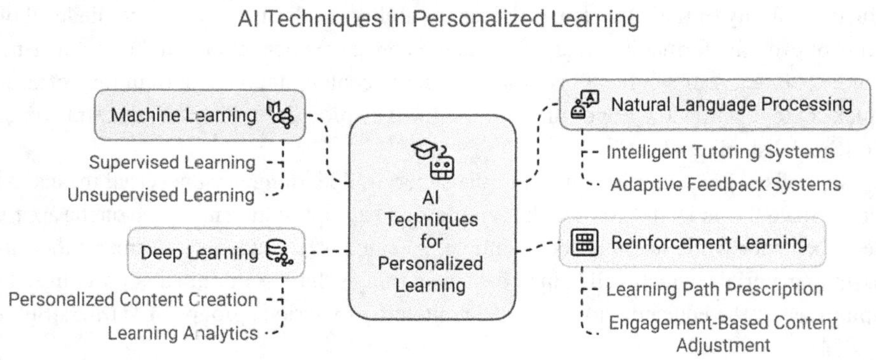

DEEP LEARNING

Deep learning is a form of machine learning where complex neural networks with many layers are used to analyse a large volume of data in order to identify intricate patterns in the entire data set [Kazi, K. S. 2024]. In personalized learning, there are several ways through which deep learning is used:

Personalized learning: Specifically, the use of neural networks could develop unique content such as quizzes, assignments or any other content type that could be customized depending on the learning profile of the students. Such profiles might contain information about the student's achievement, learning rate, and preferences. The aspect of deep learning systems that can process large amounts of information makes it easier to deliver content that will suit each learner.

Student Data Assessment and Learning Analytics: Deep learning is also applied to evaluate the students' data and make recommendations through learning analytics. This involves evaluating a student's performance pattern, analyzing the findings, and even prognosis of the future behavior. Thus, the software may warn teachers about children that they believe are failing, so that proper remedial actions may be taken. In addition, the assessments that are based on artificial intelligence can generate the results that will allow grading the papers and giving the feedback immediately. In general, ML, NLP, RL, and DL are making personalized learning effective, engaging, and responsive because they adapt to learners' needs and learning styles. These not only improve the quality of learning but also make education easier and possible for everyone to achieve their educational goals[Pradhan et al 2024].

PERSONALIZED LEARNING APPROACHES USING AI

Personalized approach is designed and implemented while delivering lessons, curricular and materials to the learner based on his or her characteristics. AI has greatly impacted the field of personal learning by allowing the methods that respond to content, offer feedbacks, and engagement. There are now several applications of AI that are being applied in the teaching-learning processes as well as in online learning environments.

Adaptive Learning Systems

It is a process that varies the delivery of content depending on the learner's progress and performance. These systems work in real time and make changes in the level of difficulty, the order of lessons, and the type of activities given to a particular student. That is the reason why the idea is to provide a student with lesson that will be tailored to student's individual speed of learning and his or her comprehension abilities.

For instance, in a math learning platform if a student finds it hard to solve multiplication but easy to solve division problems the system will give the student more problems on multiplication while advancing to the next level on division. On the other hand, if the student performs well on a given topic in the course, then the system may take the student to the next level. It also assists teachers to know areas that particular students need to be instructed on hence allowing efficient use of time when teaching. Through the tracking of the learning rate and the alteration of the learning path, the adaptive learning systems guarantee that the students are neither overburdened nor under stimulated, which is the best learning scenario for any learner.

Recommendation Systems

The use of recommendation systems in personalized learning is quite popular these days as it helps in recommending materials based on the student's learning style and aptitude. These systems track activities associated with students' engagement in learning activities within learning platforms, including time spent on certain topics, performance in quizzes, and usage of different resources. Based on this data, AI suggests the content in the form of videos, articles, exercises, quizzes, etc., that would be beneficial to the learner at the moment. For instance, when a student is unable to grasp a certain concept in a particular discipline, the system will recommend additional videos or explanations that are more basic to the concept in question. In the same way, if the student has performed well in a certain topic, the recommendation system is likely to present more difficult problems in the same area to encourage the student to learn more. Thus, students can easily navigate through the supply of materials and find only relevant information which makes their learning process much more effective.

Figure 2. AI-driven personalized learning approaches

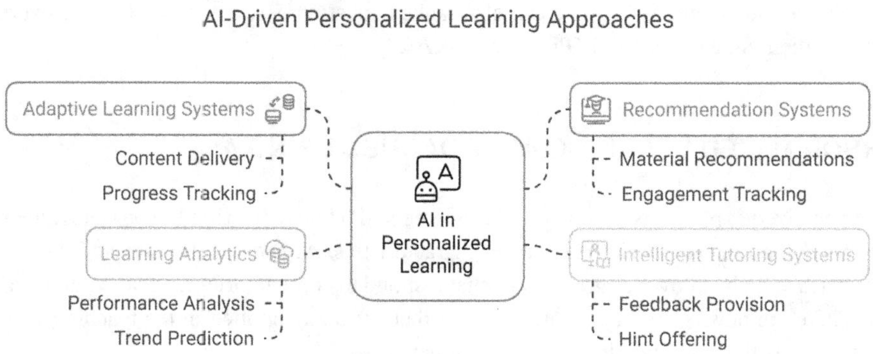

Intelligent Tutoring Systems (ITS)

Intelligent Tutoring System (ITS) is a method of personalized and computer supported tutoring system that gives hints, instructions, and graded feedback to the student. There is one called 'ITS' that uses natural language processing, machine learning, and data analytics to provide a virtual tutor that emulates the human tutor experience with the student for practice. They also offer feedback immediately after a student has completed a question and offer more support based on the score that the student has been given. For example, if a student is learning a language and he constructs a sentence in the wrong manner the ITS will then give a hint, restate the question in a different way or give more examples. Gradually, the ITS is able to adapt to the student's responses and the level of difficulty and the amount of help provided increases or decreases accordingly. This cycle assists the students in identifying their limitations and areas of strength besides enhancing learning. It also improves the student involvement by making a dynamic learning environment that responds to the individual student.

Learning Analytics

Learning analytics is the process of collecting data regarding student's activities, performance, and participation in his/her learning process. Learning analytics technologies can also gather a lot of data relative to the students' performance, their attendance, time spent on exercises, and their usage of learning materials. This information is then used to get an understanding of the student performance and to foresee the future trends. For instance, learning analytics can discover the student's tendencies as to whether the student has difficulties with some specific types of questions or takes more time to grasp certain concepts. These features help educators to prevent the student from being left behind and requiring additional support or changing the approach. Furthermore, learning analytics can be used to estimate the success of the students, find out who is likely to fail and then provide appropriate solutions to the problem. They can prove most useful in large classrooms or in online teaching environments where the teacher cannot afford to pay individual attention to all the students.

Adaptive learning systems, recommendation systems, intelligent tutoring systems and learning analytics, which are some of the approaches to applying artificial intelligence in the learning process of students, are revolutionizing education. These technologies make the learning process more individual, interesting, and effective due to the possibility to adapt lessons, provide the student with feedbacks and analyze the results. These approaches are likely to develop more advanced in the future as AI advances, thus improving the efficiency of education and the learning process for all the learners.

Benefits of AI in Personalized Learning

The incorporation of AI into the learning environment has been beneficial in creating positive impacts, particularly to the learning process and the results achieved. These features make it easier for the students to learn, and the fact that the AI can also give out assessments on the go makes it easier for the students to know what they are good at or not good at. The advantages of the use of AI in personalized learning include better results, engagement, expansion, and feedback.

Improved Learning Outcomes

Another advantage of using AI in personalized learning is the learning outcome that a student is bound to achieve. AI makes learning more effective as it is done with regard to the needs of each learner. This way, students can learn at their own level and can grasp well what has been taught before they are introduced to other levels of learning. For example, AI systems can provide the student with challenging material if she is ready for it and with simple material if she is not ready for more challenging tasks. AI also simplifies learning by detecting areas of ignorance and providing solutions and answers to questions from them. In cases where a student is unable to grasp a certain concept, the system will offer more information, examples or exercises as many times as the student needs to grasp the concept. This way, it is possible to stop a student from proceeding with misconceptions and establishes a solid base for the following classes. Therefore, students who engage in learning through the use of AI-based learning solutions are likely to have better retention of the content and mastery of the learning content.

Figure 3. Benefits of AI in personalized learning

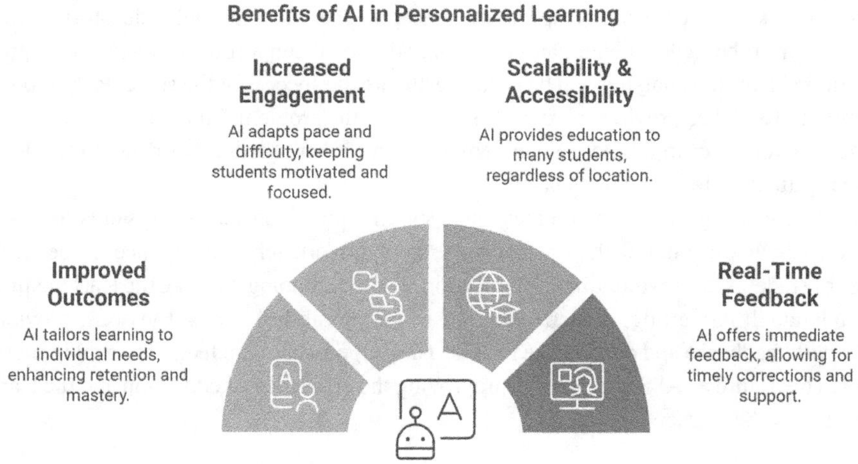

Increased Student Engagement

Another factor that may be highly beneficial for a student is the AI's capacity to learn at the pace of every learner. Teaching in a face-to-face classroom setting is always challenging as the curriculum is set to suit all the students but it does not cater to each learner's needs. AI-based systems, nevertheless, control the speed and level of difficulty of the lessons in relation to the specific performance and learning abilities of the student.

It also keeps the students focused by offering them material that is not too challenging and not too simple that it bores the student. It is important to feed students with content that is neither too hard for them nor too easy for them to handle; this will help them be motivated. Also, the AI systems can integrate the features of a game or quiz in order to make the learning process more enjoyable. The constant feedback and the changes that occur from time to time make the students to have an active role in the learning process hence making it more engaging and interesting.

Scalability and Accessibility

AI in personalized learning also has an added bonus of scalability and accessibility. It is very limited when it comes to the number of students in a class, the available resources and the possibility of addressing every student individually. That is why, the AI-powered platforms, on the contrary, can address students in large quantities at the same time offering them personalized learning options regardless of their geographical location. Another benefit of using AI in education is the aspect of scalability. AI systems are capable of providing education to as many students as possible without any limitation of geographical location, the level of education required etc. This brings personalized learning to students in the lowly and remote areas where they can hardly get access to quality learning materials. The professor demonstrated that AI enhances educational equal opportunity and availability across distance learning platforms or a traditional physical classroom to make a proper individualized learning. In addition, AI makes it possible for educators to reach out to more students at once since they do not have to spend a lot of their time doing administrative work, which is usually repetitive, in addition to the time they spend teaching and interacting with each student, as the AI systems can track the students' progress and adapt the content to suit each learner.

Real-Time Feedback and Assessment

The opportunity to give immediate feedback is one of the most significant advantages of AI in personalization of learning. AI systems can provide feedback in real time and thus, it is possible to determine the performance of a student after an activity or an assignment. This makes it easier for students to correct their thinking whenever they are wrong and this is much better than to continue with the wrong thinking pattern for some time. Real-time feedback also enables educators to intervene as they are monitoring the students. If an AI system identifies that a student has difficulties with some concepts, it can notify a teacher so that the latter would be able to help or change the approach. This capability is especially useful in large classrooms or online learning environment where individual students' learning needs may not easily be identified. Finally, AI-based assessments can be more diverse and complex than conventional methods of testing, which makes it possible to get more comprehensive information about the student's performance and his/her weak points. The possibility to provide timely and individualised feedback fosters the process of constant learning and makes a student feel that he is not alone. Such a kind of feedback loop leads to positive attitude development toward learning and helps students feel that they are capable in terms of academic performance. Several advantages come with the integration of artificial intelligence in learning, which enhances the approach to learning as more adaptive, fun and effective. AI application in education ensures that content is delivered in a way that is relevant to the learner hence increases the rate of learning and retention. It enhances students learning since it allows for flexibility in the pace at which knowledge is delivered with a view of catering for the more complex learner. In addition, AI also increases the scalability of the learning process and makes education more accessible since the class can include a large number of students regardless of whether they are in the same physical space or not. Last but not least, feedback and assessment in real-time help to identify learners' needs and promptly address them. Considering the current progression of AI technology in the educational system, the role of AI in the learning process will expand and enhance the learning process in terms of efficiency, accessibility and effectiveness.

CHALLENGES AND LIMITATIONS OF AI IN PERSONALIZED LEARNING

As much as there are advantages of using AI in personalized learning, there are also some disadvantages and constraints in its use. All these challenges have to be dealt with so that the incorporation of AI in education is done in a responsible and efficient manner. Challenges are as follows: Regulatory and security concerns stemming from the management and storage of data; captive defining in reference to the use of AI algorithms; technological challenges; and ethical issue arising from the over centralization of AI in teaching processes causing less interaction between human beings.

Data Privacy and Security

The use of AI in the learning platforms involves the gathering of large amount of personal information to deliver personalized learning which raises issues of data privacy and security. Personal data, academic performance data, and behavioral data are the core data that is used by the AI-based systems. The risk arises when this data is not protected from cyber criminals, unauthorized personnel or being used in the wrong way. For example, the violation of data privacy can result in information that is not supposed to be released getting into the wrong hands like the scores of a test or one's preferences. Second, the vast amount of data collected from students leads to concerns on the aspect of consent, whereby, the students or their guardians may not fully comprehend the use or storage of their data. The absence of clear policies on use of data might cost the credibility of the AI-based learning platforms and especially in the regions that have strong data protection laws. To this end, it is crucial that AI platforms use provincial encryption procedures and security checks as well as ensure the consent of their users is clear before collecting their data. As for the use of personal data, it is necessary to be as open as possible and follow the rules of personal data protection in order to protect both the students and the institutions.

Bias in AI Algorithms

Bias is not a phenomenon that is unique to humans, it can also be found in AI algorithms, and in the context of education, it can be expressed in several ways. These biases are usually as a result of the data fed into the AI models that are used in the AI systems. In case the data used is not a good sample or if it mimics the society's discrimination, bias will be imposed on the algorithms. For instance, an artificial intelligent system that is trained to learn from data would have the potential of passing gender, racial, or socio-economic biases in learning content, assessment, or recommendations that it provides. Prejudice in AI algorithms leads to discrimination in various ways, for instance, in grading or provision of learning materials. Some students will be provided with less relevant information or more difficulty level content while others will be favored. This leads to a major problem of making certain that systems that deploy artificial intelligence to make decisions are fair. In order to tackle this problem, developers of AI systems should be more cautious with the data used in the model. In order to reduce bias, it is necessary to have a great variety and variety of datasets. In this case, there should be periodic checks of the algorithms to ensure that they are fair and if not then corrective measures have to be taken. It is crucial that the developers bring about the principles of technical interpretability in the resulting AI systems in order to enable the stakeholders to comprehend the decision-making processes that the AI system employs and also to ensure that no particular group is being harmed by the AI system.

Technological Barriers

Another challenge is that personalized learning is based on the use of high-quality technology infrastructure, which can be a problem in the context of a lack of funds. Some students may not get equal opportunities to access fast internet connection, advanced computing devices and

AI software as may be required for effective use of AI learning tools in their region or at their school. Schools in many developing countries or rural areas may not have adequate resources to support AI platforms which include devices, internet connection and human resource to manage AI systems. It may widen the gap in education resulting into the underserved student's missing out an opportunity of what AI can offer. To address this issue, there is a need for huge investment in technology infrastructure from the governments and private companies. To ensure that this opportunity is made available to all the students in the educational institutions, there is the need for the institutions to help reduce the technology divide.

Ethical Considerations

Another issue, which is worth discussing regarding the application of AI in personalized learning, is that of concern over the overuse of technology in education. The main disadvantage of AI systems is that there is increasing reliance on such systems in students and educators, leading to the reduction of the use of human wisdom and lodgement. Traditionally, education is not just passing of knowledge but also involves attitudes, perceptions, and skills including thinking skills and social skills. Something perhaps, as AI provides customized and adapted learning experiences for users, it lacks social insight and concern as given by human tutors. The problem is that if AI is taken to the ultimate extent and used extensively in educational settings, it could be detrimental for the human factor which is so crucial for creative and personal development of students. Further, the use of AI in the evaluation of the students may also pose a number of issues on fairness and the extent of the evaluation. Therefore, AI systems can be considered utilizing information where outcome-based performance assessments may leave out such factors as motivation, effort, and emotional endurance in students.

This means that leaving the whole responsibility of student assessment to AI might end up neglecting these aspects of learning and viewing the progress of the student in a very limited way. Therefore, it is very vital that we look at the challenges and drawbacks of AI that is prevalent in the education sector with reference to personalized learning. Therefore, the following considerations are important in order to use AI appropriately by addressing data privacy, lack of bias, technological challenges, and pro-ethics of education. By addressing these issues, the AI can become an instrument for improving education that will not erode fairness and human interaction with others.

FUTURE DIRECTIONS AND RESEARCH IN AI-DRIVEN PERSONALIZED LEARNING

use of AI in adapting education to learners through multi-modal data have a great potential to revolutionize education. Such developments do not only aim at improving the experience of learning, but also at making education accessible, interesting and fruitful for all learners.

Advancements in AI

The direction of deep learning and other developing AI is one promising areas of personal learning in the future. Deep learning is a category of machine learning, which has been demonstrated to be highly effective in dealing with data in the form of images, speech, and texts. In the case of personalized learning, deep learning could further take advantage of the student's engagement with the content to be more effective in identifying the specific areas of needs to address and support the students better. For instance, deep learning algorithms could assess how children and young people read, use logic, or interact with media and video resources not only for what they comprehend but how they comprehend it to adapt the learning environment and satisfy the learner's particular thought patterns. Furthermore, the development of other forms of AI like the reinforcement learning could help in the enhancement of customized learning models. Reinforcement learning could provide reinforcement to the AI system by making it more flexible depending on the performance and the progress of the students in order to offer immediate feedback and content changes. This might create a continuous learning feedback cycle that would likely to increase learners' participation and retention leading to better learning.

AI Integration with Other Educational Technologies

When integrated with other modern trends in education, such as AR and VR, AI will be even more effective in terms of student-centered learning. When it comes to the use of AI and AR/VR, learning can be enriched through active engagement with the content in ways that are impossible with a textbook or even with most technology-based tools[Aswini, J et al 2023][Siva Subramanian R et al 2024]. For instance, it is possible to immerse students in virtual scenarios where they could apply real-life skills, for instance, carrying out a scientific experiment or studying history from the real-life view. Together with its AI element, these technologies would be able to make the learning environment personalized for the individual learner. It can observe students' activity in the virtual environment, evaluate their performance, and modify the course of events depending on the learners' abilities and development, which enhances the learning process. For example, when a student is studying the solar system, he/she can travel through space, touch planets, and get feedback from the AI system depending on the student's actions. This integration is useful in learning because it helps bring abstract concepts to life and improve the understanding of topics.

Improving Personalization through Multi-modal Data

Another future perspective to be explored in relation to personal learning is regarding multimodal data to personalization. At the present time, the data used in most AI systems include text data in forms of quiz scores, written responses, and interaction logs. However, the future AI system which will be used in the context of the education process will utilize text, video, audio, and biological data in order to get more significant information about the processes occurring in the learning activities of the learner. For instance, the data in the form of videos and audios can give the AI systems the information about the fluency of the particular student's speech and the biometric data like eye movement, facial expressions, or the pulse rate can tell about the level of interest of the particular student. Collectively, it would then be easier to quantify and monitor student engagement, anxiety or interest so that the AI system can make appropriate adjustments on what to deliver. For example, if a student looks bored while solving a particular problem, AI can identify such signals through facial or other physical cue s and provide a less complicated task. On the other hand, if the student is performing well and appears to be bored, the system may present additional material to keep the student interested. Such a level of individual engagement would be significantly more complex than the text-based approaches and provide a more holistic way of learning.

In turn, multi-modal data could solve the flexibility of AI systems by providing different forms of learning. This is because some students may be inclined to learn through watching and observing while others may be able to grasp concepts better through touching and feeling or even through listening to instructions. In this way, AI can work with different types of data, which helps to meet these preferences and provide the possibility of learning to a greater number of people. From the standpoint of the AI advance, there are incredible opportunities for applying deep learning, enlarging the usage of AR/VR, and using multi-modal data in the sphere of personalized learning[Varun, C. M. et al 2024]. With the advancement of AI technology in the future, it becomes possible to prove the highly dynamic, interactive and modular environment of learning that can be easily adjusted to learner needs[Sanjeera et al 2024]. Such innovations will also help to improve access to education, equity, and effectiveness in the teaching and learning process. AI will supplement other advanced technologies and information sources to enhance the concept of personalized learning and make it more effective in addressing future challenges for students.

CONCLUSION

The incorporation of AI in personalized learning has brought about significant change in education systems, which can be considered as strengths and weaknesses. Some of the points that have been discussed in this discussion include the following: The important roles of AI techniques including machine learning, natural language processing, and reinforcement learning in offering differential learning experiences to the students. However, the integration of AI in education also poses various issues such as privacy, algorithmic bias, technological usage, and the ethical issues in using the AI in education. It is important to address these issues so as to eliminate any negative impact that AI may have on the learning process. In the following years, the application of AI technology will become even more acute in the field of education. The advancements in learning technologies are expected the following: integration of artificial intelligence and AR/VR in the educational process, use of multimodal data for enhanced personalization, and the further development of the deep learning technologies to make the tailored educational experience even better. The following will be the implications for educators, students, and policymakers. The future classroom will be more student-centered, and the teacher will have to become a facilitator and use AI tools in the process of education. Teachers will provide improved teaching that focuses on delivering different content based on the abilities of the learners. Government and other authorities need to pay attention to the development of policies that would provide equal opportunities for the integration of AI in education, as well as to the ethical aspects of AI use in education, so that this technology would support equality and fairness. In conclusion, the experience of the development of the role of AI in education indicates that the process can bring numerous changes and improvements to facilitate the learning process for students across the world.

REFERENCES

Aswini, J., Malarvizhi, N., Subramanian, S., & Gayathri, A. (2023). Augmented reality and virtual reality in e-governance: An immersive technology application and its challenges. In *AI, IoT, and Blockchain Breakthroughs in E-Governance* (pp. 138-153). IGI Global.

Chen, L., Chen, P., & Lin, Z. (2020). Artificial intelligence in education: A review. *IEEE Access : Practical Innovations, Open Solutions*, *8*, 75264–75278. DOI: 10.1109/ACCESS.2020.2988510

Chowdhary, K., & Chowdhary, K. R. (2020). Natural language processing. *Fundamentals of artificial intelligence*, 603-649.

Hu, K., Li, M., Song, Z., Xu, K., Xia, Q., Sun, N., & Xia, M. (2024). A review of research on reinforcement learning algorithms for multi-agents. *Neurocomputing*, *599*, 128068. DOI: 10.1016/j.neucom.2024.128068

Kazi, K. S. (2024). Computer-aided diagnosis in ophthalmology: A technical review of deep learning applications. *Transformative Approaches to Patient Literacy and Healthcare Innovation*, 112-135.

Lakumarapu, S., Nithyanandhan, R., Bhargavi, V. S., Anish, T. P., & Nalini, M. (2024, August). Machine Learning Approaches for Liver Disease Prediction: A Comparative Analysis. In *2024 5th International Conference on Electronics and Sustainable Communication Systems (ICESC)* (pp. 159-164). IEEE. DOI: 10.1109/ICESC60852.2024.10689974

Pajila, P. B., Sudha, K., Selvi, D. K., Kumar, V. N., Gayathri, S., & Subramanian, R. S. (2023, July). A survey on natural language processing and its applications. In *2023 4th International Conference on Electronics and Sustainable Communication Systems (ICESC)* (pp. 996-1001). IEEE.

Pradhan, T., Nimkar, P., & Jhajharia, K. (2024). Machine Learning and Deep Learning for Big Data Analysis. In *Big Data Analytics Techniques for Market Intelligence* (pp. 209–240). IGI Global Scientific Publishing. DOI: 10.4018/979-8-3693-0413-6.ch008

Roayaei, M. (2024). Comprehensive Survey of Adaptive and Intelligent Education System Using Reinforcement Learning. *AI-Enhanced Teaching Methods*, 176-197.

Roll, I., & Wylie, R. (2016). Evolution and revolution in artificial intelligence in education. *International Journal of Artificial Intelligence in Education*, *26*(2), 582–599. DOI: 10.1007/s40593-016-0110-3

Sanjeera, S. K., Jevin, J. A., Pajila, B., & Kumari, R. (2024). Exploring the Applications of Augmented Reality and Virtual Reality in Medicine: A Comprehensive Overview. *Navigating the Augmented and Virtual Frontiers in Engineering*, 212-222.

Siva Subramanian, R., Nalini, M., & Aswini, J. (Eds.). (2024 Jul 22). *Navigating the Augmented and Virtual Frontiers in Engineering*. IGI Global. DOI: 10.4018/979-8-3693-5613-5

Sreelakshmi, S., Babu, A. A., Lakshmipriya, C., Gracious, L. A., Nalini, M., & Subramanian, R. S. (2024, October). Enhancing Intrusion Detection Systems with Machine Learning. In *2024 2nd International Conference on Self Sustainable Artificial Intelligence Systems (ICSSAS)* (pp. 557-564). IEEE. DOI: 10.1109/ICSSAS64001.2024.10760341

Subha, S., Balakrishnan, C., & Anish, T. P. (2024, August). Optimizing Machine Learning Algorithms for Heart Disease Prediction in Healthcare: A Comparative Study. In *2024 5th International Conference on Electronics and Sustainable Communication Systems (ICESC)* (pp. 866-872). IEEE. DOI: 10.1109/ICESC60852.2024.10689877

Varun, C. M., Kumar, R. A., Gokila, E., Gayathri, S., Nalini, M., & Subramanian, R. S. (2024, October). Virtual Frontiers Navigating the Impact and Potential of AR and VR. In *2024 2nd International Conference on Self Sustainable Artificial Intelligence Systems (ICSSAS)* (pp. 1559-1565). IEEE. DOI: 10.1109/ICSSAS64001.2024.10760749

Chapter 17
Transformative AI Tools for Inclusive and Holistic Learning Environments:
Enhancing Accessibility, Equity, and Emotional Intelligence

Ryan Le
https://orcid.org/0009-0006-8239-3830
Newrizons Academy, USA

ABSTRACT

This chapter explores how artificial intelligence (AI) tools reshape inclusive and holistic educational environments. The authors examine how adaptive learning platforms, emotional recognition systems, and AI-powered chatbots can address diversity, equity, and inclusion (DEI) in both K–12 and higher education settings. Case studies from institutions such as Georgia Tech and the University of Michigan highlight the transformative potential of AI in increasing accessibility, fostering psychological safety, and enhancing cultural competency. The chapter also addresses AI implementation's ethical concerns, including bias, data privacy, and the digital divide. Emphasis is placed on the importance of maintaining human-centered pedagogy alongside technological innovation.

INTRODUCTION

The educational environment transforms through artificial intelligence because it enables customized learning experiences that support inclusivity and emotional support. Educational institutions moving toward greater diversity find artificial intelligence to offer innovative methods for serving students from underrepresented groups and people with disabilities. According to Niemi & Liu (2021), educational institutions can develop supportive learning environments

DOI: 10.4018/979-8-3373-5097-4.ch017

through artificial intelligence tools, which enhance student academic success and create psychological safety, equity, and holistic development.

The most promising educational application of artificial intelligence is its ability to create customized student learning experiences. The adaptive learning platforms DreamBox and Khan Academy use real-time data analytics to adjust the difficulty level of their instructional materials. The technology delivers customized instruction matching each student's learning pace (Smith, 2021). The educational method supports students who feel left out in traditional classrooms, especially those from low-income families and students with learning differences.

Artificial intelligence (AI) enhances accessibility while supporting diversity, equity, and inclusion (DEI) initiatives by developing content that responds to different cultures. NLP algorithms analyze multiple cultural perspectives to generate content that helps students see their identities reflected in educational curricula (Dede & Grotner, 2019). The artificial intelligence-based writing tools Grammarly and Quill assist non-native speakers to overcome language barriers, which lead to increased inclusivity and better communication confidence (Samarakou et al., 2015).

Artificial intelligence significantly impacts holistic learning, which focuses on complete individual development. Students can use SEL tools, including chatbots and emotion recognition software, to reflect on their emotions and develop resilience through self-reflection. The platform Replika helps users develop self-awareness and emotional regulation skills that align with holistic education goals (Duffy & Azevedo, 2015).

AI-driven tutoring systems create psychological safety because they deliver continuous feedback without any form of judgment, enabling students to take intellectual risks. The systems decrease student anxiety about mistakes by letting students retry without public exposure (Julien, 2024). According to Ali and Morozov (2023), sentiment analysis tools help teachers detect student distress and provide timely intervention.

Despite its advantages, implementing AI in education faces multiple obstacles. Using AI algorithms with biased systems maintains existing social inequalities because training data sets do not contain diverse information (White, 2021). The accuracy of facial recognition systems decreases when they are used to identify people from specific racial backgrounds. The development of AI systems requires developers to establish transparent systems and perform regular audits while ensuring they include all users (Zawacki-Richter et al., 2019).

The protection of student data stands as an essential matter of concern. Educational institutions must establish strong governance systems to safeguard student information because AI requires extensive data sets to provide customized learning experiences (Ismail & Aloshi, 2025). The General Data Protection Regulation (GDPR) and the Family Educational Rights and Privacy Act (FERPA) establish essential guidelines for using data responsibly.

Through their case studies, the University of Michigan and Georgia Tech demonstrate how AI technology has already produced significant results. According to Holmes et al. (2021), the AI tutors at Georgia Tech have boosted computer science course retention, particularly for women and minority students. The University of Michigan implemented an AI-based captioning system that allows students with hearing disabilities to join classroom discussions (Barnes, Hutson & Perry, 2024).

The future development of AI in education will succeed through joint efforts between educational professionals, technology experts, and governmental authorities. Professional development programs will be essential to equip teachers with the skills needed to integrate AI effectively.

Research conducted by multiple disciplines will help us understand how AI supports different learning requirements while solving ethical and practical issues (Binns, 2018).

The educational sector will experience a transformative shift through AI technology, which provides new ways to improve learning experiences and increase inclusivity. The achievement of this potential depends on ethical practices alongside continuous collaboration and a focus on student development. The chapter provides educators with the necessary knowledge and resources to understand this new educational frontier, which will establish inclusive learning spaces that are both equitable and transformative (Spikol et al., 2018).

CREATING PSYCHOLOGICAL SAFETY IN LEARNING SPACES

Psychological safety is a foundational element in any learning environment, enabling students to take intellectual risks, ask questions without fear of judgment, and engage in meaningful dialogue (White, 2021). As education continues to evolve, especially with the integration of Artificial Intelligence (AI), ensuring that technology supports, not undermines, this sense of emotional security becomes increasingly important. AI tools offer promising solutions by creating nonjudgmental feedback systems, personalized learning experiences, and real-time emotional support mechanisms that enhance psychological safety in classrooms.

Non-Judgmental Feedback Systems

The most important way artificial intelligence (AI) supports psychological safety in education involves its ability to deliver fast and unbiased personalized feedback, which helps create safe learning environments. Student stress levels increase when they experience subjective grading and public performance because these methods create fear of negative peer and instructor judgments. The AI-powered tutoring systems evaluate students through data-based assessments which remain unbiased and free from human emotional influences (Hernandez, 2021). The systems enable students to practice mistakes independently while allowing multiple attempts at tasks which promote growth mindset development. The lack of social monitoring allows students to try new approaches and fail without consequences and continue their work which strengthens their academic perseverance and internal drive (Steenbergen-Hu & Cooper, 2014). The protective mechanism of AI systems benefits students with learning differences and anxiety disorders because it protects them from disengaging in traditional classroom settings.

The adaptive learning technology of Knewton and Carnegie Learning and Squirrel AI demonstrates how AI systems create customized educational paths through real-time student performance analysis. These platforms modify their instructional content difficulty levels, pacing, and material types to match individual student learning profiles, minimizing boredom and overwhelming experiences (Baran, Aleman, & Dilek, 2025). AI tools maintain student-specific feedback adjustments, which avoid the uniform instructional approach of traditional teaching methods. Students develop both confidence in handling complex material and self-directed control of their learning process. The customized feedback system enables students to develop self-directed learning behaviors, leading to better academic results and improved emotional health (Reich, 2020). AI platforms create new learning experiences by reducing performance stress while giving learners complete control over their digital and hybrid classroom activities.

Emotional Recognition and Support

The implementation of AI sentiment analysis tools into educational settings over the past years has transformed educators' capacity to detect and respond to student emotions. The combination of natural language processing (NLP) with voice recognition and computer vision algorithms enables these tools to analyze text input, vocal tones, and facial expressions in real time and deliver actionable emotional data to educators (Hinojo-Lucena et al., 2019). Detecting subtle writing indicators, including tone changes and hesitation patterns or negative emotions, allows AI systems to identify overwhelmed, confused, or disengaged students. Early intervention becomes possible because educators can detect emotional discomfort before it develops into academic performance problems or behavioral challenges. The tools operate without intrusion, protecting student privacy while creating transparent emotional engagement within digital spaces.

The capabilities of these systems prove most beneficial in hybrid and online learning settings since they operate without the need for physical body language signals. Teachers conducting remote learning face challenges in measuring student engagement because it is harder to provide suitable student support. The technology of affective computing provides continuous assessment of student engagement and emotional signals to help teachers detect students who need help (Kay, Leung, & Tang, 2023). Digital educational platforms like Emotuit and Affectiva use their platforms to assess students' cognitive and emotional states before modifying lesson delivery based on the assessment results. These systems identify learner emotional responses to boredom, anxiety, and frustration so educators can adjust their teaching approach by either slowing down instruction, redefining content, or offering emotional support. The feedback loop based on student responses enables educators to build empathetic learning spaces that maintain personalized support despite the lack of physical student-teacher interaction.

Affective AI systems align with the current educational understanding that emotional intelligence is a fundamental factor for academic success. According to research findings, students' educational success depends on emotional support and psychological safety (Henriksen et al., 2025). Through AI-driven emotion recognition, teachers gain the ability to better understand their students' mental state, which helps them build classrooms that promote student self-awareness and motivation, along with interpersonal connections. Sentiment analysis through AI creates supportive individual learning experiences while building a positive classroom environment, leading to better student engagement and retention rates. The complete potential of this technology depends on ethical implementation, which requires obtaining informed consent and implementing algorithmic fairness alongside data privacy safeguards according to Zawacki-Richter et al. (2019). Thoughtful implementation of AI-driven emotional monitoring creates a strong supportive mechanism to develop educational spaces that promote inclusivity and supportiveness.

Inclusive Moderation of Discussions

The intelligent moderation function of AI technology significantly affects how discussions develop and collaborative learning processes function. AI tools from the NLP subfield monitor and analyze student interactions during both live and delayed learning sessions, according to Ali (2020). These tools monitor discussions for inappropriate language while automatically detecting profanity, discriminatory terms, and exclusionary language and producing real-time alerts for teacher evaluation. AI moderation systems establish secure communication spaces through digital civility rules to protect students from interpersonal conflicts so they can maintain focus on their learning objectives. The automated management of large-scale online courses (MOOCs) becomes possible because manual discussion supervision becomes unfeasible, according to Kay, Leung, and Tang (2023).

AI moderation tools enable equitable student participation through their ability to detect group discussion patterns. The tools use this information to help instructors detect active speakers from silent participants so they can take measures to encourage quieter students to contribute (Castañeda & Selwyn, 2018). Real-time equity metrics available through these platforms enable educators to use this data for better group composition decisions as well as discussion design and follow-up intervention planning. AI functions as both a discourse etiquette protector and an inclusion facilitator to create opportunities for students from different linguistic, cultural, and socio-economic backgrounds to participate equally. Intelligent systems remove participation obstacles that have traditionally affected students who are English language learners and those with communication fears, according to Dede (2019).

The implementation of AI moderation systems helps students understand different cultures and develop digital empathy skills, which are essential for 21st-century learning. The different backgrounds of students in classrooms produce misunderstandings because they communicate differently and unintentionally use incorrect language. NLP tools translate content in real-time to provide alternative language options that enhance clarity and inclusiveness (Hinojo-Lucena et al., 2019). AI tools alert students about emotionally charged language and suggest alternative phrases to minimize misunderstandings, leading to a respectful and considerate communication environment. These systems build collaborative digital environments that merge academic standards with social responsibility through ethical and transparent usage, resulting in better student satisfaction and retention and enhanced engagement (Zawacki-Richter et al., 2019).

Fair Assessment Practices

AI technology delivers dual benefits, which boost classroom engagement as well as establish fair and equitable assessment methods. Traditional grading systems that depend on teacher judgment tend to introduce subconscious biases, which result in adverse impacts on students from minority groups. Teachers demonstrate unintentional score discrepancies in student work through racial and gender identity, socioeconomic status, and language proficiency characteristics, even when work quality remains constant, according to Kaplan & Haenlein (2019). The continuous bias within these grading systems maintains systemic inequality while deterring student involvement and damaging trust in academic assessment procedures. These grading issues grow more severe when rubric inconsistencies and teacher judgment differences occur throughout large or diverse student populations (Castañeda & Selwyn, 2018).

AI assessment systems provide an answer through consistent, transparent, and unbiased grading systems. The evaluation process of these systems uses standardized algorithms to analyze student work regardless of the student's background or their communication style. AI-assisted grading modules from Gradescope and Turnitin's AI-assisted grading systems examine written assignments through structural evaluation, grammar analysis, argument coherence assessment, and rubric element compliance while avoiding personal bias (Schildkamp, 2020). These assessment tools give students quick, detailed feedback to help them learn from their errors. AI systems' transparent assessment methods enable students who faced biased grading to trust academic evaluations more strongly, which leads to improved motivation and increased involvement with their schoolwork.

Educators can use AI to generate immediate performance data to detect assessment differences and prevent their occurrence. Data showing that particular student groups perform poorly on specific assignments prompts educators to investigate possible structural challenges and content delivery issues. Schools can track student performance over time by using AI systems, which help them monitor both equity and effectiveness throughout multiple years (Steenbergen-Hu & Cooper, 2014). The ethical use of these systems requires periodic bias audits as well as educator involvement in final grading decisions, especially when context and nuance are necessary. The responsible implementation of AI technology both enhances assessment fairness and preserves essential human judgment for complete educational development.

Mental Health Support

Education benefits from artificial intelligence (AI) technology through mental health support as a growing concern for K–12 and college students. Most students experience emotional challenges such as stress, anxiety, depression, or loneliness, but hesitate to seek help because of stigma, fear of judgment, or insufficient access to on-campus mental health resources. The emergence of AI mental health chatbots, Woebot and Wysa, provides valuable solutions for connecting students who need assistance. Students can receive confidential 24/7 support through AI-powered conversational interfaces, which create empathy and understanding (Inkster et al., 2018). AI mental health tools support student emotional safety and empowerment through their ability to allow users to share their feelings while keeping their information confidential. The platforms specifically support students who come from communities that view mental health discussions as forbidden.

The AI companions use cognitive-behavioral therapy principles to direct users through proven mental health techniques. The chat-based approach of Woebot allows users to experience reflective conversations, which help them recognize cognitive distortions, transform negative thoughts, and learn mindfulness-based stress reduction approaches (Fitzpatrick, Darcy, & Vierhile, 2017). Wysa integrates mood tracking with journaling prompts alongside self-help exercises that help users manage their emotions. The user-friendly conversation design enables real-time personalized interaction through the combination of emotional tone detection, input pattern analysis, and psychological risk indicator monitoring. These tools function as initial intervention platforms that provide students with immediate coping resources while they develop resilience before their distress worsens.

The accessibility of AI mental health tools extends to students in underserved schools or remote learning environments where few professional mental health services exist. These tools solve three main barriers to healthcare access: extended waiting times, restricted appointment availability, and geographic limitations. The anonymous nature of these chatbots enables students to reveal their emotions, which otherwise stay hidden (Inkster et al., 2018). Users of AI mental health tools report high satisfaction rates, trust, and continued engagement because they experience nonjudgmental and supportive interfaces (Naslund et al., 2020). Educational institutions should implement ethical, evidence-based AI mental health tools to create a transformative impact on emotional wellness and psychological safety for their diverse student population.

Human-AI Collaboration

Artificial intelligence (AI) in education offers multiple advantages, like scalable systems, individualized learning, and immediate analytical capabilities, yet it should operate as a supplementary tool to human relationships. AI tools demonstrate conversational abilities, adapt to user feedback, and detect emotional signals, but they do not possess human educator capabilities for authentic empathy, moral insight, or intuitive understanding. Teachers perform beyond content delivery because they establish trust-based bonds and provide guidance while understanding individual emotional and cultural requirements that artificial intelligence systems cannot match (Perin & Lauterbach, 2018). Emotional intelligence functions as a fundamental human ability that allows people to detect and understand emotional responses and develop appropriate reactions for creating safe learning spaces that support inclusion.

Studies indicate that powerful relationships between teachers and students produce better student involvement, together with better academic results and emotional health. AI systems fail to duplicate the complete foundations of trust, respect, and belonging that human relationships establish in educational settings (Hattie, 2009). Teachers demonstrate behaviors like empathy and patience alongside resilience and social awareness, which students need to develop, although AI systems struggle to deliver these skills independently. Teachers respond to student distress by modifying their voice, body language, and speech patterns, which exceed the capabilities of state-of-the-art AI systems. AI systems should use their capabilities to improve learning speed and offer additional educational support while leaving fundamental human-centered teaching methods unmodified.

Education benefits from AI integration through a teaching model that relies on human teachers to guide students while they interpret AI results. AI systems can detect student disengagement through sentiment analysis, but teachers must analyze these alerts for proper emotional and pedagogical interventions (Luckin, 2018). The human-in-the-loop approach establishes an ethical framework for AI use that maintains contextual understanding and emotional sensitivity. Teachers need professional development to grasp AI tools to evaluate AI outputs effectively while teaching them with both awareness and discrimination. AI exists to support teachers in their work by decreasing administrative tasks and delivering practical information, which enables them to dedicate their time to the essential task of student development as a whole person.

Ethical Implementation

Finally, ethical considerations must guide the implementation of AI in educational settings. Transparency in how AI systems operate, informed consent for data collection and ongoing evaluation of algorithmic fairness are necessary to ensure that these tools do not inadvertently harm students or reinforce systemic inequities (Zawacki-Richter et al., 2019). Collaborative efforts among educators, technologists, and policymakers are essential to create guidelines that prioritize student well-being while leveraging AI's transformative potential.

Conclusively, AI presents powerful opportunities to strengthen psychological safety in learning spaces. Through personalized feedback, emotional recognition, inclusive moderation, and mental health support, AI tools can help cultivate emotionally secure and intellectually engaging classrooms. When implemented ethically and thoughtfully, AI becomes a valuable ally in shaping inclusive and holistic learning environments. While fostering psychological safety addresses students' individual emotional needs, promoting diversity, equity, and inclusion ensures these supportive practices are extended across all learner populations.

AI AS A CATALYST FOR DIVERSITY, EQUITY, AND INCLUSION (DEI)

The deployment of AI in education can be a powerful catalyst for promoting diversity, equity, and inclusion (DEI). By leveraging adaptive learning technologies, language translation tools, and bias detection algorithms, AI has the potential to create a more inclusive and equitable educational environment for all learners (Spikol et al., 2018).

Adaptive Learning Technologies: Personalizing Education for All

A principal mechanism by which artificial intelligence promotes diversity, equity, and inclusion (DEI) is by implementing adaptive learning technologies. These tools adapt the pace and complexity of instructional materials according to the distinct needs of individual learners, thereby facilitating equitable access to the curriculum for all students, irrespective of their backgrounds or learning preferences. Adaptive learning platforms utilize data analytics to assess various factors, including student performance, engagement metrics, and individual learning preferences, in order to customize educational experiences (Akavova, Temirkhanova, & Lorsanova, 2023; Reich, 2020).

For example, artificial intelligence tools such as DreamBox and Socrative leverage data analytics to evaluate students' individual strengths and weaknesses, thereby personalizing instructional content to facilitate their progress at a self-determined pace. This personalized approach facilitates the success of students with diverse learning requirements, including those with disabilities, in ways that conventional one-size-fits-all methodologies frequently fail to achieve (Castañeda & Selwyn, 2018). By engaging students at their current level of understanding, these technologies facilitate the closing of gaps in comprehension and contribute to the mitigation of disparities in academic achievement.

Furthermore, adaptive learning facilitates assistance for students from underrepresented groups by providing customized resources to address their particular requirements. Students from low-income backgrounds frequently encounter barriers to accessing high-quality educational resources. Artificial intelligence-driven platforms possess the capability to identify existing educational deficiencies and deliver targeted interventions, including supplemental lessons or additional practice exercises, aimed at promoting equity in learning outcomes (Holmes, Bialik, & Fadel, 2021). This approach improves learning outcomes and cultivates a sense of belonging and empowerment among students who may otherwise experience marginalization.

Breaking Down Language Barriers

Language barriers have historically constituted a considerable impediment to attaining inclusivity within educational settings. Artificial Intelligence possesses the capacity to address these challenges by utilizing sophisticated language translation technologies. Applications such as Google Translate and Microsoft Translator employ neural machine translation, a subset of artificial intelligence, to facilitate real-time language translation. This functionality allows students from various linguistic backgrounds to access educational resources in their native languages (Amershi et al., 2019).

For instance, a student proficient in the Spanish language may utilize AI-enhanced translation tools to interact with English-language textbooks, participate in classroom discussions, and complete assignments, thereby mitigating feelings of exclusion. Similarly, educators can leverage these tools to engage with non-English-speaking students and their families, thereby promoting a more inclusive school environment (Samarakou et al., 2015)

Artificial Intelligence (AI) facilitates multilingual education by providing adaptive platforms that assist students in acquiring new languages. Applications such as Duolingo and Rosetta Stone employ artificial intelligence algorithms to tailor language instruction according to individual user progress, pacing, and learning preferences. This customization enhances both accessibility and retention of language skills (Hinojo-Lucena et al., 2019). By fostering linguistic diversity and enhancing cultural understanding, these platforms contribute to the establishment of a more inclusive educational environment.

Addressing Unconscious Bias in Education

Unconscious bias may be exhibited in educational settings through disparities in grading practices, representation, and access to opportunities. Artificial intelligence presents promising methodologies for the identification and alleviation of these biases. For instance, algorithms can analyze grading data for patterns that reveal disparities associated with demographic characteristics. This analysis can motivate educators to investigate and address systemic issues (Kaplan & Haenlein, 2019; Schildkamp, 2020).

Artificial intelligence is capable of identifying bias within instructional materials. Natural language processing (NLP) algorithms can analyze academic materials, including textbooks, assignments, and lecture content, to detect exclusionary language and the underrepresentation of marginalized groups. This analytical process can aid educational institutions in crafting content that more accurately reflects diverse social realities (Zawacki-Richter et al., 2019). These characteristics facilitate reflecting and validating students' identities within their educational environments.

Furthermore, artificial intelligence-driven recruitment tools can potentially mitigate bias in the admissions processes of higher education institutions. When utilized with anonymized data, these tools can concentrate exclusively on merit and potential, thereby minimizing the influence of subjective factors such as name, gender, or socioeconomic status. These instruments facilitate equity and contribute to developing a more diverse and dynamic learning environment (Binns, 2018; Baker, 2016).

Supporting Students with Disabilities

AI offers powerful tools to enhance education for students with disabilities. For instance, speech-to-text and text-to-speech applications enable students with auditory or visual impairments to access instructional content in usable formats. Tools like Grammarly, voice recognition software, and predictive text also support students with cognitive and physical challenges, allowing greater independence in classroom tasks (Duffy & Azevedo, 2015).

Beyond assistive technologies, AI can automatically caption videos, create audio descriptions, and adjust digital interfaces to meet accessibility standards—ensuring equitable access to learning resources (Barnes, Hutson, & Perry, 2024). These advancements allow students with disabilities to engage with materials at the same level as their peers.

Educators also benefit from AI-powered insights into how students with disabilities interact with course content. These analytics help instructors identify areas where students need additional support, enabling responsive, inclusive pedagogy (Henriksen et al., 2025; Steenbergen-Hu & Cooper, 2014). In this way, AI becomes a partner in building learning environments where all students can thrive.

Enhancing Cultural Competency

Cultural competency is essential to diversity, equity, and inclusion (DEI) within the educational sphere. Artificial Intelligence (AI) can potentially enhance cultural competency development by facilitating exposure to a wide array of perspectives and lived experiences for both students and educators. The integration of artificial intelligence (AI) with virtual reality (VR) and augmented reality (AR) technologies facilitates the development of immersive learning environments that enable students to engage with diverse cultures, historical narratives, and worldviews. This potential is highlighted in the work of Hinojo-Lucena et al. (2019). These experiences facilitate the development of empathy, intercultural understanding, and respect for diversity by allowing learners to engage in the perspectives of others within virtual environments (Zawacki-Richter et al., 2019)

Furthermore, artificial intelligence has the potential to enhance cross-cultural collaboration by establishing connections among students and educators from diverse geographical and cultural backgrounds. Online learning platforms that leverage artificial intelligence to align users according to shared interests and educational objectives facilitate the initiation of substantive dialogues and promote peer-to-peer knowledge exchange across geographical and cultural divides (Amershi et al., 2019; Holmes et al., 2021). These interactions foster the development of global citizenship and equip students with the skills necessary to succeed in an interconnected and multicultural environment—competencies that are increasingly recognized as invaluable in both academic and professional domains (Henriksen et al., 2025).

Challenges and Considerations

While the potential of AI to promote DEI in education is immense, it is essential to recognize and address the ethical concerns and risks associated with its deployment. A primary concern is algorithmic bias, wherein AI systems unintentionally replicate existing societal inequities due to biased training data or flawed assumptions in model design (Kaplan & Haenlein, 2019). If left unchecked, these biases can reinforce disparities rather than alleviate them, disproportionately affecting historically marginalized groups. To mitigate this, developers must build AI systems using diverse, inclusive datasets, and educators must critically assess AI outputs in context (Binns, 2018; Perin & Lauterbach, 2018).

Another persistent issue is the digital divide, which refers to the gap in access to digital tools and high-speed internet between well-resourced and under-resourced communities. Students in rural or low-income households often face connectivity issues that prevent them from benefiting from AI-driven platforms (UNESCO, 2023). Bridging this divide requires a multi-stakeholder effort among policymakers, educators, and technology providers to ensure equitable infrastructure and device access (Zawacki-Richter et al., 2019). Without such efforts, AI may exacerbate existing inequalities rather than promote inclusive education.

Privacy and data protection also remain critical concerns. Since AI in education relies heavily on student data to personalize content and generate insights, there is a heightened risk of misuse or breaches if robust security measures are not enforced (Samarakou et al., 2015). Institutions must adhere to legal standards such as FERPA and GDPR and promote transparent, ethical data use policies that protect student information while enabling beneficial innovation (Ali, 2020).

Despite these challenges, the transformational potential of AI in education is clear. By leveraging adaptive learning platforms, AI-assisted translation tools, bias detection algorithms, and inclusive assistive technologies, educators can address long-standing structural barriers to access, inclusion, and achievement (Reich, 2020; Castañeda & Selwyn, 2018). AI's strength lies in its scalability and responsiveness—when developed ethically and used responsibly, it can become a powerful tool for educational equity.

However, intentional design and implementation are crucial to fully realize this potential. Educational stakeholders must commit to inclusive AI practices—from system design to classroom integration—that prioritize DEI values at every stage. By tackling concerns around bias, connectivity, and data ethics, we can build an ecosystem where AI enhances—not replaces—human-centered, culturally responsive education (Luckin, 2018; Holmes et al., 2021).

As we look to the future of learning, AI must be guided by ethical frameworks that center diversity, equity, and inclusion. In doing so, we ensure that AI not only delivers innovation but also empowers all learners—regardless of background—to reach their full potential and contribute to a more just and inclusive society.

FOSTERING HOLISTIC LEARNING THROUGH AI

Holistic learning extends beyond traditional academic knowledge to encompass the development of emotional intelligence, social skills, and overall well-being. AI technology enables the integration of emotional and social learning (SEL) into educational experiences, supporting these aspects of education. Through AI implementation, educators can establish learning spaces that support students' complete development by focusing on their intellectual, emotional, and social dimensions (Markoff, 2015).

AI and Emotional Intelligence

Emotional intelligence (EI) is an important part of integral education, teaching such things as self-awareness, emotional regulation, motivation, empathy, and social skills (Goleman, 1995, cited by Holmes et al., 2021). Artificial intelligence technologies can facilitate EI development by tracking the students' emotional states and offering data associated with their social-emotional growth. Artificial intelligence-driven tools such as Affectiva and Cogito interpret facial expressions, speech tones, and other behavioral cues to detect signs of emotional distress or disengagement (Hinojo-Lucena et al., 2019; Amershi et al., 2019). Such insights enable instructors to determine which students are likely in need of dealing with emotions, thus facilitating early intervention, support, or modification of the learning environment.

In addition, tools such as Cerego utilize cognitive science principles to enhance retention, self-knowledge, and time management and goal-setting behaviors. These features assist learners in developing self-regulation skills and emotional toughness—key elements of emotional intelligence (Henriksen et al., 2025). For instance, learners who procrastinate or stress out may need prompt reminders and feedback delivered to boost task persistence and reduce anxiety. By activating personalized prompts, students are guided into more fruitful learning habits, improving their mental wellbeing and increasing their sense of academic control (Steenbergen-Hu & Cooper, 2014).

Artificial intelligence has the potential to maximize peer interaction through emotionally intelligent strategies. AI-powered virtual collaboration tools can pair learners according to their learning style, interest, or emotional characteristics, thus facilitating effective collaborations and partnerships (Ali, 2020). These systems enable students to build empathy, active listening, and communication by facilitating group work that appreciates different opinions. Thus, artificial intelligence can act as both mirror tool and mentor figure—offering feedback and counsel to support emotional and social development.

AI and Social Learning

Social learning—the process of acquiring knowledge through observation, interaction, and collaboration—is foundational to holistic education. AI technologies have expanded the possibilities of social learning by offering platforms that facilitate peer engagement and shared problem-solving. Learning management systems (LMS) such as Canvas, Blackboard, and Google Classroom integrate AI features like intelligent discussion moderation, automated group assignments, and sentiment analysis to promote meaningful digital dialogue (Castañeda & Selwyn, 2018; Holmes et al., 2021). These features help instructors monitor participation and foster inclusive environments where students learn collaboratively.

AI can further optimize social learning by providing data-driven insights into group dynamics. For example, AI algorithms embedded in collaborative tools can track speaking time, task completion rates, and responsiveness among group members, thereby identifying imbalances and suggesting strategies to promote equitable participation (Samarakou et al., 2015; Henriksen et al., 2025). Teachers can use this feedback to ensure that all students are actively engaged and to redesign group configurations that maximize peer learning.

Additionally, AI-powered VR and AR platforms provide immersive environments where students practice social learning in simulated settings. Whether collaborating in a virtual science lab, engaging in a digital role-play, or participating in a historical reenactment, students can develop critical social competencies such as conflict resolution, cooperative problem-solving, and teamwork (Hinojo-Lucena et al., 2019; Zawacki-Richter et al., 2019). These technologies create dynamic and interactive spaces that model real-world social experiences, supporting the development of social fluency in a safe and structured format.

Mindfulness and Well-Being Programs

Implementing artificial intelligence technology enables schools to create personalized resources for mindfulness and student well-being through individualized approaches. Classroom integration of apps like Headspace and Calm allows students to practice mindfulness while reducing anxiety and developing emotional strength (Markoff, 2015; Duffy & Azevedo, 2015). These tools guide students to pause their activities, to check their emotional state, and to learn stress management techniques.

AI technology provides immediate information about student mental health conditions. Wearable devices equipped with AI, such as Fitbit and Apple Watch, can track physiological indicators like sleep quality and heart rate, creating a comprehensive picture of students' wellness. Educational systems connected to this data enable teachers and counselors to identify struggling students, allowing for prompt, individualized support.

AI tools serve as instruments to reduce the social discrimination faced by mental health patients. Students can use chatbots like Woebot and Wysa as anonymous platforms to share their feelings without fear of judgment, receiving emotional support in a safe environment. These virtual tools function as extensions of traditional counseling services, aiding students who avoid face-to-face counseling sessions (Brynjolfsson & McAfee, 2017).

Personalized Learning Experiences

The holistic educational approach delivers purposeful learning activities linked to students' core beliefs and individual targets. AI tools enable personalized education by matching students with content and activities that align with their interests, thus creating meaningful learning experiences. AI algorithms in platforms like Edmodo and Khan Academy analyze student preferences and performance to generate customized recommendations for individual needs (Reich, 2020).

Combining personalized learning approaches leads to better academic results and helps students develop self-directed learning abilities. When students connect their educational content to personal goals and life experiences, they maintain deep engagement and study persistence. AI systems help students discover their strengths and passions by linking them to relevant opportunities, including internships, mentorship programs, and extracurricular activities that match their objectives (Reich, 2020).

AI-powered project-based learning focuses on practical applications and combined solutions from different subjects. Platforms like Project Pals and PBLWorks provide tools for creating, managing, and evaluating collaborative projects. Through these platforms, students can explore their personal interests while building essential competencies in creativity, communication, and teamwork (Zheng et al., 2024).

Bridging Gaps in Equity and Access

Implementing holistic learning must overcome institutional obstacles that prevent students from achieving their full educational potential. AI technology can eliminate educational inequalities by delivering personalized educational resources that meet the requirements of disadvantaged student groups. AI-based adaptive learning systems identify learning deficiencies in students from low-income families, providing appropriate support for their academic success (Kozlowski, 2022).

A major obstacle to achieving holistic education arises from language differences among students. AI-powered translation tools like Google Translate and Microsoft Translator enable students from diverse linguistic backgrounds to access educational materials in their native language. This inclusive approach removes language as a learning barrier, allowing all students to fully engage in their educational process (Amershi et al., 2019).

The growing integration of educational technology offers significant benefits for students with disabilities by facilitating access to various assistive tools. Students with visual or hearing impairments can enhance their comprehension of lessons by utilizing speech-to-text conversion and text-to-speech reading functionalities. Those with physical or cognitive disabilities can significantly improve their educational engagement through assistive technologies such as screen-reading software, voice-activated commands, and typing aids that offer word predictions during writing tasks. To demonstrate the practical outcomes of AI's role in inclusive and holistic learning, we now turn to several impactful case studies from educational institutions.

CASE STUDIES AND SUCCESS STORIES

Georgia Tech's AI-Powered Tutoring System

The educational infrastructure at the Georgia Institute of Technology has experienced a significant transformation due to the incorporation of artificial intelligence (AI) technologies specifically designed to promote student success in the STEM (Science, Technology, Engineering, and Mathematics) fields. A notable innovation is implementing an AI-powered tutoring system, developed specifically to assist students in foundational computer science courses. This system utilizes machine learning algorithms to conduct ongoing analyses of student performance data, monitoring various metrics including response accuracy, completion times, and levels of engagement. Based on this analysis, the system provides tailored instructional feedback congruent with individual students' learning styles and pacing. Technology in educational settings enhances traditional classroom instruction and facilitates real-time adjustments based on individual student progress, thereby fostering a more personalized and practical learning experience.

One of the AI tutor's most significant advantages lies in its ability to provide real-time academic assistance in intricate and specialized disciplines, including algorithm design and programming. Students who encounter difficulties with foundational topics can benefit from personalized, on-demand explanations and systematic problem-solving strategies. Providing immediate support mitigates the frustration and disengagement frequently linked with STEM courses, contributing directly to enhanced learning outcomes. Consequently, there has been a significant increase in course retention rates, particularly among students who would have likely struggled academically without timely support. The AI tutor functions as both an educational facilitator and a promoter of self-efficacy, fostering an environment that encourages learners to engage in inquiry, persist following setbacks, and undertake academic risks within a low-pressure context.

In addition to its academic advantages, the artificial intelligence tutoring system at Georgia Tech has made noteworthy progress in enhancing diversity and inclusion within science, technology, engineering, and mathematics (STEM). Research indicates that underrepresented student demographics, encompassing women and minority populations, frequently encounter supplemental challenges in technical disciplines attributable to implicit bias and insufficient personalized academic support. The artificial intelligence system mitigates this issue by discerning individual learning requirements and customizing content delivery to facilitate equitable access to educational instruction. The establishment of inclusive learning environments is facilitated by removing comparative pressures and providing anonymized, unbiased support (Holmes, Bialik, & Fadel, 2021). This approach fosters a more equitable academic environment, enabling students from diverse backgrounds to excel in competitive STEM disciplines. Consequently, it enhances both their performance and persistence within the field.

The University of Michigan's AI-Driven Accessibility Initiative

Accessibility serves as a fundamental component of equitable education, particularly for students with disabilities who encounter systemic obstacles to learning within traditional classroom settings. The University of Michigan has significantly advanced in this domain by implementing a progressive, artificial intelligence-driven accessibility initiative. The program facilitates the integration of advanced artificial intelligence technologies within the academic infrastructure, aimed at providing support for students with hearing impairments and those facing language barriers. A key component of this initiative is the implementation of real-time captioning, which facilitates the instantaneous transcription of spoken content. This technological advancement enables students with hearing impairments to fully engage with lectures and discussions (Barnes, Hutson, & Perry, 2024). This initiative underscores the potential of technology to bridge historical accessibility gaps, enabling all learners to engage meaningfully with course content.

The initiative's influence has transcended its primary focus on students with hearing impairments, affecting a broader population. By providing real-time language translation services, the program offers significant advantages to international students and non-native English speakers who may encounter challenges in comprehending course materials presented in English. These tools facilitate the automatic translation of lectures and classroom communications, thereby enabling multilingual learners to access academic content in their preferred language while ensuring the continuity of instructional flow. In this manner, the AI-driven platform cultivates a multilingual and multicultural learning environment; ensuring linguistic diversity does not hinder participation or performance. This functionality holds particular significance within diverse academic institutions, where the student population comprises individuals from various linguistic and cultural backgrounds.

Ultimately, the University of Michigan program is a pertinent illustration of how scalable artificial intelligence solutions can enhance accessibility and inclusivity for diverse learning needs. By mitigating the communication barriers that frequently inhibit the participation of specific groups in classroom engagement; this initiative fosters equitable opportunities for academic achievement. The extensive incorporation of these technologies substantiates the notion that inclusion should not be regarded as a specialized service but an inherent aspect of educational design. This case exemplifies a framework for other institutions aiming to utilize artificial intelligence to enhance inclusivity, equity, and responsiveness in learning environments, thereby addressing the diverse needs of contemporary students.

AI-Powered Learning Platforms in K–12 Education

Artificial intelligence (AI) systems are increasingly utilized to address the diverse needs of learners within K–12 education by means of intelligent and adaptive learning platforms. Among these resources, DreamBox Learning is distinguished as one of the most extensively utilized educational tools in the United States for elementary and middle educational institutions. This platform uses real-time data derived from student interactions, including response accuracy, the amount of time allocated to questions, inputting patterns to dynamically modify the difficulty and nature of the instructional content. Whether students engage with mathematical problems or solve logical puzzles, the system analyzes their performance and adjusts instructional pathways accordingly (Castañeda & Selwyn, 2018). The ability to adapt in real-time facilitates the provision of either scaffolded support or enrichment opportunities, contingent upon students' individual progress. This approach fosters a highly responsive and customized learning experience.

One of the most significant advantages of DreamBox is its efficacy in educational environments characterized by a diverse spectrum of learner abilities. Students requiring supplementary assistance receive immediate, systematic guidance that facilitates mastery of concepts before progression. Conversely, more advanced students are offered rigorous and engaging challenges designed to sustain their academic momentum. This dual function facilitates educators in attending to the diverse learning needs of students while avoiding the categorization of learners into inflexible ability groups. Research indicates that Title I school districts, which serve many low-income families, experienced a 16% increase in mathematics test scores following one year of implementation. This improvement was particularly pronounced among English language learners and students from historically underserved backgrounds (Reich, 2020). The findings of this study highlight the capabilities of artificial intelligence platforms to not only improve educational outcomes but also to function as instruments for mitigating disparities in academic achievement.

In addition to enhancing student performance, DreamBox provides considerable advantages for educators by facilitating instructional planning and alleviating the challenges associated with lesson differentiation. Educators can evaluate individual and collective classroom progress by utilizing data dashboards, which offer comprehensive insights into students' strengths, weaknesses, and levels of engagement. Rather than dedicating extensive hours to developing multiple lesson tracks, educators can leverage the capabilities of artificial intelligence systems to automate the process of personalization. This approach allows for the maintenance of control over the pacing of instruction and ensures alignment with established curriculum standards. This integration preserves instructional quality while promoting inclusivity while advancing equity and efficiency within the classroom environment. As educational institutions endeavor to implement innovative strategies that accommodate the diverse needs of all learners while minimizing the burden on staff, AI-driven tools such as DreamBox offer a scalable, evidence-based approach to promoting both educational quality and inclusivity.

Singapore's National AI-Driven Education Program

The Ministry of Education in Singapore shows the world how to implement AI in education through its AI in Education (AIEd) initiative. The initiative features AI tutors alongside multilingual platforms and predictive analytics that help identify students who need academic or socio-emotional support early. The centralized platform School Cockpit aggregates student data points such as attendance records, academic marks, and well-being indicators through AI systems to identify students who need academic or socio-emotional support.

Singapore's AI policy requires culturally sensitive content development to match the nation's multiracial characteristics. The 2022 government report shows that schools implementing the AIEd system reduced their technical education dropout rates by 23% (Ministry of Education Singapore, 2022). This case illustrates why national coordination between different departments and policy alignment becomes necessary to expand equitable AI-driven solutions.

Brazil's EduAI Initiative in Rural Schools

Brazil implemented EduAI through governmental collaboration with NGOs and edtech companies to deliver the program to rural schools that lack sufficient resources. The program installed offline-capable AI tools, including adaptive math and literacy platforms, for schools without internet access.

EduAI tools delivered substantial results because, according to UNESCO (2023), primary schools in Ceará state achieved a 12% rise in literacy rates during two years. Teachers used the educational analytics system to adapt lesson plans and detect students who needed extra support. EduAI represents a successful approach to deploying AI equally across diverse settings through its adaptation to rural needs and offline functionality.

KEY TAKEAWAYS FROM CASE STUDIES

The discussed examples demonstrate how artificial intelligence (AI) can address specific equity, inclusion, and accessibility challenges across different educational environments. These cases demonstrate the essential role of customizing artificial intelligence applications to meet the demands of different local educational environments through real-time STEM support, assistive technologies for disabled students, and data-driven solutions in underprivileged regions. The case studies highlight how human supervision, ethical technology design, and educator preparation function as essential components to maximize technological influence. Educators and policymakers can obtain valuable lessons about scaling artificial intelligence ethically and effectively by studying successful implementations from both the Global North and the Global South. Artificial intelligence (AI) shows remarkable application promise in educational settings ranging from top-ranking universities to remote classrooms. The educational experience becomes more personalized and accessible through AI when developers implement it with deliberate thoughtfulness and purpose.

ETHICAL CONSIDERATIONS AND CHALLENGES

The application of artificial intelligence (AI) in schools has several challenges and ethical issues that must be considered carefully. Careful consideration of the issues is required to promote the responsible and fair application of AI technologies in schools. The issues must be resolved to ensure that artificial intelligence technologies benefit all learners. This essay considers some of the most important problems related to using artificial intelligence in education, such as algorithmic bias, privacy, and the digital divide. It also discusses means of counteracting these problems and facilitating the ethical implementation of AI in schools.

Algorithmic Bias in AI Systems

One of the most significant issues with implementing artificial intelligence in education is the possibility of creating algorithmic bias. Artificial intelligence programs are created through training on big data sets, and the integrity of the data sets used plays a critical role in determining the performance and equity of the resulting AI tools (Baker, 2016). If the training data reflects historic inequities or biases, the systems will reproduce and entrench such biases by default. For example, artificial intelligence (AI) programs used in grading and assessment exercises can have biased inclinations towards certain demographic groups in cases where datasets used in training the AI programs are imbued with implicit biases in society.

To address this challenge, developers and educators must prioritize fairness and equity in the design and implementation of AI systems (Baker, 2016). This involves several key steps:

1. **Using Diverse and Representative Data Sets:** Ensuring that training data includes a wide range of student demographics, learning styles, and cultural contexts is essential to creating fair AI tools. Diverse datasets help minimize the risk of bias and ensure that AI systems are effective for all learners.
2. **Regular Auditing and Testing for Bias:** AI systems should be routinely audited to identify and address any biases that may emerge. This includes analyzing the outcomes of AI-driven tools to ensure they are equitable across different student groups.
3. **Transparency and Accountability:** Educators and developers should be transparent about how AI tools are designed, how they function, and the data they rely on. Clear communication about the limitations and potential biases of AI systems can help build trust and ensure their responsible use.
4. **Involving Diverse Stakeholders:** Including voices from underrepresented groups in the development and implementation of AI tools can help identify potential biases and create more inclusive solutions.

Privacy and Data Security

One of the serious ethical concerns pertaining to AI-based education systems is privacy and data security. AI tools tend to gather vast amounts of information regarding students' learning habits, emotional status, and academic development. Confidentiality and security of these types of data are essential to maintaining students' trust and preventing the violation of their rights (Steenbergen-Hu & Cooper, 2014; VanLEHN, 2011).

Schools and technology vendors need to have proper data governance policies in place to safeguard student data while simultaneously facilitating the ethical application of AI systems. Regulatory frameworks such as the General Data Protection Regulation (GDPR) in Europe and the Family Educational Rights and Privacy Act (FERPA) in the United States offer significant guidelines for safeguarding student privacy in an increasingly digitalized context.

Key measures to address privacy concerns include:

1. **Data Minimization:** AI tools should only collect the data necessary to achieve their educational objectives. Limiting the scope of data collection reduces the risk of misuse and ensures that students' privacy is respected.
2. **Secure Data Storage:** Educational institutions and technology providers must implement strong security measures to protect student data from breaches or unauthorized access. This includes using encryption, secure servers, and regular security audits.
3. **Informed Consent:** Students and their families should be fully informed about what data is being collected, how it will be used, and who will have access to it. Obtaining informed consent ensures that students and parents are aware of and agree to the use of AI tools.
4. **Compliance with Legal and Ethical Standards:** AI systems in education must comply with data protection laws such as the General Data Protection Regulation (GDPR) and the Family Educational Rights and Privacy Act (FERPA). Adhering to these regulations ensures that student data is handled responsibly and ethically.
5. **Transparency in Data Use:** Educators and developers should clearly communicate how student data is used to improve AI tools and enhance learning outcomes. Transparency builds trust and ensures that data is used for the benefit of students.

The Digital Divide

The digital divide remains a major obstacle to the fair integration of artificial intelligence into the educational system. Many students lack proper technological devices to fully exploit AI-augmented tools, thus having unequal learning opportunities. This disparity is especially recorded in poor neighborhoods and rural settings where high-speed internet, contemporary computing hardware, and technical assistance are not readily accessible (White, 2021).

Addressing the digital divide is critical to ensuring that AI-driven educational tools benefit all students. Strategies to bridge this gap include:

1. **Investing in Infrastructure:** Governments and educational institutions must invest in the infrastructure needed to provide all students with access to AI-powered tools. This includes expanding broadband access, providing affordable devices, and ensuring that schools are equipped with the necessary technology.
2. **Providing Training and Support:** Teachers and students in underserved areas may require additional training and support to effectively use AI tools. Professional development programs and technical assistance can help educators integrate AI into their classrooms and maximize its potential.
3. **Developing Low-Cost Solutions:** Technology providers should prioritize the development of affordable and accessible AI tools that can be used in resource-constrained settings. Simplified versions of AI systems designed for use on basic devices can help bridge the gap for students without access to high-end technology.
4. **Collaborating with Community Organizations:** Partnerships with community organizations can help provide students with access to technology and support outside of school. Libraries and community centers can serve as hubs for accessing AI-powered educational tools.

5. **Policy Advocacy:** Policymakers play a crucial role in addressing the digital divide. Advocating for policies that promote digital equity, such as funding for technology in schools and subsidies for low-income families, can help ensure that all students have the opportunity to benefit from AI-driven education.

Ethical Design and Implementation of AI Tools

Beyond responding to particular issues like bias, privacy, and the digital divide, there is also a need to look at the general ethical considerations of artificial intelligence in learning contexts. Designing and implementing AI tools ethically involves adhering to inclusivity, transparency, and accountability (Baker, 2016).

1. **Inclusivity:** AI systems should be designed to meet the needs of all learners, including those with disabilities, language barriers, or other challenges. This includes incorporating features such as real-time captioning, multilingual support, and adaptive interfaces.
2. **Transparency:** Developers and educators should provide clear explanations of how AI tools work, what data they use, and the outcomes they produce. Transparency fosters trust and ensures that stakeholders can make informed decisions about the use of AI in education.
3. **Accountability:** Institutions and technology providers must take responsibility for the ethical use of AI tools. This includes addressing unintended consequences, such as bias or privacy violations, and taking corrective action when necessary.
4. **Human Oversight:** While AI can enhance education, it should not replace the human connection between educators and students. Teachers play a vital role in creating a supportive and empathetic learning environment, and their presence cannot be substituted by technology. Instead, AI should be viewed as a complementary tool that enhances teachers' ability to meet students' needs rather than replacing human interaction.
5. **Ethical Training for Educators:** Educators should receive training on the ethical use of AI tools, including how to identify and address potential biases, protect student privacy, and promote equity.

Though AI can potentially transform education, its effective application rests on surmounting the ethical issues and concerns associated with its application. Educators and policymakers can make AI a positive force in education by transcending concerns about algorithmic bias, privacy, and the digital divide. As we move forward in uncovering the potential of AI, our eyes need to stay fixed on the vision of developing fair and just learning spaces where all students have the opportunity to excel. With the revolutionary potential and the fear it inspires, it is important to examine how schools and educators can responsibly engage with AI integration.

CONCLUSION

The educational landscape is experiencing rapid transformation through Artificial Intelligence (AI) because this technology delivers multiple educational tools that support diverse learning environments. The combination of AI tools, which includes adaptive learning platforms alongside intelligent tutoring systems, emotional recognition tools, and AI-powered mental health chatbots, enables educators to provide support for various academic, social, and emotional requirements of present-day students. AI technologies prove most advantageous for student populations, including those with disabilities and multilingual learners, as well as students from low-income families. AI has already demonstrated positive educational outcomes through the implementation of Georgia Tech's AI tutor and the University of Michigan's accessibility initiative, as well as DreamBox's K–12 adaptive learning platform, which improves student retention, access, and engagement across educational levels and contexts.

The complete utilization of AI in education needs a long-term approach, together with ethical standards and collaborative partnerships beyond basic technological advancement. A sustainable implementation plan needs to focus on four essential components which include digital infrastructure investment to close digital gaps (1) alongside the creation of inclusive AI models trained on diverse data sets (2) followed by routine bias audits for enhanced transparency (3) and strong data privacy measures that follow GDPR and FERPA guidelines (Ismail & Aloshi, 2025). The success of this roadmap depends on empowering educators through continuous professional development. Teachers need training to operate AI systems, but most importantly, they need training to use these tools ethically and critically for promoting student emotional and cognitive development (Luckin, 2018). Educational institutions need to provide certified training programs about AI implementation, together with data analysis techniques and culturally sensitive teaching practices, to maintain human connection in educational settings.

Future research must investigate three essential areas regarding AI's impact on neurodiverse students, trauma-sensitive education, and extended emotional development. The creation of emotionally intelligent AI tools that combine pedagogical effectiveness with cultural competency requires ongoing collaboration between educators, technologists, psychologists, and policymakers. The combination of affective computing with immersive virtual environments creates fresh opportunities to enhance student participation while boosting cultural understanding and belonging when students learn from SEL frameworks.

AI should serve as a driving force to enhance education rather than being considered the sole solution to educational challenges. AI functions best as a tool to improve existing teaching methods by providing instant feedback and detecting knowledge deficiencies, and enabling personalized student involvement at an educational scale. The advantages of AI become achievable only through ethical operation and active human supervision. Teachers continue to serve as essential figures because they create personal relationships and display emotional intelligence skills while reading students' contextual needs. AI must function within educational systems grounded in human-centered principles by establishing emotional safety as a base while ensuring cultural inclusivity and providing equal learning opportunities.

The main objective of integrating AI in education extends beyond improving test scores and automating administrative work because it aims to develop students who are capable and confident while being compassionate leaders for an interconnected world. AI transforms education through diversity-focused principles, which create inclusive learning spaces that support every student's growth and success.

REFERENCES

Akavova, A., Temirkhanova, Z., & Lorsanova, Z. (2023). Adaptive learning and artificial intelligence in the educational space. *E3S Web of Conferences, 451,* 06011. https://doi.org/DOI: 10.1051/e3sconf/202345106011

Ali, M. (2020). Ensuring equity in AI-enabled classrooms. *Education and Information Technologies, 25*(6), 5423–5439. DOI: 10.1007/s10639-020-10250-x

Amershi, S.. (2019). Guidelines for human-AI interaction. *Proceedings of the ACM on Human-Computer Interaction, 3* (CSCW), 1–13. https://doi.org/DOI: 10.1145/3290607.3312959

Baker, R. S. (2016). Stupid tutoring systems, intelligent humans. *International Journal of Artificial Intelligence in Education, 26*(2), 600–614. DOI: 10.1007/s40593-016-0105-0

Baran, E., Aleman, E., & Dilek, M. (2025). AI literacy in teacher education: Empowering educators through critical co-discovery. *Journal of Teacher Education, 76*(3), 294–311. Advance online publication. DOI: 10.1177/00224871251325083

Barnes, E., Hutson, J., & Perry, K. (2024). Ethical imperatives and challenges: Review of the use of machine learning for predictive analytics in higher education. [IJMCER]. *International Journal of Multidisciplinary and Current Educational Research, 6*(3), 200–208. https://www.researchgate.net/publication/381117221

Binns, R. (2018). Fairness in machine learning: Lessons from political philosophy. In *Proceedings of the 2018 ICML Workshop on Human Interpretability in Machine Learning.*

Bond, M., Bedenlier, S., Marín, V. I., & Händel, M. (2021). Emergency remote teaching in higher education: Mapping the first global online semester. *International Journal of Educational Technology in Higher Education, 18*(1), 50. DOI: 10.1186/s41239-021-00282-x PMID: 34778537

Brynjolfsson, E., & McAfee, A. (2017). *Machine, platform, and crowd: Harnessing our digital future.* W. W. Norton & Company.

Castañeda, L., & Selwyn, N. (2018). More than tools? Making sense of the ongoing digitizations of higher education. *International Journal of Educational Technology in Higher Education, 15*(22), 22. Advance online publication. DOI: 10.1186/s41239-018-0109-y

Dede, C. (2019). *The role of digital technologies in deeper learning.* Harvard Graduate School of Education.

Duffy, M. C., & Azevedo, R. (2015). Motivation matters: Interactions between achievement goals and agent scaffolding for self-regulated learning within an intelligent tutoring system. *Computers in Human Behavior, 52*, 338–348. DOI: 10.1016/j.chb.2015.05.041

Henriksen, D., Creely, E., Gruber, N., & Leahy, S. (2025). Social-emotional learning and generative AI: A critical literature review and framework for teacher education. *Journal of Teacher Education, 76*(3), 312–328. Advance online publication. DOI: 10.1177/00224871251325058

Hernandez, K. (2021). *Understanding AI ethics and safety.* Oxford Internet Institute Report.

Hinojo-Lucena, F.-J., Aznar-Díaz, I., Cáceres-Reche, M.-P., & Romero-Rodríguez, J.-M. (2019). Artificial intelligence in higher education: A bibliometric study on its impact in the scientific literature. *Education Sciences*, *9*(1), 51. DOI: 10.3390/educsci9010051

Holmes, W., Bialik, M., & Fadel, C. (2021). *Artificial intelligence in education: Promises and implications for teaching and learning*. Center for Curriculum Redesign.

Inkster, B., Sarda, S., & Subramanian, V. (2018). An empathy-driven, conversational artificial intelligence agent (Wysa) for digital mental well-being: Real-world data evaluation. *JMIR mHealth and uHealth*, *6*(11), e12106. DOI: 10.2196/12106 PMID: 30470676

Ismail, I. A., & Aloshi, J. (2025). Data privacy in AI-driven education: An in-depth exploration into the data privacy concerns and potential solutions. In *AI applications and strategies in teacher education* (pp. 223–252). IGI Global., DOI: 10.4018/979-8-3693-5443-8.ch008

Julien, G. (2024). How artificial intelligence (AI) impacts inclusive education. *Educational Research Review*, *19*(6), 95–103. DOI: 10.5897/ERR2024.4404

Kaplan, A., & Haenlein, M. (2019). Siri, Siri, in my hand: Who's the fairest in the land? On the interpretations, illustrations, and implications of artificial intelligence. *Business Horizons*, *62*(1), 15–25. DOI: 10.1016/j.bushor.2018.08.004

Kay, R. H., Leung, S., & Tang, H. (2023). Artificial intelligence in K–12 education: A review of empirical research (2010–2022). *British Journal of Educational Technology*, *54*(1), 24–47. DOI: 10.1111/bjet.13260

Kozlowski, D. (2022). Ethical considerations in AI-driven education. *Cambridge Journal of Education*, *52*(2), 197–214. DOI: 10.1080/0305764X.2021.1968309

Luckin, R. (2018). *Machine learning and human intelligence: The future of education for the 21st century*. UCL IOE Press.

Markoff, J. (2015). *Machines of loving grace: The quest for common ground between humans and robots*. Harper Perennial.

Ministry of Education Singapore. (2022). *AI in education: Transforming learning with technology*. Government of Singapore. https://www.tech.gov.sg/media/technews/ai-in-education-transforming-singapore-education-system-with-student-learning-space/

Niemi, H., & Liu, Y. (2021). AI in learning: Preparing grounds for future learning. *Journal of Pacific Rim Psychology*, *15*, 1–12. DOI: 10.1177/18344909211038105

Perin, D., & Lauterbach, M. (2018). Assessing text-based writing of low-skilled college students. *International Journal of Artificial Intelligence in Education*, *28*(1), 56–78. DOI: 10.1007/s40593-016-0122-z

Reich, J. (2020). *Failure to disrupt: Why technology alone can't transform education*. Harvard University Press., DOI: 10.22329/jtl.v16i1.7033

Samarakou, M., Fylladitakis, E. D., Früh, W. G., Hatziapostolou, A., & Gelegenis, J. J. (2015). An advanced eLearning environment developed for engineering learners. *International Journal of Emerging Technologies in Learning, 10*(3), 22–33. DOI: 10.3991/ijet.v10i3.4484

Schildkamp, K. (2020). How AI can support the use of assessment data. *Educational Assessment, Evaluation and Accountability, 32*, 217–235. DOI: 10.1007/s11092-019-09312-4

Selwyn, N. (2021). *Should robots replace teachers? AI and the future of education.* Polity Press.

Spikol, D., Ruffaldi, E., Dabisias, G., & Cukurova, M. (2018). Supervised machine learning in multimodal learning analytics for estimating success in project-based learning. *Journal of Computer Assisted Learning, 34*(4), 366–377. DOI: 10.1111/jcal.12263

Steenbergen-Hu, S., & Cooper, H. (2014). A meta-analysis of the effectiveness of intelligent tutoring systems on college students' academic learning. *Journal of Educational Psychology, 106*(2), 331–347. DOI: 10.1037/a0034752

Tuomi, I. (2018). *The impact of artificial intelligence on learning, teaching, and education: Policies for the future* (JRC Technical Report). European Commission.

UNESCO. (2023). *Artificial intelligence and the future of learning: AI in education in Latin America.* United Nations Educational, Scientific and Cultural Organization. https://www.unesco.org/en/articles/unesco-highlights-role-artificial-intelligence-education-congreso-futuro-2025

VanLehn, K. (2011). The relative effectiveness of human tutoring, intelligent tutoring systems, and other tutoring systems. *Educational Psychologist, 46*(4), 197–221. DOI: 10.1080/00461520.2011.611369

West, D. M. (2018). *The future of work: Robots, AI, and automation.* Brookings Institution Press.

White, H. (2021). Global case studies in AI and education. *Comparative Education Studies, 59*(2), 89–101.

Williamson, B. (2017). *Big data in education: Power, complexity and accountability.* EdTech Series., DOI: 10.4135/9781529714920

Zawacki-Richter, O., Marín, V. I., Bond, M., & Gouverneur, F. (2019). Systematic review of research on artificial intelligence in education. *International Journal of Educational Technology in Higher Education, 16*(1), 1–27. DOI: 10.1186/s41239-019-0171-0

Zheng, C., Yuan, K., Guo, B., Mogavi, R. H., Peng, Z., Ma, S., & Ma, X. (2024). Charting the future of AI in project-based learning: A co-design exploration with students. arXiv. https://arxiv.org/abs/2401.14915 DOI: 10.1145/3613904.3642807

Chapter 18
Chatbots and AI Tutors:
Enhancing Student Engagement and Learning Management

Parihar Suresh Dahake
https://orcid.org/0000-0002-2286-4120
Ramdeobaba University, India

Nihar Suresh Dahake
https://orcid.org/0009-0007-8971-9247
G. H. Raisoni College of Engineering, India

Vasco Santos
https://orcid.org/0000-0002-3535-9377
ISLA Santarém, Portugal

ABSTRACT

In recent years, India has witnessed a transformative shift in educational methodologies, largely driven by the integration of chatbots and AI tutors. This advancement is reshaping student engagement and learning management, fostering an educational environment where technology plays a pivotal role in both instruction and interaction. Chatbots, equipped with natural language processing capabilities, offer students personalized learning experiences by addressing individual queries, providing instant feedback, and facilitating continuous communication beyond traditional classroom settings. These tools not only enhance accessibility to educational resources but also enable educators to focus on more complex pedagogical tasks by automating routine administrative functions.

INTRODUCTION

In recent years, the educational landscape in India has undergone a significant transformation, largely driven by the integration of technology in classrooms. Digital technology in higher education positively impacts student engagement, with behavioral engagement being the most frequently identified dimension, followed by affective and cognitive engagement(Bond et al., 2020). Notably, chatbots and AI tutors stand at the forefront of this technological revolution,

DOI: 10.4018/979-8-3373-5097-4.ch018

offering innovative solutions to enhance student engagement and streamline learning management systems. In a country where the education system is often challenged by high student-to-teacher ratios and resource scarcity, AI-driven tools present a compelling potential to bridge gaps in accessibility and personalized learning experiences. Social robots in education can effectively increase cognitive and affective outcomes, with their physical presence enhancing learning outcomes compared to traditional learning technologies(Belpaeme et al., 2018). These cutting-edge technologies are designed to mimic human interaction, providing students with instant feedback, personalized learning paths, and round-the-clock academic support.

Figure 1. Chatboat system for learning and engagement

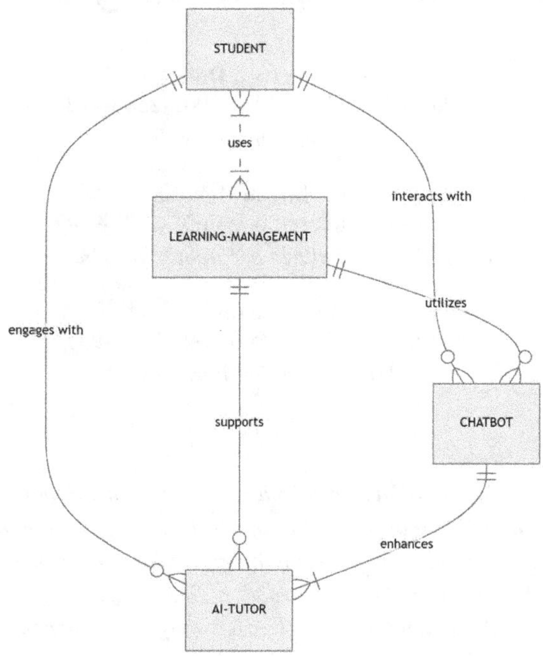

AI in education has significantly improved administration, instruction, and learning by enhancing efficiency, fostering student retention, and enhancing curriculum personalization(Chen et al., 2020) and The implementation of chatbots and AI tutors facilitates an interactive and adaptive learning environment, catering to individual student needs and learning styles. Furthermore, these AI-powered solutions can alleviate some of the burdens on educators, allowing them to focus on more complex tasks that require human insight and expertise. By automating routine tasks such as grading and responding to frequently asked questions, AI tools enable teachers to allocate more time to nurturing critical thinking and creativity among students. Moreover, the adoption of AI in education heralds a new era of data-driven decision-making. Chatbots' information and service quality positively influence users' satisfaction, with perceived enjoyment, usefulness, and ease of use being significant predictors of continuance intention(Ashfaq et al., 2020). AI systems can analyze vast amounts of data to identify learning patterns and predict student performance, thereby enabling educators to implement timely interventions. This data-centric approach not only enhances the quality of education but also supports a more efficient resource allocation within educational institutions. As India strives to provide equitable and high-quality education for its burgeoning population, integrating chatbots and AI tutors points towards a paradigm shift in educational delivery, promising to redefine traditional learning experiences through technological empowerment. the transformation of educational landscapes in India has become increasingly evident with advancements in technology, particularly through the integration of chatbots and AI tutors. These tools have been heralded for their potential to enhance student engagement and streamline learning management systems. New AI-powered technologies significantly transform the human experience, impacting each stage of the shopping journey and creating experiential value(Hoyer et al., 2020). However, despite their widespread acclaim, significant gaps persist that hinder their effective deployment and utilization in Indian educational settings. Recognizing and addressing these gaps is crucial for maximizing the impact of AI-driven tools on student learning and overall academic achievement. One prominent gap lies in the uneven distribution of technological resources across different regions and educational institutions in India. While urban centers and prestigious schools may enjoy access to robust digital infrastructure, students in rural areas often face significant barriers, including limited internet connectivity and a lack of adequately equipped facilities. This digital divide not only hinders the equitable distribution of technological benefits but also exacerbates existing educational inequalities. Many students who could benefit from AI-driven tools are unable to access them, resulting in a disparate educational experience across the country. Moreover, the development and personalization of AI tutors and chatbots tailored to the diverse linguistic and cultural context of India present another challenge. India's multilingual and multicultural landscape requires AI systems capable of understanding and adapting to diverse educational needs, dialects, and learning styles. Currently, gap identification must focus on understanding how these technologies can be customized to offer personalized learning experiences that respect and integrate linguistic diversity. Furthermore, the need for training educators and administrators in the effective implementation and management of these AI tools is critical. Without comprehensive professional development and support, educators may struggle to leverage these technologies fully to enhance students' learning outcomes. Finally, the absence of comprehensive data privacy and security frameworks within educational institutions raises concerns about the deployment of AI tools. As chatbots and AI tutors collect vast amounts of personal data to provide personalized learning experiences, safeguarding student information becomes imperative. Establishing clear, stringent policies to address privacy concerns is vital to foster trust among students, parents, and educators, and to ensure the ethical use of AI technology in education. Closing these gaps will not only enhance the efficacy of AI tools in Indian education but also pave the way for a more inclusive and secure digital learning environment. Hence In a rapidly digitalizing world, education systems are evolving to meet the complex needs of diverse learners, necessitating innovative approaches to academic engagement and management. India, with its expansive and heterogeneous student demographic, presents both unique opportunities and profound challenges for educational development. Traditional teaching methodologies, often constrained by limited teacher-to-student ratios and resource disparities, struggle to cater to personalized learning needs while fostering meaningful engagement. This shortfall becomes more pronounced when factors such as geographic diversity, linguistic variability, and socio-economic disparities are considered, all of which exert a significant influence on how students access and absorb knowledge. Amid these challenges, there arises an acute need for technologically centered interventions that go beyond standard practices, bridging gaps in learning environments and offering scalable, inclusive, and effective solutions.Chatbots and AI-driven tutors emerge as promising tools that align seamlessly with India's educational ambitions. These technologies possess the potential to mitigate pressing issues by enabling personalized, adaptive learning experiences tailored to individual student needs. Unlike traditional systems, AI tutors can deliver instant feedback, clarify doubts, and provide subject-specific assistance at any hour, effectively transcending the constraints of time and space. Furthermore, chatbots, characterized by their conversational interfaces, promote interactive engagement, simplifying administrative processes while bolstering cognitive learning. The need for this technological adoption becomes especially pronounced in resource-strapped regions, where AI models can democratize education by supplementing scarce teaching staff and addressing inequities in access to quality instruction. By integrating these intelligent tools into the education ecosystem, India could substantially enhance its student learning outcomes, heighten engagement levels, and foster a culture of continuous learning that is resilient to the constraints of traditional pedagogy.

REVIEW OF LITERATURE

In the realm of educational technology, keywords analysis proves indispensable for understanding evolving trends and emerging themes, particularly in fields like chatbot development and AI tutors in India. A sophisticated visualization tool empowers researchers to explore bibliometric data through constructing and analyzing networks of keywords. This software facilitates a granular review of scholarly publications, providing insights into the dominance and distribution of specific terminologies within the academic discourse. Analyzing keywords yields valuable information, revealing which concepts are gaining traction or experiencing shifts due to new technological advances or pedagogical strategies.

Figure 2. All keywords analysis by Vosviewer

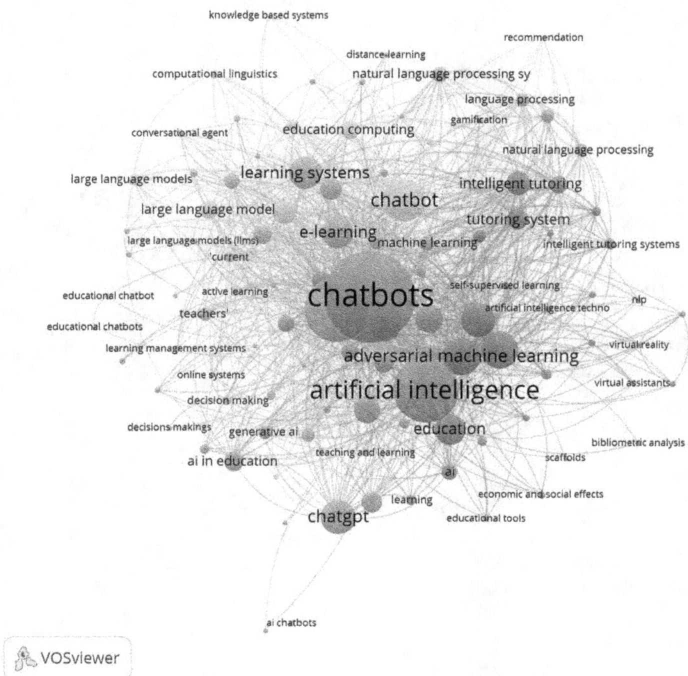

Figure 3. Author keywords analysis by Vosviewer

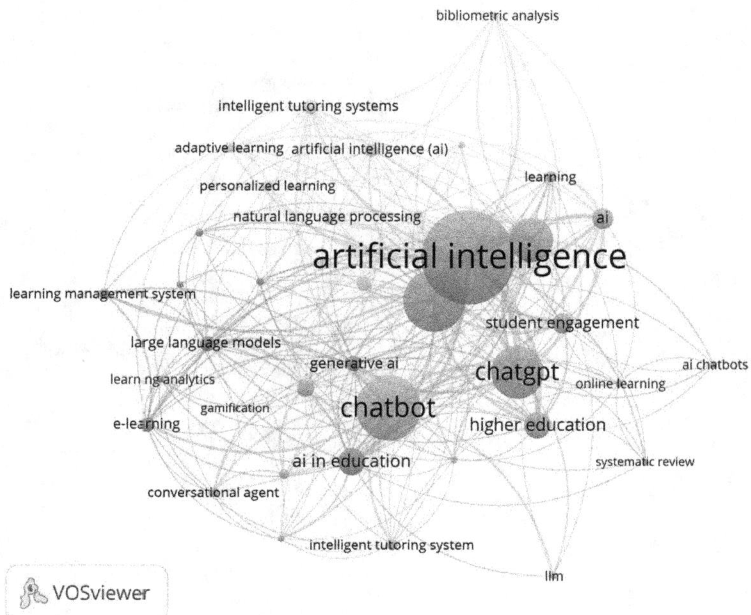

Figure 4. Index keywords analysis by Vosviewer

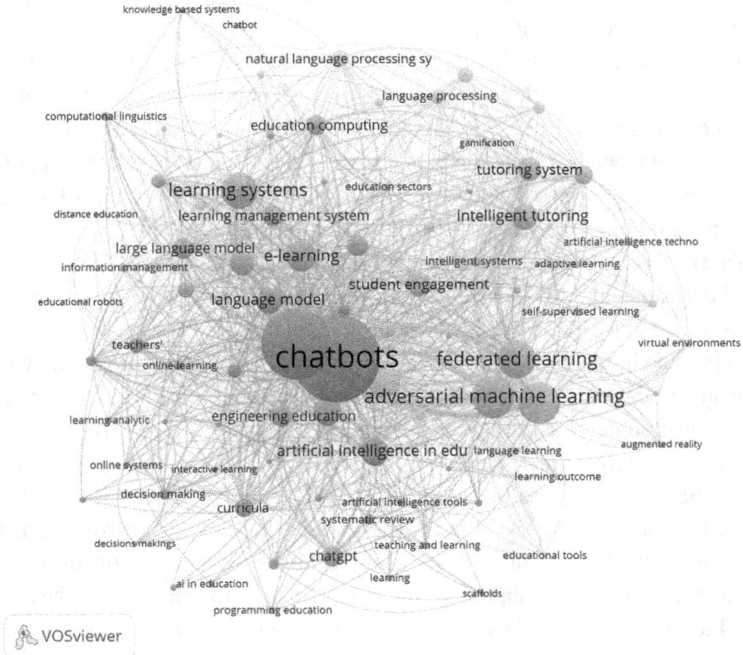

To begin with, the tool performs a thorough examination of keyword occurrences and co-occurrences to depict a comprehensive map of intellectual influence in literature relating to AI in education. Utilizing its algorithms, users can discern patterns in how certain ideas interconnect, thereby highlighting the extent of studies into chatbots and AI tutors specifically, and their application in educational settings. This examination involves processing keyword data from scientific papers and assembling intuitive visualizations that reflect how frequently and effectively these terms are discussed and related in literature. By understanding trending keywords, educators and developers can adapt their strategies to include cutting-edge methods for engaging students and managing learning processes more effectively.

Furthermore, in the context of India, where educational transformation through digital mediums is rapidly accelerating, analysing keywords can identify localized adaptations and innovations responding to unique systemic challenges. By mapping regional terminologies and narratives around AI-driven learning tools, the analysis provides stakeholders with a clearer picture of national priorities in education technology. This localized keyword analysis not only informs researchers of current paradigms but also guides the development of more relevant applications specifically tailored for the Indian educational landscape, ensuring that both technology integration and pedagogical modifications are optimally aligned with student needs and institutional goals.The literature surrounding the integration of chatbots and AI tutors in educational contexts, particularly in India, reveals a growing recognition of their potential to enhance student engagement and improve learning management. The journey begins with (J. Yang &

Zhang, 2019), who provide a systematic review of intelligent tutoring robots (ITRs), highlighting the significance of AI in personalizing education and enriching teaching methodologies. Their work underscores the foundational role of AI in creating interactive educational environments that foster individualized learning experiences.

In the subsequent years, (Schiff, 2021)expands on this notion by exploring the broader applications of AI in educational settings, particularly through intelligent tutoring systems (ITS). He emphasizes the adaptability of these systems and their ability to simulate teaching and learning processes, thereby enhancing educational outcomes. This evolution is further supported by(Hemachandran et al., 2022), who discuss various AI models that cater to students' knowledge levels and teaching methodologies, indicating a shift towards more personalized educational experiences.

The impact of AI chatbots became particularly pronounced during the COVID-19 pandemic, as evidenced by(Han et al., 2022), who examine the effectiveness of an AI chatbot educational program in non-face-to-face classes. Their findings reveal that chatbots can facilitate self-directed learning and provide immediate feedback, thus addressing the challenges posed by remote education. (Martín-Núñez et al., 2023)further contribute to this discourse by investigating the role of intrinsic motivation in AI learning, suggesting that AI tools can optimize teaching tasks and enhance student engagement, particularly during challenging times like the pandemic.

Recent studies, such as those by (Shaik et al., 2023)and (Mallik & Gangopadhyay, 2023), delve into the technical aspects of AI in education, focusing on personalized learning systems and the importance of adaptive engagement. They highlight the necessity of considering student interactions and feedback in developing effective AI-driven educational tools. The exploration of generative AI tools, as articulated by(Latif et al., 2023), emphasizes their potential in providing tailored learning experiences that align with diverse student needs, reinforcing the idea that AI can significantly contribute to achieving inclusive education.

As the discourse continues, studies by (Chukwuere, 2024) and (Krause et al., 2024)illustrate the transformative impact of generative AI chatbots on higher education. They advocate for the integration of AI tools to enhance student support, streamline administrative tasks, and foster a more connected academic environment. The ongoing research into the pedagogical implications of AI, as discussed by (Faruqui et al., 2024), reflects a commitment to understanding how these technologies can be harnessed to improve educational practices.

In conclusion, the literature collectively underscores the transformative potential of AI and chatbots in education, particularly in enhancing student engagement and learning management. As these technologies continue to evolve, ongoing research will be critical to fully realize their capabilities and address the challenges associated with their implementation in diverse educational contexts.

Extensive research highlights the benefits of chatbots in educational settings, including immediate feedback and constant availability, which facilitate continuous learning beyond the classroom. Particularly important is the role these technologies play in managing the routine aspects of student inquiries and administrative tasks, freeing human educators to focus on more complex pedagogical processes. The literature also explores the challenges in implementing AI in education, such as infrastructure limitations and socioeconomic disparities across urban and rural regions in India. Discussions on these barriers offer insights into strategies to overcome them, such as collaborative efforts between government bodies and educational institutions.

Furthermore, empirical studies stress the importance of cultural and linguistic adaptability of AI systems to meet the unique needs of Indian students, suggesting that the success of these technologies largely depends on their customization to local contexts. The literature suggests a significant degree of optimism regarding the future of AI in education, urging educational stakeholders in India to embrace these innovations while also considering ethical implications and data privacy concerns. Ultimately, this body of research provides a foundational understanding of how chatbots and AI tutors can transform educational landscapes, create more inclusive learning experiences, and contribute to the holistic development of students across India.

THE EVOLUTION OF CHATBOTS IN EDUCATION

The integration of chatbots in education has emerged as a transformative force, evolving from simple automated response systems to sophisticated digital tutors capable of enhancing the educational experience. Initially, chatbots in the educational sector were limited in functionality, primarily designed for answering frequently asked questions related to administrative tasks, such as enrollment procedures or deadlines. However, with the rapid advancements in artificial intelligence and natural language processing technologies, these chatbots have undergone a significant transformation, extending their capabilities to support personalized learning experiences. AI in education can enhance teaching and learning experiences, addressing intractable problems and promoting better outcomes for all, but requires a collaborative approach, smart funding, and a focus on pedagogy, technology, and system change(Krause et al., 2024).as the Social chatbots must focus on user engagement and emotional connection to achieve widespread adoption and benefit society(Shum et al., 2018).Above all Generative AI chatbots can improve student support, administrative efficiency, and research processes(Chukwuere, 2024).This is very important to note that the Chatbots can be useful in education, information retrieval, business, and e-commerce, beyond just mimicking human conversation and entertainment(Abu Shawar & Atwell, 2007).

Figure 5. The evolution of chatbots in education

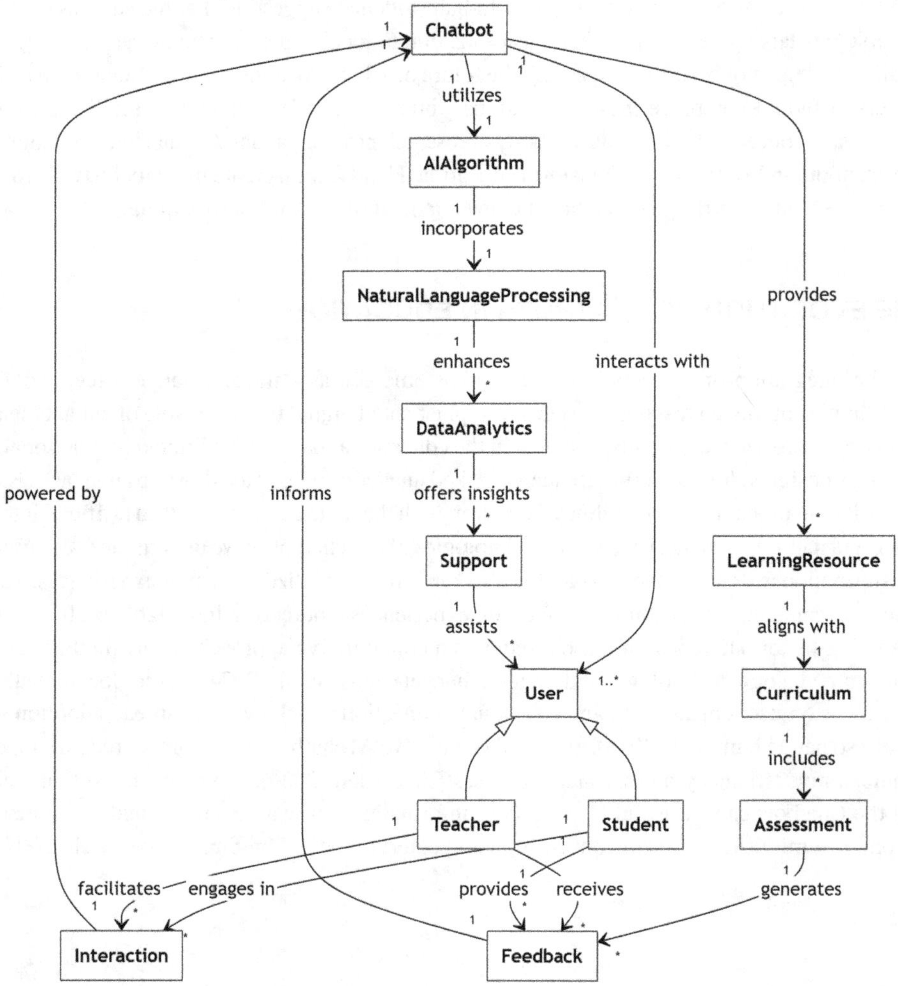

This technological evolution reflects a broader trend towards creating responsive, interactive educational environments tailored to individual student needs. Modern educational chatbots have become pivotal in reshaping teaching and learning paradigms. By leveraging AI, chatbots can now simulate human-like interactions, providing students with instant feedback, addressing queries in real-time, and offering additional explanations for complex subject matter. Students using Ai Diagram Creator, Solution Finder, Gemini, Deep Seek Chatgpt etc, and ChatGPT can increase access to information, facilitate personalized learning, and decrease teaching workload, but its weaknesses include potential bias, discrimination, and declining high-order cognitive skills(Farrokhnia et al., 2024).This interactive capability not only augments the traditional classroom environment but also supports a self-paced learning model, where students can explore topics beyond curriculum confines at their convenience. However, ChatGPT's performance in education varies across subject domains, with potential benefits for instructors and students, but challenges like incorrect information and plagiarism need to be addressed(Lo, 2023). In India, where diverse linguistic and cultural contexts present unique educational challenges, chatbots are increasingly being deployed to bridge learning gaps by delivering content in multiple languages and accommodating various learning styles.ChatGPT has revolutionized scientific research and has wide-ranging applications across industries, but ethical concerns and data biases require balancing AI-assisted innovation with human expertise(Ray, 2023). ChatGPT enhances personalized learning but poses ethical challenges—clear guidelines and evaluation are essential for effective use(Su ( ) & Yang ( ), 2023) Furthermore, as educational institutions strive to manage learning more effectively, chatbots play a crucial role in enhancing student engagement and facilitating seamless learning management. ChatGPT influences student engagement across behavioral, emotional, and cognitive dimensions(Lo et al., 2024) By integrating with learning management systems, chatbots act as virtual teaching assistants, offering personalized assistance and tracking student progress .Universities can effectively address concerns about academic dishonesty and cheating in higher education by adopting proactive and ethical strategies, such as developing policies, training, and using various methods(Cotton et al., 2024). This integration enables educators in India to monitor learning outcomes more efficiently and adjust teaching strategies accordingly. As these technologies continue to advance, they promise to democratize education by providing access to quality learning resources, regardless of geographical or socio-economic barriers, supporting India's goal towards achieving universal education and digital literacy.

AI TUTORS: DEFINITION AND FUNCTIONALITY

AI tutors, a subset of artificial intelligence applications, are designed to mimic the interactions of human tutors while leveraging the vast computational capabilities of modern machines. By using sophisticated algorithms and machine learning techniques, these digital entities provide personalized and adaptive learning experiences for students. AI tutors can assess a learner's current level of understanding, adapt content delivery to their learning pace, and provide instant feedback. They draw from extensive databases of knowledge to offer a variety of explanations and learning paths, thus catering to diverse learning styles and preferences. This customization ensures that students remain engaged and motivated, facilitating deeper understanding and retention of academic material. AI-driven education enhances personalized learning, accessibility, and engagement while raising ethical and socio-economic concerns(Tapalova & Zhiyenbayeva, 2022). Functionality of AI tutors is founded on a multi-layered approach to education, encompassing content delivery, assessment, feedback, and interaction. These systems utilize natural language processing to facilitate intuitive conversations, enabling them to interpret and respond to student queries in real-time. By analyzing vast quantities of data generated during these interactions, AI tutors can refine their responses and identify areas where a student may be struggling, offering targeted practice exercises or alternative explanations. Furthermore, they can incorporate multimedia tools such as videos, simulations, and interactive quizzes, enriching the learning environment and making complex topics more accessible. Moreover, AI tutors contribute to the democratization of education in India by providing affordable and scalable solutions, especially in regions where access to quality education is limited. By bridging geographical and socioeconomic gaps, these tutors can deliver standardized education and supplement traditional teaching methods. As AI technology continues to advance, these tutors are becoming increasingly sophisticated in their functionality, offering potential transformations in educational delivery and management, thus playing an essential role in enhancing student engagement and learning outcomes in the Indian education landscape.

CURRENT TRENDS IN EDTECH IN INDIA

The landscape of educational technology in India is undergoing a significant transformation, driven by the rapid adoption of digital tools and innovative teaching methodologies. The integration of artificial intelligence and machine learning is one of the most pronounced trends, redefining the approach to personalized learning. Educational platforms are increasingly employing AI-driven analytics to tailor content and learning paths to the individual needs of students. This customization not only enhances student engagement but also improves learning outcomes by addressing diverse learning styles and paces. As a result, platforms offer adaptive learning experiences, which are proving instrumental in bridging educational gaps and ensuring that students receive a holistic education irrespective of their geographical location or socio-economic background. Teacher support enhances AI chatbot learning, boosting motivation and competence while balancing autonomy and relatedness needs(Chiu et al., 2023).Another emerging trend is the proliferation of gamification in educational settings. EdTech companies, recognizing the potential of game-based learning, are integrating elements such as leaderboards, badges, and interactive challenges to make learning more engaging and competitive. This approach capitalizes on the innate human desire for achievement and recognition, especially among younger learners, fostering a more immersive and participatory educational experience. Additionally, the surge in mobile learning applications tailored for the Indian market highlights a shift towards on-the-go, anytime, anywhere learning. With widespread smartphone penetration and affordable internet access, these applications are democratizing education, enabling students in remote and underserved areas to access quality educational resources.

Furthermore, the rise of augmented reality and virtual reality technologies is transforming traditional pedagogical methods into immersive experiences that provide students with a deeper understanding of complex concepts. By simulating real-world scenarios, these technologies offer experiential learning opportunities that transcend the limitations of conventional classroom environments. AI in education depends on performance expectancy, effort, motivation, and learning value, with moderating factors(Foroughi et al., 2024).This is complemented by the growing acceptance of hybrid learning models, where online and offline methodologies converge to offer a flexible, student-centric approach. The push towards digital literacy and initiatives emphasizes the integration of technology in education, aiming to equip students with 21st-century skills. Collectively, these trends highlight the dynamic evolution of EdTech in India, underscoring its potential to revolutionize how education is delivered and perceived across the nation.

BENEFITS OF CHATBOTS IN EDUCATION

In the evolving landscape of education in India, chatbots are increasingly seen as transformative tools. By leveraging artificial intelligence, chatbots offer a plethora of benefits that enhance student engagement and streamline learning management. One of the foremost advantages is increased accessibility. Chatbots have evolved from generative ideas to present-day applications, with pattern matching and machine learning being essential technologies, and a general architectural design highlighting crucial issues(Adamopoulou & Moussiades, 2020). Educational chatbots break down barriers, providing students with an interface that supports language diversity and varying learning paces. Students, irrespective of geographical constraints or socio-economic status, gain access to educational resources and assistance anytime, anywhere. Schools and educational institutions confronted with limited human resources find great value in deploying chatbots, as they ensure a consistent and uniform delivery of information and instructional support to a broader student base. Furthermore, chatbots offer round-the-clock assistance, negating the traditional limitations of rigid school hours and availability of educators. Students often require help beyond usual classroom times due to the diverse schedules and some inclination towards nocturnal study habits. Chatbots serve as a tireless academic companion, catering immediately to queries and academic help needs, thus significantly reducing delays in learning and support. Their ability to provide instant responses not only satisfies the students' need for immediate information but also boosts their engagement and motivation to learn, as they are less likely to become frustrated or lose momentum while studying independently. ChatGPT aids academic writing but requires updated policies to ensure integrity, originality, and responsible AI use(Imran & Almusharraf, 2023) hence, Personalized learning experiences represent perhaps one of the most impactful contributions of chatbots in the education sector. By analyzing individual students' interactions, chatbots can adapt to cater to specific learning styles, preferences, and progress levels. This tailored approach enables more effective learning, as students receive customized feedback and recommendations that align with their unique learning objectives and challenges. The personalization process facilitated by chatbots empowers educators to track student performance with greater precision while providing students with a more nuanced and supportive learning journey. Consequently, the integration of chatbots in education not only facilitates a more inclusive and accessible learning environment but also fosters an adaptive landscape that accentuates the individual learner's journey toward educational success.

Figure 6. Benefits of chatbots in education

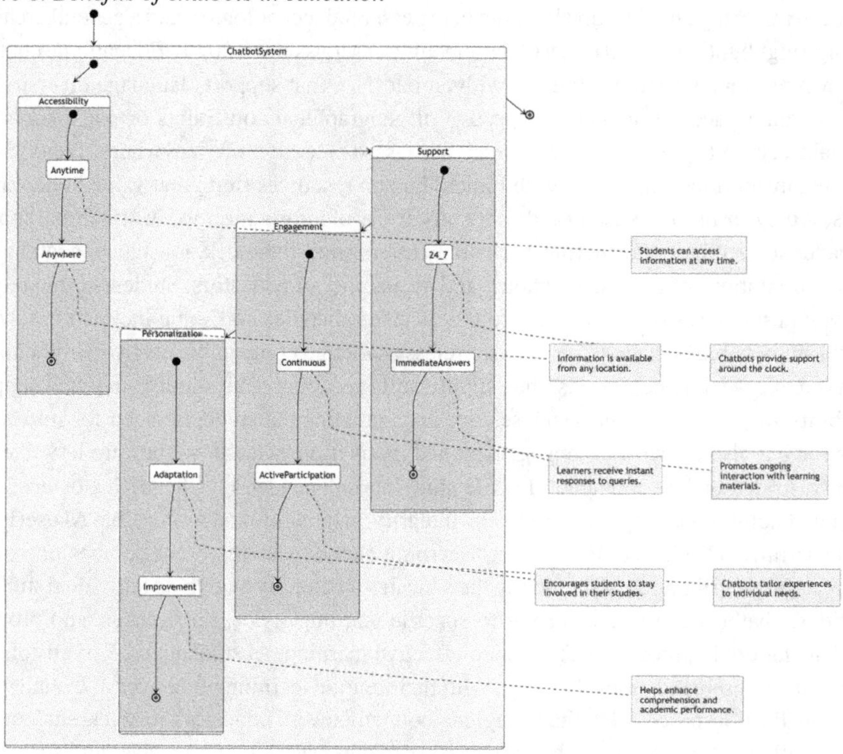

Increased Accessibility

In the vast and dynamic educational landscape of India, the integration of chatbots and AI tutors is redefining accessibility, offering unprecedented opportunities for students across diverse regions and socioeconomic backgrounds. Embracing technological advancements, these digital tools bridge the gap between learners and information, democratizing access to educational resources in ways that traditional systems often fall short. Unlike conventional models that may restrict access due to geographical limitations, financial constraints, or resource availability, AI-driven solutions expand the reach of quality education by enabling students to engage with sophisticated learning materials and expert guidance, all from the comfort of their own devices.

The proliferation of smartphones and internet accessibility across India has set the stage for this transformative shift. Chatbots and AI tutors, equipped with Natural Language Processing capabilities, adeptly communicate with students in various regional languages, further ensuring inclusivity across the linguistic diversity of Indian society. This multilingual adaptability fosters a more engaging and conducive learning environment, where students can access information and clarifications in their native tongues—an essential feature in a country with over 1,600 spoken languages. This approach not only simplifies complex academic concepts but also empowers students to learn without the barriers imposed by traditional language instruction, nurturing an educational ecosystem that resonates with each learner.Chatbots enhance learner engagement through negotiation, improving personalized learning but requiring careful implementation strategies(Kerly et al., 2007).Moreover, these AI-powered tools are fine-tuned to accommodate the unique learning trajectories of each student, allowing for personalized instructional strategies that transcend the limitations of standardized curricula. By continuously analyzing user interactions and feedback, chatbots can offer tailored responses and suggestions that cater specifically to individual learning styles, pace, and interests. This increased accessibility ensures that students, irrespective of their location, economic background, or previous educational experiences, can experience a level of educational inclusivity and support that was once an aspirational goal. As such, chatbots and AI tutors not only enhance learning management but also play a pivotal role in realizing equitable and accessible education for all in India.

24/7 Support

Chatbots and AI tutors have revolutionized the concept of student support services by providing round-the-clock assistance, eliminating the time restrictions traditionally associated with human-led educational support systems. AI enhances international student learning through personalized support but requires ethical safeguards for effective integration(Wang et al., 2023). This innovation ensures students in India can access help whenever needed, transcending the confines of classroom hours and conventional institutional working schedules. Whether it is answering doubts about course material, guiding students in exam preparation, or offering mental health resources, 24/7 chatbots foster an educational environment where learning becomes seamless and uninterrupted. Furthermore, this perpetual availability proves especially beneficial for students juggling personal commitments or employment alongside their studies, as it ensures equitable access regardless of individual schedules. AI enhances education through automation and personalization but requires ethical safeguards for responsible implementation(Alam, 2021). At the heart of this 24/7 support system lies advanced natural language processing technology that enables chatbots to interpret diverse queries and address them with contextual accuracy. These AI-driven systems can simulate one-on-one communication, providing speedy, relevant responses while adapting to the needs of individual learners. In addition to responding to direct questions, they are equipped to proactively identify areas where students may need guidance, offering recommendations on additional resources, tutorials, or study strategies. This functionality empowers learners to progress autonomously while maintaining a sense of connectedness with a virtual guide. For institutions, this around-the-clock service not only minimizes the workload on human faculty but also significantly enhances the overall efficiency of managing large student bodies. India's educational landscape, which is marked by its vast number of learners and varied socioeconomic contexts, stands to particularly benefit from such support systems. By bridging the gap between geographically dispersed students and quality educational resources, AI-powered 24/7 tools democratize learning opportunities, fostering inclusivity while enhancing engagement. Additionally, such systems mitigate learning roadblocks caused by time-zone differences, regional disparities, or institutional constraints, aligning perfectly with the modern demand for scalability and flexibility in education delivery. This shift from reactive, schedule-bound assistance to proactive, continuous aid exemplifies how chatbots are spearheading a transformation in learning management and support, offering an endless cycle of engagement for the benefit of every student.

Personalized Learning Experiences

The advent of chatbots and AI tutors in the educational landscape of India is profoundly transforming how personalized learning experiences are crafted and delivered. Central to this transformation is the ability of chatbots to recognize and adapt to individual learning styles, preferences, and paces, thereby fostering a more tailored educational journey for each student. They achieve this through robust algorithms and machine learning techniques, continuously analyzing students' interactions, responses, and performance to gauge their strengths and weaknesses. AI chatbots enhance children's reading engagement by fostering social connection and sustained situational interest in books(Liu et al., 2022).This analytic ability allows for the dynamic adjustment of the curriculum and the provision of targeted resources that cater to each student's unique learning path, ensuring that educational delivery moves beyond the traditional one-size-fits-all model. Moreover, these AI-driven platforms not only personalize content but also create an engaging and interactive environment that encourages students to take ownership of their learning process. By simulating human-like interactions, chatbots provide timely feedback and motivational prompts, thus reducing the intimidation that many students feel in traditional classroom settings. This virtual support can be particularly impactful in India, where large class sizes and resource constraints often limit personalized attention from human educators. Through gamification elements, customized quizzes, and interactive exercises, students are more likely to remain engaged, improving retention and comprehension rates. Furthermore, these platforms collect and analyze data to identify patterns that help in anticipating learning difficulties and proactively addressing them, ensuring a smoother learning curve for students. The integration of chatbots in personalized learning also opens up new avenues for lifelong learning, allowing students to revisit topics and master concepts at their own pace even beyond the formal education system. This is crucial in catering to diverse educational needs across India's varied socio-economic landscape, where access to quality education can be uneven. Thus, AI tutors not only broaden educational access but also substantially enhance the quality of learning experiences, ensuring that education is inclusive, flexible, and more attuned to the rapidly evolving demands of the 21st-century learner. This paradigm shifts towards personalization in education, catalysed by chatbot technology, holds the promise of nurturing more autonomous, confident, and competent learners capable of thriving in a competitive global environment.

CHALLENGES IN IMPLEMENTING CHATBOTS AND AI TUTORS

Implementing chatbots and AI tutors in India presents several multifaceted challenges. Firstly, technical limitations pose significant hurdles. Many institutions in India continue to struggle with inadequate infrastructure, such as limited access to high-speed internet and modern computing resources, which is crucial for the seamless integration of AI technologies.AI chatbots in higher education enhance personalized learning but require ethical safeguards and institutional support(S. Yang & Evans, 2019). Furthermore, the sophistication of current chatbot algorithms may not fully meet the diverse linguistic landscape in India. This inadequacy impedes the ability of AI tutors to effectively understand and interact with students across various dialects and languages spoken nationwide. Moreover, the current chatbots often rely on existing databases and learning algorithms that may not be specifically tailored to the Indian educational context, thereby limiting their effectiveness in fostering meaningful educational interactions. Cultural barriers also present substantial challenges. The Indian educational system has traditionally emphasized a teacher-centric model, which may conflict with the student-focused approach that AI tutors promote. This shift may encounter resistance from educators who are accustomed to conventional methods and may perceive AI as a threat rather than a tool. AI in education enhances personalized learning and research but requires ethical safeguards to prevent misinformation and bias("Chatbots and AI in Education (AIEd) Tools," 2023).Furthermore, the diverse cultural landscape of India requires AI systems to be culturally sensitive and adaptable, ensuring that they respect and accommodate the various cultural nuances that influence teaching and learning practices. Chatbot-based formative assessment boosts student engagement, especially among girls, improving task completion rates significantly(Benotti et al., 2018).Creating an AI system that is both intuitive and adaptive to these diverse needs remains a complex challenge. Data privacy concerns further complicate the implementation of chatbots and AI tutors. The data-driven nature of these technologies necessitates the collection and analysis of sensitive student data. In India, there is growing awareness and scrutiny about how personal data is handled and protected, magnified by global orientations toward stringent privacy measures. Ensuring compliance with evolving data protection laws is vital to maintaining trust and ensuring the ethical use of AI technologies in education. The challenges of implementing chatbots and AI tutors in India thus encompass a blend of technological, cultural, and ethical considerations that require comprehensive strategies to navigate effectively.

Figure 7. Challenges in implementing chatbots and AI tutors

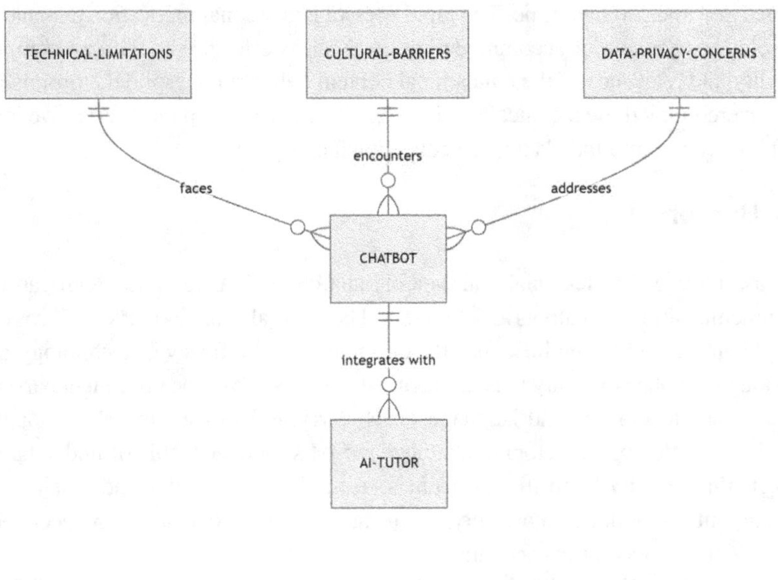

Technical Limitations

The adoption of chatbots and AI tutors in India's educational landscape promises innovative ways to enhance student engagement and manage learning, yet several technical limitations hinder their full potential. One significant limitation is the natural language processing capabilities of these systems. While advances have been made in conversational AI, most chatbots still struggle with understanding and responding to nuanced human language and diverse dialects prevalent across India. This results in interactions that may lack depth, personalization, and contextual understanding—critical elements needed for effective learning assistance. Additionally, the integration of AI tutors requires robust data infrastructure to support real-time processing and analytics, which is not uniformly available across Indian schools, particularly those in remote or under-resourced areas. Consequently, the disparity in technological infrastructure creates varying levels of accessibility and functionality, constraining equitable educational advances across different demographics. AI in education enhances personalized learning, research, and collaboration("Chatbots and AI in Education (AIEd) Tools," 2023).

Another technical constraint is the adaptability of AI systems to specific curricula and learning styles. The current models often require extensive customization to align with the pedagogical objectives and teaching methods unique to Indian educational institutions. This customization can be resource-intensive, involving substantial time and effort from educators and developers to identify learning objectives, curate relevant content, and ensure proper alignment with examination requirements. Furthermore, AI systems must continuously evolve with unexpected changes in curricula and learning materials, representing challenges in how these systems are programmed and updated over time. The rapid pace of educational innovation demands equally agile AI solutions capable of accommodating these shifts effortlessly, without compromising on the quality and relevance of the educational content delivered. Despite the promise of AI in education, overcoming these technical barriers remains a pivotal step for its effective implementation and integration into India's diverse educational ecosystem.

Cultural Barriers

In the vast and diverse educational landscape of India, cultural barriers pose significant challenges to the implementation of chatbots and AI tutors. The cultural nuances that vary across different regions and communities often influence the acceptance and efficacy of technology-enhanced learning tools. Language diversity must be acknowledged as one of the prominent barriers. India is home to numerous dialects and languages, each carrying its own cultural connotations and educational terminologies. Developing chatbots and AI systems capable of understanding and responding to this complex linguistic spectrum is a formidable task. It demands not just linguistic programming but also cultural sensitivity, ensuring that these technologies respect and reflect the cultural richness inherent in each language.

Moreover, traditional attitudes towards education also play a crucial role in shaping cultural barriers. In many regions, the conventional teacher-student dynamic is deeply ingrained, with a high reliance on face-to-face interaction and human mentorship. This traditional perception can lead to hesitancy or skepticism towards AI-based educational tools, which are perceived as impersonal and devoid of emotional intelligence. Overcoming such barriers requires a strategic approach that integrates AI technology with local educational practices, fostering trust and acceptance among users. Additionally, socio-economic factors may also contribute to cultural resistance, as access to technology isn't uniformly distributed, and the perceived value of AI tools might be questioned in communities where traditional educational practices are deeply valued.

The integration of chatbots and AI tutors must therefore be carried out with an acute awareness of India's cultural diversity. ChatGPT enhances management education by improving accessibility and engagement but requires ethical safeguards for responsible use(Dahake et al., 2024). Initiatives need to be culturally adaptive, ensuring educational content resonates with regional values, beliefs, and practices. Collaborations with local educators and stakeholders can help align these technologies with culturally specific pedagogies. By fostering an inclusive educational ecosystem, and ensuring these tools complement rather than replace traditional methodologies, the acceptance and effectiveness of AI in education can be enhanced. Ultimately, bridging cultural barriers not only elevates technological engagement but also ensures that digital learning empowers students across varied cultural contexts in India.

Data Privacy Concerns

The integration of chatbots and AI tutors in Indian education systems is ushering in a new era of personalized learning and student engagement. However, this technological revolution brings the pivotal challenge of data privacy concerns to the fore. As these AI-driven tools collect vast amounts of data to tailor educational content, they simultaneously raise critical questions regarding how this sensitive information is stored, utilized, and protected. The primary concern is the potential exposure of students' personal data, which may include academic records, behavioral assessments, and even demographic information, to unauthorized entities. Such breaches could have far-reaching consequences, impacting students' privacy and trust in digital educational tools.

To further complicate matters, the legal frameworks governing data privacy in India, while evolving, are not yet fully equipped to address the specific challenges posed by AI and advanced data analytics in education. The Personal Data Protection Bill, although a step in the right direction, requires robust implementation strategies to ensure strong security measures and accountability of educational platforms utilizing AI. Institutions and developers of AI tutors need to prioritize the integration of privacy-by-design principles in their systems, ensuring that data encryption, anonymization, and rigorous access controls are in place to safeguard the integrity and confidentiality of student data. These precautionary measures are vital, not only in fostering a secure learning environment but also in gaining the trust of students, parents, and educators alike.

Moreover, fostering digital literacy among students and educators becomes an integral part of addressing data privacy concerns. Educating users about the rights over their digital information, understanding consent, and recognizing the signs of potential data misuse are crucial steps towards empowering them to make informed decisions. As AI-driven educational tools continue to advance, balancing innovation with stringent data privacy safeguards will be essential to maintaining the integrity of the educational experience. Emphasizing transparent data practices, alongside developing robust policies aligned with international standards, can significantly contribute to mitigating privacy concerns and ensuring that AI technology remains a trusted partner in education.

USER EXPERIENCE AND ENGAGEMENT METRICS

User experience and engagement metrics serve as critical barometers for evaluating the success of chatbots and AI tutors in fostering student interaction and academic performance in India. These insights go beyond assessing simple usability and provide comprehensive data on how students interact with AI-driven systems, revealing their effectiveness in cultivating engagement and meeting educational goals. Central to this process is the measurement of both qualitative and quantitative metrics, such as session duration, task completion rates, dropout rates, sentiment analysis, and frequency of chatbot usage.AI chatbots help preservice teachers refine questioning skills, improving responsive teaching through iterative design enhancements(Lee & Yeo, 2022) These indicators collectively demonstrate how seamless the interface is, the degree of personalization achieved, and the extent to which the AI meets students' day-to-day learning needs. In India's nuanced and diverse educational ecosystem, these metrics must also account for socio-economic disparities, factoring in conditions such as internet access, language barriers, and digital literacy levels to ensure inclusive and meaningful engagement for all students. Achieving high user satisfaction and engagement with AI tutors hinges on several design considerations and iterative performance tracking. A pivotal element lies in crafting intuitive navigation, adaptive learning pathways, and culturally relevant content that resonates with Indian learners. Moreover, engagement is significantly amplified by AI systems that leverage natural language processing to deliver conversational fluency and personalized learning support. Student chatbot adoption depends on performance expectancy, effort, and habit, guiding future AI integration strategies(Almahri et al., 2020). Metrics such as response accuracy and user retention are particularly indicative of how effectively the chatbot fosters a sense of trust and utility. AI in sustainable education by addressing personalized learning and educational accessibility(Alshahrani, 2023) Emotional engagement, captured through sentiment analysis or real-time feedback mechanisms, can shed light on whether students feel motivated and supported while using the tool. Continuous improvement cycles driven by data analytics and student performance reviews help refine these interactions, ensuring that the AI evolves in alignment with learner expectations and pedagogical objectives. By systematically evaluating user experience and engagement metrics, educational institutions can derive actionable insights to bridge gaps in learning outcomes and maximize the educational potential of AI. In the Indian context, where disparities in access and quality of education persist, such metrics are indispensable in tailoring AI systems to accommodate diverse user groups. Creating a dynamic feedback loop between user data and system design not only enhances learning outcomes but also fosters sustained, multidimensional student engagement ultimately contributing to a more inclusive and effective digital learning environment.

FUTURE OF AI IN EDUCATION

As the educational landscape in India continues to evolve, the future of AI in this sector holds immense potential to revolutionize learning experiences and management systems. The integration of AI technologies is expected to bring about a transformative shift, enhancing personalization in education like never before. Traditional one-size-fits-all approaches are giving way to individualized learning experiences wherein AI-driven tools can assess a student's strengths, weaknesses, and preferences. AI in English language teaching enhances learning(Hockly, 2023)

These insights allow for the customization of learning paths, offering resources and guidance tailored to individual needs. Such personalized learning can greatly enhance student engagement, efficacy, and outcomes. Moreover, AI is poised to play a crucial role in automating administrative tasks, thus allowing educators to dedicate more time to teaching and interacting with students. By leveraging AI tools for grading, student performance analytics, and even administrative paperwork, schools can significantly improve efficiency and focus resources on core teaching activities. The potential of AI extends to virtual classrooms as well, where it facilitates seamless integration of interactive and immersive technologies such as augmented reality and virtual reality. These tools can provide students with hands-on experiences, stimulating creativity and deeper understanding of complex subjects. The evolution of AI in education is a continuous process, demanding collaboration between technologists and educators to ensure ethical considerations are addressed and technologies are accessible to all students. In this progression, AI also opens pathways for adaptive assessment, enabling dynamic evaluation of student performance, and providing real-time feedback. Such systems can assess not only academic knowledge but also life skills and emotional intelligence, offering a holistic view of student development. Furthermore, AI-driven communication platforms are likely to foster better student-teacher-parent interactions, ensuring transparency and facilitating collaborative learning environments. As AI innovations become more sophisticated, the challenge remains to balance technology integration with the human touch that is fundamental in education. The future of AI in education thus lies in its ability to complement human efforts, fostering environments where technology and pedagogy harmoniously enhance the learning journey in Indian schools and universities.

Predicted Trends

As India embraces the digital transformation of its educational landscape, the integration of AI-powered chatbots and virtual tutors continues to evolve rapidly, setting the stage for transformative trends in the future. One of the most significant predicted shifts is the widespread personalization of learning experiences. AI systems are poised to leverage data on student behavior, learning patterns, and preferences to deliver tailored educational content. This shift will redefine the one-size-fits-all approach traditionally seen in Indian education, offering dynamic adaptation to individual learner needs. By 2030, it is anticipated that AI will not only analyze performance metrics in real-time but also provide predictive insights into areas where students are likely to struggle, thus enabling early intervention and fostering better outcomes. The ability of AI tutors to incorporate regional nuances such as multilingual capabilities and cultural relevance in their interactions will further enhance their adoption across diverse socio-economic groups in the country.

Another trend shaping the future is the integration of AI with emerging technologies such as augmented reality and virtual reality. This convergence promises to create immersive learning environments that extend beyond textual or video-based engagement. Students will be able to virtually enter historical landmarks, conduct simulated science experiments, or practice real-world problem-solving in controlled digital spaces. These advancements align with India's push toward adopting experiential and skill-based education. Furthermore, the role of AI in redefining assessments will be pivotal. Instead of conventional exams, AI systems could evaluate competencies through continuous, task-based interaction, emphasizing critical thinking and creativity.

Generative AI chatbots enhance student engagement but require ethical safeguards and structured implementation in higher education(Ilieva et al., 2023).

Equally impactful is the projected rise in AI-driven platforms for teacher collaboration and training. In a country where teacher shortages persist, AI will assist educators by automating administrative functions, suggesting teaching strategies based on classroom data, and offering professional development through adaptive learning modules. This trend signals an essential step toward bridging educational gaps in underserved regions and making quality education more accessible nationwide. However, these developments will require robust infrastructure, ethical considerations, and regulatory frameworks to ensure equitable implementation. The road ahead promises an era wherein AI will coexist with human educators, not as replacements but as indispensable allies in reshaping learning experiences for millions of students.

Potential Innovations

In the realm of educational technology, potential innovations linking chatbots and AI tutors to learning management systems signify a seismic shift in how education can be tailored and delivered in India. At the forefront is the creation of highly personalized learning experiences that extend beyond static content delivery. By harnessing AI's adaptive capabilities, educational platforms can intelligently assess students' strengths and weaknesses, adapting instructional strategies in real-time. Chatbots enhance mature student engagement by fostering peer interaction, reducing isolation, and improving sense of belonging(Abbas et al., 2022).These AI-driven systems could offer personalized recommendations for learning materials, practice exercises, and alternative explanations, ensuring that each student's unique learning trajectory is comprehensively supported. Moreover, AI tutors possess the potential to transcend language barriers, a particularly significant challenge in India's multilingual landscape. By incorporating advanced natural language processing technology, AI systems can provide real-time translation and contextual explanations in various regional languages. CALMsystem improves student self-assessment through chatbot negotiation, enhancing reflection and metacognitive learning skills(Kerly et al., 2008). This ability ensures equitable access to quality education, regardless of linguistic background. Additionally, the integration of speech recognition technology can enable students to interact with learning materials using voice commands, thus supporting learners with visual impairments or other disabilities, and making educational resources universally accessible. AI-powered chatbots improve academic library services but require careful integration and privacy safeguards for adoption(Kaushal & Yadav, 2022). Furthermore, the use of chatbots and AI tutors can significantly streamline administrative tasks within educational institutions. These virtual assistants can manage routine inquiries, schedule classes, and provide instant feedback, thereby freeing educators' valuable time to focus on pedagogical tasks that require human intervention. They can also effectively monitor academic progress and alert educators to students who may need additional support. As AI continues to evolve, it may even offer predictive analytics to foresee academic challenges and recommend intervention strategies. Such innovations not only enhance student engagement but also establish a robust framework for managing learning environments efficiently, fortifying India's educational infrastructure for a future thriving with technological advancements.

ROLE OF EDUCATORS IN AI-DRIVEN ENVIRONMENTS

In AI-driven educational environments, the role of educators evolves from traditional instruction to becoming facilitators of deeper learning experiences. As artificial intelligence tools like chatbots and AI tutors become more prevalent in the classroom, teachers are increasingly required to integrate these technologies into their pedagogical practices effectively.

Educators are tasked with guiding students in navigating and utilizing AI resources, ensuring that these digital tools enrich rather than overwhelm the learning experience. This shift necessitates a multifaceted approach that combines technical proficiency with pedagogical expertise, empowering teachers to evaluate the efficacy of AI applications, tailor educational interactions, and foster a participatory culture that encourages critical thinking and collaboration. Furthermore, educators in AI-driven settings assume a pivotal role in interpreting the data generated by AI systems. With access to analytics that capture students' learning patterns and progress, teachers can develop personalized learning pathways that cater to individual students' needs and potential. This data-driven approach enables educators to identify gaps in understanding, modify instructional strategies, and implement timely interventions to support student success.

Figure 8. Role of educators in AI-driven environments

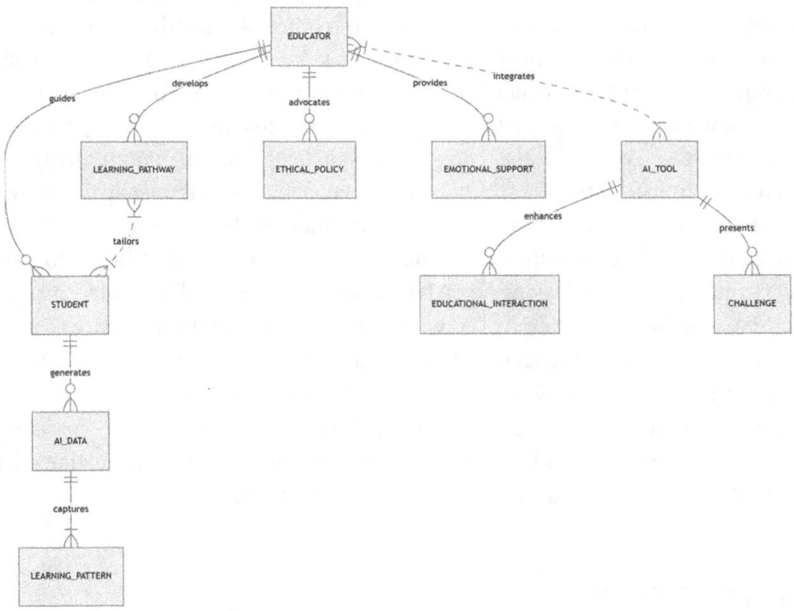

In doing so, teachers become adept analysts, capable of utilizing AI insights to enhance educational outcomes. Though AI technologies offer numerous advantages, they also present challenges that educators must address, such as data privacy concerns and ensuring equitable access to technological resources. Teachers are therefore crucial in advocating for ethical implementation and usage policies within educational institutions, ensuring that students derive maximum benefit from AI without compromising their privacy or personal development. Moreover, educators maintain the essential human element in educational interactions, providing empathy, emotional support, and mentorship—qualities that remain irreplaceable by technology. As AI continues to reshape the educational landscape, the role of educators will remain indispensable, yet transformed, as they embrace new tools and methodologies to enrich student engagement and learning management.

ETHICAL CONSIDERATIONS IN AI EDUCATION

Ethical considerations in AI education encompass a broad spectrum of issues that fundamentally reshape how learning environments function in India. As AI technologies increasingly permeate educational settings, the ethical facets of their deployment cannot be overlooked. One primary concern is the accuracy and impartiality of data used in AI systems, which influences the quality of interaction students have with AI tutors. It is crucial to scrutinize the algorithms employed by educational chatbots and AI systems to ensure that they do not perpetuate biases or reinforce inequalities. Bias in algorithms can undermine educational objectives by skewing educational content and experiences, thereby affecting students' learning pathways. This bias might stem from a lack of diversity in the data sets used to train these algorithms, leading to outputs that disproportionately favor certain groups over others. Hence, there's an exigent need for comprehensive auditing of AI algorithms to ensure they foster inclusive learning environments.

Moreover, the advent of AI in educational contexts raises substantive questions concerning the impact on employment within the sector. As AI systems become more adept at performing tasks traditionally undertaken by educators, there is both a challenge and an opportunity in redefining roles within educational frameworks. While AI can enhance learning management by offering personalized educational experiences, thereby complementing human efforts, it also risks displacing jobs. Educators and institutional staff may find themselves having to adapt to new roles or acquire additional skills to work alongside AI technologies. An ethical approach entails devising strategies to balance the incorporation of AI with sustainable employment practices, ensuring that the human workforce is neither rendered obsolete nor marginalized. This balance involves policy interventions, retraining programs, and fostering a culture of collaboration between humans and AI in educational contexts. Addressing these ethical concerns is vital not only for safeguarding equitable educational experiences but also for fostering a forward-looking educational landscape that harmonizes technological advancement with human values.

BIAS IN ALGORITHMS

In the domain of AI education, bias in algorithms emerges as a pressing concern, primarily because algorithms form the backbone of AI-driven applications and tools. These algorithms, often perceived as impartial and objective, are in fact shaped by the data on which they are trained. This data, reflecting real-world scenarios, inherently carries the biases, stereotypes, and disparities present in society. When algorithms are trained on biased data, they may unintentionally propagate or even amplify existing inequalities, affecting decision-making processes in education systems. For instance, if an AI tutor is trained on a biased dataset, it may favor students from certain backgrounds over others, thereby reinforcing inequalities rather than bridging educational gaps. In India, where diversity, in terms of language, culture, and socioeconomic status, is vast, the implications of algorithmic bias are even more pronounced. Educational technologies utilizing AI must be scrutinized to ensure they recognize and respect this diversity. This involves not only the integration of diverse datasets during the training of AI models but also regular audits and updates to algorithms to mitigate potential biases. Furthermore, the development and implementation of AI in education require the involvement of educators, technologists, and policymakers to collaboratively address and mitigate bias-related challenges. By fostering interdisciplinary collaborations, stakeholders can work towards creating AI systems in education that are equitable and inclusive, ultimately enhancing learning outcomes for students across various socio-cultural contexts in India. To tackle bias in educational algorithms, transparency is key. Educators, students, and data scientists must have open channels of communication to comprehend how algorithmic decisions are made. Employing explainable AI can help demystify decision-making processes, allowing stakeholders to identify and rectify biased outcomes more effectively. Such endeavors not only contribute to improved AI tools but also build trust in AI systems in education. By ensuring that AI in education supports fairness and equity, India can leverage technology to universally enhance student engagement and learning management, without succumbing to the pitfalls of bias in algorithms.

STUDENT PERSPECTIVES ON AI TUTORS

The integration of artificial intelligence (AI) tutors in educational systems has emerged as a transformative force in India, reshaping how students perceive learning. Students across diverse regions and educational backgrounds have expressed varied perspectives on these digital assistants, highlighting both opportunities and challenges. Many students appreciate the personalized learning experience offered by AI tutors, which adapts to their individual learning pace and preferences. This customization fosters a more engaging and interactive learning environment, allowing students to focus on areas where they require additional support while advancing quickly through topics they grasp more easily. AI tutors also provide timely feedback, enhancing understanding and retention of new information, thus acting as a catalyst for deeper learning. Online students value learner-to-learner, learner-to-instructor, and learner-to-content engagement strategies, with icebreaker discussions, collaborative work, and regular reminders being most beneficial(Martin & Bolliger, 2018).

However, despite these advantages, students have also raised valid concerns regarding the use of AI in education. A significant apprehension is the potential reduction in human interaction, as some students still value the interpersonal connections and insights offered by human teachers. The lack of emotional engagement and empathy, which a human tutor typically provides, cannot be replicated by AI, leading students to fear that education could become overly mechanized. Moreover, concerns about data privacy and the ethical use of their personal learning data further complicate the acceptance of AI tutors. These apprehensions highlight the need for a balanced approach that integrates AI with traditional teaching methods, fostering an educational environment that benefits from technological advancements while preserving the human touch. AI can enhance human engagement by standardizing routine tasks, personalizing data-rich services, and fostering relationships(Huang & Rust, 2021).

In addressing these divergent perspectives, educational institutions in India are tasked with the challenge of effectively integrating AI tutors into the traditional framework. Schools and universities must ensure that these tools complement rather than replace human educators. One solution is to encourage collaborative learning paradigms where AI serves as an adjunct to teacher-led instruction, thereby enriching the educational experience. As AI tutors become more prevalent, understanding student perspectives is crucial in designing systems that are equitable, inclusive, and aligned with the varied needs of Indian students. By acknowledging the nuanced views of learners, educators can harness the potential of AI while mitigating its drawbacks, ultimately fostering a more holistic educational landscape.

PARENTAL INVOLVEMENT IN AI EDUCATION

Parental involvement in AI education is pivotal in shaping students' learning experiences and outcomes, especially in a diverse and rapidly developing educational landscape like India. With AI technologies increasingly integrated into educational frameworks, parents play a critical role in fostering an environment that encourages curiosity and adaptability in their children. In the context of AI tutors and chatbots, parents are not merely observers but active participants who can influence how these tools are perceived and used by students. By engaging with AI-driven educational platforms, parents can better understand the technological landscape their children are navigating, enabling them to offer guidance and support effectively. Furthermore, the collaboration between parents, educators, and AI technologies can significantly enhance the learning process. When parents are informed and involved, they can provide valuable feedback to educational institutions, contributing to the development of more tailored and effective AI tools. This partnership can also help demystify AI technologies, alleviating fears and misconceptions that may exist within families about the use of such technologies in learning. By equipping parents with the knowledge and skills required to engage with AI tools, educational systems can ensure that learners receive the full benefits of these innovations, promoting a more inclusive and participative form of education. Moreover, parental involvement can extend to advocating for equitable access to AI educational tools, ensuring that all students benefit from enhanced learning opportunities regardless of their socioeconomic background. As AI continues to transform education in India, parents have the power to influence policy decisions and the integration of AI tools in schools. They can push for transparency in data usage and privacy concerns associated with AI platforms, advocating for ethical and responsible use of technology in learning environments. In essence, empowering parents with AI literacy not only supports their children's education but also contributes significantly to the broader goal of fostering a technologically informed society. By actively participating in AI education, parents become collaborators in their children's learning journey, as well as shapers of the future educational landscape.

INTEGRATION WITH EXISTING LEARNING MANAGEMENT SYSTEMS

The integration of chatbots and AI tutors into existing Learning Management Systems (LMS) represents a pivotal advancement in the digitization of education, offering functionalities that augment both the operational efficiency of such platforms and the overall learning experience for students. By seamlessly embedding these AI-driven tools within LMS platforms, institutions can transform static repositories of content into dynamic, interactive learning ecosystems. This integration leverages the existing databases, communication channels, and assessment tools of an LMS while incorporating adaptive learning mechanisms powered by artificial intelligence. The result is a more personalized learning experience, where AI tutors can identify individual student strengths and weaknesses, recommend tailored resources, and provide timely assistance, thus ensuring that students remain engaged and supported throughout their academic journey.

Technologically, this integration often relies on robust APIs, which allow AI systems to interface with LMS platforms. Through these interfaces, chatbots can automate several administrative tasks that were previously labor-intensive, including grade tracking, assignment reminders, and course enrollment assistance. For educators, this translates into reduced administrative burden and more time to focus on instructional design and student interaction. Furthermore, AI tutors equipped with natural language processing capabilities can facilitate real-time communication with students directly through the LMS, providing instant clarification of doubts, step-by-step explanations, or recommendations for supplementary materials all without leaving the platform interface. This creates a centralized, unified learning environment where student queries, notifications, and course engagement are streamlined.In the context of India's education sector, where the scale of student populations and variance in tech literacy levels often pose challenges, such integrations can democratize access to quality educational support. AI tutors bring consistency to instruction and can bridge gaps in teacher-to-student ratios, particularly in under-resourced schools and institutions. The ability to integrate language-specific conversational interfaces ensures inclusivity, making learning materials and support available to students in their native languages. As a result, the synthesis of AI tools with LMS platforms not only enhances the educational process but also addresses systemic challenges, fostering a future-ready, equitable educational landscape in India.

CULTURAL ADAPTATION OF AI TOOLS

In the context of Indian education, cultural adaptation of AI tools is paramount to ensure relevance and engagement among students. India is a tapestry of diverse languages, traditions, and learning styles, necessitating AI-driven educational tools that are not only linguistically inclusive but also culturally sensitive. This cultural congruence begins with the integration of local languages and dialects into AI interfaces, facilitating enhanced accessibility and relatability. Such adaptations help bridge the gap between standardized AI systems and the nuanced demands of a diverse educational landscape, where one-size-fits-all solutions often fall short. Furthermore, incorporating culturally specific examples, references, and contextual knowledge into the AI's learning modules can strengthen students' connection with the content, making it more meaningful and engaging.

Beyond language and content, cultural adaptation involves recognizing and aligning with prevalent social norms and values. In India, the educational ethos often emphasizes respect for authority, collective learning, and communal success. AI tools that effectively blend these cultural elements into their operations are more likely to resonate with students, fostering increased interaction and acceptance. For instance, AI tutors can incorporate social learning elements, encouraging collaboration among students, reflecting traditional Indian pedagogy that values shared knowledge and discussion. Additionally, considering cultural attitudes towards technology and its role in education is crucial. By aligning AI tools with localized values and educational expectations, developers can create systems that not only teach but also inspire and motivate within the culturally rich Indian context. This comprehensive approach to cultural adaptation ensures that AI tools not only meet educational objectives but also enhance overall student engagement, paving the way for transformational learning experiences.

FEEDBACK MECHANISMS FOR CONTINUOUS IMPROVEMENT

Feedback mechanisms in the integration of chatbots and AI tutors in educational management systems are pivotal for fostering a cycle of continuous improvement and maintaining the efficacy of these digital tools. In the context of Indian education, where diverse learning challenges and opportunities exist, establishing robust feedback loops ensures that the AI systems remain relevant and adaptive to students' evolving needs. Feedback mechanisms encompass both quantitative and qualitative data, enabling educators and developers to refine AI functionalities continually. They serve as a vital tool not only in measuring the success of AI interventions but also in identifying areas for enhancement. These mechanisms typically involve direct feedback from users students, teachers, and administrators—via surveys, performance analytics, and usage metrics that provide insights into the interaction patterns and effectiveness of AI tutors and chatbots. Additionally, AI systems themselves can collect and analyze data about students' progress and engagement, providing valuable insights that can lead to personalized learning experiences. By leveraging machine learning techniques, AI can process feedback data to discern trends, thereby adjusting its algorithms to better address distinct educational needs and preferences. Moreover, regular feedback collection encourages an iterative development approach, where AI systems are frequently updated and improved based on user experience and technological advancements. Educators can use feedback to tailor their teaching methods, ensuring that the digital tutoring and assistance provided through AI are effectively supplementing traditional educational strategies. In doing so, feedback mechanisms not only heighten the performance and user satisfaction of AI tools but also contribute to the broader aim of enhancing student engagement in India's education landscape. Balancing technological innovation with human input remains quintessential in creating a harmonious learning environment that thrives on adaptability and responsiveness.

SCALABILITY OF AI SOLUTIONS IN EDUCATION

Scalability, a critical metric for assessing the viability of AI solutions in education, involves the capacity to expand and adapt these technologies to accommodate an increasing number of students and diverse educational settings without compromising performance or diminishing the quality of the learning experience. This facet of AI applications highlights their potential to address the unique challenges faced by India's education sector, characterized by large class sizes and varying access to resources. AI-driven platforms, through their versatility, offer a scalable approach to personalized learning, tailoring educational experiences to individual student's needs, irrespective of class size or demographic diversity. A key factor in the scalability of AI solutions is the modularity and adaptability of the underlying algorithms, which enable the systems to learn from large volumes of data and continuously enhance their performance over time. This dynamic learning process ensures that AI tools can effectively manage increased loads, incorporating more students and broader curricula seamlessly. With advanced data analytics and machine learning capabilities, AI systems can identify and respond to patterns in student behavior and learning outcomes, thus offering timely interventions to support student success. Moreover, cloud-based infrastructures amplify the scalability prospects of AI in education by providing the necessary computational power and storage to support substantial growth in user base and data handling. Such platforms allow educational institutions to deploy AI solutions ubiquitously, enabling access to educational resources and tools across various geographic locations in India, including underserved and rural areas. These solutions not only accommodate the existing infrastructural constraints but also open avenues for integrating AI seamlessly into traditional education systems, thereby democratizing access to quality education and fostering an inclusive learning environment. As AI solutions continue to evolve, their scalability will be paramount in transforming India's educational landscape, ensuring that every student has the opportunity to benefit from innovative learning strategies and resources.

RESULT & DISCUSSION BASED ON THE LITERATURE

Research and literature indicate that the integration of chatbots and AI tutors within the educational framework in India holds significant promise for enhancing student engagement and improving learning management. Such technological tools are not only pivotal in providing round-the-clock assistance and personalized learning experiences but also in bridging the gap between students and educators. Students' AI chatbot adoption in higher education depends on gender, academic field, and familiarity with technology(Stöhr et al., 2024), Numerous studies highlight the effectiveness of chatbots in facilitating instant access to educational content, answering queries, and providing an adaptive learning environment that caters to individual student needs. Negotiation-driven chatbots enhance metacognitive skills by fostering self-reflection, improving learner engagement and assessment accuracy(Suleman et al., 2016).This responsiveness plays a critical role in sustaining student interest and commitment, especially in a diverse educational landscape like India, where students come from varied socioeconomic and linguistic backgrounds. Generative AI in higher education enhances pedagogy but raises concerns about ethics, bias, and commercialization(Rudolph et al., 2024). Moreover, the deployment of AI tutors has shown marked improvements in student learning outcomes. AI systems equipped with machine learning algorithms analyze data patterns from students' interactions to tailor educational resources and support according to their proficiency levels.A user-centric framework enhances chatbot-based distance learning by addressing engagement, privacy, pedagogy, and ethical concerns(Bahja et al., 2020), By doing so, these systems contribute to a more personalized and efficient learning journey. The literature underscores the importance of personalization in education, as it leads to increased student motivation and better academic performance. Furthermore, AI tutors provide valuable feedback to educators, offering insights into areas where students struggle, thereby enabling educators to modify their teaching strategies accordingly. However, challenges remain regarding the full-scale integration of chatbots and AI tutors in the Indian educational system. Issues such as technological infrastructure, access to digital devices, and varying levels of digital literacy among students and teachers must be addressed to fully harness the potential of these tools. Intelligent tutoring chatbots enhance education by reducing teacher dependency and improving adaptive, AI-driven learning experiences(Ashfaque et al., 2020). Nevertheless, the overall implications of existing research underline the transformative impact of these technologies, suggesting that they could act as vital instruments in modernizing education, making it more accessible and effective for learners across the nation. Personas-based chatbots enhance student engagement by tailoring interactions using machine learning-driven persona development(Ali Amer Jid Almahri et al., 2019).AI chatbots enhance student engagement in higher education but require ethical safeguards and institutional support for success(Nguyen et al., 2024). This literature consistently showcases that while challenges exist, the benefits of adopting AI-driven educational solutions vastly outweigh the drawbacks, marking a progressive step towards a more engaging and managed learning environment.

CONCLUSION

The journey through the implementation and integration of chatbots and AI tutors in India's educational landscape reveals a transformative potential for enhancing student engagement and learning management. As the digital age continues to unfold, these technological advancements provide compelling opportunities to address some of the traditional challenges that educators and learners face. AI in higher education research mainly focuses on profiling, assessment, and personalization, but there is a need for more critical reflection on challenges, risks, and ethical approaches(Zawacki-Richter et al., 2019). By leveraging the capabilities of artificial intelligence, educational institutions in India are poised to offer personalized learning experiences, thereby bridging gaps in comprehension and engagement that have historically hindered progress. Intelligent interactive tutors can revolutionize e-learning by assessing students' knowledge and adapting to their learning needs, revolutionizing the educational process(Woolf, 2008). Chatbots enhance high school student engagement in computer science, improving retention and interest, especially among girls(Benotti et al., 2014), ChatGPT aids programming education by enhancing learning efficiency but raises concerns about dependency and ethical use(Silva et al., 2024). Incorporating AI-driven tools in the classroom extends beyond mere augmentation of existing educational practices; it redefines the pedagogical approach by enabling real-time feedback, fostering autonomous learning, and encouraging inquiry-driven exploration. These intelligent systems can cater to diverse learning styles, instantly adapting to individual student needs and allowing for a tailored educational quest that aligns with each learner's pace and preferences. This personalized interaction not only motivates students but empowers educators to focus more deeply on facilitating conceptual understanding rather than routine administrative tasks. However, this integration is not without its challenges. Key concerns such as data privacy, the digital divide, and the potential for technology-induced isolation require careful consideration. Strategies to mitigate these concerns must prioritize equitable access to technology, robust data security measures, and the promotion of human interaction alongside technological solutions. By addressing these issues comprehensively, the benefits of AI in education can be maximized, ensuring that the digital transformation translates into equitable, enhanced learning outcomes for all students. In conclusion, chatbots and AI tutors present an exciting frontier in India's educational reform, promising to enrich the teaching and learning experience. By intelligently addressing individual needs and providing innovative solutions to educational challenges, these tools markedly contribute to the broader goal of enhancing educational quality and accessibility in India. This technological evolution demands a thoughtful, inclusive approach, ensuring that every student's journey is both empowering and enlightening in a rapidly changing world.

FUTURE SCOPE OF THE STUDY

Over the coming years, the landscape of education in India is poised for transformative changes driven by the integration of chatbots and AI tutors. These technologies offer novel opportunities for enhancing student engagement and optimizing learning management systems. As educators continue to explore their potential, several key areas emerge where AI can significantly impact the education sector. Firstly, personalization stands as a promising frontier. AI-powered systems can analyze vast amounts of data to discern individual learning styles, preferences, and needs. By providing tailored educational experiences, they can help each student progress at an optimal pace, thereby improving outcomes. This capability makes education more inclusive, allowing students who may otherwise fall behind due to standardized teaching methods to receive customized support. Additionally, chatbots, equipped with natural language processing capabilities, can facilitate real-time doubt resolution and feedback, creating a more responsive learning environment.

Another dimension of future exploration in this field is scalability. AI tutors and chatbots can make quality education accessible to a vast number of students at a fraction of the cost compared to traditional methods. The economic efficiency and reach offered by these technologies are especially pertinent in a country like India, where the demand for educational resources far exceeds the supply. With the government and private sector increasingly investing in digital infrastructure, the integration of AI-driven educational tools could address the shortage of qualified teachers and improve educational outcomes in rural and underserved areas. As these technologies mature, they could also evolve to encompass multilingual capabilities, addressing language barriers that often hinder education in India's diverse linguistic landscape.

Lastly, the ethical implications and data privacy concerns associated with AI in education must be meticulously addressed. As chatbots and AI tutors become more prevalent, safeguarding students' personal information remains paramount. Establishing transparent data governance policies and ensuring the ethical use of AI will facilitate trust and uptake among educators, students, and parents alike. In conclusion, while challenges persist, the future scope of AI-driven educational innovations in India is vast and varied, promising to reshape how education is delivered and experienced across the country. With careful implementation and continuous innovation, these technologies can revolutionize educational accessibility, quality, and personalization, thereby fostering a more equitable and effective learning ecosystem.

REFERENCES

Abbas, N., Whitfield, J., Atwell, E., Bowman, H., Pickard, T., & Walker, A. (2022). Online chat and chatbots to enhance mature student engagement in higher education. *International Journal of Lifelong Education, 41*(3), 308–326. DOI: 10.1080/02601370.2022.2066213

Abu Shawar, B., & Atwell, E. (2007). Chatbots: Are they Really Useful? *Journal for Language Technology and Computational Linguistics, 22*(1), 29–49. DOI: 10.21248/jlcl.22.2007.88

Adamopoulou, E., & Moussiades, L. (2020). Chatbots: History, technology, and applications. *Machine Learning with Applications, 2*, 100006. DOI: 10.1016/j.mlwa.2020.100006

Alam, A. (2021). Should Robots Replace Teachers? Mobilisation of AI and Learning Analytics in Education. *2021 International Conference on Advances in Computing, Communication, and Control (ICAC3)*, 1–12. DOI: 10.1109/ICAC353642.2021.9697300

Ali Amer Jid Almahri, F., Bell, D., & Arzoky, M. (2019). Personas Design for Conversational Systems in Education. *Informatics (MDPI), 6*(4), 46. DOI: 10.3390/informatics6040046

Almahri, F. A. J., Bell, D., & Merhi, M. (2020). Understanding Student Acceptance and Use of Chatbots in the United Kingdom Universities: A Structural Equation Modelling Approach. *2020 6th International Conference on Information Management (ICIM)*, 284–288. DOI: 10.1109/ICIM49319.2020.244712

Alshahrani, A. (2023). The impact of ChatGPT on blended learning: Current trends and future research directions. *International Journal of Data and Network Science, 7*(4), 2029–2040. DOI: 10.5267/j.ijdns.2023.6.010

Ashfaq, M., Yun, J., Yu, S., & Loureiro, S. M. C. (2020). I, Chatbot: Modeling the determinants of users' satisfaction and continuance intention of AI-powered service agents. *Telematics and Informatics, 54*, 101473. DOI: 10.1016/j.tele.2020.101473

Ashfaque, M. W., Tharewal, S., Iqhbal, S., & Kayte, C. N. (2020). A Review on Techniques, Characteristics and approaches of an intelligent tutoring Chatbot system. *2020 International Conference on Smart Innovations in Design, Environment, Management, Planning and Computing (ICSIDEMPC)*, 258–262. DOI: 10.1109/ICSIDEMPC49020.2020.9299583

Bahja, M., Hammad, R., & Butt, G. (2020). A User-Centric Framework for Educational Chatbots Design and Development. In Stephanidis, C., Kurosu, M., Degen, H., & Reinerman-Jones, L. (Eds.), *HCI International 2020—Late Breaking Papers: Multimodality and Intelligence* (Vol. 12424, pp. 32–43). Springer International Publishing., DOI: 10.1007/978-3-030-60117-1_3

Belpaeme, T., Kennedy, J., Ramachandran, A., Scassellati, B., & Tanaka, F. (2018). Social robots for education: A review. *Science Robotics, 3*(21), eaat5954. Advance online publication. DOI: 10.1126/scirobotics.aat5954 PMID: 33141719

Benotti, L., Martínez, M. C., & Schapachnik, F. (2014). Engaging high school students using chatbots. *Proceedings of the 2014 Conference on Innovation & Technology in Computer Science Education - ITiCSE '14*, 63–68. DOI: 10.1145/2591708.2591728

Benotti, L., Martinez, M. C., & Schapachnik, F. (2018). A Tool for Introducing Computer Science with Automatic Formative Assessment. *IEEE Transactions on Learning Technologies, 11*(2), 179–192. DOI: 10.1109/TLT.2017.2682084

Bond, M., Buntins, K., Bedenlier, S., Zawacki-Richter, O., & Kerres, M. (2020). Mapping research in student engagement and educational technology in higher education: A systematic evidence map. *International Journal of Educational Technology in Higher Education, 17*(1), 2. DOI: 10.1186/s41239-019-0176-8

Chatbots and AI in Education (AIEd) tools: The good, the bad, and the ugly. (2023). *Journal of Applied Learning & Teaching, 6*(2). DOI: 10.37074/jalt.2023.6.2.29

Chen, L., Chen, P., & Lin, Z. (2020). Artificial Intelligence in Education: A Review. *IEEE Access : Practical Innovations, Open Solutions, 8*, 75264–75278. DOI: 10.1109/ACCESS.2020.2988510

Chiu, T. K. F., Moorhouse, B. L., Chai, C. S., & Ismailov, M. (2023). Teacher support and student motivation to learn with Artificial Intelligence (AI) based chatbot. *Interactive Learning Environments*, •••, 1–17. DOI: 10.1080/10494820.2023.2172044

Chukwuere, J. E. (2024). *The future of generative AI chatbots in higher education* (Version 1). arXiv. DOI: 10.48550/ARXIV.2403.13487

Cotton, D. R. E., Cotton, P. A., & Shipway, J. R. (2024). Chatting and cheating: Ensuring academic integrity in the era of ChatGPT. *Innovations in Education and Teaching International, 61*(2), 228–239. DOI: 10.1080/14703297.2023.2190148

Dahake, P. S., Mohare, R. V., & Dahake, N. S. (2024). Enhancing Management Education Through ChatGPT: A Novel Method for Ease and Efficacy. In Inder, S., Min, B., & Sharma, S. (Eds.), (pp. 161–178). Advances in Business Strategy and Competitive Advantage. IGI Global., DOI: 10.4018/979-8-3693-1734-1.ch012

Farrokhnia, M., Banihashem, S. K., Noroozi, O., & Wals, A. (2024). A SWOT analysis of ChatGPT: Implications for educational practice and research. *Innovations in Education and Teaching International, 61*(3), 460–474. DOI: 10.1080/14703297.2023.2195846

Faruqui, S. H. A., Tasnim, N., Basith, I. I., Obeidat, S., & Yildiz, F. (2024). *Integrating A.I. in Higher Education: Protocol for a Pilot Study with "SAMCares: An Adaptive Learning Hub"* (Version 1). arXiv. DOI: 10.48550/ARXIV.2405.00330

Foroughi, B., Senali, M. G., Iranmanesh, M., Khanfar, A., Ghobakhloo, M., Annamalai, N., & Naghmeh-Abbaspour, B. (2024). Determinants of Intention to Use ChatGPT for Educational Purposes: Findings from PLS-SEM and fsQCA. *International Journal of Human-Computer Interaction, 40*(17), 4501–4520. DOI: 10.1080/10447318.2023.2226495

Han, J.-W., Park, J., & Lee, H. (2022). Analysis of the effect of an artificial intelligence chatbot educational program on non-face-to-face classes: A quasi-experimental study. *BMC Medical Education, 22*(1), 830. DOI: 10.1186/s12909-022-03898-3 PMID: 36457086

Hemachandran, K., Verma, P., Pareek, P., Arora, N., Rajesh Kumar, K. V., Ahanger, T. A., Pise, A. A., & Ratna, R. (2022). Artificial Intelligence: A Universal Virtual Tool to Augment Tutoring in Higher Education. *Computational Intelligence and Neuroscience*, *2022*, 1–8. DOI: 10.1155/2022/1410448 PMID: 35586099

Hockly, N. (2023). Artificial Intelligence in English Language Teaching: The Good, the Bad and the Ugly. *RELC Journal*, *54*(2), 445–451. DOI: 10.1177/00336882231168504

Hoyer, W. D., Kroschke, M., Schmitt, B., Kraume, K., & Shankar, V. (2020). Transforming the Customer Experience through New Technologies. *Journal of Interactive Marketing*, *51*(1), 57–71. DOI: 10.1016/j.intmar.2020.04.001

Huang, M.-H., & Rust, R. T. (2021). Engaged to a Robot? The Role of AI in Service. *Journal of Service Research*, *24*(1), 30–41. DOI: 10.1177/1094670520902266

Ilieva, G., Yankova, T., Klisarova-Belcheva, S., Dimitrov, A., Bratkov, M., & Angelov, D. (2023). Effects of Generative Chatbots in Higher Education. *Information (Basel)*, *14*(9), 492. DOI: 10.3390/info14090492

Imran, M., & Almusharraf, N. (2023). Analyzing the role of ChatGPT as a writing assistant at higher education level: A systematic review of the literature. *Contemporary Educational Technology*, *15*(4), ep464. DOI: 10.30935/cedtech/13605

Kaushal, V., & Yadav, R. (2022). The Role of Chatbots in Academic Libraries: An Experience-based Perspective. *Journal of the Australian Library and Information Association*, *71*(3), 215–232. DOI: 10.1080/24750158.2022.2106403

Kerly, A., Ellis, R., & Bull, S. (2008). CALMsystem: A Conversational Agent for Learner Modelling. *Knowledge-Based Systems*, *21*(3), 238–246. DOI: 10.1016/j.knosys.2007.11.015

Kerly, A., Hall, P., & Bull, S. (2007). Bringing chatbots into education: Towards natural language negotiation of open learner models. *Knowledge-Based Systems*, *20*(2), 177–185. DOI: 10.1016/j.knosys.2006.11.014

Krause, S., Panchal, B. H., & Ubhe, N. (2024). *The Evolution of Learning: Assessing the Transformative Impact of Generative AI on Higher Education* (Version 1). arXiv. DOI: 10.48550/ARXIV.2404.10551

Latif, E., Mai, G., Nyaaba, M., Wu, X., Liu, N., Lu, G., Li, S., Liu, T., & Zhai, X. (2023). *AGI: Artificial General Intelligence for Education* (Version 5). arXiv. DOI: 10.48550/ARXIV.2304.12479

Lee, D., & Yeo, S. (2022). Developing an AI-based chatbot for practicing responsive teaching in mathematics. *Computers & Education*, *191*, 104646. DOI: 10.1016/j.compedu.2022.104646

Liu, C.-C., Liao, M.-G., Chang, C.-H., & Lin, H.-M. (2022). An analysis of children' interaction with an AI chatbot and its impact on their interest in reading. *Computers & Education*, *189*, 104576. DOI: 10.1016/j.compedu.2022.104576

Lo, C. K. (2023). What Is the Impact of ChatGPT on Education? A Rapid Review of the Literature. *Education Sciences*, *13*(4), 410. DOI: 10.3390/educsci13040410

Lo, C. K., Hew, K. F., & Jong, M. S. (2024). The influence of ChatGPT on student engagement: A systematic review and future research agenda. *Computers & Education, 219*, 105100. DOI: 10.1016/j.compedu.2024.105100

Mallik, S., & Gangopadhyay, A. (2023). Proactive and reactive engagement of artificial intelligence methods for education: A review. *Frontiers in Artificial Intelligence, 6*, 1151391. DOI: 10.3389/frai.2023.1151391 PMID: 37215064

Martin, F., & Bolliger, D. U. (2018). Engagement Matters: Student Perceptions on the Importance of Engagement Strategies in the Online Learning Environment. *Online Learning : the Official Journal of the Online Learning Consortium, 22*(1). Advance online publication. DOI: 10.24059/olj.v22i1.1092

Martín-Núñez, J. L., Ar, A. Y., Fernández, R. P., Abbas, A., & Radovanović, D. (2023). Does intrinsic motivation mediate perceived artificial intelligence (AI) learning and computational thinking of students during the COVID-19 pandemic? *Computers and Education: Artificial Intelligence, 4*, 100128. DOI: 10.1016/j.caeai.2023.100128

Nguyen, A., Kremantzis, M., Essien, A., Petrounias, I., & Hosseini, S. (2024). Editorial: Enhancing Student Engagement Through Artificial Intelligence (AI): Understanding the Basics, Opportunities, and Challenges. *Journal of University Teaching & Learning Practice, 21*(06). Advance online publication. DOI: 10.53761/caraaq92

Ray, P. P. (2023). ChatGPT: A comprehensive review on background, applications, key challenges, bias, ethics, limitations and future scope. *Internet of Things and Cyber-Physical Systems, 3*, 121–154. DOI: 10.1016/j.iotcps.2023.04.003

Rudolph, J., Mohamed Ismail, F. M., & Popenici, S. (2024). Higher Education's Generative Artificial Intelligence Paradox: The Meaning of Chatbot Mania. *Journal of University Teaching & Learning Practice, 21*(06). Advance online publication. DOI: 10.53761/54fs5e77

Schiff, D. (2021). Out of the laboratory and into the classroom: The future of artificial intelligence in education. *AI & Society, 36*(1), 331–348. DOI: 10.1007/s00146-020-01033-8 PMID: 32836908

Shaik, T., Tao, X., Li, Y., Dann, C., Mcdonald, J., Redmond, P., & Galligan, L. (2023). *A Review of the Trends and Challenges in Adopting Natural Language Processing Methods for Education Feedback Analysis*. DOI: 10.48550/ARXIV.2301.08826

Shum, H., He, X., & Li, D. (2018). From Eliza to XiaoIce: Challenges and opportunities with social chatbots. *Frontiers of Information Technology & Electronic Engineering, 19*(1), 10–26. DOI: 10.1631/FITEE.1700826

Silva, C. A. G. D., Ramos, F. N., De Moraes, R. V., & Santos, E. L. D. (2024). ChatGPT: Challenges and Benefits in Software Programming for Higher Education. *Sustainability (Basel), 16*(3), 1245. DOI: 10.3390/su16031245

Stöhr, C., Ou, A. W., & Malmström, H. (2024). Perceptions and usage of AI chatbots among students in higher education across genders, academic levels and fields of study. *Computers and Education: Artificial Intelligence, 7*, 100259. DOI: 10.1016/j.caeai.2024.100259

Su, J., & Yang, W. (2023). Unlocking the Power of ChatGPT: A Framework for Applying Generative AI in Education. *ECNU Review of Education, 6*(3), 355–366. DOI: 10.1177/20965311231168423

Suleman, R. M., Mizoguchi, R., & Ikeda, M. (2016). A New Perspective of Negotiation-Based Dialog to Enhance Metacognitive Skills in the Context of Open Learner Models. *International Journal of Artificial Intelligence in Education, 26*(4), 1069–1115. DOI: 10.1007/s40593-016-0118-8

Tapalova, O., & Zhiyenbayeva, N. (2022). Artificial Intelligence in Education: AIEd for Personalised Learning Pathways. *Electronic Journal of e-Learning, 20*(5), 639–653. DOI: 10.34190/ejel.20.5.2597

Wang, T., Lund, B. D., Marengo, A., Pagano, A., Mannuru, N. R., Teel, Z. A., & Pange, J. (2023). Exploring the Potential Impact of Artificial Intelligence (AI) on International Students in Higher Education: Generative AI, Chatbots, Analytics, and International Student Success. *Applied Sciences (Basel, Switzerland), 13*(11), 6716. DOI: 10.3390/app13116716

Woolf, B. P. (2008). *Building Intelligent Interactive Tutors: Student-centered strategies for revolutionizing e-learning*. Morgan Kaufmann Publishers Inc.

Yang, J., & Zhang, B. (2019). Artificial Intelligence in Intelligent Tutoring Robots: A Systematic Review and Design Guidelines. *Applied Sciences (Basel, Switzerland), 9*(10), 2078. DOI: 10.3390/app9102078

Yang, S., & Evans, C. (2019). Opportunities and Challenges in Using AI Chatbots in Higher Education. *Proceedings of the 2019 3rd International Conference on Education and E-Learning*, 79–83. DOI: 10.1145/3371647.3371659

Zawacki-Richter, O., Marín, V. I., Bond, M., & Gouverneur, F. (2019). Systematic review of research on artificial intelligence applications in higher education – where are the educators? *International Journal of Educational Technology in Higher Education, 16*(1), 39. DOI: 10.1186/s41239-019-0171-0

About the Contributors

Viktor Wang, is a globally recognized professor and leader in the field of Education in the Department of Educational Leadership and Technology at California State University, San Bernardino. His distinguished career is marked by innovation, scholarship, and mentorship. With more than 240 peer-reviewed publications, Dr. Wang has made transformative contributions to academic research and thought leadership. His work has inspired over 200 scholarly articles and more than 1,500 book chapters contributed to his edited volumes and journals by scholars around the world. His publications are widely respected and housed in top-tier institutions, including Stanford University Libraries and other globally renowned academic collections. Dr. Wang has received numerous prestigious honors, including the 2016 Presidential Award for Exceptional and Innovative Leadership from the American Association for Adult and Continuing Education (AAACE), as well as institutional recognition such as the Distinguished Faculty and Scholarly Achievement Award from CSULB. A dedicated mentor, Dr. Wang has successfully guided more than 80 doctoral students through dissertation completion. His leadership has also driven measurable institutional outcomes, including enrollment growth, the launch of innovative academic programs, and the establishment of international educational partnerships.

***

Otmane Azeroual is a leading expert in data science, artificial intelligence, and digital transformation. With a PhD in computer science, specializing in databases, information systems, AI, and digitalization, Dr. Azeroual has made significant contributions to both academia and industry. He holds senior positions in research institutions and the private sector, where he has developed cutting-edge AI solutions. As an educator, Dr. Azeroual teaches AI and data science courses at the University of Hagen, shaping the next generation of experts in the field. His research focuses on big data, data quality management, and the integration of digital technologies. His work has been widely published in prestigious journals and presented at international conferences. Recognized for bridging the gap between academic research and real-world applications, Dr. Azeroual's expertise continues to drive innovation and digital transformation across industries. As a sought-after speaker, he is committed to advancing the global conversation on AI and fostering collaboration in digital innovation.

Bao Kham is a lecturer at Faculty of English, University of Foreign Languages & International Studies, Hue University, Viet Nam. His research interests include technology in language teaching, curriculum design and development, and language teacher education.

Patcha Bhujanga Rao is a distinguished professional with a stellar reputation in the realms of human resources (HR) and soft skills development. With over two decades of experience and an extensive academic background encompassing degrees such as M.Com., DCFA., M.Phil., Ph.D., MBA (HR), M.Sc (Psychology), and LL.B, he possesses a comprehensive understanding of multiple disciplines. Currently serving as a professor at Jain Deemed-to-Be University in Bengaluru, Dr. Rao is highly regarded for his expertise in HR management, which has been instrumental in shaping the careers of numerous professionals. His commitment to nurturing essential skills such as effective communication, leadership, and interpersonal abilities reflects his dedication to facilitating personal and professional growth. Dr. Rao's contributions have earned him widespread respect and admiration within the HR and soft skills domains, positioning him as a respected authority and mentor for aspiring professionals seeking to excel in their respective fields.

Mei Rianto Chandra is a lecturer and researcher in the Chinese Studies Program at BINUS University, Jakarta. His work focuses on Chinese-Indonesian translation, technology-enhanced language learning, and the evaluation of AI-based translation systems.

Angela Crevar received her Ph.D. in Educational Leadership and Policy from Texas Tech University, Angela served as postdoctoral researcher at Texas Tech University, and she previously served as a high school school principal for ten years. Her research is focused in the nexus of high school to college and career with a focus on pathways through education to student success. These pathways include career technical education, hybrid education, and the impact of teacher quality. Her work has been published in the Journal of Higher Education and Policy and Leadership Studies and Early Education and Development. Dr. Crevar has presented research papers at several national research conferences such as Association for Public Policy Analysis and Management, American Educational Research Association, Association for Education Finance and Policy, University Council for Educational Administration, and the Society for Research on Educational Effectiveness and is currently working on multiple grants.

Nihar Suresh Dahake is currently serving as an Assistant Professor in the Department of MBA at G H Raisoni College of Engineering, Nagpur. He holds a B.Com, M.Com, and MBA from Rashtrasant Tukdoji Maharaj Nagpur University and earned his Ph.D. from Sant Gadge Baba Amravati University, Amravati. In addition to his academic qualifications, Dr. Dahake has successfully qualified the State Eligibility Test (SET) in both Commerce and Management, demonstrating his strong foundation in these disciplines. With a rich academic background, he brings 14 years of teaching experience and 8 years of dedicated research experience to his role. Throughout his career, he has consistently contributed to academic excellence and research development. Dr. Dahake's areas of expertise include Financial Accounting, Consumer Behavior, Marketing Management, and Financial Management. His multidisciplinary knowledge allows him to effectively engage with a wide range of topics in business and management studies. Passionate about both teaching and research, he strives to inspire students while also contributing meaningfully to the academic community through his scholarly work. His professional journey reflects a deep commitment to education, research, and the advancement of management studies in higher education institutions.

Parihar Suresh Dahake is an accomplished academician and researcher with over 15 years of experience in teaching and research in the fields of Commerce and Management. Currently serving as an Assistant Professor at the School of Management, Ramdeobaba University, Nagpur, he holds a diverse educational background, including B.Tech (Applied Electronics), MBA (Marketing & Financial Management), M.Com, PGDIBO, M.A. (Psychology), and a Ph.D. in Business Management. Dr. Dahake's research interests span Business Analytics, Consumer Behavior, Predictive Analytics, and Marketing Communication. A recognized Ph.D. supervisor, he guides multiple doctoral candidates under the faculty of Commerce. He has published extensively in peer-reviewed, Scopus, and ABDC-indexed journals and authored books on Marketing Management and Consumer Behavior. He also holds a patent in wage sheet automation and actively contributes as a reviewer for prestigious journals. A recipient of multiple accolades, including the Young Researcher and Research Excellence Awards, Dr. Dahake is also a sought-after speaker and trainer. His commitment to academic excellence and innovative pedagogy has made significant contributions to management education, research, and institutional development in Central India.

Praveen Dubey is an Assistant Professor of Education and Director of Clinical Experiences and Partnerships at Montana State University Northern. His research interest focuses in the areas of Multicultural/Immigrant Education, Diversity, Equity, & Inclusivity, Leadership and Change, Technology in Education (Digital Equity & AI), STEM education, Comparative and International Education, Teacher Quality, and Teacher Choice for diverse classrooms. In his research, he uses the statistical tools of Structural Education Modelling (SEM), Mediation & Moderation, and R programming to address the issues that intersect in improving the learning experiences of diverse student population, immigrant/refugee students, and minority students. He has presented research papers at several national research conferences such as AERA, UCIE, AEFP, SREE, etc. and is currently working on different projects and grants.

Marvin Espinoza, M.Ed., is a seasoned educational leader and community advocate with over 25 years of experience in program management and leadership across the nonprofit sector and higher education. Currently a doctoral candidate at California State University, San Bernardino, he has dedicated his career to advancing educational outcomes and expanding services for underserved communities. His expertise spans teaching, strategic planning, youth development, community engagement, grant writing, program development, and quality assurance. As the Chief Operating Officer at the Girls Club of Los Angeles, Mr. Espinoza ensures that the organization's mission aligns with its operations, driving significant community impact. His leadership extends to higher education, where he has been an adjunct faculty member at East Los Angeles College for 18 years, contributing to in-person and online learning. Mr. Espinoza holds a Master of Arts in Education and a Bachelor of Arts in Liberal Studies and Child Development from California State University, Dominguez Hills, and an Associate of Arts in Child Development from Los Angeles Southwest College. His professional development includes certifications such as a Leadership Certificate from the Executive Directors Leadership Institute and a Project Grantsmanship Certificate from The Grantsmanship Center. His work has been recognized with several awards, including the City of Los Angeles Commendation Award, LAUSD Outstanding Director, and County of Los Angeles Commendation. Marvin Espinoza remains committed to empowering children and families through innovative programs and strategic partnerships, contributing significantly to educational leadership and community development.

L. A. Anto Gracious is an accomplished academic professional in Information Technology and Computer Science, known for his dedication to education, technology, and research. He holds a B.Tech in IT from C.S.I Institute of Technology (2006), an MBA in Technology Management, and an M.Tech in IT from Francis Xavier Engineering College (2011). He began his career as a Programmer at Software Solutions Integrated Limited, later transitioning to academia in 2011 as an Assistant Professor at Marthandam College of Engineering and Technology. Over eight years, he excelled in teaching, led the Software Development Cell, and earned multiple awards for his contributions. He later served at St. Xavier's Catholic College of Engineering and currently holds a position at R.M.K. College of Engineering and Technology. A prolific researcher, Anto focuses on machine learning, wireless sensor networks, and healthcare technologies. His work is widely published, and he has received accolades such as the Best Paper Award and multiple Best Faculty Awards.

Ryan Le is a distinguished scholar and dynamic educational leader whose career bridges the fields of engineering, business, healthcare, and education. With an impressive academic portfolio that includes multiple master's and doctoral degrees—spanning an MBA in Human Resource Management, an MSc in International Business, a Doctorate in Healthcare Administration (DHA), and an EdD in Educational Leadership and Innovation—Dr. Le exemplifies the ethos of lifelong learning. He holds advanced teaching certificates from Ivy League institutions, including Harvard, Columbia, and Cornell, reflecting his deep commitment to pedagogical excellence. As Director of Newrizons Academy, Dr. Le leads with innovation and inclusion, designing forward-thinking programs that prepare learners to thrive in a rapidly evolving world. His leadership is grounded in a belief that education should empower not just academic growth, but personal and professional transformation. Recognized for his impactful contributions to academic leadership, Dr. Le is dedicated to creating collaborative, student-centered environments that foster curiosity, resilience, and visionary thinking. His work inspires the next generation of learners and educators to pursue excellence, embrace innovation, and lead with purpose.

Raj Madhu is a Research Scholar at the Central University of Jammu, Department of Educational Studies. He holds a Master's degree in Education from the University of Kalyani. His research interests lie in the areas of Educational Philosophy, Inclusive Education, and Educational Technology, with a focus on bridging theoretical frameworks and practical applications to enhance educational equity and innovation.

James A. Martinez is the Vice President of Data Science at DB Legal Support, Inc. | McCune Law Group, where he leads enterprise strategies for cloud-based analytics, AI-driven legal technologies, and data governance. He holds a doctorate in Health and Behavioral Studies from Columbia University and has over 15 years of experience integrating Geographic Information Systems (GIS), public health informatics, and machine learning in both academic and applied settings. As a faculty member at Loma Linda University and California State University, San

Bernardino, Dr. Martinez teaches graduate-level courses in geospatial data integration, workforce education, and the ethical use of AI in professional practice. He has authored and co-authored book chapters and research articles focused on AI literacy, technological innovation in education, and interdisciplinary workforce development. Dr. Martinez is also a mentor and community advocate, promoting STEM access and real-world learning opportunities for underrepresented students.

Dalbin Osorio is a seasoned non-profit leader bringing over two decades of experience dedicated to advancing social justice and cultural equity. Throughout their extensive career, Dalbin has consistently championed impactful initiatives designed to foster robust community engagement and amplify marginalized voices. A deep-seated passion for literature and the arts fuels their commitment to promoting diverse narratives and creating vital platforms for underrepresented communities to share their unique stories and perspectives. In their role as Senior Advisor for Policy and Community Impact at NYEC, Dalbin has demonstrated exceptional leadership and fundraising acumen, securing over $2 million in revenue to support the organization's mission. Their strategic guidance has been instrumental in leading initiatives aimed at decreasing recidivism, expanding access to crucial educational resources, and improving mental health outcomes for vulnerable populations. Dalbin possesses a proven ability to build, mentor, and lead high-performing teams, cultivate strategic partnerships across sectors, and drive innovative programming that delivers measurable and meaningful community impact. Dalbin Osorio's unwavering dedication to social justice, combined with a remarkable capacity to inspire and mobilize diverse groups, distinguishes them as a truly transformative leader. They are driven to leverage their extensive experience and forward-thinking vision to contribute significantly to building a more equitable and inclusive world, harnessing the power of storytelling and community collaboration to effect lasting change.

R. Balakrishna is an Associate Professor in the Department of Computer Science and Engineering at Vels Institute of Science, Technology and Advanced Studies (VISTAS). He is dedicated to teaching, research, and guiding students in core areas of computer science. His academic interests include advanced computing technologies and innovative research methodologies.

Siva Subramanian R is an Associate Professor in the Department of Computer Science and Engineering at R.M.K. College of Engineering and Technology, Puduvoyal. He is actively involved in teaching, research, and academic development in the domain of computer science. His interests include emerging technologies and fostering innovation through collaborative research.

Mattius Rischard is an Assistant Professor of English at Montana State University-Northern. He received his MA and PhD at the University of Arizona from the Department of English and Social, Cultural, and Critical Theory Programs. He has taught writing, literature, and digital/ visual culture and methods for the University of Arizona, Pima Community College, and as a Writing Assessment Specialist for the University of Texas. He is the author of Street, Text, and Representation in African American Literature (Routledge, 2024), and publishes and presents on sociohistorical, phenomenological, and computational methods of literary and cultural analysis. Winner of the 2020 New Directions in the Humanities International Award, he has written widely in the fields of writing pedagogy, assessment, and digital humanities research for journals including Writing Spaces, Texas Studies in Literature and Language, and The International Journal of Critical Cultural Studies.

S. Dhivya Devi is an Assistant Professor in the Faculty of Management at SRM Institute of Science and Technology, Kattankulathur. She specializes in management studies with a focus on academic research and student development. Her contributions span teaching, research publications, and active involvement in institutional academic activities.

Vasco Santo, Polytechnic University of Tomar, Portugal Adjunct Professor at the Polytechnic University of Tomar (IPT) and member of the Research and Innovation Support Office (GAII). He has a Habilitation in Management (European University, Lisbon), a PhD in Business Sciences (Fernando Pessoa University, Porto), a PhD in Tourism (University of Seville, Spain) and a Post-Doctorate in Innovation Management (University of Aveiro). Specialises in Hotel and Restaurant Management. Integrated researcher at NECE-UI and collaborating researcher at GOVCOPP (University of Aveiro), TECHN&ART (Polytechnic University of Tomar) and CITUR (Polytechnic of Leiria). Editor-in-Chief of the scientific journal 'International Journal of Digital Marketing, Management, and Innovation (IJDMMI)'. Author and reviewer for indexed scientific journals. Author of Book Chapters in IGI Global. Editor of Books in IGI Global.

Ratan Sarkar is an Assistant Professor of Education (Stage II) at the Department of Teachers' Training (B.Ed.) and the former Head of the Department of Education at Prabhat Kumar College, Contai (affiliated to Vidyasagar University), West Bengal. Dr. Sarkar holds a Ph.D. in Education from Pondicherry University (A Central University) and an M.Phil. and M.Ed. in Special Education (ID) from Ramakrishna Mission Vivekananda Educational and Research Institute. He has an M.A. in Education and Technology from Tata Institute of Social Sciences, Mumbai, an M.Sc. in Applied Psychology from Bharathiar University, an M.A. in Education from JRN Rajasthan Vidyapeeth, and an M.A. in English Language & Linguistics from Madurai Kamaraj University, where he also completed a Post B.Ed. Diploma in School Administration. His undergraduate qualifications include a B.Ed. in Special Education (ID) from Jadavpur University and a B.A. in English (Hons) from Siliguri College (University of North Bengal). Dr. Sarkar has over a decade of teaching and research experience. He has also served as a guest faculty for B.Ed. Special Education (ID), M.Ed. Special Education (ID), and M.A. in Education offered by Netaji Subhash Open University, National Institute for Empowerment of Persons with Intellectual Disabilities - Regional Centre (NIEPID-RC), Kolkata, and the University of Kalyani. As a Core Committee Member of the 'Inclusive Education for CwSN Project' led by Jagadish Bose National Science Talent Search (JBNSTS), Kolkata, and the Department of School Education, Govt. of W.B., he has significantly contributed to inclusive education initiatives, teacher training, policy advocacy, and accessibility projects across the state. He has also completed a research project funded by the Ministry of Education, Govt of India under the PMMMNMTT scheme. He has received UGC-National Fellowship (JRF & SRF), the National Merit-Cum-Means Scholarship, Suhashchandra Talukdar Smriti Medha Britti, multiple Best Paper Presenter Awards, and published extensively in Scopus-indexed journals, authored several books, and secured multiple patents in artificial intelligence-driven assistive technology. As a Ph.D. supervisor, he mentors scholars in inclusive education and policy research, establishing himself as a leading voice in disability-inclusive education in India.

Erhan Sur completed his undergraduate studies in 2007 at Gazi University, Faculty of Industrial Arts Education, Department of Computer Education. He earned his master's degree in 2011 from the Institute of Informatics at the same university, with a thesis focusing on a comparative study of mobile learning and web-based learning methods. In 2024, he received his Ph.D. in Management Information Systems from the Institute of Informatics at Gazi University. His doctoral dissertation proposed an innovative service quality measurement model based on sentiment analysis and text mining techniques. His research interests include artificial intelligence, text mining, sentiment analysis, digital service quality, and bibliometric analysis. In 2024, he gained notable attention with his original article titled "Digital Service Quality Measurement Model Proposal and Prototype Development", published in the SCI-indexed journal Sustainability. He has also authored several book chapters on AI-supported service quality measurement models, social media data analysis, and social network analysis. His work titled "Bibliometric Analysis of AI Studies Affiliated with Turkey (1992–2024)" stands out as a significant contribution to the literature in the field.

T. Selva Banu Priya is an Assistant Professor at Panimalar Engineering College. She is committed to fostering academic excellence and student growth in the field of engineering education. Her areas of interest include emerging technologies and effective teaching methodologies.

T. Thilagam is an Assistant Professor (Senior Grade) in the Department of Computer Science and Engineering at Vel Tech Rangarajan Dr. Sagunthala R\&D Institute of Science and Technology. She is actively engaged in teaching, research, and mentoring students in the field of computer science. Her academic interests include software engineering, data analytics, and innovative pedagogical practices.

Ayşin Gaye Üstün is an Asst. Prof. at Vocational School at Sinop University, Turkey. She earned her doctoral degree from the Department of Computer Education and Instructional Technology at Atatürk University, Turkey. Her academic interest areas are open and distance eucation environments, educational technologies and instructional design.

Sathya V is an Assistant Professor in the Department of Computer Science and Engineering at Vel Tech Rangarajan Dr. Sagunthala R&D Institute of Science and Technology, Chennai. She actively contributes to academic research and education in the field of computer science. Her work focuses on innovation, technology development, and student engagement in research.

Index

A

E

P

R

S

T

U

V

W

www.ingramcontent.com/pod-product-compliance
Lightning Source LLC
LaVergne TN
LVHW080352011026
849161LV00009B/2283
* 9 7 9 8 3 3 7 3 5 0 9 7 4 *